Vauxhall/Opel Astra
Owners Workshop Manual

John S. Mead

Models covered

(4733 - 352)

Hatchback, Sport Hatch & Estate with turbo-diesel engines, including special/limited editions
1.3 litre (1248cc), 1.7 litre (1686cc) & 1.9 litre (1910cc)

Does NOT cover TwinTop models or 'Easytronic' transmission
For coverage of petrol models, see manual no. 4732

© Haynes Publishing 2008

ABCDE
FGHIJ
KLMNO
PQRST

A book in the **Haynes Owners Workshop Manual Series**

ISBN **978 1 84425 733 1**

British Library Cataloguing in Publication Data
A catalogue record for this book is available from the British Library.

Printed in the USA

Haynes Publishing
Sparkford, Yeovil, Somerset BA22 7JJ, England

Haynes North America, Inc
861 Lawrence Drive, Newbury Park, California 91320, USA

Haynes Publishing Nordiska AB
Box 1504, 751 45 UPPSALA, Sverige

Contents

LIVING WITH YOUR VAUXHALL/OPEL ASTRA

Roadside Repairs

Weekly Checks

Lubricants and fluids

Tyre pressures

MAINTENANCE

Routine Maintenance and Servicing

Contents

REPAIRS AND OVERHAUL

Engine and Associated Systems

Transmission

Brakes and suspension

Body equipment

REFERENCE

Index

Advanced driving

Many people see the words 'advanced driving' and believe that it won't interest them or that it is a style of driving beyond their own abilities. Nothing could be further from the truth. Advanced driving is straightforward safe, sensible driving - the sort of driving we should all do every time we get behind the wheel.

An average of 10 people are killed every day on UK roads and 870 more are injured, some seriously. Lives are ruined daily, usually because somebody did something stupid. Something like 95% of all accidents are due to human error, mostly driver failure. Sometimes we make genuine mistakes - everyone does. Sometimes we have lapses of concentration. Sometimes we deliberately take risks.

For many people, the process of 'learning to drive' doesn't go much further than learning how to pass the driving test because of a common belief that good drivers are made by 'experience'.

Learning to drive by 'experience' teaches three driving skills:

☐ Quick reactions. (Whoops, that was close!)
☐ Good handling skills. (Horn, swerve, brake, horn).
☐ Reliance on vehicle technology. (Great stuff this ABS, stop in no distance even in the wet...)

Drivers whose skills are 'experience based' generally have a lot of near misses and the odd accident. The results can be seen every day in our courts and our hospital casualty departments.

Advanced drivers have learnt to control the risks by controlling the position and speed of their vehicle. They avoid accidents and near misses, even if the drivers around them make mistakes.

The key skills of advanced driving are **concentration,** effective all-round **observation, anticipation** and **planning.** When **good vehicle handling** is added to

these skills, all driving situations can be approached and negotiated in a safe, methodical way, leaving nothing to chance.

Concentration means applying your mind to safe driving, completely excluding anything that's not relevant. Driving is usually the most dangerous activity that most of us undertake in our daily routines. It deserves our full attention.

Observation means not just looking, but seeing and seeking out the information found in the driving environment.

Anticipation means asking yourself what is happening, what you can reasonably expect to happen and what could happen unexpectedly. (One of the commonest words used in compiling accident reports is 'suddenly'.)

Planning is the link between seeing something and taking the appropriate action. For many drivers, planning is the missing link.

If you want to become a safer and more skilful driver and you want to enjoy your driving more, contact the Institute of Advanced Motorists at www.iam.org.uk, phone 0208 996 9600, or write to IAM House, 510 Chiswick High Road, London W4 5RG for an information pack.

Working on your car can be dangerous. This page shows just some of the potential risks and hazards, with the aim of creating a safety-conscious attitude.

General hazards

Scalding

• Don't remove the radiator or expansion tank cap while the engine is hot.
• Engine oil, automatic transmission fluid or power steering fluid may also be dangerously hot if the engine has recently been running.

Burning

• Beware of burns from the exhaust system and from any part of the engine. Brake discs and drums can also be extremely hot immediately after use.

Crushing

• When working under or near a raised vehicle, always supplement the jack with axle stands, or use drive-on ramps. *Never venture under a car which is only supported by a jack.*
• Take care if loosening or tightening high-torque nuts when the vehicle is on stands. Initial loosening and final tightening should be done with the wheels on the ground.

Fire

• Fuel is highly flammable; fuel vapour is explosive.
• Don't let fuel spill onto a hot engine.
• Do not smoke or allow naked lights (including pilot lights) anywhere near a vehicle being worked on. Also beware of creating sparks (electrically or by use of tools).
• Fuel vapour is heavier than air, so don't work on the fuel system with the vehicle over an inspection pit.
• Another cause of fire is an electrical overload or short-circuit. Take care when repairing or modifying the vehicle wiring.
• Keep a fire extinguisher handy, of a type suitable for use on fuel and electrical fires.

Electric shock

• Ignition HT voltage can be dangerous, especially to people with heart problems or a pacemaker. Don't work on or near the ignition system with the engine running or the ignition switched on.

• Mains voltage is also dangerous. Make sure that any mains-operated equipment is correctly earthed. Mains power points should be protected by a residual current device (RCD) circuit breaker.

Fume or gas intoxication

• Exhaust fumes are poisonous; they often contain carbon monoxide, which is rapidly fatal if inhaled. Never run the engine in a confined space such as a garage with the doors shut.
• Fuel vapour is also poisonous, as are the vapours from some cleaning solvents and paint thinners.

Poisonous or irritant substances

• Avoid skin contact with battery acid and with any fuel, fluid or lubricant, especially antifreeze, brake hydraulic fluid and Diesel fuel. Don't syphon them by mouth. If such a substance is swallowed or gets into the eyes, seek medical advice.
• Prolonged contact with used engine oil can cause skin cancer. Wear gloves or use a barrier cream if necessary. Change out of oil-soaked clothes and do not keep oily rags in your pocket.
• Air conditioning refrigerant forms a poisonous gas if exposed to a naked flame (including a cigarette). It can also cause skin burns on contact.

Asbestos

• Asbestos dust can cause cancer if inhaled or swallowed. Asbestos may be found in gaskets and in brake and clutch linings. When dealing with such components it is safest to assume that they contain asbestos.

Special hazards

Hydrofluoric acid

• This extremely corrosive acid is formed when certain types of synthetic rubber, found in some O-rings, oil seals, fuel hoses etc, are exposed to temperatures above 400°C. The rubber changes into a charred or sticky substance containing the acid. *Once formed, the acid remains dangerous for years. If it gets onto the skin, it may be necessary to amputate the limb concerned.*
• When dealing with a vehicle which has suffered a fire, or with components salvaged from such a vehicle, wear protective gloves and discard them after use.

The battery

• Batteries contain sulphuric acid, which attacks clothing, eyes and skin. Take care when topping-up or carrying the battery.
• The hydrogen gas given off by the battery is highly explosive. Never cause a spark or allow a naked light nearby. Be careful when connecting and disconnecting battery chargers or jump leads.

Air bags

• Air bags can cause injury if they go off accidentally. Take care when removing the steering wheel and/or facia. Special storage instructions may apply.

Diesel injection equipment

• Diesel injection pumps supply fuel at very high pressure. Take care when working on the fuel injectors and fuel pipes.

⚠ *Warning: Never expose the hands, face or any other part of the body to injector spray; the fuel can penetrate the skin with potentially fatal results.*

Remember...

DO

• Do use eye protection when using power tools, and when working under the vehicle.

• Do wear gloves or use barrier cream to protect your hands when necessary.

• Do get someone to check periodically that all is well when working alone on the vehicle.

• Do keep loose clothing and long hair well out of the way of moving mechanical parts.

• Do remove rings, wristwatch etc, before working on the vehicle – especially the electrical system.

• Do ensure that any lifting or jacking equipment has a safe working load rating adequate for the job.

DON'T

• Don't attempt to lift a heavy component which may be beyond your capability – get assistance.

• Don't rush to finish a job, or take unverified short cuts.

• Don't use ill-fitting tools which may slip and cause injury.

• Don't leave tools or parts lying around where someone can trip over them. Mop up oil and fuel spills at once.

• Don't allow children or pets to play in or near a vehicle being worked on.

The Vauxhall/Opel Astra-H model was introduced in the UK in May 2004 as a replacement for the previous Astra, the 'G' model. It is available in 3- and 5-door Hatchback and Estate versions with 1.3, 1.7 and 1.9 litre diesel engines and various petrol engines (not covered in this manual). The 1.3 and 1.7 litre engines are all DOHC 16-valve units, whereas the 1.9 litre engines are available in either SOHC 8-valve, or DOHC 16-valve form.

According to engine type, the manual gear-box is of the five- or six-speed all synchromesh type, with a six-speed electronically-controlled automatic transmission optionally available on 1.9 litre SOHC 8-valve models.

All models have front-wheel-drive with fully-independent front suspension, and semi-independent rear suspension with a torsion beam and trailing arms.

A wide range of standard and optional equipment is available within the Astra range to suit most tastes, including electro/hydraulic power steering, air conditioning, remote central locking, electric windows, electric sunroof, anti-lock braking system, electronic alarm system and supplemental restraint systems.

For the home mechanic, the Astra is a relatively straightforward vehicle to maintain, and most of the items requiring frequent attention are easily accessible.

Your Vauxhall/Opel Astra manual

The aim of this manual is to help you get the best value from your vehicle. It can do so in several ways. It can help you decide what work must be done (even should you choose to get it done by a garage), provide information on routine maintenance and servicing, and give a logical course of action and diagnosis when random faults occur. However, it is hoped that you will use the manual by tackling the work yourself. On simpler jobs, it may even be quicker than booking the car into a garage and going there twice, to leave and collect it. Perhaps most important, a lot of money can be saved by avoiding the costs a garage must charge to cover its labour and overheads.

The manual has drawings and descriptions to show the function of the various components, so that their layout can be understood. Then the tasks are described and photographed in a clear step-by-step sequence.

References to the 'left' or 'right' are in the sense of a person in the driver's seat, facing forward.

Project vehicles

The main vehicle used in the preparation of this manual, and which appears in many of the photographic sequences, was a Vauxhall Astra Estate with a 1.7 litre DOHC engine. Additional work was carried out on an Astra Hatchback with a 1.9 litre DOHC engine.

Acknowledgements

Thanks are also due to Draper Tools Limited, who provided some of the workshop tools, and to all those people at Sparkford who helped in the production of this manual.

We take great pride in the accuracy of information given in this manual, but vehicle manufacturers make alterations and design changes during the production run of a particular vehicle of which they do not inform us. No liability can be accepted by the authors or publishers for loss, damage or injury caused by any errors in, or omissions from, the information given.

Vauxhall Astra 1.9 litre DOHC

The following pages are intended to help in dealing with common roadside emergencies and breakdowns. You will find more detailed fault finding information at the back of the manual, and repair information in the main chapters.

If your car won't start and the starter motor doesn't turn

☐ If it's a model with automatic transmission, make sure the selector is in P or N.
☐ Open the bonnet and make sure that the battery terminals are clean and tight.
☐ Switch on the headlights and try to start the engine. If the headlights go very dim when you're trying to start, the battery is probably flat. Get out of trouble by jump starting (see next page) using a friend's car.

If your car won't start even though the starter motor turns as normal

☐ Is there fuel in the tank?
☐ Is there moisture on electrical components under the bonnet? Switch off the ignition, then wipe off any obvious dampness with a dry cloth. Spray a water-repellent aerosol product (WD-40 or equivalent) on ignition and fuel system electrical connectors like those shown in the photos. (Note that diesel engines don't usually suffer from damp).

1 Check that the airflow meter wiring is connected securely.

2 Check the security and condition of the battery connections.

3 Check all multiplugs and wiring connectors for security.

Check that electrical connections are secure (with the ignition switched off) and spray them with a water-dispersant spray like WD-40 if you suspect a problem due to damp

4 Check that all fuses are still in good condition and none have blown.

Jump starting

When jump-starting a car using a booster battery, observe the following precautions:

✔ Before connecting the booster battery, make sure that the ignition is switched off.

✔ Ensure that all electrical equipment (lights, heater, wipers, etc) is switched off.

✔ Take note of any special precautions printed on the battery case.

✔ Make sure that the booster battery is the same voltage as the discharged one in the vehicle.

✔ If the battery is being jump-started from the battery in another vehicle, the two vehicles MUST NOT TOUCH each other.

✔ Make sure that the transmission is in neutral (or PARK, in the case of automatic transmission).

 Jump starting will get you out of trouble, but you must correct whatever made the battery go flat in the first place. There are three possibilities:

1 *The battery has been drained by repeated attempts to start, or by leaving the lights on.*

2 *The charging system is not working properly (alternator drivebelt slack or broken, alternator wiring fault or alternator itself faulty).*

3 *The battery itself is at fault (electrolyte low, or battery worn out).*

1 Connect one end of the red jump lead to the positive (+) terminal of the flat battery

2 Connect the other end of the red lead to the positive (+) terminal of the booster battery.

3 Connect one end of the black jump lead to the negative (-) terminal of the booster battery

4 Connect the other end of the black jump lead to a bolt or bracket on the engine block, well away from the battery, on the vehicle to be started.

5 Make sure that the jump leads will not come into contact with the fan, drive-belts or other moving parts of the engine.

6 Start the engine using the booster battery and run it at idle speed. Switch on the lights, rear window demister and heater blower motor, then disconnect the jump leads in the reverse order of connection. Turn off the lights etc.

Wheel changing

 Warning: Do not change a wheel in a situation where you risk being hit by other traffic. On busy roads, try to stop in a lay-by or a gateway. Be wary of passing traffic while changing the wheel – it is easy to become distracted by the job in hand.

Preparation

☐ When a puncture occurs, stop as soon as it is safe to do so.

☐ Park on firm level ground, if possible, and well out of the way of other traffic.

☐ Use hazard warning lights if necessary.

☐ If you have one, use a warning triangle to alert other drivers of your presence.

☐ Apply the handbrake and engage first or reverse gear (or Park on models with automatic transmission).

☐ Chock the wheel diagonally opposite the one being removed – a couple of large stones will do for this.

☐ If the ground is soft, use a flat piece of wood to spread the load under the jack.

Changing the wheel

1 Lift the floor covering and unscrew the spare wheel clamp nut. Lift out the spare wheel.

2 Remove the tools from the carrier stored beneath the spare wheel.

3 On models with steel wheels, use the special tool to pull the wheel trim from the wheel. On models with alloy wheels, use the screwdriver provided inserted at the wheel bolt holes to prise off the trim.

4 Slacken each wheel bolt by half a turn.

5 Locate the jack head below the jacking point nearest the wheel to be changed; the jacking point is indicated by an arrow in the sill. Turn the handle until the base of the jack touches the ground ensuring that the jack is vertical. Raise the vehicle until the wheel is clear of the ground. If the tyre is flat make sure that the vehicle is raised sufficiently to allow the spare wheel to be fitted.

6 Remove the bolts and lift the wheel from the vehicle. Place it beneath the sill as a precaution against the jack failing. Fit the spare wheel and tighten the bolts moderately with the wheel brace.

Finally . . .

☐ Remove the wheel chocks.

☐ Stow the jack and tools in the correct locations in the car.

☐ Check the tyre pressure on the wheel just fitted. If it is low, or if you don't have a pressure gauge with you, drive slowly to the nearest garage and inflate the tyre to the correct pressure.

☐ Have the damaged tyre or wheel repaired as soon as possible, or another puncture will leave you stranded.

7 Lower the vehicle to the ground, then finally tighten the wheel bolts in a diagonal sequence. Refit the wheel trim. Note that the wheel bolts should be tightened to the specified torque at the earliest opportunity.

Identifying leaks

Puddles on the garage floor or drive, or obvious wetness under the bonnet or underneath the car, suggest a leak that needs investigating. It can sometimes be difficult to decide where the leak is coming from, especially if the engine bay is very dirty already. Leaking oil or fluid can also be blown rearwards by the passage of air under the car, giving a false impression of where the problem lies.

 Warning: Most automotive oils and fluids are poisonous. Wash them off skin, and change out of contaminated clothing, without delay.

 HAYNES HINT *The smell of a fluid leaking from the car may provide a clue to what's leaking. Some fluids are distinctively coloured. It may help to clean the car carefully and to park it over some clean paper overnight as an aid to locating the source of the leak.*
Remember that some leaks may only occur while the engine is running.

Sump oil

Engine oil may leak from the drain plug...

Oil from filter

...or from the base of the oil filter.

Gearbox oil

Gearbox oil can leak from the seals at the inboard ends of the driveshafts.

Antifreeze

Leaking antifreeze often leaves a crystalline deposit like this.

Brake fluid

A leak occurring at a wheel is almost certainly brake fluid.

Power steering fluid

Power steering fluid may leak from the pipe connectors on the steering rack.

Towing

When all else fails, you may find yourself having to get a tow home – or of course you may be helping somebody else. Long-distance recovery should only be done by a garage or breakdown service. For shorter distances, DIY towing using another car is easy enough, but observe the following points:

☐ Use a proper tow-rope – they are not expensive. The vehicle being towed must display an ON TOW sign in its rear window.

☐ Always turn the ignition key to the 'On' position when the vehicle is being towed, so that the steering lock is released, and the direction indicator and brake lights work.

☐ Only attach the tow-rope to the towing eye provided with the tool kit in the luggage compartment. To fit the towing eye, remove the circular cover from the front or rear bumper, as required, then screw in the towing eye anti-clockwise as far as it will go using the handle of the wheel brace to turn the eye. **Note that the towing eye has a left-hand thread.**

☐ Before being towed, release the handbrake and select neutral on the transmission. On models with automatic transmission, special precautions apply. If in doubt, do not tow, or transmission damage may result.

☐ Note that greater-than-usual pedal pressure will be required to operate the brakes, since the vacuum servo unit is only operational with the engine running.

☐ The driver of the car being towed must keep the tow-rope taut at all times to avoid snatching.

☐ Make sure that both drivers know the route before setting off.

☐ Only drive at moderate speeds and keep the distance towed to a minimum. Drive smoothly and allow plenty of time for slowing down at junctions.

Introduction

There are some very simple checks which need only take a few minutes to carry out, but which could save you a lot of inconvenience and expense.

These *Weekly checks* require no great skill or special tools, and the small amount of time they take to perform could prove to be very well spent, for example:

☐ Keeping an eye on tyre condition and pressures, will not only help to stop them wearing out prematurely, but could also save your life.

☐ Many breakdowns are caused by electrical problems. Battery-related faults are particularly common, and a quick check on a regular basis will often prevent the majority of these.

☐ If your car develops a brake fluid leak, the first time you might know about it is when your brakes don't work properly. Checking the level regularly will give advance warning of this kind of problem.

☐ If the oil or coolant levels run low, the cost of repairing any engine damage will be far greater than fixing the leak, for example.

Underbonnet check points

◀ 1.3 litre

1 *Engine oil level dipstick*

2 *Engine oil filler cap*

3 *Coolant reservoir (expansion tank)*

4 *Hydraulic fluid reservoir*

5 *Washer fluid reservoir*

6 *Battery*

◀ 1.7 litre

1 *Engine oil level dipstick*

2 *Engine oil filler cap*

3 *Coolant reservoir (expansion tank)*

4 *Hydraulic fluid reservoir*

5 *Washer fluid reservoir*

6 *Battery*

◀ **1.9 litre (DOHC)**

1 *Engine oil level dipstick*
2 *Engine oil filler cap*
3 *Coolant reservoir (expansion tank)*
4 *Hydraulic fluid reservoir*
5 *Washer fluid reservoir*
6 *Battery*

Engine oil level

Before you start

✔ Make sure that the car is on level ground.
✔ Check the oil level before the car is driven, or at least 5 minutes after the engine has been switched off.

 If the oil is checked immediately after driving the vehicle, some of the oil will remain in the upper engine components, resulting in an inaccurate reading on the dipstick.

The correct oil

Modern engines place great demands on their oil. It is very important that the correct oil for your car is used (see *Lubricants and fluids*).

Car care

● If you have to add oil frequently, you should check whether you have any oil leaks. Place some clean paper under the car overnight, and check for stains in the morning. If there are no leaks, then the engine may be burning oil, or the oil may only be leaking when the engine is running.
● Always maintain the level between the upper and lower dipstick marks (see photo 3). If the level is too low, severe engine damage may occur. Oil seal failure may result if the engine is overfilled by adding too much oil.

1 The dipstick is brightly coloured for easy identification (see *Underbonnet check points* for exact location). Withdraw the dipstick.

2 Using a clean rag or paper towel remove all oil from the dipstick. Insert the clean dipstick into the tube as far as it will go, then withdraw it again.

3 Note the level on the end of the dipstick, which should be between the upper (MAX) mark and lower (MIN) mark. Approximately 1.0 litre of oil will raise the level from the lower mark to the upper mark.

4 Oil is added through the filler cap. Unscrew the cap and top-up the level. A funnel may help to reduce spillage. Add the oil slowly, checking the level on the dipstick frequently. Avoid overfilling (see *Car care*).

Coolant level

Warning: Do not attempt to remove the expansion tank pressure cap when the engine is hot, as there is a very great risk of scalding. Do not leave open containers of coolant about, as it is poisonous.

Car Care

● With a sealed-type cooling system, adding coolant should not be necessary on a regular basis. If frequent topping-up is required, it is likely there is a leak. Check the radiator, all hoses and joint faces for signs of staining or wetness, and rectify as necessary.

● It is important that antifreeze is used in the cooling system all year round, not just during the winter months. Don't top up with water alone, as the antifreeze will become diluted.

1 The coolant level varies with the temperature of the engine. When the engine is cold, the coolant level should be slightly above the KALT/COLD mark on the side of the tank. When the engine is hot, the level will rise.

2 If topping-up is necessary, **wait until the engine is cold**. Slowly unscrew the expansion tank cap, to release any pressure present in the cooling system, and remove it.

3 Add a mixture of water and antifreeze to the expansion tank until the coolant is up to the KALT/COLD level mark. Refit the cap and tighten it securely.

Brake and clutch fluid level

Warning: Brake fluid can harm your eyes and damage painted surfaces, so use extreme caution when handling and pouring it. Do not use fluid which has been standing open for some time, as it absorbs moisture from the air, which can cause a dangerous loss of braking effectiveness.

Before you start

✔ Make sure that the car is on level ground.
✔ Cleanliness is of great importance when dealing with the braking system, so take care to clean around the reservoir cap before topping-up. Use only clean brake fluid.

Safety first!

● If the reservoir requires repeated topping-up, this is an indication of a fluid leak somewhere in the system, which should be investigated immediately.
● If a leak is suspected, the car should not be driven until the braking system has been checked. Never take any risks where brakes are concerned.

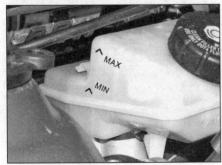

1 The MAX and MIN marks are indicated on the side of the reservoir. The fluid level must be kept between the marks at all times.

2 If topping-up is necessary, first wipe clean the area around the filler cap to prevent dirt entering the hydraulic system. Unscrew the reservoir cap.

3 Carefully add fluid, taking care not to spill it onto the surrounding components. Use only the specified fluid; mixing different types can cause damage to the system. After topping-up to the correct level, securely refit the cap and wipe off any spilt fluid.

Tyre condition and pressure

It is very important that tyres are in good condition, and at the correct pressure - having a tyre failure at any speed is highly dangerous. Tyre wear is influenced by driving style - harsh braking and acceleration, or fast cornering, will all produce more rapid tyre wear. As a general rule, the front tyres wear out faster than the rears. Interchanging the tyres from front to rear ("rotating" the tyres) may result in more even wear. However, if this is completely effective, you may have the expense of replacing all four tyres at once! Remove any nails or stones embedded in the tread before they penetrate the tyre to cause deflation. If removal of a nail does reveal that

the tyre has been punctured, refit the nail so that its point of penetration is marked. Then immediately change the wheel, and have the tyre repaired by a tyre dealer.

Regularly check the tyres for damage in the form of cuts or bulges, especially in the sidewalls. Periodically remove the wheels, and clean any dirt or mud from the inside and outside surfaces. Examine the wheel rims for signs of rusting, corrosion or other damage. Light alloy wheels are easily damaged by "kerbing" whilst parking; steel wheels may also become dented or buckled. A new wheel is very often the only way to overcome severe damage.

New tyres should be balanced when they are fitted, but it may become necessary to re-balance them as they wear, or if the balance weights fitted to the wheel rim should fall off. Unbalanced tyres will wear more quickly, as will the steering and suspension components. Wheel imbalance is normally signified by vibration, particularly at a certain speed (typically around 50 mph). If this vibration is felt only through the steering, then it is likely that just the front wheels need balancing. If, however, the vibration is felt through the whole car, the rear wheels could be out of balance. Wheel balancing should be carried out by a tyre dealer or garage.

1 Tread Depth - visual check
The original tyres have tread wear safety bands (B), which will appear when the tread depth reaches approximately 1.6 mm. The band positions are indicated by a triangular mark on the tyre sidewall (A).

2 Tread Depth - manual check
Alternatively, tread wear can be monitored with a simple, inexpensive device known as a tread depth indicator gauge.

3 Tyre Pressure Check
Check the tyre pressures regularly with the tyres cold. Do not adjust the tyre pressures immediately after the vehicle has been used, or an inaccurate setting will result.

Tyre tread wear patterns

Shoulder Wear

Underinflation (wear on both sides)
Under-inflation will cause overheating of the tyre, because the tyre will flex too much, and the tread will not sit correctly on the road surface. This will cause a loss of grip and excessive wear, not to mention the danger of sudden tyre failure due to heat build-up.
Check and adjust pressures
Incorrect wheel camber (wear on one side)
Repair or renew suspension parts
Hard cornering
Reduce speed!

Centre Wear

Overinflation
Over-inflation will cause rapid wear of the centre part of the tyre tread, coupled with reduced grip, harsher ride, and the danger of shock damage occurring in the tyre casing.
Check and adjust pressures

If you sometimes have to inflate your car's tyres to the higher pressures specified for maximum load or sustained high speed, don't forget to reduce the pressures to normal afterwards.

Uneven Wear

Front tyres may wear unevenly as a result of wheel misalignment. Most tyre dealers and garages can check and adjust the wheel alignment (or "tracking") for a modest charge.
Incorrect camber or castor
Repair or renew suspension parts
Malfunctioning suspension
Repair or renew suspension parts
Unbalanced wheel
Balance tyres
Incorrect toe setting
Adjust front wheel alignment
Note: The feathered edge of the tread which typifies toe wear is best checked by feel.

Washer fluid level

● Screenwash additives not only keep the windscreen clean during bad weather, they also prevent the washer system freezing in cold weather – which is when you are likely to need it most. Don't top-up using plain water, as the screenwash will become diluted, and will freeze in cold weather.

 Warning: On no account use engine coolant antifreeze in the screen washer system – this may damage the paintwork.

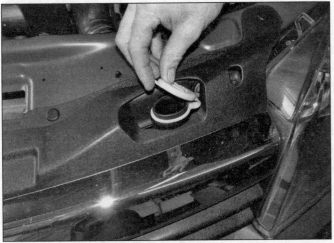

1 The reservoir for the windscreen, rear window and headlight (where applicable) washer systems is located on the front left-hand side of the engine compartment. If topping-up is necessary, open the filler cap.

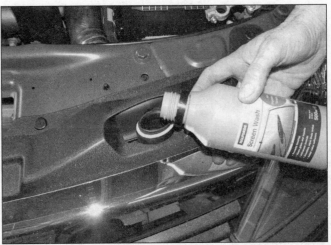

2 When topping-up the reservoir a screenwash additive should be added in the quantities recommended on the bottle.

Wiper blades

1 Check the condition of the wiper blades; if they are cracked or show any signs of deterioration, or if the glass swept area is smeared, renew them. Wiper blades should be renewed annually.

2 To remove a windscreen wiper blade, pull the arm fully away from the screen until it locks. Swivel the blade through 90°, then lift it off the pivot peg on the wiper arm. Don't forget to check the tailgate wiper blade as well which is removed in the same way.

Battery

Caution: Before carrying out any work on the vehicle battery, read the precautions given in 'Safety first!' at the start of this manual. If the battery is to be disconnected, refer to 'Disconnecting the battery' in the Reference Chapter, before proceeding.

✔ Make sure that the battery tray is in good condition, and that the clamp is tight. Corrosion on the tray, retaining clamp and the battery itself can be removed with a solution of water and baking soda. Thoroughly rinse all cleaned areas with water. Any metal parts damaged by corrosion should be covered with a zinc-based primer, then painted.

✔ Periodically (approximately every three months), check the charge condition of the battery as described in Chapter 5A.

✔ If the battery is flat, and you need to jump start your vehicle, see *Roadside Repairs*.

HAYNES HiNT

Battery corrosion can be kept to a minimum by applying a layer of petroleum jelly to the clamps and terminals after they are reconnected.

1 The battery is located at the front, left-hand side of the engine compartment. Where fitted, open the insulation jacket around the battery, then check the tightness of battery clamps to ensure good electrical connections. You should not be able to move them. Also check each cable for cracks and frayed conductors.

2 If corrosion (white, fluffy deposits) is evident, remove the cables from the battery terminals, clean them with a small wire brush, then refit them. Automotive stores sell a tool for cleaning the battery post . . .

3 . . . as well as the battery cable clamps

Electrical systems

✔ Check all external lights and the horn. Refer to the appropriate Sections of Chapter 12 for details if any of the circuits are found to be inoperative.

✔ Visually check all accessible wiring connectors, harnesses and retaining clips for security, and for signs of chafing or damage.

HAYNES HiNT *If you need to check your brake lights and indicators unaided, back up to a wall or garage door and operate the lights. The reflected light should show if they are working properly.*

1 If a single indicator light, stop-light or headlight has failed, it is likely that a bulb has blown and will need to be renewed. Refer to Chapter 12 for details. If both stop-lights have failed, it is possible that the switch has failed (see Chapter 9).

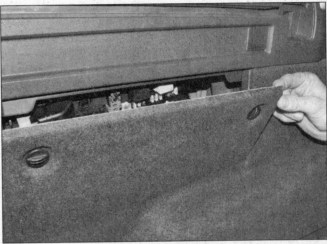

2 If more than one indicator light or headlight has failed, it is likely that either a fuse has blown or that there is a fault in the circuit (see Chapter 12). The main fuses are located behind the trim panel on the left-hand side of the luggage compartment. Turn the catches and open the cover for access to the fuses.

3 Additional fuses and relays are located in the fuse/relay box on the left-hand side of the engine compartment. Refer to the wiring diagrams at the end of Chapter 12 for details of the fuse locations and circuits protected.

4 To renew a blown fuse, remove it, where applicable, using the plastic tool provided. Fit a new fuse of the same rating, available from car accessory shops. It is important that you find the reason that the fuse blew (see *Electrical fault finding* in Chapter 12).

Lubricants and fluids

Engine	Multigrade engine oil, viscosity SAE 0W/30, 0W/40, 5W/30, 5W/40 to specification ACEA B3, ACEA A3/B3 or ACEA A3/B3/B4 or higher
Manual transmission	Vauxhall/Opel gear oil (09 120 541)
Automatic transmission	Vauxhall/Opel automatic transmission fluid (93 165 147)
Power steering reservoir	Vauxhall/Opel steering fluid (90 544 116)
Cooling system	Vauxhall/Opel silicate-free coolant (93 170 402)
Brake/clutch fluid reservoir	Hydraulic fluid to DOT 4

Tyre pressures (cold)

Note: *Pressures apply to original-equipment tyres, and may vary if any other make or type of tyre is fitted; check with the tyre manufacturer or supplier for correct pressures if necessary.*

Normal load (up to 3 passengers)	Front	Rear
1.3 litre models		
185/65 R 15, 195/60 R 15	2.3 bar (33 psi)	2.1 bar (30 psi)
195/65 R 15, 205/55 R 16	2.1 bar (30 psi)	2.1 bar (30 psi)
1.7 litre (Z17DTL engine) models		
185/65 R 15, 195/60 R 15, 215/45 R 17, 225/40 R 18	2.3 bar (33 psi)	2.1 bar (30 psi)
195/65 R 15, 205/55 R 16, 225/45 R 17	2.1 bar (30 psi)	2.1 bar (30 psi)
1.7 litre (Z17DTH engine) models		
195/65 R 15, 205/55 R 16, 225/45 R 17	2.1 bar (30 psi)	2.1 bar (30 psi)
215/45 R 17, 225/40 R 18	2.5 bar (36 psi)	2.3 bar (33 psi)
1.9 litre models		
205/55 R 16, 225/45 R 17	2.3 bar (33 psi)	2.1 bar (30 psi)
215/45 R 17, 225/40 R 18	2.7 bar (39 psi)	2.5 bar (36 psi)
Fully laden		
1.3 litre models		
All tyre sizes	2.5 bar (36 psi)	2.9 bar (42 psi)
1.7 litre (Z17DTL engine) models		
All tyre sizes	2.5 bar (36 psi)	2.9 bar (42 psi)
1.7 litre (Z17DTH engine) models		
195/65 R 15, 205/55 R 16, 225/45 R 17	2.5 bar (36 psi)	2.9 bar (42 psi)
215/45 R 17, 225/40 R 18	2.6 bar (38 psi)	3.0 bar (44 psi)
1.9 litre models		
205/55 R 16, 225/45 R 17	2.5 bar (36 psi)	2.9 bar (42 psi)
215/45 R 17, 225/40 R 18	2.8 bar (41 psi)	3.1 bar (45 psi)
Space-saver temporary spare tyre		
All models	4.2 bar (61 psi)	4.2 bar (61 psi)

Chapter 1
Routine maintenance and servicing

Contents

Degrees of difficulty

| Easy, suitable for novice with little experience | | Fairly easy, suitable for beginner with some experience | | Fairly difficult, suitable for competent DIY mechanic | | Difficult, suitable for experienced DIY mechanic | | Very difficult, suitable for expert DIY or professional | |

Lubricants and fluids................................. Refer to *Weekly checks* on page 0•18

Capacities

Engine oil (including oil filter)
1.3 litre engines .... 3.2 litres
1.7 litre (Z17DTL) engines................................. 4.5 litres
1.7 litre (Z17DTH) engines .... 5.0 litres
1.9 litre engines .... 4.3 litres
Difference between MIN and MAX dipstick marks.............. 1.0 litre

Cooling system
1.3 litre engines .... 7.6 litres
1.7 litre engines .... 6.8 litres
1.9 litre (Z19DT and Z19DTL) engines .... 7.0 litres
1.9 litre (Z19DTH) engines .... 6.2 litres

Transmission
Manual transmission:
   F17+ transmission .... 1.6 litres
   F23 transmission .... 1.75 litres
   M20 and M32 transmissions .... 2.4 litres
Automatic transmission (at fluid change)..................... 3.0 (approximately)

Washer fluid reservoir
Without headlight washers................................... 2.4 litres
With headlight washers .... 4.0 litres

Fuel tank .... 52 litres

Cooling system
Antifreeze mixture:
   50% antifreeze .... Protection down to -40°C

Brakes
Friction material minimum thickness:
   Front brake pads .... 2.0 mm
   Rear brake pads... 2.0 mm

Torque wrench settings

	Nm	lbf ft
Engine oil filter:		
1.3 and 1.7 litre engines	25	18
1.9 litre engines:		
Z19DT and Z19DTH engines	25	18
Z19DTL engines	15	11
Fuel filter housing cover retaining ring (1.3 and 1.9 litre engines)	30	22
Fuel filter housing cover centre bolt (1.7 litre engines)	6	4
Roadwheel bolts	110	81
Sump drain plug:		
1.3 and 1.9 litre engines	20	15
1.7 litre engines	78	58

Maintenance schedule

The maintenance intervals in this manual are provided with the assumption that you, not the dealer, will be carrying out the work. These are the minimum maintenance intervals based on the standard service schedule recommended by the manufacturer for vehicles driven daily. If you wish to keep your vehicle in peak condition at all times, you may wish to perform some of these procedures more often. We encourage

frequent maintenance, because it enhances the efficiency, performance and resale value of your vehicle.

If the vehicle is driven in dusty areas, used to tow a trailer, or driven frequently at slow speeds (idling in traffic) or on short journeys, more frequent maintenance intervals are recommended.

When the vehicle is new, it should be

serviced by a dealer service department (or other workshop recognised by the vehicle manufacturer as providing the same standard of service) in order to preserve the warranty. The vehicle manufacturer may reject warranty claims if you are unable to prove that servicing has been carried out as and when specified, using only original equipment parts or parts certified to be of equivalent quality.

Every 250 miles or weekly

☐ Refer to *Weekly checks*

Every 9000 miles or 6 months – whichever comes first

☐ Renew the engine oil and filter (Section 3)

Note: *Vauxhall/Opel recommend that the engine oil and filter are changed every 18 000 miles or 12 months if the vehicle is being operated under the standard service schedule. However, oil and filter changes are good for the engine and we recommend that the oil and filter are renewed more frequently, especially if the vehicle is used on a lot of short journeys.*

Every 18 000 miles or 12 months – whichever comes first

☐ Check all underbonnet and underbody components, pipes and hoses for leaks (Section 4)
☐ Drain the water from the fuel filter (Section 5)
☐ Check the power steering fluid level (Section 6)
☐ Check the condition of the brake pads (renew if necessary), the calipers and discs (Section 7)
☐ Check the condition of all brake fluid pipes and hoses (Section 8)
☐ Check the condition of the front suspension and steering components, particularly the rubber gaiters and seals (Section 9)
☐ Check the condition of the driveshaft joint gaiters, and the driveshaft joints (Section 10)
☐ Check the condition of the exhaust system components (Section 11)
☐ Check the condition of the rear suspension components (Section 12)
☐ Check the bodywork and underbody for damage and corrosion, and check the condition of the underbody corrosion protection (Section 13)
☐ Check the tightness of the roadwheel bolts (Section 14)
☐ Lubricate all door, bonnet and tailgate hinges and locks (Section 15)
☐ Check the operation of the horn, all lights, and the wipers and washers (Section 16)
☐ Carry out a road test (Section 17)
☐ Reset the service interval indicator (Section 18)

Every 36 000 miles or 2 years – whichever comes first

☐ Renew the pollen filter (Section 19)
☐ Renew the fuel filter (Section 20)
☐ Check the auxiliary drivebelt and tensioner (Section 21)
☐ Check, and if necessary adjust, the valve clearances – 1.9 litre SOHC engines (Section 22)
☐ Check the operation of the handbrake and adjust if necessary (Section 23)
☐ Check the headlight beam alignment (Section 24)

Every 2 years, regardless of mileage

☐ Renew the battery for the remote control handset (Section 25)
☐ Renew the brake and clutch fluid (Section 26)
☐ Renew the coolant (Section 27)*
☐ Exhaust emission test (Section 28)

* Note: *Vehicles using Vauxhall/Opel silicate-free coolant do not need the coolant renewed on a regular basis.*

Every 36 000 miles or 4 years – whichever comes first

☐ Renew the air cleaner filter element (Section 29)
☐ Renew the timing belt, tensioner and idler pulleys – 1.7 and 1.9 litre engines (Section 30)*

* Note: *The normal interval for timing belt renewal is 60 000 miles or 10 years for the 1.7 litre Z17DTH engines, or 90 000 miles or 10 years for all other engines. However, it is strongly recommended that the interval used is 36 000 miles on vehicles which are subjected to intensive use, ie, mainly short journeys or a lot of stop-start driving. The actual belt renewal interval is therefore very much up to the individual owner, but bear in mind that severe engine damage will result if the belt breaks.*

Every 48 000 miles or 6 years – whichever comes first

☐ Renew the automatic transmission fluid (Section 31)

Every 72 000 miles or 10 years – whichever comes first

☐ Renew the auxiliary drivebelt – 1.9 litre engines (Section 32)

Every 90 000 miles or 10 years – whichever comes first

☐ Check, and if necessary adjust, the valve clearances – 1.7 litre engines (Section 33)
☐ Renew the auxiliary drivebelt – 1.3 and 1.7 litre engines (Section 34)

Underbonnet view of a 1.3 litre engine model

1 Engine oil level dipstick
2 Engine oil filler cap
3 Air cleaner assembly
4 Front suspension strut upper mounting
5 Washer fluid reservoir
6 Airflow meter
7 Brake (and clutch) fluid reservoir
8 Fuel filter
9 Coolant expansion tank
10 Battery
11 Fuse/relay box

Underbonnet view of a 1.7 litre engine model

1 Engine oil level dipstick
2 Engine oil filler cap
3 Air cleaner assembly
4 Front suspension strut upper mounting
5 Washer fluid reservoir
6 Airflow meter
7 Brake (and clutch) fluid reservoir
8 Fuel filter
9 Power steering fluid reservoir
10 Coolant expansion tank
11 Battery
12 Fuse/relay box

Underbonnet view of a 1.9 litre DOHC engine model

1 Engine oil level dipstick
2 Engine oil filler cap
3 Air cleaner assembly
4 Front suspension strut upper mounting
5 Washer fluid reservoir
6 Airflow meter
7 Brake (and clutch) fluid reservoir
8 Fuel filter
9 Coolant expansion tank
10 Battery
11 Fuse/relay box

Front underbody view

1 Exhaust front pipe
2 Steering track rods
3 Front suspension lower arms
4 Front brake calipers
5 Engine mounting front torque link
6 Engine mounting rear torque link
7 Right-hand driveshaft/ intermediate shaft
8 Manual transmission
9 Engine oil drain plug
10 Alternator
11 Front subframe

Rear underbody view

1 Exhaust tailpipe and silencer
2 Rear suspension torsion beam and trailing arms
3 Fuel tank
4 Handbrake cables
5 Spare wheel well
6 Rear coil springs
7 Rear shock absorber lower mountings

Maintenance procedures

1 General information

1 This Chapter is designed to help the home mechanic maintain his/her vehicle for safety, economy, long life and peak performance.
2 The Chapter contains a master maintenance schedule, followed by Sections dealing specifically with each task in the schedule. Visual checks, adjustments, component renewal and other helpful items are included. Refer to the accompanying illustrations of the engine compartment and the underside of the vehicle for the locations of the various components.
3 Servicing your vehicle in accordance with the mileage/time maintenance schedule and the following Sections will provide a planned maintenance programme, which should result in a long and reliable service life. This is a comprehensive plan, so maintaining some items but not others at the specified service intervals, will not produce the same results.
4 As you service your vehicle, you will discover that many of the procedures can – and should – be grouped together, because of the particular procedure being performed, or because of the proximity of two otherwise-unrelated components to one another. For example, if the vehicle is raised for any reason, the exhaust can be inspected at the same time as the suspension and steering components.
5 The first step in this maintenance programme

is to prepare yourself before the actual work begins. Read through all the Sections relevant to the work to be carried out, then make a list and gather all the parts and tools required. If a problem is encountered, seek advice from a parts specialist, or a dealer service department.

2 Regular maintenance

1 If, from the time the vehicle is new, the routine maintenance schedule is followed closely, and frequent checks are made of fluid levels and high-wear items, as suggested throughout this manual, the engine will be kept in relatively good running condition, and the need for additional work will be minimised.
2 It is possible that there will be times when the engine is running poorly due to the lack of regular maintenance. This is even more likely if a used vehicle, which has not received regular and frequent maintenance checks, is purchased. In such cases, additional work may need to be carried out, outside of the regular maintenance intervals. ·
3 If engine wear is suspected, a compression test (refer to the appropriate part of Chapter 2) will provide valuable information regarding the overall performance of the main internal components. Such a test can be used as a basis to decide on the extent of the work to be carried out. If, for example, a compression test indicates serious

internal engine wear, conventional maintenance as described in this Chapter will not greatly improve the performance of the engine, and may prove a waste of time and money, unless extensive overhaul work is carried out first.
4 The following series of operations are those most often required to improve the performance of a generally poor-running engine:

Primary operations

a) Clean, inspect and test the battery (refer to Weekly checks).
b) Check all the engine-related fluids (refer to Weekly checks).
c) Check the condition and tension of the auxiliary drivebelt (Section 21).
d) Check the condition of the air cleaner element and renew if necessary (Section 29).
e) Renew the fuel filter (Section 20).
f) Check the condition of all hoses, and check for fluid leaks (Section 4).

5 If the above operations do not prove fully effective, carry out the following secondary operations:

Secondary operations

All items listed under *Primary operations*, plus the following:
a) Check the charging system (refer to Chapter 5).
b) Check the pre/post-heating system (refer to Chapter 5).
c) Check the fuel, exhaust and emission control systems (refer to the appropriate Parts of Chapter 4).

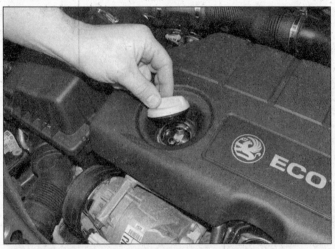

3.3 Removing the oil filler cap

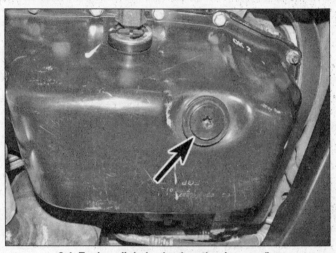

3.4 Engine oil drain plug location (arrowed) – 1.3 litre engines

Every 9000 miles or 6 months

3 Engine oil and filter renewal

HAYNES HiNT *Frequent oil and filter changes are the most important preventative maintenance procedures which can be undertaken by the DIY owner. As engine oil ages, it becomes diluted and contaminated, which leads to premature engine wear.*

1 Before starting this procedure, gather together all the necessary tools and materials. Also make sure that you have plenty of clean rags and newspapers handy to mop-up any spills. Ideally, the engine oil should be warm, as it will drain more easily, and more built-up sludge will be removed with it. Take care not to touch the exhaust or any other hot parts of the engine when working under the vehicle. To avoid any possibility of scalding, and to protect yourself from possible skin irritants and other harmful contaminants in used engine oils, it is advisable to wear gloves when carrying out this work.

2 Access to the underside of the vehicle will be greatly improved if it can be raised on a lift, driven onto ramps, or jacked up and supported on axle stands (see *Jacking and vehicle support*). Whichever method is chosen, make sure that the vehicle remains level, or if it is at an angle, that the drain plug is at the lowest point. Where fitted, remove the screws and clips and remove the engine undertray for access.

3 Remove the oil filler cap from the camshaft cover (twist it through a quarter-turn anti-clockwise and withdraw it) **(see illustration)**.

4 Using a spanner, or preferably a suitable socket and bar, slacken the drain plug about half a turn **(see illustration)**. Position the draining container under the drain plug, then remove the plug completely **(see Haynes Hint)**.

5 Allow some time for the oil to drain, noting that it may be necessary to reposition the container as the oil flow slows to a trickle.

6 Position another container under the oil filter. On 1.3 litre engines the oil filter is located at the front of the engine and is accessible from above. On 1.7 litre engines the oil filter is located at the rear of the engine and is also accessible from above. On 1.9 litre engines, the oil filter is located at the rear of the engine and is accessible from under the car. Proceed as described under the following sub-Sections, according to engine.

1.3 and 1.7 litre engines

7 On 1.3 litre engines, undo the nut and two screws and remove the metal heat shield located over the filter housing **(see illustration)**.

8 Using a large socket, unscrew the cover and remove it from the top of the oil filter housing **(see illustration)**. Lift out the old filter element.

9 Wipe clean the oil filter cover and the filter housing.

10 Lubricate the sealing rings of the new filter with clean engine oil, then insert the filter into the housing or cover **(see illustrations)**.

11 Renew the sealing ring on the oil filter cover, and lubricate the new sealing ring with

HAYNES HiNT

As the drain plug releases from the threads, move it away quickly so that the stream of oil running out of the sump goes into the drain pan and not up your sleeve.

3.7 Undo the nut and two screws (arrowed) and remove the metal heat shield located over the filter housing – 1.3 litre engines

3.8 Unscrew the cover and remove it from the top of the oil filter housing

3.10a Lubricate the sealing rings of the new filter . . .

3.10b . . . then insert the filter into the housing – 1.3 litre engines . . .

3.10c . . . or cover – 1.7 litre engines

3.11a Renew the sealing ring on the oil filter cover . . .

3.11b . . . and lubricate the new sealing ring

3.12a Unscrew the filter cap and withdraw it together with the element . . .

clean engine oil **(see illustrations)**. Refit the oil filter cover and tighten it to the specified torque. On 1.3 litre engines, refit the heat shield over the filter housing.

1.9 litre engines

12 Unscrew the filter housing cover and withdraw it, together with the element, then separate the element, and remove the two O-ring seals from the cover **(see illustrations)**.
13 Use a clean rag to remove all oil, dirt and sludge from the oil filter housing and cover.
14 Locate the new O-ring seals in their grooves on the housing cover, then locate the new element in the cover and insert them both in the filter housing. Screw on the cover and tighten to the specified torque.

All engines

15 After all the oil has drained, wipe the drain plug and the sealing washer/O-ring with a clean rag. Examine the condition of the sealing washer/O-ring, and renew it if it shows signs of damage which may prevent an oil-tight seal. Clean the area around the drain plug opening, and refit the plug complete with the washer/O-ring. Tighten the plug to the specified torque, using a torque wrench.
16 Remove the old oil and all tools from under the vehicle then refit the undertray (where applicable) and lower the vehicle to the ground.
17 Fill the engine through the filler hole in the camshaft cover, using the correct grade and type of oil (refer to *Weekly checks* for details of topping-up). Pour in half the specified quantity of oil first, then wait a few minutes for the oil to drain into the sump. Continue to add oil, a small quantity at a time, until the level is up to the lower mark on the dipstick. Adding

approximately a further 1.0 litre will bring the level up to the upper mark on the dipstick.
18 Start the engine and run it until it reaches normal operating temperature. While the engine is warming-up, check for leaks around the oil filter and the sump drain plug.
19 Stop the engine, and wait at least five minutes for the oil to settle in the sump once more. With the new oil circulated and the filter now completely full, recheck the level on the dipstick, and add more oil as necessary.
20 Dispose of the used engine oil and filter safely, with reference to *General repair procedures* in the Reference Chapter of this manual. Do not discard the old filter with domestic household waste. The facility for waste oil disposal provided by many local council refuse tips and/or recycling centres generally has a filter receptacle alongside.

3.12b . . . then separate the element from the cap . . .

3.12c . . . and remove the two O-ring seals – 1.9 litre engines

Every 18 000 miles or 12 months

4 Hose and fluid leak check

1 Visually inspect the engine joint faces, gaskets and seals for any signs of water or oil leaks. Pay particular attention to the areas around the camshaft cover, cylinder head, oil filter and sump joint faces. Similarly, check the transmission and (where applicable) the air conditioning compressor for oil leakage. Bear in mind that, over a period of time, some very slight seepage from these areas is to be expected; what you are really looking for is any indication of a serious leak. Should a leak be found, renew the offending gasket or oil seal by referring to the appropriate Chapters in this manual.

2 Also check the security and condition of all the engine-related pipes and hoses. Ensure that all cable ties or securing clips are in place, and in good condition. Clips which are broken or missing can lead to chafing of the hoses pipes or wiring, which could cause more serious problems in the future.

3 Carefully check the radiator hoses and heater hoses along their entire length. Renew any hose which is cracked, swollen or deteriorated. Cracks will show up better if the hose is squeezed. Pay close attention to the hose clips that secure the hoses to the cooling system components. Hose clips can pinch and puncture hoses, resulting in cooling system leaks. If wire-type hose clips are used, it may be a good idea to update them with screw-type clips.

4 Inspect all the cooling system components (hoses, joint faces, etc) for leaks. Where any problems of this nature are found on system components, renew the component or gasket with reference to Chapter 3 **(see Haynes Hint)**.

5 Where applicable, inspect the automatic transmission fluid cooler hoses for leaks or deterioration.

6 With the vehicle raised, inspect the fuel tank and filler neck for punctures, cracks and other damage. The connection between the filler neck and tank is especially critical. Sometimes, a rubber filler neck or connecting hose will leak due to loose retaining clamps or deteriorated rubber.

7 Carefully check all rubber hoses and metal or plastic fuel lines leading away from the fuel tank. Check for loose connections, deteriorated hoses, crimped lines and other damage. Pay particular attention to the vent pipes and hoses, which often loop up around the filler neck and can become blocked or crimped. Follow the lines to the front of the vehicle, carefully inspecting them all the way. Renew damaged sections as necessary. Similarly, whilst the vehicle is raised, take the opportunity to inspect all underbody brake fluid pipes and hoses.

8 From within the engine compartment, check the security of all fuel hose attachments and pipe unions, and inspect the fuel hoses and vacuum hoses for kinks, chafing and deterioration.

5 Fuel filter water draining

Caution: Before starting any work on the fuel filter, wipe clean the filter assembly and the area around it; it is essential that no dirt or other foreign matter is allowed into the system. Obtain a suitable container into which the filter can be drained and place rags or similar material under the filter assembly to catch any spillages. Do not allow diesel fuel to contaminate components such as the alternator and starter motor, the coolant hoses and engine mountings, and any wiring.

1 The fuel filter is located at the rear of the engine compartment, in the centre of the bulkhead.

2 Disconnect the heater element wiring connector from the fuel filter cover and, where fitted, the water level sensor wiring connector from the base of the filter housing **(see illustrations)**.

3 Using a screwdriver inserted from the right-hand side, depress the retaining clip and lift the filter from the crash box **(see**

A leak in the cooling system will usually show up as white- or antifreeze-coloured deposits on the area adjoining the leak.

illustration). It may be necessary to release the fuel hoses from their support clips to provide sufficient clearance to lift out the filter.

4 In addition to taking the precautions noted above to catch any fuel spillages, connect a tube to the drain screw on the base of the fuel filter **(see illustration)**. Place the other end of the tube in a clean jar or can.

5 Loosen the drain screw approximately one complete turn and allow the filter to drain until clean fuel, free of dirt or water, emerges from the tube (approximately 100 cc is usually sufficient). Note that on 1.7 litre engines, it maybe necessary to slacken the filter housing cover bolt to allow the fuel to drain.

6 Remove the drain tube, then tighten the drain screw, and where necessary the housing cover screw, securely.

5.2a Disconnect the heater element wiring connector from the fuel filter cover . . .

5.2b . . . and the water level sensor wiring connector from the base of the filter housing

5.3 Depress the retaining clip and lift the filter from the crash box

5.4 Fuel filter drain screw (arrowed)

6.2 Power steering fluid reservoir filler cap (arrowed)

7 Insert the filter in the crash box making sure that the retaining clip engages.
8 Reconnect the wiring and secure the fuel hoses in their support clips (if disturbed).
9 On completion, dispose of the drained fuel safely. Check all disturbed components to ensure that there are no leaks (of air or fuel) when the engine is restarted.

6 Power steering fluid level check

1 The power steering fluid reservoir is located on RHD vehicles on the left-hand side of the engine compartment between the transmission and the bulkhead. On LHD vehicles, the reservoir is located between the engine and bulkhead on the right-hand side of the engine compartment. The fluid level should be checked with the cold.
2 Wipe clean the reservoir and filler cap, then unscrew the filler cap from the top of the reservoir **(see illustration)**. The filler cap has a bayonet fitting and has a dipstick incorporated into it.
3 Wipe all fluid from the dipstick with a clean rag. Refit the dipstick, then remove it again. Note the fluid level on the dipstick which should be up to the MAX mark **(see illustration)**.
4 If topping-up is necessary, obtain a clean funnel and a long length of flexible pipe to fit the end of the funnel. Insert the pipe

For a quick check, the thickness of friction material remaining on the inner brake pad can be measured through the aperture in the caliper body.

6.3 The fluid level should be up to the MAX mark (arrowed) on the dipstick

down behind the engine and into the top of the reservoir **(see illustration)**. Using power steering fluid of the specified type (see *Lubricants and fluids*), top-up the reservoir by means of the funnel and tube until the level is up to the MAX mark on the dipstick. Do this slowly and carefully, checking the level with the dipstick frequently. Take care not to overfill the reservoir.
5 When the level is correct, remove the funnel and tube and refit the reservoir filler cap.

7 Brake pad and disc check

1 Firmly apply the handbrake, then jack up the front and rear of the vehicle and support it securely on axle stands (see *Jacking and vehicle support*). Remove the roadwheels.
2 For a quick check, the pad thickness can be carried out via the inspection hole on the caliper **(see Haynes Hint)**. Using a steel rule, measure the thickness of the pad friction linings. This must not be less than that indicated in the Specifications.
3 The view through the caliper inspection hole gives a rough indication of the state of the brake pads. For a comprehensive check, the brake pads should be removed and cleaned. The operation of the caliper can then also be checked, and the condition of the brake disc itself can be fully examined on both sides. Chapter 9 contains a detailed description of how the brake disc should be checked for wear and/or damage.

9.4 Check for wear in the hub bearings by grasping the wheel and trying to rock it

6.4 Use a clean funnel and a long length of flexible pipe to top-up the reservoir

4 If any pad's friction material is worn to the specified thickness or less, *all four pads must be renewed as a set*. Refer to Chapter 9 for details.
5 On completion, refit the roadwheels and lower the vehicle to the ground.

8 Brake fluid pipe and hose check

1 The brake hydraulic system includes a number of metal pipes, which run from the master cylinder to the hydraulic modulator of the anti-lock braking system (ABS) and then to the front and rear brake assemblies. Flexible hoses are fitted between the pipes and the front and rear brake assemblies, to allow for steering and suspension movement.
2 When checking the system, first look for signs of leakage at the pipe or hose unions, then examine the flexible hoses for signs of cracking, chafing or deterioration of the rubber. Bend the hoses sharply between the fingers (but do not actually bend them double, or the casing may be damaged) and check that this does not reveal previously-hidden cracks, cuts or splits. Check that the pipes and hoses are securely fastened in their clips.
3 Carefully working along the length of the metal pipes, look for dents, kinks, damage of any sort, or corrosion. Light corrosion can be polished off, but if the depth of pitting is significant, the pipe must be renewed.

9 Front suspension and steering check

1 Apply the handbrake, then raise the front of the vehicle and securely support it on axle stands (see *Jacking and vehicle support*).
2 Inspect the balljoint dust covers and the steering gear gaiters for splits, chafing or deterioration.
3 Any wear of these components will cause loss of lubricant, and may allow water to enter the components, resulting in rapid deterioration of the balljoints or steering gear.
4 Grasp each roadwheel at the 12 o'clock and 6 o'clock positions, and try to rock it **(see illustration)**. Very slight free play may

be felt, but if the movement is appreciable, further investigation is necessary to determine the source. Continue rocking the wheel while an assistant depresses the footbrake. If the movement is now eliminated or significantly reduced, it is likely that the hub bearings are at fault. If the free play is still evident with the footbrake depressed, then there is wear in the suspension joints or mountings.

5 Now grasp each wheel at the 9 o'clock and 3 o'clock positions, and try to rock it as before. Any movement felt now may again be caused by wear in the hub bearings or the steering track rod end balljoints. If the track rod end balljoint is worn, the visual movement will be obvious.

6 Using a large screwdriver or flat bar, check for wear in the suspension mounting bushes by levering between the relevant suspension component and its attachment point. Some movement is to be expected, as the mountings are made of rubber, but excessive wear should be obvious. Also check the condition of any visible rubber bushes, looking for splits, cracks or contamination of the rubber.

7 Check for any signs of fluid leakage around the suspension struts, or from the rubber gaiters around the piston rods. Should any fluid be noticed, the suspension strut is defective internally, and should be renewed. **Note:** *Suspension struts should always be renewed in pairs on the same axle.*

8 With the vehicle standing on its wheels, have an assistant turn the steering wheel back-and-forth about an eighth of a turn each way. There should be very little, if any, lost movement between the steering wheel and roadwheels. If this is not the case, closely observe the joints and mountings previously described. In addition, check the steering column universal joints for wear, and also check the rack-and-pinion steering gear itself.

9 The efficiency of each suspension strut may be checked by bouncing the vehicle at each front corner. Generally speaking, the body will

return to its normal position and stop after being depressed. If it rises and returns on a rebound, the suspension strut is probably suspect. Also examine the suspension strut upper mountings for any signs of wear.

10 Driveshaft check

1 Firmly apply the handbrake, then jack up the front of the car and support it securely on axle stands (see *Jacking and vehicle support*).

2 Turn the steering onto full lock then slowly rotate the roadwheel. Inspect the condition of the outer constant velocity (CV) joint rubber gaiters while squeezing the gaiters to open out the folds **(see illustration)**. Check for signs of cracking, splits or deterioration of the rubber which may allow the grease to escape and lead to water and grit entry into the joint. Also check the security and condition of the retaining clips. Repeat these checks on the inner CV joints. If any damage or deterioration is found, the gaiters should be renewed as described in Chapter 8.

3 At the same time, check the general condition of the CV joints themselves by first holding the driveshaft and attempting to rotate the wheel. Repeat this check by holding the inner joint and attempting to rotate the driveshaft. Any appreciable movement indicates wear in the joints, wear in the driveshaft splines or loose driveshaft retaining nut.

11 Exhaust system check

1 With the engine cold (at least an hour after the vehicle has been driven), check the complete exhaust system from the engine to

the end of the tailpipe. The exhaust system is most easily checked with the vehicle raised on a hoist, or suitably-supported on axle stands, so that the exhaust components are readily visible and accessible (see *Jacking and vehicle support*).

2 Check the exhaust pipes and connections for evidence of leaks, severe corrosion and damage. Make sure that all brackets and mountings are in good condition, and that all relevant nuts and bolts are tight. Leakage at any of the joints or in other parts of the system will usually show up as a black sooty stain in the vicinity of the leak.

3 Rattles and other noises can often be traced to the exhaust system, especially the brackets and mountings **(see illustration)**. Try to move the pipes and silencers. If the components are able to come into contact with the body or suspension parts, secure the system with new mountings. Otherwise separate the joints (if possible) and twist the pipes as necessary to provide additional clearance.

12 Rear suspension check

1 Chock the front wheels, then jack up the rear of the vehicle and support securely on axle stands (see *Jacking and vehicle support*).

2 Inspect the rear suspension components for any signs of obvious wear or damage. Pay particular attention to the rubber mounting bushes, and renew if necessary (see Chapter 10).

3 Grasp each roadwheel at the 12 o'clock and 6 o'clock positions **(see illustration 9.4)**, and try to rock it. Any excess movement indicates wear in the wheel bearings. Wear may also be accompanied by a rumbling sound when the wheel is spun, or a noticeable roughness if the wheel is turned slowly. The wheel bearing can be renewed as described in Chapter 10.

10.2 Check the condition of the driveshaft gaiters (1) and the retaining clips (2)

11.3 Exhaust mountings

4 Check for any signs of fluid leakage around the shock absorber bodies. Should any fluid be noticed, the shock absorber is defective internally, and should be renewed. **Note:** *Shock absorbers should always be renewed in pairs on the same axle.*

5 With the vehicle standing on its wheels, the efficiency of each shock absorber may be checked by bouncing the vehicle at each rear corner. Generally speaking, the body will return to its normal position and stop after being depressed. If it rises and returns on a rebound, the shock absorber is probably suspect.

13 Bodywork and underbody condition check

Note: *This work should be carried out by a Vauxhall/Opel dealer in order to validate the vehicle warranty. The work includes a thorough inspection of the vehicle paintwork and underbody for damage and corrosion.*

Bodywork check

1 Once the car has been washed, and all tar spots and other surface blemishes have been cleaned off, carefully check all paintwork, looking closely for chips or scratches. Pay particular attention to vulnerable areas such as the front panels (bonnet and spoiler), and around the wheel arches. Any damage to the paintwork must be rectified as soon as possible, to comply with the terms of the manufacturer's anti-corrosion warranties; check with a Vauxhall/Opel dealer for details.

2 If a chip or light scratch is found which is recent and still free from rust, it can be touched-up using the appropriate touch-up stick which can be obtained from Vauxhall/Opel dealers. Any more serious damage, or rusted stone chips, can be repaired as described in Chapter 11, but if damage or corrosion is so severe that a panel must be renewed, seek professional advice as soon as possible.

3 Always check that the door and ventilation opening drain holes and pipes are completely clear, so that water can drain out.

Corrosion protection check

4 The wax-based underbody protective coating should be inspected annually, preferably just prior to Winter, when the underbody should be washed down as thoroughly as possible without disturbing the protective coating. Any damage to the coating should be repaired using a suitable wax-based sealer. If any of the body panels are disturbed for repair or renewal, do not forget to re-apply the coating. Wax should be injected into door cavities, sills and box sections, to maintain the level of protection provided by the vehicle manufacturer – seek the advice of a Vauxhall/Opel dealer.

14 Roadwheel bolt tightness check

1 Where applicable, remove the wheel trims from the wheels.
2 Using a torque wrench on each wheel bolt in turn, ensure that the bolts are tightened to the specified torque.
3 Where applicable, refit the wheel trims on completion, making sure they are fitted correctly.

15 Hinge and lock lubrication

1 Work around the vehicle and lubricate the hinges of the bonnet, doors, boot lid and tailgate with a light machine oil.
2 Lightly lubricate the bonnet release mechanism and exposed section of inner cable with a smear of grease.
3 Check the security and operation of all hinges, latches and locks, adjusting them where required. Check the operation of the central locking system.
4 Check the condition and operation of the bonnet and tailgate support struts, renewing them both if either is leaking or no longer able to support the bonnet/tailgate securely when raised.

16 Electrical systems check

1 Check the operation of all the electrical equipment, ie, lights, direction indicators, horn, etc. Refer to the appropriate sections of Chapter 12 for details if any of the circuits are found to be inoperative.
2 Note that the stop-light switch is described in Chapter 9.
3 Check all accessible wiring connectors, harnesses and retaining clips for security, and for signs of chafing or damage. Rectify any faults found.

17 Road test

Instruments and electrical equipment

1 Check the operation of all instruments, warning lights and electrical equipment.
2 Make sure that all instruments read correctly, and switch on all electrical equipment in turn, to check that it functions properly.

Steering and suspension

3 Check for any abnormalities in the steering, suspension, handling or road 'feel'.
4 Drive the vehicle, and check that there are no unusual vibrations or noises.

5 Check that the steering feels positive, with no excessive 'sloppiness', or roughness, and check for any suspension noises when cornering and driving over bumps.

Drivetrain

6 Check the performance of the engine, clutch, transmission and driveshafts.
7 Listen for any unusual noises from the engine, clutch and transmission.
8 Make sure that the engine runs smoothly when idling, and that there is no hesitation when accelerating.
9 Check that, where applicable, the clutch action is smooth and progressive, that the drive is taken up smoothly, and that the pedal travel is not excessive. Also listen for any noises when the clutch pedal is depressed.
10 Check that all gears can be engaged smoothly without noise, and that the gear lever action is smooth and not abnormally vague or 'notchy'.
11 On automatic transmission models, make sure that all gearchanges occur smoothly, without snatching, and without an increase in engine speed between changes. Check that all of the gear positions can be selected with the vehicle at rest. If any problems are found, they should be referred to a Vauxhall/Opel dealer.
12 Listen for a metallic clicking sound from the front of the vehicle, as the vehicle is driven slowly in a circle with the steering on full-lock. Carry out this check in both directions. If a clicking noise is heard, this indicates wear in a driveshaft joint (see Chapter 8).

Braking system

13 Make sure that the vehicle does not pull to one side when braking.
14 Check that there is no vibration through the steering when braking.
15 Check that the handbrake operates correctly, without excessive movement of the lever, and that it holds the vehicle stationary on a slope.
16 Test the operation of the brake servo unit as follows. Depress the footbrake four or five times to exhaust the vacuum, then start the engine. As the engine starts, there should be a noticeable 'give' in the brake pedal as vacuum builds-up. Allow the engine to run for at least two minutes, and then switch it off. If the brake pedal is now depressed again, it should be possible to detect a hiss from the servo as the pedal is depressed. After about four or five applications, no further hissing should be heard, and the pedal should feel considerably harder.

18 Service interval indicator reset

1.3 and 1.7 litre engines

1 With the ignition switched off, the display on the instrument panel must show the trip odometer.

2 With the ignition still switched off, depress and hold the trip odometer reset button located on the instrument panel.
3 With the reset button depressed, switch on the ignition, wait until the service interval display changes (approximately 10 seconds).
4 After approximately 10 seconds the display will show the service symbol and the maximum mileage before the next required service, followed by 'InSP'. When '- - -' appears in the display, release the reset button and switch off

the ignition. When the button is released, the odometer reading will appear again.

1.9 litre engines

5 With the ignition switched off, the display on the instrument panel must show the trip odometer.
6 With the ignition still switched off, depress and hold the trip odometer reset button located on the instrument panel. The service interval indicator will appear after approximately 2 seconds.

7 With the reset button still depressed, also depress the brake pedal, then switch on the ignition. 'InSP - - -' will appear in the display.
8 After approximately 10 seconds the display will show 'InSP' and the maximum mileage before the next required service. Release the reset button and switch off the ignition. When the button is released, the odometer reading will appear again.

Every 36 000 miles or 2 years

19 Pollen filter renewal

1 Remove the glovebox as described in Chapter 11.
2 Undo the two screws and remove the facia lower panel below the glovebox **(see illustration)**.
3 Release the expanding rivet and remove the passenger's side footwell air duct **(see illustration)**.
4 Undo the three screws and remove the pollen filter access cover from the side of the heater/ventilation air distribution housing **(see illustration)**.
5 Withdraw the pollen filter from the housing **(see illustration)**.
6 Fit the new filter using a reversal of the removal procedure; make sure that the filter is

fitted the correct way up, as indicated on the edge of the filter.

20 Fuel filter renewal

Caution: Before starting any work on the fuel filter, wipe clean the filter assembly and the area around it; it is essential that no dirt or other foreign matter is allowed into the system. Obtain a suitable container into which the filter can be drained and place rags or similar material under the filter assembly to catch any spillages. Do not allow diesel fuel to contaminate components such as the starter motor, the coolant hoses and engine mountings, and any wiring.

1.3 and 1.9 litre engines

Note: *Vauxhall/Opel special tool EN-46784-010,*

or a suitable alternative will be required to unscrew the filter housing cover retaining ring.
1 The fuel filter is located at the rear of the engine compartment, in the centre of the bulkhead.
2 Disconnect the heater element wiring connector from the fuel filter cover, and the water level sensor wiring connector from the base of the filter housing **(see illustrations 5.2a and 5.2b)**.
3 Detach the two fuel hose quick-release connectors and remove the hoses from the fuel filter housing and cover. A Vauxhall/Opel special tool (KM-796-A) is available to disconnect the hose connectors, but provided care is taken, the connections can be released using two screwdrivers, a pair of long-nosed pliers, or similar, to depress the retaining tangs **(see illustrations)**. Suitably cover or plug the open hose connections to prevent dirt entry.
4 Using a screwdriver inserted from the

19.2 Undo the two screws and remove the facia lower panel below the glovebox

19.3 Release the expanding rivet and remove the passenger's side footwell air duct

19.4 Undo the three screws and remove the pollen filter access cover from the side of the air distribution housing

19.5 Withdraw the pollen filter from the housing

20.3a Depress the quick-release connector retaining tangs and . . .

20.3b . . . remove the hoses from the fuel filter housing cover – 1.3 and 1.9 litre engines

20.7 Using a home-made tool to slacken the filter housing cover retaining ring – 1.3 and 1.9 litre engines

20.9a Unscrew and remove the cover retaining ring . . .

20.9b . . . then lift the cover together with the filter element . . .

20.9c . . . and recover the O-ring seal – 1.3 and 1.9 litre engines

20.10 Turn the filter element approximately 50° anti-clockwise to release it from the cover – 1.3 and 1.9 litre engines

right-hand side, depress the retaining clip and lift the filter housing from the crash box.

5 Loosen the drain screw on the base of the filter housing one complete turn and drain the fuel into a suitable container. Tighten the drain screw securely once the filter has drained.

6 Lay the filter on its side and clamp the two filter housing mounting lugs in a soft-jawed vice. Take great care not to damage the lugs and only tighten the vice sufficiently to hold the housing while the cover retaining ring is slackened.

7 Slacken the filter housing cover retaining ring using the Vauxhall/Opel special tool or a suitable alternative (see illustration).

8 Reposition the filter housing vertically in the vice and tighten the vice lightly.

9 Fully unscrew the cover retaining ring, then lift the cover together with the filter element from the housing. Recover the O-ring seal (see illustrations).

10 Turn the filter element approximately 50° anti-clockwise to release it from the cover (see illustration).

11 Empty the fuel from the filter housing, then thoroughly clean the housing and cover with a lint-free cloth.

12 Align the arrow on the new filter element with the corresponding arrow on the cover then push the filter onto the cover until it locks in position (see illustrations).

13 Locate a new O-ring seal on the filter housing, then fit the element and cover to the housing (see illustrations).

14 Lubricate the threads of the retaining ring with a little diesel fuel then screw the ring onto the housing. Reposition the housing horizontally in the vice as before, and tighten

20.12a Align the arrow on the new filter element with the corresponding arrow on the cover . . .

20.12b . . . then push the filter onto the cover until it locks in position – 1.3 and 1.9 litre engines

20.13a Locate a new O-ring seal on the filter housing . . .

20.13b . . . then fit the element and cover to the housing – 1.3 and 1.9 litre engines

20.19 Disconnect the heater element wiring connector (arrowed) from the fuel filter cover – 1.7 litre engines

20.20 Disconnect the fuel hoses from the fuel filter housing cover – 1.7 litre engines

the retaining ring to the specified torque using the special tool or alternative.

15 Insert the filter assembly into the crash box, making sure that the retaining clip engages. Reconnect the fuel hoses and the wiring connectors.

16 Bleed the fuel system as described in Chapter 4A and check all disturbed components to ensure that there are no leaks (of air or fuel) when the engine is restarted.

17 On completion, safely dispose of the drained fuel.

1.7 litre engines

18 The fuel filter is located at the rear of the engine compartment, in the centre of the bulkhead.

19 Disconnect the heater element wiring connector from the fuel filter cover (see illustration).

20 Suitably identify the fitted position of the fuel hoses at their filter attachments to avoid confusion when refitting. Detach the two fuel hose quick-release connectors and remove the hoses from the filter housing cover. A Vauxhall/Opel special tool (KM-796-A) is available to disconnect the hose connectors, but provided care is taken, the connections can be released using two screwdrivers, a pair of long-nosed pliers, or similar, to depress the retaining tangs (see illustration). Suitably cover or plug the open hose connections to prevent dirt entry.

21 Depress the retaining clip and lift the filter housing from the crash box.

22 Unscrew the centre bolt and remove the cover from the filter housing (see illustration). Collect the cover sealing ring.

23 Remove the filter element, then empty the fuel from the filter housing. Thoroughly clean the housing and cover with a lint-free cloth.

24 Fit a new sealing ring to the centre bolt and filter housing, then place the new element in the housing.

25 Fill the filter housing with fresh diesel fuel until the level is just below the rim of the housing.

26 Refit the cover to the housing then refit the centre bolt, tightening it to the specified torque. **Do not** overtighten the cover screw, as the housing is easily damaged.

27 Insert the filter assembly into the crash box, making sure that the retaining clip engages. Reconnect the fuel hoses in their correct locations as noted during removal, and reconnect the heater element wiring connector.

28 Reattach the two fuel hoses to their retaining clips on the bulkhead.

29 Bleed the fuel system as described in Chapter 4A and check all disturbed components to ensure that there are no leaks (of air or fuel) when the engine is restarted.

30 On completion, safely dispose of the drained fuel.

21 Auxiliary drivebelt condition check

Checking

1 Due to their function and material make-up, drivebelts are prone to failure after a long period of time and should therefore be inspected regularly.

2 Apply the handbrake, then jack up the front of the vehicle and support it on axle stands (see Jacking and vehicle support). Remove the right-hand front roadwheel and the wheel arch liner cover for access to the right-hand side of the engine.

3 With the engine stopped, inspect the full length of the drivebelt for cracks and separation of the belt plies. It will be necessary to turn the engine (using a spanner or socket and bar on the crankshaft pulley bolt) so that the belt can be inspected thoroughly. Twist the belt between the pulleys so that both sides can be viewed. Also check for fraying, and glazing which gives the belt a shiny appearance. Check the pulleys for nicks, cracks, distortion and corrosion. If the belt shows signs of wear or damage, it should be renewed as a precaution against breakage in service.

Renewal

Note: The manufacturers recommend that the tensioner roller is checked and if necessary renewed at the same time as the drivebelt.

4 If not already done, apply the handbrake, then jack up the front of the vehicle and support it on axle stands (see Jacking and

H46358

20.22 Fuel filter and housing components – 1.7 litre engines

1 Centre bolt	4 Filter housing
2 Centre bolt sealing ring	cover sealing ring
3 Filter housing cover	5 Filter element
	6 Filter housing

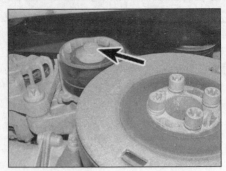

21.7a Turn the drivebelt tensioner using a spanner on the pulley centre bolt (arrowed) . . .

21.7b . . . then lock the tensioner by inserting a drill bit (arrowed) through the hole on the underside of the tensioner – 1.9 litre engines . . .

21.7c . . . or on the top of the tensioner – 1.3 and 1.7 litre engines

vehicle support). Remove the right-hand front roadwheel and the wheel arch liner cover for access to the right-hand side of the engine.

5 For additional working clearance, remove the air cleaner housing as described in Chapter 4A.

6 If the drivebelt is to be re-used, mark it to indicate its normal running direction.

7 Using a spanner on the pulley centre bolt, turn the tensioner against the spring tension. Hold the tensioner in this position by inserting a suitable locking pin or drill bit through the special hole provided **(see illustrations)**.

8 Slip the drivebelt from the pulleys.

9 Locate the new drivebelt on the pulleys in the correct routing. If the drivebelt is being re-used, make sure it is fitted the correct way around.

10 Turn back the tensioner and remove the locking pin/drill bit, then release it, making sure that the drivebelt ribs locate correctly on each of the pulley grooves.

11 Refit the air cleaner housing (if removed), then refit the wheel arch liner and roadwheel, and lower the vehicle to the ground.

22 Valve clearance check and adjustment – 1.9 litre SOHC engines

Refer to the procedures contained in Chapter 2C.

23 Handbrake operation and adjustment check

1 With the vehicle on a slight slope, apply the handbrake lever by up to 3 clicks of the ratchet, and check that it holds the vehicle stationary, then release the lever and check that there is no resistance to movement of the vehicle.

2 If necessary, adjust the handbrake as follows.

3 Chock the front wheels then jack up the rear of the car and securely support it on axle stands (see *Jacking and vehicle support*).

4 From inside the vehicle, unclip and remove the access panel in the centre console, beneath the handbrake lever **(see illustration)**.

5 The handbrake cable adjuster nut is situated is situated by the handbrake lever inside the vehicle, unclip the cover from around the handbrake lever **(see illustration)**.

6 Move the handbrake lever to the fully released position, then turn the cable adjuster nut anti-clockwise to remove all tension from the cables **(see illustration)**.

7 Depress the footbrake five times, then fully apply and release the handbrake lever five times.

8 With the handbrake lever set on the second

notch of the ratchet mechanism, rotate the adjuster nut clockwise until a reasonable amount of force is required to turn each wheel. **Note:** *The force required should be equal for each wheel.*

9 Now pull the handbrake lever up to the third notch of the ratchet mechanism and check that both rear wheels are locked. Once this is so, fully release the handbrake lever and check that the wheels rotate freely. Check the adjustment by applying the handbrake fully whilst counting the clicks emitted from the handbrake ratchet and, if necessary, re-adjust.

10 On completion of adjustment, refit the handbrake lever cover and centre console access panel, then lower the vehicle to the ground.

24 Headlight beam alignment check

1 Accurate adjustment of the headlight beam is only possible using optical beam-setting equipment, and this work should therefore be carried out by a Vauxhall/Opel dealer or service station with the necessary facilities. Refer to Chapter 12 for further information.

23.4 Unclip and remove the centre console access panel

23.5 Unclip the cover from around the handbrake lever . . .

23.6 . . . for access to the handbrake cable adjuster nut (arrowed)

Every 2 years, regardless of mileage

25 Remote control battery renewal

1 Using a screwdriver, prise the battery cover from the ignition key fob **(see illustrations)**.
2 Note how the circular battery is fitted, then carefully remove it from the contacts.
3 Fit the new battery (type CR 20 32) and refit the cover making sure that it clips fully onto the base.
4 After changing the battery, lock and unlock the driver's door with the key in the lock to synchronise the remote control unit.

26 Hydraulic fluid renewal

⚠ Warning: Hydraulic fluid can harm your eyes and damage painted surfaces, so use extreme caution when handling and pouring it. Do not use fluid that has been standing open for some time, as it absorbs moisture from the air. Excess moisture can cause a dangerous loss of braking effectiveness.

Note: *The brake and clutch hydraulic systems share a common reservoir.*

1 The procedure is similar to that for the bleeding of the hydraulic system as described in Chapters 9 (brake) and 6 (clutch).
2 Working as described in Chapter 9, open the first bleed screw in the sequence, and pump the brake pedal gently until nearly all the old fluid has been emptied from the master cylinder reservoir. Top-up to the MAX level with new fluid, and continue pumping until only the new fluid remains in the reservoir, and new fluid can be seen emerging from the bleed screw. Tighten the screw, and top the reservoir level up to the MAX level line.

Old hydraulic fluid is invariably much darker in colour than the new, making it easy to distinguish the two.

3 Work through all the remaining bleed screws in the sequence until new fluid can be seen at all of them. Be careful to keep the master cylinder reservoir topped-up to above the MIN level at all times, or air may enter the system and greatly increase the length of the task.
4 Bleed the fluid from the clutch hydraulic system as described in Chapter 6.
5 When the operation is complete, check that all bleed screws are securely tightened, and that their dust caps are refitted. Wash off all traces of spilt fluid, and recheck the master cylinder reservoir fluid level.
6 Check the operation of the brakes and clutch before taking the car on the road.

27 Coolant renewal

Note: *Vauxhall/Opel do not specify renewal intervals for the antifreeze mixture, as the mixture used to fill the system when the vehicle is new is designed to last the lifetime of the vehicle. However, it is strongly recommended that the coolant is renewed at the intervals specified in the 'Maintenance schedule', as a precaution against possible engine corrosion problems. This is particularly advisable if the coolant has been renewed using an antifreeze other than that specified by Vauxhall/Opel. With many antifreeze types, the corrosion inhibitors become progressively less effective with age. It is up to the individual owner whether or not to follow this advice.*

⚠ Warning: Wait until the engine is cold before starting this procedure. Do not allow antifreeze to come in contact with your skin, or with the painted surfaces of the vehicle. Rinse off spills immediately with plenty of water. Never leave antifreeze lying around in an open container, or in a puddle in the driveway or on the garage floor. Children and pets are attracted by its sweet smell, but antifreeze can be fatal if ingested.

Cooling system draining

1 To drain the cooling system, first cover the expansion tank cap with a wad of rag, and slowly turn the cap anti-clockwise to relieve the pressure in the cooling system (a hissing sound will normally be heard). Wait until any pressure remaining in the system is released, then continue to turn the cap until it can be removed.
2 Remove the engine undertray (where fitted), then position a suitable container beneath the right-hand side of the radiator.
3 The coolant drain plug is located at the bottom of the radiator right-hand end tank. Unscrew the drain plug and allow the coolant to drain..
4 When the flow of coolant stops, refit and tighten the drain plugs.

5 As no cylinder block drain plug is fitted, it is not possible to drain all of the coolant. Due consideration must be made for this when refilling the system, in order to maintain the correct concentration of antifreeze.
6 If the coolant has been drained for a reason other than renewal, then provided it is clean and less than two years old, it can be re-used.

Cooling system flushing

7 If coolant renewal has been neglected, or if the antifreeze mixture has become diluted, then in time, the cooling system may gradually lose efficiency, as the coolant passages become restricted due to rust, scale deposits, and other sediment. The cooling system efficiency can be restored by flushing the system clean.
8 The radiator should be flushed independently of the engine, to avoid unnecessary contamination.

Radiator flushing

9 Disconnect the top and bottom hoses and any other relevant hoses from the radiator, with reference to Chapter 3.
10 Insert a garden hose into the radiator top inlet. Direct a flow of clean water through the radiator, and continue flushing until clean water emerges from the radiator bottom outlet.
11 If after a reasonable period, the water still does not run clear, the radiator can be flushed with a good proprietary cleaning agent. It is important that the manufacturer's instructions are followed carefully. If the contamination is particularly bad, remove the radiator, insert the hose in the radiator bottom outlet, and reverse-flush the radiator.

Engine flushing

12 To flush the engine, the thermostat must be removed, because it will be shut, and would otherwise prevent the flow of water around the engine. The thermostat can be removed as described in Chapter 3. Take care not to introduce dirt or debris into the system if this approach is used.
13 With the bottom hose disconnected from the radiator, insert a garden hose into

25.1a Prise off the battery cover . . .

25.1b . . . and remove the circular battery

27.18 On 1.9 litre engines, open the bleed screw (arrowed) in the coolant pipe above the exhaust manifold

the thermostat opening. Direct a clean flow of water through the engine, and continue flushing until clean water emerges from the radiator bottom hose.

14 On completion of flushing, refit the thermostat with reference to Chapter 3, and reconnect the hoses.

Cooling system filling

15 Before attempting to fill the cooling system, make sure that all hoses and clips are in good condition, and that the clips are tight. Note that an antifreeze mixture must be used all year round, to prevent corrosion of the engine components.

16 Remove the expansion tank filler cap.

17 Fill the system by slowly pouring the coolant into the expansion tank until it is up to the filler neck.

18 On 1.9 litre engines, open the bleed screw in the coolant pipe above the exhaust manifold **(see illustrations)**. Close the coolant pipe bleed screw as soon as coolant emerges.

19 Top-up the expansion tank until the coolant level is up to the KALT/COLD mark on the side of the tank.

20 Refit and tighten the expansion tank filler cap.

21 Start the engine and run it at 2000 to 2500 rpm until the cooling fan switches on. Continue running the engine at between 2000 and 2500 rpm for a further 2 minutes.

22 Stop the engine, and allow it to cool, then recheck the coolant level with reference to *Weekly checks*. Top-up the level if necessary and refit the expansion tank filler cap. Refit the engine undertray (where applicable).

Antifreeze mixture

23 Always use an ethylene-glycol based antifreeze which is suitable for use in mixed-metal cooling systems. **Note:** *Vauxhall/ Opel recommend the use of silicate-free 'red' coolant (93 170 402).* The quantity of antifreeze and level of protection is given in the Specifications.

24 Before adding antifreeze, the cooling system should be completely drained, preferably flushed, and all hoses checked for condition and security.

25 After filling with antifreeze, a label should be attached to the expansion tank, stating the type and concentration of antifreeze used, and the date installed. Any subsequent topping-up should be made with the same type and concentration of antifreeze.

26 Do not use engine antifreeze in the windscreen/tailgate washer system, as it will cause damage to the vehicle paintwork. A screenwash additive should be added to the washer system in the quantities stated on the bottle.

28 Exhaust emission check

1 The exhaust emission check is carried out initially after 3 years, then every 2 years, however, on vehicles which are subject to intensive use (eg, taxis/hire cars/ambulances) it must be carried out annually. The check involves checking the engine management system operation by plugging an electronic tester into the system diagnostic socket to check the electronic control unit (ECU) memory for faults (see Chapter 4A).

2 In reality, if the vehicle is running correctly and the engine management warning light in the instrument panel is functioning normally, then this check need not be carried out.

Every 36 000 miles or 4 years

29.2 Disconnect the wiring connector from the airflow meter

29.3a Undo the retaining screws . . .

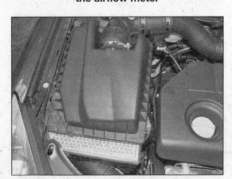

29.3b . . . lift off the air cleaner cover . . .

29.3c . . . then lift out the filter element

29 Air cleaner element renewal

1 The air cleaner is located in the front right-hand corner of the engine compartment.

2 Disconnect the wiring connector from the side of the airflow meter **(see illustration)**.

3 Undo the screws and lift off the air cleaner cover, then lift out the filter element **(see illustrations)**.

4 Wipe out the casing and the cover.

5 Fit the new filter, noting that the rubber locating flange should be uppermost, and secure the cover with the screws.

6 Reconnect the airflow meter wiring connector.

30 Timing belt, tensioner and idler pulley renewal – 1.7 and 1.9 litre engines

Refer to the procedures contained in the relevant Part of Chapter 2.

Every 48 000 miles or 6 years

31 Automatic transmission fluid renewal

Refer to the procedures contained in Chapter 7B.

Every 72 000 miles or 10 years

32 Auxiliary drivebelt renewal –
1.9 litre engines

Refer to the procedures contained in Section 21.

Every 90 000 miles or 10 years

33 Valve clearance check and adjustment –
1.7 litre engines

34 Auxiliary drivebelt renewal –
1.3 and 1.7 litre engines

Refer to the procedures contained in Chapter 2B.

Refer to the procedures contained in Section 21.

Chapter 2 Part A:
1.3 litre engine in-car repair procedures

Contents

Degrees of difficulty

Easy, suitable for novice with little experience	**Fairly easy,** suitable for beginner with some experience	**Fairly difficult,** suitable for competent DIY mechanic	**Difficult,** suitable for experienced DIY mechanic	**Very difficult,** suitable for expert DIY or professional

Specifications

General

Engine type...	Four-cylinder, in-line, water-cooled. Chain-driven double overhead camshafts, 16 valves
Manufacturer's engine code...............................	Z13DTH
Bore	69.6 mm
Stroke...	82.0 mm
Capacity...	1248 cc
Firing order..	1-3-4-2 (No 1 cylinder at timing chain end)
Direction of crankshaft rotation	Clockwise (viewed from timing chain end of engine)
Compression ratio	18.0:1

Compression pressures

Maximum difference between any two cylinders..................	1.5 bar

Lubrication system

Oil pump type...	Gear-type, driven directly from crankshaft
Oil pressure at 80°C (approximate)	1.4 bars at idle speed
Oil pump clearances:	
Outer rotor-to-body clearance	0.10 to 0.23 mm
Rotor endfloat..	0.050 to 0.075 mm

Torque wrench settings

	Nm	lbf ft
Auxiliary drivebelt tensioner to cylinder block	50	37
Big-end bearing cap nuts*:		
Stage 1	20	15
Stage 2	Angle-tighten a further 40°	
Camshaft drivegear bolts	150	111
Camshaft housing closure bolts.............................	15	11
Camshaft housing to cylinder head:		
M8 stud bolts	25	18
M7 bolts	18	13

Torque wrench settings (continued)

	Nm	lbf ft
Camshaft position sensor retaining bolt	7	5
Camshaft sprocket bolt	150	111
Catalytic converter support bracket to sump reinforcement bracket	25	18
Catalytic converter-to-turbocharger nuts	25	18
Coolant pipe-to-heat exchanger bolts	9	7
Coolant pump nuts	9	7
Crankshaft pulley hub to crankshaft†	230	170
Crankshaft pulley to pulley hub	25	18
Cylinder block baseplate bolts*:		
M10 bolts:		
Stage 1	20	15
Stage 2	Angle-tighten a further 90°	
M8 bolts	30	22
Cylinder head bolts*:		
Stage 1	40	30
Stage 2	Angle-tighten a further 90°	
Stage 3	Angle-tighten a further 90°	
Engine/transmission mountings:		
Front mounting/torque link:		
Mounting to subframe bracket	55	41
Bracket to transmission	80	59
Left-hand:		
Mounting-to-body bolts	20	15
Mounting bracket to transmission bracket	55	41
Rubber mounting through-bolt	55	41
Transmission bracket to transmission	60	44
Rear mounting/torque link:		
Mounting to subframe	55	41
Mounting-to-transmission bracket through-bolt	55	41
Transmission bracket to transmission	80	59
Right-hand:		
Engine bracket-to-engine bolts	60	44
Mounting-to-body bolts	35	26
Mounting-to-engine bracket bolts	55	41
Engine-to-transmission bolts	60	44
Flywheel bolts*	44	32
Fuel rail mounting bracket to camshaft housing	25	18
Fuel rail-to-mounting bracket bolts	25	18
Oil cooler/heat exchanger to oil filter housing	9	7
Oil filter housing cover	25	18
Oil filter housing to cylinder block	9	7
Sump drain plug	20	15
Roadwheel bolts	110	81
Sump reinforcement bracket bolts	30	22
Sump to cylinder block baseplate	9	7
Timing chain guide rail bolts	9	7
Timing chain tensioner bolts	9	7
Timing chain tensioner rail pivot bolt	9	7
Timing cover retaining nuts/bolts	9	7
Turbocharger oil supply pipe banjo union bolts	12	9

* *Use new fasteners*
† *Left-hand thread*

---

1 General information

How to use this Chapter

This Part of Chapter 2 describes the repair procedures which can reasonably be carried out on the engine while it remains in the vehicle. If the engine has been removed from the vehicle and is being dismantled as described in Chapter 2E, any preliminary dismantling procedures can be ignored.

Note that, while it may be possible physically to overhaul items such as the piston/connecting rod assemblies while the engine is in the vehicle, such tasks are not usually carried out as separate operations, and usually require the execution of several additional procedures (not to mention the cleaning of components and of oilways); for this reason, all such tasks are classed as major overhaul procedures, and are described in Chapter 2E.

Chapter 2E describes the removal of the engine/transmission unit from the vehicle, and the full overhaul procedures which can then be carried out.

Engine description

The 1.3 litre common-rail diesel engine is of sixteen-valve, in-line four-cylinder, double overhead camshaft (DOHC) type, mounted transversely at the front of the car with the transmission attached to its left-hand end.

The crankshaft runs in five main bearings. Thrustwashers are fitted to No 3 main bearing shell (upper half) to control crankshaft endfloat.

The cylinder block is made of cast iron and the cylinder bores are an integral part of the block. On this type of engine the cylinder bores are sometimes referred to as having dry liners. An aluminium baseplate is bolted to the cylinder block and forms the lower half of the crankcase.

The connecting rods rotate on horizontally-split bearing shells at their big-ends. The pistons are attached to the connecting rods by gudgeon pins, which are a sliding fit in the connecting rod small-end eyes and retained by circlips. The aluminium-alloy pistons are fitted with three piston rings – two compression rings and an oil control ring.

The camshafts are situated in a separate housing bolted to the top of the cylinder head. The exhaust camshaft is driven by the crankshaft by a hydraulically-tensioned timing chain and drives the inlet camshaft via a spur gear. Each cylinder has four valves (two inlet and two exhaust), operated via rocker arms which are supported at their pivot ends by hydraulic self-adjusting valve lifters (tappets). One camshaft operates the inlet valves, and the other operates the exhaust valves.

The inlet and exhaust valves are each closed by a single valve spring, and operate in guides pressed into the cylinder head.

A rotor-type oil pump is located in the timing cover attached to the cylinder block, and is driven directly from the crankshaft. An oil cooler (heat exchanger) is fitted to keep the oil temperature stable under arduous operating conditions.

The coolant pump is located externally on the timing cover, and is driven by the auxiliary drivebelt.

Operations with engine in place

The following operations can be carried out without having to remove the engine from the vehicle.

a) Removal and refitting of the cylinder head.
b) Removal and refitting of the timing cover.
c) Removal and refitting of the timing chain, tensioner, sprockets and guide rails.
d) Removal and refitting of the camshaft housing.
e) Removal and refitting of the hydraulic tappets and rocker arms.
f) Removal and refitting of the camshafts.
g) Removal and refitting of the sump.
h) Removal and refitting of the big-end bearings, connecting rods, and pistons*.
i) Removal and refitting of the oil pump.
j) Removal and refitting of the oil cooler/ heat exchanger.
k) Renewal of the crankshaft oil seals.
l) Renewal of the engine mountings.
m) Removal and refitting of the flywheel.

* Although the operation marked with an asterisk can be carried out with the engine in the vehicle (after removal of the sump), it is preferable for the engine to be removed, in the interests of cleanliness and improved access. For this reason, the procedure is described in Chapter 2E.

2 Compression test – description and interpretation

Compression test

Note: *A compression tester specifically designed for diesel engines must be used for this test.*

1 When engine performance is down, or if misfiring occurs which cannot be attributed to the fuel system, a compression test can provide diagnostic clues as to the engine's condition. If the test is performed regularly, it can give warning of trouble before any other symptoms become apparent.

2 A compression tester specifically intended for diesel engines must be used, because of the higher pressures involved. The tester is generally connected to an adapter which screws into the glow plug or injector hole. On these models, an adapter suitable for use in the injector holes will be required. It is unlikely to be worthwhile buying such a tester for occasional use, but it may be possible to borrow or hire one – if not, have the test performed by a garage.

3 Unless specific instructions to the contrary are supplied with the tester, observe the following points:
a) The battery must be in a good state of charge, the air filter must be clean, and the engine should be at normal operating temperature.
b) All the fuel injectors must be removed before starting the test (see Chapter 4A).
c) Open the cover on the engine compartment fuse/relay box and remove the fuel pump relay (see illustrations).

4 Screw the compression tester and adapter in to the fuel injector hole of No 1 cylinder.

5 With the help of an assistant, crank the engine on the starter motor; after one or two revolutions, the compression pressure should build-up to a maximum figure, and then stabilise. Record the highest reading obtained.

6 Repeat the test on the remaining cylinders, recording the pressure in each.

7 All cylinders should produce very similar pressures; any difference greater than that specified indicates the existence of a fault. Note that the compression should build-up quickly in a healthy engine; low compression on the first stroke, followed by gradually-increasing pressure on successive strokes, indicates worn piston rings. A low compression reading on the first stroke, which does not build-up during successive strokes, indicates leaking valves or a blown head gasket (a cracked head could also be the cause). **Note:** *The cause of poor compression is less easy to establish on a diesel engine than on a petrol one. The effect of introducing oil into the cylinders ('wet' testing) is not conclusive, because there is a risk that the oil will sit in the recess on the piston crown instead of passing to the rings.*

8 On completion of the test, refit the fuel pump relay, then refit the fuel injectors as described in Chapter 4A.

Leakdown test

9 A leakdown test measures the rate at which compressed air fed into the cylinder is lost. It is an alternative to a compression test, and in many ways it is better, since the escaping air provides easy identification of where pressure loss is occurring (piston rings, valves or head gasket).

10 The equipment needed for leakdown testing is unlikely to be available to the home mechanic. If poor compression is suspected, have the test performed by a dealership.

3 Engine assembly/ valve timing holes – general information and usage

Note: *Do not attempt to rotate the engine whilst the camshafts are locked in position. If the engine is to be left in this state for a long period of time, it is a good idea to place suitable warning notices inside the car, and in the engine compartment. This will reduce the possibility of the engine being accidentally*

2.3a Open the cover on the fuse/relay box . . .

2.3b . . . and remove the fuel pump relay (arrowed)

3.2 Camshaft timing slot (arrowed) for use with the camshaft locking tools

3.3a Inserting the Vauxhall/Opel crankshaft locking tool through the timing hole in the bellhousing

3.3b Using a drill bit (arrowed) to lock the crankshaft through the additional timing hole provided in the flywheel

cranked on the starter motor, which is likely to cause damage with the locking tools in place.

1 To accurately set the valve timing for all operations requiring removal and refitting of the timing chain, timing slots are machined in the camshafts and corresponding holes are drilled in the camshaft housing. Timing holes are also drilled in the flywheel, and transmission bellhousing. The holes are used in conjunction with camshaft and crankshaft locking tools to lock the camshafts and crankshaft when all the pistons are positioned at the mid-point of their stroke. This arrangement prevents the possibility of the valves contacting the pistons when refitting the cylinder head or timing chain, and also ensures that the correct valve timing can be obtained. The design of the engine is such that there are no conventional timing marks on the crankshaft or camshaft sprockets to indicate the normal TDC position. Therefore, for any work on the timing chain, camshafts or cylinder head, the locking tools must be used.

2 The Vauxhall/Opel special tool for locking the camshafts comprises a spring-loaded plunger free to slide in the bore of the tool body. The tool body is screwed into the camshaft housing timing hole (after removal of a closure plug) so that the sliding plunger contacts the exhaust camshaft. The plunger is retained in contact with the camshaft by the spring. The crankshaft is then rotated by means of the crankshaft pulley bolt until a machined slot in the camshaft aligns with the tool plunger **(see illustration)**. The spring then forces the plunger into engagement with the slot, locking the camshaft in the timing position. To accurately check the valve timing,

or for any work that entails removal of the camshafts or their drivegears, two of these tools will be required, one for each camshaft.

3 The Vauxhall/Opel special tool for locking the crankshaft is simply a 6 mm diameter pin which is inserted through a hole in the bellhousing to engage with a corresponding hole in the rim of the flywheel. An additional hole is provided in the inner face of the flywheel with a corresponding hole in the cylinder block, for use when the transmission has been removed **(see illustrations)**.

4 The tool numbers are as follows:
Camshaft locking tools: EN-46781
Crankshaft locking tool (bellhousing into flywheel): EN-46785
Crankshaft locking tool (flywheel into cylinder block): EN-46778

5 Although the Vauxhall/Opel camshaft locking tools (or aftermarket equivalents) are relatively inexpensive and should be readily available, it is possible to fabricate suitable alternatives, with the help of a local machine shop, as described below. Once the tools have been made up, their usage is described in the relevant Sections of this Chapter where the tools are required.

Camshaft locking tool

6 Lift off the plastic cover over the top of the engine.

7 Unscrew the three bolts securing the plastic wiring harness guide to the top of the camshaft housing.

8 Release the locking catches securing the wiring connectors to the four injectors, then disconnect the injector wiring, while at the

same time moving the wiring harness guide forward **(see illustration)**.

9 Unscrew the closure bolt from the valve timing checking hole on the front face of the camshaft housing. The bolt is located above, and just between, Nos 2 and 3 glow plugs.

10 Using the closure bolt as a pattern, obtain a length of threaded dowel rod, or suitable bolt to screw into the closure bolt hole. With the help of a machine shop or engineering works, make up the camshaft locking tool by having the dowel rod or bolt machined **(see illustrations)**. Note that for some of the procedures described in this Chapter, two locking tools will be needed, one for each camshaft.

11 To refit the closure bolt, thoroughly clean the bolt threads and apply suitable thread-locking compound. Screw the bolt into the camshaft housing and tighten to the specified torque.

12 Securely reconnect the injector wiring connectors, then refit and tighten the three wiring harness guide retaining bolts. Refit the engine cover on completion.

Crankshaft locking tools

13 Suitable drill bits or dowel rods can be used as alternatives for the Vauxhall/Opel special tools described previously. Their respective diameters are as follows:
Crankshaft locking tool (bellhousing into flywheel): 6.0 mm diameter
Crankshaft locking tool (flywheel into cylinder block): 9.0 mm diameter

3.8 Disconnect the injector wiring then, move the wiring harness guide forward

3.10a To make an alternative camshaft locking tool . . .

3.10b . . . have suitable dowel rods or bolts machined to the dimensions shown

4.8 Undo the three bolts and remove the engine lifting bracket and fuel rail mounting bracket from the camshaft housing

4 Valve timing – checking and adjustment

Note: *Certain special tools will be required for this operation. Read through the entire procedure to familiarise yourself with the work involved, then either obtain the manufacturer's special tools, or use the alternatives described. New gaskets and sealing rings will also be required for all disturbed components.*

Checking

1 Disconnect the battery negative terminal (refer to *Disconnecting the battery* in the Reference Chapter).

2 Remove the turbocharger charge air pipe as described in Chapter 4A.

3 Disconnect the wiring connector at the camshaft position sensor on the top of the camshaft housing.

4 Disconnect the wiring connectors at the four glow plugs.

5 Unscrew the three bolts securing the plastic wiring harness guide to the top of the camshaft housing.

6 Release the locking catches securing the wiring connectors to the four injectors, then disconnect the injector wiring, while at the same time moving the wiring harness guide forward **(see illustration 3.8)**.

7 Undo the two retaining bolts securing the fuel rail to the mounting bracket.

8 Undo the three bolts and remove the engine lifting bracket and fuel rail mounting bracket from the camshaft housing **(see illustration)**. After removal of the mounting bracket, take care not to apply any force to the fuel rail otherwise damage could be caused to the high-pressure fuel pipes.

9 Unscrew the closure bolt from the valve timing checking hole on each side of the camshaft housing **(see illustration)**.

10 The camshafts must now be set to the timing position, to enable a camshaft locking tool to be inserted (see Section 3).

11 If the Vauxhall/Opel camshaft locking tools or similar alternatives are available, screw one of the tools into each of the valve timing checking holes. Ensure that the mark on the tool plunger is facing upwards **(see**

4.9 Unscrew the closure bolt from the valve timing checking hole on each side of the camshaft housing

illustration). Using a socket or spanner on the crankshaft pulley hub bolt, turn the crankshaft in the normal direction of rotation (clockwise as viewed from the right-hand side of the car) until the spring-loaded plungers of the locking tools slide into engagement with the slot on each camshaft. There will be an audible click from each tool when this happens and the plungers will be seen to move in, towards the camshafts.

12 If the home-made locking tools described in Section 3 are being used, insert a screwdriver through the valve timing checking hole on the front of the camshaft housing, and into contact with the exhaust camshaft. Using a socket or spanner on the crankshaft pulley hub bolt, turn the crankshaft in the normal direction of rotation (clockwise as viewed from the right-hand side of the car) until the screwdriver can be felt to engage with the slot in the camshaft. Screw the tool into the camshaft housing until resistance is felt, then turn the crankshaft slightly until the camshaft

4.11 If the Vauxhall/Opel camshaft locking tools (1) are being used, screw the tools into the valve timing checking holes. Ensure that the mark on the tool plunger (arrowed) is facing upwards

slot is correctly aligned, and the tool can be screwed fully in **(see illustrations)**. Repeat this procedure for the inlet camshaft.

13 Firmly apply the handbrake, then jack up the front of the car and support it securely on axle stands (see *Jacking and vehicle support*).

14 Insert the Vauxhall/Opel crankshaft locking tool or suitable alternative (see Section 3) into the timing hole at the base of the transmission bellhousing and into engagement with the flywheel **(see illustrations)**. It may be

4.12a If the home-made tools are being used, screw one of the tools (arrowed) into each timing hole in the camshaft housing . . .

4.12b . . . so the end of the tool engages with the slot in the camshaft (shown with camshaft removed)

4.14a Insert the camshaft locking tool through the bellhousing into engagement with the flywheel. Hold the tool in place with the spring

necessary to turn the crankshaft very slightly one way or the other (within the limits of any slack afforded by the timing chain/tensioner) to allow the tool to fully engage.

15 If the crankshaft locking tool has engaged fully, then the valve timing is correct. Refit the disturbed components as described in the following paragraphs. If it is not possible to fully insert the crankshaft locking tool, then it will be necessary to adjust the valve timing as described in paragraphs 24 to 33.

16 Remove the camshaft locking tools from both sides of the camshaft housing.

17 Thoroughly clean the closure bolt threads and apply suitable thread locking compound. Screw the bolts into the camshaft housing and tighten to the specified torque.

18 Place the engine lifting bracket and fuel rail mounting bracket in position on the camshaft housing. Refit the three retaining bolts and tighten to the specified torque.

19 Locate the fuel rail on the mounting bracket, insert the two bolts and tighten to the specified torque.

20 Reconnect the fuel injector wiring connectors and secure with the locking catches.

21 Refit the three bolts securing the plastic wiring harness guide to the top of the camshaft housing.

22 Reconnect the wiring connectors at the four glow plugs and at the camshaft position sensor.

23 Refit the turbocharger charge air pipe as

4.14b Alternatively, use a suitable drill bit . . .

described in Chapter 4A, then reconnect the battery and lower the car to the ground.

Adjustment

24 Remove the crankshaft pulley as described in Section 5.

25 It will now be necessary to hold the crankshaft pulley hub to enable the retaining bolt to be removed. Vauxhall/Opel special tool KM-662-C is available for this purpose, however, a home-made tool can easily be fabricated **(see Tool Tip)**.

26 Using the Vauxhall/Opel tool or the home-made alternative, hold the pulley hub stationary and unscrew the retaining bolt. **Note:** *The pulley hub retaining bolt has a **left-hand thread** and is unscrewed by turning it clockwise.*

27 Withdraw the pulley hub from the crankshaft and refit the retaining bolt sufficiently tight to allow the crankshaft to be turned.

28 Using a socket or spanner on the crankshaft pulley hub bolt, turn the crankshaft as necessary, until it is possible to fully insert the crankshaft locking tool into engagement with the flywheel.

29 Undo the bolt, refit the crankshaft pulley hub, and refit the bolt.

30 Hold the pulley hub using the holding tool and tighten the bolt to the specified torque.

31 Remove the crankshaft locking tool.

32 Refit the crankshaft pulley as described in Section 5.

33 Refit the disturbed components as described in paragraphs 16 to 23.

5 Crankshaft pulley – removal and refitting

Removal

1 Apply the handbrake, then jack up the front of the vehicle and support it on axle stands (see *Jacking and vehicle support*). Remove the right-hand front roadwheel and the inner wheel arch liner for access to the crankshaft pulley.

2 Remove the auxiliary drivebelt as described in Chapter 1. Prior to removal, mark the direction of rotation on the belt to ensure the belt is refitted the same way around.

4.14c . . . and hold it in place with an elastic band

3 Slacken and remove the four retaining bolts securing the pulley to the pulley hub. If necessary, prevent the crankshaft from turning by holding the pulley hub retaining bolt with a socket.

Refitting

4 Refit the crankshaft pulley to the pulley hub. Refit the pulley retaining bolts, tightening them to the specified torque.

5 Refit the auxiliary drivebelt as described in Chapter 1 using the mark made prior to removal to ensure the belt is fitted the correct way around.

6 Refit the wheel arch liner and roadwheel, then lower the car to the ground and tighten the wheel bolts to the specified torque.

6 Timing cover – removal and refitting

Note: *The special tools described in Section 3, together with additional tools will be required for this operation. Read through the entire procedure and also the procedures contained in Section 3 to familiarise yourself with the work involved, then either obtain the manufacturer's special tools, or use the alternatives described, where applicable. New gaskets and sealing rings will be needed for all disturbed components, together with a tube of suitable gasket sealant.*

Removal

1 Disconnect the battery negative terminal (refer to *Disconnecting the battery* in the Reference Chapter).

2 Referring to the procedures contained in Chapter 1, drain the engine oil and the cooling

TOOL TiP

To make a sprocket holding tool, obtain two lengths of steel strip about 6 mm thick by about 30 mm wide or similar, one 600 mm long, the other 200 mm long (all dimensions are approximate). Bolt the two strips together to form a forked end, leaving the bolt slack so that the shorter strip can pivot freely. At the other end of each 'prong' of the fork, drill a suitable hole and fit a nut and bolt to allow the tool to be bolted to the crankshaft pulley hub.

6.13 Undo nut and two bolts (arrowed) and remove the oil filter heat shield

6.14 Undo the two bolts (arrowed) securing the coolant pipe to the heat exchanger

6.15 Unscrew the turbocharger oil supply pipe banjo union bolt (arrowed) from the oil filter housing

system. Refit the drain plug, using a new seal, when the oil has drained. Close the cooling system when the coolant has drained.

3 Remove the crankshaft pulley as described in Section 5.

4 Remove the air cleaner assembly and the turbocharger charge air pipe and charge air hose as described in Chapter 4A.

5 Disconnect the wiring connector at the camshaft position sensor on the top of the camshaft housing.

6 Disconnect the wiring connectors at the four glow plugs.

7 Unscrew the three bolts securing the plastic wiring harness guide to the top of the camshaft housing.

8 Release the locking catches securing the wiring connectors to the four injectors, then disconnect the injector wiring, while at the same time moving the wiring harness guide forward **(see illustration 3.8)**.

9 Unscrew the closure bolt from the valve timing checking hole on the exhaust camshaft side of the camshaft housing **(see illustration 4.9)**.

10 If the Vauxhall/Opel camshaft locking tool or similar alternative is available (see Section 3), screw the tool into the valve timing checking hole. Ensure that the mark on the tool plunger is facing upwards. Using a socket or spanner on the crankshaft pulley hub bolt, turn the crankshaft in the normal direction of rotation (clockwise as viewed from the right-hand side of the car) until the spring-loaded plunger of the locking tool slides into engagement with the slot on the camshaft. There will be an audible click from the tool when this happens, and the

plunger will be seen to move in, towards the camshaft.

11 If the home-made locking tool described in Section 3 is being used, insert a screwdriver through the valve timing checking hole on the front of the camshaft housing, and into contact with the exhaust camshaft. Using a socket or spanner on the crankshaft pulley hub bolt, turn the crankshaft in the normal direction of rotation (clockwise as viewed from the right-hand side of the car) until the screwdriver can be felt to engage with the slot in the camshaft. Screw the tool into the camshaft housing until resistance is felt, then turn the crankshaft slightly until the camshaft slot is correctly aligned, and the tool can be screwed fully in **(see illustrations 4.12a and 4.12b)**.

12 Referring to the procedures contained in Chapter 4A, separate the exhaust system front section from the catalytic converter.

13 Undo the upper nut and two lower bolts and remove the oil filter heat shield **(see illustration)**.

14 Undo the two bolts securing the coolant pipe to the heat exchanger on the oil filter housing **(see illustration)**. Release the retaining clip securing the other end of the pipe to the hose on the thermostat housing. Undo the pipe support bracket bolt, release the wiring harness from the retaining clip and remove the coolant pipe from the engine. Recover the gasket noting that a new one will be required for refitting.

15 Unscrew the banjo union bolt and release the turbocharger oil supply pipe from the oil filter housing **(see illustration)**. Recover the two copper washers from the banjo union, and

suitably cover the end of the pipe to prevent dirt entry. Note that new copper washers will be required for refitting.

16 Slacken the retaining clip and disconnect the radiator bottom hose from the outlet at the base of the oil filter housing.

17 Undo the three bolts securing the heat shield support bracket to the heat exchanger on the oil filter housing **(see illustration)**.

18 Undo the remaining bolt and remove the oil filter housing and heat exchanger assembly from the cylinder block. Recover the rubber seal from the rear of the housing. Note that a new seal will be required for refitting.

19 From under the car, undo the bolt securing the catalytic converter support bracket to the sump reinforcement bracket.

20 Suitably support the weight of the catalytic converter on blocks or on a jack. Bend back the locking plate tabs and unscrew the three bolts securing the catalytic converter flange to the turbocharger **(see illustration)**. Remove the bolts and locking plate, noting that a new locking plate will be required for refitting.

21 Separate the catalytic converter from the turbocharger and recover the gasket **(see illustration)**. Carefully lower the converter and remove it from under the car. Note that a new gasket will be required for refitting.

22 It will now be necessary to hold the crankshaft pulley hub to enable the retaining bolt to be removed. Vauxhall/Opel special tool KM-662-C is available for this purpose, however, a home-made tool can easily be fabricated (refer to the **Tool Tip** in Section 4).

23 Using the Vauxhall/Opel tool or the home-

6.17 Undo the three bolts (arrowed) securing the heat shield support bracket to the heat exchanger

6.20 Unscrew the three bolts (arrowed) securing the catalytic converter to the turbocharger

6.21 Separate the catalytic converter from the turbocharger and recover the gasket

6.26 Remove the sump reinforcement bracket from the cylinder block baseplate and transmission bellhousing

6.27 Disconnect the oil level sensor wiring connector

6.30 Right-hand engine mounting retaining bolts (arrowed)

6.31 Undo the four bolts (arrowed) and remove the engine bracket

6.33 Release the wiring harness from the timing cover support clips

6.34 Undo the retaining bolt and detach the crankcase ventilation hose attachment

made alternative, hold the pulley hub stationary and unscrew the retaining bolt. **Note:** *The pulley hub retaining bolt has a **left-hand thread** and is unscrewed by turning it clockwise.*

24 Withdraw the pulley hub from the crankshaft and refit the retaining bolt sufficiently tight to allow the crankshaft to be turned.

25 Insert the Vauxhall/Opel crankshaft locking tool or suitable alternative (see Section 3) into the timing hole at the base of the transmission bellhousing and into engagement with the flywheel **(see illustrations 4.14a, 4.14b and 4.14c)**. It may be necessary to turn the crankshaft very slightly one way or the other, by means of the pulley retaining bolt, to allow the tool to fully engage.

26 Undo the five bolts securing the sump reinforcement bracket to the cylinder block baseplate and transmission bellhousing and remove the bracket **(see illustration)**. Note

the locations of the different length bolts to aid refitting.

27 Disconnect the oil level sensor wiring connector at the rear of the sump **(see illustration)**.

28 Undo the thirteen bolts and two nuts securing the sump to the cylinder block baseplate and timing cover. Using a wide-bladed scraper or similar tool inserted between the sump and baseplate, carefully break the joint, then remove the sump from under the car.

29 Connect a suitable hoist and lifting tackle to the right-hand end of the engine and support its weight. If available, the type of support bar which locates in the engine compartment side channels is to be preferred. Alternatively, support the engine on a jack with a block of wood positioned between the jack head and cylinder block baseplate.

30 Mark the bolt positions for correct refitting, then undo the three bolts securing the right-hand engine mounting to the body and the three bolts securing the mounting to the engine bracket **(see illustration)**. Remove the mounting.

31 Undo the four bolts securing the engine bracket to the cylinder block and cylinder head and remove the engine bracket **(see illustration)**.

32 Undo the centre retaining bolt and remove the auxiliary drive belt tensioner from the timing cover.

33 Release the wiring harness from the support clips on the timing cover and move the harness to one side **(see illustration)**.

34 Undo the retaining bolt and detach the crankcase ventilation hose attachment at the timing cover **(see illustration)**.

35 Working through the apertures in the pulley, unscrew and remove the four coolant pump retaining nuts **(see illustration)**.

36 Withdraw the coolant pump from the cylinder block studs. **Note:** *Coolant which is trapped in the cylinder block will leak out when the pump is removed.*

37 Recover the pump sealing ring, and discard it; a new one must be used on refitting.

38 Undo the retaining bolt and remove the wiring harness support clip bracket from the top of the timing cover **(see illustration)**.

39 Undo the fourteen bolts and three nuts securing the timing cover to the cylinder block, cylinder block baseplate, cylinder head and camshaft housing. Using a flat-bladed screwdriver inserted behind the lugs on the

6.35 Working through the pulley apertures, unscrew and remove the coolant pump retaining nuts

6.38 Undo the retaining bolt (arrowed) and remove the wiring harness support clip bracket

6.39a Using a flat-bladed screwdriver inserted behind the lugs on the edge of the timing cover . . .

6.39b . . . carefully prise the cover free and remove it from the engine

6.43 Apply a bead of sealant across the housing joints

edge of the timing cover, carefully prise the cover free and remove it from the engine **(see illustrations)**. Recover the timing cover gasket, a new gasket will be required for refitting.

40 Thoroughly clean the timing cover and remove all traces of gasket and sealant from all the mating surfaces. Similarly clean the cylinder block baseplate, cylinder block, cylinder head and camshaft housing mating surfaces. Ensure that all traces of old sealant are removed, particularly from the joint areas between these components.

6.45 Timing cover tightening sequence. Arrows indicate the location of the three nuts

41 Obtain all new gaskets and components as necessary ready for refitting. In addition, a new crankshaft oil seal will be required together with a tube of Loctite 5900 sealant, or equivalent. Vauxhall/Opel special tool EN-46775, or a suitable alternative, will be required to centralise the timing cover during refitting.

Refitting

42 Prior to refitting the timing cover, ensure that the face of the timing chain sprocket on the crankshaft is free from oil or grease.
43 Apply a 2 mm bead of Loctite 5900 across the camshaft housing-to-cylinder head joint, the cylinder head-to-cylinder block joint and the cylinder block-to-baseplate joint **(see illustration)**.
44 Place the new gasket in position on the engine then locate the timing cover over the gasket. Insert the Vauxhall/Opel tool (EN-46775) or a suitable equivalent, over the crankshaft and into engagement with the timing cover.
45 Refit the fourteen bolts and three nuts securing the timing cover to the engine, and tighten them to the specified torque, in the sequence shown **(see illustration)**.
46 Remove the cantering tool and carefully prise out the old crankshaft oil seal with a screwdriver or similar hooked tool. Clean the oil seal seat with a wooden or plastic scraper.
47 Tap a new crankshaft oil seal into position until it is flush with the outer face of the timing cover, using a suitable socket or tube, or a wooden block.
48 Refit the wiring harness support clip bracket to the top of the timing cover.
49 Ensure that the coolant pump and cylinder block mating surfaces are clean and dry. Fit a new sealing ring to the pump, and install the pump in the cylinder block.
50 Refit the pump retaining nuts, tightening them to the specified torque.
51 Insert the crankcase ventilation hose attachment to the timing cover and secure with the retaining bolt.
52 Refit the wiring harness to the support clips on the timing cover.
53 Thoroughly clean the crankshaft pulley hub, ensuring that the timing chain sprocket contact face is free from oil or grease.
54 Refit the pulley hub to the crankshaft, then refit the retaining bolt. Using the method

employed on removal to hold the pulley hub stationary, tighten the retaining bolt to the specified torque.
55 Refit the auxiliary drivebelt tensioner ensuring that the lug on the tensioner body engages with the hole in the cylinder block **(see illustration)**. Refit the retaining bolt and tighten the bolt to the specified torque.
56 Locate the engine bracket in position, refit the four retaining bolts and tighten to the specified torque.
57 Refit the right-hand engine mounting and secure the mounting to the body and engine bracket with the six retaining bolts. Tighten the bolts to the specified torque. Remove the hoist or jack used to support the engine.
58 Thoroughly clean the inside and outside of the sump ensuring that all traces of old sealant are removed from the mating face. Also clean the cylinder block baseplate mating face to remove all traces of old sealant.
59 Apply a 2 mm bead of Loctite 5900 to the sump mating face, ensuring the sealant bead runs around the inside of the bolt holes **(see illustration)**. Position the sump on the cylinder block baseplate, then refit the thirteen bolts and two nuts. Progressively tighten the bolts/nuts to the specified torque. Reconnect the oil level sensor wiring connector.
60 Refit the sump reinforcement bracket to the cylinder block baseplate and transmission bellhousing and secure with the five bolts, tightened to the specified torque.
61 Using a new gasket, position the catalytic converter on the turbocharger. Insert the three retaining bolts, with a new locking plate and

6.55 Refit the auxiliary drivebelt tensioner ensuring that the lug (arrowed) engages with the hole in the cylinder block

6.59 Apply a bead of sealant to the sump mating face, ensuring the bead runs around the inside of the bolt holes

tighten the bolts to the specified torque. Bent over the tabs of the locking plate to retain the bolts.

62 From under the car, refit the bolt securing the catalytic converter support bracket to the sump reinforcement bracket and tighten the bolt to the specified torque.

63 Place a new rubber seal on the oil filter housing, ensuring the seal is fully engaged with the housing grooves (see illustration).

64 Position the oil filter housing on the cylinder block and fit the lower left retaining bolt finger tight. Place the heat shield support bracket in position and fit the remaining three retaining bolts. Tighten the four bolts to the specified torque.

65 Connect the radiator bottom hose to the outlet at the base of the oil filter housing and secure with the retaining clip.

66 Using a new copper washer on each side of the banjo union, refit the turbocharger oil supply pipe and screw in the banjo union bolt. Tighten the bolt to the specified torque.

6.63 Place a new rubber seal on the oil filter housing, ensuring it fully engages with the housing grooves

67 Locate a new gasket over the heat exchanger coolant pipe and bend over the tabs of the gasket to retain it on the flange (see illustration).

68 Engage the coolant pipe with the hose on the thermostat housing, then position the pipe flange on the heat exchanger. Refit the two bolts and tighten them to the specified torque. At the other end of the pipe, tighten the hose retaining clip, refit and tighten the pipe support bracket bolt and secure the wiring harness with the retaining clip.

69 Place the heat shield over the oil filter, refit the two lower bolts and tighten them finger tight. Refit the two upper nuts securing the heat shield(s), then tighten the engine lifting bracket bolt, the manifold heat shield upper nuts and the oil filter heat shield lower bolts securely.

70 Refit the exhaust system components with reference to Chapter 4A.

71 Refit the crankshaft pulley as described in Section 5.

72 Remove the camshaft and crankshaft locking tools. Turn the engine through two complete revolutions, then check that the locking tools can be reinserted. Remove the locking tools.

73 Thoroughly clean the threads of the closure bolt and apply suitable thread locking compound. Screw the bolt into the camshaft housing and tighten to the specified torque.

74 Reconnect the fuel injector wiring connectors and secure with the locking catches.

75 Refit the three bolts securing the plastic

6.67 Locate a new gasket over the heat exchanger coolant pipe and bend over the tabs to retain it on the flange

wiring harness guide to the top of the camshaft housing.

76 Reconnect the camshaft position sensor wiring connector.

77 Reconnect the glow plug wiring connectors.

78 Refit the air cleaner assembly and the turbocharger charge air pipe and charge air hose as described in Chapter 4A.

79 Refill the engine with fresh oil with reference to Chapter 1.

80 Refill the cooling system as described in Chapter 1, then reconnect the battery negative terminal.

81 Refit the wheel arch liner and roadwheel, then lower the car to the ground and tighten the wheel bolts to the specified torque.

7 Timing chain, sprockets, tensioner and guide rails – removal and refitting

Removal

1 Remove the timing cover as described in Section 6.

2 Push the timing chain tensioner plunger back into its bore and insert a suitable drill bit or similar tool to retain it in the released position (see illustration).

3 Undo the two retaining bolts and remove the tensioner from the cylinder head (see illustration).

4 Undo the lower pivot bolt and remove the chain tensioner rail (see illustrations).

7.2 Push the timing chain tensioner plunger back into its bore and retain it using a suitable drill bit (arrowed)

7.3 Undo the two bolts and remove the tensioner from the cylinder head

7.4a Undo the lower pivot bolt . . .

7.4b . . . and remove the chain tensioner rail

5 Slide the crankshaft sprocket off the end of the crankshaft. Slip the chain off the camshaft sprocket and remove it together with the crankshaft sprocket **(see illustration)**.

6 It will now be necessary to hold the camshaft sprocket to enable the retaining bolt to be removed. Vauxhall/Opel special tools KM-956-1 and KM-6347 are available for this purpose, however, a home-made tool can easily be fabricated **(see Tool Tip)**.

7 Using the holding tool to prevent rotation of the camshaft, slacken the sprocket retaining bolt. Remove the holding tool, unscrew the retaining bolt and remove the sprocket **(see illustrations)**.

8 Undo the two retaining bolts and remove the timing chain guide rail **(see illustration)**.

9 Inspect the timing chain, sprockets, tensioner rail and guide rail for any sign of wear or deformation, and renew any suspect components as necessary.

10 Push the timing chain tensioner plunger into the tensioner body and remove the locking drill bit. Check that the tensioner plunger is free to move in out of the tensioner body with no trace of binding. If any binding or sticking of the plunger is felt, renew the tensioner assembly. On completion of the check, or if a new tensioner is being fitted, Compress the plunger and refit the locking drill bit.

Refitting

11 Locate the timing chain guide rail in position, refit the two retaining bolts and tighten the bolts to the specified torque.

12 Fit the sprocket to the camshaft and

7.5 Slip the chain off the camshaft sprocket and remove it together with the crankshaft sprocket

screw in the retaining bolt. Using the method employed on removal to hold the sprocket, tighten the retaining bolt to the specified torque.

13 Thoroughly clean the crankshaft and crankshaft sprocket, ensuring that there is no oil or grease on the contact faces.

14 Place the crankshaft sprocket in the timing chain, then engage the chain over the camshaft sprocket. Slide the crankshaft sprocket over the end of the crankshaft.

15 Refit the timing chain tensioner rail, screw in the lower pivot bolt and tighten the bolt to the specified torque.

16 Refit the timing chain tensioner and tighten the two retaining bolts to the specified torque. Depress the tensioner plunger, withdraw the locking drill bit and release the plunger.

17 Refit the timing cover as described in Section 6.

8 Camshaft housing – removal and refitting

Removal

1 Refer to the procedures contained in Chapter 4A, and remove the following components:
   a) *High-pressure fuel pump.*
   b) *Fuel rail.*
   c) *Fuel injectors.*

2 Disconnect the engine wiring harness at the following connectors, if not already done:
   a) *Crankshaft speed/position sensor.*
   b) *Manifold pressure sensor.*

To make a sprocket holding tool, obtain two lengths of steel strip about 6 mm thick by about 30 mm wide or similar, one 600 mm long, the other 200 mm long (all dimensions are approximate). Bolt the two strips together to form a forked end, leaving the bolt slack so that the shorter strip can pivot freely. At the other end of each 'prong' of the fork, drill a suitable hole and fit a nut and bolt. The bolts can be engaged with the holes in the sprocket to hold the sprocket stationary.

   c) *EGR valve.*
   d) *Starter/alternator.*

3 Move the disconnected wiring harness to one side.

4 Remove the timing cover as described in Section 6.

5 Remove the timing chain, sprockets and tensioner as described in Section 7.

6 Undo the three bolts and remove the engine lifting bracket and fuel rail mounting bracket from the camshaft housing.

7 Undo the sixteen bolts, and two stud bolts, securing the camshaft housing to the cylinder head.

8 Lift the camshaft housing off the cylinder head and recover the gasket.

9 Thoroughly clean the mating faces of the cylinder head and camshaft housing and obtain a new gasket for refitting.

Refitting

10 Check that all the hydraulic tappets and rocker arms are correctly positioned in the cylinder head and none have been disturbed.

7.7a Using the holding tool to prevent rotation, slacken the camshaft sprocket retaining bolt . . .

7.7b . . . then unscrew the bolt and remove the sprocket

7.8 Undo the two retaining bolts (arrowed) and remove the timing chain guide rail

8.11a Place a new gasket on the cylinder head . . .

8.11b . . . locate the camshaft housing in position . . .

8.11c . . . then refit the two stud bolts to align the assembly

8.15 Camshaft housing retaining bolt tightening sequence

11 Place a new gasket on the cylinder head, then locate the camshaft housing in position. Refit the two stud bolts to align the assembly but only tighten them finger tight at this stage **(see illustrations)**.

12 Using a straight-edge, align the front face of the camshaft housing with the front face of the cylinder head. Lightly tighten the two stud bolts to retain the housing and maintain the alignment.

13 Refit the sixteen camshaft housing retaining bolts, noting that the longer bolt is fitted at the flywheel end of the housing between the high-pressure fuel pump and vacuum pump locations. Progressively screw in the retaining bolts to gradually draw the housing down and into contact with the cylinder head.

14 Using the straight-edge, check the alignment of the camshaft housing and cylinder head once more and correct if necessary.

15 Working in sequence, tighten the camshaft housing retaining bolts to the specified torque **(see illustration)**. Note that the torque setting for the two stud bolts is different from the other bolts.

16 Refit the engine lifting bracket and fuel rail mounting bracket to the camshaft housing. Refit the three retaining bolts and tighten to the specified torque.

17 Refit the timing chain, sprockets and tensioner as described in Section 7.

18 Refit the timing cover as described in Section 8.

19 Reconnect the engine wiring harness to the connectors listed in paragraph 2.

20 Refit the fuel injectors, fuel rail and high-pressure fuel pump as described in Chapter 4A.

9 Camshafts – removal, inspection and refitting

Note: *An additional camshaft locking tool (two in total) will be required for this operation (see Section 3).*

Removal

1 Carry out the operations described in Section 8, paragraphs 1 to 6.

2 Before removing the camshaft housing completely, the retaining bolts for the camshaft drivegears and sprocket should be slackened as follows.

3 It will be necessary to hold the camshaft sprocket to enable the drivegear and sprocket retaining bolts to be slackened. Vauxhall/Opel special tools KM-956-1 and KM-6347 are available for this purpose, however, a home-made tool can easily be fabricated (see Tool Tip in Section 7).

4 Working through the vacuum pump aperture, and using the holding tool to prevent rotation of the camshaft, slacken the inlet camshaft drivegear retaining bolt. Working through the high-pressure fuel pump aperture, slacken the exhaust camshaft drivegear retaining bolt in the same way.

5 Again, using the holding tool, slacken the camshaft sprocket retaining bolt.

6 Continue with the camshaft housing removal procedure as described in Section 8, paragraphs 7 to 9.

7 With the camshaft housing removed, unscrew the retaining bolt and withdraw the camshaft position sensor from the top of the housing.

8 Turn the housing over and remove the camshaft locking tool.

9 Unscrew the previously-slackened retaining bolt, lift off the drivegear and carefully withdraw the inlet camshaft from the camshaft housing **(see illustrations)**. Using quick-drying paint, correction fluid or a label, suitably mark the sprocket and camshaft to identify them as the inlet components.

10 At the exhaust camshaft, unscrew the previously-slackened retaining bolt and lift off the camshaft sprocket. Unscrew the retaining bolt, lift off the drivegear and carefully

9.9a Unscrew the previously-slackened retaining bolt . . .

9.9b . . . lift off the drivegear . . .

9.9c . . . and carefully withdraw the inlet camshaft from the camshaft housing

withdraw the exhaust camshaft from the camshaft housing **(see illustrations)**. Using quick-drying paint, correction fluid or a label, suitably mark the sprocket and camshaft to identify them as the exhaust components.

Inspection

11 Examine the camshaft bearing surfaces and cam lobes for signs of wear ridges and scoring. Renew the camshaft if any of these conditions are apparent. Examine the condition of the bearing surfaces in the camshaft housing. If the any wear or scoring is evident, the camshaft housing will need to be renewed.

12 If either camshaft is being renewed, it will be necessary to renew all the rocker arms and tappets for that particular camshaft also (see Section 10).

13 Check the condition of the camshaft drive-gears and sprocket for chipped or damaged teeth, wear ridges and scoring. Renew any components as necessary.

Refitting

14 Prior to refitting, thoroughly clean all components and dry with a lint-free cloth. Ensure that all traces of oil and grease are removed from the contact faces of the drivegears, sprocket and camshafts.

15 Lubricate the exhaust camshaft bearing journals in the camshaft housing and carefully insert the exhaust camshaft. Ensuring that the contact faces are clean and dry, refit the drivegear to the camshaft and insert the retaining bolt. Screw in the bolt two or three turns at this stage.

16 Locate the sprocket on the exhaust camshaft with the writing on the sprocket facing away from the camshaft housing. Insert the retaining bolt and screw in the bolt two or three turns at this stage.

17 Lubricate the inlet camshaft bearing journals in the camshaft housing and carefully insert the inlet camshaft. Ensuring that the contact faces are clean and dry, refit the drivegear to the camshaft and insert the retaining bolt. Screw in the bolt two or three turns at this stage.

18 Turn each camshaft to align the timing slot with the valve timing checking hole in the camshaft housing. Insert the camshaft locking tools (either the Vauxhall/Opel tool or the home-made equivalent described in Section 3)

9.18 Insert the locking tools (arrowed) to lock the camshafts in the timing position

ensuring that the tools fully engage with the camshaft slots **(see illustration)**.

19 With the camshafts locked in the timing position, tighten the drivegear retaining bolts and the sprocket retaining bolt to 20 Nm (15 lbf ft). Note that this is only an initial setting to retain the components. Final tightening is carried out after the camshaft housing has been refitted to the cylinder head.

20 Refit the camshaft position sensor to the camshaft housing and tighten the retaining bolt securely.

21 Refit the camshaft housing to the cylinder head as described in Section 8, paragraphs 10 to 15.

22 With the camshaft housing installed, final tightening of the drivegear and sprocket retaining bolts can be carried out.

23 Using the method employed on removal to hold the sprocket, tighten the sprocket retaining bolt to the specified torque **(see illustration)**.

9.10a Unscrew the previously-slackened retaining bolt and lift off the exhaust camshaft sprocket

9.10c . . . lift off the drivegear . . .

9.23 Hold the sprocket with the tool and tighten the retaining bolt to the specified torque

9.10b Unscrew the retaining bolt . . .

9.10d . . . and carefully withdraw the exhaust camshaft from the camshaft housing

24 While still holding the sprocket with the tool, tighten the exhaust camshaft drivegear retaining bolt to the specified torque followed by the inlet camshaft drivegear retaining bolt **(see illustration)**.

25 Remove the locking tool from the inlet camshaft, but leave the exhaust camshaft locking tool in place.

26 Continue with the camshaft housing refitting procedure as described in Section 8, paragraphs 16 to 20.

10 Hydraulic tappets and rocker arms – removal, inspection and refitting

Removal

1 Remove the camshaft housing as described in Section 8.

9.24 While still holding the sprocket with the tool, tighten the drivegear retaining bolt on each camshaft

10.3a Withdraw each rocker arm and hydraulic tappet in turn . . .

2 Obtain sixteen small, oil-tight clean plastic containers, and number them inlet 1 to 8 and exhaust 1 to 8; alternatively, divide a larger container into sixteen compartments and number each compartment accordingly.

3 Withdraw each rocker arm and hydraulic tappet in turn, unclip the rocker arm from the tappet, and place them in their respective container **(see illustrations)**. Do not interchange the rocker arms and tappets, or the rate of wear will be much increased. Fill each container with clean engine oil and ensure that the tappet is submerged.

Inspection

4 Examine the rocker arm and hydraulic tappet bearing surfaces for wear ridges and scoring. Renew any rocker arm or tappet on which these conditions are apparent.

5 If any new hydraulic tappets are obtained, they should be immersed in a container of clean engine oil prior to refitting.

Refitting

6 Liberally oil the cylinder head hydraulic tappet bores and the tappets. Working on one assembly at a time, clip the rocker arm back onto the tappet, then refit the tappet to the cylinder head, ensuring that it is refitted to its original bore. Lay the rocker arm over its respective valve.

7 Refit the remaining tappets and rocker arms in the same way.

8 With all the tappets and rocker arms in place, refit the camshaft housing as described in Section 8.

11.6 Undo the two bolts (arrowed) and free the oil separator from the inlet manifold

10.3b . . . then unclip the rocker arm from the tappet

11 Cylinder head – removal and refitting

Note: *New cylinder head retaining bolts will be required for refitting.*

Removal

1 Remove the camshaft housing as described in Section 8, and the hydraulic tappets and rocker arms as described in Section 10.

2 Remove the turbocharger charge air pipe as described in Chapter 4A.

3 Remove the exhaust gas recirculation (EGR) valve as described in Chapter 4B.

4 Withdraw the engine oil dipstick, then undo the retaining bolt securing the dipstick guide tube to the inlet manifold.

5 Using a small screwdriver, lift up the locking catch and disconnect the manifold pressure sensor wiring connector.

6 Undo the two bolts and free the crankcase ventilation system oil separator from the inlet manifold **(see illustration)**.

7 Working in the **reverse** of the tightening sequence **(see illustration 11.27b)**, progressively slacken the cylinder head bolts by half a turn at a time, until all bolts can be unscrewed by hand. Note that an M12 RIBE socket bit will be required to unscrew the bolts. Remove the cylinder head bolts and recover the washers.

8 Engage the help of an assistant and lift the cylinder head from the cylinder block. Take care as it is a bulky and heavy assembly.

11.16 Cylinder head gasket thickness identification hole (arrowed)

9 Remove the gasket and keep it for identification purposes (see paragraph 16).

10 If the cylinder head is to be dismantled for overhaul, then refer to Part E of this Chapter.

Preparation for refitting

11 The mating faces of the cylinder head and cylinder block/crankcase must be perfectly clean before refitting the head. Use a hard plastic or wood scraper to remove all traces of gasket and carbon; also clean the piston crowns. Take particular care, as the surfaces are damaged easily. Also, make sure that the carbon is not allowed to enter the oil and water passages – this is particularly important for the lubrication system, as carbon could block the oil supply to any of the engine's components. Using adhesive tape and paper, seal the water, oil and bolt holes in the cylinder block/crankcase. To prevent carbon entering the gap between the pistons and bores, smear a little grease in the gap. After cleaning each piston, use a small brush to remove all traces of grease and carbon from the gap, then wipe away the remainder with a clean rag. Clean all the pistons in the same way.

12 Check the mating surfaces of the cylinder block/crankcase and the cylinder head for nicks, deep scratches and other damage. If slight, they may be removed carefully with a file, but if excessive, machining may be the only alternative to renewal.

13 Ensure that the cylinder head bolt holes in the crankcase are clean and free of oil. Syringe or soak up any oil left in the bolt holes. This is most important in order that the correct bolt tightening torque can be applied and to prevent the possibility of the block being cracked by hydraulic pressure when the bolts are tightened.

14 The cylinder head bolts must be discarded and renewed, regardless of their apparent condition.

15 If warpage of the cylinder head gasket surface is suspected, use a straight-edge to check it for distortion. Refer to Part E of this Chapter if necessary.

16 On this engine, the cylinder head-to-piston clearance is controlled by fitting different thickness head gaskets. The gasket thickness can be determined by looking at the left-hand front corner of the gasket and checking on the number of holes **(see illustration)**.

Holes in gasket	Gasket thickness
No holes	0.67 to 0.77 mm
One hole	0.77 to 0.87 mm
Two holes	0.87 to 0.97 mm

The correct thickness of gasket required is selected by measuring the piston protrusions as follows.

17 Remove the crankshaft locking tool from the base of the bellhousing and temporarily refit the crankshaft pulley retaining bolt to enable the crankshaft to be turned.

18 Mount a dial test indicator securely on the block so that its pointer can be easily pivoted between the piston crown and block mating surface. Turn the crankshaft to bring No 1 piston roughly to the TDC position. Move the dial test indicator probe over and in contact with No 1 piston. Turn the crankshaft back-and-forth slightly until the highest reading is shown on the gauge, indicating that the piston is at TDC.

19 Zero the dial test indicator on the gasket surface of the cylinder block then carefully move the indicator over No 1 piston. Measure its protrusion at the highest point between the valve cut-outs, and then again at its highest point between the valve cut-outs at 90° to the first measurement (see illustration). Repeat this procedure with No 4 piston.

20 Rotate the crankshaft half a turn (180°) to bring No 2 and 3 pistons to TDC. Ensure the crankshaft is accurately positioned then measure the protrusions of No 2 and 3 pistons at the specified points. Once all pistons have been measured, rotate the crankshaft to position all the pistons at their mid-stroke and refit the crankshaft locking tool. If the tool will not engage the hole in the flywheel, turn the crankshaft one complete turn and try again.

21 Select the correct thickness of head gasket required by determining the largest amount of piston protrusion, and using the following table.

Piston protrusion measurement	Gasket thickness required
0.028 to 0.127 mm	0.67 to 0.77 mm (no holes)
0.128 to 0.227 mm	0.77 to 0.87 mm (one hole)
0.228 to 0.327 mm	0.87 to 0.97 mm (two holes)

Refitting

22 Wipe clean the mating surfaces of the cylinder head and cylinder block/crankcase. Place the new gasket in position with the words ALTO/TOP uppermost.

23 If not already done, rotate the crankshaft to position all the pistons at their mid-stroke and refit the crankshaft locking tool. If the

tool will not engage the hole in the flywheel, turn the crankshaft one complete turn and try again. Once the tool is in place, remove the crankshaft pulley hub retaining bolt.

24 With the aid of an assistant, carefully refit the cylinder head assembly to the block, aligning it with the locating dowels.

25 Apply a thin film of engine oil to the bolt threads and the underside of the bolt heads. Carefully enter each new cylinder head bolt into its relevant hole (do not drop them in). Screw all bolts in, by hand only, until finger-tight.

26 Using a straight-edge, align the front face of the cylinder head with the front face of the cylinder block (see illustration). Lightly tighten the cylinder head bolts to retain the head and maintain the alignment.

27 Working progressively in sequence, tighten the cylinder head bolts to their Stage 1 torque setting, using a torque wrench and suitable socket (see illustrations).

28 Once all bolts have been tightened to the Stage 1 torque, working again in the same sequence, go around and tighten all bolts through the specified Stage 2 angle, then through the specified Stage 3 angle using an angle-measuring gauge (see illustration).

29 Refit the crankcase ventilation system oil

11.19 Using a dial test indicator to measure piston protrusion

separator to the inlet manifold and secure with the two bolts.

30 Reconnect the manifold pressure sensor wiring connector.

31 Refit the dipstick guide tube to the inlet manifold, refit and tighten the retaining bolt, then insert the dipstick.

32 Refit the exhaust gas recirculation (EGR) valve as described in Chapter 4B.

33 Refit the turbocharger charge air pipe as described in Chapter 4A.

34 Refit the hydraulic tappets and rocker arms as described in Section 10 and the camshaft housing as described in Section 8.

11.26 Using a straight-edge, align the front face of the cylinder head with the front face of the cylinder block

11.27a Working in sequence, tighten the cylinder head bolts to their Stage 1 torque, using a torque wrench

11.27b Cylinder head bolt tightening sequence

11.28 Tighten the bolts through the Stage 2 and Stage 3 angle using an angle-measuring gauge

13.2a Remove the oil pick-up pipe from the oil pump cover . . .

13.2b . . . then remove the rubber seal from the pick-up pipe

13.3 Remove the screws and withdraw the oil pump cover from the rear of the timing cover

12 Sump –
removal and refitting

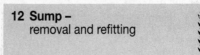

Removal

1 Disconnect the battery negative terminal (refer to *Disconnecting the battery* in the Reference Chapter).
2 Apply the handbrake, then jack up the front of the vehicle and support it on axle stands (see *Jacking and vehicle support*).
3 Drain the engine oil as described in Chapter 1, then fit a new sealing ring and refit the drain plug, tightening it to the specified torque. It is also recommended that the oil filter is renewed at the same time.
4 Referring to the relevant procedures contained in Chapter 4A, remove the catalytic converter from the turbocharger.

5 Undo the five bolts securing the sump reinforcement bracket to the cylinder block baseplate and transmission bellhousing and remove the bracket **(see illustration 6.26)**. Note the locations of the different length bolts to aid refitting.
6 Disconnect the oil level sensor wiring connector at the rear of the sump **(see illustration 6.27)**.
7 Undo the thirteen bolts and two nuts securing the sump to the cylinder block baseplate and timing cover. Using a wide-bladed scraper or similar tool inserted between the sump and baseplate, carefully break the joint, then remove the sump from under the car.

Refitting

8 Thoroughly clean the inside and outside of the sump ensuring that all traces of old sealant are removed from the mating face. Also clean

the cylinder block baseplate mating face to remove all traces of old sealant.
9 Apply a 2 mm bead of Loctite 5900 to the sump mating face, ensuring the sealant bead runs around the inside of the bolt holes **(see illustration 6.59)**. Position the sump on the cylinder block baseplate, then refit the thirteen bolts and two nuts. Progressively tighten the bolts/nuts to the specified torque. Reconnect the oil level sensor wiring connector.
10 Refit the sump reinforcement bracket to the cylinder block baseplate and transmission bellhousing and secure with the five bolts, tightened to the specified torque.
11 Refit the catalytic converter to the turbocharger as described in the relevant procedures contained in Chapter 4A.
12 Lower the vehicle to the ground then fill the engine with fresh oil, with reference to Chapter 1.
13 Refill the cooling system as described in Chapter 1, then reconnect the battery terminal.

13 Oil pump –
removal, inspection and refitting

Removal

1 Remove the timing cover as described in Section 6.
2 Undo the two retaining bolts and remove the oil pick-up pipe from the oil pump cover on the rear of the timing cover. Remove the rubber seal from the pick-up pipe, noting that a new seal will be required for refitting **(see illustrations)**.
3 Remove the securing screws and withdraw the oil pump cover from the rear of the timing cover **(see illustration)**.
4 Remove the inner and outer rotor from the timing cover and wipe them clean. Also clean the rotor location in the timing cover **(see illustrations)**.
5 The oil pressure relief valve components can also be removed from the timing cover by unscrewing the cap. Withdraw the cap, the spring and the plunger **(see illustrations)**.

Inspection

6 Check for any signs of scoring, pitting,

13.4a Remove the oil pump inner rotor . . .

13.4b . . . and outer rotor from the timing cover

13.5a Unscrew the oil pressure relief valve cap . . .

13.5b . . . then withdraw the spring . . .

scuffing or general wear on the rotors or their location in the timing cover. Renew any components as necessary. If the pump components are satisfactory, check the rotor clearances as follows.

7 Locate the inner and outer rotor back in the timing cover. Check the clearance between the end faces of the gears and the housing (endfloat) using a straight-edge and a feeler gauge **(see illustration)**.

8 Check the outer rotor-to-body clearance using a feeler gauge **(see illustration)**.

9 If the clearances are outside the specified limits, renew the components as necessary.

10 Examine the pressure relief valve spring and plunger, and renew if any sign of damage or wear is evident.

11 Ensure that the rotor location in the interior of the timing cover is scrupulously clean before commencing reassembly.

Refitting

12 Thoroughly clean the pressure relief valve components, and lubricate them with clean engine oil before refitting. Insert the plunger and spring, then apply thread-locking compound to the cap threads and refit the cap. Tighten the cap securely.

13 Ensure that the rotors are clean, then lubricate them with clean engine oil. Locate the inner and outer rotor back in the timing cover, with the dot marks aligned and facing away from the timing cover **(see illustration)**.

14 Ensure that the mating faces of the rear cover and the pump housing are clean, then refit the rear cover. Refit and tighten the securing screws securely.

15 Fit a new rubber seal to the oil pick-up pipe and locate the pipe on the oil pump cover. Refit the two retaining bolts and tighten securely.

16 Refit the timing cover as described in Section 6.

---

14 Crankshaft oil seals –
renewal

Timing cover oil seal

Note: *The design of the engine is such that, once the crankshaft pulley hub bolt is undone the valve timing will be lost unless suitable locking tools are used to retain the camshafts and crankshaft in the timing position. Refer to the information contained in Section 3 for further details and obtain the tools described.*

1 Remove the crankshaft pulley as described in Section 5.

2 Disconnect the wiring connector at the camshaft position sensor on the top of the camshaft housing.

3 Disconnect the wiring connectors at the four glow plugs.

4 Unscrew the three bolts securing the plastic wiring harness guide to the top of the camshaft housing.

13.5c . . . and the plunger

13.8 Checking the oil pump outer rotor-to-body clearance

5 Release the locking catches securing the wiring connectors to the four injectors, then disconnect the injector wiring, while at the same time moving the wiring harness guide forward **(see illustration 3.8)**.

6 Unscrew the closure bolt from the valve timing checking hole on the exhaust camshaft side of the camshaft housing **(see illustration 4.9)**.

7 If the Vauxhall/Opel camshaft locking tool or similar alternative is available (see Section 3), screw the tool into the valve timing checking hole. Ensure that the mark on the tool plunger is facing upwards. Using a socket or spanner on the crankshaft pulley hub bolt, turn the crankshaft in the normal direction of rotation (clockwise as viewed from the right-hand side of the car) until the spring-loaded plunger of the locking tool slides into engagement with the slot on the camshaft. There will be an audible click from the tool when this happens, and the plunger will be seen to move in, towards the camshaft.

8 If the home-made locking tool described in Section 3 is being used, insert a screwdriver through the valve timing checking hole on the front of the camshaft housing, and into contact with the exhaust camshaft. Using a socket or spanner on the crankshaft pulley hub bolt, turn the crankshaft in the normal direction of rotation (clockwise as viewed from the right-hand side of the car) until the screwdriver can be felt to engage with the slot in the camshaft. Screw the tool into the camshaft housing until resistance is felt, then turn the crankshaft slightly until the camshaft slot is correctly aligned, and the tool can be screwed fully in **(see illustrations 4.12a and 4.12b)**.

13.7 Checking the oil pump rotor endfloat

13.13 Locate the rotors in the timing cover with the dot marks (arrowed) aligned and facing away from the timing cover

9 Once the camshaft is locked in position, insert the Vauxhall/Opel crankshaft locking tool or suitable alternative (see Section 3) into the timing hole at the base of the transmission bellhousing and into engagement with the flywheel **(see illustrations 4.14a, 4.14b and 4.14c)**. It may be necessary to turn the crankshaft very slightly one way or the other (within the limits of any slack afforded by the timing chain/tensioner) to allow the tool to fully engage.

10 It will now be necessary to hold the crankshaft pulley hub to enable the retaining bolt to be removed. Vauxhall/Opel special tool KM-662-C is available for this purpose, however, a home-made tool can easily be fabricated (see **Tool Tip** in Section 4).

11 Using the Vauxhall/Opel tool or the home-made alternative, hold the pulley hub stationary and unscrew the retaining bolt. **Note:** *The pulley hub retaining bolt has a **left-hand thread** and is unscrewed by turning it clockwise.*

12 Withdraw the pulley hub from the crankshaft.

13 Carefully prise out the old crankshaft oil seal with a screwdriver or similar hooked tool. Clean the oil seal seat with a wooden or plastic scraper.

14 Tap the new oil seal into position until it is flush with the outer face of the timing cover, using a suitable socket or tube, or a wooden block.

15 Thoroughly clean the crankshaft pulley hub, ensuring that the timing chain sprocket contact face is free from oil or grease.

16 Refit the pulley hub to the crankshaft,

14.29 Fit the oil seal to the fitting tool, so that the seal lip is spread open toward the crankshaft side

14.30a Position the seal, together with the fitting tool over the end of the crankshaft . . .

15 Oil cooler/heat exchanger – removal and refitting

14.30b . . . then tap the seal into position using a suitable wooden block or similar

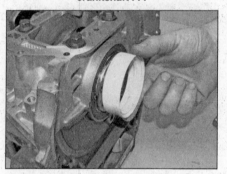

14.31 Once the seal is in position, remove the fitting tool

then refit the retaining bolt. Using the method employed on removal to hold the pulley hub stationary, tighten the retaining bolt to the specified torque.

17 Refit the crankshaft pulley to the pulley hub. Refit the pulley retaining bolts, tightening them to the specified torque.

18 Remove the camshaft and crankshaft locking tools.

19 Thoroughly clean the threads of the closure bolt and apply suitable thread-locking compound. Screw the bolt into the camshaft housing and tighten to the specified torque.

20 Reconnect the fuel injector wiring connectors and secure with the locking catches.

21 Reconnect the wiring connector at the camshaft position sensor.

22 Reconnect the wiring connectors at the four glow plugs.

23 Refit the three bolts securing the plastic wiring harness guide to the top of the camshaft housing.

24 Refit the auxiliary drivebelt as described in Chapter 1 using the mark made prior to removal to ensure the belt is fitted the correct way around.

25 Refit the wheel arch liner and roadwheel, then lower the car to the ground and tighten the wheel bolts to the specified torque.

Transmission end oil seal

Note: *Vauxhall/Opel special tools EN-4677-10 and EN-4677-20 or a suitable equivalent*

oil seal fitting tool will be required for this operation.

26 Remove the flywheel as described in Section 16.

27 Carefully prise out the old seal from its location using a screwdriver or similar hooked tool.

28 Clean the oil seal seat with a wooden or plastic scraper.

29 Fit the new seal to the Vauxhall/Opel tool, or equivalent fitting tool, so that the seal lip is spread open toward the crankshaft side (see illustration).

30 Position the seal, together with the fitting tool over the end of the crankshaft, then tap the seal into position using a suitable socket or tube, or a wooden block, until it is flush with the outer faces of the cylinder block and baseplate (see illustrations).

15.11 Undo the three bolts (arrowed) and withdraw the heat exchanger from the oil filter housing

31 Once the seal is in position, remove the fitting tool (see illustration).

32 Refit the flywheel as described in Section 16.

Removal

1 Disconnect the battery negative terminal (refer to *Disconnecting the battery* in the Reference Chapter).

2 Referring to the procedures contained in Chapter 4A, separate the exhaust system front section from the catalytic converter.

3 Drain the cooling system as described in Chapter 1.

4 Remove the turbocharger charge air hose as described in Chapter 4A.

5 Undo the upper nut and two lower bolts and remove the oil filter heat shield (see illustration 6.13).

6 Undo the two bolts securing the coolant pipe to the oil filter housing (see illustration 6.14). Recover the gasket noting that a new one will be required for refitting.

7 Unscrew the banjo union bolt and release the turbocharger oil supply pipe from the oil filter housing (see illustration 6.15). Recover the two copper washers from the banjo union, and suitable cover the end of the pipe to prevent dirt entry. Note that new copper washers will be required for refitting.

8 Slacken the retaining clip and disconnect the radiator bottom hose from the outlet at the base of the oil filter housing.

9 Undo the three bolts securing the heat shield support bracket to the heat exchanger on the oil filter housing (see illustration 6.17).

10 Undo the remaining bolt and remove the oil filter housing and heat exchanger assembly from the cylinder block. Recover the rubber seal from the rear of the housing. Note that a new seal will be required for refitting.

11 Undo the three retaining bolts and withdraw the heat exchanger from the oil filter housing (see illustration). Recover the four sealing rings, noting that new sealing rings will be required for refitting.

Refitting

12 Thoroughly clean the heat exchanger and oil filter housing, then fit the four new sealing rings to the filter housing.

13 Place the heat exchanger in position and secure with the three retaining bolts, securely tightened.

14 Place a new rubber seal on the oil filter housing, ensuring the seal is fully engaged with the housing grooves (see illustration 6.63).

15 Position the oil filter housing on the cylinder block and fit the lower left retaining bolt finger tight. Place the heat shield support bracket in position and fit the remaining three retaining bolts. Tighten the four bolts to the specified torque.

16.3 Flywheel retaining bolts (arrowed)

17.8 Right-hand engine mounting retaining bolts (arrowed)

16 Connect the radiator bottom hose to the outlet at the base of the oil filter housing and secure with the retaining clip.

17 Using a new copper washer on each side of the banjo union, refit the turbocharger oil supply pipe and screw in the banjo union bolt. Tighten the bolt to the specified torque.

18 Locate a new gasket over the coolant pipe and bend over the tabs of the gasket to retain it on the flange.

19 Position the coolant pipe on the heat exchanger/oil filter housing. Refit the two bolts and tighten them to the specified torque.

20 Place the heat shield over the oil filter and secure with the two lower bolts and upper nut.

21 Refit the turbocharger charge air hose as described in Chapter 4A.

22 Refit the exhaust system components with reference to Chapter 4A.

23 Lower the vehicle to the ground, then reconnect the battery negative terminal.

24 Refill the cooling system as described in Chapter 1.

16 Flywheel – removal, inspection and refitting

Note: *New flywheel retaining bolts will be required on refitting.*

Removal

1 Remove the transmission as described in Chapter 7A then remove the clutch assembly as described in Chapter 6.

2 Prevent the flywheel from turning by inserting one of the bellhousing-to-engine retaining bolts. Rest a large screwdriver against the bolt with its end in contact with the flywheel ring gear teeth.

3 Slacken and remove the retaining bolts and remove the flywheel **(see illustration)**. Do not drop it, as it is very heavy.

Inspection

4 Examine the flywheel for wear or chipping of the ring gear teeth. Renewal of the ring gear is possible but is not a task for the home mechanic; renewal requires the new ring gear to be heated (up to 180° to 230ºC) to allow it to be fitted.

5 Examine the flywheel for scoring of the clutch face. If the clutch face is scored, the flywheel may be surface-ground, but renewal is preferable.

6 If there is any doubt about the condition of the flywheel, seek the advice of a Vauxhall/Opel dealer or engine reconditioning specialist. They will be able to advise if it is possible to recondition it or whether renewal is necessary.

Refitting

7 Clean the mating surfaces of the flywheel and crankshaft.

8 Apply a drop of locking compound to the threads of each of the new flywheel retaining bolts (unless they are already precoated) then refit the flywheel and install the new bolts.

9 Lock the flywheel using the method employed on removal then, working in a diagonal sequence, evenly and progressively tighten the retaining bolts to the specified torque setting.

10 Refit the clutch as described in Chapter 6, then refit the transmission as described in Chapter 7A.

17 Engine/transmission mountings – inspection and renewal

Inspection

1 To improve access, firmly apply the handbrake, then jack up the front of the vehicle and support it on axle stands (see *Jacking and vehicle support*).

2 Check the mounting blocks (rubbers) to see if they are cracked, hardened or separated from the metal at any point. Renew the mounting block if any such damage or deterioration is evident.

3 Check that all the mounting securing nuts and bolts are securely tightened, using a torque wrench to check if possible.

4 Using a large screwdriver, or a similar tool, check for wear in the mounting blocks by carefully levering against them to check for free play. Where this is not possible, enlist the aid of an assistant to move the engine/gearbox unit back-and-forth, and from side-to-side, while you observe the mountings. While some free play is to be expected, even from new components, excessive wear should be obvious. If excessive free play is found, check first to see that the securing nuts and bolts are correctly tightened, then renew any worn components as described in the following paragraphs.

Renewal

Note: *Before slackening any of the engine mounting bolts/nuts, the relative positions of the mountings to their various brackets should be marked to ensure correct alignment upon refitting.*

Right-hand mounting

5 Apply the handbrake, then jack up the front of the vehicle and support it on axle stands (see *Jacking and vehicle support*).

6 Remove the air cleaner assembly as described in Chapter 4A.

7 Attach a suitable hoist and lifting tackle to the engine lifting brackets on the cylinder head, and support the weight of the engine.

8 Mark the position of the six mounting bracket bolts, then undo the three bolts securing the mounting to the body and the three bolts securing the mounting to the engine bracket **(see illustration)**. Remove the mounting.

17.16 Front mounting/torque link

9 If necessary, undo the four bolts securing the engine bracket to the cylinder block and cylinder head and remove the engine bracket **(see illustration 6.31)**.

10 If removed, refit the engine mounting bracket and tighten the bolts to the specified torque

11 Place the engine mounting in position and refit the six retaining bolts. Align the mounting in its original position, then tighten the bolts to the specified torque.

12 Remove the hoist, then refit the air cleaner as described in Chapter 4A.

13 On completion, lower the vehicle to the ground.

Front mounting/torque link

14 Apply the handbrake, then jack up the front of the vehicle and support it on axle stands (see *Jacking and vehicle support*).

15 Attach a suitable hoist and lifting tackle to the engine lifting brackets on the cylinder head, and support the weight of the engine.

16 Slacken and remove the nut and washer securing the mounting to the subframe bracket. Withdraw the bolt **(see illustration)**.

17 Undo the bolts securing the mounting bracket to the transmission, then manoeuvre the mounting and bracket out of position.

18 Check all components for signs of wear or damage, and renew as necessary.

19 On reassembly, refit the mounting bracket (aligning the previously-made marks) and tighten its bolts to the specified torque.

20 Locate the mounting in the subframe, ensuring it is fitted the correct way up, and manoeuvre the engine/transmission into position. Refit the mounting bolts and new nuts. Tighten them to the specified torque.

21 Lower the vehicle to the ground.

Left-hand mounting

22 Apply the handbrake, then jack up the front of the vehicle and support it on axle stands (see *Jacking and vehicle support*). Remove the left-hand roadwheel and the plastic wheel arch liner.

23 Remove the battery and battery tray as described in Chapter 5.

24 Attach a suitable hoist and lifting tackle to the engine lifting brackets on the cylinder head, and support the weight of the engine.

25 Working under the wheel arch undo the nut securing the lower rear corner of the mounting to the body, then withdraw the bolt from within the engine compartment.

26 Undo the three bolts securing the mounting bracket to the transmission bracket.

27 Undo the three remaining bolts securing the mounting to the body and the three bolts securing the transmission bracket to the transmission.

28 Slightly lower the engine, then unclip the clutch hydraulic line from the mounting bracket. Remove the mounting assembly from the car.

29 If necessary, undo the through-bolt and separate the rubber mounting from the mounting bracket.

30 If removed, refit the rubber mounting to the mounting bracket and tighten the through-bolt to the specified torque.

31 Locate the mounting brackets in position and clip the clutch hydraulic line onto the bracket.

32 Raise the engine and insert the bolts/nut, then tighten them to the specified torque.

33 Disconnect the hoist and lifting tackle, refit the wheel arch liner and roadwheel, then lower the vehicle to the ground.

34 Refit the battery and battery tray as described in Chapter 5.

Rear mounting/torque link

35 Apply the handbrake, then jack up the front of the vehicle and support it on axle stands (see *Jacking and vehicle support*).

36 Attach a suitable hoist and lifting tackle to the engine lifting brackets on the cylinder head, and support the weight of the engine.

37 Working under the vehicle, remove the centre nut and bolt securing the mounting to the transmission bracket.

38 Remove the two bolts securing the mounting to the subframe, and withdraw the mounting/torque link.

39 If necessary, unbolt the bracket from the transmission. **Note:** *The bracket bolts and link bolts are of different lengths.*

40 Refit the bracket to the transmission and tighten the bolts to the specified torque.

41 Locate the new mounting/link in position ensuring that the lug on the top of the mounting engages with the slot in the transmission bracket. Insert the bolts, screw on the nut and tighten to the specified torque.

42 Remove the hoist and lower the vehicle to the ground.

Chapter 2 Part B:
1.7 litre engine in-car repair procedures

Contents

Degrees of difficulty

Easy, suitable for novice with little experience	Fairly easy, suitable for beginner with some experience	Fairly difficult, suitable for competent DIY mechanic	Difficult, suitable for experienced DIY mechanic	Very difficult, suitable for expert DIY or professional

Specifications

General

Engine type	Four-cylinder, in-line, water-cooled. Belt-driven double overhead camshaft, 16 valves
Manufacturer's engine codes	Z17DTL and Z17DTH
Bore	79.0 mm
Stroke	86.0 mm
Capacity	1686 cc
Firing order	1-3-4-2 (No 1 cylinder at timing belt end)
Direction of crankshaft rotation	Clockwise (viewed from timing belt end of engine)
Compression ratio	18.4:1

Compression pressures

Maximum difference between any two cylinders	1.5 bar

Valve clearances

Engine cold:	
Inlet and exhaust	0.4 ± 0.05 mm

Lubrication system

	Standard	Service limit
Oil pump type	Rotor-type, driven by timing belt	
Oil pressure at 80°C (approximate)	1.3 bars at idle speed	
Oil pump clearances:		
Outer rotor-to-body clearance	0.24 to 0.36 mm	0.40 mm
Inner-to-outer rotor clearance	0.13 to 0.15 mm	0.20 mm
Rotor endfloat	0.035 to 0.100 mm	0.150 mm

Torque wrench settings

	Nm	lbf ft
Auxiliary belt tensioner to alternator support	50	37
Auxiliary belt guide roller to alternator support	38	28
Baffle plate-to-cylinder block bolts	19	14
Camshaft bearing cap nuts:		
M8 nuts	21	15
M10 nuts	27	20
Camshaft cover bolts	10	7

Torque wrench settings (continued)

	Nm	lbf ft
Camshaft housing to cylinder head:		
M8 bolts	21	15
M10 bolts	27	20
Camshaft sprocket bolt	64	47
Charge air pipe to throttle housing and inlet manifold	25	18
Coolant pump pulley bolts	12	9
Coolant pipe to cylinder block	95	70
Connecting rod big-end bearing cap nuts*:		
Stage 1	25	18
Stage 2	Angle-tighten a further 100°	
Stage 3	Angle-tighten a further 15°	
Crankshaft oil seal housing bolts	10	7
Crankshaft pulley bolts	20	15
Crankshaft sprocket bolt	196	145
Cylinder head bolts*:		
Stage 1	40	30
Stage 2	Angle-tighten a further 60°	
Stage 3	Angle-tighten a further 60°	
Engine/transmission mounting bolts:		
Front mounting/torque link:		
Mounting-to-transmission bolts	80	59
Mounting to subframe	55	41
Left-hand mounting:		
Mounting-to-body bolts	20	15
Bracket-to-transmission bolts	55	41
Mounting-to-bracket bolts	55	41
Rear mounting/torque link:		
Mounting-to-bracket bolts	55	41
Mounting-to-subframe bolts	55	41
Bracket-to-transmission bolts	80	59
Right-hand mounting:		
Bracket-to-engine bolts	55	41
Mounting-to-body nuts	35	26
Mounting-to-bracket bolt	55	41
Engine-to-transmission unit bolts:		
M10 bolts	40	30
M12 bolts	60	44
Flywheel bolts*:		
Z17DTL engines:		
Stage 1	30	22
Stage 2	Angle-tighten a further 60°	
Stage 3	Angle-tighten a further 15°	
Z17DTH engines:		
Stage 1	85	63
Stage 2	Angle-tighten a further 30°	
Stage 3	Angle-tighten a further 15°	
Fuel injector upper seal plate bolts:		
Stage 1	10	7
Stage 2	20	15
High-pressure fuel pipe union nuts	25	18
High-pressure fuel pump sprocket nut	68	50
Main bearing cap bolts*	88	65
Oil dipstick guide tube bolts	10	7
Oil cooler/filter housing to cylinder block	25	18
Oil pressure relief valve bolt	30	22
Oil pump cover retaining bolts	10	7
Oil pump sprocket nut	44	32
Oil pump pick-up/strainer bolts	19	14
Sump bolts:		
Main casting-to-block bolts	10	7
Sump pan-to-main casting bolts	10	7
Drain plug	78	58
Roadwheel bolts	110	81
Timing belt cover bolts	10	7
Timing belt idler pulley bolt	80	59
Timing belt tensioner pulley bolt	38	28

* Use new fasteners

1 General information

How to use this Chapter

This Part of Chapter 2 describes the repair procedures which can reasonably be carried out on the engine while it remains in the vehicle. If the engine has been removed from the vehicle and is being dismantled as described in Chapter 2E, any preliminary dismantling procedures can be ignored.

Note that, while it may be possible physically to overhaul items such as the piston/connecting rod assemblies while the engine is in the vehicle, such tasks are not usually carried out as separate operations, and usually require the execution of several additional procedures (not to mention the cleaning of components and of oilways); for this reason, all such tasks are classed as major overhaul procedures, and are described in Chapter 2E.

Chapter 2E describes the removal of the engine/transmission unit from the vehicle, and the full overhaul procedures which can then be carried out.

Engine description

The 1.7 litre common-rail diesel engine is of the sixteen-valve, in-line four-cylinder, double overhead camshaft (DOHC) type, mounted transversely at the front of the car with the transmission attached to its left-hand end.

The crankshaft runs in five main bearings. Thrustwashers are fitted to No 2 main bearing shell (upper half) to control crankshaft endfloat.

The connecting rods rotate on horizontally-split bearing shells at their big-ends. The pistons are attached to the connecting rods by gudgeon pins, which are a sliding fit in the connecting rod small-end eyes and retained by circlips. The aluminium-alloy pistons are fitted with three piston rings – two compression rings and an oil control ring.

The cylinder block is made of cast iron and the cylinder bores are an integral part of the block. On this type of engine the cylinder bores are sometimes referred to as having dry liners.

The inlet and exhaust valves are each closed by coil springs, and operate in guides pressed into the cylinder head.

The inlet camshaft is driven by the crankshaft by a timing belt and rotates directly in the camshaft housing. The exhaust camshaft is driven by the inlet camshaft via a spur gear. The camshafts operate the valves via followers, which are situated directly below the camshafts. Valve clearances are adjusted using camshaft followers of different thickness.

Lubrication is by means of an oil pump, which is driven by the timing belt. It draws oil through a strainer located in the sump, and then forces it through an externally-mounted filter into galleries in the cylinder block/crankcase. From there, the oil is distributed to the crankshaft (main bearings) and camshaft. The big-end bearings are supplied with oil via internal drillings in the crankshaft, while the camshaft bearings also receive a pressurised supply. The camshaft lobes and valves are lubricated by splash, as are all other engine components. An oil cooler is fitted to keep the oil temperature stable under arduous operating conditions.

Operations with engine in place

The following operations can be carried out without having to remove the engine from the vehicle.
a) Compression pressure testing.
b) Camshaft cover – removal and refitting.
c) Timing belt cover – removal and refitting.
d) Timing belt – removal and refitting.
e) Timing belt tensioner and sprockets – removal and refitting.
f) Valve clearances – checking and adjustment.
g) Camshaft and followers – removal, inspection and refitting.
h) Cylinder head – removal and refitting.
i) Connecting rods and pistons – removal and refitting*.
j) Sump – removal and refitting.
k) Oil pump – removal, overhaul and refitting.
l) Oil cooler – removal and refitting.
m) Crankshaft oil seals – renewal.
n) Engine/transmission mountings – inspection and renewal.
o) Flywheel – removal, inspection and refitting.
p) Camshaft housing – removal and refitting.
* Although the operation marked with an asterisk can be carried out with the engine in the car after removal of the sump, it is better for the engine to be removed, in the interests of cleanliness and improved access. For this reason, the procedure is described in Chapter 2E.

2 Compression and leakdown tests – general information

Compression test

1 When engine performance is down, or if misfiring occurs which cannot be attributed to the fuel system, a compression test can provide diagnostic clues as to the engine's condition. If the test is performed regularly, it can give warning of trouble before any other symptoms become apparent.

2 Due to the design of the electronic control system used on these engines, a compression test can only be carried out with the engine management electronic control unit connected to Vauxhall/Opel Tech2 diagnostic test equipment, or a compatible alternative unit. Without the test equipment, it is not possible to prevent the high-pressure fuel pump from supplying fuel to the fuel rail and injectors when the engine is cranking. When connected, the test equipment communicates with the engine management ECU to inhibit the fuel supply.

3 As the equipment needed for the compression test is unlikely to be available to the home mechanic, it is recommended that the test is performed by a Vauxhall/Opel dealer, or suitably-equipped garage.

Leakdown test

4 A leakdown test measures the rate at which compressed air fed into the cylinder is lost. It is an alternative to a compression test, and in many ways it is better, since the escaping air provides easy identification of where pressure loss is occurring (piston rings, valves or head gasket).

5 As the equipment needed for the compression test is also unlikely to be available to the home mechanic, it is recommended that the test is performed by a Vauxhall/Opel dealer, or suitably-equipped garage.

3 Top dead centre (TDC) for No 1 piston – locating

Note: If the engine is to be locked in position with No 1 piston at TDC on its compression stroke then a M6 and M8 bolt will be required.

1 In its travel up-and-down its cylinder bore, Top Dead Centre (TDC) is the highest point that each piston reaches as the crankshaft rotates. While each piston reaches TDC both at the top of the compression stroke and again at the top of the exhaust stroke, for the purpose of timing the engine, TDC refers to the piston position (usually number 1) at the top of its compression stroke.

2 Number 1 piston (and cylinder) is at the right-hand (timing belt) end of the engine, and its TDC position is located as follows. Note that the crankshaft rotates clockwise when viewed from the right-hand side of the car.

3 Disconnect the battery negative terminal (refer to Disconnecting the battery in the Reference Chapter).

4 Firmly apply the handbrake, then jack up the front of the car and support it securely on axle stands (see Jacking and vehicle support). Remove the right-hand front roadwheel.

5 Remove the timing belt upper cover as described in Section 6.

6 Using a socket and extension bar on the crankshaft sprocket bolt, rotate the crankshaft until the notch on the crankshaft pulley rim is aligned with the pointer on the base of the oil pump cover (see illustration). Once the mark is correctly aligned, No 1 and 4 pistons are at TDC.

7 To determine which piston is at TDC on its compression stroke, check the position of the timing holes in the camshaft and high-pressure

3.6 Align the timing mark on the crankshaft pulley with the pointer on the oil pump cover to bring No 1 piston to TDC

3.8a The camshaft sprocket can be locked using a 6 mm bolt (arrowed) . . .

3.8b . . . and the high-pressure fuel pump sprocket by an 8 mm bolt (arrowed)

fuel pump sprockets. When No 1 piston is at TDC on its compression stroke, both sprocket holes will be aligned with the threaded holes in the cylinder head/block, and both exhaust camshaft lobes for cylinder No 1 are pointing upwards if viewed through the oil filler hole. If the timing holes are out of alignment, continue rotating the crankshaft until they align. Note that because the sprockets are of different diameters, it may take up to six revolutions of the crankshaft to achieve alignment.

8 With No 1 piston at TDC on its compression stroke, if necessary, the camshaft and high-pressure fuel pump sprockets can be locked in position. Secure the camshaft sprocket in position by screwing a M6 bolt into the hole in the cylinder head and lock the high-pressure fuel pump sprocket in position by screwing a M8 bolt into the cylinder block **(see illustrations)**.

4 Camshaft cover – removal and refitting

> **Warning: Refer to the information contained in Chapter 4A, Section 2, before proceeding.**

Removal

1 Disconnect the battery negative terminal (refer to *Disconnecting the battery* in the Reference Chapter).

2 Remove the engine oil filler cap, then lift off the plastic cover over the top of the engine. Refit the oil filler cap.

3 Remove the air cleaner assembly and intake duct as described in Chapter 4A.

4 Release the wiring harness support clips

from the plastic charge air pipe over the top of the engine **(see illustration)**.

5 Slacken the retaining clips securing the charge air pipe to the turbocharger.

6 Release the retaining clip and disconnect the crankcase ventilation hose from the camshaft cover **(see illustration)**.

7 Open the clip and detach the fuel hose from the charge air pipe, then undo the two charge air pipe retaining bolts. Disengage the pipe from the turbocharger, then remove the pipe from the top of the engine **(see illustration)**.

8 Undo the six bolts securing the rear charge air pipe to the throttle housing and inlet manifold. Remove the charge air pipe and recover the gaskets **(see illustrations)**.

9 Release the locking catches securing the wiring connectors to the four fuel injectors then disconnect the injector wiring **(see illustrations)**.

4.4 Release the wiring harness support clips from the charge air pipe

4.6 Disconnect the crankcase ventilation hose from the camshaft cover

4.7 Remove the charge air pipe from the top of the engine

4.8a Undo the six bolts then remove the rear charge air pipe . . .

4.8b . . . and recover the gaskets

4.9a Release the wiring connector locking catches . . .

4.9b . . . and disconnect the wiring connectors at the fuel injectors

4.10 Squeeze the connectors and disconnect the wiring at the four glow plugs

4.11a Undo the two bolts (arrowed) securing the wiring harness guide to the camshaft cover . . .

4.11b . . . then move the wiring harness to one side

10 Disconnect the wiring from the glow plugs by squeezing the connectors with thumb and forefinger, and pulling them from the plugs **(see illustration)**.

11 Undo the two bolts securing the wiring harness guide to the camshaft cover, then move the wiring harness to one side **(see illustrations)**.

12 Thoroughly clean the fuel pipe unions on the fuel injectors and fuel rail. Using an open-ended spanner, unscrew the union nuts securing the high-pressure fuel pipes to the injectors and fuel rail. Withdraw the high-pressure fuel pipes and plug or cover the open unions to prevent dirt entry **(see illustrations)**.

13 Disconnect the fuel leak-off hose connection at each injector by pushing in the locking clip and lifting out the hose fitting **(see illustration)**. Suitably plug or cover the open unions to prevent dirt entry.

4.12a Unscrew the union nuts securing the high-pressure fuel pipes to the injectors and fuel rail . . .

14 Unscrew the nut and two bolts securing the injector leak-off hose assembly to the camshaft cover and inlet manifold and move the hose assembly to one side **(see illustration)**.

15 Unscrew the two bolts and remove the

4.12c . . . and plug or cover the open unions to prevent dirt entry

4.12b . . . withdraw the high-pressure fuel pipes . . .

left-hand engine lifting bracket from the rear of the camshaft cover. Similarly, release the wiring harness support clip, undo the retaining bolt and remove the right-hand engine lifting bracket **(see illustrations)**.

16 Unclip the vacuum hose from the oil

4.13 Push in the locking clip and lift out the leak-off hose fitting on each injector

4.14 Unscrew the nut and two bolts (arrowed) and move the leak-off hose assembly to one side

4.15a Unscrew the bolts and remove the left-hand engine lifting bracket . . .

4.15b . . . and right-hand engine lifting bracket

4.16a Unclip the vacuum hose from the oil dipstick guide tube support bracket . . .

4.16b . . . release the dipstick guide tube from the bracket and undo the two bolts (arrowed) . . .

4.16c . . . then remove the bracket from the camshaft cover

4.17a Undo the two bolts . . .

4.17b . . . and remove the outer seal plate from each fuel injector

4.18 Undo the two bolts and remove the upper seal plate from each fuel injector

dipstick guide tube support bracket, and release the dipstick guide tube from the bracket. Undo the two bolts and remove the bracket from the camshaft cover **(see illustrations)**.

17 Undo the two bolts and remove the

4.20 Unscrew the retaining bolts and lift away the camshaft cover, complete with rubber seal

4.23 Fit the new rubber seal to the camshaft cover ensuring it is fully seated in the cover groove

outer seal plate from each fuel injector **(see illustrations)**. Note that new seal plates will be required for refitting.

18 Undo the two bolts and remove the upper seal plate from each fuel injector **(see illustration)**. Note that new seal plates will be required for refitting.

19 Unscrew the two bolts securing the timing belt upper cover to the camshaft cover.

20 Unscrew the nine retaining bolts, noting the different bolt lengths, and lift away the camshaft cover, complete with rubber seal **(see illustration)**. Note that a new rubber seal will be required for refitting.

21 Prior to refitting, obtain four new injector

4.24a Apply sealant to areas (1) and (2) in the camshaft housing . . .

upper seal plates, four new injector outer seal plates, a new camshaft cover rubber seal and a tube of Vauxhall/Opel sealant compound (white), part no 90 511 124.

Refitting

22 Thoroughly clean the camshaft cover and the mating surfaces of the cover and camshaft housing ensuring that all traces of oil are removed from the mating surfaces.

23 Fit the new rubber seal to the camshaft cover ensuring it is fully seated in the cover groove **(see illustration)**.

24 Apply Vauxhall/Opel sealant compound to the camshaft housing mating surfaces at the end of each camshaft. Ensure that the oil borehole at the right-hand end of the exhaust camshaft is not covered in sealant **(see illustrations)**.

25 Carefully lower the cover into position, ensuring the seal remains correctly seated.

4.24b . . . ensuring the borehole (arrowed) is not covered in sealant

Refit the timing belt upper cover and camshaft cover retaining bolts and tighten them progressively to the specified torque.

26 Locate the fuel injector upper seal plates in position on the camshaft cover ensuring they are centralised over each injector. Apply Vauxhall/Opel sealant compound to the underside of the bolt heads and screw in the bolts finger tight.

27 Hold the upper seal plates in position by hand, while tightening the retaining bolts to the specified torque in the two stages given in the Specifications.

28 The remainder of the reassembly procedure is a reversal of removal, noting the following points:

a) *Ensure all nuts, bolts and pipe unions are tightened to the correct torque setting where specified.*

b) *The injector outer seal plates are marked 'up' or 'upper' and 'outside' on their outer surface. Fit the seals and make sure that the centre of the seal is pushed over the injector taper (see illustration).*

c) *After starting the engine, check for leaks.*

5 Crankshaft pulley – removal and refitting

Removal

1 Firmly apply the handbrake, then jack up the front of the car and support it securely on axle stands (see *Jacking and vehicle support*). Remove the right-hand roadwheel.

5.3 Remove the bolts (arrowed) securing the crankshaft pulley to the sprocket

6.5 Undo the six securing bolts and remove the right-hand engine mounting

2 Remove the auxiliary drivebelt as described in Chapter 1. Prior to removal, mark the direction of rotation on the belt to ensure the belt is refitted the same way around.

3 Slacken and remove the small retaining bolts securing the pulley to the crankshaft sprocket and remove the pulley from the engine **(see illustration)**. If necessary, prevent crankshaft rotation by holding the sprocket retaining bolt with a suitable socket.

Refitting

4 Refit the pulley to the crankshaft sprocket, aligning the pulley hole with the sprocket locating pin **(see illustrations)**. Refit the pulley retaining bolts, tightening them to the specified torque.

5 Refit the auxiliary drivebelt as described in Chapter 1 using the mark made prior to removal to ensure the belt is fitted the correct way around.

6 Refit the roadwheel, then lower the car to the ground and tighten the wheel bolts to the specified torque.

6 Timing belt covers – removal and refitting

Removal

Upper cover

1 Disconnect the battery negative terminal (refer to *Disconnecting the battery* in the Reference Chapter).

5.4a Refit the pulley to the crankshaft sprocket, aligning the pulley hole (arrowed) . . .

6.6 Undo the bolts and separate the engine mounting support bracket from the mounting adapter

4.28 The injector outer seal plates are marked 'up' or 'upper' and 'outside' on their outer surface

2 Remove the engine oil filler cap, then lift off the plastic cover over the top of the engine. Refit the oil filler cap.

3 Remove the air cleaner assembly and intake duct as described in Chapter 4A.

4 Support the weight of the engine using a trolley jack with a block of wood placed on its head.

5 Mark the position of the right-hand engine mounting to the support bracket, then undo the six securing bolts and remove the mounting **(see illustration)**.

6 Undo the retaining bolts and separate the engine mounting support bracket from the engine block mounting adapter **(see illustration)**.

7 Disconnect the camshaft sensor wiring connector, then undo the sensor bracket retaining bolt and remove the sensor **(see illustrations)**.

5.4b . . . with the sprocket locating pin (arrowed)

6.7a Disconnect the camshaft sensor wiring connector . . .

6.7b . . . then undo the sensor bracket retaining bolt (arrowed) . . .

6.7c . . . and remove the sensor

6.8a Undo the bolt (arrowed) securing the wiring trough to the camshaft housing . . .

6.8b . . . and release the trough, wiring harness and vacuum pipe from the timing belt cover

6.9 Release the lower vacuum pipe from the clips at the base of the timing belt cover

6.10 Undo the eight upper cover retaining bolts and withdraw the cover

8 Undo the bolt securing the wiring trough to the camshaft housing, and release the trough, wiring harness and vacuum pipe from the timing belt cover **(see illustrations)**.

9 Release the lower vacuum pipe from the clips at the base of the timing belt cover **(see illustration)**.

10 Undo the eight upper cover retaining bolts and withdraw the cover **(see illustration)**. Note the cover bolts are of different lengths.

Lower cover

11 Firmly apply the handbrake, then jack up the front of the car and support it securely on axle stands (see *Jacking and vehicle support*). Remove the right-hand roadwheel.

12 Remove the auxiliary drivebelt as described in Chapter 1. Prior to removal, mark the direction of rotation on the belt to ensure the belt is refitted the same way around.

13 Remove the timing belt upper cover as described previously.

14 Slacken and remove the small retaining bolts securing the crankshaft pulley to the crankshaft sprocket and remove the pulley from the engine **(see illustration 5.3)**. If necessary, prevent crankshaft rotation by holding the sprocket retaining bolt with a suitable socket.

15 Undo the three retaining bolts and remove the coolant pump pulley.

16 Undo the three retaining bolts, and remove the lower cover from the oil pump housing, then manoeuvre the engine mounting adapter out from the timing belt area **(see illustrations)**.

Rear cover

17 Remove timing belt as described in Section 7.

18 With reference to Section 8, remove the timing belt guide roller, camshaft sprocket and high-pressure fuel pump sprocket.

19 Undo the five retaining bolts, and remove the rear timing belt cover.

Refitting

20 Refitting is the reverse of removal, ensuring all retaining bolts are tightened to the specified torque.

7 Timing belt – removal and refitting

Note: *The timing belt must be removed and refitted with the engine cold.*

Removal

1 Position No 1 cylinder at TDC on its compression stroke as described in Section 3. Lock the camshaft and injection pump sprockets in position by screwing the bolts into the threaded holes in the cylinder head/block.

2 Remove the crankshaft pulley as described in Section 5.

3 Unbolt and remove the timing belt upper and lower covers with reference to Section 6.

4 Slacken the timing belt tensioner retaining bolt, then turn the tensioner anti-clockwise to relieve the belt tension, using a suitable hexagon bit or Allen key engaged with the hole provided in the tensioner front plate **(see illustration)**. Hold the tensioner in this position and tighten the retaining bolt.

6.16a Undo the three retaining bolts, and remove the lower cover from the oil pump housing . . .

6.16b . . . then manoeuvre the engine mounting adapter out from the timing belt area

7.4 Slacken the timing belt tensioner retaining bolt (arrowed) then turn the tensioner anti-clockwise to relieve the belt tension

7.7 Align the notch on the crankshaft sprocket with the pointer on the oil pump cover (arrowed)

5 Slide the timing belt off its sprockets and remove it from the engine. If the belt is to be re-used, use white paint or similar to mark the direction of rotation on the belt. **Do not** rotate the crankshaft until the timing belt has been refitted.

6 Check the timing belt carefully for any signs of uneven wear, splitting or oil contamination, and renew it if there is the slightest doubt about its condition. If the engine is undergoing an overhaul and is approaching the specified interval for belt renewal (see Chapter 1) renew the belt as a matter of course, regardless of its apparent condition. If signs of oil contamination are found, trace the source of the oil leak and rectify it, then wash down the engine timing belt area and all related components to remove all traces of oil.

Refitting

7 On reassembly, thoroughly clean the timing belt sprockets and ensure the camshaft and high-pressure fuel pump sprockets are locked correctly in position. Temporarily refit the crankshaft pulley to the sprocket and check that the pulley cut-out is still aligned with the pointer on the oil pump cover; the mark on the crankshaft sprocket should also be aligned with the mark on the oil pump cover **(see illustration)**.

8 Remove the pulley and fit the timing belt over the crankshaft, oil pump, high-pressure fuel pump and camshaft sprockets, ensuring that the belt rear run is taut (ie, all slack is on the tensioner pulley side of the belt). Do not twist the belt sharply while refitting it. Ensure that the belt teeth are correctly seated centrally in the sprockets, and that the timing marks remain in alignment. If a used belt is being refitted, ensure that the arrow mark made on removal points in the normal direction of rotation, as before.

9 Tension the belt by slackening the tensioner retaining bolt and allowing the tensioner to automatically take up the slack in the belt.

10 Check that the crankshaft sprocket timing mark is still correctly positioned then unscrew

the locking bolts from the high-pressure fuel pump and camshaft sprockets.

11 With the tensioner pulley retaining bolt still slackened, rotate the crankshaft pulley approximately 60° **backwards** (anti-clockwise) to automatically adjust the timing belt tension. Hold the crankshaft pulley stationary and tighten the tensioner pulley retaining bolt to the specified torque.

12 Rotate the crankshaft through six complete turns in the normal direction of rotation to settle the timing belt in position. Realign the crankshaft sprocket timing mark and check that the camshaft and high-pressure fuel pump sprocket locking bolts can be refitted. If it is not possible to fit the locking bolts with the crankshaft sprocket timing mark aligned, repeat the belt refitting procedure.

13 Refit the timing belt covers and the crankshaft pulley as described in Sections 5 and 6.

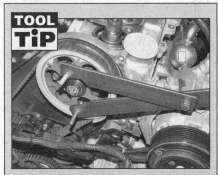

TOOL TIP

To make a sprocket holding tool, obtain two lengths of steel strip about 6 mm thick by about 30 mm wide or similar, one 600 mm long, the other 200 mm long (all dimensions are approximate). Bolt the two strips together to form a forked end, leaving the bolt slack so that the shorter strip can pivot freely. At the other end of each 'prong' of the fork, drill a suitable hole and fit a nut and bolt to allow the tool to engage with the spokes in the sprocket.

8 Timing belt tensioner and sprockets – removal and refitting

Camshaft sprocket

Removal

1 Remove the timing belt as described in Section 7. Prior to attempting to unscrew the sprocket retaining bolt, turn the crankshaft 60° **backwards** (anti-clockwise) to prevent any accidental piston-to-valve contact.

2 Remove the locking bolt securing the camshaft sprocket in the TDC position.

3 It will now be necessary to hold the camshaft sprocket to enable the retaining bolt to be removed. Vauxhall/Opel special tools KM-956-1 and KM-6347 are available for this purpose, however, a home-made tool can easily be fabricated **(see Tool Tip)**.

4 Using the holding tool to prevent rotation of the camshaft, slacken the sprocket retaining bolt. Remove the holding tool, unscrew the retaining bolt and remove the sprocket, noting which way round it is fitted **(see illustration)**. If the sprocket locating pin is a loose fit, remove it from the camshaft end and store it with the sprocket for safe-keeping.

8.4 Using the holding tool to prevent rotation of the camshaft, slacken the sprocket retaining bolt

8.12 Using a sprocket holding tool to prevent rotation as the high-pressure fuel pump sprocket nut is slackened

8.13 Using a puller to remove the high-pressure fuel pump sprocket

8.14 Align the keyway in the sprocket with the Woodruff key in the shaft

Refitting

5 Ensure the locating pin is in position then refit the sprocket to the camshaft end aligning its locating hole with the pin.

6 Refit the sprocket retaining bolt, then tighten the bolt to the specified torque using the holding tool to prevent rotation.

7 Turn the camshaft sprocket slightly, as necessary, then refit the locking bolt to secure the sprocket in the TDC position.

8 Rotate the crankshaft 60° **forwards** (clockwise) until the groove in the crankshaft timing belt sprocket is at '12 o'clock' and aligns with the cast-in mark on the oil pump cover.

9 Refit the timing belt as described in Section 7.

High-pressure fuel pump sprocket

Removal

10 Remove the timing belt as described in Section 7.

11 Remove the locking bolt securing the high-pressure fuel pump sprocket in the TDC position.

12 Refer to the information contained in paragraph 3 and hold the sprocket, then slacken and remove the sprocket retaining nut **(see illustration)**.

13 Remove the sprocket from the fuel pump shaft, noting which way around it is fitted. If the Woodruff key is a loose fit in the pump shaft, remove it and store it with the sprocket for safe-keeping. **Note:** *The sprocket is a tapered-fit on the fuel pump shaft and in some cases a suitable puller*

may be needed to free it from the shaft (see illustration).

Refitting

14 Ensure the Woodruff key is correctly fitted to the pump shaft then refit the sprocket, aligning the sprocket groove with the key **(see illustration)**.

15 Refit the retaining nut and tighten it to the specified torque whilst using the holding tool to prevent rotation.

16 If not already done, align the sprocket timing hole with the threaded hole in the cylinder block and screw in the locking bolt.

17 Refit the timing belt as described in Section 7.

Crankshaft sprocket

Removal

18 Remove the timing belt as described in Section 7.

19 Slacken the crankshaft sprocket retaining bolt. To prevent crankshaft rotation, have an assistant select top gear and apply the brakes firmly. If the engine is removed from the vehicle it will be necessary to lock the flywheel (see Section 18).

20 Unscrew the retaining bolt and washer and remove the crankshaft sprocket from the end of the crankshaft **(see illustration)**. If the sprocket is a tight fit, draw it off of the crankshaft using a suitable puller. If the Woodruff key is a loose fit in the crankshaft, remove it and store it with the sprocket for safe-keeping.

21 Slide the flanged spacer off of the crankshaft, noting which way around it is fitted.

Refitting

22 Refit the flanged spacer to the crankshaft with its convex surface facing away from the oil pump housing **(see illustration)**.

23 Ensure the Woodruff key is correctly fitted then slide on the crankshaft sprocket aligning its groove with the key.

24 Refit the retaining bolt and washer then lock the crankshaft by the method used on removal, and tighten the sprocket retaining bolt to the specified torque setting **(see illustration)**.

25 Refit the timing belt as described in Section 7.

Oil pump sprocket

Removal

26 Remove the timing belt as described in Section 7.

27 Prevent the oil pump sprocket from rotating using a socket and extension bar fitted to one of the oil pump cover bolts then slacken and remove the sprocket retaining nut.

28 Remove the sprocket from the oil pump shaft, noting which way around it is fitted.

Refitting

29 Refit the sprocket, aligning it with the flat on the pump shaft, and fit the retaining nut. Tighten the sprocket retaining nut to the specified torque, using the socket and extension bar to prevent rotation **(see illustration)**.

8.20 Slide the sprocket from the shaft

8.22 Fit the flanged spacer with the convex side away from the oil pump cover

8.24 Refit the sprocket retaining bolt and washer

30 Refit the timing belt as described in Section 7.

Tensioner assembly

Removal

31 Remove the timing belt as described in Section 7.

32 Unscrew the retaining bolt and remove the tensioner assembly from the engine. Disengage the tension spring from its locating stud as the tensioner is removed.

Refitting

33 Fit the tensioner assembly to the engine, engaging the tension spring over the stud. Screw in the tensioner retaining bolt, then turn the tensioner anti-clockwise using a suitable hexagon bit or Allen key engaged with the hole provided in the tensioner front plate. Hold the tensioner in this position and tighten the retaining bolt.

34 Refit the timing belt as described in Section 7.

Idler pulley

Removal

35 Remove the timing belt as described in Section 7.

36 Slacken and remove the retaining bolt and remove the idler pulley from the engine **(see illustration)**.

Refitting

37 Refit the idler pulley and tighten the retaining bolt to the specified torque.

38 Refit the timing belt as described in Section 7.

---

9 Camshaft oil seal – renewal

1 Remove the camshaft sprocket as described in Section 8.

2 Carefully punch or drill a small hole in the oil seal. Screw in a self-tapping screw, and pull on the screw with pliers to extract the seal **(see illustration)**.

3 Clean the seal housing, and polish off any burrs or raised edges which may have caused the seal to fail in the first place.

8.29 Use a socket and extension bar on one of the oil pump cover bolts to prevent the sprocket from turning

4 Press the new seal into position using a suitable tubular drift (such as a socket) which bears only on the hard outer edge of the seal. Take care not to damage the seal lips during fitting; note that the seal lips should face inwards **(see illustration)**.

5 Refit the camshaft sprocket as described in Section 8.

---

10 Valve clearances – checking and adjustment

Checking

1 The importance of having the valve clearances correctly adjusted cannot be overstressed, as they vitally affect the performance of the engine. The engine must be cold for the check to be accurate. The clearances are checked as follows.

2 Apply the handbrake, then jack up the front of the car and support it on axle stands. Remove the right-hand front roadwheel to gain access to the crankshaft pulley.

3 Remove the camshaft cover as described in Section 4, and with reference to Chapter 4A, remove the fuel injectors.

4 Using a socket and extension on the crankshaft sprocket bolt, rotate the crankshaft in the normal direction of rotation (clockwise when viewed from the right-hand end of the engine) until the notch on the crankshaft pulley is correctly aligned with the pointer on the base of the oil pump cover.

8.36 Timing belt idler pulley retaining bolt

5 Now rotate the crankshaft in the normal direction (clockwise) until the inlet camshaft lobes for No 1 cylinder (nearest the timing belt end of the engine) and the exhaust camshaft lobes for No 3 cylinder are pointing away from the followers. This indicates that these valves are completely closed, and the clearances can be checked.

6 On a piece of paper, draw the outline of the engine with the cylinders numbered from the timing belt end. Show the position of each valve, together with the specified valve clearance. Note that the clearance for both the inlet and exhaust valves is the same.

7 With the cam lobes positioned as described in paragraph 5, using feeler blades, measure the clearance between the base of both No 1 cylinder inlet cam lobes and No 3 cylinder exhaust cam lobes and their followers. Record the clearances on the paper **(see illustration)**.

8 Rotate the crankshaft pulley through a half a turn (180º) to position No 3 cylinder inlet camshaft lobes and No 4 cylinder exhaust camshaft lobes pointing away from their followers. Measure the clearance between the base of the camshaft lobes and their followers and record the clearances on the paper.

9 Rotate the crankshaft pulley through a half a turn (180º) to position No 2 cylinder exhaust camshaft lobes and No 4 inlet camshaft lobes pointing away from their followers. Measure the clearance between the base of the camshaft lobes and their followers and record the clearances on the paper.

10 Rotate the crankshaft pulley through a half a turn (180º) to position No 1 cylinder

9.2 Pull the screw to extract the seal

9.4 Press the oil seal into position using a tubular drift such as a socket

10.7 With the camshaft lobe pointing away from the follower measure the clearance

10.14 Carefully depress the follower and slide the shim out

10.15 The thickness of each shim should be stamped on one of its surfaces

exhaust camshaft lobes and No 2 cylinder inlet camshaft lobes pointing away from their followers. Measure the clearance between the base of the camshaft lobes and their followers and record the clearances on the paper.

11 If all the clearances are correct, refit the cylinder head cover (see Section 4), and injectors (see Chapter 4A), then refit the roadwheel, lower the vehicle to the ground and tighten the wheel bolts to the specified torque. If any clearance measured is not correct, adjustment must be carried out as described in the following paragraphs.

Adjustment

12 Rotate the crankshaft pulley until the lobe of the valve to be adjusted is pointing directly away from the follower. **Note:** *Ensure that the crankshaft is not positioned at TDC, as when a valve follower is depressed to remove the shim, the valve will strike the piston.*

13 Rotate the follower until the groove on its upper edge is facing towards the front of the engine (exhaust followers), or rear of the engine (inlet followers).

14 In the absence of the special Vauxhall/Opel tool (KM-6090), position a large flat-bladed screwdriver between the edge of the follower and the base of the camshaft. Use the screwdriver to carefully depress the follower until there is enough clearance to allow the shim to be slid out from between the follower and camshaft (a magnetic tool is particularly useful for this task) **(see illustration)**.

15 Clean the shim, and measure its thickness with a micrometer. The shims carry thickness markings, but wear may have reduced the

original thickness, so be sure to check **(see illustration)**.

16 Add the measured clearance of the valve to the thickness of the original shim then subtract the specified valve clearance from this figure. This will give you the thickness of the shim required. For example:

Valve clearance measured:	0.35 mm
Plus thickness of the original shim:	2.70 mm
Equals:	3.05 mm
Minus clearance required:	0.40 mm
Thickness of shim required:	2.65 mm

17 Obtain the correct thickness of shim required and lubricate it with clean engine oil. Carefully depress the follower and slide the shim into position, with the thickness number downwards, ensuring it is correctly located.

> **HAYNES HINT** *It may be possible to correct the clearances by moving the shims around between the valves, but don't rotate the engine with any shims missing. Keep a note of all the shim thicknesses to assist valve clearance adjustment when they need to be done again.*

18 Repeat the procedure given in paragraphs 12 to 17 on the remaining valves which require adjustment.

19 Rotate the crankshaft a few times to settle all shims in position then recheck the valve clearances before refitting the fuel injectors (Chapter 4A) and the camshaft cover (Section 4).

20 Refit the roadwheel then lower the vehicle

11.5 Insert a screw through the fixed gear and into the backlash compensating gear (arrowed)

11.9 Lift out the cam followers and shims

to the ground and tighten the wheel bolts to the specified torque.

11 Camshaft and followers – removal, inspection and refitting

Removal

1 Remove the camshaft cover as described in Section 4.

2 Remove the fuel injectors as described in Chapter 4A.

3 Remove the camshaft sprocket as described in Section 8.

4 Undo the nuts and remove the No 5 bearing cap from the left-hand (gearbox) end of the camshafts.

5 The exhaust camshaft gear incorporates a backlash compensating gear. This must now be locked to the fixed exhaust camshaft gear by inserting a suitably-sized bolt/rod into the hole on the inboard face of the fixed gear, and through into the backlash compensating gear. This prevents the spring preload of the compensating gear being lost when either camshaft is removed **(see illustration)**.

6 Working in a spiral pattern from the outside in, slacken the remaining camshaft bearing cap retaining nuts by one turn at a time, to relieve the pressure of the valve springs on the bearing caps gradually and evenly. Once the valve spring pressure has been relieved, the nuts can be fully unscrewed and removed.

Caution: If the bearing cap nuts are carelessly slackened, the bearing caps might break. If any bearing cap breaks then the complete cylinder head assembly must be renewed; the bearing caps are matched to the head and are not available separately.

7 Remove the bearing caps, noting each caps correct fitted location. The bearing caps are numbered 1 to 5 and the arrow on each cap points towards the timing belt end of the engine.

8 Lift the camshafts out of the cylinder head.

9 Obtain sixteen small, clean plastic containers, and label them for identification. Alternatively, divide a larger container into compartments. Lift the followers and shims out from the top of the cylinder head and store each one in its respective fitted position. Make sure the followers and shims are not mixed to ensure the valve clearances remain correctly adjusted on refitting **(see illustration)**.

Inspection

10 Examine the camshaft bearing surfaces and camshaft lobes for signs of wear ridges and scoring. Renew the camshaft if any of these conditions are apparent.

11 Examine the condition of the bearing surfaces both on the camshaft journals and in the cylinder head. If the head bearing surfaces are worn excessively, the cylinder head will need to be renewed.

11.13 Ensure each shim is correctly located

11.14 Align the camshaft gear marks (arrowed)

11.16 Apply a smear of sealant to the No 1 camshaft-bearing cap

12 Examine the followers and their bores in the cylinder head for signs of wear or damage. If any follower is visibly worn it should be renewed.

Refitting

13 Where removed, lubricate the followers with clean engine oil and carefully insert each one into its original location in the cylinder head. Ensure each shim is correctly located in the top of the its relevant follower **(see illustration)**.

14 Rotate the crankshaft approximately 60° **backwards** (anti-clockwise) as a precaution against accidental piston-to-valve contact. Lubricate the camshaft followers with clean engine oil then lay the camshafts in position. Check that the exhaust camshaft backlash compensating gear is still locked to the fixed gear. Ensure that the mark on the outer face exhaust camshaft gear lies between the two marks on the outer face of the inlet camshaft gear, and that the marks are approximately level with the upper edge of the camshaft housing **(see illustration). Note:** *If the exhaust camshaft is being renewed, it will be necessary to obtain Vauxhall/Opel tool No KM 6092, and pretension the backlash compensating gear prior to installation.*

15 Ensure the mating surfaces of the bearing caps and camshaft housing are clean and dry

and lubricate the camshaft journals and lobes with clean engine oil.

16 Apply a smear of suitable sealant (available from Vauxhall/Opel dealers) to the areas of the camshaft housing No 1 bearing cap mating surface **(see illustration)**.

17 Refit the No 1 to 4 camshaft bearing caps in their original locations on the cylinder head. The caps are numbered 1 to 5 (No 1 cap being at the timing belt end of the engine) and the arrow cast onto the top of each cap should point towards the timing belt end of the engine **(see illustration)**.

18 Refit the No 1 to 4 bearing cap nuts, tightening them by hand only.

19 Remove the bolt/rod locking the backlash compensating gear to the exhaust camshaft fixed gear, and refit the No 5 camshaft bearing cap.

20 Working in sequence, tighten the nuts by one turn at a time to gradually impose the pressure of the valve springs evenly on the bearing caps **(see illustration)**. Repeat this sequence until all bearing caps are in contact with the cylinder head then go around in sequence and tighten them to the specified torque.

Caution: If the bearing cap bolts are carelessly tightened, the bearing caps might break. If any bearing cap breaks then the complete cylinder head assembly

must be renewed; the bearing caps are matched to the head and are not available separately.

21 Fit a new camshaft oil seal as described in Section 9.

22 Refit the camshaft sprocket and timing belt as described in Sections 7 and 8.

23 Check the valve clearances as described in Section 10, then refit the fuel injectors as described in Chapter 4A and the camshaft cover as described in Section 4.

12 Camshaft housing – removal and refitting

Removal

1 Remove the camshaft sprocket as described in Section 8, and the camshaft cover as described in Section 4. Remove the two bolts securing the rear timing belt cover to the camshaft housing **(see illustration)**.

2 With reference to Chapter 4A, remove the fuel injectors and the throttle housing.

3 Undo the retaining bolt(s) and remove the throttle housing mounting bracket.

4 Undo the retaining bolt and detach the EGR valve heat exchanger bracket from the front of the camshaft housing.

11.17 The arrows on the camshaft bearing caps should point towards the timing belt end of the engine

11.20 Camshaft bearing cap tightening sequence

J44603

12.1 Remove the two bolts securing the rear timing belt cover to the camshaft housing

12.6a Tie the compressor to the slam panel . . .

12.6b . . . and remove the compressor mounting bracket

12.8 Remove the gasket

12.11 Camshaft housing bolts tightening sequence

H32428

5 Undo the retaining bolt and remove the engine lifting bracket from the front of the camshaft housing.

6 Release the refrigerant hoses from the retaining clip on the right-hand side inner wing. Without undoing the refrigerant pipes, disconnect the wiring plug, unbolt the air conditioning compressor from its support bracket (3 bolts), and position it clear of the engine. Use a cable tie or similar to tie the compressor to the bonnet slam panel out of the way. Undo the three bolts and remove the air conditioning compressor support bracket (see illustrations).

7 Slacken the camshaft housing retaining bolts 1/2 turn at a time in the **reverse** of the sequence shown in illustration 12.11.

8 Undo the bolts completely and remove the camshaft housing. Remove and discard the gasket (see illustration).

Refitting

9 Ensure all mating surfaces are clean and free from any gasket or sealant residue.

10 Prior to refitting the housing, check that the camshaft gears are correctly aligned, with the mark on the outer face of the exhaust gear between the marks on the outer face of the inlet gear (see Section 11, paragraph 14)

11 With a new gasket in place, position the camshaft housing on to the cylinder head, and tighten the housing bolts evenly and gradually to the specified torque, in sequence (see illustration).

12 The remainder of refitting is a reversal of removal. noting the following points:
   a) Check the valve clearances and adjust if necessary (see Section 10).
   b) Refit the fuel injectors and throttle housing as described in Chapter 4A.
   c) Refit the camshaft cover as described in Section 4.
   d) Refit the camshaft sprocket (Section 8) then refit and tension the timing belt as described in Section 7.

13 Cylinder head – removal and refitting

Caution: Be careful not to allow dirt into the fuel injection pump or injector pipes during this procedure.

Note: New cylinder head bolts will be required on refitting.

Removal

1 Drain the engine oil and cooling system as described in Chapter 1.

2 Remove the camshaft housing as described in Section 12.

3 As a precaution, obtain sixteen small, clean plastic containers, and label them for identification. Alternatively, divide a larger container into compartments.

4 Lift the followers out from the top of the cylinder head and store each one in its respective fitted position (see illustration).

13.4 Store the followers the correct way up

13.13 Lift the cylinder head off the block

13.20 Cylinder head gasket identification hole – type 1 gasket (arrowed)

5 Release the retaining clips and disconnect the upper and lower coolant hoses from the EGR valve heat exchanger. Undo the two bolts at each end of the metal EGR pipe, securing the pipe flanges to the exhaust manifold and EGR valve housing. Remove the EGR valve heat exchanger/pipe assembly from the engine and collect the two flange gaskets.

6 Remove the exhaust manifold and turbocharger as described in Chapter 4A.

7 Disconnect the wiring connector from the rear of the EGR valve.

8 Release the retaining clip and disconnect the coolant hose from the EGR valve housing. Undo the two bolts and remove the EGR valve and housing from the cylinder head.

9 Release the retaining clips and disconnect the coolant hoses from the thermostat housing and cylinder head.

10 Disconnect the wiring connectors at the charge pressure sensor and inlet manifold switch-over valve solenoid. Disconnect the vacuum hose at the switch-over valve vacuum unit.

11 Working in a spiral sequence starting at the outside and working inwards, progressively slacken the cylinder head bolts by half a turn at a time, until all bolts can be unscrewed by hand.

12 Lift out the cylinder head bolts and recover the washers.

13 Lift the cylinder head away; seek assistance if possible, as it is a heavy assembly **(see illustration)**. Remove the gasket, noting the two locating dowels fitted to the top of the cylinder block. If they are a loose fit, remove the locating dowels and store them with the head for safe-keeping. Keep the head gasket for identification purposes (see paragraph 20).

14 If the cylinder head is to be dismantled for overhaul, then refer to Part E of this Chapter.

Preparation for refitting

15 The mating faces of the cylinder head and cylinder block/crankcase must be perfectly clean before refitting the head. Use a hard plastic or wood scraper to remove all traces of gasket and carbon; also clean the piston crowns. Take particular care, as the surfaces are damaged easily. Also, make sure that the carbon is not allowed to enter the oil and water passages – this is particularly important

for the lubrication system, as carbon could block the oil supply to any of the engine's components. Using adhesive tape and paper, seal the water, oil and bolt holes in the cylinder block/crankcase. To prevent carbon entering the gap between the pistons and bores, smear a little grease in the gap. After cleaning each piston, use a small brush to remove all traces of grease and carbon from the gap, then wipe away the remainder with a clean rag. Clean all the pistons in the same way.

16 Check the mating surfaces of the cylinder block/crankcase and the cylinder head for nicks, deep scratches and other damage. If slight, they may be removed carefully with a file, but if excessive, machining may be the only alternative to renewal.

17 Ensure that the cylinder head bolt holes in the crankcase are clean and free of oil. Syringe or soak up any oil left in the bolt holes. This is most important in order that the correct bolt tightening torque can be applied and to prevent the possibility of the block being cracked by hydraulic pressure when the bolts are tightened.

18 The cylinder head bolts must be discarded and renewed, regardless of their apparent condition.

19 If warpage of the cylinder head gasket surface is suspected, use a straight-edge to check it for distortion. Refer to Part E of this Chapter if necessary.

20 On this engine, the cylinder head-to-piston clearance is controlled by fitting different thickness head gaskets. Two different types of gasket are supplied by Vauxhall/Opel

13.21 Measure the piston projection at the highest points between the valve cut-outs

parts stockists, with each type being available in three different thicknesses. The gasket thickness can be determined by looking at the left-hand front corner of the gasket (type 1) or front centre of the gasket (type 2) and checking on the number of holes **(see illustration)**.

Holes in gasket		Gasket thickness
Type 1	Type 2	
No holes	One hole	1.45 mm
One hole	Two holes	1.50 mm
Two holes	Three holes	1.55 mm

The correct thickness of gasket required is selected by measuring the piston protrusions as follows.

21 Ensure that the crankshaft is still correctly positioned in the TDC position. Mount a dial test indicator securely on the block so that its pointer can be easily pivoted between the piston crown and block mating surface. Zero the dial test indicator on the gasket surface of the cylinder block then carefully move the indicator over No 1 piston and measure the its protrusion at its highest point between the valve cut-outs, and then again at its highest point between the valve cut-outs at 90° to the first measurement **(see illustration)**.

22 Rotate the crankshaft half a turn (180°) to bring No 2 and 3 pistons to TDC. Ensure the crankshaft is accurately positioned then measure the protrusions of No 2 and 3 pistons at the specified points. Once both pistons have been measured, rotate the crankshaft through a further one and a half turns (540°) to bring No 1 and 4 pistons back to TDC.

23 Select the correct thickness of head gasket required by determining the largest amount of piston protrusion, and using the following table.

Piston protrusion measurement	Gasket thickness required
0.630 to 0.696 mm	1.45 mm
0.697 to 0.763 mm	1.50 mm
0.764 to 0.830 mm	1.55 mm

Refitting

24 Wipe clean the mating surfaces of the cylinder head and cylinder block/crankcase.

25 Check that the two locating dowels are in position then fit a new gasket to the cylinder block **(see illustration)**.

26 If not already positioned at TDC, rotate

13.25 Check the locating dowels are in place

13.29 Tighten the bolts to the Stage 1 torque setting . . .

13.30 . . . then through the Stage 2 and 3 angles

the crankshaft so that No 1 piston is at its highest point in the cylinder. Now turn the crankshaft 60° **backwards** (anti-clockwise). This is to ensure that whist the cylinder head and camshafts are being refitted, there is little chance of accidental piston-to-valve contact.

27 With the aid of an assistant, carefully refit the cylinder head assembly to the block, aligning it with the locating dowels.

28 Carefully enter each new cylinder head bolt into its relevant hole (*do not drop them in*). Screw all bolts in, by hand only, until finger-tight.

29 Working progressively in a spiral sequence starting at the centre and working outwards, tighten the cylinder head bolts to their Stage 1 torque setting, using a torque wrench and suitable socket **(see illustration)**.

30 Once all bolts have been tightened to the Stage 1 torque, working again in sequence, go around and tighten all bolts through the specified Stage 2 and Stage 3 angles. It is recommended that an angle-measuring gauge is used to ensure accuracy **(see illustration)**. If a gauge is not available, use white paint to make alignment marks prior to tightening; the marks can then be used to check that the bolt has been rotated through the correct angle.

31 The remainder of refitting is a reversal of removal, bearing in mind the following points:

a) *Prior to refitting the timing belt, turn the crankshaft 60° in the normal direction of rotation (clockwise) to TDC on No 1 cylinder until the groove in the crankshaft sprocket aligns with the cast-in mark on the oil pump housing* **(see illustration 7.7)**.

b) *Ensure all wiring is correctly routed secured*

c) *Check the valve clearances as described in Section 10.*

d) *On completion, refill the engine with fresh oil and coolant as described in Chapter 1.*

14 Sump – removal and refitting

Removal

1 Disconnect the battery negative terminal (refer to *Disconnecting the battery* in the Reference Chapter).

2 Firmly apply the handbrake, then jack up the front of the car and support it securely on axle stands (see *Jacking and vehicle support*).

3 Drain the engine oil as described in Chapter 1, then fit a new sealing washer and refit the drain plug, tightening it to the specified torque.

4 Slacken and remove the bolts securing the sump lower pan to the main casting then remove the sump pan from underneath the vehicle **(see illustration)**.

5 To remove the main casting from the engine, remove the exhaust system front pipe as described in Chapter 4A.

6 Undo the two bolts securing the oil dipstick guide tube to the main sump casting.

7 Progressively slacken and remove the nuts and bolts securing the main casting to the base of the cylinder block/oil pump cover and transmission. Break the joint by striking the

casting with the palm of the hand, or using a wide plastic spatula carefully inserted in the joint between the sump and cylinder block. Lower the casting away from the engine and withdraw it from underneath the vehicle.

8 While the sump main casting is removed, take the opportunity to check the oil pump pick-up/strainer for signs of clogging or splitting. If necessary, unbolt the pick-up/strainer and remove it from the engine along with its sealing ring **(see illustration)**. The strainer can then be cleaned easily in solvent or renewed.

Refitting

9 Remove all traces of dirt, oil and sealant from the mating surfaces of the sump main casting and pan, the cylinder block and (where removed) the pick-up/strainer.

10 Where necessary, fit a new sealing ring to the oil pump pick-up/strainer and fit the strainer to the base of the cylinder block **(see illustration)**. Refit the strainer retaining bolt and tighten it to the specified torque.

11 Ensure the main casting and cylinder block mating surfaces are clean and dry, and apply a coat of suitable sealant (available from Vauxhall/Opel dealers) to the upper mating surface of the casting.

12 Position a new dipstick guide tube rubber seal on the main casting **(see illustration)**.

13 Offer up the main casting and loosely refit all the retaining nuts and bolts **(see illustration)**. Note that the four long bolts correspond with the bolts holes at the rear of the casting. If the sump is being fitted with the engine removed from the vehicle and separated from the

14.4 If the lower pan is stuck to the main casting, carefully ease it away using a wide-bladed scraper

14.8 Remove the oil pick-up pipe and strainer

14.10 Fit a new oil pick-up pipe sealing ring

14.12 Position a new oil dipstick guide tube sealing ring

14.13 Refit the sump main casting

14.17 Apply a bead of sealant and refit the pan to the sump main casting

transmission, ensure that the rear face of the casting is flush with the transmission mounting face of the cylinder block. Working out from the centre in a diagonal sequence, progressively tighten the main casting retaining bolts to the specified torque setting.

14 Refit the bolts securing the main casting to the transmission housing and tighten them to the specified torque.

15 Ensure that the oil dipstick guide tube is correctly positioned, refit the retaining bolts, and tighten to the specified torque.

16 Refit the exhaust front pipe as described in Chapter 4A.

17 Ensure the main casting and sump pan mating surfaces are clean and dry and apply a coat of suitable sealant (available from Vauxhall/Opel dealers) to the upper mating surface of the pan. Refit the pan to the base of the main casting and tighten its retaining bolts to the specified torque **(see illustration)**.

18 Lower the vehicle to the ground then fill the engine with fresh oil, with reference to Chapter 1.

15 Oil pump –
removal, inspection and refitting

Removal

1 Remove the timing belt as described in Section 7.

2 Remove the oil pump and crankshaft timing belt sprockets as described in Section 8.

3 Remove the sump main casting as described in Section 14.

4 Slacken and remove the retaining bolts then slide the oil pump cover off of the end of the crankshaft, taking great care not to lose the locating dowels. Remove the sealing ring, which is fitted around the oil pump housing section of the cover, and discard it.

5 Using a suitable marker pen, mark the surface of the pump outer rotor; the mark can then be used to ensure the rotor is refitted the correct way around.

6 Remove the oil pump inner and outer rotors from the cylinder block **(see illustrations)**.

7 If necessary, unscrew the oil pressure relief valve assembly from the rear of the cylinder block. Remove the sealing ring.

Inspection

8 Clean the components, and carefully examine the rotors, pump housing and cover for any signs of scoring or wear. Renew any component which shows signs of wear or damage. If the pump housing in the cylinder block is marked then seek the advice of a Vauxhall/Opel dealer on the best course of action.

9 If the components appear serviceable, fit the rotors into the housing and measure the clearance between the outer rotor and pump housing, and the inner rotor tip-to-outer rotor clearance using feeler blades **(see illustration)**. Also measure the rotor endfloat, and check the flatness of the end cover. If the clearances exceed the specified tolerances, renew the worn components.

10 If the relief valve has been removed, check that the valve piston is free to move easily and return smoothly under spring pressure. If not renew the valve assembly.

Refitting

11 Where removed, fit a new sealing ring to the oil pressure relief valve then refit the valve assembly to the cylinder block and tighten it to the specified torque setting.

12 Lubricate the pump rotors with clean engine oil and refit them to the pump housing, using the mark made prior to removal to ensure the outer rotor is fitted the correct way around.

13 Prior to refitting, carefully lever out the crankshaft and oil pump oil seals using a flat-bladed screwdriver. Fit the new oil seals, ensuring that each seals sealing lip is facing inwards, and press them squarely into the housing using a tubular drift which bears only on the hard outer edge of the seal. Press each seal into position so that it is flush with the housing **(see illustration)**.

14 Ensure the mating surfaces of the oil pump and cylinder block are clean and dry and the

15.6a Remove the oil pump inner rotor . . .

15.6b . . . and outer rotor

15.9 Measure the inner rotor tip-to-outer rotor clearance

15.13 The seal fits flush with the housing

15.15 Fit a new seal to the oil pump cover

16.2 Pull the screw to extract the seal

locating dowels are in position. Remove all traces of sealant from the threads of the pump cover bolts.

15 Fit a new seal into the groove around the oil pump housing section of the cover, and apply a bead of suitable sealant (available from Vauxhall/Opel dealers) to the pump cover mating surface **(see illustration)**.

16 Carefully manoeuvre the oil pump cover into position, taking great care not to damage the oil seal lips on the crankshaft and inner rotor shaft. Locate the cover on the dowels making sure the pump sealing ring remains correctly positioned.

17 Apply a smear of sealant to the threads of each cover retaining bolt then refit all bolts and tighten them to the specified torque. Note that the longer bolt corresponds to the lower left-hand bolt hole in the cover.

18 Refit the timing belt sprockets and belt as described in Sections 7 and 8 then refit the sump as described in Section 13.

19 On completion refill the engine with fresh oil as described in Chapter 1.

16 Oil pump seal – renewal

1 Remove the oil pump sprocket as described in Section 8.

2 Carefully punch or drill a small hole in the oil seal. Screw a self-tapping screw into the seal, and pull on the screw with pliers to extract the seal **(see illustration)**.

Caution: Great care must be taken to avoid damage to the oil pump.

3 Clean the seal housing, and polish off any burrs or raised edges which may have caused the seal to fail in the first place.

4 Press the new seal into position using a suitable tubular drift (such as a socket) which bears only on the hard outer edge of the seal. Take care not to damage the seal lips during fitting; note that the seal lips should face inwards.

5 Refit the oil pump sprocket as described in Section 8.

17 Oil cooler – removal and refitting

Removal

1 The oil cooler and integral oil filter housing is situated on the rear left-hand side of the cylinder block. Firmly apply the handbrake, then jack up the front of the car and support it securely on axle stands (see *Jacking and vehicle support*).

2 Drain the cooling system as described in Chapter 1. Alternatively, clamp the oil cooler coolant hoses directly above the cooler, and be prepared for some coolant loss as the hoses are disconnected. To improve access to the coolant hoses, remove the charge air pipe/hose.

3 Position a suitable container beneath the oil filter. Undo the oil cooler return hose union/ release the retaining clip and disconnect the return hose.

4 Release the clips and disconnect the coolant hoses from the oil cooler, and release the wiring loom retaining clip.

5 Remove the single bolt securing the oil filter housing to the cylinder block. Discard the sealing ring; a new one must be used on refitting.

Refitting

6 Fit a new sealing ring to the recess in the rear of the cooler, then offer the cooler to the cylinder block **(see illustration)**.

7 Ensure that the oil cooler return hose union is correctly positioned, ensure that the lug of the oil filter housing engages correctly, then refit the centre bolt and tighten it to the specified torque **(see illustration)**.

8 Reconnect the coolant hoses to the cooler and secure them in position with the retaining clips.

9 Lower the vehicle to the ground. Top-up the engine oil level as described in Chapter 1.

10 If removed, refit the charge air pipe/ hose.

11 Refill or top-up the cooling system and engine oil as described in Chapter 1. Start the engine, and check the oil cooler for signs of leakage.

18 Flywheel – removal, inspection and refitting

Note: *New flywheel retaining bolts will be required on refitting.*

Removal

1 Remove the transmission as described in Chapter 7A then remove the clutch assembly as described in Chapter 6.

2 Prevent the flywheel from turning by locking the ring gear teeth **(see illustration)**. Alternatively, bolt a strap between the flywheel and the cylinder block/crankcase. Make alignment marks between the flywheel and crankshaft using paint or a suitable marker pen.

3 Slacken and remove the retaining bolts and plate, then remove the flywheel **(see illustration)**. Do not drop it, as it is very heavy.

17.6 Fit a new sealing ring to the recess in the oil cooler

17.7 Ensure that the lug of the oil filter housing engages, then refit the centre bolt

18.2 Fabricate a locking tool to retain the flywheel

Inspection

4 Examine the flywheel for wear or chipping of the ring gear teeth. Renewal of the ring gear is possible but is not a task for the home mechanic; renewal requires the new ring gear to be heated (up to 180° to 230°C) to allow it to be fitted.

5 Examine the flywheel for scoring of the clutch face. If the clutch face is scored, the flywheel may be surface-ground, but renewal is preferable.

6 If there is any doubt about the condition of the flywheel, seek the advice of a Vauxhall/Opel dealer or engine reconditioning specialist. They will be able to advise if it is possible to recondition it or whether renewal is necessary.

Refitting

7 Clean the mating surfaces of the flywheel and crankshaft.

8 Apply a drop of locking compound to the threads of each of the new flywheel retaining bolts then refit the flywheel and retaining plate and install the new bolts. If the original is being refitted align the marks made prior to removal.

9 Lock the flywheel using the method employed on dismantling then, working in a diagonal sequence, evenly and progressively tighten the retaining bolts to the specified Stage 1 torque setting.

10 Once all bolts have been tightened to the Stage 1 torque, go around and tighten all bolts through the specified Stages 2 and 3 angles. It is recommended that an angle-measuring gauge is used during the final stages of the tightening, to ensure accuracy. If a gauge is not available, use white paint to make alignment marks prior to tightening; the marks can then be used to check that the bolt has been rotated through the correct angle.

11 Refit the clutch as described in Chapter 6 then remove the locking tool and refit the transmission as described in Chapter 7A.

19 Crankshaft oil seals – renewal

Timing belt end oil seal

1 Remove the crankshaft sprocket as described in Section 8.

2 Carefully punch or drill two small holes opposite each other in the oil seal. Screw a self-tapping screw into each and pull on the screws with pliers to extract the seal.

3 Clean the seal housing and polish off any burrs or raised edges which may have caused the seal to fail in the first place.

4 Ease the new seal into position on the end of the crankshaft. Press the seal squarely into position until it is flush with the housing. If necessary, a suitable tubular drift which bears only on the hard outer edge of the seal can be used to tap the seal into position. Take great

18.3 Remove the flywheel bolts and recover the plate

care not to damage the seal lips during fitting and ensure that the seal lips face inwards.

5 Wash off any traces of oil, then refit the crankshaft sprocket as described in Section 8.

Transmission end oil seal

6 Remove the flywheel as described in Section 18.

7 Renew the seal as described in paragraphs 2 to 4 **(see illustration)**.

8 Refit the flywheel as described in Section 18.

20 Engine/transmission mountings – inspection and renewal

Inspection

1 If improved access is required, raise the front of the car and support it securely on axle stands. Where necessary, undo the retaining bolts and remove the undertray from beneath the engine/transmission unit.

2 Check the mounting rubber to see if it is cracked, hardened or separated from the metal at any point; renew the mounting if any such damage or deterioration is evident.

3 Check that all the mountings' fasteners are securely tightened; use a torque wrench to check if possible.

4 Using a large screwdriver or a pry bar, check for wear in the mounting by carefully levering against it to check for free-play; where this is not possible, enlist the aid of an assistant to move the engine/transmission unit back-and-forth, or from side-to-side, while you

20.7 Remove the bolts securing the right-hand mounting to the support bracket

19.7 The seal fits flush with the housing

watch the mounting. While some free play is to be expected even from new components, excessive wear should be obvious. If excessive free play is found, check first that the fasteners are correctly secured, then renew any worn components as described below.

Renewal

Note: *Before slackening any of the engine mounting bolts/nuts, the relative positions of the mountings to their various brackets should be marked to ensure correct alignment upon refitting.*

Right-hand mounting

5 With reference to Chapter 4A, remove the air cleaner housing.

6 Support the weight of the engine using a trolley jack with a block of wood placed on its head.

7 Remove the three bolts securing the right-hand engine mounting to the engine mounting support bracket **(see illustration)**.

8 Undo the bolts securing the mounting to the body, and withdraw the bracket with the mounting.

9 If required, the mounting can be separated by undoing the single bolt in the centre of the rubber element.

10 Refitting is a reversal of removal. Tighten the bolts to the specified torque.

Front mounting/torque link

11 Firmly apply the handbrake, then jack up the front of the car and support it securely on axle stands (see *Jacking and vehicle support*).

12 Support the weight of the engine/transmission using a trolley jack with a block of wood placed on its head.

13 Slacken and remove the nut and washer securing the mounting to the subframe. Withdraw the bolt **(see illustration)**.

14 Undo the bolts securing the mounting bracket to the transmission, then manoeuvre the mounting and bracket out of position.

15 Check all components for signs of wear or damage, and renew as necessary.

16 On reassembly, refit the mounting bracket (aligning the previously-made marks) and tighten its bolts to the specified torque.

17 Locate the mounting in the subframe, ensuring it is fitted the correct way up, and manoeuvre the engine/transmission into

20.13 Front engine mounting/torque link bolts

20.21 Unscrew the two rear engine mounting/torque link retaining bolts

20.26 Undo the three bolts and remove the mounting bracket

20.27 Remove the four bolts and manoeuvre the mounting out from the inner wing

position. Refit the mounting bolts and new nuts. Tighten them to the specified torque.

18 Lower the vehicle to the ground.

Rear mounting/torque link

19 Firmly apply the handbrake, then jack up the front of the car and support it securely on axle stands (see *Jacking and vehicle support*).

20 Support the weight of the engine/ transmission using a trolley jack with a block of wood placed on its head. Position the jack underneath the transmission and raise the transmission slightly to remove all load from the rear mounting.

21 Slacken and remove the two bolts securing the rear mounting to the subframe, and the nut securing the mounting to the transmission bracket, then manoeuvre the assembly out from underneath the vehicle **(see illustration)**.

22 On refitting, manoeuvre the mounting into position and refit the bolts/nuts securing it to the subframe. Ensure that the mounting is correctly engaged with the transmission bracket and fit the mounting-to-bracket retaining nut. Tighten the mounting bolts/ nuts to their specified torque settings. Remove the jack from underneath the engine/ transmission.

23 Lower the vehicle to the ground.

Left-hand mounting

24 Remove the battery and battery tray as described in Chapter 5.

25 Support the weight of the transmission using a trolley jack with a block of wood placed on its head.

26 Undo the three retaining bolts, and withdraw the mounting bracket from the transmission **(see illustration)**.

27 Slacken and remove the four bolts and manoeuvre the mounting out from the inner wing **(see illustration)**.

28 If required, separate the rubber element from the bracket by unscrewing the single retaining bolt.

29 Refitting is a reversal of removal. Ensure all bolts/nuts are tightened to their specified torques.

Chapter 2 Part C:
1.9 litre SOHC engine in-car repair procedures

Contents

Degrees of difficulty

Easy, suitable for novice with little experience	**Fairly easy,** suitable for beginner with some experience	**Fairly difficult,** suitable for competent DIY mechanic	**Difficult,** suitable for experienced DIY mechanic	**Very difficult,** suitable for expert DIY or professional

Specifications

General

Engine type. . . . . Four-cylinder, in-line, water-cooled. Single overhead camshaft, belt-driven
Manufacturer's engine code. . . . . Z19DT and Z19DTL
Bore . . . . 82.0 mm
Stroke. . . . . 90.4 mm
Capacity. . . . . 1910 cc
Compression ratio 18.0:1
Firing order . . . . 1-3-4-2 (No 1 cylinder at timing belt end of engine)
Direction of crankshaft rotation . . . . Clockwise (viewed from timing belt end of engine)

Compression pressures

Maximum difference between any two cylinders. . . . . 1.5 bar

Valve clearances

Engine cold:
   Inlet and exhaust . . . . 0.30 to 0.40 mm

Lubrication system

Minimum oil pressure at 100°C . . . . 1.0 bar at idle speed
Oil pump type. . . . . Rotor-type, driven by crankshaft pulley/vibration damper from crankshaft

Torque wrench settings

	Nm	lbf ft
Air conditioning compressor mounting bracket to cylinder block/sump	50	37
Auxiliary drivebelt idler pulley bolt	50	37
Auxiliary drivebelt tensioner assembly bolts	50	37
Camshaft bearing cap bolts.	15	11
Camshaft cover bolts.	10	7
Camshaft sprocket bolt*.	120	89
Connecting rod big-end bearing cap bolt*:		
Stage 1	25	18
Stage 2	Angle-tighten a further 60°	
Crankshaft oil seal housing	9	7
Crankshaft pulley/vibration damper bolts	25	18
Crankshaft sprocket bolt*†.	340	251

Torque wrench settings (continued)

	Nm	lbf ft
Cylinder head bolts*:		
Stage 1	20	15
Stage 2	65	48
Stage 3	Angle-tighten a further 90°	
Stage 4	Angle-tighten a further 90°	
Stage 5	Angle-tighten a further 90°	
Engine/transmission mountings:		
Front mounting/torque link:		
Mounting to subframe bracket	55	41
Bracket to transmission	80	59
Left-hand:		
Mounting-to-body bolts	25	18
Mounting bracket to transmission bracket	80	59
Rubber mounting through-bolt	55	41
Transmission bracket to transmission	55	41
Rear mounting/torque link:		
Mounting to subframe	55	41
Mounting-to-transmission bracket through-bolt	55	41
Transmission bracket to transmission	80	59
Right-hand:		
Engine bracket-to-engine bolts:		
Lower bolts (M8)	25	18
Upper bolts (M10)	50	37
Mounting-to-body bolts	35	26
Mounting-to-engine bracket bolts	55	41
Engine-to-transmission unit bolts:		
M10 bolts	40	30
M12 bolts	60	44
Flywheel/driveplate bolts*	160	118
High-pressure fuel pump sprocket nut*	50	37
Intermediate shaft bearing housing support bracket bolts	55	41
Main bearing cap bolts*:		
Stage 1	25	18
Stage 2	Angle-tighten a further 100°	
Oil filter housing to cylinder block	50	37
Oil pump housing to cylinder block	9	7
Oil pump pick-up/strainer bolts	9	7
Roadwheel bolts	110	81
Sump bolts:		
M6 bolts	9	7
M8 bolts	25	18
M10 bolts	40	30
Sump drain plug	20	15
Timing belt idler pulley bolt	50	37
Timing belt tensioner bolt	30	22
Timing belt upper cover bolts:		
M6 bolts	9	7
M8 bolts	25	18

* Use new nuts/bolts
† Left-hand thread

1 General information

How to use this Chapter

This Part of Chapter 2 describes the repair procedures which can reasonably be carried out on the engine while it remains in the vehicle. If the engine has been removed from the vehicle and is being dismantled as described in Chapter 2E, any preliminary dismantling procedures can be ignored.

Note that, while it may be possible physically to overhaul items such as the piston/connecting rod assemblies while the engine is in the vehicle, such tasks are not usually carried out as separate operations, and usually require the execution of several additional procedures (not to mention the cleaning of components and of oilways); for this reason, all such tasks are classed as major overhaul procedures, and are described in Chapter 2E.

Chapter 2E describes the removal of the engine/transmission unit from the vehicle, and the full overhaul procedures which can then be carried out.

Engine description

The 1.9 litre SOHC diesel engine is of the eight-valve, in-line four-cylinder, single overhead camshaft type, mounted transversely at the front of the car, with the transmission on its left-hand end.

The crankshaft is supported within the cylinder block on five shell-type main bearings. Thrustwashers are fitted to number 3 main bearing, to control crankshaft endfloat.

The connecting rods rotate on horizontally-split bearing shells at their big-ends. The pistons are attached to the connecting rods by gudgeon pins, which are retained by circlips. The aluminium-alloy pistons are fitted with three piston rings – two compression rings and scraper-type oil control ring.

The camshaft runs directly in the cylinder head, and is driven by the crankshaft via a toothed composite rubber timing belt (which also drives the high-pressure fuel pump and the coolant pump). The camshaft operates each valve via a camshaft follower with adjustment shim.

Lubrication is by pressure-feed from a rotor-type oil pump, which is mounted on the right-hand end of the crankshaft. The pump draws oil through a strainer located in the sump, and then forces it through an externally mounted full-flow cartridge-type filter. The oil flows into galleries in the cylinder block/crankcase, from where it is distributed to the crankshaft (main bearings) and camshaft. The big-end bearings are supplied with oil via internal drillings in the crankshaft, while the camshaft bearings also receive a pressurised supply. The camshaft lobes and valves are lubricated by splash, as are all other engine components.

A semi-closed crankcase ventilation system is employed; crankcase fumes are drawn from the oil separator (integral with the camshaft cover), and passed via a hose to the inlet manifold.

Operations with engine in place

The following operations can be carried out without having to remove the engine from the vehicle.

a) Removal and refitting of the camshaft cover.
b) Adjustment of the valve clearances.
c) Removal and refitting of the cylinder head.
d) Removal and refitting of the timing belt, tensioner, idler pulleys and sprockets.
e) Renewal of the camshaft oil seal.
f) Removal and refitting of the camshaft and followers.
g) Removal and refitting of the sump.
h) Removal and refitting of the connecting rods and pistons*.
i) Removal and refitting of the oil pump.
j) Removal and refitting of the oil filter housing.
k) Renewal of the crankshaft oil seals.
l) Renewal of the engine mountings.
m) Removal and refitting of the flywheel.

* Although the operation marked with an asterisk can be carried out with the engine in the car (after removal of the sump), it is preferable for the engine to be removed, in the interests of cleanliness and improved access. For this reason, the procedure is described in Chapter 2E.

2 Compression and leakdown tests – description and interpretation

Compression test

Note: *A compression tester specifically designed for diesel engines must be used for this test.*

1 When engine performance is down, or if misfiring occurs which cannot be attributed to the fuel system, a compression test can provide diagnostic clues as to the engine's condition. If the test is performed regularly, it can give warning of trouble before any other symptoms become apparent.

2 A compression tester specifically intended for diesel engines must be used, because of the higher pressures involved. The tester is connected to an adapter which screws into the injector holes. It is unlikely to be worthwhile buying such a tester for occasional use, but it may be possible to borrow or hire one – if not, have the test performed by a Vauxhall/Opel dealer, or suitably-equipped garage.

3 Unless specific instructions to the contrary are supplied with the tester, observe the following points:

a) The battery must be in a good state of charge, the air filter must be clean, and the engine should be at normal operating temperature.
b) All the fuel injectors must be removed before starting the test (see Chapter 4A).
c) Open the cover on the engine compartment fuse/relay box and remove the fuel pump relay **(see illustrations)**.

4 Screw the compression tester and adapter in to the fuel injector hole of No 1 cylinder.

5 With the help of an assistant, crank the engine on the starter motor; after one or two revolutions, the compression pressure should build-up to a maximum figure, and then stabilise. Record the highest reading obtained.

6 Repeat the test on the remaining cylinders, recording the pressure in each.

7 All cylinders should produce very similar pressures; any difference greater than the maximum figure given in the Specifications indicates the existence of a fault. Note that the compression should build-up quickly in a healthy engine; low compression on the first stroke, followed by gradually-increasing pressure on successive strokes, indicates worn piston rings. A low compression reading on the first stroke, which does not build-up during successive strokes, indicates leaking valves or a blown head gasket (a cracked head could also be the cause). **Note:** *The cause of poor compression is less easy to establish on a diesel engine than on a petrol one. The effect of introducing oil into the cylinders ('wet' testing) is not conclusive, because there is a risk that the oil will sit in the recess in the piston crown instead of passing to the rings.*

8 On completion of the test, refit the fuel pump relay, then refit the fuel injectors as described in Chapter 4A.

Leakdown test

9 A leakdown test measures the rate at which compressed air fed into the cylinder is lost. It is an alternative to a compression test, and in many ways it is better, since the escaping air provides easy identification of where pressure loss is occurring (piston rings, valves or head gasket).

10 The equipment needed for leakdown testing is unlikely to be available to the home mechanic. If poor compression is suspected, have the test performed by a Vauxhall/Opel dealer, or suitably-equipped garage.

3 Top dead centre (TDC) for No 1 piston – locating

Note: *To accurately determine the TDC position for No 1 piston, it will be necessary to use Vauxhall/Opel special tool EN-46788 (or suitable equivalents) to set the crankshaft at the TDC position* **(see illustration)**.

1 In its travel up-and-down its cylinder bore, Top Dead Centre (TDC) is the highest point that each piston reaches as the crankshaft rotates. While each piston reaches TDC both at the top of the compression stroke and again at the top of the exhaust stroke, for the

2.3a Open the cover on the fuse/relay box . . .

2.3b . . . and remove the fuel pump relay (arrowed)

3.0 Vauxhall/Opel special tool EN-46788 (or equivalent) is required to set the TDC position for No 1 piston

3.3a Remove the engine oil filler cap . . .

3.3b . . . undo the two retaining bolts (arrowed) . . .

3.3c . . . release the hose support clip . . .

3.3d . . . then lift off the plastic cover over the top of the engine

3.5 Undo the central mounting bolt (arrowed), and remove the auxiliary drivebelt tensioner assembly

purpose of timing the engine, TDC refers to the piston position of No 1 cylinder at the top of its compression stroke.

2 Number 1 piston (and cylinder) is at the right-hand (timing belt) end of the engine, and its TDC position is located as follows. Note that the crankshaft rotates clockwise when viewed from the right-hand side of the car.

3 Remove the engine oil filler cap, undo the two retaining bolts, release the hose support clip, then lift off the plastic cover over the top of the engine **(see illustrations)**. Refit the oil filler cap.

4 Remove the crankshaft pulley/vibration damper as described in Section 6.

5 Undo the central mounting bolt, and remove the auxiliary drivebelt tensioner assembly from the engine **(see illustration)**.

6 Remove the air cleaner assembly and air intake duct as described in Chapter 4A.

7 Place a trolley jack beneath the right-hand end of the engine with a block of wood on the jack head. Raise the jack until it is supporting the weight of the engine.

8 Mark the bolt positions for correct refitting, then undo the three bolts securing the right-

hand engine mounting to the engine bracket, and the three bolts securing the mounting to the body. Remove the mounting **(see illustration)**.

9 Unclip the wiring harness from the top and side of the upper timing belt cover. Unscrew the six retaining bolts and lift off the upper timing belt cover **(see illustration)**.

10 Using a socket and extension bar on the crankshaft sprocket bolt, rotate the crankshaft in the normal direction of rotation until the mark on the camshaft sprocket is aligned with the pointer on the camshaft cover **(see illustration)**.

3.8 Undo the retaining bolts and remove the right-hand engine mounting

3.9 Upper timing belt cover retaining bolts (arrowed)

3.10 Rotate the crankshaft to align the mark on the camshaft sprocket (arrowed) with the pointer on the camshaft cover

3.11 Screw the fastening stud of special tool EN-46788 into the oil pump housing

3.12 Positioning ring of tool EN-46788 (arrowed) attached to the fastening stud and crankshaft sprocket

11 Unscrew the bolt from the lower left-hand side of the oil pump housing and screw in the fastening stud of Vauxhall/Opel special tool EN-46788 **(see illustration)**.

12 Fit the positioning ring of tool EN-46788 over the fastening stud and engage it with the crankshaft sprocket. Ensure that the hole in the positioning ring engages with the lug on the sprocket. Secure the tool in position with the retaining bolt and nut **(see illustration)**.

13 With the crankshaft positioning ring in place and the mark on the camshaft sprocket aligned with the pointer on the camshaft cover, the engine is positioned with No 1 piston at TDC on compression.

5.2 Undo the retaining bolt(s) to release the vacuum lines from the camshaft cover

5.3a Release the retaining clips and disconnect the breather hoses from the front . . .

4 Valve timing – checking and adjustment

1 Position No 1 cylinder at TDC on its compression stroke as described in Section 3.

2 With the crankshaft positioning ring in place, check that the mark on the camshaft sprocket is aligned with the pointer on the camshaft cover; if so, the valve timing is correct.

3 If the mark on the camshaft sprocket is not aligned with the pointer on the camshaft cover, readjust the timing belt position as described in Section 7.

5 Camshaft cover – removal and refitting

Removal

1 Remove the engine oil filler cap, undo the two retaining bolts, release the hose support clip, then undo the two bolts and lift off the plastic cover over the top of the engine **(see illustrations 3.3a to 3.3d)**. Refit the oil filler cap.

2 Undo the retaining bolt(s) to release the

vacuum lines running over the top of the camshaft cover **(see illustration)**.

3 Release the retaining clips and disconnect the breather hoses from the front and rear of the camshaft cover **(see illustrations)**.

4 Disconnect the fuel leak-off hose connection at No 2 and No 3 injector by extracting the locking clip and lifting out the hose fitting. Refit the locking clips to the injectors after disconnecting the hose fitting.

5 Undo the seven retaining bolts securing the camshaft cover to the cylinder head **(see illustration)**.

5.3b . . . and rear of the camshaft cover

5.5 Undo the seven bolts (arrowed) securing the camshaft cover to the cylinder head

5.6 Move the leak-off hose assembly rearward, then lift the camshaft cover from the cylinder head

5.7 Fit the seal to the camshaft cover groove

6.3 Crankshaft pulley/vibration damper retaining bolts (arrowed)

6 Carefully move the disconnected leak-off hose assembly rearward, then lift the camshaft cover from the cylinder head **(see illustration)**.

Refitting

7 Ensure the cover and cylinder head surfaces are clean and dry then fit the seal to the cover groove **(see illustration)**.
8 Move the leak-off hose assembly to the rear and carefully lower the cover into position. Screw in the retaining bolts and lightly tighten them. Once all bolts are hand-tight, go around and tighten them all to the specified torque setting.
9 Reconnect the leak-off hose fittings to the injectors by pushing in the locking clip, attaching the fitting, then releasing the locking clip. Ensure that each fitting is securely connected and retained by the clip.

10 Reconnect the breather hoses to the cover.
11 Refit and tighten the bolts securing the vacuum lines.
12 Refit the plastic cover to the top of the engine, tighten the two retaining bolts and resecure the hose.

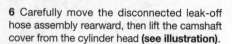

6 Crankshaft pulley/ vibration damper – removal and refitting

Removal

1 Apply the handbrake, then jack up the front of the vehicle and support it on axle stands (see *Jacking and vehicle support*). Remove the right-hand front roadwheel.

2 Remove the auxiliary drivebelt as described in Chapter 1. Prior to removal, mark the direction of rotation on the belt to ensure the belt is refitted the same way around.
3 Undo the four bolts securing the pulley to the crankshaft sprocket and remove the pulley from the sprocket **(see illustration)**.

Refitting

4 Locate the crankshaft pulley on the sprocket, ensuring that the hole on the rear face of the pulley engages with the lug on the sprocket.
5 Refit the four retaining bolts and tighten them progressively to the specified torque.
6 Refit the auxiliary drivebelt as described in Chapter 1 using the mark made prior to removal to ensure the belt is fitted the correct way around.
7 Refit the roadwheel, then lower the car to the ground and tighten the wheel bolts to the specified torque.

7 Timing belt – removal and refitting

Note: *The timing belt must be removed and refitted with the engine cold.*

Removal

1 Position No 1 cylinder at TDC on its compression stroke as described in Section 3.
2 Undo the retaining bolt and remove the auxiliary drivebelt idler pulley from the engine bracket **(see illustration)**.
3 Undo the two lower bolts, and the three upper bolts, and remove the engine bracket from the engine **(see illustrations)**.
4 Undo the nut and bolt and remove the crankshaft positioning tool (EN-46788) from the crankshaft sprocket.
5 Slacken the timing belt tensioner retaining bolt and allow the tensioner to retract, relieving the tension on the timing belt.
6 Slide the timing belt from its sprockets and remove it from the engine. If the belt is to be re-used, use white paint or similar to mark the direction of rotation on the belt. **Do not** rotate the crankshaft or camshafts until the timing belt has been refitted.

7.2 Undo the bolt (arrowed) and remove the auxiliary drivebelt idler pulley from the engine bracket

7.3a Undo the two lower bolts (arrowed) . . .

7.3b . . . and the three upper bolts (arrowed) . . .

7.3c . . . and remove the engine bracket from the engine

7 Check the timing belt carefully for any signs of uneven wear, splitting or oil contamination, and renew it if there is the slightest doubt about its condition. If the engine is undergoing an overhaul and is approaching the interval for belt renewal (see Chapter 1) renew the belt as a matter of course, regardless of its apparent condition. If signs of oil contamination are found, trace the source of the oil leak and rectify it, then wash down the engine timing belt area and all related components to remove all traces of oil.

Refitting

8 On reassembly, thoroughly clean the timing belt sprockets and tensioner/idler pulleys.
9 Place the timing belt in position over the crankshaft sprocket. If the original belt is being refitted, ensure that the arrow mark made on removal points in the normal direction of rotation, as before.
10 Check that the camshaft and crankshaft are still correctly positioned with No 1 piston at TDC on compression as described in Section 3, and refit the crankshaft positioning tool.
11 Fit the timing belt over the crankshaft, camshaft and fuel pump sprockets and around the idler pulleys, ensuring that the belt front run is taut (ie, all slack is on the tensioner side of the belt), then fit the belt over the coolant pump sprocket and tensioner pulley. Do not twist the belt sharply while refitting it. Ensure that the belt teeth are correctly seated centrally in the sprockets, and that the timing mark on the camshaft sprocket remain in alignment.
12 Screw in a suitable bolt, approximately 50 mm in length, into the threaded hole directly below the timing belt tensioner. Using a screwdriver resting on the bolt as a pivot, move the adjusting lever on the tensioner until the tensioner pointer is aligned with the mark on the backplate. Hold the tensioner in this position and tighten the tensioner retaining bolt (see illustrations).
13 Remove the crankshaft positioning tool.
14 Using a socket on the crankshaft sprocket bolt, rotate the crankshaft smoothly through two complete turns (720°) in the normal direction of rotation to settle the timing belt in position. At the end of the second turn, align the mark on the camshaft sprocket with the pointer on the camshaft cover.
15 Refit the positioning ring of tool EN-46788 over the fastening stud and engage it with the crankshaft sprocket. Ensure that the hole in the positioning ring engages with the lug on the sprocket. Secure the tool in position with the retaining bolt and nut.
16 Slacken the timing belt tensioner retaining bolt and, using a screwdriver resting on the pivot bolt as before, move the adjusting lever on the tensioner until the tensioner pointer is once again aligned with the mark on the backplate. Hold the tensioner in this position and tighten the tensioner retaining bolt to the specified torque.
17 Remove all the positioning tools and

7.12a Using a screwdriver resting on a pivot bolt (arrowed), move the adjusting lever on the tensioner . . .

7.12b . . . until the tensioner pointer (arrowed) is aligned with the mark on the backplate

again rotate the crankshaft smoothly through two complete turns (720°) in the normal direction of rotation. Check that the timing belt tensioner pointer is still aligned with the mark on the backplate. If not, repeat the procedure described in paragraph 16.
18 When all is correct, remove the tensioner position pivot bolt. Refit the bolt removed from the oil pump housing and tighten it to the specified torque.
19 Place the engine bracket in position and refit the two lower bolts, and the three upper bolts. Tighten the bolts to the specified torque. Refit the auxiliary drivebelt idler pulley to the engine bracket and tighten the retaining bolt to the specified torque.
20 Refit the upper timing belt cover and tighten the retaining bolts to the specified torque. Clip the wiring harness back into position.
21 Place the right-hand engine mounting assembly in position and refit the three bolts securing the mounting to the body. Tighten the bolts to the specified torque. Align the

To make a sprocket holding tool, obtain two lengths of steel strip about 6 mm thick by about 30 mm wide or similar, one 600 mm long, the other 200 mm long (all dimensions are approximate). Bolt the two strips together to form a forked end, leaving the bolt slack so that the shorter strip can pivot freely. At the other end of each 'prong' of the fork, drill a suitable hole and fit a nut and bolt to allow the tool to engage with the spokes in the sprocket.

mounting in its original position, then fit and tighten the three mounting bracket bolts to the specified torque. Remove the jack from under the engine.
22 Refit the air cleaner assembly and air intake duct as described in Chapter 4A.
23 Place the auxiliary drivebelt tensioner assembly in position ensuring that the locating peg on the tensioner mounting surface engages correctly with the corresponding hole in the mounting bracket. Tighten the tensioner central mounting bolt to the specified torque.
24 Refit the crankshaft pulley/vibration damper as described in Section 6, then refit the auxiliary drivebelt as described in Chapter 1.
25 Refit the plastic cover to the top of the engine and tighten the retaining bolts.
26 Refit the roadwheel, then lower the car to the ground and tighten the wheel bolts to the specified torque.

---

8 Timing belt sprockets, tensioner and idler pulley – removal and refitting

Note: Certain special tools will be required for the removal and refitting of the sprockets. Read through the entire procedure to familiarise yourself with the work involved, then either obtain the manufacturer's special tools, or use the alternatives described.

Camshaft sprocket

Note: A new sprocket retaining bolt will be required for refitting.

Removal

1 Remove the timing belt as described in Section 7.
2 It will now be necessary to hold the camshaft sprocket to enable the retaining bolt to be removed. Vauxhall/Opel special tools EN-46787 and KM-956-1 are available for this purpose, however, a home-made tool can easily be fabricated (see Tool Tip).
3 Engage the tool with the holes in the camshaft sprocket, taking care not to damage the camshaft sensor located behind the sprocket
4 Unscrew the retaining bolt and remove the sprocket from the end of the camshaft.

8.12a Remove the bolt and washer . . .

8.12b . . . and slide the sprocket off the end of the crankshaft

8.18 Engage the holding tool with the holes in the fuel pump sprocket and undo the retaining nut

Refitting

5 Prior to refitting check the oil seal for signs of damage or leakage. If necessary, renew as described in Section 9.

6 Refit the sprocket to the camshaft end, aligning its cut-out with the locating peg, and fit the new retaining bolt.

7 Retain the sprocket using the holding tool, and tighten the retaining bolt to the specified torque.

8 Refit the timing belt as described in Section 7.

Crankshaft sprocket

Note 1: *The crankshaft sprocket retaining bolt is extremely tight. Ensure that the holding tool used to prevent rotation as the bolt is slackened is of sturdy construction and securely attached.*

Note 2: *A new sprocket retaining bolt will be required for refitting.*

Removal

9 Remove the timing belt as described in Section 7.

10 It will now be necessary to hold the crankshaft sprocket to enable the retaining bolt to be removed. Vauxhall/Opel special tools EN-47630 and KM-956-1 are available for this purpose, however, a home-made tool similar to that described in paragraph 2, can easily be fabricated.

11 Using the crankshaft pulley retaining bolts, securely attach the tool to the crankshaft sprocket. With the help of an assistant, hold

the sprocket stationary and unscrew the retaining bolt. **Note:** *The sprocket retaining bolt has a **left-hand thread** and is unscrewed by turning it clockwise.*

12 Remove the bolt and washer and slide the sprocket off the end of the crankshaft **(see illustrations)**. Note that a new bolt will be required for refitting.

Refitting

13 Align the sprocket location key with the crankshaft groove and slide the sprocket into position. Fit the new retaining bolt and washer.

14 Hold the sprocket stationary using the holding tool and tighten the retaining bolt to the specified torque. Remove the holding tool.

15 Refit the timing belt as described in Section 7.

High-pressure fuel pump sprocket

Note: *A new sprocket retaining nut will be required for refitting.*

Removal

16 Remove the timing belt as described in Section 7.

17 It will now be necessary to hold the fuel pump sprocket to enable the retaining nut to be removed. Vauxhall/Opel special tools KM-6347 and KM-956-1 are available for this purpose, however, a home-made tool similar to that described in paragraph 2, can easily be fabricated.

18 Engage the tool with the holes in the fuel pump sprocket and undo the sprocket retaining nut **(see illustration)**. Note that a new nut will be required for refitting.

19 Attach a suitable puller to the threaded holes in the fuel pump sprocket using bolts and washers similar to the arrangement shown **(see illustration)**.

20 Tighten the puller centre bolt to release the sprocket from the taper on the pump shaft. Once the taper releases, remove the puller and withdraw the sprocket. Collect the Woodruff key from the pump shaft **(see illustrations)**.

Refitting

21 Clean the fuel pump shaft and the sprocket hub ensuring that all traces of oil or grease are removed.

22 Refit the Woodruff key to the pump shaft, then locate the sprocket in position. Fit the new retaining nut.

23 Hold the sprocket stationary using the holding tool and tighten the retaining nut to the specified torque. Remove the holding tool.

24 Refit the timing belt as described in Section 7.

Tensioner assembly

Removal

25 Remove the timing belt as described in Section 7.

26 Slacken and remove the retaining bolt and remove the tensioner assembly from the engine **(see illustration)**.

8.19 Use a suitable puller to release the fuel pump sprocket taper

8.20a Once the taper releases, withdraw the sprocket . . .

8.20b . . . and collect the Woodruff key from the pump shaft

Refitting

27 Fit the tensioner to the engine, making sure that the slot on the tensioner backplate is correctly located over the peg on the engine bracket **(see illustration)**.

28 Clean the threads of the retaining bolt and apply thread-locking compound to the bolt threads. Screw in the retaining bolt, set the tensioner in the retracted position and tighten the retaining bolt.

29 Refit the timing belt as described in Section 7.

Idler pulley

Removal

30 Remove the timing belt as described in Section 7.

31 Slacken and remove the retaining bolt and remove the idler pulley from the engine.

Refitting

32 Refit the idler pulley and tighten the retaining bolt to the specified torque.

33 Refit the timing belt as described in Section 7.

9 Camshaft oil seal – renewal

1 Remove the camshaft sprocket as described in Section 8.

2 Carefully punch or drill a small hole in the oil seal. Screw in a self-tapping screw, and pull on the screw with pliers to extract the seal.

3 Clean the seal housing, and polish off any burrs or raised edges which may have caused the seal to fail in the first place.

4 Press the new seal into position using a suitable tubular drift (such as a socket) which bears only on the hard outer edge of the seal. Take care not to damage the seal lips during fitting; note that the seal lips should face inwards.

5 Refit the camshaft sprocket as described in Section 8.

10 Valve clearances – checking and adjustment

Note: *Vauxhall/Opel special tools EN-46797 and EN-46799 (or suitable equivalents) will be required if adjustment is necessary.*

Checking

1 The importance of having the valve clearances correctly adjusted cannot be overstressed, as they vitally affect the performance of the engine. The engine must be cold for the check to be accurate. The clearances are checked as follows.

2 Apply the handbrake, then jack up the front of the vehicle and support it on axle stands (see *Jacking and vehicle support*). Remove the right-hand front roadwheel.

8.26 Slacken and remove the retaining bolt and remove the timing belt tensioner assembly

3 Remove the camshaft cover as described in Section 5.

4 Using a socket and extension on the crankshaft pulley bolt, rotate the crankshaft in the normal direction of rotation (clockwise when viewed from the right-hand end of the engine) until camshaft lobes 1 and 6 are pointing upward **(see illustration)**.

5 On a piece of paper, draw the outline of the engine with the cylinders numbered from the timing belt end. Show the position of each valve, together with the specified valve clearance. Note that the clearance for both the inlet and exhaust valves is the same.

6 With the cam lobes positioned as described in paragraph 4, using feeler blades, measure the clearance between the base of camshaft lobes 1 and 6 and the adjustment shim located on the top of the camshaft follower **(see illustration)**. Record the clearances on the paper.

7 Rotate the crankshaft until camshaft lobes 5 and 8 are pointing upward. Measure the clearance between the base of the camshaft lobes and the shims on their followers and record the clearances on the paper.

8 Rotate the crankshaft until camshaft lobes 4 and 7 are pointing upward. Measure the clearance between the base of the camshaft lobes and the shims on their followers and record the clearances on the paper.

9 Rotate the crankshaft until camshaft lobes 2 and 3 are pointing upward. Measure the clearance between the base of the camshaft lobes and the shims on their followers and record the clearances on the paper.

10.6 Valve clearance measurement

8.27 The slot on the tensioner backplate must locate over the peg (arrowed) on the engine bracket

10 If all the clearances are correct, refit the camshaft cover as described in Section 5. Refit the roadwheel and engine undertray, then lower the car to the ground and tighten the wheel bolts to the specified torque.

11 If any clearance measured is not correct, adjustment must be carried out as described in the following paragraphs.

Adjustment

12 Rotate the crankshaft clockwise until camshaft lobes 1 and 6 are once again pointing upward. With the camshaft in this position, valve No 1 and valve No 6 can be adjusted as follows.

13 Rotate the follower until the groove on its upper edge is facing towards the front of the engine **(see illustration)**.

14 Insert Vauxhall/Opel special tool EN-46797

10.4 Camshaft positioned with No 1 and No 6 cam lobes (arrowed) pointing upward

10.13 Rotate the follower until the groove (arrowed) is facing towards the front of the engine

10.16 The thickness of each shim should be stamped on one of its surfaces

between the base of the camshaft lobe and the shim and lever downward to open the valve. Now insert Vauxhall/Opel special tool EN-46799 between the edge of the follower and the base of the camshaft to hold the valve open. Take care when doing this as it is possible for the valve to contact the piston. If any resistance is felt as the valve is opened, remove the tool and rotate the crankshaft slightly to move the piston down its bore.

15 Using a small screwdriver inserted in the groove on the edge of the follower, lift up the shim, then slide it out from between the follower and camshaft.

16 Clean the shim, and measure its thickness with a micrometer. The shims carry thickness markings, but wear may have reduced the original thickness, so be sure to double-check **(see illustration)**.

17 Add the measured clearance of the valve to the thickness of the original shim then subtract the specified valve clearance from this figure. This will give you the thickness of the shim required. For example:

Measured valve clearance	0.45 mm
Plus thickness of the original shim	2.70 mm
Equals	3.15 mm
Minus clearance required	0.40 mm
Thickness of shim required	2.75 mm

18 Obtain the correct thickness of shim required and lubricate it with clean engine oil. With the valve still held open with the special tool, slide the shim into position, with the thickness number downwards, ensuring it is correctly located.

19 Using the first special tool, lever down on the shim and remove the second special tool.

11.6 Camshaft bearing cap retaining bolts (arrowed)

Allow the valve to close and remove the first special tool. Check that the valve clearance is within limits.

> **HAYNES HINT** *It may be possible to correct the clearances by moving the shims around between the valves, but don't rotate the crankshaft with any shims missing. Keep a note of all the shim thicknesses to assist valve clearance adjustment when they need to be done again.*

20 Rotate the crankshaft clockwise until camshaft lobes 5 and 8 are once again pointing upward. Adjust No 5 and No 8 valve clearances as described in paragraphs 13 to 19.

21 Rotate the crankshaft clockwise until camshaft lobes 4 and 7 are once again pointing upward. Adjust No 4 and No 7 valve clearances as described in paragraphs 13 to 19.

22 Rotate the crankshaft clockwise until camshaft lobes 2 and 3 are once again pointing upward. Adjust No 2 and No 3 valve clearances as described in paragraphs 13 to 19.

23 On completion, refit the camshaft cover as described in Section 5 . Refit the roadwheel, then lower the car to the ground and tighten the wheel bolts to the specified torque.

11 Camshaft and followers – removal, inspection and refitting

Removal

1 Remove the timing belt as described in Section 7.

2 Remove the camshaft sprocket as described in Section 8.

3 Remove the camshaft cover as described in Section 5.

4 Remove the braking system vacuum pump as described in Chapter 9.

5 Check for identification markings on the camshaft bearing caps. If no markings can be seen, make suitable identification marks on the caps, to indicate their number and which way round they are fitted.

6 Working in a spiral pattern from the outside inwards, slacken the twelve camshaft bearing

11.7 Carefully release the oil pipe (arrowed) from its location in the cylinder head

cap retaining bolts by half a turn at a time, to relieve the pressure of the valve springs on the bearing caps gradually and evenly **(see illustration)**. Once the valve spring pressure has been relieved, the bolts can be fully unscrewed and removed.

Caution: If the bearing cap bolts are carelessly slackened, the bearing caps might break. If any bearing cap breaks then the complete cylinder head assembly must be renewed; the bearing caps are matched to the head and are not available separately.

7 Carefully release the oil supply pipe from its location in the cylinder head, then lift the pipe off the bearing caps **(see illustration)**.

8 Remove the bearing caps, then lift the camshaft out of the cylinder head and slide off the oil seal.

9 Obtain eight small, clean plastic containers, and label them for identification. Alternatively, divide a larger container into compartments. Lift the followers and shims out from the top of the cylinder head and store each one in its respective fitted position. Make sure the followers and shims are not mixed up, to ensure the valve clearances remain correct on refitting.

Inspection

10 Examine the camshaft bearing surfaces and cam lobes for signs of wear ridges and scoring. Renew the camshaft if any of these conditions are apparent. Examine the condition of the bearing surfaces both on the camshaft journals and in the cylinder head. If the head bearing surfaces are worn excessively, the cylinder head will need to be renewed.

11 Check the camshaft followers and their bores in the cylinder head for signs of wear or damage. If any follower is thought to be faulty or is visibly worn it should be renewed.

Refitting

12 Commence refitting by turning the crankshaft anti-clockwise by 90°. This will position all the pistons half-way down their bores, and prevent any chance of the valves touching the piston crowns as the camshaft is being fitted.

13 Lubricate the camshaft followers with clean engine oil and carefully insert each one (together with its adjusting shim) into its original location in the cylinder head.

14 Lubricate the camshaft follower shims, and the bearing journals with clean engine oil, then lay the camshaft in position.

15 Apply a smear of sealant to the mating surfaces of both the No 1 and No 5 camshaft bearing caps. Using the marks made on removal as a guide, refit the camshaft bearing caps in their original locations on the cylinder head.

16 Carefully engage the oil supply pipe into its location in the cylinder head, then place the pipe in position on the bearing caps.

17 Refit the bearing cap retaining bolts and

tighten them by hand until they just contact the bearing caps.

18 Working in a spiral pattern from the centre outwards, tighten the bolts by half a turn at a time to gradually impose the pressure of the valve springs on the bearing caps. Repeat this sequence until all bearing caps are in contact with the cylinder head then go around and tighten the camshaft bearing cap bolts to the specified torque.

Caution: If the bearing cap bolts are carelessly tightened, the bearing caps might break. If any bearing cap breaks then the complete cylinder head assembly must be renewed; the bearing caps are matched to the head and are not available separately.

19 Fit a new camshaft oil seal as described in Section 9.

20 Refit the braking system vacuum pump as described in Chapter 9.

21 Refit the camshaft cover as described in Section 5.

22 Refit the camshaft sprocket as described in Section 8. Rotate the camshaft until the mark on the camshaft sprocket is aligned with the pointer on the camshaft cover (see Section 3).

23 Turn the crankshaft clockwise by 90° to bring No 1 and 4 pistons to approximately the TDC position.

24 Refit the timing belt as described in Section 7.

25 If any new components have been fitted, check, and if necessary adjust, the valve clearances as described in Section 10.

12 Cylinder head –
removal and refitting

Note: *New cylinder head bolts will be required on refitting.*

Removal

1 Disconnect the battery negative terminal (refer to *Disconnecting the battery* in the Reference Chapter).

2 Drain the cooling system as described in Chapter 1.

3 Remove the timing belt as described in Section 7.

4 Disconnect the wiring harness connectors from the following components with reference to the Chapters indicated:
  a) *Coolant temperature sensor (Chapter 3).*
  b) *Fuel pressure sensor (Chapter 4A).*
  c) *Fuel pressure regulating valve (Chapter 4A).*
  d) *Throttle housing (Chapter 4A).*
  e) *Fuel injectors (Chapter 4A).*
  f) *Air conditioning compressor (Chapter 3).*
  g) *EGR valve (Chapter 4B).*
  h) *Inlet manifold pressure sensor (Chapter 4A).*
  i) *High-pressure fuel pump (Chapter 4A).*
  j) *Camshaft sensor (Chapter 4A).*

5 Undo the wiring harness support bracket bolts, release the retaining clips and move the harness to one side **(see illustration)**.

6 Remove the inlet and exhaust manifolds as described in Chapter 4A.

7 Remove the camshaft cover as described in Section 5.

8 Remove the braking system vacuum pump as described in Chapter 9.

9 Make a final check to ensure that all relevant hoses, pipes and wires have been disconnected.

10 Working in the **reverse** of the tightening sequence **(see illustration 12.28)**, progressively slacken the cylinder head bolts by half a turn at a time, until all bolts can be unscrewed by hand. Note that an M14 RIBE socket bit will be required to unscrew the bolts. Remove the cylinder head bolts and recover the washers.

11 Engage the help of an assistant and lift the cylinder head from the cylinder block. Take care as it is a bulky and heavy assembly.

Caution: Do not lay the head on its lower mating surface; support the head on wooden blocks, ensuring each block only contacts the head mating surface.

12 Remove the gasket and keep it for identification purposes (see paragraph 19).

13 If the cylinder head is to be dismantled for overhaul, then refer to Part E of this Chapter.

Preparation for refitting

14 The mating faces of the cylinder head and cylinder block/crankcase must be perfectly clean before refitting the head. Use a hard plastic or wood scraper to remove all traces of gasket and carbon; also clean the piston crowns. Take particular care, as the surfaces are damaged easily. Also, make sure that the carbon is not allowed to enter the oil and water passages – this is particularly important for the lubrication system, as carbon could block the oil supply to any of the engine's components. Using adhesive tape and paper, seal the water, oil and bolt holes in the cylinder block/crankcase. To prevent carbon entering the gap between the pistons and bores, smear a little grease in the gap. After cleaning each piston, use a small brush to remove all traces of grease and carbon from the gap, then wipe away the remainder with a clean rag. Clean all the pistons in the same way.

15 Check the mating surfaces of the cylinder block/crankcase and the cylinder head for nicks, deep scratches and other damage. If slight, they may be removed carefully with a file, but if excessive, machining may be the only alternative to renewal.

16 Ensure that the cylinder head bolt holes in the crankcase are clean and free of oil. Syringe or soak up any oil left in the bolt holes. This is most important in order that the correct bolt tightening torque can be applied and to prevent the possibility of the block being cracked by hydraulic pressure when the bolts are tightened.

17 The cylinder head bolts must be discarded and renewed, regardless of their apparent condition.

18 If warpage of the cylinder head gasket

12.5 Undo the support bracket bolts (arrowed), release the retaining clips and move the wiring harness to one side

surface is suspected, use a straight-edge to check it for distortion. Refer to Part E of this Chapter if necessary.

19 On this engine, the cylinder head-to-piston clearance is controlled by fitting different thickness head gaskets. The gasket thickness can be determined by looking at the holes stamped on the edge of the gasket **(see illustration)**.

Number of holes	Gasket thickness
No holes	0.77 to 0.87 mm
One hole	0.87 to 0.97 mm
Two holes	0.97 to 1.07 mm

The correct thickness of gasket required is selected by measuring the piston protrusions as follows.

20 Mount a dial test indicator securely on the block so that its pointer can be easily pivoted between the piston crown and block mating surface. Turn the crankshaft to bring No 1 piston roughly to the TDC position. Move the dial test indicator probe over and in contact with No 1 piston. Turn the crankshaft back-and-forth slightly until the highest reading is shown on the gauge, indicating that the piston is at TDC.

21 Zero the dial test indicator on the gasket surface of the cylinder block then carefully move the indicator over No 1 piston. Measure its protrusion at the highest point between the valve cut-outs, and then again at its highest point between the valve cut-outs at 90° to the first measurement **(see illustration)**. Repeat this procedure with No 4 piston.

22 Rotate the crankshaft half a turn (180°) to bring No 2 and 3 pistons to TDC. Ensure

12.19 Cylinder head gasket thickness identification hole (arrowed)

12.21 Using a dial test indicator to measure piston protrusion

12.24 Place the new gasket in position with the words ALTO/TOP uppermost

the crankshaft is accurately positioned then measure the protrusions of No 2 and 3 pistons at the specified points. Once all pistons have been measured, rotate the crankshaft to position all the pistons at their mid-stroke.

23 Select the correct thickness of head gasket required by determining the largest amount of piston protrusion, and using the following table.

Piston protrusion measurement (mm)	Gasket thickness required (mm)
0.020 to 0.100	0.77 to 0.87 (no holes)
0.101 to 0.200	0.87 to 0.97 (one hole)
0.201 to 0.295	0.97 to 1.07 (two holes)

Refitting

24 Wipe clean the mating surfaces of the cylinder head and cylinder block/crankcase. Place the new gasket in position with the words ALTO/TOP uppermost **(see illustration)**.

25 If not already done, rotate the crankshaft to position all the pistons at their mid-stroke.

26 With the aid of an assistant, carefully refit the cylinder head assembly to the block, aligning it with the locating dowels.

27 Apply a thin film of engine oil to the bolt threads and the underside of the bolt heads. Carefully enter each new cylinder head bolt into its relevant hole (*do not drop them in*). Screw all bolts in, by hand only, until finger-tight.

28 Working progressively in sequence, tighten the cylinder head bolts to their Stage 1 torque setting, using a torque wrench and suitable socket **(see illustration)**. Working again in the same sequence, go around and tighten all bolts through the specified Stage 2 torque setting.

29 Once all bolts have been tightened to the Stage 2 torque, working again in the same sequence, go around and tighten all bolts through the specified Stage 3 angle, then through the specified Stage 4 angle, and finally through the specified Stage 5 angle using an angle-measuring gauge.

30 Refit the braking system vacuum pump as described in Chapter 9.

31 Refit the camshaft cover as described in Section 5.

32 Refit the inlet and exhaust manifolds as described in Chapter 4A.

33 Reconnect the wiring harness connectors to the components listed in paragraph 4, then refit the wiring harness support bracket bolts, and secure the harness with the retaining clips.

34 Refit the timing belt as described in Section 7.

35 On completion, reconnect the battery negative terminal, then refill the cooling system as described in Chapter 1.

13 Sump –
removal and refitting

Removal

1 Disconnect the battery negative terminal (refer to *Disconnecting the battery* in the Reference Chapter).

2 Apply the handbrake, then jack up the front of the vehicle and support it on axle stands (see *Jacking and vehicle support*). Remove the right-hand front roadwheel.

3 Remove the right-hand driveshaft and the intermediate shaft as described in Chapter 8.

4 Undo the three bolts securing the intermediate shaft bearing housing support bracket to the cylinder block and remove the support bracket **(see illustration)**.

5 Remove the exhaust system as described in Chapter 4A.

6 Undo the three bolts and remove the support bracket from the catalytic converter and sump.

7 Remove the crankshaft pulley/vibration damper as described in Section 6.

8 Disconnect the wiring connector from the air conditioning compressor. Undo the three bolts securing the air conditioning compressor to the mounting bracket and suitably support the compressor on the front subframe.

9 Undo the four bolts securing the compressor mounting bracket to the cylinder block and sump **(see illustration)**. Unclip the wiring harness and remove the mounting bracket.

10 Drain the engine oil as described in Chapter 1. When the oil has completely drained, refit the drain plug with new sealing washer, and tighten to the specified torque.

11 Undo the upper bolt securing the oil dipstick guide tube to the coolant pipe. Undo the lower bolt securing the guide tube to the sump flange, then unclip the wiring harness and withdraw the tube from the sump flange sealing grommet.

12.28 Cylinder head bolt tightening sequence

13.4 intermediate shaft bearing housing support bracket retaining bolts (arrowed)

13.9 Air conditioning compressor mounting bracket retaining bolts (arrowed)

13.17 Removing the oil baffle plate from inside the sump

13.18 Renew the pick-up/strainer sealing ring prior to refitting

12 Disconnect the wiring connector from the oil level sensor, then release the retaining clip and disconnect the oil return hose.

13 Undo the two bolts securing the sump flange to the transmission bellhousing.

14 Using a socket and extension on the crankshaft pulley bolt, rotate the crankshaft in the normal direction of rotation (clockwise when viewed from the right-hand end of the engine) until the opening in the flywheel is positioned to allow access to one of the rear sump retaining bolts. Undo and remove the bolt, then rotate the crankshaft again until the flywheel allow access to the second rear retaining bolt. Undo and remove the bolt.

15 Progressively slacken and remove the remaining twelve bolts securing the sump to the base of the cylinder block and oil pump housing. Using a wide-bladed scraper or similar tool inserted between the sump and cylinder block, carefully break the joint to release the sump.

16 Manoeuvre the sump out from under the car. Clearance is extremely limited between the sump and subframe, and it may be necessary to release the oil pump pick-up/strainer, by undoing its two retaining bolts, to enable the sump to be removed.

17 If required, undo the retaining bolts and remove the oil baffle plate from inside the sump **(see illustration)**.

18 While the sump is removed, take the opportunity to check the oil pump pick-up/strainer for signs of clogging or splitting. If not already done, unbolt the oil pump pick-up/strainer and remove it from the engine along with its sealing ring. The strainer can then be cleaned easily in solvent or renewed. Renew the pick-up/strainer sealing ring prior to refitting **(see illustration)**.

Refitting

19 Thoroughly clean the sump and remove all traces of silicone sealer and oil from the mating surfaces of the sump and cylinder block. If removed, refit the oil baffle plate and tighten its retaining bolts securely.

20 If clearance allows, refit the oil pump pick-up/strainer using a new sealing ring, and tighten its two retaining bolts securely. If it was necessary to unbolt the pick-up/strainer to allow the sump to be removed,

place the unit in position and loosely screw in the bolt securing it to the main bearing cap. It must still be possible for the forward end of the pipe to be moved to the rear as the sump is refitted.

21 Apply a continuous bead of silicone sealing compound (available from your Vauxhall/Opel dealer) at approximately 1.0 mm from the inner edge of the sump **(see illustration)**. The bead of sealant should be between 2.0 and 2.5 mm in diameter.

22 Locate the sump over the pick-up/strainer then, where applicable, fit the forward end of the pick-up/strainer to the oil pump housing and fit the retaining bolt. Tighten both retaining bolts securely.

23 Engage the sump with the cylinder block and loosely refit all the retaining bolts.

24 Working out from the centre in a diagonal sequence, progressively tighten the bolts securing the sump to the cylinder block and oil pump housing. Tighten all the bolts to their specified torque setting.

25 Tighten the two bolts securing the sump flange to the transmission bellhousing to their specified torque settings.

26 Reconnect the wiring connector to the oil level sensor, then refit the oil return hose and secure with the retaining clip.

27 Refit the oil dipstick guide tube and secure with the two bolts tightened securely.

28 Locate the air conditioning compressor mounting bracket in position and refit the four retaining bolts. Tighten the bolts to the specified torque. Clip the wiring harness back into position on the bracket.

13.21 Apply a continuous bead of silicone sealing compound to the sump flange

29 Position the air conditioning compressor on the mounting bracket. Fit and tighten the three retaining bolts to the specified torque (see Chapter 3), then reconnect the compressor wiring connector.

30 Refit the crankshaft pulley/vibration damper as described in Section 6.

31 Refit the catalytic converter support bracket and securely tighten the three bolts.

32 Refit the exhaust system as described in Chapter 4A.

33 Position the intermediate shaft bearing housing support bracket on the cylinder block and secure with the three retaining bolts tightened to the specified torque.

34 Refit the intermediate shaft and right-hand driveshaft as described in Chapter 8.

35 Refit the roadwheel, then lower the car to the ground and tighten the wheel bolts to the specified torque.

36 Fill the engine with fresh engine oil as described in Chapter 1.

37 On completion, reconnect the battery negative terminal.

14 Oil pump –
removal, overhaul and refitting

Removal

1 Remove the timing belt as described in Section 7.

2 Remove the crankshaft sprocket as described In Section 8.

3 Remove the sump and oil pump pick-up/strainer as described in Section 13.

4 Slacken and remove the seven retaining bolts then slide the oil pump housing assembly off of the end of the crankshaft **(see illustration)**. Remove the housing gasket and discard it.

Overhaul

5 Undo the retaining screws and lift off the pump cover from the rear of the housing **(see illustration)**.

6 Check the inner and outer rotors for identification dots indicating which way round they are fitted **(see illustration)**. If no marks are visible, use a suitable marker pen to mark

14.4 Oil pump housing retaining bolts (arrowed)

14.5 Undo the retaining screws and lift off the oil pump cover

14.6 Oil pump inner and outer rotor identification dots (arrowed)

14.8a Unscrew the oil pressure relief valve bolt . . .

14.8b . . . and withdraw the spring . . .

14.8c . . . and plunger

the surface of both the pump inner and outer rotors.

7 Lift out the inner and outer rotors from the pump housing.

8 Unscrew the oil pressure relief valve bolt from the base of the housing and withdraw the spring and plunger, noting which way around the plunger is fitted (**see illustrations**). Remove the sealing washer from the valve bolt.

9 Clean the components, and carefully examine the rotors, pump body and relief valve plunger for any signs of scoring or wear. If any damage or wear is noticed, it will be necessary to renew the complete pump assembly.

10 If the pump is satisfactory, reassemble the components in the reverse order of removal, noting the following.

a) Ensure both rotors are fitted the correct way around.
b) Fit a new sealing ring to the pressure relief valve bolt and securely tighten the bolt.
c) Apply a little locking compound to the threads, and securely tighten the pump cover screws.
d) On completion prime the oil pump by filling it with clean engine oil whilst rotating the inner rotor (**see illustration**).

Refitting

11 Prior to refitting, carefully lever out the crankshaft oil seal using a flat-bladed screwdriver. Fit the new oil seal, ensuring its sealing lip is facing inwards, and press it squarely into the housing using a tubular drift which bears only on the hard outer edge of

the seal. Press the seal into position so that it is flush with the housing and lubricate the oil seal lip with clean engine oil.

12 Ensure the mating surfaces of the oil pump and cylinder block are clean and dry.

13 Fit a new gasket to the oil pump housing and bend down the tabs on the edge of the gasket to retain it on the pump housing (**see illustration**).

14 Locate the pump housing over the end of the crankshaft and into position on the cylinder block.

15 Refit the pump housing retaining bolts and tighten them to the specified torque.

16 Refit the oil pump pick-up/strainer and sump as described in Section 13.

17 Refit the crankshaft sprocket as described in Section 8.

18 Refit the timing belt as described in Section 7.

19 On completion, fit a new oil filter and fill the engine with clean oil as described in Chapter 1.

15 Oil filter housing – removal and refitting

Removal

1 The oil filter housing with integral oil cooler is located at the rear of the cylinder block, above the right-hand driveshaft.

2 Disconnect the battery negative terminal (refer to *Disconnecting the battery* in the Reference Chapter).

14.10 Prime the oil pump by filling it with clean engine oil whilst rotating the inner rotor

14.13 Bend down the tabs on the edge of the gasket to retain it on the oil pump housing

15.10 Oil filter housing retaining bolts (arrowed)

15.11a Fit a new sealing ring to the oil filter housing supply channel . . .

3 Apply the handbrake, then jack up the front of the vehicle and support it on axle stands (see *Jacking and vehicle support*). Remove the right-hand front roadwheel.

4 Drain the cooling system as described in Chapter 1.

5 Remove the engine oil filter element as described in Chapter 1.

6 Remove the right-hand driveshaft and the intermediate shaft as described in Chapter 8.

7 Undo the three bolts securing the intermediate shaft bearing housing support bracket to the cylinder block and remove the support bracket **(see illustration 13.4)**.

8 Disconnect the wiring connector from the oil pressure switch.

9 Release the retaining clips and disconnect the two coolant hoses from the oil cooler on the oil filter housing.

10 Undo the three retaining bolts and remove the oil filter housing from the cylinder block **(see illustration)**. Recover the two rubber seals from the rear of the housing. Note that new seals will be required for refitting.

Refitting

11 Thoroughly clean the oil filter housing, then fit the two new sealing rings **(see illustrations)**.

12 Position the oil filter housing on the cylinder block and refit the retaining bolts. Tighten the bolts to the specified torque.

13 Refit the two coolant hoses and secure with their retaining clips. Reconnect the oil pressure switch wiring connector.

14 Position the intermediate shaft bearing housing support bracket on the cylinder block and secure with the three retaining bolts tightened to the specified torque.

15 Refit the intermediate shaft and right-hand driveshaft as described in Chapter 8.

16 Fit a new oil filter element as described in Chapter 1.

17 Refit the roadwheel, then lower the car to the ground and tighten the wheel bolts to the specified torque.

18 Refill the cooling system as described in Chapter 1.

19 Check, and if necessary, top-up the engine oil as described in *Weekly checks*.

20 On completion, reconnect the battery negative terminal.

16 Crankshaft oil seals – renewal

Timing belt end oil seal

1 Remove the crankshaft sprocket as described in Section 8.

2 Carefully punch or drill a small hole in the oil seal. Screw in a self-tapping screw and pull on the screw with pliers to extract the seal **(see illustration)**.

3 Clean the seal housing and polish off any burrs or raised edges which may have caused the seal to fail in the first place.

4 Ease the new seal into position on the end of the crankshaft. Press the seal squarely into position until it is flush with the housing. If necessary, a suitable tubular drift which bears only on the hard outer edge of the seal can be used to tap the seal into position **(see illustration)**. Take great care not to damage

15.11b . . . and to the return channel

the seal lips during fitting and ensure that the seal lips face inwards.

5 Wash off any traces of oil, then refit the crankshaft sprocket as described in Section 8.

Transmission end oil seal

6 Remove the flywheel/driveplate as described in Section 17.

7 Remove the sump as described in Section 13.

8 Undo the five bolts and remove the rear oil seal housing. Note that the oil seal and the housing are a single assembly.

9 Clean the crankshaft and polish off any

16.2 Screw in a self-tapping screw and pull on the screw with pliers to extract the oil seal

16.4 Using a socket as a tubular drift to fit the new oil seal

16.10 Fitting the new oil seal housing, with integral oil seal over the crankshaft

16.12 After fitting, remove the protector sleeve from the housing

burrs or raised edges which may have caused the seal to fail in the first place.

10 Position the new oil seal housing, complete with seal over the crankshaft and into position on the cylinder block **(see illustration)**. Note that the new oil seal housing is supplied with a protector sleeve over the oil seal. Leave the sleeve in position as the housing is fitted.

11 Refit the five retaining bolts and tighten to the specified torque.

12 Remove the protector sleeve from the housing **(see illustration)**.

13 Refit the sump as described in Section 13.

14 Refit the flywheel/driveplate as described in Section 17.

17 Flywheel/driveplate –
removal, inspection and refitting

Note: *New flywheel/driveplate retaining bolts will be required on refitting.*

Removal

Manual transmission models

1 Remove the transmission as described in Chapter 7A, then remove the clutch assembly as described in Chapter 6.

2 Prevent the flywheel from turning by locking the ring gear teeth with a similar arrangement to that shown **(see illustration)**.

3 Slacken and remove the retaining bolts and remove the flywheel **(see illustration)**. Do not drop it, as it is very heavy.

Automatic transmission models

4 Remove the transmission as described in Chapter 7B then remove the driveplate as described in paragraphs 2 and 3.

Inspection

5 If there is any doubt about the condition of the flywheel/driveplate, seek the advice of a Vauxhall/Opel dealer or engine reconditioning specialist. They will be able to advise if it is possible to recondition it or whether renewal is necessary.

Refitting

Manual transmission models

6 Clean the mating surfaces of the flywheel and crankshaft.

7 Offer up the flywheel and engage it over the positioning dowel on the crankshaft. Apply a drop of locking compound to the threads of each new flywheel retaining bolt (unless they are already precoated) and install the new bolts.

8 Lock the flywheel by the method used on removal then, working in a diagonal sequence,

evenly and progressively tighten the retaining bolts to the specified torque.

9 Refit the clutch as described in Chapter 6 then remove the locking tool, and refit the transmission as described in Chapter 7A.

Automatic transmission models

10 Refit the driveplate as described in paragraphs 6 to 8.

11 Remove the locking tool, and refit the transmission as described in Chapter 7B.

18 Engine/transmission mountings –
inspection and renewal

Inspection

1 If improved access is required, firmly apply the handbrake, then jack up the front of the car and support it securely on axle stands (see *Jacking and vehicle support*).

2 Check the mounting rubber to see if it is cracked, hardened or separated from the metal at any point; renew the mounting if any such damage or deterioration is evident.

3 Check that all the mounting's fasteners are securely tightened; use a torque wrench to check if possible.

4 Using a large screwdriver or a pry bar, check for wear in the mounting by carefully levering against it to check for free play; where this is not possible, enlist the aid of an assistant to move the engine/transmission unit back-and-forth, or from side-to-side, while you watch the mounting. While some free play is to be expected even from new components, excessive wear should be obvious. If excessive free play is found, check first that the fasteners are correctly secured, then renew any worn components as described below.

Renewal

Note: *Before slackening any of the engine mounting bolts/nuts, the relative positions of*

17.2 Prevent the flywheel from turning by locking the ring gear teeth

17.3 Flywheel retaining bolts (arrowed)

18.6 Front mounting/torque link through-bolt (A) and mounting bracket-to-transmission bolts (B)

18.15 Unscrew the two rear mounting/torque link retaining bolts

the mountings to their various brackets should be marked to ensure correct alignment upon refitting.

Front mounting/torque link

5 Apply the handbrake, then jack up the front of the vehicle and support it on axle stands (see *Jacking and vehicle support*).

6 Slacken and remove the nut securing the mounting to the subframe bracket. Withdraw the through-bolt **(see illustration)**.

7 Undo the bolts securing the mounting bracket to the transmission, then manoeuvre the mounting and bracket out of position.

8 Check all components for signs of wear or damage, and renew as necessary.

9 Locate the mounting in the subframe, refit the through-bolt and nut, then tighten the nut finger-tight at this stage.

10 Refit the mounting bracket to the transmission and tighten its bolts to the specified torque.

11 Tighten the through-bolt nut to the specified torque.

12 On completion, lower the vehicle to the ground.

Rear mounting/torque link

13 Apply the handbrake, then jack up the front of the vehicle and support it on axle stands (see *Jacking and vehicle support*).

14 Working under the vehicle, remove the centre nut and bolt securing the mounting to the transmission bracket.

15 Remove the two bolts securing the mounting to the subframe, and withdraw the mounting/torque link **(see illustration)**.

16 If necessary, unbolt the bracket from the transmission. **Note:** *The bracket bolts and link bolts are of different lengths.*

17 Refit the bracket to the transmission and tighten the bolts to the specified torque.

18 Locate the new mounting/link in position ensuring that the lug on the top of the mounting engages with the slot in the transmission bracket. Insert the bolts, screw on the nut and tighten to the specified torque.

19 On completion, lower the vehicle to the ground.

Right-hand mounting

19 Apply the handbrake, then jack up the front of the vehicle and support it on axle stands (see *Jacking and vehicle support*).

20 Remove the air cleaner as described in Chapter 4A.

21 Place a trolley jack beneath the right-hand end of the engine with a block of wood on the jack head. Raise the jack until it is supporting the weight of the engine.

22 Mark the position of the three bolts securing the mounting bracket to the engine bracket and undo the bolts. Undo the three bolts securing the mounting to the body and remove the mounting assembly **(see illustration)**.

23 Place the mounting assembly in position and refit the three bolts securing the mounting to the body. Tighten the bolts to the specified torque. Align the mounting in its original position, then tighten the three mounting bracket bolts to the specified torque.

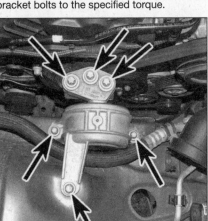

18.22 Right-hand mounting retaining bolts (arrowed)

24 Remove the support jack, then refit the air cleaner as described in Chapter 4A.

25 On completion, lower the vehicle to the ground.

Left-hand mounting

26 Apply the handbrake, then jack up the front of the vehicle and support it on axle stands (see *Jacking and vehicle support*). Remove the left-hand roadwheel and the plastic wheel arch liner.

27 Remove the battery and battery tray as described in Chapter 5.

28 Attach a suitable hoist and lifting tackle to the engine lifting brackets on the cylinder head, and support the weight of the engine.

29 Working under the wheel arch undo the nut securing the lower rear corner of the mounting to the body, then withdraw the bolt from within the engine compartment.

30 Undo the three bolts securing the mounting bracket to the transmission bracket **(see illustration)**.

31 Undo the three remaining bolts securing the mounting to the body **(see illustration)**.

18.30 Left-hand mounting bracket-to-transmission bracket retaining bolts (arrowed)

18.31 Left-hand mounting-to-body retaining bolts (arrowed) – shown with engine/transmission removed

32 Where applicable, unclip the clutch hydraulic line from the mounting bracket. Remove the mounting assembly from the car.
33 If necessary, undo the through-bolt and separate the rubber mounting from the mounting bracket.
34 If removed, refit the rubber mounting to the mounting bracket and tighten the through-bolt to the specified torque.
35 Locate the mounting brackets in position and, where applicable, clip the clutch hydraulic line onto the bracket.
36 Insert the bolts/nut, then tighten them to the specified torque.
37 Disconnect the hoist and lifting tackle.
38 Refit the wheel arch liner and roadwheel, then lower the vehicle to the ground.
39 Refit the battery tray and battery as described in Chapter 5.

Chapter 2 Part D:
1.9 litre DOHC engine in-car repair procedures

Contents

Degrees of difficulty

Easy, suitable for novice with little experience	Fairly easy, suitable for beginner with some experience	Fairly difficult, suitable for competent DIY mechanic	Difficult, suitable for experienced DIY mechanic	Very difficult, suitable for expert DIY or professional

Specifications

General
Engine type	Four-cylinder, in-line, water-cooled. Double overhead camshaft, belt-driven
Manufacturer's engine code	Z19DTH
Bore	82.0 mm
Stroke	90.4 mm
Capacity	1910 cc
Compression ratio	17.5:1
Firing order	1-3-4-2 (No 1 cylinder at timing belt end of engine)
Direction of crankshaft rotation	Clockwise (viewed from timing belt end of engine)

Compression pressures
Maximum difference between any two cylinders	1.5 bar

Lubrication system
Minimum oil pressure at 100°C	1.0 bar at idle speed
Oil pump type	Rotor-type, driven by crankshaft pulley/vibration damper from crankshaft

Torque wrench settings
	Nm	lbf ft
Air conditioning compressor mounting bracket to cylinder block/sump	50	37
Auxiliary drivebelt idler pulley bolt	50	37
Auxiliary drivebelt tensioner assembly bolts	50	37
Camshaft drivegear bolts	120	89
Camshaft housing bolts	25	18
Camshaft housing closure bolts	16	12
Camshaft sprocket bolt*	120	89
Connecting rod big-end bearing cap bolt*:		
Stage 1	25	18
Stage 2	Angle-tighten a further 60°	
Crankshaft oil seal housing	9	7
Crankshaft pulley/vibration damper bolts	25	18

Torque wrench settings (continued)

	Nm	lbf ft
Crankshaft sprocket bolt*†	340	251
Cylinder head bolts*:		
Stage 1	20	15
Stage 2	65	48
Stage 3	Angle-tighten a further 90°	
Stage 4	Angle-tighten a further 90°	
Stage 5	Angle-tighten a further 90°	
Engine/transmission mountings:		
Front mounting/torque link:		
Mounting to subframe bracket	55	41
Bracket to transmission	80	59
Left-hand:		
Mounting-to-body bolts	25	18
Mounting bracket to transmission bracket	80	59
Rubber mounting through-bolt	55	41
Transmission bracket to transmission	55	41
Rear mounting/torque link:		
Mounting to subframe	55	41
Mounting-to-transmission bracket through-bolt	55	41
Transmission bracket to transmission	80	59
Right-hand:		
Engine bracket-to-engine bolts:		
Lower bolts (M8)	25	18
Upper bolts (M10)	50	37
Mounting-to-body bolts	35	26
Mounting-to-engine bracket bolts	55	41
Engine-to-transmission unit bolts:		
M10 bolts	40	30
M12 bolts	60	44
Flywheel bolts*	160	118
High-pressure fuel pump sprocket nut*	50	37
Intermediate shaft bearing housing support bracket bolts	55	41
Main bearing cap bolts*:		
Stage 1	25	18
Stage 2	Angle-tighten a further 100°	
Oil filler housing bolts	9	7
Oil filter housing to cylinder block	50	37
Oil pump housing to cylinder block	9	7
Oil pump pick-up/strainer bolts	9	7
Roadwheel bolts	110	81
Sump bolts:		
M6 bolts	9	7
M8 bolts	25	18
M10 bolts	40	30
Sump drain plug	20	15
Timing belt idler pulley bolt	50	37
Timing belt tensioner bolt	30	22
Timing belt upper cover bolts:		
M6 bolts	9	7
M8 bolts	25	18

* Use new nuts/bolts
† Left-hand thread

1 General information

How to use this Chapter

This Part of Chapter 2 describes the repair procedures which can reasonably be carried out on the engine while it remains in the vehicle. If the engine has been removed from the vehicle and is being dismantled as described in Chapter 2E, any preliminary dismantling procedures can be ignored.

Note that, while it may be possible physically to overhaul items such as the piston/connecting rod assemblies while the engine is in the vehicle, such tasks are not usually carried out as separate operations, and usually require the execution of several additional procedures (not to mention the cleaning of components and of oilways); for this reason, all such tasks are classed as major overhaul procedures, and are described in Chapter 2E.

Chapter 2E describes the removal of the engine/transmission unit from the vehicle, and the full overhaul procedures which can then be carried out.

Engine description

The 1.9 litre DOHC diesel engine is of the sixteen-valve, in-line four-cylinder, double overhead camshaft type, mounted transversely at the front of the car, with the transmission on its left-hand end.

The crankshaft is supported within the cylinder block on five shell-type main bearings. Thrustwashers are fitted to number 3 main bearing, to control crankshaft endfloat.

The connecting rods rotate on horizontally-split bearing shells at their big-ends. The pistons are attached to the connecting rods by gudgeon pins, which are retained by circlips. The aluminium-alloy pistons are fitted with three piston rings – two compression rings and scraper-type oil control ring.

The camshafts are situated in a separate housing bolted to the top of the cylinder head. The exhaust camshaft is driven by the crankshaft via a toothed composite rubber timing belt (which also drives the high-pressure fuel pump and the coolant pump). The exhaust camshaft drives the inlet camshaft via a spur gear. Each cylinder has four valves (two inlet and two exhaust), operated via followers which are supported at their pivot ends by hydraulic self-adjusting tappets. One camshaft operates the inlet valves, and the other operates the exhaust valves.

The inlet and exhaust valves are each closed by a single valve spring, and operate in guides pressed into the cylinder head.

Lubrication is by pressure-feed from a rotor-type oil pump, which is mounted on the right-hand end of the crankshaft. The pump draws oil through a strainer located in the sump, and then forces it through an externally mounted full-flow cartridge-type filter. The oil flows into galleries in the cylinder block/ crankcase, from where it is distributed to the crankshaft (main bearings) and camshafts. The big-end bearings are supplied with oil via internal drillings in the crankshaft, while the camshaft bearings also receive a pressurised supply. The camshaft lobes and valves are lubricated by splash, as are all other engine components.

A semi-closed crankcase ventilation system is employed; crankcase fumes are drawn from the oil separator attached to the cylinder block via a hose to the camshaft housing. The fumes are then passed via a hose to the inlet manifold.

Operations with engine in place

The following operations can be carried out without having to remove the engine from the vehicle.

a) Removal and refitting of the cylinder head.
b) Removal and refitting of the timing belt, tensioner, idler pulleys and sprockets.

c) Renewal of the camshaft oil seal.
d) Removal and refitting of the camshaft housing.
e) Removal and refitting of the camshafts and followers.
f) Removal and refitting of the sump.
g) Removal and refitting of the connecting rods and pistons*.
h) Removal and refitting of the oil pump.
i) Removal and refitting of the oil filter housing.
j) Renewal of the crankshaft oil seals.
k) Renewal of the engine mountings.
l) Removal and refitting of the flywheel/ driveplate.

* Although the operation marked with an asterisk can be carried out with the engine in the car (after removal of the sump), it is preferable for the engine to be removed, in the interests of cleanliness and improved access. For this reason, the procedure is described in Chapter 2E.

2 Compression and leakdown tests – description and interpretation

Compression test

Note 1: A compression tester specifically designed for diesel engines must be used for this test.

Note 2: The battery must be in a good state of charge, the air filter must be clean, and the engine should be at normal operating temperature.

1 When engine performance is down, or if misfiring occurs which cannot be attributed to the fuel system, a compression test can provide diagnostic clues as to the engine's condition. If the test is performed regularly, it can give warning of trouble before any other symptoms become apparent.

2 A compression tester specifically intended for diesel engines must be used, because of the higher pressures involved. The tester is connected to an adapter which screws into the glow plug holes. It is unlikely to be worthwhile buying such a tester for occasional use, but it may be possible to borrow or hire one – if not, have the test performed by a Vauxhall/ Opel dealer, or suitably-equipped garage. If

the necessary equipment is available, proceed as follows.

3 Remove the glow plugs as described in Chapter 5, then open the cover on the engine compartment fuse/relay box and remove the fuel pump relay **(see illustrations)**.

4 Screw the compression tester adapter in to the glow plug hole of No 1 cylinder.

5 With the help of an assistant, crank the engine on the starter motor; after one or two revolutions, the compression pressure should build-up to a maximum figure, and then stabilise. Record the highest reading obtained.

6 Repeat the test on the remaining cylinders, recording the pressure in each.

7 All cylinders should produce very similar pressures; any difference greater than the maximum figure given in the Specifications indicates the existence of a fault. Note that the compression should build-up quickly in a healthy engine; low compression on the first stroke, followed by gradually-increasing pressure on successive strokes, indicates worn piston rings. A low compression reading on the first stroke, which does not build-up during successive strokes, indicates leaking valves or a blown head gasket (a cracked head could also be the cause). **Note:** The cause of poor compression is less easy to establish on a diesel engine than on a petrol one. The effect of introducing oil into the cylinders ('wet' testing) is not conclusive, because there is a risk that the oil will sit in the recess on the piston crown instead of passing to the rings.

8 On completion of the test, refit the fuel pump relay, then refit the glow plugs as described in Chapter 5.

Leakdown test

9 A leakdown test measures the rate at which compressed air fed into the cylinder is lost. It is an alternative to a compression test, and in many ways it is better, since the escaping air provides easy identification of where pressure loss is occurring (piston rings, valves or head gasket).

10 The equipment needed for leakdown testing is unlikely to be available to the home mechanic. If poor compression is suspected, have the test performed by a Vauxhall/Opel dealer, or suitably-equipped garage.

2.3a Open the cover on the fuse/relay box . . .

2.3b . . . and remove the fuel pump relay (arrowed)

3.0a Vauxhall/Opel special tool EN-46788 (or equivalent) is required to set the TDC position for No 1 piston . . .

3 Top dead centre (TDC) for No 1 piston – locating

Note: *To accurately determine the TDC position for No 1 piston, it will be necessary to use Vauxhall/Opel special tool EN-46788 (or suitable equivalent) to set the crankshaft at the TDC position, together with the camshaft positioning tool, Vauxhall/Opel special tool EN-46789 (or suitable equivalent) (see illustrations).*

1 In its travel up-and-down its cylinder bore, Top Dead Centre (TDC) is the highest point that each piston reaches as the crankshaft rotates. While each piston reaches TDC both at the top of the compression stroke and again at the top of the exhaust stroke, for the purpose of timing the engine, TDC refers to

3.8 Undo the retaining bolts and remove the right-hand engine mounting

3.10 Undo the bolt (arrowed) and release the engine oil dipstick guide tube from the coolant pipe

3.0b . . . together with Vauxhall/Opel special tool EN-46789 (or equivalent) to set the camshaft position

the piston position of No 1 cylinder at the top of its compression stroke.

2 Number 1 piston (and cylinder) is at the right-hand (timing belt) end of the engine, and its TDC position is located as follows. Note that the crankshaft rotates clockwise when viewed from the right-hand side of the car.

3 Disconnect the battery negative terminal (refer to *Disconnecting the battery* in the Reference Chapter), then lift off the plastic cover over the top of the engine.

4 Remove the crankshaft pulley/vibration damper as described in Section 5.

5 Undo the central mounting bolt, and remove the auxiliary drivebelt tensioner assembly from the engine **(see illustration)**.

6 Remove the air cleaner assembly and air intake duct as described in Chapter 4A.

7 Place a trolley jack beneath the right-hand end of the engine with a block of wood on the

3.9 Engine breather pipe retaining bolts (arrowed)

3.11 Unscrew the closure bolt from the valve timing checking hole in the camshaft housing

3.5 Undo the central mounting bolt (arrowed), and remove the auxiliary drivebelt tensioner assembly

jack head. Raise the jack until it is supporting the weight of the engine.

8 Mark the bolt positions for correct refitting, then undo the three bolts securing the right-hand engine mounting to the engine bracket, and the three bolts securing the mounting to the body. Remove the mounting **(see illustration)**.

9 Release the retaining clip securing the engine breather hose to the breather pipe adjacent to the engine oil dipstick. Undo the two bolts securing the breather pipe to the cylinder head, and disconnect the pipe from the hose **(see illustration)**.

10 Undo the bolt and release the engine oil dipstick guide tube from the coolant pipe **(see illustration)**.

11 Unscrew the closure bolt from the valve timing checking hole in the camshaft housing **(see illustration)**.

12 Screw the camshaft positioning tool (Vauxhall/Opel special tool EN-46789) into the valve timing checking hole.

13 Using a socket and extension bar on the crankshaft sprocket bolt, rotate the crankshaft in the normal direction of rotation until the spring-loaded plunger of the positioning tool slides into engagement with the slot in the camshaft. There will be an audible click from the tool when this happens.

14 Unscrew the bolt from the lower left-hand side of the oil pump housing and screw in the fastening stud of Vauxhall/Opel special tool EN-46788 **(see illustration)**.

15 Fit the positioning ring of tool EN-46788 over the fastening stud and engage it with the

3.14 Screw the fastening stud of special tool EN-46788 into the oil pump housing

crankshaft sprocket. Ensure that the hole in the positioning ring engages with the lug on the sprocket. Secure the tool in position with the retaining bolt and nut **(see illustration)**.

16 With the crankshaft positioning ring in place and the camshaft positioning tool engaged with the slot in the camshaft, the engine is positioned with No 1 piston at TDC on compression.

4 Valve timing – checking and adjustment

Note: *To check and adjust the valve timing, it will be necessary to use Vauxhall/Opel special tool EN-46788 (or suitable equivalent) to set the crankshaft at the TDC position. Additionally, it will be necessary to use Vauxhall/Opel special tools EN-46789 and EN46789-100 (or suitable equivalents) to lock the camshafts in the TDC position.*

Checking

1 Disconnect the battery negative terminal (refer to *Disconnecting the battery* in the Reference Chapter), then lift off the plastic cover over the top of the engine.
2 Release the retaining clip securing the engine breather hose to the breather pipe adjacent to the engine oil dipstick. Undo the two bolts securing the breather pipe to the cylinder head, and disconnect the pipe from the hose **(see illustration 3.9)**.
3 Undo the bolt and release the engine oil dipstick guide tube from the coolant pipe **(see illustration 3.10)**.
4 Unscrew the closure bolt from the valve timing checking hole in the exhaust side of camshaft housing **(see illustration 3.11)**.
5 Screw the exhaust camshaft positioning tool (Vauxhall/Opel special tool EN-46789) into the valve timing checking hole.
6 Unscrew the closure bolt from the valve timing checking hole in the inlet side of the camshaft housing. The closure bolt is located below the fuel pressure regulating valve on the fuel rail.
7 Screw the inlet camshaft positioning tool (Vauxhall/Opel special tool EN-46789-100) into the valve timing checking hole.
8 Using a socket and extension bar on the crankshaft sprocket bolt, rotate the crankshaft in the normal direction of rotation until the spring-loaded plungers of the positioning tools slide into engagement with the slots in the camshafts. There will be an audible click from the tools when this happens.
9 Remove the crankshaft pulley/vibration damper as described in Section 5.
10 Unscrew the bolt from the lower left-hand side of the oil pump housing and screw in the fastening stud of Vauxhall/Opel special tool EN-46788 **(see illustration 3.14)**.
11 Fit the positioning ring of tool EN-46788 over the fastening stud and engage it with the crankshaft sprocket. Ensure that the hole in the positioning ring engages with the lug on the

3.15 Positioning ring of tool EN-46788 (arrowed) attached to the fastening stud and crankshaft sprocket

sprocket. Secure the tool in position with the retaining bolt and nut **(see illustration 3.15)**.
12 If it is not possible to fit the positioning ring of tool EN-46788 as described, or if the camshaft positioning tools did not engage with the camshaft slots, adjust the valve timing as follows.

Adjustment

13 Remove the timing belt as described in Section 6.
14 Using a socket and extension bar on the crankshaft sprocket bolt, rotate the crankshaft anti-clockwise by 90°. This will position all the pistons half-way down their bores, and prevent any chance of the valves touching the piston crowns during the following procedure.
15 Remove the inlet and exhaust camshaft positioning tools from the valve timing checking holes.
16 Using a suitable tool engaged with the timing belt sprocket on the exhaust camshaft, rotate the sprocket approximately 90° clockwise. Vauxhall/Opel special tools EN-46787 and KM-956-1 are available for this purpose, however, a home-made tool can easily be fabricated **(see Tool Tip in Section 7)**. Take care not to damage the camshaft sensor with the tool as the sprocket is rotated.
17 Screw the inlet camshaft positioning tool (Vauxhall/Opel special tool EN-46789-100) into the valve timing checking hole.
18 Rotate the camshaft sprocket clockwise until the spring-loaded plunger of the positioning tool slides into engagement with the slot in the inlet camshaft. There will be an

5.3 Crankshaft pulley/vibration damper retaining bolts (arrowed)

audible click from the tool when this happens.
19 Release the two retaining clips and disconnect the charge air hose from the throttle body/housing, and intercooler charge air pipe.
20 Release the clip and disconnect the crankcase ventilation hose from the engine oil filler housing.
21 Disconnect the wiring connector from the coolant temperature sensor, then undo the three retaining bolts and remove the oil filler housing.
22 Remove the braking system vacuum pump as described in Chapter 9.
23 Working through the oil filler housing aperture, and using the holding tool to prevent rotation of the camshaft, slacken the inlet camshaft drivegear retaining bolt. Working through the vacuum pump aperture, slacken the exhaust camshaft drivegear retaining bolt in the same way.
24 Screw the exhaust camshaft positioning tool (Vauxhall/Opel special tool EN-46789) into the valve timing checking hole.
25 Rotate the camshaft sprocket clockwise until the spring-loaded plunger of the positioning tool slides into engagement with the slot in the exhaust camshaft. There will be an audible click from the tool when this happens.
26 Hold the camshaft sprocket with the tool and tighten both drivegear retaining bolts to the specified torque.
27 Remove the positioning tool from the inlet camshaft and refit the closure bolt. Tighten the bolt to the specified torque.
28 Refit the oil filler housing to the camshaft housing using a new gasket, refit the retaining bolts and tighten the bolts to the specified torque. Reconnect the coolant temperature sensor wiring connector, and reconnect the crankcase ventilation hose.
29 Refit the braking system vacuum pump as described in Chapter 9.
30 Refit the charge air hose to the throttle body/housing, and intercooler charge air pipe and secure with the retaining clips.
31 Refit the timing belt as described in Section 6.

5 Crankshaft pulley/ vibration damper – removal and refitting

Removal

1 Apply the handbrake, then jack up the front of the vehicle and support it on axle stands (see *Jacking and vehicle support*). Remove the right-hand front roadwheel.
2 Remove the auxiliary drivebelt as described in Chapter 1. Prior to removal, mark the direction of rotation on the belt to ensure the belt is refitted the same way around.
3 Undo the four bolts securing the pulley to the crankshaft sprocket and remove the pulley from the sprocket **(see illustration)**.

6.2 Upper timing belt cover retaining bolts (arrowed)

6.3 Undo the bolt (arrowed) and remove the auxiliary drivebelt idler pulley from the engine bracket

6.4a Undo the two lower bolts (arrowed) . . .

6.4b . . . and the three upper bolts (arrowed) . . .

6.4c . . . and remove the engine bracket from the engine

Refitting

4 Locate the crankshaft pulley on the sprocket, ensuring that the hole on the rear face of the pulley engages with the lug on the sprocket.

5 Refit the four retaining bolts and tighten them progressively to the specified torque.

6 Refit the auxiliary drivebelt as described in Chapter 1 using the mark made prior to removal to ensure the belt is fitted the correct way around.

7 Refit the roadwheel, then lower the car to the ground and tighten the wheel bolts to the specified torque.

6 Timing belt – removal and refitting

Note: The timing belt must be removed and refitted with the engine cold.

Removal

1 Position No 1 cylinder at TDC on its compression stroke as described in Section 3.

2 Unclip the wiring harness from the side of the upper timing belt cover. Unscrew the seven retaining bolts and lift off the upper timing belt cover **(see illustration)**.

3 Undo the retaining bolt and remove the auxiliary drivebelt idler pulley from the engine bracket **(see illustration)**.

4 Undo the two lower bolts, and the three upper bolts, and remove the engine bracket from the engine **(see illustrations)**.

5 Undo the nut and bolt and remove the crankshaft positioning tool (EN-46788) from the crankshaft sprocket.

6 Slacken the timing belt tensioner retaining bolt and allow the tensioner to retract, relieving the tension on the timing belt.

7 Slide the timing belt from its sprockets and remove it from the engine. If the belt is to be

re-used, use white paint or similar to mark the direction of rotation on the belt. **Do not** rotate the crankshaft or camshafts until the timing belt has been refitted.

8 Check the timing belt carefully for any signs of uneven wear, splitting or oil contamination, and renew it if there is the slightest doubt about its condition. If the engine is undergoing an overhaul and is approaching the interval for belt renewal (see Chapter 1) renew the belt as a matter of course, regardless of its apparent condition. If signs of oil contamination are found, trace the source of the oil leak and rectify it, then wash down the engine timing belt area and all related components to remove all traces of oil.

Refitting

9 On reassembly, thoroughly clean the timing belt sprockets and tensioner/idler pulleys.

10 Place the timing belt in position over the crankshaft sprocket. If the original belt is being refitted, ensure that the arrow mark made on removal points in the normal direction of rotation, as before.

11 Check that the camshaft and crankshaft are still positioned with No 1 piston at TDC on compression as described in Section 3, and with the camshaft positioning tool still in place. Now refit the crankshaft positioning tool.

12 Fit the timing belt over the crankshaft, camshaft and fuel pump sprockets and around the idler pulleys, ensuring that the belt front run is taut (ie, all slack is on the tensioner side of the belt), then fit the belt over the coolant pump sprocket and tensioner pulley. Do not twist the belt sharply while refitting it. Ensure that the belt teeth are correctly seated centrally in the sprockets.

13 Screw in a suitable bolt, approximately 50 mm in length, into the threaded hole directly below the timing belt tensioner. Using a screwdriver resting on the bolt as a pivot, move the adjusting lever on the tensioner until the tensioner pointer is aligned with the mark on the backplate. Hold the tensioner in this position and tighten the tensioner retaining bolt **(see illustrations)**.

14 Remove the crankshaft and camshaft positioning tools.

15 Using a socket on the crankshaft sprocket

6.13a Using a screwdriver resting on a pivot bolt (arrowed), move the adjusting lever on the tensioner . . .

6.13b . . . until the tensioner pointer (arrowed) is aligned with the mark on the backplate

bolt, rotate the crankshaft smoothly through two complete turns (720º) in the normal direction of rotation to settle the timing belt in position. Stop rotating the crankshaft just before completing the second turn.

16 Refit the camshaft positioning tool and continue turning the crankshaft until the camshaft positioning tool engages.

17 Refit the positioning ring of tool EN-46788 over the fastening stud and engage it with the crankshaft sprocket. Ensure that the hole in the positioning ring engages with the lug on the sprocket. Secure the tool in position with the retaining bolt and nut.

18 Slacken the timing belt tensioner retaining bolt and, using a screwdriver resting on the pivot bolt as before, move the adjusting lever on the tensioner until the tensioner pointer is once again aligned with the mark on the backplate. Hold the tensioner in this position and tighten the tensioner retaining bolt to the specified torque.

19 Remove all the positioning tools and again rotate the crankshaft smoothly through two complete turns (720º) in the normal direction of rotation. Check that the timing belt tensioner pointer is still aligned with the mark on the backplate. If not, repeat the procedure described in paragraph 18.

20 When all is correct, remove the tensioner position pivot bolt. Refit the bolt removed from the oil pump housing and tighten it to the specified torque. Refit the closure plug to the camshaft housing and tighten to the specified torque.

21 Place the engine bracket in position and refit the two lower bolts, and the three upper bolts. Tighten the bolts to the specified torque. Refit the auxiliary drivebelt idler pulley to the engine bracket and tighten the retaining bolt to the specified torque.

22 Refit the upper timing belt cover and tighten the retaining bolts to the specified torque. Clip the wiring harness back into position.

23 Place the right-hand engine mounting assembly in position and refit the three bolts securing the mounting to the body. Tighten the bolts to the specified torque. Align the mounting in its original position, then fit and tighten the three mounting bracket bolts to the specified torque. Remove the jack from under the engine.

24 Refit the air cleaner assembly and air intake duct as described in Chapter 4A.

25 Place the auxiliary drivebelt tensioner assembly in position ensuring that the locating peg on the tensioner mounting surface engages correctly with the corresponding hole in the mounting bracket. Tighten the tensioner central mounting bolt to the specified torque.

26 Refit the crankshaft pulley/vibration damper as described in Section 5, then refit the auxiliary drivebelt as described in Chapter 1.

27 Move the engine oil dipstick guide tube back into position. Refit the bolt securing the guide tube to the coolant pipe and tighten the bolt securely.

28 Attach the engine breather hose to the breather pipe and secure with the retaining clip. Secure the breather pipe to the cylinder head with the two bolts securely tightened.

29 Refit the plastic cover to the top of the engine.

30 Refit the roadwheel, then lower the car to the ground and tighten the wheel bolts to the specified torque.

7 Timing belt sprockets, tensioner and idler pulley – removal and refitting

Note: *Certain special tools will be required for the removal and refitting of the sprockets. Read through the entire procedure to familiarise yourself with the work involved, then either obtain the manufacturer's special tools, or use the alternatives described.*

Camshaft sprocket

Note: *A new sprocket retaining bolt will be required for refitting.*

Removal

1 Remove the timing belt as described in Section 6, then remove camshaft positioning tool from the valve timing checking hole.

2 It will now be necessary to hold the camshaft sprocket to enable the retaining bolt to be removed. Vauxhall/Opel special tools EN-46787 and KM-956-1 are available for this purpose, however, a home-made tool can easily be fabricated (see Tool Tip).

3 Engage the tool with the holes in the camshaft sprocket, taking care not to damage the camshaft sensor located behind the sprocket

4 Unscrew the retaining bolt and remove the sprocket from the end of the camshaft.

Refitting

5 Prior to refitting check the oil seal for signs of damage or leakage. If necessary, renew as described in Section 8.

6 Refit the sprocket to the camshaft end, aligning its cut-out with the locating peg, and fit the new retaining bolt finger-tight only at this stage. Final tightening is carried out after the timing belt has been fitted and tensioned.

7 Refit the camshaft positioning tool to the valve timing checking hole. If necessary, rotate the camshaft slightly, by means of the sprocket, until the tool audibly engages.

8 Proceed with the timing belt refitting procedure as described in Section 6, paragraphs 9 to 14.

9 Retain the camshaft sprocket using the holding tool, and tighten the retaining bolt to the specified torque.

10 Continue with the timing belt refitting procedure as described in Section 6, paragraphs 15 to 30.

Crankshaft sprocket

Note 1: *The crankshaft sprocket retaining bolt is extremely tight. Ensure that the holding tool used to prevent rotation as the bolt*

To make a sprocket holding tool, obtain two lengths of steel strip about 6 mm thick by about 30 mm wide or similar, one 600 mm long, the other 200 mm long (all dimensions are approximate). Bolt the two strips together to form a forked end, leaving the bolt slack so that the shorter strip can pivot freely. At the other end of each 'prong' of the fork, drill a suitable hole and fit a nut and bolt to allow the tool to engage with the spokes in the sprocket.

is slackened is of sturdy construction and securely attached.

Note 2: *A new sprocket retaining bolt will be required for refitting.*

Removal

11 Remove the timing belt as described in Section 6.

12 It will now be necessary to hold the crankshaft sprocket to enable the retaining bolt to be removed. Vauxhall special tools EN-47630 and KM-956-1 are available for this purpose, however, a home-made tool similar to that described in paragraph 2, can easily be fabricated.

13 Using the crankshaft pulley retaining bolts, securely attach the tool to the crankshaft sprocket. With the help of an assistant, hold the sprocket stationary and unscrew the retaining bolt. **Note:** *The sprocket retaining bolt has a **left-hand thread** and is unscrewed by turning it clockwise.*

14 Remove the bolt and washer and slide the sprocket off the end of the crankshaft (see illustrations). Note that a new bolt will be required for refitting.

7.14a Remove the bolt and washer . . .

7.14b ... and slide the sprocket off the end of the crankshaft

7.20 Engage the holding tool with the holes in the fuel pump sprocket and undo the retaining nut

7.21 Use a suitable puller to release the fuel pump sprocket taper

Refitting

15 Align the sprocket location key with the crankshaft groove and slide the sprocket into position. Fit the new retaining bolt and washer.

16 Hold the sprocket stationary using the holding tool and tighten the retaining bolt to the specified torque. Remove the holding tool.

17 Refit the timing belt as described in Section 6.

High-pressure fuel pump sprocket

Note: *A new sprocket retaining nut will be required for refitting.*

Removal

18 Remove the timing belt as described in Section 6.

19 It will now be necessary to hold the fuel

pump sprocket to enable the retaining nut to be removed. Vauxhall special tools KM-6347 and KM-956-1 are available for this purpose, however, a home-made tool similar to that described in paragraph 2, can easily be fabricated.

20 Engage the tool with the holes in the fuel pump sprocket and undo the sprocket retaining nut **(see illustration)**. Note that a new nut will be required for refitting.

21 Attach a suitable puller to the threaded holes in the fuel pump sprocket using bolts and washers similar to the arrangement shown **(see illustration)**.

22 Tighten the puller centre bolt to release the sprocket from the taper on the pump shaft. Once the taper releases, remove the puller and withdraw the sprocket. Collect the Woodruff key from the pump shaft **(see illustrations)**.

Refitting

23 Clean the fuel pump shaft and the sprocket hub ensuring that all traces of oil or grease are removed.

24 Refit the Woodruff key to the pump shaft, then locate the sprocket in position. Fit the new retaining nut.

25 Hold the sprocket stationary using the holding tool and tighten the retaining nut to the specified torque. Remove the holding tool.

26 Refit the timing belt as described in Section 6.

Tensioner assembly

Removal

27 Remove the timing belt as described in Section 6.

28 Slacken and remove the retaining bolt and remove the tensioner assembly from the engine **(see illustrations)**.

Refitting

29 Fit the tensioner to the engine, making sure that the slot on the tensioner backplate is correctly located over the peg on the engine bracket **(see illustration)**.

30 Clean the threads of the retaining bolt and apply thread-locking compound to the bolt threads. Screw in the retaining bolt, set the tensioner in the retracted position and tighten the retaining bolt.

31 Refit the timing belt as described in Section 6.

7.22a Once the taper releases, withdraw the sprocket ...

7.22b ... and collect the Woodruff key from the pump shaft

7.28a Slacken and remove the retaining bolt ...

7.28b ... and remove the timing belt tensioner assembly

7.29 The slot on the tensioner backplate must locate over the peg (arrowed) on the engine bracket

7.33 Slacken and remove the retaining bolt and remove the idler pulley from the engine

Idler pulley

Removal

32 Remove the timing belt as described in Section 6.

33 Slacken and remove the retaining bolt and remove the idler pulley from the engine **(see illustration)**.

Refitting

34 Refit the idler pulley and tighten the retaining bolt to the specified torque.

35 Refit the timing belt as described in Section 6.

8 Camshaft oil seal – renewal

1 Remove the camshaft sprocket as described in Section 7.

2 Carefully punch or drill a small hole in the oil seal. Screw in a self-tapping screw, and pull on the screw with pliers to extract the seal.

3 Clean the seal housing, and polish off any burrs or raised edges which may have caused the seal to fail in the first place.

4 Press the new seal into position using a suitable tubular drift (such as a socket) which bears only on the hard outer edge of the seal. Take care not to damage the seal lips during fitting; note that the seal lips should face inwards.

5 Refit the camshaft sprocket as described in Section 7.

9 Camshaft housing – removal and refitting

Removal

1 Remove the timing belt as described in Section 6.

2 Disconnect the wiring harness connectors from the following components **(see illustrations)**:

    a) *Fuel injectors.*

    b) *Fuel pressure regulating valve.*

    c) *Fuel pressure sensor.*

9.2a Disconnect the wiring connectors at the fuel injectors . . .

9.2c . . . fuel pressure sensor . . .

    d) *Camshaft sensor.*

    e) *Air conditioning compressor.*

3 Release the air conditioning compressor wiring harness from the clip on the oil dipstick guide tube. Undo the two bolts securing the plastic wiring harness guide to the camshaft

9.2e . . . and air conditioning compressor (arrowed)

9.3b . . . and move the disconnected wiring harness to one side

9.2b . . . fuel pressure regulating valve . . .

9.2d . . . camshaft sensor . . .

housing and move the disconnected wiring harness to one side **(see illustrations)**.

4 Disconnect the two vacuum hoses from the vacuum pipe assembly on top of the camshaft housing. Undo the two retaining bolts and move the pipe assembly to one side **(see illustration)**.

9.3a Undo the two bolts (arrowed) securing the wiring harness guide to the camshaft housing . . .

9.4a Disconnect the two vacuum hoses from the vacuum pipe assembly . . .

9.4b ... then undo the two retaining bolts (arrowed) and move the pipe assembly to one side

9.6 Release the retaining clips and remove the charge air hose

9.7 Disconnect the vacuum hose quick-release fitting from the braking system vacuum pump

9.8 Disconnect the crankcase ventilation hose from the engine oil filler housing

9.11 Lift the camshaft housing off the cylinder head and recover the gasket

5 Remove the fuel injectors and the fuel rail as described in Chapter 4A.

6 Release the two retaining clips and disconnect the charge air hose from the throttle body/housing, and intercooler charge air pipe **(see illustration)**.

7 Disconnect the vacuum hose quick-release fitting from the braking system vacuum pump **(see illustration)**.

8 Release the clip and disconnect the crankcase ventilation hose from the engine oil filler housing **(see illustration)**.

9 Undo the retaining bolts and remove the two engine lifting brackets from the left-hand end of the camshaft housing. Undo the bolt securing the turbocharger charge air pipe to the right-hand end of the camshaft housing

10 Working in a spiral pattern from the outside inwards, progressively slacken, then remove, the sixteen bolts, securing the camshaft housing to the cylinder head. Ensure that the housing releases evenly from the cylinder block.

11 Lift the camshaft housing off the cylinder head and recover the gasket **(see illustration)**.

12 Thoroughly clean the mating faces of the cylinder head, camshaft housing and vacuum pump and obtain a new gasket for refitting.

Refitting

13 Check that all the hydraulic tappets and rocker arms are correctly positioned in the cylinder head and none have been disturbed.

14 Commence refitting by turning the crankshaft anti-clockwise by 90°. This will

position all the pistons half-way down their bores, and prevent any chance of the valves touching the piston crowns as the camshaft housing is being fitted.

15 Place a new gasket on the cylinder head, then locate the camshaft housing in position aligning it with the locating dowels.

16 Refit the sixteen camshaft housing retaining bolts. Progressively screw in the bolts to gradually draw the housing down and into contact with the cylinder head.

17 Working in a spiral pattern from the inside outwards, progressively tighten the sixteen bolts to the specified torque.

18 Refit the two engine lifting brackets to the left-hand end of the camshaft housing and tighten the retaining bolts securely. Refit and tighten the charge air pipe retaining bolt.

19 Reconnect the crankcase ventilation hose to the engine oil filler housing.

20 Reconnect the vacuum hose quick-release

10.3 Undo the three retaining bolts and remove the oil filler housing

fitting to the braking system vacuum pump ensuring that the fitting audibly engages.

21 Refit the charge air hose to the throttle body/housing, and intercooler charge air pipe and secure with the retaining clips.

22 Refit the fuel rail and fuel injectors as described in Chapter 4A.

23 Place the vacuum pipe assembly in position on the top of the camshaft housing and refit the two retaining bolts. Tighten the bolts securely, then reconnect the two vacuum hoses.

24 Lay the plastic wiring harness guide in position on the camshaft housing, then refit and tighten the two retaining bolts.

25 Reconnect the wiring harness connectors to the components listed in paragraph 2, ensuring that the harness is secured by all the relevant retaining clips.

26 Turn the crankshaft clockwise by 90° to bring No 1 and 4 pistons to approximately the TDC position.

27 Refit the timing belt as described in Section 6.

10 Camshafts – removal, inspection and refitting

Note: *An additional camshaft positioning tool Vauxhall/Opel special tool EN-46789 (or suitable equivalent) will be required for this operation – two in total (see Section 3).*

Removal

1 Carry out the operations described in Section 9, paragraphs 1 to 8.

2 Remove the braking system vacuum pump as described in Chapter 9.

3 Disconnect the wiring connector from the coolant temperature sensor, then undo the three retaining bolts and remove the oil filler housing **(see illustration)**.

4 Undo the retaining bolt and remove the camshaft sensor from the right-hand end of the camshaft housing.

5 Before removing the camshaft housing completely, the retaining bolts for the camshaft drivegears and sprocket should be slackened as follows.

6 Remove the exhaust camshaft positioning tool from the valve timing checking hole.

10.8a Slacken the inlet camshaft drivegear retaining bolt . . .

10.8b . . . and the exhaust camshaft drivegear retaining bolt

10.12a Unscrew and remove the two previously-slackened retaining bolts . . .

7 It will be necessary to hold the camshaft sprocket to enable the drivegear and sprocket retaining bolts to be slackened. Vauxhall special tools EN-46787 and KM-956-1 are available for this purpose, however, a home-made tool can easily be fabricated (see **Tool Tip in Section 7**).

8 Working through the oil filler housing aperture, and using the holding tool to prevent rotation of the camshaft, slacken the inlet camshaft drivegear retaining bolt. Working through the vacuum pump aperture, slacken the exhaust camshaft drivegear retaining bolt in the same way (see illustrations).

9 Again, using the holding tool, slacken the camshaft sprocket retaining bolt.

10 Continue with the camshaft housing removal procedure as described in Section 9, paragraphs 9 to 11.

11 With the camshaft housing placed upside down on the bench, unscrew and remove the previously-slackened retaining bolt, and remove the timing belt sprocket from the exhaust camshaft.

12 At the other end of the housing, unscrew and remove the two previously-slackened retaining bolts, and lift off the drivegears from the inlet and exhaust camshafts (see illustrations).

13 Carefully prise out the exhaust camshaft oil seal with a screwdriver or similar hooked tool. Carefully withdraw the exhaust camshaft out from the timing belt end of the camshaft housing (see illustration).

14 Using a wooden dowel or similar, carefully tap the end of the inlet camshaft toward the timing belt end of the housing, to release the blanking cap. Remove the cap, then carefully

10.12b . . . then lift out the exhaust camshaft drivegear . . .

withdraw the inlet camshaft from the housing (see illustration).

Inspection

15 Examine the camshaft bearing surfaces and cam lobes for signs of wear ridges and scoring. Renew the camshaft(s) if any of these conditions are apparent. Examine the condition of the bearing surfaces in the camshaft housing. If the any wear or scoring is evident, the camshaft housing will need to be renewed.

16 If either camshaft is being renewed, it will be necessary to renew all the rocker arms and tappets for that particular camshaft also (see Section 11).

17 Check the condition of the camshaft drivegears and sprocket for chipped or damaged teeth, wear ridges and scoring. Renew any components as necessary.

Refitting

18 Prior to refitting, thoroughly clean all

10.12c . . . and the inlet camshaft drivegear

components and dry with a lint-free cloth. Ensure that all traces of oil and grease are removed from the contact faces of the drivegears, sprocket and camshafts.

19 Lubricate the camshaft bearing journals in the camshaft housing and carefully insert the inlet and exhaust camshafts.

20 Ensuring that the contact faces are clean and dry, refit the drivegear to each camshaft. Note that the gear with the vacuum pump drive dogs is fitted to the exhaust camshaft, and the plain gear is fitted to the inlet camshaft.

21 Screw in a new drivegear retaining bolt for each camshaft and tighten both bolts finger-tight only at this stage.

22 Refit the camshaft positioning tool to the valve timing checking hole of the exhaust camshaft. If necessary, rotate the exhaust camshaft slightly, until the tool audibly engages (see illustration).

23 Unscrew and remove the closure bolt

10.13 Withdraw the exhaust camshaft . . .

10.14 . . . and inlet camshaft from the camshaft housing

10.22 Refit the camshaft positioning tool to the valve timing checking hole of the exhaust camshaft

10.23a Unscrew the closure bolt from the inlet camshaft side of the camshaft housing . . .

10.23b . . . and fit a camshaft positioning tool for the inlet camshaft

10.24 With both camshafts locked, tighten both drivegear retaining bolts to the specified torque

10.26a Fit a new inlet camshaft blanking cap to the camshaft housing . . .

10.26b . . . and tap it into position until it is flush with the outer face of the housing

10.27 Similarly, fit a new exhaust camshaft oil seal to the camshaft housing

from the inlet camshaft side of the camshaft housing and fit a second camshaft positioning tool **(see illustrations)**. If necessary, rotate the camshaft slightly, until the tool audibly engages.

24 With both camshafts locked by means of the positioning tools, tighten both drivegear retaining bolts to the specified torque **(see illustration)**. It may be beneficial to have an assistant securely support the camshaft housing as the bolts are tightened.

25 Remove the positioning tool from the inlet camshaft and refit the closure bolt. Tighten the bolt to the specified torque.

26 Fit a new inlet camshaft blanking cap to the timing belt end of the camshaft housing and tap it into position until it is flush with the outer face of the housing, using a suitable socket or tube, or a wooden block **(see illustrations)**.

27 Similarly, fit a new exhaust camshaft oil

seal to the timing belt end of the camshaft housing and tap it into position until it is flush with the outer face of the housing, using a suitable socket or tube, or a wooden block **(see illustration)**.

28 Refit the timing belt sprocket to the exhaust camshaft, aligning its cut-out with the locating peg, and fit the new retaining bolt finger-tight only at this stage. Final tightening is carried out after the timing belt has been fitted and tensioned.

29 Refit the camshaft sensor to the camshaft housing and tighten the retaining bolt securely.

30 Refit the oil filler housing to the camshaft housing using a new gasket, refit the retaining bolts and tighten the bolts to the specified torque. Reconnect the coolant temperature sensor wiring connector.

31 Refit the braking system vacuum pump as described in Chapter 9.

32 Thoroughly clean the mating faces of the cylinder head and camshaft housing.

33 Refit the camshaft housing to the cylinder head as described in Section 9, paragraphs 13 to 26.

34 Commence refitting of the timing belt as described in Section 6, paragraphs 9 to 14.

35 Retain the camshaft sprocket using the holding tool, and tighten the retaining bolt to the specified torque.

36 Continue refitting of the timing belt as described in Section 6, paragraphs 15 to 30.

11 Camshaft followers and hydraulic tappets – removal, inspection and refitting

Removal

1 Remove the camshaft housing as described in Section 9.

2 Obtain sixteen small, oil-tight clean plastic containers, and number them inlet 1 to 8 and exhaust 1 to 8; alternatively, divide a larger container into sixteen compartments and number each compartment accordingly.

3 Withdraw each camshaft follower and hydraulic tappet in turn, unclip the follower from the tappet, and place them in their respective container **(see illustrations)**. Do not interchange the followers and tappets, or the rate of wear will be much increased. Fill each container with clean engine oil and ensure that the tappet is submerged.

11.3a Withdraw each camshaft follower . . .

11.3b . . . and hydraulic tappet in turn, and place them in their respective container

Inspection

4 Examine the followers and hydraulic tappet bearing surfaces for wear ridges and scoring. Renew any follower or tappet on which these conditions are apparent.

5 If any new hydraulic tappets are obtained, they should be immersed in a container of clean engine oil prior to refitting.

Refitting

6 Liberally oil the cylinder head hydraulic tappet bores and the tappets. Working on one assembly at a time, clip the follower back onto the tappet, then refit the tappet to the cylinder head, ensuring that it is refitted to its original bore. Lay the follower over its respective valve **(see illustrations)**.

7 Refit the remaining tappets and followers in the same way.

8 With all the tappets and followers in place, refit the camshaft housing as described in Section 9.

| 12 Cylinder head – removal and refitting |

Note: *New cylinder head bolts will be required for refitting.*

Removal

1 Disconnect the battery negative terminal (refer to *Disconnecting the battery* in the Reference Chapter).

2 Drain the cooling system as described in Chapter 1.

3 Remove the camshaft housing as described in Section 9.

4 Remove the camshaft followers and hydraulic tappets as described in Section 11.

5 Remove the inlet and exhaust manifolds as described in Chapter 4A.

6 Release the clips and disconnect the remaining two coolant hoses at the thermostat housing, and the coolant hose at the EGR valve heat exchanger **(see illustration)**.

7 Release the coolant pipe from the stud at the base of the thermostat housing **(see illustration)**.

8 Undo the bolt securing the high-pressure fuel pump mounting bracket to the cylinder head **(see illustration)**.

9 Make a final check to ensure that all relevant hoses, pipes and wires have been disconnected.

10 Working in the **reverse** of the tightening sequence **(see illustration 12.27)**, progressively slacken the cylinder head bolts by half a turn at a time, until all bolts can be unscrewed by hand. Note that an M14 RIBE socket bit will be required to unscrew the bolts. Remove the cylinder head bolts and recover the washers.

11 Engage the help of an assistant, if necessary, and lift the cylinder head from the cylinder block **(see illustration)**.

Caution: Do not lay the head on its lower

11.6a Clip the follower back onto the tappet . . .

mating surface; support the head on wooden blocks, ensuring each block only contacts the head mating surface.

12 Remove the gasket and keep it for identification purposes (see paragraph 19).

13 If the cylinder head is to be dismantled for overhaul, then refer to Part E of this Chapter.

Preparation for refitting

14 The mating faces of the cylinder head and cylinder block/crankcase must be perfectly clean before refitting the head. Use a hard plastic or wood scraper to remove all traces of gasket and carbon; also clean the piston crowns. Take particular care, as the surfaces are damaged easily. Also, make sure that the carbon is not allowed to enter the oil and water passages – this is particularly important for the lubrication system, as carbon could

11.6b . . . then refit the tappet to its original bore, and lay the follower over its respective valve

block the oil supply to any of the engine's components. Using adhesive tape and paper, seal the water, oil and bolt holes in the cylinder block/crankcase. To prevent carbon entering the gap between the pistons and bores, smear a little grease in the gap. After cleaning each piston, use a small brush to remove all traces of grease and carbon from the gap, then wipe away the remainder with a clean rag. Clean all the pistons in the same way.

15 Check the mating surfaces of the cylinder block/crankcase and the cylinder head for nicks, deep scratches and other damage. If slight, they may be removed carefully with a file, but if excessive, machining may be the only alternative to renewal.

16 Ensure that the cylinder head bolt holes in the crankcase are clean and free of oil. Syringe or soak up any oil left in the bolt holes.

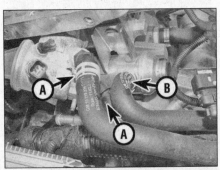

12.6 Disconnect the coolant hoses at the thermostat housing (A), and at the EGR valve heat exchanger (B)

12.7 Release the coolant pipe from the stud (arrowed) at the base of the thermostat housing

12.8 Undo the bolt (arrowed) securing the high-pressure fuel pump mounting bracket to the cylinder head

12.11 Lift the cylinder head from the cylinder block

12.19 Cylinder head gasket thickness identification hole (arrowed)

12.21 Using a dial test indicator to measure piston protrusion

This is most important in order that the correct bolt tightening torque can be applied and to prevent the possibility of the block being cracked by hydraulic pressure when the bolts are tightened.

17 The cylinder head bolts must be discarded and renewed, regardless of their apparent condition.

18 If warpage of the cylinder head gasket surface is suspected, use a straight-edge to check it for distortion. Refer to Part E of this Chapter if necessary.

19 On this engine, the cylinder head-to-piston clearance is controlled by fitting different thickness head gaskets. The gasket thickness can be determined by looking at the holes stamped on the edge of the gasket **(see illustration)**.

Number of holes	Gasket thickness
No holes	0.77 to 0.87 mm
One hole	0.87 to 0.97 mm
Two holes	0.97 to 1.07 mm

The correct thickness of gasket required is selected by measuring the piston protrusions as follows.

20 Mount a dial test indicator securely on the block so that its pointer can be easily pivoted between the piston crown and block mating surface. Turn the crankshaft to bring No 1 piston roughly to the TDC position. Move the dial test indicator probe over and in contact with No 1 piston. Turn the crankshaft back-and-forth slightly until the highest reading is shown on the gauge, indicating that the piston is at TDC.

21 Zero the dial test indicator on the gasket surface of the cylinder block then carefully move the indicator over No 1 piston. Measure its protrusion at the highest point between the valve cut-outs, and then again at its highest point between the valve cut-outs at 90° to the first measurement **(see illustration)**. Repeat this procedure with No 4 piston.

22 Rotate the crankshaft half a turn (180°) to bring No 2 and 3 pistons to TDC. Ensure the crankshaft is accurately positioned then measure the protrusions of No 2 and 3 pistons at the specified points. Once all pistons have been measured, rotate the crankshaft to position all the pistons at their mid-stroke.

23 Select the correct thickness of head gasket required by determining the largest amount of piston protrusion, and using the following table.

Piston protrusion measurement (mm)	Gasket thickness required (mm)
0.020 to 0.100	0.77 to 0.87 (no holes)
0.101 to 0.200	0.87 to 0.97 (one hole)
0.201 to 0.295	0.97 to 1.07 (two holes)

Refitting

24 Wipe clean the mating surfaces of the cylinder head and cylinder block/crankcase. Place the new gasket in position with the words ALTO/TOP uppermost **(see illustration)**.

25 Carefully refit the cylinder head assembly to the block, aligning it with the locating dowels.

26 Apply a thin film of engine oil to the bolt threads and the underside of the bolt heads. Carefully enter each new cylinder head bolt into its relevant hole (*do not drop them in*). Screw all bolts in, by hand only, until finger-tight.

27 Working progressively in sequence, tighten the cylinder head bolts to their Stage 1 torque setting, using a torque wrench and suitable socket **(see illustration)**. Working again in the same sequence, go around and tighten all bolts through the specified Stage 2 torque setting.

28 Once all bolts have been tightened to the Stage 2 torque, working again in the same sequence, go around and tighten all bolts through the specified Stage 3 angle, then through the specified Stage 4 angle, and finally through the specified Stage 5 angle using an angle-measuring gauge.

29 Refit the bolt securing the high-pressure fuel pump mounting bracket to the cylinder head and tighten the bolt securely.

30 Engage the coolant pipe with the stud on the thermostat housing, then reconnect the coolant hoses to the thermostat housing and EGR valve heat exchanger.

31 Refit the inlet and exhaust manifolds as described in Chapter 4A.

32 Refit the camshaft followers and hydraulic tappets as described in Section 11.

33 Refit the camshaft housing as described in Section 9.

34 On completion, reconnect the battery negative terminal, then refill the cooling system as described in Chapter 1.

12.24 Place the new gasket in position with the words ALTO/TOP uppermost

12.27 Cylinder head bolt tightening sequence

13.4 intermediate shaft bearing housing support bracket retaining bolts (arrowed)

13.9 Air conditioning compressor mounting bracket retaining bolts (arrowed)

13.17 Removing the oil baffle plate from inside the sump

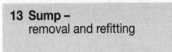

13 Sump –
removal and refitting

Removal

1 Disconnect the battery negative terminal (refer to *Disconnecting the battery* in the Reference Chapter).

2 Apply the handbrake, then jack up the front of the vehicle and support it on axle stands (see *Jacking and vehicle support*). Remove the right-hand front roadwheel.

3 Remove the right-hand driveshaft and the intermediate shaft as described in Chapter 8.

4 Undo the three bolts securing the intermediate shaft bearing housing support bracket to the cylinder block and remove the support bracket **(see illustration)**.

5 Remove the exhaust system as described in Chapter 4A.

6 Undo the three bolts and remove the support bracket from the catalytic converter and sump.

7 Remove the crankshaft pulley/vibration damper as described in Section 5.

8 Disconnect the wiring connector from the air conditioning compressor. Undo the three bolts securing the air conditioning compressor to the mounting bracket and suitably support the compressor on the front subframe.

9 Undo the four bolts securing the compressor mounting bracket to the cylinder block and sump **(see illustration)**. Unclip the wiring harness and remove the mounting bracket.

10 Drain the engine oil as described in Chapter 1. When the oil has completely drained, refit the drain plug with new sealing washer, and tighten to the specified torque.

11 Undo the upper bolt securing the oil dipstick guide tube to the coolant pipe. Undo the lower bolt securing the guide tube to the sump flange, then unclip the wiring harness and withdraw the tube from the sump flange sealing grommet.

12 Disconnect the wiring connector from the oil level sensor, then release the retaining clip and disconnect the oil return hose.

13 Undo the two bolts securing the sump flange to the transmission bellhousing.

14 Using a socket and extension on the

crankshaft pulley bolt, rotate the crankshaft in the normal direction of rotation (clockwise when viewed from the right-hand end of the engine) until the opening in the flywheel is positioned to allow access to one of the rear sump retaining bolts. Undo and remove the bolt, then rotate the crankshaft again until the flywheel allows access to the second rear retaining bolt. Undo and remove the bolt.

15 Progressively slacken and remove the remaining twelve bolts securing the sump to the base of the cylinder block and oil pump housing. Using a wide-bladed scraper or similar tool inserted between the sump and cylinder block, carefully break the joint to release the sump.

16 Manoeuvre the sump out from under the car. Clearance is extremely limited between the sump and subframe, and it may be necessary to release the oil pump pick-up/strainer, by undoing its two retaining bolts, to enable the sump to be removed.

17 If required, undo the retaining bolts and remove the oil baffle plate from inside the sump **(see illustration)**.

18 While the sump is removed, take the opportunity to check the oil pump pick-up/strainer for signs of clogging or splitting. If not already done, unbolt the oil pump pick-up/strainer and remove it from the engine along with its sealing ring. The strainer can then be cleaned easily in solvent or renewed. Renew the pick-up/strainer sealing ring prior to refitting **(see illustration)**.

Refitting

19 Thoroughly clean the sump and remove all traces of silicone sealer and oil from the mating surfaces of the sump and cylinder block. If removed, refit the oil baffle plate and tighten its retaining bolts securely.

20 If clearance allows, refit the oil pump pick-up/strainer using a new sealing ring, and tighten its two retaining bolts securely. If it was necessary to unbolt the pick-up/strainer to allow the sump to be removed, place the unit in position and loosely screw in the bolt securing it to the main bearing cap. It must still be possible for the forward end of the pipe to be moved to the rear as the sump is refitted.

21 Apply a continuous bead of silicone sealing compound (available from your Vauxhall/Opel dealer) at approximately 1.0 mm from the inner edge of the sump **(see illustration)**. The bead of sealant should be between 2.0 and 2.5 mm in diameter.

22 Locate the sump over the pick-up/strainer then, where applicable, fit the forward end of the pick-up/strainer to the oil pump housing and fit the retaining bolt. Tighten both retaining bolts securely.

23 Engage the sump with the cylinder block and loosely refit all the retaining bolts.

24 Working out from the centre in a diagonal sequence, progressively tighten the bolts securing the sump to the cylinder block and oil pump housing. Tighten all the bolts to their specified torque setting.

25 Tighten the two bolts securing the sump

13.18 Renew the pick-up/strainer sealing ring prior to refitting

13.21 Apply a continuous bead of silicone sealing compound to the sump flange

14.4 Oil pump housing retaining bolts (arrowed)

14.5 Undo the retaining screws and lift off the oil pump cover

14.6 Oil pump inner and outer rotor identification dots (arrowed)

14.8a Unscrew the oil pressure relief valve bolt . . .

14.8b . . . and withdraw the spring . . .

14.8c . . . and plunger

flange to the transmission bellhousing to their specified torque settings.

26 Reconnect the wiring connector to the oil level sensor, then refit the oil return hose and secure with the retaining clip.

27 Refit the oil dipstick guide tube and secure with the two bolts tightened securely.

28 Locate the air conditioning compressor mounting bracket in position and refit the four retaining bolts. Tighten the bolts to the specified torque. Clip the wiring harness back into position on the bracket.

29 Position the air conditioning compressor on the mounting bracket. Fit and tighten the three retaining bolts to the specified torque (see Chapter 3), then reconnect the compressor wiring connector.

30 Refit the crankshaft pulley/vibration damper as described in Section 5.

31 Refit the catalytic converter support bracket and securely tighten the three bolts.

32 Refit the exhaust system as described in Chapter 4A.

33 Position the intermediate shaft bearing housing support bracket on the cylinder block and secure with the three retaining bolts tightened to the specified torque.

34 Refit the intermediate shaft and right-hand driveshaft as described in Chapter 8.

35 Refit the roadwheel, then lower the car to the ground and tighten the wheel bolts to the specified torque.

36 Fill the engine with fresh engine oil as described in Chapter 1.

37 On completion, reconnect the battery negative terminal.

14 Oil pump –
removal, overhaul and refitting

Removal

1 Remove the timing belt as described in Section 6.

2 Remove the crankshaft sprocket as described In Section 7.

3 Remove the sump and oil pump pick-up/strainer as described in Section 13.

4 Slacken and remove the seven retaining bolts then slide the oil pump housing assembly off of the end of the crankshaft **(see illustration)**. Remove the housing gasket and discard it.

Overhaul

5 Undo the retaining screws and lift off the

14.10 Prime the oil pump by filling it with clean engine oil whilst rotating the inner rotor

pump cover from the rear of the housing **(see illustration)**.

6 Check the inner and outer rotors for identification dots indicating which way round they are fitted **(see illustration)**. If no marks are visible, use a suitable marker pen to mark the surface of both the pump inner and outer rotors.

7 Lift out the inner and outer rotors from the pump housing.

8 Unscrew the oil pressure relief valve bolt from the base of the housing and withdraw the spring and plunger, noting which way around the plunger is fitted **(see illustrations)**. Remove the sealing washer from the valve bolt.

9 Clean the components, and carefully examine the rotors, pump body and relief valve plunger for any signs of scoring or wear. If any damage or wear is noticed, it will be necessary to renew the complete pump assembly.

10 If the pump is satisfactory, reassemble the components in the reverse order of removal, noting the following.

a) Ensure both rotors are fitted the correct way around.

b) Fit a new sealing ring to the pressure relief valve bolt and securely tighten the bolt.

c) Apply a little locking compound to the threads, and securely tighten the pump cover screws.

d) On completion prime the oil pump by filling it with clean engine oil whilst rotating the inner rotor **(see illustration)**.

Refitting

11 Prior to refitting, carefully lever out the crankshaft oil seal using a flat-bladed screwdriver. Fit the new oil seal, ensuring its sealing lip is facing inwards, and press it squarely into the housing using a tubular drift which bears only on the hard outer edge of the seal. Press the seal into position so that it is flush with the housing and lubricate the oil seal lip with clean engine oil.

12 Ensure the mating surfaces of the oil pump and cylinder block are clean and dry.

13 Fit a new gasket to the oil pump housing and bend down the tabs on the edge of the gasket to retain it on the pump housing (**see illustration**).

14 Locate the pump housing over the end of the crankshaft and into position on the cylinder block.

15 Refit the pump housing retaining bolts and tighten them to the specified torque.

16 Refit the oil pump pick-up/strainer and sump as described in Section 13.

17 Refit the crankshaft sprocket as described in Section 7.

18 Refit the timing belt as described in Section 6.

19 On completion, fit a new oil filter and fill the engine with clean oil as described in Chapter 1.

15 Oil filter housing –
removal and refitting

Removal

1 The oil filter housing with integral oil cooler is located at the rear of the cylinder block, above the right-hand driveshaft.

2 Disconnect the battery negative terminal (refer to *Disconnecting the battery* in the Reference Chapter).

3 Apply the handbrake, then jack up the front of the vehicle and support it on axle stands (see *Jacking and vehicle support*). Remove the right-hand front roadwheel.

4 Drain the cooling system as described in Chapter 1.

5 Remove the engine oil filter element as described in Chapter 1.

6 Remove the right-hand driveshaft and the intermediate shaft as described in Chapter 8.

7 Undo the three bolts securing the intermediate shaft bearing housing support bracket to the cylinder block and remove the support bracket (**see illustration 13.4**).

8 Disconnect the wiring connector from the oil pressure switch.

9 Release the retaining clips and disconnect the two coolant hoses from the oil cooler on the oil filter housing.

10 Undo the three retaining bolts and remove the oil filter housing from the cylinder block (**see illustration**). Recover the two rubber seals from the rear of the housing. Note that new seals will be required for refitting.

14.13 Bend down the tabs on the edge of the gasket to retain it on the oil pump housing

Refitting

11 Thoroughly clean the oil filter housing, then fit the two new sealing rings (**see illustrations**).

12 Position the oil filter housing on the cylinder block and refit the retaining bolts. Tighten the bolts to the specified torque.

13 Refit the two coolant hoses and secure with their retaining clips. Reconnect the oil pressure switch wiring connector.

14 Position the intermediate shaft bearing housing support bracket on the cylinder block and secure with the three retaining bolts tightened to the specified torque.

15 Refit the intermediate shaft and right-hand driveshaft as described in Chapter 8.

16 Fit a new oil filter element as described in Chapter 1.

17 Refit the roadwheel, then lower the car to the ground and tighten the wheel bolts to the specified torque.

18 Refill the cooling system as described in Chapter 1.

19 Top-up the engine oil as described in *Weekly checks*.

20 On completion, reconnect the battery negative terminal.

16 Crankshaft oil seals –
renewal

Timing belt end oil seal

1 Remove the crankshaft sprocket as described in Section 7.

2 Carefully punch or drill a small hole in the oil seal. Screw in a self-tapping screw and pull on the screw with pliers to extract the seal (**see illustration**).

3 Clean the seal housing and polish off any burrs or raised edges which may have caused the seal to fail in the first place.

4 Ease the new seal into position on the end of the crankshaft. Press the seal squarely into position until it is flush with the housing. If necessary, a suitable tubular drift which bears only on the hard outer edge of the seal can be used to tap the seal into position (**see illustration**). Take great care not to damage the seal lips during fitting and ensure that the seal lips face inwards.

5 Wash off any traces of oil, then refit the crankshaft sprocket as described in Section 7.

15.10 Oil filter housing retaining bolts (arrowed)

15.11a Fit a new sealing ring to the oil filter housing supply channel . . .

15.11b . . . and to the return channel

16.2 Screw in a self-tapping screw and pull on the screw with pliers to extract the oil seal

16.4 Using a socket as a tubular drift to fit the new oil seal

16.10 Fitting the new oil seal housing, with integral oil seal over the crankshaft

16.12 After fitting, remove the protector sleeve from the housing

Flywheel end oil seal

6 Remove the flywheel as described in Section 17.

7 Remove the sump as described in Section 13.

8 Undo the five bolts and remove the oil seal housing. Note that the oil seal and the housing are a single assembly.

9 Clean the crankshaft and polish off any burrs or raised edges which may have caused the seal to fail in the first place.

10 Position the new oil seal housing, complete with seal over the crankshaft and into position on the cylinder block **(see illustration)**. Note that the new oil seal housing is supplied with a protector sleeve over the oil seal. Leave the sleeve in position as the housing is fitted.

11 Refit the five retaining bolts and tighten to the specified torque.

12 Remove the protector sleeve from the housing **(see illustration)**.

13 Refit the sump as described in Section 13.

14 Refit the flywheel as described in Section 17.

17 Flywheel – removal, inspection and refitting

Note: *New flywheel retaining bolts will be required on refitting.*

Removal

1 Remove the transmission as described in Chapter 7A, then remove the clutch assembly as described in Chapter 6.

2 Prevent the flywheel from turning by locking the ring gear teeth with a similar arrangement to that shown **(see illustration)**.

3 Slacken and remove the retaining bolts and remove the flywheel **(see illustration)**. Do not drop it, as it is very heavy.

Inspection

4 If there is any doubt about the condition of the flywheel, seek the advice of a Vauxhall/Opel dealer or engine reconditioning specialist. They will be able to advise if it is

possible to recondition it or whether renewal is necessary.

Refitting

5 Clean the mating surfaces of the flywheel and crankshaft.

6 Offer up the flywheel and engage it over the positioning dowel on the crankshaft. Apply a drop of locking compound to the threads of each new flywheel retaining bolt (unless they are already precoated) and install the new bolts.

7 Lock the flywheel by the method used on removal then, working in a diagonal sequence, evenly and progressively tighten the retaining bolts to the specified torque.

8 Refit the clutch as described in Chapter 6 then remove the locking tool, and refit the transmission as described in Chapter 7A.

18 Engine/transmission mountings – inspection and renewal

Refer to Chapter 2C, Section 18.

17.2 Prevent the flywheel from turning by locking the ring gear teeth

17.3 Flywheel retaining bolts (arrowed)

Chapter 2 Part E:
Engine removal and overhaul procedures

Contents

Degrees of difficulty

Easy, suitable for novice with little experience 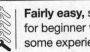 | **Fairly easy,** suitable for beginner with some experience | **Fairly difficult,** suitable for competent DIY mechanic | **Difficult,** suitable for experienced DIY mechanic | **Very difficult,** suitable for expert DIY or professional

Specifications

Engine type

1.3 litre (1248 cc) DOHC 16-valve engines	
1.7 litre (1686 cc) DOHC 16-valve engines	
1.9 litre (1910 cc) SOHC 8-valve engines.	
1.9 litre (1910 cc) DOHC 16-valve engines	

Manufacturer's engine code

Z13DTH
Z17DTL and Z17DTH
Z19DT and Z19DTL
Z19DTH

1.3 litre DOHC engines (Z13DTH)

Note: *Where specifications are given as N/A, no information was available at the time of writing. Refer to your Vauxhall/Opel dealer for the latest information available.*

Cylinder head

Maximum gasket face distortion	0.10 mm
Cylinder head (sealing surface-to-sealing surface)	105.45 to 105.55 mm
Valve seat angle	45°
Valve seat width	1.5 to 1.7 mm

Valves and guides

Stem diameter (inlet and exhaust)	5.90 to 5.94 mm
Valve head diameter	22.0 mm
Valve length	107.95 mm
Maximum permissible valve stem play in guide	0.028 to 0.064 mm
Valve clearances	Automatic adjustment by hydraulic valve lifters

Cylinder block

Maximum gasket face distortion	N/A
Cylinder bore diameter	69.600 to 69.630 mm (nominal)
Maximum cylinder bore ovality	0.005 mm
Maximum cylinder bore taper	0.001 mm

Crankshaft and bearings

Number of main bearings	5
Main bearing journal diameter:	
Standard size	50.855 to 51.000 mm (nominal)
Big-end bearing journal diameter:	
Standard size	42.455 to 42.600 mm (nominal)
Crankshaft endfloat	0.055 to 0.265 mm

Pistons

Piston diameter	69.520 to 69.550 mm (nominal)

Piston rings

Number of rings (per piston)	2 compression, 1 oil control
Ring end gap:	
Top compression ring	0.20 to 0.30 mm
Second compression ring	1.00 to 1.50 mm
Oil control ring	0.25 to 0.50 mm

Torque wrench settings

Refer to Chapter 2A Specifications

1.7 litre DOHC engines (Z17DTL and Z17DTH)

Note: *Where specifications are given as N/A, no information was available at the time of writing. Refer to your Vauxhall/Opel dealer for the latest information available.*

Cylinder head

Maximum gasket face distortion	0.10 mm
Cylinder head height (sealing surface-to-sealing surface)	94.95 to 95.05 mm
Valve seat angle	45°
Valve seat width:	
Inlet	1.6 to 1.8 mm
Exhaust	1.4 to 1.6 mm

Valves and guides

Stem diameter (inlet and exhaust)	5.96 to 5.97 mm
Valve head diameter:	
Inlet	27.5 mm
Exhaust	26.5 mm
Valve length:	
Inlet	98.45 mm
Exhaust	98.10 mm
Maximum permissible valve stem play in guide:	
Inlet	0.019 mm
Exhaust	0.021 mm
Valve clearances (cold):	
Inlet and exhaust	0.4 ± 0.05 mm

1.7 litre DOHC engines (Z17DTL and Z17DTH) (continued)

Cylinder block
Maximum gasket face distortion . . . . N/A
Cylinder bore diameter. . . . . 79.000 to 79.030 mm (nominal)
Maximum cylinder bore ovality. . . . . N/A
Maximum cylinder bore taper. . . . . N/A

Crankshaft and bearings
Number of main bearings. 5
Main bearing journal diameter:
   Standard size . . . . 51.918 to 51.938 mm (nominal)
Big-end bearing journal (crankpin) diameter . . . . N/A
Crankshaft endfloat . . . . 0.030 to 0.120 mm

Pistons
Piston diameter . . . . 78.930 to 78.959 mm (nominal)

Piston rings
Number of rings (per piston). . . . . 2 compression, 1 oil control
Ring end gap:
   Top compression . . . . 0.25 to 0.35 mm
   Second compression . . . . 0.20 to 0.30 mm
   Oil control . . . . 0.20 to 0.40 mm

Torque wrench settings
Refer to Chapter 2B Specifications

1.9 litre SOHC engines (Z19DT and Z19DTL)

Note: *Where specifications are given as N/A, no information was available at the time of writing. Refer to your Vauxhall/Opel dealer for the latest information available.*

Cylinder head
Maximum gasket face distortion . . . . 0.10 mm
Cylinder head height (sealing surface-to-sealing surface). . . . . 140.85 to 141.15 mm
Valve seat angle . . . . N/A
Valve seat width . . . . N/A

Valves and guides
Stem diameter (inlet and exhaust) . . . . 7.974 to 7.992 mm
Valve head diameter. . . . . N/A
Valve length . . . . N/A
Maximum permissible valve stem play in guide. . . . . N/A
Valve clearances (cold). . . . . 0.30 to 0.40 mm

Cylinder block
Maximum gasket face distortion . . . . 0.15 mm
Cylinder bore diameter. . . . . 82.000 to 82.030 mm (nominal)
Maximum cylinder bore ovality. . . . . 0.050 mm
Maximum cylinder bore taper. . . . . 0.005 mm

Crankshaft and bearings
Number of main bearings. 5
Main bearing journal diameter:
   Standard size . . . . 59.855 to 60.000 mm (nominal)
Big-end bearing journal diameter:
   Standard size . . . . 50.660 to 50.805 mm (nominal)
Crankshaft endfloat . . . . 0.049 to 0.211 mm

Pistons
Piston diameter . . . . 81.920 to 81.950 mm (nominal)

Piston rings
Number of rings (per piston). . . . . 2 compression, 1 oil control
Ring end gap:
   Top compression . . . . 0.25 to 0.40 mm
   Second compression . . . . 0.25 to 0.50 mm
   Oil control . . . . 0.25 to 0.50 mm

Torque wrench settings
Refer to Chapter 2C Specifications

1.9 litre DOHC engines (Z19DTH)

Note: *Where specifications are given as N/A, no information was available at the time of writing. Refer to your Vauxhall/Opel dealer for the latest information available.*

Cylinder head

Maximum gasket face distortion	0.10 mm
Cylinder head height	106.95 to 107.05 mm
Valve seat angle in cylinder head	N/A
Valve seat width in cylinder head	N/A

Valves and guides

Stem diameter:	
Inlet valve	5.982 to 6.000 mm
Exhaust valve	5.972 to 5.990 mm
Valve head diameter	N/A
Valve length	N/A
Maximum permissible valve stem play in guide	N/A
Valve clearances	Automatic adjustment by hydraulic cam followers

Cylinder block

Maximum gasket face distortion	0.15 mm
Cylinder bore diameter	82.000 to 82.030 mm (nominal)
Maximum cylinder bore ovality	0.050 mm
Maximum cylinder bore taper	0.005 mm

Crankshaft and bearings

Number of main bearings	5
Main bearing journal diameter:	
Standard size	59.855 to 60.000 mm (nominal)
Big-end bearing journal diameter:	
Standard size	50.660 to 50.805 mm (nominal)
Crankshaft endfloat	0.049 to 0.211 mm

Pistons

Piston diameter	81.920 to 81.950 mm (nominal)

Piston rings

Number of rings (per piston)	2 compression, 1 oil control
Ring end gap:	
Top compression	0.20 to 0.35 mm
Second compression	0.60 to 0.80 mm
Oil control	0.25 to 0.50 mm

Torque wrench settings

Refer to Chapter 2D Specifications

---

1 General information

Included in this Part of Chapter 2 are details of removing the engine/transmission from the car and general overhaul procedures for the cylinder head, cylinder block/crankcase and all other engine internal components.

The information given ranges from advice concerning preparation for an overhaul and the purchase of parts, to detailed step-by-step procedures covering removal, inspection, renovation and refitting of engine internal components.

After Section 5, all instructions are based on the assumption that the engine has been removed from the car. For information concerning in-car engine repair, as well as the removal and refitting of those external components necessary for full overhaul, refer to Part A, B, C or D of this Chapter (as applicable) and to Section 5. Ignore any preliminary dismantling operations described in Part A, B, C or D that are no longer relevant once the engine has been removed from the car.

Apart from torque wrench settings, which are given at the beginning of Part A, B, C, or D (as applicable), all specifications relating to engine overhaul are at the beginning of this Part of Chapter 2.

2 Engine overhaul – general information

It is not always easy to determine when, or if, an engine should be completely overhauled, as a number of factors must be considered.

High mileage is not necessarily an indication that an overhaul is needed, while low mileage does not preclude the need for an overhaul. Frequency of servicing is probably the most important consideration. An engine which has had regular and frequent oil and filter changes, as well as other required maintenance, should give many thousands of miles of reliable service. Conversely, a neglected engine may require an overhaul very early in its life.

Excessive oil consumption is an indication that piston rings, valve seals and/or valve guides are in need of attention. Make sure that oil leaks are not responsible before deciding that the rings and/or guides are worn. Have a compression test performed (refer to Part A, B, C or D of this Chapter), to determine the likely cause of the problem.

Check the oil pressure with a gauge fitted in place of the oil pressure switch, and compare it with that specified. If it is extremely low, the main and big-end bearings, and/or the oil pump, are probably worn out.

Loss of power, rough running, knocking or metallic engine noises, excessive valve gear noise, and high fuel consumption may also point to the need for an overhaul, especially if they are all present at the same time. If a complete service does not cure the situation, major mechanical work is the only solution.

A full engine overhaul involves restoring all internal parts to the specification of a new engine. During a complete overhaul, the pistons and the piston rings are renewed, and the cylinder bores are reconditioned. New main and big-end bearings are generally fitted; if necessary, the crankshaft may be reground, to compensate for wear in the journals. The valves are also serviced as well, since they are usually in less-than-perfect condition at this point. Always pay careful attention to the condition of the oil pump when overhauling the engine, and renew it if there is any doubt as to its serviceability. The end result should be an as-new engine that will give many trouble-free miles.

Critical cooling system components such as the hoses, thermostat and coolant pump should be renewed when an engine is overhauled. The radiator should also be checked carefully, to ensure that it is not clogged or leaking.

Before beginning the engine overhaul, read through the entire procedure, to familiarise yourself with the scope and requirements of the job. Check on the availability of parts and make sure that any necessary special tools and equipment are obtained in advance. Most work can be done with typical hand tools, although a number of precision measuring tools are required for inspecting parts to determine if they must be renewed.

The services provided by an engineering machine shop or engine reconditioning specialist will almost certainly be required, particularly if major repairs such as crankshaft regrinding or cylinder reboring are necessary. Apart from carrying out machining operations, these establishments will normally handle the inspection of parts, offer advice concerning reconditioning or renewal and supply new components such as pistons, piston rings and bearing shells. It is recommended that the establishment used is a member of the Federation of Engine Re-Manufacturers, or a similar society.

Always wait until the engine has been completely dismantled, and until all components (especially the cylinder block/ crankcase and the crankshaft) have been inspected, before deciding what service and repair operations must be performed by an engineering works. The condition of these components will be the major factor to consider when determining whether to overhaul the original engine, or to buy a reconditioned unit. Do not, therefore, purchase parts or have overhaul work done on other components until they have been thoroughly inspected. As a general rule, time is the primary cost of an overhaul, so it does not pay to fit worn or sub-standard parts.

As a final note, to ensure maximum life and minimum trouble from a reconditioned engine, everything must be assembled with care, in a spotlessly-clean environment.

3 Engine removal – methods and precautions

If you have decided that the engine must be removed for overhaul or major repair work, several preliminary steps should be taken.

Engine/transmission removal is extremely complicated and involved on these vehicles. It must be stated, that unless the vehicle can be positioned on a ramp, or raised and supported on axle stands over an inspection pit, it will be very difficult to carry out the work involved.

Cleaning the engine compartment and engine/transmission before beginning the removal procedure will help keep tools clean and organised.

An engine hoist will also be necessary. Make sure the equipment is rated in excess of the combined weight of the engine and transmission. Safety is of primary importance, considering the potential hazards involved in removing the engine/transmission from the car.

The help of an assistant is essential. Apart from the safety aspects involved, there are many instances when one person cannot simultaneously perform all of the operations required during engine/transmission removal.

Plan the operation ahead of time. Before starting work, arrange for the hire of or obtain all of the tools and equipment you will need. Some of the equipment necessary to perform engine/transmission removal and installation safely (in addition to an engine hoist) is as follows: a heavy duty trolley jack, complete sets of spanners and sockets as described in the rear of this manual, wooden blocks, and plenty of rags and cleaning solvent for mopping-up spilled oil, coolant and fuel. If the hoist must be hired, make sure that you arrange for it in advance, and perform all of the operations possible without it beforehand. This will save you money and time.

Plan for the car to be out of use for quite a while. An engineering machine shop or engine reconditioning specialist will be required to perform some of the work which cannot be accomplished without special equipment. These places often have a busy schedule, so it would be a good idea to consult them before removing the engine, in order to accurately estimate the amount of time required to rebuild or repair components that may need work.

During the engine/transmission removal procedure, it is advisable to make notes of the locations of all brackets, cable ties, earthing points, etc, as well as how the wiring harnesses, hoses and electrical connections are attached and routed around the engine and engine compartment. An effective way of doing this is to take a series of photographs of the various components before they are disconnected or removed; the resulting photographs will prove invaluable when the engine/transmission is refitted.

Always be extremely careful when removing and refitting the engine/transmission. Serious injury can result from careless actions. Plan ahead and take your time, and a job of this nature, although major, can be accomplished successfully.

On all Astra models, the engine must be removed complete with the transmission as an assembly. There is insufficient clearance in the engine compartment to remove the engine leaving the transmission in the vehicle. The assembly is removed by raising the front of the vehicle, and lowering the assembly from the engine compartment.

4 Engine and transmission unit – removal, separation and refitting

Note 1: *The engine can be removed from the car only as a complete unit with the transmission; the two are then separated for overhaul. The engine/transmission unit is lowered out of position, and withdrawn from under the vehicle. Bearing this in mind, and also bearing in mind the information contained in Section 3, ensure the vehicle is raised sufficiently so that there is enough clearance between the front of the vehicle and the floor to allow the engine/transmission unit to be slid out once it has been lowered out of position.*
Note 2: *Such is the complexity of the power unit arrangement on these vehicles, and the variations that may be encountered according to model and optional equipment fitted, that the following should be regarded as a guide to the work involved, rather than a step-by-step procedure. Where differences are encountered, or additional component disconnection or removal is necessary, make notes of the work involved as an aid to refitting.*

Removal

1 On models equipped with air conditioning, have the air conditioning system fully discharged by an air conditioning specialist.
2 Position the vehicle as described in Section 3, paragraph 2, and remove both front roadwheels.
3 Remove the bonnet and the front bumper as described in Chapter 11.
4 Remove the plastic cover from the top of the engine.
5 Remove the battery and battery tray as described in Chapter 5.
6 Carry out the following operations as described in Chapter 1:
  a) Drain the engine oil.
  b) Drain the cooling system.
  c) Remove the auxiliary drivebelt.
7 Remove the air cleaner assembly, intake ducts and charge air pipes/hoses as described in Chapter 4A.
8 Lift off the cover from the wiring junction box at the left-hand rear corner of the

4.8 Disconnect the two positive cables (arrowed) from the junction box terminals

4.23a Release the selector inner cable end fittings from the transmission selector levers . . .

engine compartment. Undo the two nuts and disconnect the two positive cables from the junction box terminals (see illustration).

9 Disconnect the wiring harness connector at the side of the junction box. Release the wiring harness from the retaining clips and cable ties so that it is free to be removed with the engine.

10 Undo the two bolts and disconnect the two earth cables from the battery negative terminal clamp.

11 Undo the bolt and disconnect the positive cable from the battery positive terminal clamp.

12 Disconnect the wiring harness connector located in front of the engine compartment fuse/relay box. Undo the nut securing the earth lead to the stud below the battery box location. Release the disconnected wiring harness from the retaining clips and cable ties so that it is free to be removed with the engine.

13 Disconnect the wiring block connector from the cooling fan module adjacent to the cooling fan. Release the wiring harness from the retaining bolt and clips.

14 Disconnect the oxygen sensor wiring connector.

15 Working under the front, left-hand side of the car, release the locking lever catch,

then lift the locking levers and disconnect the two wiring connectors from the engine management system ECU. Free the wiring harness from the retaining clips and cable ties.

16 Remove the air conditioning system compressor as described in Chapter 3.

17 Disconnect the brake vacuum servo hose from the vacuum pump.

18 On 1.3 and 1.9 litre engines, detach the fuel supply hose quick-release connector and remove the hose from the high-pressure fuel pump. A Vauxhall/Opel special tool (KM-796-A) is available to disconnect the hose connectors, but provided care is taken, the connections can be released using two screwdrivers, a pair of long-nosed pliers, or similar, to depress the retaining tangs. Suitably cover or plug the open hose connections to prevent dirt entry. Similarly disconnect the fuel return hose from the fuel rail.

19 On 1.7 litre engines, release the retaining clips and detach the fuel supply and return hoses at the high-pressure fuel pump. Suitably cover or plug the open hose connections to prevent dirt entry.

20 Loosen the clips and remove the upper and lower radiator hoses.

21 Release the clips and disconnect the coolant hoses at the coolant expansion tank.

22 Release the quick-release connectors by sliding them forward, and disconnect the two heater hoses from the heater matrix pipe stubs.

23 On manual transmission models, using a suitable forked tool, release the gear-change selector cable end fittings from the transmission selector levers. Pull back the retaining sleeves and detach the outer cables from the mounting bracket on the transmission (see illustrations).

24 On automatic transmission models, use a forked tool or flat-bladed screwdriver, and carefully lever off the gear selector inner cable end fitting from the balljoint on the selector lever position switch. Pull back the retaining sleeve and detach the outer cable from the mounting bracket on the transmission.

25 Drain the manual transmission oil or automatic transmission fluid as described in Chapter 7A or 7B, as applicable.

26 Remove both driveshafts as described in Chapter 8.

27 Position the steering with the front roadwheels straight-ahead, and lock the steering by removing the ignition key.

28 Unscrew the nut and remove the bolt securing the steering column intermediate shaft to the steering gear pinion shaft. Separate the intermediate shaft from the pinion shaft by pulling the intermediate shaft upwards (see illustration).

Caution: To prevent damage to the airbag wiring contact unit, the steering lock must remain locked until the intermediate shaft is re-attached to the pinion shaft.

29 On manual transmission models, remove the filler cap from the brake/clutch fluid reservoir on the bulkhead, then tighten it onto a piece of polythene. This will reduce the loss of fluid when the clutch hydraulic hose is disconnected. Alternatively, fit a hose clamp to the flexible hose next to the clutch hydraulic connection on the transmission housing.

30 Place some cloth rags beneath the hose, then prise out the retaining clip securing the

4.23b . . . then pull back the retaining sleeves and detach the outer cables from the transmission mounting bracket

4.28 Unscrew the nut and remove the bolt (arrowed) securing the steering column intermediate shaft to the steering gear pinion shaft

4.30a Prise out the clip securing the clutch hydraulic hose to the end fitting on the transmission bellhousing . . .

4.30b . . . then detach the hose from the end fitting

4.34 Right-hand engine mounting bracket-to-engine bracket retaining bolts (arrowed)

clutch hydraulic hose to the end fitting on top of the transmission bellhousing. Detach the hose from the end fitting (see illustrations). Gently squeeze the two legs of the retaining clip together and re-insert the retaining clip back into position in the end fitting. Discard the sealing ring from the hose end; a new sealing ring must be used on refitting. Plug/cover both the end fitting and hose end to minimise fluid loss and prevent the entry of dirt into the hydraulic system. Note: Whilst the hose is disconnected, do not depress the clutch pedal.

31 On automatic transmission models, unscrew the central retaining bolt (or nut) and detach the fluid cooler pipes from the transmission. Suitably cover the pipe ends and plug the transmission orifices to prevent dirt entry.

32 Attach a suitable hoist and lifting tackle to the engine lifting brackets on the cylinder head, and support the weight of the engine/transmission.

33 Remove the front subframe as described in Chapter 10.

34 Mark the position of the three bolts securing the right-hand engine mounting bracket to the engine bracket and undo the bolts (see illustration). Note: There is no need to remove the mounting, since the engine/transmission is lowered from the engine compartment.

35 Mark the position of the three bolts securing the left-hand engine mounting to the transmission bracket (see illustration).

36 Make a final check to ensure that all relevant pipes and hoses have been disconnected, and that they are positioned clear of the engine and transmission. Check that all wiring connectors have been disconnected and that the main engine harness is free to be removed with the engine.

37 With the help of an assistant, carefully lower the engine/transmission assembly to the ground. Make sure that the surrounding components in the engine compartment are not damaged. Ideally, the assembly should be lowered onto a trolley jack or low platform with castors, so that it can easily be withdrawn from under the car.

38 Ensure that the assembly is adequately supported, then disconnect the engine hoist and lifting tackle, and withdraw the engine/transmission assembly from under the front of the vehicle.

39 Clean away any external dirt using paraffin or a water-soluble solvent and a stiff brush.

40 With reference to Chapter 7A or 7B, unbolt the transmission from the engine. Carefully withdraw the transmission from the engine. On manual transmission models, ensure that its weight is not allowed to hang on the input shaft while engaged with the clutch friction disc. On automatic transmission models, ensure that the torque converter is removed together with the transmission so that it remains engaged with the oil pump. Note that the transmission locates on dowels positioned in the rear of the cylinder block.

Refitting

41 With reference to Chapter 7A or 7B, refit the transmission to the engine and tighten the bolts to the specified torque.

42 With the front of the vehicle raised and supported on axle stands, move the engine/transmission assembly under the vehicle, ensuring that the assembly is adequately supported.

43 Reconnect the hoist and lifting tackle to the engine lifting brackets, and carefully raise the engine/transmission assembly up into the engine compartment with the help of an assistant.

44 Reconnect the right- and left-hand engine/transmission mountings and tighten the bolts to the specified torque given in Chapter 2A, 2B, 2C or 2D, as applicable. Ensure that the marks made on removal are correctly aligned when tightening the retaining bolts.

45 Refit the front subframe as described in Chapter 10.

46 Disconnect the hoist and lifting tackle from the engine lifting brackets.

47 Refit the driveshafts as described in Chapter 8.

48 On manual transmission models, refill the transmission with correct quantity and type of oil, as described in Chapter 7A.

49 Reconnect the steering column intermediate shaft to the steering gear pinion shaft and tighten the bolt and nut with reference to Chapter 10.

50 On automatic transmission models,

reconnect the fluid cooler pipes together with new O-ring seals to the transmission.

51 On manual transmission models, reconnect and bleed the clutch hydraulic connection at the transmission with reference to Chapter 6.

52 Refit the gearchange/selector outer cable(s) to the mounting bracket on the transmission. Engage the inner cable end fitting(s) with the selector lever balljoint, squeezing them together with pliers if necessary.

53 Push the heater hoses back onto the matrix pipe stubs. Ensure that the quick-release connectors securely lock the hoses in position.

54 Reconnect the upper and lower radiator hoses and expansion tank hoses.

55 Reconnect the brake vacuum servo hose to the vacuum pump, and the fuel hoses and wiring connectors at the high-pressure fuel pump and fuel rail.

56 Reconnect the two wiring connectors to the engine management system ECU.

57 Refit the air conditioning system compressor as described in Chapter 3, then refit the auxiliary drivebelt as described in Chapter 1.

58 Reconnect the wiring block connector to the cooling fan module.

59 Reconnect the earth lead to the stud under the battery box location and secure with the retaining nut.

60 Reconnect the positive and negative wiring terminals to the battery positive and negative terminal clamps.

61 Reconnect the positive cable connections to the engine compartment junction box.

4.35 Left-hand engine mounting-to-transmission bracket retaining bolts (arrowed)

6.2 Using a valve spring compressor, compress the valve spring to relieve the pressure on the collets

62 Reconnect all remaining wiring connectors and secure the wiring and harness with the cable clips or new cable ties.

63 Refit the air cleaner assembly, intake ducts and charge air pipes/hoses as described in Chapter 4A.

64 Refit the battery tray and battery as described in Chapter 5.

65 Refit the bonnet and the front bumper as described in Chapter 11.

66 Refit both front roadwheels, then lower the vehicle to the ground.

67 Make a final check to ensure that all relevant hoses, pipes and wires have been correctly reconnected.

68 Refill the engine with oil with reference to Chapter 1.

69 On automatic transmission models, refill the transmission with correct quantity and type of fluid, as described in Chapter 7B.

70 Refill and bleed the cooling system with reference to Chapter 1.

71 On models equipped with air conditioning, have the air conditioning system evacuated, charged and leak-tested by the specialist who discharged it.

5 Engine overhaul – dismantling sequence

1 It is much easier to dismantle and work on the engine if it is mounted on a portable engine stand. These stands can often be hired from a tool hire shop. Before the engine is mounted on a stand, the flywheel/driveplate

6.4 Extract the two split collets by hooking them out using a small screwdriver

should be removed, so that the stand bolts can be tightened into the end of the cylinder block/crankcase.

2 If a stand is not available, it is possible to dismantle the engine with it blocked up on a sturdy workbench, or on the floor. Be extra careful not to tip or drop the engine when working without a stand.

3 If you are going to obtain a reconditioned engine, all the external components must be removed first, to be transferred to the new engine (just as they will if you are doing a complete engine overhaul yourself). These components include the following:

a) *Engine wiring harness and supports.*
b) *Alternator and air conditioning compressor mounting brackets (as applicable).*
c) *Coolant pump (where applicable) and inlet/outlet housings.*
d) *Dipstick tube.*
e) *Fuel system components.*
f) *All electrical switches and sensors.*
g) *Inlet and exhaust manifolds and turbocharger.*
h) *Oil filter and oil cooler/heat exchanger.*
i) *Flywheel/driveplate.*

Note: *When removing the external components from the engine, pay close attention to details that may be helpful or important during refitting. Note the fitted position of gaskets, seals, spacers, pins, washers, bolts, and other small items.*

4 If you are obtaining a 'short' engine (which consists of the engine cylinder block/crankcase, crankshaft, pistons and connecting rods all assembled), then the cylinder head, sump, oil pump, and timing belt/chains (as applicable) will have to be removed also.

5 If you are planning a complete overhaul, the engine can be dismantled, and the internal/external components removed, in the order given below.

a) *Inlet and exhaust manifolds (see Chapter 4A).*
b) *Timing belt, sprockets, tensioner and idler pulleys – 1.7 and 1.9 litre engines (see Chapter 2B, 2C or 2D).*
c) *Coolant pump (see Chapter 3).*
d) *Cylinder head (see Chapter 2A, 2B, 2C or 2D).*
e) *Flywheel/driveplate (see Chapter 2A, 2B, 2C or 2D).*

6.5a Remove the valve spring cap . . .

f) *Sump (see Chapter 2A, 2B, 2C or 2D).*
g) *Oil pump (see Chapter 2A, 2B, 2C or 2D).*
h) *Timing chains and sprockets – 1.3 litre engines (see Chapter 2A).*
i) *Piston/connecting rod assemblies (see Section 9).*
j) *Crankshaft (see Section 10).*

6 Before beginning the dismantling and overhaul procedures, make sure that you have all of the correct tools necessary. See *Tools and working facilities* for further information.

6 Cylinder head – dismantling

Note: *New and reconditioned cylinder heads are available from the manufacturer, and from engine overhaul specialists. Due to the fact that some specialist tools are required for the dismantling and inspection procedures, and new components may not be readily available, it may be more practical and economical for the home mechanic to purchase a reconditioned head rather than to dismantle, inspect and recondition the original head. A valve spring compressor tool will be required for this operation.*

1 With the cylinder head removed as described in the relevant Part of this Chapter, clean away all external dirt, and remove the following components as applicable, if not already done:

a) *Manifolds (see Chapter 4A).*
b) *Cooling system components (see Chapter 3).*
c) *Glow plugs (see Chapter 5).*
d) *Camshafts and and associated valve train components (see Chapter 2A, 2B, 2C or 2D).*
e) *Fuel injectors (see Chapter 4A).*
f) *Engine lifting brackets.*

2 To remove a valve, fit a valve spring compressor tool. Ensure that the arms of the compressor tool are securely positioned on the head of the valve and the spring cap **(see illustration)**. The valves are often deeply recessed, and a suitable extension piece may be required for the spring compressor.

3 Compress the valve spring to relieve the pressure of the spring cap acting on the collets.

 HAYNES HINT *If the spring cap sticks to the valve stem, support the compressor tool, and give the end a light tap with a soft-faced mallet to help free the spring cap.*

4 Extract the two split collets by hooking them out using a small screwdriver, then slowly release the compressor tool **(see illustration)**.

5 Remove the valve spring cap and the spring, then withdraw the valve through the combustion chamber. Using pliers, remove the valve stem oil seal, which also incorporates the spring seat on most engines **(see illustrations)**.

If the spring seat is not part of the valve stem oil seal, hook it out using a small screwdriver.

6 Repeat the procedure for the remaining valves, keeping all components in strict order so that they can be refitted in their original positions, unless the components are to be renewed. If the components are to be kept and used again, place each valve assembly in a labelled polythene bag or a similar small container **(see illustration)**. Note that as with cylinder numbering, the valves are normally numbered from the timing chain or timing belt end of the engine. Make sure that the valve components are identified as inlet and exhaust, as well as numbered.

6.5b . . . and the spring . . .

6.5c . . . then withdraw the valve through the combustion chamber

7 Cylinder head and valves – cleaning and inspection

1 Thorough cleaning of the cylinder head and valve components, followed by a detailed inspection, will enable you to decide how much valve service work must be carried out during the engine overhaul. **Note:** *If the engine has been severely overheated, it is best to assume that the cylinder head is warped – check carefully for signs of this.*

Cleaning

2 Scrape away all traces of old gasket material from the cylinder head.

3 Scrape away the carbon from the combustion chambers and ports, then wash the cylinder head thoroughly with paraffin or a suitable solvent.

4 Scrape off any heavy carbon deposits that may have formed on the valves, then use a power-operated wire brush to remove deposits from the valve heads and stems.

Inspection

Note: *Be sure to perform all the following inspection procedures before concluding that the services of a machine shop or engine overhaul specialist are required. Make a list of all items that require attention.*

Cylinder head

5 Inspect the head very carefully for cracks, evidence of coolant leakage, and other damage. If cracks are found, a new cylinder head should be obtained.

6 Use a straight-edge and feeler gauge blade to check that the cylinder head surface is not distorted **(see illustration)**. If it is, it may be possible to resurface it, provided that the cylinder head is not reduced to less than the minimum specified height.

7 Examine the valve seats in each of the combustion chambers. If they are severely pitted, cracked or burned, then they will need to be recut by an engine overhaul specialist. If they are only slightly pitted, this can be removed by grinding-in the valve heads and seats with fine valve-grinding compound, as described below.

8 If the valve guides are worn, indicated by

6.5d Using pliers, remove the valve stem oil seal, which also incorporates the spring seat on most engines

a side-to-side motion of the valve, oversize valve guides are available, and valves with oversize stems can be fitted. This work is best carried out by an engine overhaul specialist. A dial gauge may be used to determine whether the amount of side play of a valve exceeds the specified maximum.

9 Check the tappet bores in the cylinder head for wear. If excessive wear is evident, the cylinder head must be renewed. Also check the tappet oil holes in the cylinder head for obstructions.

Valves

10 Examine the head of each valve for pitting, burning, cracks and general wear, and check the valve stem for scoring and wear ridges. Rotate the valve, and check for any obvious indication that it is bent. Look for pitting and excessive wear on the tip of each valve stem. Renew any valve that shows any such signs of wear or damage.

6.6 Place each valve assembly in a labelled polythene bag or similar container

11 If the valve appears satisfactory at this stage, measure the valve stem diameter at several points using a micrometer **(see illustration)**. Any significant difference in the readings obtained indicates wear of the valve stem. Should any of these conditions be apparent, the valve(s) must be renewed.

12 If the valves are in satisfactory condition, they should be ground (lapped) into their respective seats, to ensure a smooth gas-tight seal. If the seat is only lightly pitted, or if it has been recut, fine grinding compound **only** should be used to produce the required finish. Coarse valve-grinding compound should **not** be used unless a seat is badly burned or deeply pitted; if this is the case, the cylinder head and valves should be inspected by an expert to decide whether seat recutting, or even the renewal of the valve or seat insert, is required.

7.6 Using a straight-edge and feeler gauge to check cylinder head surface distortion

7.11 Using a micrometer to measure valve stem diameter

7.14 Grinding-in a valve

8.1 Lubricate the valve stem with engine oil and insert the valve into the correct guide

8.2a Fit the spring seat . . .

8.2b . . . then fit the seal protector (where supplied) to the valve . . .

8.2c . . . and install the new valve stem oil seal . . .

8.2d . . . pressing it onto the valve guide with a suitable socket

13 Valve grinding is carried out as follows. Place the cylinder head upside-down on a bench, with a block of wood at each end to give clearance for the valve stems.
14 Smear a trace of the appropriate grade of valve-grinding compound on the seat face,

8.3 Refit the valve spring and fit the spring cap

8.4 Compress the valve and locate the collets in the recess on the valve stem

and press a suction grinding tool onto the valve head. With a semi-rotary action, grind the valve head to its seat, lifting the valve occasionally to redistribute the grinding compound **(see illustration)**. A light spring placed under the valve head will greatly ease this operation.
15 If coarse grinding compound is being used, work only until a dull, matt even surface is produced on both the valve seat and the valve, then wipe off the used compound and repeat the process with fine compound. When a smooth unbroken ring of light grey matt finish is produced on both the valve and seat, the grinding operation is complete. **Do not** grind in the valves any further than absolutely necessary, or the seat will be prematurely sunk into the cylinder head.
16 When all the valves have been ground-in, carefully wash off all traces of grinding compound using paraffin or a suitable solvent before reassembly of the cylinder head.

Use a little dab of grease to hold the collets in position on the valve stem while the spring compressor is released.

Valve components

17 Examine the valve springs for signs of damage and discoloration; if possible; also compare the existing spring free length with new components.
18 Stand each spring on a flat surface, and check it for squareness. If any of the springs are damaged, distorted or have lost their tension, obtain a complete new set of springs.

8 Cylinder head – reassembly

1 Lubricate the stems of the valves, and insert them into their original locations **(see illustration)**. If new valves are being fitted, insert them into the locations to which they have been ground.
2 Working on the first valve, refit the spring seat if it is not an integral part of the valve stem oil seal. Dip the new valve stem seal in fresh engine oil, then carefully locate it over the valve and onto the guide. Take care not to damage the seal as it is passed over the valve stem. Use a suitable socket or metal tube to press the seal firmly onto the guide. **Note:** *If genuine seals are being fitted, use the oil seal protector which is supplied with the seals; the protector fits over the valve stem and prevents the oil seal lip being damaged on the valve (see illustrations).*
3 Locate the spring on the seat and fit the spring cap **(see illustration)**.
4 Compress the valve spring, and locate the split collets in the recess in the valve stem **(see illustration and Haynes Hint)**. Release

the compressor, then repeat the procedure on the remaining valves.

5 With all the valves installed, support the cylinder head on blocks on the bench and, using a hammer and interposed block of wood, tap the end of each valve stem to settle the components.

6 Refit the components removed in Section 6, paragraph 1.

9 Pistons/connecting rods – removal

Note: *New connecting rod big-end cap bolts/ nuts will be needed on refitting.*

1 Referring to the relevant Part of this Chapter, remove the cylinder head and sump. Where applicable, unbolt the pick-up/strainer from the base of the oil pump and the oil baffle plate from the base of the cylinder block.

2 On all models, if there is a pronounced wear ridge at the top of any bore, it may be necessary to remove it with a scraper or ridge reamer, to avoid piston damage during removal. Such a ridge indicates excessive wear of the cylinder bore.

3 If the connecting rods and big-end caps are not marked to indicate their positions in the cylinder block (ie, marked with cylinder numbers), suitably mark both the rod and cap with quick-drying paint or similar **(see illustration)**. Note which side of the engine the marks face and accurately record this also. There may not be any other way of identifying which way round the cap fits on the rod, when refitting.

4 Turn the crankshaft to bring pistons 1 and 4 to BDC (bottom dead centre).

5 Unscrew the bolts/nuts from No 1 piston big-end bearing cap, then take off the cap and recover the bottom half-bearing shell **(see illustration)**. If the bearing shells are to be re-used, tape the cap and the shell together.

Caution: On some engines, the connecting rod/bearing cap mating surfaces are not machined flat; the big-end bearing caps are 'cracked' off from the rod during production and left untouched to ensure the cap and rod mate perfectly. Where this type of connecting rod is fitted, great

9.3 The connecting rods and big-end caps should be marked to indicate their positions in the cylinder block – 1.3 litre engines

care must be taken to ensure the mating surfaces of the cap and rod are not marked or damaged in anyway. Any damage to the mating surfaces will adversely affect the strength of the connecting rod and could lead to premature failure.

6 Using a hammer handle, push the piston up through the bore, and remove it from the top of the cylinder block. Recover the bearing shell, and tape it to the connecting rod for safe-keeping.

7 Loosely refit the big-end cap to the connecting rod, and secure with the nuts/ bolts – this will help to keep the components in their correct order.

8 Remove No 4 piston assembly in the same way.

9 Turn the crankshaft through 180° to bring pistons 2 and 3 to BDC, and remove them in the same way.

10 Crankshaft – removal

1.3 litre engines

Note: *New cylinder block baseplate retaining bolts will be required for refitting.*

1 Working as described in Part A of this Chapter, remove the flywheel.

2 Remove the piston and connecting rod assemblies as described in Section 9. If no work is to be done on the pistons and connecting rods, unbolt the caps and push

9.5 Take off the big-end bearing cap and recover the bottom half bearing shell – 1.3 litre engines

the pistons far enough up the bores that the connecting rods are positioned clear of the crankshaft journals.

3 Before removing the crankshaft, check the endfloat using a dial gauge in contact with the end of the crankshaft. Push the crankshaft fully one way, and then zero the gauge. Push the crankshaft fully the other way, and check the endfloat **(see illustration)**. The result should be compared with the specified limit, and will give an indication as to the size of the main bearing shell thrust journal width which will be required for reassembly.

4 If a dial gauge is not available, a feeler gauge can be used to measure crankshaft endfloat. Push the crankshaft fully towards one end of the crankcase, and insert a feeler gauge between the thrust flange of the main bearing shell and the machined surface of the crankshaft web **(see illustration)**. Before measuring, ensure that the crankshaft is fully forced towards one end of the crankcase, to give the widest possible gap at the measuring location. **Note:** *Measure at the bearing with the thrustwasher (see Section 17).*

5 Working in a diagonal sequence, progressively slacken the outer (M8) bolts securing the cylinder block baseplate to the cylinder block.

6 When all the outer bolts have been slackened, repeat the procedure on the inner (M10) retaining bolts.

7 Remove all the bolts and lift the cylinder block baseplate off the cylinder block **(see illustration)**. If the baseplate is initially tight to remove, carefully tap it free using a soft-faced

10.3 Check the crankshaft endfloat using a dial gauge . . .

10.4 . . . or a feeler gauge

10.7 Lift the cylinder block baseplate off the cylinder block – 1.3 litre engines

10.21a Main bearing cap identification marks (arrowed) . . .

10.21b . . . and the lug at the base of the cap (arrowed) is used to identify the inlet manifold side of the engine – 1.9 litre engines

mallet. Alternatively, use a spatula to break the seal between the baseplate and cylinder block.

8 As the baseplate is withdrawn check that the lower main bearing shells come away with the baseplate. If they remain on the crankshaft journals, lift them off and refit them to their respective locations in the baseplate.

9 Lift the crankshaft from the cylinder block and remove the crankshaft oil seal.

10 Extract the upper bearing shells, and identify them for position if they are to be re-used.

1.7 litre engines

Note: *New main bearing cap bolts will be required on refitting.*

11 Working as described in Part B of this Chapter, remove the flywheel, main sump casting, oil pump cover and oil pick-up pipe.

12 Unbolt the crankshaft oil seal housing and remove it from the cylinder block. If the housing locating dowels are a loose fit, remove them and store them with the housing for safe-keeping.

13 Remove the piston and connecting rod assemblies as described in Section 9. If no work is to be done on the pistons and connecting rods, unbolt the caps and push the pistons far enough up the bores that the connecting rods are positioned clear of the crankshaft journals.

14 Before removing the crankshaft, check the endfloat as described in paragraphs 3 and 4.

15 Unscrew the main bearing cap bolts and

11.3 Unscrew the retaining bolts and remove the piston oil spray nozzles from the cylinder block

remove the bearing caps. Note that the caps should are numbered 1 to 5, Number 1 cap being at the timing belt end, and the arrow on each cap should point towards the timing belt end of the engine. Ensure that the lower main bearing shell remains in position in the cap

16 Carefully remove the crankshaft, and recover the thrustwasher halves from the sides of Number 2 main bearing.

17 Recover the upper bearing shells and tape them to their respective caps for safe-keeping.

1.9 litre engines

Note: *New main bearing cap bolts will be required on refitting.*

18 Working as described in Part C or D of this Chapter (as applicable), remove the flywheel/driveplate, oil pump and the crankshaft left-hand oil seal housing.

19 Remove the piston and connecting rod assemblies as described in Section 9. If no work is to be done on the pistons and connecting rods, unbolt the caps and push the pistons far enough up the bores that the connecting rods are positioned clear of the crankshaft journals.

20 Before removing the crankshaft, check the endfloat as described in paragraphs 3 and 4.

21 Check the main bearing caps for identification markings. Normally, No 1 bearing cap (timing belt end) is not marked and the remaining caps are numbered I, II, III, IIII. The lug at the base of the cap is used to identify the inlet manifold side of the engine **(see illustrations)**. If the bearing caps are not marked, using a hammer and punch or a suitable marker pen, number the caps from 1 to 5 from the timing belt end of the engine and mark each cap to indicate its correct fitted direction to avoid confusion on refitting.

22 Working in a diagonal sequence, evenly and progressively slacken the ten main bearing cap retaining bolts by half a turn at a time until all bolts are loose. Remove all the bolts.

23 Carefully remove each cap from the cylinder block, ensuring that the lower main bearing shell remains in position in the cap.

24 Carefully lift out the crankshaft, taking care not to displace the upper main bearing shells.

25 Recover the upper bearing shells and the thrustwashers from the cylinder block, and tape them to their respective caps for safe-keeping.

---

11 Cylinder block –
cleaning and inspection

Cleaning

1 For complete cleaning, remove all external components (senders, sensors, brackets, oil pipes, coolant pipes, etc) from the cylinder block.

2 Scrape all traces of gasket and/or sealant from the cylinder block and baseplate (where applicable), taking particular care not to damage the mating faces.

3 Remove all oil gallery plugs, where fitted. The plugs are usually very tight – they may have to be drilled out and the holes retapped. Use new plugs when the engine is reassembled. Where fitted, undo the retaining bolts and remove the piston oil spray nozzles from inside the cylinder block **(see illustration)**.

4 If the block and baseplate (where applicable) are extremely dirty, they should be steam-cleaned.

5 If the components have been steam-cleaned, clean all oil holes and oil galleries one more time on completion. Flush all internal passages with warm water until the water runs clear. Dry the block and, where necessary, the baseplate thoroughly and wipe all machined surfaces with a light oil. If you have access to compressed air, use it to speed-up the drying process, and to blow out all the oil holes and galleries.

> ⚠ **Warning: Wear eye protection when using compressed air.**

6 If the block and baseplate are relatively clean, an adequate cleaning job can be achieved with hot soapy water and a stiff brush. Take plenty of time, and do a thorough job. Regardless of the cleaning method used, be sure to clean all oil holes and galleries very thoroughly, dry everything completely, and coat all cast-iron machined surfaces with light oil.

7 The threaded holes in the cylinder block must be clean, to ensure accurate torque readings when tightening fixings during reassembly. Run the correct-size tap (which can be determined from the size of the relevant bolt) into each of the holes to remove rust, corrosion, thread sealant or other contamination, and to restore damaged threads. If possible, use compressed air to clear the holes of debris produced by this operation. Do not forget to clean the threads of all bolts and nuts which are to be re-used, as well.

8 Where applicable, apply suitable sealant to the new oil gallery plugs, and insert them into the relevant holes in the cylinder block.

Tighten the plugs securely. Where applicable, refit the oil spray nozzles into the block and secure with the retaining bolts tightened securely.

9 If the engine is to be left dismantled for some time, cover the cylinder block with a large plastic bag to keep it clean and prevent corrosion. Where applicable, refit the baseplate and tighten the bolts finger-tight.

Inspection

10 Visually check the block for cracks, rust and corrosion. Look for stripped threads in the threaded holes. It's also a good idea to have the block checked for hidden cracks by an engine reconditioning specialist that has the equipment to do this type of work, especially if the vehicle had a history of overheating or using coolant. If defects are found, have the block repaired, if possible, or renewed.

11 If in any doubt as to the condition of the cylinder block, have it inspected and measured by an engine reconditioning specialist. If the bores are worn or damaged, they will be able to carry out any necessary reboring (where possible), and supply appropriate oversized pistons, etc.

12 Pistons/connecting rods – inspection

1 Before the inspection process can begin, the piston/connecting rod assemblies must be cleaned, and the original piston rings removed from the pistons. **Note:** *Always use new piston rings when the engine is reassembled.*

2 Carefully expand the old rings over the top of the pistons. The use of two or three old feeler gauges will be helpful in preventing the rings dropping into empty grooves **(see illustration)**. Take care, however, as piston rings are sharp.

3 Scrape away all traces of carbon from the top of the piston. A hand-held wire brush, or a piece of fine emery cloth, can be used once the majority of the deposits have been scraped away.

4 Remove the carbon from the ring grooves in the piston, using an old ring. Break the ring in half to do this (be careful not to cut your fingers – piston rings are sharp). Be very careful to remove only the carbon deposits – do not remove any metal, and do not nick or scratch the sides of the ring grooves.

5 Once the deposits have been removed, clean the piston/connecting rod assembly with paraffin or a suitable solvent, and dry thoroughly. Make sure that the oil return holes in the ring grooves are clear.

6 If the pistons and cylinder bores are not damaged or worn excessively, and if the cylinder block does not need to be rebored, the original pistons can be refitted. Normal piston wear shows up as even vertical wear on the piston thrust surfaces, and slight

looseness of the top ring in its groove. New piston rings should always be used when the engine is reassembled.

7 Carefully inspect each piston for cracks around the skirt, at the gudgeon pin bosses, and at the piston ring lands (between the ring grooves).

8 Look for scoring and scuffing on the thrust faces of the piston skirt, holes in the piston crown, and burned areas at the edge of the crown. If the skirt is scored or scuffed, the engine may have been suffering from overheating, and/or abnormal combustion ('pinking') which caused excessively-high operating temperatures. The cooling and lubrication systems should be checked thoroughly. A hole in the piston crown, or burned areas at the edge of the piston crown indicates that abnormal combustion (pre-ignition, 'pinking', knocking or detonation) has been occurring. If any of the above problems exist, the causes must be investigated and corrected, or the damage will occur again.

9 Corrosion of the piston, in the form of pitting, indicates that coolant has been leaking into the combustion chamber and/or the crankcase. Again, the cause must be corrected, or the problem may persist in the rebuilt engine.

10 If in any doubt as to the condition of the pistons and connecting rods, have them inspected and measured by an engine reconditioning specialist. If new parts are required, they will be able to supply and fit appropriate-sized pistons/rings, and rebore (where possible) or hone the cylinder block.

13 Crankshaft – inspection

1 Clean the crankshaft using paraffin or a suitable solvent, and dry it, preferably with compressed air if available. Be sure to clean the oil holes with a pipe cleaner or similar probe, to ensure that they are not obstructed.

⚠️ **Warning: Wear eye protection when using compressed air.**

2 Check the main and big-end bearing journals for uneven wear, scoring, pitting and cracking.

3 Big-end bearing wear is accompanied by distinct metallic knocking when the engine is running (particularly noticeable when the engine is pulling from low revs), and some loss of oil pressure.

4 Main bearing wear is accompanied by severe engine vibration and rumble – getting progressively worse as engine revs increase – and again by loss of oil pressure.

5 Check the bearing journal for roughness by running a finger lightly over the bearing surface. Any roughness (which will be accompanied by obvious bearing wear) indicates that the crankshaft requires regrinding.

12.2 Using a feeler blade to remove a piston ring

6 If the crankshaft has been reground, check for burrs around the crankshaft oil holes (the holes are usually chamfered, so burrs should not be a problem unless regrinding has been carried out carelessly). Remove any burrs with a fine file or scraper, and thoroughly clean the oil holes as described previously.

7 Have the crankshaft journals measured by an engine reconditioning specialist. If the crankshaft is worn or damaged, they may be able to regrind the journals and supply suitable undersize bearing shells. If no undersize shells are available and the crankshaft has worn beyond the specified limits, it will have to be renewed. Consult your Vauxhall/Opel dealer or engine reconditioning specialist for further information on parts availability.

8 If a new crankshaft is to be fitted, undo the screws securing the crankshaft speed/position sensor pulse pick-up ring to the crankshaft, and transfer the ring to the new crankshaft **(see illustration)**.

14 Main and big-end bearings – inspection

1 Even though the main and big-end bearings should be renewed during the engine overhaul, the old bearings should be retained for close examination, as they may reveal valuable information about the condition of the engine.

2 Bearing failure occurs because of lack of lubrication, the presence of dirt or other foreign particles, overloading the engine, or

13.8 Transfer the crankshaft speed/position sensor pulse pick-up ring to the new crankshaft

FATIGUE FAILURE — CRATERS OR POCKETS

IMPROPER SEATING — BRIGHT (POLISHED) SECTIONS

SCRATCHED BY DIRT — DIRT EMBEDDED INTO BEARING MATERIAL

LACK OF OIL — OVERLAY WIPED OUT

EXCESSIVE WEAR — OVERLAY WIPED OUT

TAPERED JOURNAL — RADIUS RIDE

H 28395

14.2 Typical bearing failures

corrosion (see illustration). If a bearing fails, the cause must be found and eliminated before the engine is reassembled, to prevent the failure from happening again.

3 To examine the bearing shells, remove them from the cylinder block, the main bearing caps or cylinder block lower casing, the connecting rods and the big-end bearing caps, and lay them out on a clean surface in the same order as they were fitted to the engine. This will enable any bearing problems to be matched with the corresponding crankshaft journal.

4 Dirt and other foreign particles can enter the engine in a variety of ways. Contamination may be left in the engine during assembly, or it may pass through filters or the crankcase ventilation system. Normal engine wear produces small particles of metal, which can eventually cause problems. If particles find their way into the lubrication system, it is likely that they will eventually be carried to the bearings. Whatever the source, these foreign particles often end up embedded in the soft bearing material, and are easily recognised. Large particles will not embed in the bearing, and will score or gouge the bearing and journal. To prevent possible contamination, clean all parts thoroughly, and keep everything spotlessly-clean during engine assembly. Once the engine has been installed in the vehicle, ensure that engine oil and filter changes are carried out at the recommended intervals.

5 Lack of lubrication (or lubrication breakdown) has a number of interrelated causes. Excessive heat (which thins the oil), overloading (which squeezes the oil from the bearing face), and oil leakage (from excessive bearing clearances, worn oil pump or high engine speeds) all contribute to lubrication breakdown. Blocked oil passages, which may be the result of misaligned oil holes in a

bearing shell, will also starve a bearing of oil and destroy it. When lack of lubrication is the cause of bearing failure, the bearing material is wiped or extruded from the steel backing of the bearing. Temperatures may increase to the point where the steel backing turns blue from overheating.

6 Driving habits can have a definite effect on bearing life. Full-throttle, low-speed operation (labouring the engine) puts very high loads on bearings, which tends to squeeze out the oil film. These loads cause the bearings to flex, which produces fine cracks in the bearing face (fatigue failure). Eventually the bearing material will loosen in places, and tear away from the steel backing. Regular short journeys can lead to corrosion of bearings, because insufficient engine heat is produced to drive off the condensed water and corrosive gases which form inside the engine. These products collect in the engine oil, forming acid and sludge. As the oil is carried to the bearings, the acid attacks and corrodes the bearing material.

7 Incorrect bearing installation during engine assembly will also lead to bearing failure. Tight-fitting bearings leave insufficient bearing lubrication clearance, and will result in oil starvation. Dirt or foreign particles trapped behind a bearing shell results in high spots on the bearing which can lead to failure.

8 Do not touch any shell's bearing surface with your fingers during reassembly; there is a risk of scratching the delicate surface, or of depositing particles of dirt on it.

9 As mentioned at the beginning of this Section, the bearing shells should be renewed as a matter of course during engine overhaul; to do otherwise is false economy.

15 Engine overhaul – reassembly sequence

1 Before reassembly begins, ensure that all necessary new parts have been obtained (particularly gaskets, and various bolts which must be renewed), and that all the tools required are available. Read through the entire procedure to familiarise yourself with the work involved, and to ensure that all items necessary for reassembly of the engine are to hand. In addition to all normal tools and materials, a thread-locking compound will be required. A tube of suitable sealant will be required to seal certain joint faces which are not fitted with gaskets.

2 In order to save time and avoid problems, engine reassembly can be carried out in the following order:

1.3 litre engines

a) Piston rings (see Section 16).
b) Crankshaft (see Section 17).
c) Pistons/connecting rod assemblies (see Section 18).
d) Flywheel (see Chapter 2A).

e) Inlet and exhaust manifolds (see Chapter 4A).
f) Cylinder head (see Chapter 2A).
g) Camshaft housing (see Chapter 2A).
h) Oil pump (see Chapter 2A).
i) Timing chain and sprockets (see Chapter 2A).
j) Coolant pump (see Chapter 3).
k) Sump (see Chapter 2A).
l) Engine external components.

1.7 litre engines

a) Piston rings (see Section 16).
b) Crankshaft (see Section 17).
c) Piston/connecting rod assemblies (see Section 18).
d) Oil pump (see Chapter 2B).
e) Sump including baffle plate (see Chapter 2B).
f) Flywheel (see Chapter 2B).
g) Cylinder head (see Chapter 2B).
h) Coolant pump (see Chapter 3).
i) Timing belt, sprockets, tensioner and idler pulleys (see Chapter 2B).
j) Inlet and exhaust manifolds (Chapter 4A).
k) Engine external components.

1.9 litre engines

a) Piston rings (see Section 16).
b) Crankshaft (see Section 17).
c) Pistons/connecting rod assemblies (see Section 18).
d) Cylinder head (see Chapter 2C or 2D).
e) Oil pump (see Chapter 2C or 2D).
f) Sump (see Chapter 2C or 2D).
g) Flywheel/driveplate (see Chapter 2C or 2D).
h) Coolant pump (see Chapter 3).
i) Timing belt, sprockets, tensioner and idler pulleys (see Chapter 2C or 2D).
j) Inlet and exhaust manifolds (see Chapter 4A).
k) Engine external components.

3 At this stage, all engine components should be absolutely clean and dry, with all faults repaired. The components should be laid out (or in individual containers) on a completely clean work surface.

16 Piston rings – refitting

1 Before refitting the new piston rings, the ring end gaps must be checked as follows.

2 Lay out the piston/connecting rod assemblies and the new piston ring sets, so that the ring sets will be matched with the same piston and cylinder during the end gap measurement and subsequent engine reassembly.

3 Insert the top ring into the first cylinder, and push it down the bore slightly using the top of the piston. This will ensure that the ring remains square with the cylinder walls. Push the ring down into the bore until it is positioned 15 to 20 mm down from the top edge of the bore, then withdraw the piston.

4 Measure the end gap using feeler gauges, and compare the measurements with the figures given in the Specifications **(see illustration)**.

5 If the gap is too small (unlikely if genuine Vauxhall/Opel parts are used), it must be enlarged or the ring ends may contact each other during engine operation, causing serious damage. Ideally, new piston rings providing the correct end gap should be fitted, but as a last resort, the end gap can be increased by filing the ring ends very carefully with a fine file. Mount the file in a vice equipped with soft jaws, slip the ring over the file with the ends contacting the file face, and slowly move the ring to remove material from the ends – take care, as piston rings are sharp, and are easily broken.

6 With new piston rings, it is unlikely that the end gap will be too large. If they are too large, check that you have the correct rings for your engine and for the particular cylinder bore size.

7 Repeat the checking procedure for each ring in the first cylinder, and then for the rings in the remaining cylinders. Remember to keep rings, pistons and cylinders matched up.

8 Once the ring end gaps have been checked and if necessary corrected, the rings can be fitted to the pistons.

9 The oil control ring (lowest one on the piston) is composed of three sections, and should be installed first. Fit the lower steel ring, then the spreader ring, followed by the upper steel ring **(see illustration)**.

10 With the oil control ring components installed, the second (middle) ring can be fitted. It is usually stamped with a mark (TOP) which must face up, towards the top of the piston. **Note:** *Always follow the instructions supplied with the new piston ring sets – different manufacturers may specify different procedures. Do not mix up the top and middle rings, as they have different cross-sections.* Using two or three old feeler blades, as for removal of the old rings, carefully slip the ring into place in the middle groove.

11 Fit the top ring in the same manner, ensuring that, where applicable, the mark on the ring is facing up. If a stepped ring is being fitted, fit the ring with the smaller diameter of the step uppermost.

12 Repeat the procedure for the remaining pistons and rings.

17 Crankshaft – refitting

Note: *It is recommended that new main bearing shells are fitted regardless of the condition of the original ones.*

1 Refitting the crankshaft is the first step in the engine reassembly procedure. It is assumed at this point that the cylinder block, cylinder block baseplate (where applicable) and crankshaft have been cleaned,

16.4 Measuring a piston ring end gap using a feeler gauge

inspected and repaired or reconditioned as necessary.

2 Position the cylinder block with the sump/baseplate mating face uppermost.

3 Clean the bearing shells and the bearing recesses in both the cylinder block and the baseplate/caps. If new shells are being fitted, ensure that all traces of the protective grease are cleaned off using paraffin. Wipe the shells dry with a clean lint-free cloth.

4 Note that the crankshaft endfloat is controlled by thrustwashers located on one of the main bearing shells. The thrustwashers may be separate or incorporated into, or attached to, the bearing shells themselves.

5 If the original bearing shells are being re-used, they must be refitted to their original locations in the block and baseplate, or caps.

6 Fit the upper main bearing shells in place in the cylinder block, ensuring that the tab on each shell engages in the notch in the cylinder

17.6 Fitting a main bearing shell to the cylinder block

17.7b . . . and lower the crankshaft into position – 1.3 litre engines

16.9 Fitting the oil control spreader ring

block **(see illustration)**. Where separate thrustwashers are fitted, use a little grease to stick them to each side of their respective bearing upper location; ensure that the oilway grooves on each thrustwasher face outwards (away from the block).

1.3 litre engines

Note: *New cylinder block baseplate bolts must be used when refitting the crankshaft. A tube of sealant (Loctite 5900 or equivalent) will be required when fitting the baseplate to the cylinder block.*

7 Liberally lubricate each bearing shell in the cylinder block, and lower the crankshaft into position **(see illustrations)**.

8 If necessary, seat the crankshaft using light taps from a soft-faced mallet on the crankshaft balance webs.

9 Fit the bearing shells in the baseplate **(see illustration)**.

17.7a Liberally lubricate each bearing shell in the cylinder block . . .

17.9 Fit the bearing shells in the baseplate . . .

17.10 ... then lubricate the crankshaft journals, and the bearing shells – 1.3 litre engines

17.11a Apply a bead of sealant to the cylinder block mating face ...

17.11b ... ensuring the sealant is applied around the inside of the bolt holes as shown – 1.3 litre engines

10 Lubricate the crankshaft journals, and the bearing shells in the baseplate (see illustration).

11 Ensure that the cylinder block and baseplate mating surfaces are clean and dry, then apply a 2.5 mm diameter bead of sealant to the cylinder block face (see illustrations).

12 Locate the baseplate over the crankshaft and onto the cylinder block.

13 Fit the new baseplate retaining bolts, then working progressively and in sequence, tighten the inner (M10) bolts to the specified torque, then through the specified angle, in the two stages given in the Specifications. Now similarly tighten the outer (M8) retaining bolts to the specified torque in sequence (see illustrations).

14 Check that the crankshaft is free to rotate smoothly; if excessive force is required to turn the crankshaft, investigate the cause before proceeding further.

15 Check the crankshaft endfloat with reference to Section 10.

16 Refit/reconnect the piston connecting rod assemblies to the crankshaft as described in Section 18.

17 Referring to Part A of this Chapter, fit a new left-hand crankshaft oil seal, then refit the flywheel.

1.7 litre engines

18 Place the upper bearing shells in their locations as described above in paragraph 6. If new shells are being fitted, ensure that all traces of the protective grease are cleaned off using paraffin. Wipe dry the shells and caps with a lint-free cloth.

19 Using a little grease, stick the thrust-washers to each side of the Number 2 main bearing upper location; ensure that the oilway

17.13a Tightening sequence for cylinder block baseplate inner (M10) bolts ...

17.13b ... and outer (M8) bolts – 1.3 litre engines

17.13c Tighten the M10 bolts to the specified torque ...

17.13d ... then through the specified angle ...

17.13e ... and tighten the outer M8 bolts to the specified torque – 1.3 litre engines

17.19 Fit the thrust washers to the No 2 main bearing with the oil grooves facing outwards – 1.7 litre engines

17.20 Lower the crankshaft into position – 1.7 litre engines

17.22 Fit the bearing caps with the arrows towards the timing belt end of the engine – 1.7 litre engines

grooves on each thrustwasher face outwards **(see illustration)**.

20 Lubricate the upper shells with clean engine oil then lower the crankshaft into position **(see illustration)**.

21 Ensure the crankshaft is correctly seated then check the endfloat as described in Section 10.

22 Fit the bearing shells to the bearing caps, then lubricate the crankshaft journals and bearing shells in the caps. Refit the caps to the cylinder block **(see illustration)**. Ensure the caps are fitted in their correct locations, with Number 1 cap at the timing belt end, and are fitted the correct way around so that the arrows all point towards the timing belt end of the engine. Prior to refitting Number 1 cap, apply a smear of sealant to its mating surface.

23 Apply a smear of clean engine to oil to the threads and underneath the heads of the new main bearing cap bolts. Fit the bolts tightening them all by hand then working in a diagonal sequence from the centre outwards, evenly and progressively tighten them to the specified torque setting **(see illustration)**.

24 Check that the crankshaft is free to rotate smoothly; if excessive force is required to turn the crankshaft, investigate the cause before proceeding further.

25 Ensure that the mating surfaces of the oil seal housing and cylinder block are clean and dry. Note the correct fitted depth of the oil seal then tap/lever the seal out of the housing.

26 Apply a smear of sealant to the oil seal housing mating surface, and make sure that the locating dowels are in position **(see**

illustration). Slide the housing over the end of the crankshaft, and into position on the cylinder block. Put a drop of locking compound on the threads, then tighten the retaining bolts to the specified torque setting.

27 Referring to Part B of this Chapter, fit a new left-hand crankshaft oil seal, then refit the flywheel.

28 Fit the transmission input shaft guide into the end of the crankshaft **(see illustration)**.

29 Refit/reconnect the piston connecting rod assemblies to the crankshaft as described in Section 18.

1.9 litre engines

30 Place the upper bearing shells in their locations as described above in paragraph 6. If new shells are being fitted, ensure that all traces of the protective grease are cleaned off using paraffin. Wipe dry the shells and caps with a lint-free cloth.

31 Liberally lubricate each bearing shell in the cylinder block, and lower the crankshaft into position.

32 If necessary, seat the crankshaft using light taps from a soft-faced mallet on the crankshaft balance webs.

33 Fit the bearing shells into the bearing caps.

34 Lubricate the bearing shells in the bearing caps, and the crankshaft journals, then fit the caps ensuring they are fitted to their correct locations and the right way around. Fit and tighten the new bolts as far as possible by hand.

35 Working in a spiral pattern from the centre

outwards, tighten the main bearing cap bolts to the specified Stage 1 torque setting.

36 Once all bolts are tightened to the specified Stage 1 torque, go around again and tighten all bolts through the specified Stage 2 angle. It is recommended that an angle-measuring gauge is used during the final stages of the tightening, to ensure accuracy. If a gauge is not available, use white paint to make alignment marks between the bolt head and cap prior to tightening; the marks can then be used to check that the bolt has been rotated through the correct angle.

37 Check that the crankshaft is free to rotate smoothly; if excessive pressure is required to turn the crankshaft, investigate the cause before proceeding further.

38 Check the crankshaft endfloat with reference to Section 10.

39 Refit/reconnect the piston connecting rod assemblies to the crankshaft as described in Section 18.

40 Referring to Part C or D of this Chapter, fit a new left-hand crankshaft oil seal/housing, then refit the flywheel/driveplate.

18 Pistons/connecting rods – refitting

Note: *It is recommended that new big-end bearing shells are fitted regardless of the condition of the original ones.*

1.3 litre engines

1 Clean the backs of the big-end bearing

17.23 Tighten the main bearing cap bolts to the specified torque – 1.7 litre engines

17.26 Apply sealant to the oil seal housing mating surface – 1.7 litre engines

17.28 Fit the input shaft guide into the end of the crankshaft – 1.7 litre engines

18.2 Press the bearing shells into the connecting rods and caps in their correct positions – 1.3 litre engines

18.5a Position the piston with the arrow or notch (as applicable) pointing towards the timing chain/belt end of the engine . . .

18.5b . . . then tap the piston carefully into the cylinder bore – 1.3 litre engines

18.7a Tighten the big-end bearing cap bolts to the specified torque . . .

18.7b . . . then through the specified angle – 1.3 litre engines

18.10 Replace the big-end bolts – 1.7 litre engines

shells and the recesses in the connecting rods and big-end caps. If new shells are being fitted, ensure that all traces of the protective grease are cleaned off using paraffin. Wipe the shells, caps and connecting rods dry with a lint-free cloth.

2 Press the bearing shells into the connecting rods and caps in their correct positions **(see illustration)**. **Note:** *When finally refitting the piston/connecting rod assemblies, new big-end bearing cap bolts must be used. Ensure that the mating faces of the connecting rods and big-end bearing caps are clean before refitting.*

18.14 Piston ring end gap positions – 1.7 and 1.9 litre engines

I Top compression ring
II Second compression ring
III Oil control ring

3 Lubricate No 1 piston and piston rings, and check that the ring gaps are correctly positioned. The gaps in the upper and lower steel rings of the oil control ring should be offset by 25 to 50 mm to the right and left of the spreader ring gap. The two upper compression ring gaps should be offset by 180° to each other.

4 Liberally lubricate the cylinder bore with clean engine oil.

5 Fit a ring compressor to No 1 piston, then insert the piston and connecting rod into the cylinder bore so that the base of the compressor stands on the block. With the crankshaft big-end bearing journal positioned at its lowest point, tap the piston carefully into the cylinder bore with the wooden handle of a hammer, and at the same time guide the connecting rod onto the bearing journal. Note that the arrow or notch (as applicable) on the piston crown must point towards the timing chain end of the engine **(see illustrations)**.

6 Fit the bearing shells to the bearing caps.

7 Liberally lubricate the bearing journals and bearing shells, and fit the bearing cap in its original location. Tighten the new bearing cap bolts to the Stage 1 torque setting, then tighten all bolts through the specified angles **(see illustrations)**.

8 After refitting each piston/connecting rod assembly, rotate the crankshaft, and check that it turns freely, with no signs of binding or tight spots.

9 Refit the following components.

  a) Refit the oil baffle plate and tighten the retaining bolts securely.

  b) Refit the cylinder head as described in Chapter 2A.
  c) Refit the camshaft housing as described in Chapter 2A.
  d) Refit the timing chain, sprockets and tensioner as deccribed in Chapter 2A.
  e) Refit the timing cover (which includes the sump refitting procedure) as described in Chapter 2A.

1.7 litre engines

10 Prior to refitting, carefully tap the original bolts out from the connecting rod and install the new bolts **(see illustration)**.

11 Clean the backs of the big-end bearing shells and the recesses in the connecting rods and big-end caps. If new shells are being fitted, ensure that all traces of the protective grease are cleaned off using paraffin. Wipe the shells, caps and connecting rods dry with a lint-free cloth.

12 Press the bearing shells into the connecting rods and caps in their correct positions **(see illustration 18.2)**.

13 Lubricate the bores, the pistons and piston rings then lay out each piston/connecting rod assembly in its respective position.

14 Starting with assembly Number 1, space the ring gaps uniformly around the piston at 120° intervals, then clamp them in position with a piston ring compressor **(see illustration)**.

15 Insert the piston/connecting rod assembly into the top of cylinder No 1, ensuring that the mark (dot) on the piston crown is pointing towards the timing belt end of the engine. Using a block of wood or hammer handle

18.16 Lubricate the bearing surface and refit the bearing cap –
1.7 litre engines

18.27 The cut-out on the piston skirt (A) must be on the same
side as the oil spray jet, and the lugs on the cap and rod (B) must
be toward the timing belt end of the engine – 1.9 litre engines

against the piston crown, tap the assembly into the cylinder until the piston crown is flush with the top of the cylinder (see illustration 18.5b).

16 Taking care not to mark the cylinder bore, liberally lubricate the crankpin and both bearing shells, then pull the piston/connecting rod assembly down the bore and onto the crankpin and refit the big-end bearing cap, using the markings to ensure it is fitted the correct way around (align the previously-made marks), and fit the new retaining nuts (see illustration).

17 Tighten both bearing cap nuts to the specified Stage 1 torque setting then tighten them through the specified Stage 2 angle, and finally through the specified Stage 3 angle. It is recommended that an angle-measuring gauge is used during the final stages of the tightening, to ensure accuracy. If a gauge is not available, use white paint to make alignment marks between the nut and cap prior to tightening; the marks can then be used to check that the bolt has been rotated through the correct angle.

18 Refit the remaining three piston and connecting rod assemblies in the same way.

19 Rotate the crankshaft, and check that it turns freely, with no signs of binding or tight spots.

20 Refit the baffle plate to the base of the cylinder block and tighten its retaining bolts to the specified torque.

21 Refit the oil pump, pick-up/strainer, sump and the cylinder head as described in Part B of this Chapter.

1.9 litre engines

22 Clean the backs of the big-end bearing shells and the recesses in the connecting rods and big-end caps. If new shells are being fitted, ensure that all traces of the protective grease are cleaned off using paraffin. Wipe the shells, caps and connecting rods dry with a lint-free cloth.

23 Press the bearing shells into their locations, ensuring that the tab on each shell engages in the notch in the connecting rod and cap (see illustration 18.2). If there is no tab on the bearing shell (and no notch in the rod or cap) position the shell equidistant from each side of the rod and cap. If the original bearing shells are being used ensure they are refitted in their original locations.

24 Lubricate the bores, the pistons and piston rings then lay out each piston/connecting rod assembly in its respective position.

25 Lubricate No 1 piston and piston rings, and space the ring gaps uniformly around the piston at 120° intervals (see illustration 18.14).

26 Fit a ring compressor to No 1 piston, then insert the piston and connecting rod into the cylinder bore so that the base of the compressor stands on the block.

27 Position the piston so that the cut-out on the piston skirt is on the same side as the oil spray jet, and the lugs on the cap and rod are toward the timing belt end of the engine (see illustration).

28 With the crankshaft big-end bearing journal positioned at its lowest point, tap the piston carefully into the cylinder bore with the wooden handle of a hammer, and at the same time guide the connecting rod onto the bearing journal.

29 Liberally lubricate the bearing journals and bearing shells, and fit the bearing cap in its original location.

30 Screw in the new bearing cap retaining bolts, and tighten both bolts to the specified Stage 1 torque setting then tighten them through the specified Stage 2 angle. It is recommended that an angle-measuring gauge is used during the final stages of the tightening, to ensure accuracy. If a gauge is not available, use white paint to make alignment marks between the bolt head and cap prior to tightening; the marks can then be used to check that the bolt has been rotated through the correct angle.

31 Refit the remaining three piston and connecting rod assemblies in the same way.

32 Rotate the crankshaft, and check that it turns freely, with no signs of binding or tight spots.

33 Refit the oil pump, pick-up/strainer, sump and the cylinder head as described in Part C or D (as applicable) of this Chapter.

19 Engine –
initial start-up after overhaul

1 With the engine refitted in the vehicle, double-check the engine oil and coolant levels. Make a final check that everything has been reconnected, and that there are no tools or rags left in the engine compartment.

2 Prime and bleed the fuel system as described in Chapter 4A, then start the engine, noting that this may take a little longer than usual. Make sure that the oil pressure warning light goes out.

3 While the engine is idling, check for fuel, water and oil leaks. Don't be alarmed if there are some odd smells and smoke from parts getting hot and burning off oil deposits.

4 Assuming all is well, run the engine until it reaches normal operating temperature, then switch off the engine.

5 After a few minutes, recheck the oil and coolant levels as described in Weekly checks, and top-up as necessary.

6 Note that there is no need to retighten the cylinder head bolts once the engine has first run after reassembly.

7 If new pistons, rings or crankshaft bearings have been fitted, the engine must be treated as new, and run-in for the first 600 miles. Do not operate the engine at full-throttle, or allow it to labour at low engine speeds in any gear. It is recommended that the oil and filter be changed at the end of this period.

Notes

Chapter 3
Cooling, heating and air conditioning systems

Contents

Degrees of difficulty

Easy, suitable for novice with little experience 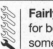	**Fairly easy,** suitable for beginner with some experience	**Fairly difficult,** suitable for competent DIY mechanic	**Difficult,** suitable for experienced DIY mechanic	**Very difficult,** suitable for expert DIY or professional

Specifications

Thermostat

Opening temperature . . . . 92°C

Air conditioning compressor

Lubricant capacity:
    1.3 litre engines . . . . 150 cc
    1.7 litre engines . . . . 120 cc
    1.9 litre engines . . . . 135 cc
Lubricant type (synthetic PAG fluid) . . . . Vauxhall part number 90 509 933/19 49 873

Torque wrench settings	**Nm**	**lbf ft**
Air conditioning compressor mounting bolts	25	18
Air conditioning refrigerant pipe block connections	20	15
Coolant pump retaining bolts:		
1.3 litre engines	10	7
1.7 litre engines	23	17
1.9 litre engines	25	18
Coolant pump pulley bolts (1.7 litre engines)	12	9
Coolant temperature sensor:		
1.3 litre engines	34	25
1.7 litre engines	23	17
1.9 litre engines	20	15
Radiator mounting brackets-to-subframe	15	11
Thermostat housing/cover:		
1.3 litre engines	25	18
1.7 litre engines	23	17
1.9 litre engines	25	18

1 General information and precautions

General information

The cooling system is of pressurised type, comprising a coolant pump, a crossflow radiator, electric cooling fan and thermostat.

On 1.3 and 1.7 litre engines, the coolant pump is driven by the auxiliary drivebelt. On 1.9 litre engines, the coolant pump is driven by the timing belt.

The system functions as follows. Cold coolant from the radiator passes through the bottom hose to the coolant pump, where it is pumped around the cylinder block, head passages and heater matrix. After cooling the cylinder bores, combustion surfaces and valve seats, the coolant reaches the underside of the thermostat, which is initially closed. The coolant passes through the heater, and is returned to the coolant pump.

When the engine is cold, the coolant circulates only through the cylinder block, cylinder head and heater. When the coolant reaches a predetermined temperature, the thermostat opens and the coolant also passes through to the radiator. As the coolant circulates through the radiator, it is cooled by the inrush of air when the car is in forward motion. Airflow is supplemented by the action of the electric cooling fan when necessary. Once the coolant has passed through the radiator, and has cooled, the cycle is repeated.

The electric cooling fan, mounted on the rear of the radiator, is controlled by the engine management system electronic control unit, in conjunction with a cooling fan module. At a predetermined coolant temperature, the fan is actuated.

An expansion tank is fitted to the left-hand side of the engine compartment to accommodate expansion of the coolant when hot. The expansion tank is connected to the top of the radiator.

Precautions

 Warning: Do not attempt to remove the expansion tank filler cap, or disturb any part of the cooling system, while the engine is hot; there is a high risk of scalding. If the cap must be removed before the engine and radiator have fully cooled (even though this is not recommended) the pressure in the cooling system must first be relieved. Cover the cap with a thick layer of cloth, to avoid scalding, and slowly unscrew the filler cap until a hissing sound can be heard. When the hissing has stopped, indicating that the pressure has reduced, slowly unscrew the filler cap until it can be removed; if more hissing sounds are heard, wait until they have stopped before unscrewing the cap completely. At all times, keep well away from the filler cap opening.

 Warning: Do not allow antifreeze to come into contact with the skin, or with the painted surfaces of the vehicle. Rinse off spills immediately, with plenty of water. Never leave antifreeze lying around in an open container, or in a puddle on the driveway or garage floor. Children and pets are attracted by its sweet smell, but antifreeze can be fatal if ingested.

 Warning: If the engine is hot, the electric cooling fan may start rotating even if the engine is not running; be careful to keep hands, hair and loose clothing well clear when working in the engine compartment.

 Warning: Refer to Section 10 for precautions to be observed when working on models equipped with air conditioning.

2 Cooling system hoses – disconnection and renewal

Note: Refer to the warnings given in Section 1 of this Chapter before proceeding. Do not attempt to disconnect any hose while the system is still hot.

1 If the checks described in Chapter 1 reveal a faulty hose, it must be renewed as follows.

2 First drain the cooling system (see Chapter 1). If the coolant is not due for renewal, it may be re-used if it is collected in a clean container.

3 Before disconnecting a hose, first note its routing in the engine compartment, and whether it is secured by any additional retaining clips or cable ties. Use a pair of pliers to release the clamp-type clips, or a screwdriver to slacken the screw-type clips, then move the clips along the hose, clear of the relevant inlet/outlet union. Carefully work the hose free.

4 Note that the radiator inlet and outlet unions are fragile; do not use excessive force when attempting to remove the hoses. If a hose proves to be difficult to remove, try to release it by rotating the hose ends before attempting to free it.

5 When fitting a hose, first slide the clips onto the hose, then work the hose into position. If clamp-type clips were originally fitted, it is a good idea to use screw-type clips when refitting the hose. If the hose is stiff, use a little soapy water (washing-up liquid is ideal) as a lubricant, or soften the hose by soaking it in hot water.

6 Work the hose into position, checking that it is correctly routed and secured. Slide each clip along the hose until it passes over the flared end of the relevant inlet/outlet union, before tightening the clips securely.

7 Refill the cooling system with reference to Chapter 1.

8 Check thoroughly for leaks as soon as possible after disturbing any part of the cooling system.

3 Radiator – removal, inspection and refitting

Removal

1 Remove the battery and battery tray as described in Chapter 5.

2 Remove the plastic cover from the top of the engine.

3 Apply the handbrake, then jack up the front of the vehicle and support it on axle stands (see *Jacking and vehicle support*).

4 Remove the front bumper as described in Chapter 11.

5 Drain the cooling system as described in Chapter 1.

6 Disconnect the cooling fan wiring harness connector from the base of the fan housing **(see illustration)**. Free the wiring harness from the cable ties.

7 On models with air conditioning, open the retaining clip and detach the air conditioning refrigerant pipe from the right-hand side of the radiator. Release the air conditioning compressor wiring harness from the retaining clip.

8 Release the clamp and disconnect the bottom hose from the radiator.

9 Unclip the two vacuum hoses from the bracket on the right-hand side of the radiator.

10 Retain the radiator in position by inserting a drill bit, or similar, through the holes provided on each of the radiator upper mounting brackets **(see illustration)**.

3.6 Disconnect the cooling fan wiring harness connector from the base of the fan housing

3.10 Insert a drill bit (arrowed) or similar, through the holes on the radiator mounting brackets (shown with radiator removed)

11 Undo the two bolts each side securing the radiator left-hand and right-hand mounting brackets to the subframe. Remove the brackets, noting their orientation **(see illustrations)**.

12 Release the clamps and disconnect the top hose and expansion tank hose from the right-hand side of the radiator.

13 Slacken the retaining clip and disconnect the turbocharger charge air hose from the intercooler and charge air pipe at the front of the engine.

14 Undo the bolt each side securing the fan housing to the top of the radiator **(see illustrations)**.

15 Unclip the charge air pipe from the upper edge of the fan housing.

16 On models with automatic transmission, detach the protective ring (where fitted) over the fluid cooler pipe unions at the radiator. Using a small screwdriver, release the quick-release fitting retaining lugs and disconnect the fitting from the radiator. Suitably cover the open unions after disconnection.

17 On models with air conditioning, secure the condenser to the bonnet crossmember with cable ties. Undo the upper and lower bolts securing the right-hand side of the condenser to the radiator. Similarly undo the upper bolt and two lower bolts securing the condenser and intercooler to the radiator **(see illustrations)**.

18 Remove the drill bits, or similar tools used to retain the radiator in position and carefully lower the radiator out from under the car.

Inspection

19 If the radiator has been removed due to suspected blockage, reverse-flush it as described in Chapter 1.

20 Clean dirt and debris from the radiator fins, using an air line (in which case, wear eye protection) or a soft brush.
Caution: Be careful, as the fins are easily damaged, and are sharp.

21 If necessary, a radiator specialist can perform a 'flow test' on the radiator, to establish whether an internal blockage exists.

22 A leaking radiator must be referred to a specialist for permanent repair. Do not attempt to weld or solder a leaking radiator.

23 In an emergency, minor leaks from the radiator can be cured by using a suitable radiator sealant (in accordance with its manufacturer's instructions) with the radiator fitted in the vehicle.

24 Inspect the radiator mounting rubbers, and renew them if necessary.

Refitting

25 Refitting is a reversal of removal, bearing in mind the following points.

  a) Ensure that all hoses are correctly reconnected, and their retaining clips securely tightened.

3.11a Undo the two bolts (arrowed) each side . . .

3.11b . . . and remove the radiator mounting brackets, noting their orientation

3.14a Undo the fan housing right-hand mounting bolt (arrowed) . . .

3.14b . . . and left-hand mounting bolt (arrowed)

  b) On completion, refill the cooling system as described in Chapter 1.
  c) On models with automatic transmission, check and if necessary top-up the

automatic transmission fluid level with reference to the 'Transmission fluid – draining and refilling' procedures contained in Chapter 7B.

3.17a Undo the condenser right-hand upper retaining bolt (arrowed) . . .

3.17b . . . right-hand lower retaining bolt (arrowed) . . .

3.17c . . . left-hand upper retaining bolt (arrowed) . . .

3.17d . . . and two left-hand lower retaining bolts (arrowed)

4.7 Undo the two retaining bolts (arrowed) and remove the thermostat housing – 1.3 litre engines

4.13 Remove the thermostat housing cover . . .

4 Thermostat –
removed and refitting

Removal

1.3 litre engines

1 The thermostat is located on the left-hand end of the cylinder head, and is integral with the housing.
2 Remove the plastic cover over the top of the engine.
3 Remove the battery and battery tray as described in Chapter 5.
4 Drain the cooling system (see Chapter 1).
5 Slacken the retaining clips, and disconnect the four coolant hoses from the thermostat housing.
6 Disconnect the coolant temperature sensor wiring connector.

5.8 Manoeuvre the fan housing assembly up and out of the engine compartment

4.8 Remove the sealing ring from the thermostat housing – 1.3 litre engines

4.14 . . . and withdraw the thermostat from the housing – 1.7 litre engines

7 Undo and remove the two retaining bolts, unclip the wiring harness and remove the thermostat housing from the engine **(see illustration)**.
8 Remove the sealing ring from the housing and discard it; a new one should be used on refitting **(see illustration)**.

1.7 litre engines

9 Remove the plastic cover over the top of the engine.
10 Drain the cooling system (see Chapter 1).
11 Remove the battery and battery tray as described in Chapter 5.
12 Loosen the clip and disconnect the top hose from the thermostat cover located on the left-hand end of the cylinder head.
13 Unscrew the bolts and remove the thermostat cover from the housing **(see illustration)**.
14 Lift the thermostat from its housing and recover the sealing ring **(see illustration)**.

5.9 Undo the three bolts (arrowed) and lift off the fan

1.9 litre engines

15 The thermostat is located on the left-hand end of the cylinder head, and is integral with the housing.
16 Remove the plastic cover over the top of the engine.
17 Remove the battery and battery tray as described in Chapter 5.
18 Drain the cooling system (see Chapter 1).
19 Release the two retaining clips and disconnect the charge air hose from the throttle housing, and intercooler charge air pipe.
20 Release the clips and disconnect the four hoses from the thermostat housing.
21 Disconnect the coolant temperature sensor wiring connector.
22 Unscrew the nut and release the coolant pipes from the stud at the base of the thermostat housing.
23 Unbolt the thermostat housing from the cylinder head. Clean away all traces of gasket from the housing and cylinder head.

Refitting

24 Refitting is a reversal of removal, but fit a new gasket/seal and tighten the mounting bolts to the specified torque (where given). Refill the cooling system as described in Chapter 1.

5 Electric cooling fan –
removal and refitting

⚠ *Warning: If the engine is hot, the cooling fan may start up at any time. Take extra precautions when working in the vicinity of the fan.*

Removal

1 Remove the battery and battery tray as described in Chapter 5.
2 Remove the plastic cover from the top of the engine.
3 Referring to Chapter 4A, release the wiring harness (where applicable), then slacken the retaining clips, undo the bolts and disconnect the charge air pipes and hoses from the intercooler, turbocharger and throttle housing as necessary to allow the fan assembly to be removed from above.
4 Unclip the radiator top hose and the coolant hoses(s) from the fan housing.
5 Disconnect the cooling fan wiring harness connector from the base of the fan housing **(see illustration 3.6)**. Free the wiring harness from the cable ties.
6 Undo the bolt each side securing the fan housing to the top of the radiator **(see illustrations 3.14a and 3.14b)**.
7 Unclip the charge air pipe from the upper edge of the fan housing.
8 Lift the fan housing from the lower guides on the radiator and manoeuvre the assembly up and out of the engine compartment **(see illustration)**.
9 To remove the fan motor, undo the three bolts and lift off the fan **(see illustration)**.

5.10a Undo the bolt (arrowed) securing the fan motor resistor to the housing . . .

5.10b . . . then undo the three bolts (arrowed) and remove the motor from the housing

10 Undo the bolt securing the fan motor resistor to the housing, then undo the three bolts and remove the motor from the housing **(see illustrations)**.

Refitting

11 Refitting is a reversal of removal.

6 Coolant temperature sensor – testing, removal and refitting

Testing

1 Testing of the coolant temperature sensor must be entrusted to a Vauxhall/Opel dealer, who will have the necessary specialist diagnostic equipment.

Removal

2 Partially drain the cooling system with reference to Chapter 1. Alternatively, it is possible to change the sensor quickly with minimal loss of coolant by first releasing any pressure from the cooling system. With the engine cold, temporarily remove the expansion tank cap.
3 Remove the plastic cover over the top of the engine.
4 Remove the battery and battery tray as described in Chapter 5.
5 On 1.9 litre engines, slacken the two retaining clips and disconnect the upper charge air hose from the throttle housing, and intercooler left-hand charge air pipe.
6 Disconnect the wiring connector from the sensor located on the thermostat housing on the left-hand end of the cylinder head **(see illustrations)**.
7 Unscrew and remove the sensor.

Refitting

8 Fit the new sensor using a reversal of the removal procedure, but tighten the sensor to the specified torque and refill the cooling system with reference to Chapter 1.

7 Coolant pump – removal and refitting

Removal

1.3 litre engines

1 Disconnect the battery negative terminal (refer to *Disconnecting the battery* in the Reference Chapter).
2 Drain the cooling system and remove the auxiliary drivebelt as described in Chapter 1.

3 Working through the apertures in the pulley, unscrew and remove the four coolant pump retaining nuts **(see illustration)**.
4 Withdraw the coolant pump from the cylinder block studs. **Note:** *Coolant which is trapped in the cylinder block will leak out when the pump is removed.*
5 Recover the pump sealing ring, and discard it; a new one must be used on refitting **(see illustration)**.
6 Note that it is not possible to overhaul the pump. If it is faulty, the unit must be renewed complete.

6.6a Coolant temperature sensor location (arrowed) on 1.3 litre engines . . .

6.6b . . . 1.7 litre engines . . .

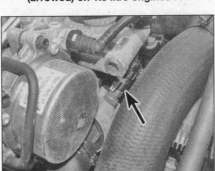

6.6c . . . and 1.9 litre engines

7.3 Working through the pulley apertures, unscrew and remove the four coolant pump retaining nuts – 1.3 litre engines

7.5 Remove the sealing ring from the coolant pump – 1.3 litre engines

7.10 Remove the pulley from the drive flange on the coolant pump – 1.7 litre engines

7.11 Unscrew and remove the coolant pump retaining bolts (arrowed) – 1.7 litre engines

7.13 Withdraw the coolant pump and remove the gasket – 1.7 litre engines

1.7 litre engines

7 Disconnect the battery negative terminal (refer to *Disconnecting the battery* in the Reference Chapter).

8 Drain the cooling system and remove the auxiliary drivebelt as described in Chapter 1.

9 Remove the air cleaner assembly and intake duct as described in Chapter 4A.

10 Hold the pump pulley stationary (if necessary using an old auxiliary drivebelt or an oil filter strap wrench), then unscrew and remove the bolts and remove the pulley from the drive flange on the coolant pump **(see illustration)**.

11 Unscrew and remove the coolant pump retaining bolts **(see illustration)**.

12 Withdraw the coolant pump from the cylinder block, noting that it may be necessary

to tap the pump lightly with a soft-faced mallet to free it.

13 Recover the gasket and discard it; a new one must be used on refitting **(see illustration)**.

14 Note that it is not possible to overhaul the pump. If it is faulty, the unit must be renewed complete.

1.9 litre engines

15 Disconnect the battery negative terminal (refer to *Disconnecting the battery* in the Reference Chapter).

16 Remove the plastic cover from the top of the engine.

17 Drain the cooling system as described in Chapter 1.

18 Remove the timing belt as described in Chapter 2C or 2D as applicable. **Note:** *The*

timing belt must not come into contact with coolant.

19 Unscrew and remove the three coolant pump securing bolts **(see illustration)**.

20 Withdraw the coolant pump from the cylinder head, noting that it may be necessary to tap the pump lightly with a soft-faced mallet to free it **(see illustration)**.

21 Recover the pump sealing ring, and discard it; a new one must be used on refitting.

22 Note that it is not possible to overhaul the pump. If it is faulty, the unit must be renewed complete.

Refitting

23 Refitting is a reversal of the removal procedure, bearing in mind the following points:

a) Ensure that the pump and cylinder block mating surfaces are clean and dry, and fit a new sealing ring/gasket to the pump.

b) Tighten all retaining bolts to the specified torque.

c) On 1.9 litre engines, refit the timing belt as described in Chapter 2C or 2D as applicable.

d) Refill the cooling system and refit the auxiliary drivebelt as described in Chapter 1.

8 Heating and ventilation system – general information

The heater/ventilation system consists of a four-speed blower motor (housed behind the facia), face-level vents in the centre and at each end of the facia, and air ducts to the front and rear footwells.

The heater controls are located in the centre of the facia, and the controls operate flap valves to deflect and mix the air flowing through the various parts of the heater/ventilation system. The flap valves are contained in the air distribution housing, which acts as a central distribution unit, passing air to the various ducts and vents.

Cold air enters the system through the grille at the rear of the engine compartment. A pollen filter is fitted to the ventilation intake, to filter out dust, soot, pollen and spores from the air entering the vehicle.

The air (boosted by the blower fan if required) then flows through the various ducts, according to the settings of the controls. Stale air is expelled through ducts at the rear of the vehicle. If warm air is required, the cold air is passed through the heater matrix, which is heated by the engine coolant.

A recirculation switch enables the outside air supply to be closed off, while the air inside the vehicle is recirculated. This can be useful to prevent unpleasant odours entering from outside the vehicle, but should only be used briefly, as the recirculated air inside the vehicle will soon deteriorate.

7.19 Undo the coolant pump retaining bolts (arrowed) . . .

7.20 . . . and remove the pump from the cylinder head – 1.9 litre engines

9.2 Undo the two screws and remove the facia lower panel below the glovebox

9.3 Remove the passenger's side footwell air duct

9.5a Undo the five retaining bolts (arrowed) . . .

9 Heater/ventilation system components – removal and refitting

Heater blower motor

Removal

1 Remove the glovebox as described in Chapter 11.

2 Undo the two screws and remove the facia lower panel below the glovebox **(see illustration)**.

3 Release the expanding rivet and remove the passenger's side footwell air duct **(see illustration)**.

4 Trace the wiring from the blower motor up to the resistor and disconnect the two wires at the resistor.

5 Undo the five bolts securing the blower motor housing to the base of the recirculating air valve housing and remove the blower motor down and out from under the facia **(see illustrations)**.

Refitting

6 Refitting is a reversal of removal.

9.5b . . . and remove the blower motor from the recirculating air valve housing

Heater blower motor resistor

Removal

7 Remove the glovebox as described in Chapter 11.

8 Carefully prise free the blower motor resistor from the air distribution housing **(see illustration)**.

9 Disconnect the main wiring connector and the two heater blower motor wiring connectors and remove the resistor **(see illustration)**.

Refitting

10 Refitting is a reversal of removal.

9.8 Heater blower motor resistor location (arrowed)

Recirculating air valve housing

Removal

11 Remove the heater blower motor as described previously.

12 Remove the water deflector at the base of the windscreen as described in Chapter 11.

13 Working in the water deflector aperture, undo the four screws and remove the recirculating air valve housing grille. With the grille removed, undo the bolt now exposed securing the top of the air valve housing to the bulkhead **(see illustration)**.

9.9 Disconnect the main wiring connector (A) and the two heater blower motor wiring connectors (B)

9.13 Undo the bolt (arrowed) securing the top of the recirculating air valve housing to the bulkhead

9.14 Undo the two retaining bolts (arrowed) and lower the housing from its location

9.15 Disconnect the wiring connector from the servo motor, then manouvre the housing out from under the facia

9.18 Recirculating air valve servo motor retaining bolts (arrowed)

9.23 Mixed air valve servo motor wiring connector (A) and retaining bolts (B)

9.27 Release the quick-release connectors (arrowed) and disconnect the heater hoses from the matrix pipe stubs

14 Undo the two retaining bolts and lower the housing from its location (see illustration).

15 Disconnect the wiring connector from the recirculating air valve servo motor, then manoeuvre the housing out from under the facia (see illustration).

Refitting

16 Refitting is a reversal of removal, ensuring that the housing seals correctly seated.

Recirculating air valve servo motor

Removal

17 Remove the recirculating air valve housing as described previously.

18 Undo the three retaining bolts and remove the motor from the housing (see illustration).

Refitting

19 Refitting is a reversal of removal.

Mixed air valve servo motor

Removal

20 Remove the glovebox as described in Chapter 11.

21 Undo the two screws and remove the facia lower panel below the glovebox (see illustration 9.2).

22 Release the expanding rivet and remove the passenger's side footwell air duct (see illustration 9.3).

23 Disconnect the wiring connector, then undo the three bolts and remove the servo motor from the side of the air distribution housing (see illustration).

Refitting

24 Refitting is a reversal of removal.

Heater matrix

Removal

25 Remove the centre console as described in Chapter 11.

9.31 Undo the two bolts (arrowed) securing the heater matrix condensation drain tube to the bulkhead

26 Working in the engine compartment, use two hose clamps to clamp the hoses leading to the heater matrix. The hoses are located on the bulkhead, just above the steering gear. Alternatively, drain the cooling system completely as described in Chapter 1.

27 Release the quick-release connectors by sliding them forward, and disconnect the two heater hoses from the heater matrix pipe stubs (see illustration).

28 Remove the water deflector at the base of the windscreen as described in Chapter 11.

29 Working in the water deflector aperture, undo the four screws and remove the recirculating air valve housing grille. With the grille removed, undo the bolt now exposed securing the top of the air valve housing to the bulkhead (see illustration 9.13).

30 Remove the engine/transmission rear mounting/torque link and transmission bracket as described in the relevant Part of Chapter 2, for access to the heater matrix condensation drain tube.

31 From under the car, unclip and carefully move aside the fuel and brake pipes in the area of the matrix condensation drain tube, then undo the two bolts securing the drain tube to the bulkhead (see illustration).

32 Working in the engine compartment, undo the four bolts securing the air

9.32a Undo the two bolts (arrowed) adjacent to the heater hoses . . .

9.32b . . . the bolt (arrowed) behind the refrigerant pipe . . .

9.32c . . . and the bolt (arrowed) adjacent to the wiper linkage, securing the air distribution housing to the bulkhead

9.34a Undo the bolts (arrowed) on each side . . .

9.34b . . . and the bolts (arrowed) at the front securing the heater matrix lower cover panel to the air distribution housing

9.34c Lift the air distribution housing as far as clearance will allow and withdraw the lower cover panel

distribution housing to the bulkhead **(see illustrations)**.

33 From inside the car, undo the bolts and remove the facia lower centre support brackets.

34 Undo the eight bolts securing the heater matrix lower cover panel to the air distribution housing. Lift the air distribution housing as far as clearance will allow and withdraw the lower cover panel **(see illustrations)**.

35 Be prepared for coolant spillage as the matrix is removed and place some cloths or absorbent material over the carpet. Pull the heater matrix from its location and remove it from the car **(see illustration)**.

Refitting

36 Refitting is a reversal of removal, bearing in mind the following:

 a) *Push the heater hoses back onto the*

matrix pipe stubs, ensuring that the quick-release connectors securely lock the hoses in position.

 b) *Refit the engine/transmission rear mounting/torque link and transmission bracket as described in the relevant Part of Chapter 2.*

 c) *If the cooling system was completely drained, refill as described in Chapter 1. If the heater hoses were clamped prior to removal, top-up the cooling system as described in 'Weekly checks'.*

Heater control assembly

Removal

37 Remove the radio/cassette/CD player as described in Chapter 12.

38 Lift up the two upper retaining catches and withdraw the heater control assembly

from the facia. Disconnect the two wiring connectors and remove the unit from the car **(see illustrations)**.

Refitting

39 Refitting is a reversal of removal.

Air distribution housing

Note: *On models with air conditioning, it is not possible to remove the air distribution housing without opening the refrigerant circuit (see Sections 10 and 11). Have the refrigerant discharged at a dealer service department or an automotive air conditioning repair facility before proceeding.*

40 Drain the cooling system as described in Chapter 1.

41 On models with air conditioning, undo the bolt securing the refrigerant pipe block connection to the expansion valve and

9.35 Pull the heater matrix from its location and remove it from the car

9.38a Lift up the two retaining catches (arrowed) and withdraw the heater control assembly from the facia

9.38b Disconnect the two wiring connectors and remove the unit from the car

9.41 Undo the bolt (arrowed) securing the refrigerant pipe block connection to the expansion valve

withdraw the refrigerant pipes from the valve **(see illustration)**. Note that new seals for the refrigerant pipes will be required for refitting. Suitably plug or cover the disconnected pipes.

42 Refit the bolt used to secure the refrigerant pipe block connection to the expansion valve and draw off the expansion valve.

43 Remove the expansion valve retaining plate.

44 Remove the engine/transmission rear mounting/torque link and transmission bracket as described in the relevant Part of Chapter 2, for access to the heater matrix condensation drain tube.

45 From under the car, unclip and carefully move aside the fuel and brake pipes in the area of the matrix condensation drain tube, then undo the two bolts securing the drain tube to the bulkhead **(see illustration 9.31)**.

46 Working in the engine compartment, use two hose clamps to clamp the hoses leading to the heater matrix. The hoses are located on the bulkhead, just above the steering gear. Alternatively, drain the cooling system completely as described in Chapter 1.

Many car accessory shops sell one-shot air conditioning recharge aerosols. These generally contain refrigerant, compressor oil, leak sealer and system conditioner. Some also have a dye to help pinpoint leaks.

⚠️ Warning: These products must only be used as directed by the manufacturer, and do not remove the need for regular maintenance.

47 Release the quick-release connectors by sliding them forward, and disconnect the two heater hoses from the heater matrix pipe stubs **(see illustration 9.27)**.

48 Remove the complete facia assembly and the facia crossmember as described in Chapter 11.

49 Remove the passenger's airbag as described in Chapter 12.

50 Remove the water deflector at the base of the windscreen as described in Chapter 11.

51 Working in the water deflector aperture, undo the four screws and remove the recirculating air valve housing grille. With the grille removed, undo the bolt now exposed securing the top of the air valve housing to the bulkhead **(see illustration 9.13)**.

52 Working in the engine compartment, undo the four bolts securing the air distribution housing to the bulkhead **(see illustrations 9.32a to 9.32c)**.

53 From inside the car, undo the bolts and remove the facia lower centre support brackets.

54 Disconnect the wiring connectors at the heater blower motor resistor.

55 Carefully withdraw the air distribution housing from the bulkhead. **Note:** *Keep the matrix unions uppermost as the housing is removed, to prevent coolant spillage.* Mop-up any spilt coolant immediately, and wipe the affected area with a damp cloth to prevent staining.

Refitting

56 Refitting is the reverse of removal. On completion, refill the cooling system as described in Chapter 1. On models with air conditioning, have the system evacuated, charged and leak-tested by the specialist who discharged it.

10 Air conditioning system – general information and precautions

General information

1 Air conditioning is standard on top of the range models, and optional on certain other models. It enables the temperature of incoming air to be lowered, and also dehumidifies the

10.6 Air conditioning system high-pressure service port (arrowed) . . .

air, which makes for rapid demisting and increased comfort.

2 The cooling side of the system works in the same way as a domestic refrigerator. Refrigerant gas is drawn into a belt-driven compressor, and passes into a condenser mounted in front of the radiator, where it loses heat and becomes liquid. The liquid passes through an expansion valve to an evaporator, where it changes from liquid under high pressure to gas under low pressure. This change is accompanied by a drop in temperature, which cools the evaporator. The refrigerant returns to the compressor, and the cycle begins again.

3 Air blown through the evaporator passes to the heater assembly, where it is mixed with hot air blown through the heater matrix, to achieve the desired temperature in the passenger compartment.

4 The heating side of the system works in the same way as on models without air conditioning (see Section 8).

5 The operation of the system is controlled electronically. Any problems with the system should be referred to a Vauxhall/Opel dealer or an air conditioning specialist **(see Tool tip)**.

Air conditioning service ports

Note: *The air conditioning service port location varies slightly according to model. The following is a general description of service port location.*

6 The high-pressure service port is the larger of the two service port connections and is located in front of the radiator. Remove the radiator grille as described in Chapter 11 for access **(see illustration)**.

7 The low-pressure service port is located at the rear right-hand side of the engine compartment **(see illustration)**.

Precautions

8 It is necessary to observe special precautions whenever dealing with any part of the system, its associated components, and any items which necessitate disconnection of the system.

⚠️ *Warning: The refrigeration circuit contains a liquid refrigerant. This refrigerant is potentially dangerous, and should only be handled by qualified persons. If it is splashed onto the*

10.7 . . . and low-pressure service port (arrowed)

skin, it can cause frostbite. It is not itself poisonous, but in the presence of a naked flame it forms a poisonous gas; inhalation of the vapour through a lighted cigarette could prove fatal. Uncontrolled discharging of the refrigerant is dangerous, and potentially damaging to the environment. Do not disconnect any part of the system unless it has been discharged by a Vauxhall/Opel dealer or an air conditioning specialist. Caution: Do not operate the air conditioning system if it is known to be short of refrigerant, as this may damage the compressor.

11 Air conditioning system components – removal and refitting

⚠️ **Warning: The air conditioning system is under high pressure. Do not loosen any fittings or remove any components until after the system has been discharged. Air conditioning refrigerant should be properly discharged into an approved type of container at a dealer service department or an automotive air conditioning repair facility capable of handling R134a refrigerant. Cap or plug the pipe lines as soon as they are disconnected, to prevent the entry of moisture. Always wear eye protection when disconnecting air conditioning system fittings.**

Note: *This Section refers to the components of the air conditioning system itself – refer to Sections 8 and 9 for details of components common to the heating/ventilation system.*

Compressor

Removal

1 Have the refrigerant discharged at a dealer service department or an automotive air conditioning repair facility.

2 Disconnect the battery negative terminal (refer to *Disconnecting the battery* in the Reference Chapter).

3 Firmly apply the handbrake, then jack up the front of the car and support it securely on axle stands (see *Jacking and vehicle support*).

4 Remove the auxiliary drivebelt as described in Chapter 1.

5 With the system discharged, undo the retaining bolt(s) and disconnect the refrigerant pipes from the compressor. Discard the O-ring seals – new ones must be used when refitting. Suitably cap the open fittings immediately to keep moisture and contamination out of the system.

6 Disconnect the compressor wiring connector.

7 Unbolt the compressor from the cylinder block/crankcase/sump, then withdraw the compressor from the vehicle.

Refitting

8 Refit the compressor in the reverse order of removal; renew all seals disturbed.

11.19 Cut off the evaporator cover on the air distribution housing, working in the groove around the cover periphery

9 If you are installing a new compressor, refer to the compressor manufacturer's instructions for adding refrigerant oil to the system.

10 Have the system evacuated, charged and leak-tested by the specialist that discharged it.

11 After installing a new compressor, always observe the following running-in procedure:
1) *Open all instrument panel air outlet flaps.*
2) *Start vehicle engine and stabilise idle speed for approximately 5 seconds.*
3) *Switch fan to maximum speed.*
4) *Switch on the air conditioning and let it run for at least 2 minutes without interruption at engine speed under 1500 rpm.*

Evaporator

Removal

12 Have the refrigerant discharged at a dealer service department or an automotive air conditioning repair facility.

13 Remove the recirculating air valve housing as described in Section 9.

14 From within the engine compartment, undo the bolt securing the refrigerant pipe block connection to the expansion valve and withdraw the refrigerant pipes from the valve **(see illustration 9.41)**. Note that new seals for the refrigerant pipes will be required for refitting. Suitably plug or cover the disconnected pipes.

15 Refit the bolt used to secure the refrigerant pipe block connection to the expansion valve and draw off the expansion valve.

16 Remove the expansion valve retaining plate.

17 Remove the pollen filter as described in Chapter 1.

18 On models equipped with a radio/glovebox cooling tube, unclip and remove the tube.

19 Using a sharp knife cut off the evaporator cover on the air distribution housing, working in the groove around the periphery of the cover **(see illustration)**. Note that a new cover will be required for refitting.

20 Carefully withdraw the evaporator from the side of the air distribution housing.

Refitting

21 Slide the evaporator in place in the air distribution housing.

22 Using a sharp knife, cut off the two internal webs in the new evaporator cover.

23 On models equipped with a radio/glovebox

11.30 Unclip the relays from the auxiliary cooling fan housing

cooling tube, lay the old evaporator cover on the new cover and mark the position of the cooling tube hole. Cut a cooling tube hole in the new cover using a suitable knife or tank cutter. Using suitable adhesive (Vauxhall/Opel part no 93160951) glue the radio/glovebox cooling tube in place on both sides.

24 Fit the new evaporator cover to the air distribution housing and secure with four screws in the holes provided on the air distribution housing.

25 The remainder of refitting is the reverse of removal ensuring that all disturbed pipe seals are renewed.

26 Have the system evacuated, charged and leak-tested by the specialist who discharged it.

Auxiliary cooling fan

Removal

27 Disconnect the battery negative terminal (refer to *Disconnecting the battery* in the Reference Chapter).

28 Apply the handbrake, then jack up the front of the vehicle and support it on axle stands (see *Jacking and vehicle support*).

29 Remove the front bumper as described in Chapter 11.

30 Unclip the relays, then release the cable ties securing the wiring harness to the auxiliary cooling fan housing **(see illustration)**.

31 Release and disconnect the wiring harness connector at the base of the fan housing.

32 Undo the two upper retaining nuts, then lift the fan and housing up and off the condenser **(see illustration)**. Remove the fan and housing from under the car.

11.32 Undo the two upper retaining nuts (arrowed), then lift the fan and housing up and off the condenser

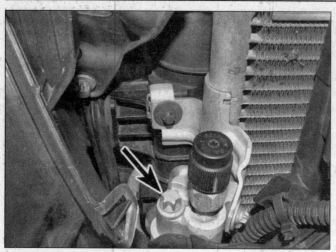

11.39a Undo the upper retaining bolt (arrowed) . . .

11.39b . . . and lower retaining bolt (arrowed) and disconnect the refrigerant pipe connector blocks from the condenser

Refitting

33 Refitting is the reverse of removal.

Condenser

Removal

34 Have the refrigerant discharged at a dealer service department or an automotive air conditioning repair facility.
35 Disconnect the battery negative terminal (refer to *Disconnecting the battery* in the Reference Chapter).
36 Apply the handbrake, then jack up the front of the vehicle and support it on axle stands (see *Jacking and vehicle support*).
37 Remove the front bumper as described in Chapter 11.
38 Remove the auxiliary cooling fan as described previously in this Section.
39 Undo the retaining bolts and disconnect the upper and lower refrigerant pipe connector blocks from the right-hand side of the condenser **(see illustrations)**. Discard the seals – new ones must be used when refitting. Suitably cap the open fittings immediately to keep moisture and contamination out of the system.

40 Disconnect the wiring connector from the pressure sensor on the right-hand side of the condenser.
41 Undo the four bolts securing the condenser to the radiator **(see illustrations 3.17a to 3.17d)**. Carefully lower the condenser and remove it from under the car.

Refitting

42 Refitting is the reverse of removal ensuring that all disturbed pipe seals are renewed.
43 Have the system evacuated, charged and leak-tested by the specialist who discharged it.

Chapter 4 Part A:
Fuel and exhaust systems

Contents

Degrees of difficulty

Easy, suitable for novice with little experience 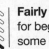	**Fairly easy,** suitable for beginner with some experience	**Fairly difficult,** suitable for competent DIY mechanic	**Difficult,** suitable for experienced DIY mechanic	**Very difficult,** suitable for expert DIY or professional

Specifications

System type

1.3 litre engines	Magneti-Marelli 6JO high-pressure direct injection 'common-rail' system electronically controlled
1.7 and 1.9 litre engines	Bosch EDC 16C9 or EDC 16C39 high-pressure direct injection 'common-rail' system, electronically controlled

Fuel system data

1.3 litre engines

Firing order.	1–3–4–2 (No 1 at timing chain end of engine)
Fuel system operating pressure.	1600 bar at 2200 rpm
Idle speed.	Controlled by ECU
Maximum speed.	Controlled by ECU
High-pressure fuel pump:	
Type	Bosch CP1H or Bosch CP3.2
Fuel supply pump:	
Type	Electric, mounted in fuel tank
Delivery pressure	3.3 bar (maximum)
Injectors:	
Type	Bosch CRIP 2-MI

Fuel system data (continued)

1.7 and 1.9 litre engines

Firing order	1–3–4–2 (No 1 at timing belt end of engine)
Fuel system operating pressure	1400 to 1600 bar at 2200 rpm
Idle speed	Controlled by ECU
Maximum speed	Controlled by ECU
High-pressure fuel pump:	
Type:	
1.7 litre engines	Bosch CP3.2
1.9 litre engines	Bosch CP1H
Fuel supply pump (1.9 litre engines):	
Type	Electric, mounted in fuel tank
Delivery pressure	3.3 bar (maximum)
Injectors:	
Type	Bosch CRIP 2-MI

Torque wrench settings

	Nm	lbf ft
1.3 litre engines		
Catalytic converter support bracket to sump reinforcement bracket	25	18
Catalytic converter-to-turbocharger nuts	25	18
Camshaft position sensor retaining bolt	7	5
Coolant pipe-to-heat exchanger bolts	9	7
Crankshaft speed/position sensor retaining bolt	9	7
EGR valve bolts	22	16
Exhaust manifold nuts*:		
Stage 1	15	11
Stage 2	Angle-tighten a further 30°	
Exhaust system clamp nuts	50	37
Fuel injector clamp bracket nuts	20	15
Fuel pressure regulator to fuel rail	60	44
Fuel pressure sensor to fuel rail	70	52
Fuel rail-to-mounting bracket bolts	25	18
Fuel rail mounting bracket-to-camshaft housing bolts	25	18
High-pressure fuel pipe unions:		
M12 union nuts	25	18
M14 union nuts	28	21
High-pressure fuel pump mounting bolts	15	11
Inlet manifold bolts	25	18
Injector retaining clamp nut	20	15
Oil filter housing to cylinder block	9	7
Throttle housing retaining bolts	9	7
Turbocharger oil return pipe bolts	9	7
Turbocharger oil supply pipe banjo union bolts	12	9
Turbocharger to exhaust manifold	25	18
1.7 litre engines		
Catalytic converter heat shield bolts	12	9
Catalytic converter-to-turbocharger nuts	25	18
EGR valve heat exchanger pipe flange bolts	28	21
EGR valve heat exchanger to camshaft housing	25	18
Exhaust manifold nuts/bolts	70	52
Exhaust system clamp nuts	50	37
Exhaust system front pipe to catalytic converter	20	15
Fuel injector clamp bracket bolt:		
Stage 1	40	30
Stage 2	Slacken bolt	
Stage 3	32	24
High-pressure fuel pipe unions	25	18
Inlet manifold nuts/bolts	25	18
Throttle housing mounting bracket bolts	25	18
Throttle housing to charge air pipe elbow	10	7
Turbocharger oil supply pipe banjo union bolts:		
Cylinder block union	28	21
Turbocharger union	20	15
Turbocharger to exhaust manifold*	27	20

Torque wrench settings (continued)

	Nm	lbf ft
1.9 litre engines		
Alternator and high-pressure fuel pump bracket bolts	25	18
Camshaft sensor retaining bolt(s).	9	7
Catalytic converter clamp bolt.	20	15
Charge (boost) pressure sensor retaining bolts	9	7
Crankshaft speed/position sensor retaining bolt	9	7
EGR valve pipe to exhaust manifold	25	18
Exhaust manifold nuts*.	25	18
Exhaust front pipe-to-catalytic converter nuts*	20	15
Exhaust system clamp nuts	50	37
Fuel injector clamp bracket nuts:		
Z19DT engines.	32	24
Z19DTH engines.	25	18
Fuel pressure regulator to fuel rail	60	44
Fuel pressure sensor to fuel rail	70	52
Fuel rail retaining nuts/bolts.	25	18
High-pressure fuel pipe unions	23	17
High-pressure fuel pump mounting nuts	25	18
Inlet manifold nuts	25	18
Injector clamp bracket nut	25	18
Throttle housing bolts:		
Z19DT engines.	25	18
Z19DTH engines.	9	7
Turbocharger oil return pipe bolts:		
M6 bolts	9	7
M8 bolts	25	18
Turbocharger oil supply pipe banjo union bolt.	15	11

* Use new fasteners

1 General information and precautions

General information

All engines are fitted with a high-pressure direct injection system which incorporates the very latest in diesel injection technology. On this system, a high-pressure fuel pump is used purely to provide the pressure required for the injection system and has no control over the injection timing (unlike conventional diesel injection systems). The injection timing is controlled by the electronic control unit (ECU) via the electrically-operated injectors. The system operates as follows.

The fuel system consists of a fuel tank (which is mounted under the rear of the car), a fuel filter with integral water separator, a high-pressure fuel pump, injectors and associated components. 1.3 and 1.9 litre engines also contain an electric fuel supply pump mounted inside the fuel tank.

Fuel is supplied to the fuel filter housing which is located in the engine compartment. The fuel filter removes all foreign matter and water and ensures that the fuel supplied to the pump is clean.

The fuel is heated to ensure no problems occur when the ambient temperature is very low. This is achieved by an electrically-operated fuel heater incorporated in the filter housing, the heater is controlled by the ECU.

The high-pressure fuel pump is driven at half-crankshaft speed by the timing belt/chain. The high-pressure required in the system (up to 1600 bar) is produced by the three pistons in the pump. The high-pressure pump supplies high-pressure fuel to the fuel rail, which acts as a reservoir for the four injectors.

The electrical control system consists of the ECU, along with the following sensors:

a) *Accelerator pedal position sensor – informs the ECU of the accelerator pedal position, and the rate of throttle opening/closing.*

b) *Coolant temperature sensor – informs the ECU of engine temperature.*

c) *Airflow meter – informs the ECU of the amount of air passing through the intake duct.*

d) *Crankshaft sensor – informs the ECU of the crankshaft position and speed of rotation.*

e) *Camshaft sensor – informs the ECU of the positions of the pistons.*

f) *Charge (boost) pressure sensor – informs ECU of the pressure in the inlet manifold.*

g) *Fuel pressure sensor – informs the ECU of the fuel pressure present in the fuel rail.*

h) *ABS control unit – informs the ECU of the vehicle speed.*

All the above signals are analysed by the ECU which selects the fuelling response appropriate to those values. The ECU controls the fuel injectors (varying the pulse width – the length of time the injectors are held open – to provide a richer or weaker mixture, as appropriate). The mixture is constantly varied by the ECU, to provide the best setting for cranking, starting (with either a hot or cold engine), warm-up, idle, cruising and acceleration.

The ECU also has full control over the fuel pressure present in the fuel rail via the high-pressure fuel regulator and third piston deactivator solenoid valve which are fitted to the high-pressure pump. To reduce the pressure, the ECU opens the high-pressure fuel regulator which allows the excess fuel to return direct to the tank from the pump. The third piston deactivator is used mainly to reduce the load on the engine, but can also be used to lower the fuel pressure. The deactivator solenoid valve relieves the fuel pressure from the third piston of the pump which results in only two of the pistons pressurising the fuel system.

The ECU also controls the exhaust gas recirculation (EGR) system, described in detail in Part B of this Chapter, the pre/post-heating system (see Chapter 5), and the engine cooling fan.

On 1.7 and 1.9 litre engines, the inlet manifold is fitted with a butterfly valve (changeover flap) arrangement to improve efficiency at low engine speeds. Each cylinder has two intake tracts in the manifold, one of which is fitted with a valve; the operation of the valve is controlled by the ECU via a vacuum solenoid (1.7 litre engines) or by an electric motor actuator drive arrangement (1.9 litre engines). At low engine speeds (below approximately 1500 rpm) the valves remain closed, meaning that air entering each cylinder is passing through only one of the two manifold tracts. At higher engine speeds, the ECU opens up each of the four valves allowing the air passing through the manifold to pass through both inlet tracts.

2.4 Typical plastic plug and cap set for sealing disconnected fuel pipes and components

A variable-vane turbocharger is fitted to increases engine efficiency. It does this by raising the pressure in the inlet manifold above atmospheric pressure. Instead of the air simply being sucked into the cylinders, it is forced in.

Between the turbocharger and the inlet manifold, the compressed air passes through an intercooler. This is an air-to-air heat exchanger mounted in front of the radiator, and supplied with cooling air from the front of the vehicle. The purpose of the intercooler is to remove some of the heat gained in being compressed from the inlet air. Because cooler air is denser, removal of this heat further increases engine efficiency.

Energy for the operation of the turbocharger comes from the exhaust gas. The gas flows through a specially-shaped housing (the turbine housing) and in so doing, spins the turbine wheel. The turbine wheel is attached to a shaft, at the end of which is another vaned wheel known as the compressor wheel. The compressor wheel spins in its own housing, and compresses the inlet air on the way to the inlet manifold. The turbo shaft is pressure-lubricated by an oil feed pipe from the main oil gallery. The shaft 'floats' on a cushion of oil. A drain pipe returns the oil to the sump. Boost pressure (the pressure in the inlet manifold) is limited by a wastegate, which diverts the exhaust gas away from the turbine wheel in response to a pressure-sensitive actuator.

2.6 Two crow-foot adapters will be necessary for tightening the fuel pipe unions

If certain sensors fail, and send abnormal signals to the ECU, the ECU has a back-up programme. In this event, the abnormal signals are ignored, and a pre-programmed value is substituted for the sensor signal, allowing the engine to continue running, albeit at reduced efficiency. If the ECU enters its back-up mode, a warning light on the instrument panel will illuminate, and a fault code will be stored in the ECU memory. This fault code can be read using suitable specialist test equipment plugged into the system's diagnostic socket.

Precautions

⚠️ *Warning: It is necessary to take certain precautions when working on the fuel system components, particularly the high-pressure side of the system. Before carrying out any operations on the fuel system, refer to the precautions given in 'Safety first!' at the beginning of this manual, and to any additional warning notes at the start of the relevant Sections. Also refer to the additional information contained in Section 2.*

Caution: Do not operate the engine if any of air intake ducts are disconnected or the filter element is removed. Any debris entering the engine will cause severe damage to the turbocharger.

Caution: To prevent damage to the turbocharger, do not race the engine immediately after start-up, especially if it is cold. Allow it to idle smoothly to give the oil a few seconds to circulate around the turbocharger bearings. Always allow the engine to return to idle speed before switching it off – do not blip the throttle and switch off, as this will leave the turbo spinning without lubrication.

Caution: Observe the recommended intervals for oil and filter changing, and use a reputable oil of the specified quality. Neglect of oil changing, or use of inferior oil, can cause carbon formation on the turbo shaft, leading to subsequent failure.

2 High-pressure diesel injection system – special information

Warnings and precautions

1 It is essential to observe strict precautions when working on the fuel system components, particularly the high-pressure side of the system. Before carrying out any operations on the fuel system, refer to the precautions given in *Safety first!* at the beginning of this manual, and to the following additional information.

• Do not carry out any repair work on the high-pressure fuel system unless you are competent to do so, have all the necessary tools and equipment required, and are aware of the safety implications involved.

• Before starting any repair work on the fuel system, wait at least 30 seconds after switching off the engine to allow the fuel circuit to return to atmospheric pressure.

• Never work on the high-pressure fuel system with the engine running.

• Keep well clear of any possible source of fuel leakage, particularly when starting the engine after carrying out repair work. A leak in the system could cause an extremely high-pressure jet of fuel to escape, which could result in severe personal injury.

• Never place your hands or any part of your body near to a leak in the high-pressure fuel system.

• Do not use steam cleaning equipment or compressed air to clean the engine or any of the fuel system components.

Repair procedures and general information

2 Strict cleanliness must be observed at all times when working on any part of the fuel system. This applies to the working area in general, the person doing the work, and the components being worked on.

3 Before working on the fuel system components, they must be thoroughly cleaned with a suitable degreasing fluid. Cleanliness is particularly important when working on the fuel system connections at the following components:

   a) Fuel filter.
   b) High-pressure fuel pump.
   c) Fuel rail.
   d) Fuel injectors.
   e) High-pressure fuel pipes.

4 After disconnecting any fuel pipes or components, the open union or orifice must be immediately sealed to prevent the entry of dirt or foreign material. Plastic plugs and caps in various sizes are available in packs from motor factors and accessory outlets, and are particularly suitable for this application **(see illustration)**. Fingers cut from disposable rubber gloves should be used to protect components such as fuel pipes, fuel injectors and wiring connectors, and can be secured in place using elastic bands. Suitable gloves of this type are available at no cost from most petrol station forecourts.

5 Whenever any of the high-pressure fuel pipes are disconnected or removed, a new pipe(s) must be obtained for refitting.

6 The torque wrench settings given in the Specifications must be strictly observed when tightening component mountings and connections. This is particularly important when tightening the high-pressure fuel pipe unions. To enable a torque wrench to be used on the fuel pipe unions, two crow-foot adapters are required. Suitable types are available from motor factors and accessory outlets **(see illustration)**.

3.1 Disconnect the wiring connector from the airflow meter – 1.7 litre engine shown

3.2 Detach the flexible air intake duct from the turbocharger charge air pipe – 1.7 litre engine shown

3.4 Undo the retaining screw (arrowed) and release the air cleaner housing mounting bracket

3 Air cleaner assembly and intake ducts – removal and refitting

Removal

1 Disconnect the wiring connector from the side of the airflow meter **(see illustration)**.

2 Slacken the retaining clip and detach the flexible air intake duct from the turbocharger charge air pipe **(see illustration)**.

3 Where applicable, unclip the vacuum hose or wiring harness from the side of the air cleaner housing.

4 Undo the retaining screw and release the mounting bracket at the rear of the air cleaner housing **(see illustration)**.

5 Detach the air intake duct at the front of the air cleaner housing **(see illustration)**.

6 Lift the housing upwards at the rear, then disengage the front mounting rubber from the body bracket.

7 When sufficient clearance exists, release the retaining clip and disconnect the water drain tube from the base of the air cleaner housing **(see illustration)**. Remove the assembly from the engine compartment.

8 The various air intake ducts and charge air pipes/hoses linking the intercooler to the manifold and turbocharger can be disconnected and removed once the retaining clips have been slackened **(see illustration)**. In some cases it will be necessary to disconnect breather hoses, vacuum pipes and wiring connectors to allow the pipe/duct to be removed; the pipe/duct may also be bolted to a support bracket.

Refitting

9 Refitting is the reverse of removal, making sure all the air intake ducts and charge air pipes/hoses are securely reconnected.

4 Accelerator pedal/ position sensor – removal and refitting

Removal

1 Disconnect the battery negative terminal (refer to *Disconnecting the battery* in the Reference Chapter).

3.5 Detach the air intake duct at the front of the air cleaner housing

3.7 Release the clip and disconnect the water drain tube from the base of the air cleaner housing

3.8 Typical air intake duct arrangement

1 Air cleaner assembly	8 Intercooler charge air pipe hose
2 Airflow meter	connection
3 Upper intake duct	10 Charge air hose
4 Inlet manifold charge air pipe	11 Resonator
5 Turbocharger charge air pipe	12 Air cleaner intake duct
6 Inlet manifold charge air pipe	13 Inlet manifold
connection hose	14 Turbocharger
7 Intercooler	

4.3 Disconnect the wiring connector (arrowed) from the accelerator pedal/ position sensor

2 Undo the two screws and remove the facia lower panel on the driver's side.

3 Working in the driver's footwell under the facia, disconnect the wiring connector from the top of the accelerator pedal/position sensor **(see illustration)**.

4 Unscrew the three mounting nuts, and withdraw the sensor from the bulkhead.

Refitting

5 Refitting is a reversal of removal.

5 Fuel system – priming and bleeding

1 After disconnecting part of the fuel supply system or running out of fuel, it is necessary to prime the fuel system and bleed off any air which may have entered the system components, as follows.

2 Prime the system by switching on the ignition three times for approximately 15 seconds each time. Operate the starter for a maximum of 30 seconds. If the engine does not start within this time, wait 5 seconds and repeat the procedure.

3 When the engine starts, run it at a fast idle speed for a minute or so to purge any trapped air from the fuel lines. After this time the engine should idle smoothly at a constant speed.

4 If the engine idles roughly, then there is still some air trapped in the fuel system. Increase the engine speed again for another minute or so then allow it to idle. Repeat this procedure as necessary until the engine is idling smoothly.

6 Fuel gauge sender unit – removal and refitting

Note 1: *Vauxhall/Opel special tool KM-797 (or suitable alternative) will be required to remove and refit the fuel pump cover locking ring, and special tool KM-6391 (or suitable alternative) will be required to remove the in-tank module from the fuel tank.*

Note 2: *A new fuel pump cover sealing ring will be required on refitting.*

Note 3: *The fuel tank should be as empty as possible when carrying out this procedure.*

Removal

1 Disconnect the battery negative terminal (refer to *Disconnecting the battery* in the Reference Chapter).

2 Remove the rear seat cushion as described in Chapter 11.

3 Lift up the sound insulation reveal the fuel tank access cover.

4 Using a screwdriver, carefully prise the plastic access cover from the floor **(see illustration)**.

5 Disconnect the wiring connector from the fuel supply pump cover, and tape the connector to the vehicle body, to prevent it disappearing behind the tank **(see illustration)**.

6 Mark the fuel hoses for identification purposes. The hoses are equipped with quick-release fittings to ease removal. To disconnect each hose, compress the clips located on each side of the fitting and ease the fitting off of its union **(see illustration)**. Plug the hose ends to minimise fuel loss.

7 Using the Vauxhall/Opel special tool, unscrew the locking ring and remove it from the tank **(see illustration)**.

8 Make identification marks on the fuel pump cover and the body to ensure that the cover is refitted in its original position. There may be an arrow stamped on the cover; if so note its direction.

9 Carefully lift the fuel pump cover away from tank and remove the cover sealing ring **(see illustration)**.

10 Disconnect the wiring connector(s) from the underside of the fuel pump cover **(see illustration)**.

11 Depress the retaining tabs and lift the fuel pump or fuel filter (according to model) out of

6.4 Carefully prise the plastic access cover from the floor

6.5 Disconnect the wiring connector from the fuel supply pump cover

6.6 Disconnect the fuel hoses at the quick-release fittings

6.7 Unscrew the locking ring and remove it from the tank

6.9 Lift the fuel pump cover away from tank and remove the cover sealing ring

6.10 Disconnect the wiring connector(s) from the underside of the fuel pump cover

6.11 Depress the retaining tabs and lift the fuel pump or fuel filter (according to model) out of the in-tank module

the in-tank module (see illustration). Place the assembly to one side.

12 To remove the in-tank module (containing the gauge sender unit) from the fuel tank, Vauxhall/Opel special tool KM-6391, or a suitable alternative will be required. The special tool consists of four metal strips that are inserted down the sides of the in-tank module, to release the module from the four tabs of the mounting bracket, which remains in the tank. In the absence of the special tool a suitable alternative can be easily made (see Tool Tip).

13 Carefully insert the four tools down through the slots on the side of the in-tank module until they engage and release the four retaining tabs in the tank mounting bracket (see illustrations). Move the float arm on the sender unit slightly when inserting the tool adjacent to the sender unit.

An in-tank module removal tool can be made from 3 mm thick steel strip, approximately 150 mm long and 26 mm wide. Cut or file a 12 mm slot in one end of the tool and put a slight bend in the tool at the other end, approximately 100 mm from the slotted end. Note that 4 of these tools will be required to remove the module.

14 Once the tabs in the tank mounting bracket are released, carefully lift the in-tank module up and out of the fuel tank (see illustration).

15 With the assembly on the bench, release the two retaining tabs and lift the fuel gauge sender unit up and out of the in-tank module (see illustrations).

Refitting

16 Refit the gauge sender unit to the in-tank module ensuring that the retaining tabs positively engage.

17 Manoeuvre the in-tank module carefully in through the tank aperture and push it down onto the retaining tabs of the tank mounting bracket. Ensure that the retaining tabs audibly engage with the module.

18 Locate the fuel pump or fuel filter into the in-tank module and engage the retaining tabs.

19 Reconnect the wiring connector(s) to the fuel pump cover, and place a new sealing ring in position on the tank. Locate the cover on the tank and align the marks, or direction arrow in the position noted during removal.

20 Refit the locking ring and tighten it with the special tool until it locks in place.

21 Reconnect the fuel hoses to the pump cover, using the marks made on removal, then reconnect the wiring connector.

22 Reconnect the battery then start the engine and check for fuel leaks. If all is well, refit the access cover and sound insulation, then refit the seat cushion.

7 Fuel supply pump (1.3 and 1.9 litre engines) – removal and refitting

1 On 1.3 and 1.9 litre engines, the diesel fuel supply pump is located in the in-tank module in the fuel tank. The removal and refitting procedures are the same as for the fuel gauge sender unit described in Section 6. The pump is integral with the in-tank module and cannot be renewed separately.

2 A fuel supply pump is not fitted to 1.7 litre engines.

6.13a Carefully insert the removal tools down through the slots on the side of the in-tank module . . .

6.13b . . . push the tools down into the slots . . .

6.13c . . . until they release the four retaining tabs (arrowed) in the tank mounting bracket (shown with in-tank module removed)

6.14 With the tabs in the mounting bracket released, lift the in-tank module up and out of the fuel tank

6.15a Release the two retaining tabs . . .

6.15b . . . and lift the fuel gauge sender unit up and out of the in-tank module

8.5 Disconnect the fuel feed and return line at the underbody quick-release connectors (arrowed)

8.6 Unclip the handbrake cables from the fuel tank retaining straps (arrowed)

Refitting

15 Refitting is the reverse of the removal procedure, noting the following points:

a) *When lifting the tank back into position, take care to ensure that none of the hoses become trapped between the tank and vehicle body. Refit the retaining straps and tighten the bolts securely.*

b) *Ensure all pipes and hoses are correctly routed and all hoses unions are securely joined.*

c) *On completion, refill the tank with a small amount of fuel, and check for signs of leakage prior to taking the vehicle out on the road.*

---

8 Fuel tank –
removed and refitting

Note 1: *Refer to the information contained in Section 2 before proceeding.*
Note 2: *The fuel tank should be as empty as possible when carrying out this procedure.*

Removal

1 Disconnect the battery negative terminal (refer to *Disconnecting the battery* in the Reference Chapter).

2 Before removing the fuel tank, all fuel must be drained from the tank. Since a fuel tank drain plug is not provided, it is therefore preferable to carry out the removal operation when the tank is nearly empty. The remaining fuel can then be syphoned or hand-pumped from the tank.

3 Remove the exhaust system and relevant heat shield(s) as described in Section 33.

4 Disconnect the wiring for the gauge sender unit and, where applicable, the fuel supply pump at the underbody connector adjacent to the fuel tank. Unclip the wiring harness from the retaining clips.

5 Disconnect the fuel feed and return line at the underbody quick-release connectors on the left-hand side of the tank **(see illustration)**. Be prepared for some loss of fuel. A Vauxhall/Opel special tool is available to release the fuel line connectors, but provided care is taken, the connectors can be released using a pair of long-nosed pliers, or a similar tool, to

depress the retaining tangs. Suitably plug the disconnected fuel and vent hoses to prevent entry of dust and dirt.

6 Unclip the handbrake cables from the fuel tank and fuel tank retaining straps **(see illustration)**.

7 Place a suitable container under the tank, then release the retaining clamps and disconnect the fuel filler connection hose from the fuel tank and fuel filler pipe. Collect the escaping fuel in the container.

8 Support the weight of the fuel tank on a jack with interposed block of wood.

9 Undo the four bolts and remove the two securing straps from the fuel tank.

10 Slowly lower the tank and when sufficient clearance exists, disconnect the fuel filler vent hose.

11 Continue to lower the tank until it can be removed from under the vehicle.

12 If necessary, remove the fuel lines and hoses, heat shield and wiring from the tank for transfer to the new tank. If a new tank is being fitted, it is recommended that the filter is renewed at the same time.

13 If the tank contains sediment or water, it may cleaned out with two or three rinses of clean fuel. Remove the fuel gauge sender unit as described in Section 6. Shake the tank vigorously, and change the fuel as necessary to remove all contamination from the tank.

14 Any repairs to the fuel tank should be carried out by a professional. Do not under any circumstances attempt any form of DIY repair to a fuel tank.

---

9 Fuel filter crash box –
removal and refitting

Removal

1 The fuel filter and crash box are located at the rear of the engine compartment, in the centre of the bulkhead.

2 Remove the water deflector at the base of the windscreen as described in Chapter 11, Section 20.

3 Disconnect the heater element wiring connector from the fuel filter cover and, where fitted, the water level sensor wiring connector from the base of the filter housing **(see illustration)**.

4 Unclip the fuel hoses and vacuum hose from the side of the crash box.

5 Using a screwdriver inserted from the right-hand side, depress the retaining clip and lift the filter from the crash box **(see illustration)**.

6 Working in the water deflector aperture, undo the two nuts securing the crash box to the bulkhead **(see illustration)**.

7 Remove the reinforcement plate and remove the crash box from the bulkhead.

Refitting

8 Refitting is the reverse of the removal procedure.

9.3 Disconnect the heater element wiring connector (arrowed) from the fuel filter cover

9.5 Lift the filter from the crash box

9.6 Undo the two nuts (arrowed) securing the crash box to the bulkhead

10 Injection system electrical components – testing

1 If a fault is suspected in the electronic control side of the system, first ensure that all the wiring connectors are securely connected and free of corrosion. Ensure that the suspected problem is not of a mechanical nature, or due to poor maintenance; ie, check that the air cleaner filter element is clean, the engine breather hoses are clear and undamaged, and that the cylinder compression pressures are correct, referring to Chapter 1 and the relevant Parts of Chapter 2.

2 If these checks fail to reveal the cause of the problem, the vehicle should be taken to a Vauxhall/Opel dealer or suitably-equipped engine management diagnostic specialist for testing.

3 A diagnostic socket is located in the centre console, to which a fault code reader or other suitable test equipment can be connected. Unclip and remove the trim panel beneath the handbrake lever for access **(see illustrations)**. By using the code reader or test equipment, the engine management ECU (and the various other vehicle system ECUs) can be interrogated, and any stored fault codes can be retrieved. This will allow the fault to be quickly and simply traced, alleviating the need to test all the system components individually, which is a time-consuming operation that carries a risk of damaging the ECU.

11 Injection system electrical components (1.3 litre engines) – removal and refitting

Airflow meter

1 Disconnect the airflow meter wiring connector **(see illustration)**.

2 Slacken the retaining clip securing the air intake duct to the airflow meter and disconnect the duct.

3 Slacken the retaining clip and remove the airflow meter from the elbow on the air cleaner housing lid.

4 Refitting is a reversal of removal, but ensure

10.3a Unclip and remove the trim panel beneath the handbrake lever . . .

that the arrow on the airflow meter points toward the throttle housing when fitted.

Throttle housing

5 Lift off the plastic cover over the top of the engine.

6 Slacken the two retaining clips and disconnect the charge air hose from the intercooler and charge air pipe elbow.

7 Undo the two bolts and remove the charge air pipe elbow from the throttle housing. Recover the seal.

8 Disconnect the vacuum hose from the throttle housing solenoid valve.

9 Undo the three retaining bolts and remove the throttle housing from the inlet manifold. Note the location of any wiring harness support brackets also secured by the retaining bolts.

10 Refitting is a reversal of removal, but thoroughly clean the mating faces and use a new seal on the charge air pipe elbow. Tighten the retaining bolts to the specified torque.

Crankshaft speed/position sensor

11 Lift off the plastic cover over the top of the engine.

12 The crankshaft speed/position sensor is located on the front of the cylinder block, in-line with the flywheel.

13 Disconnect the sensor wiring connector, then undo the retaining bolt and remove the sensor from the cylinder block **(see illustration)**.

14 Refitting is a reversal of removal, tightening the retaining bolt securely.

10.3b . . . for access to the diagnostic socket (arrowed)

Camshaft position sensor

15 Lift off the plastic cover over the top of the engine.

16 The camshaft position sensor is located on the front right-hand side of the camshaft housing, above the exhaust camshaft **(see illustration)**.

17 Disconnect the sensor wiring connector, then undo the retaining bolt and remove the sensor from the camshaft housing.

18 Refitting is a reversal of removal, tightening the retaining bolt securely.

Coolant temperature sensor

19 Refer to the procedures contained in Chapter 3.

Charge (boost) pressure sensor

20 Lift off the plastic cover over the top of the engine.

21 The charge pressure sensor is located on the upper face of the inlet manifold, near the centre. For improved access, remove the turbocharger charge air pipe.

22 Using a small screwdriver, lift up the locking catch and disconnect the sensor wiring connector **(see illustration)**.

23 Undo the retaining bolt and withdraw the sensor from the manifold. Recover the sealing O-ring.

24 Renew the sealing O-ring, then refit the sensor and tighten the retaining bolt securely. Reconnect the wiring connector and secure with the locking catch.

25 If removed, refit the charge air pipe, then refit the engine cover.

11.1 Airflow meter wiring connector (A) and retaining clips (B)

11.13 Undo the retaining bolt and remove the crankshaft speed/position sensor from the cylinder block

11.16 Camshaft position sensor location (arrowed)

11.22 Lift up the locking catch to disconnect the charge (boost) pressure sensor wiring connector

Fuel pressure regulator

26 Disconnect the battery negative terminal (refer to *Disconnecting the battery* in the Reference Chapter).

27 Lift off the plastic cover over the top of the engine.

28 Release the quick-release fitting and disconnect the crankcase ventilation hose from the turbocharger charge air pipe **(see illustration)**.

29 Disconnect the wiring connector from the fuel pressure regulator.

30 Remove the regulator from the fuel rail by unscrewing the inner nut (nearest the fuel rail) while counterholding the regulator body with a second spanner. Be prepared for some loss of fuel.

31 Refitting is the reverse of removal, tightening the regulator to the specified torque.

Fuel pressure sensor

32 Lift off the plastic cover over the top of the engine.

33 The fuel pressure sensor is located at the right-hand end of the fuel rail.

34 Disconnect the sensor wiring connector, then unscrew the sensor from the fuel rail **(see illustration 17.8a)**.

35 Refitting is a reversal of removal, tightening the sensor to the specified torque.

Electronic control unit (ECU)

Note: *If a new ECU is to be fitted, this work must be entrusted to a Vauxhall/Opel dealer or suitably-equipped specialist. It is necessary to initialise the new ECU after installation, which*

12.1 Disconnect the airflow meter wiring connector

11.28 Disconnect the crankcase ventilation hose (arrowed) from the turbocharger charge air pipe

requires the use of dedicated diagnostic equipment.

36 Disconnect the battery negative terminal (refer to *Disconnecting the battery* in the Reference Chapter).

37 Firmly apply the handbrake, then jack up the front of the car and support it securely on axle stands (see *Jacking and vehicle support*). Remove the left-hand roadwheel.

38 Undo the two bolts, remove the three plastic rivets and detach the front part of the wheel arch liner from the bumper and underbody.

39 Withdraw the locking plates, lift the locking levers and disconnect the two wiring connectors from the ECU.

40 Undo the four nuts securing the ECU to its mounting frame and remove the ECU from under the bumper.

41 Refitting is a reversal of removal, ensuring that the wiring connectors are securely connected and locked with the locking levers.

Turbocharger wastegate solenoid

42 The wastegate (charge pressure) solenoid valve is located under the front bumper on the right-hand side.

43 Firmly apply the handbrake, then jack up the front of the car and support it securely on axle stands (see *Jacking and vehicle support*).

44 Disconnect the wiring connector and the two vacuum hoses from the valve then undo the retaining nuts and remove the valve from its mounting bracket.

45 Refitting is the reverse of removal.

12.2 Slacken the clip (arrowed) securing the air intake duct to the airflow meter and disconnect the duct

Wheel speed sensors

46 Refer to the anti-lock braking system information contained in Chapter 9.

12 Injection system electrical components (1.7 litre engines) – removal and refitting

Airflow meter

1 Disconnect the airflow meter wiring connector **(see illustration)**.

2 Slacken the retaining clip securing the air intake duct to the airflow meter and disconnect the duct **(see illustration)**.

3 Slacken the retaining clip and remove the airflow meter from the elbow on the air cleaner housing lid.

4 Refitting is a reversal of removal, but ensure that the arrow on the airflow meter points toward the throttle housing when fitted.

Throttle housing

5 Lift off the plastic cover over the top of the engine.

6 Slacken the retaining clip and disconnect the charge air hose from the throttle housing.

7 Disconnect the throttle housing wiring connector **(see illustration)**.

8 Undo the bolts securing the throttle housing to the mounting bracket, and the bolts securing the mounting bracket to the camshaft housing. Remove the mounting bracket.

9 Undo the four bolts securing the throttle housing to the charge air pipe elbow and remove the housing from the engine. Recover the seal.

10 Refitting is a reversal of removal, but thoroughly clean the mating faces and use a new seal on the charge air pipe elbow. Tighten the retaining bolts to the specified torque.

Crankshaft speed/position sensor

11 The sensor is located at the rear of the cylinder block, below the starter motor. To gain access, firmly apply the handbrake, then jack up the front of the car and support it securely on axle stands (see *Jacking and vehicle support*).

12 Wipe clean the area around the crankshaft sensor then disconnect the wiring connector.

12.7 Disconnect the throttle housing wiring connector

12.13 Remove the crankshaft speed/ position sensor and recover the sealing ring

12.17a Disconnect the camshaft sensor wiring connector . . .

12.17b . . . then undo the sensor retaining bolt (arrowed) and remove the sensor from the mounting bracket

13 Slacken and remove the retaining bolt and remove the sensor from the cylinder block **(see illustration)**. Recover the sealing ring.

14 Refitting is the reverse of removal, using a new sealing ring. Tighten the sensor retaining bolt securely.

Camshaft position sensor

15 Lift off the plastic cover over the top of the engine.

16 The camshaft position sensor is located on the front right-hand side of the camshaft housing, adjacent to the exhaust camshaft sprocket.

17 Disconnect the camshaft sensor wiring connector, then undo the sensor retaining bolt and remove the sensor from the mounting bracket **(see illustrations)**.

18 Refitting is a reversal of removal, tightening the retaining bolt securely.

Coolant temperature sensor

19 Refer to the procedures contained in Chapter 3.

Charge (boost) pressure sensor

20 Lift off the plastic cover over the top of the engine.

21 The charge pressure sensor is located on the right-hand side of the inlet manifold below the changeover flap vacuum actuator.

22 Slacken the retaining clips and remove the flexible air intake hose connecting the airflow meter to the charge air pipe.

23 Release the locking catches securing the wiring connectors to the four fuel injectors then disconnect the injector wiring.

24 Disconnect the wiring from the glow plugs by squeezing the connectors with thumb and forefinger, and pulling them from the plugs.

25 Undo the two bolts securing the wiring harness guide to the camshaft cover, then move the wiring harness to one side.

26 Disconnect the fuel leak-off hose connection at each injector by pushing in the locking clip and lifting out the hose fitting. Suitably plug or cover the open unions to prevent dirt entry.

27 Unscrew the nut and two bolts securing the injector leak-off hose assembly to the camshaft cover and changeover flap vacuum actuator and move the hose assembly to one side.

28 Unscrew the two stud bolts securing the changeover flap vacuum actuator to the inlet manifold. Carefully lift the actuator upwards slightly for access to the charge pressure sensor.

29 Using a small screwdriver, lift up the locking catch and disconnect the sensor wiring connector.

30 Undo the retaining bolt and withdraw the sensor from the manifold. Recover the sealing O-ring.

31 Renew the sealing O-ring, then refit the sensor and tighten the retaining bolt securely. Reconnect the wiring connector and secure with the locking catch.

32 Place the changeover flap vacuum actuator back in position, refit the two stud bolts and tighten securely.

33 The remainder of refitting is the reverse of removal.

Fuel pressure regulator

34 Disconnect the battery negative terminal (refer to *Disconnecting the battery* in the Reference Chapter).

35 Lift off the plastic cover over the top of the engine.

36 Disconnect the wiring connector from the fuel pressure regulator, located at the rear of the high-pressure fuel pump.

37 Undo the three bolts and remove the regulator from the fuel pump.

38 Refitting is the reverse of removal. Renew the two sealing rings and tighten the regulator retaining bolts securely.

Fuel pressure sensor

39 Lift off the plastic cover over the top of the engine.

40 The fuel pressure sensor is located in the centre of the fuel rail, situated at the rear of the engine.

41 Disconnect the sensor wiring connector, then unscrew the sensor from the fuel rail.

42 Refitting is a reversal of removal, tightening the sensor securely.

Electronic control unit (ECU)

Note: *If a new ECU is to be fitted, this work must be entrusted to a Vauxhall/Opel dealer or suitably-equipped specialist. It is necessary to initialise the new ECU after installation, which requires the use of dedicated diagnostic equipment.*

43 Disconnect the battery negative terminal (refer to *Disconnecting the battery* in the Reference Chapter).

44 Firmly apply the handbrake, then jack up the front of the car and support it securely on axle stands (see *Jacking and vehicle support*). Remove the left-hand roadwheel.

45 Undo the two bolts, remove the three plastic rivets and detach the front part of the wheel arch liner from the bumper and underbody.

46 Withdraw the locking plates, lift the locking levers and disconnect the two wiring connectors from the ECU.

47 Undo the four nuts securing the ECU to its mounting frame and remove the ECU from under the bumper.

48 Refitting is a reversal of removal, ensuring that the wiring connectors are securely connected and locked with the locking levers.

Turbocharger wastegate solenoid

49 The wastegate (charge pressure) solenoid valve is located at the rear of the engine above the starter motor.

50 Firmly apply the handbrake, then jack up the front of the car and support it securely on axle stands (see *Jacking and vehicle support*).

51 Disconnect the wiring connector and the two vacuum hoses from the valve then undo the two retaining bolts and remove the valve from its location.

52 Refitting is the reverse of removal.

Changeover flap actuator solenoid

53 The solenoid valve controlling the inlet manifold changeover flap vacuum actuator is located at the rear right-hand side of the cylinder block.

54 Firmly apply the handbrake, then jack up the front of the car and support it securely on axle stands (see *Jacking and vehicle support*).

55 Mark the two vacuum hoses for correct refitting, then disconnect the hoses from the valve.

56 Disconnect the wiring connector then undo the two retaining bolts and remove the valve from its location.

57 Refitting is the reverse of removal.

13.1 Disconnect the air intake duct from the airflow meter

13.7 EGR pipe to EGR valve retaining bolts (arrowed)

13.16 The crankshaft speed/position sensor (arrowed) is located below the starter motor

Wheel speed sensors

58 Refer to the anti-lock braking system information contained in Chapter 9.

13 Injection system electrical components (1.9 litre engines) – removal and refitting

Airflow meter

1 Slacken the retaining clip securing the air intake duct to the airflow meter and disconnect the duct **(see illustration)**.
2 Disconnect the airflow meter wiring connector.
3 Slacken the retaining clip and remove the airflow meter from the air cleaner housing lid.
4 Refitting is a reversal of removal, but ensure that the arrow on the airflow meter points toward the throttle housing when fitted.

Throttle housing

Z19DT engines

5 Remove the plastic cover over the top of the engine.
6 Release the retaining clip and disconnect the charge air hose from the throttle housing.
7 Undo the four bolts and disconnect the metal EGR pipe from the EGR valve and throttle housing, noting its correct fitted position **(see illustration)**. Recover the two gaskets.
8 Undo the three retaining bolts and remove the throttle housing from the inlet manifold.

Note the location of any wiring harness support brackets also secured by the retaining bolts.
9 Refitting is a reversal of removal, but thoroughly clean the mating faces and use a new gasket/seal and new EGR pipe gaskets. Tighten the retaining bolts to the specified torque.

Z19DTH engines

10 Remove the plastic cover over the top of the engine.
11 Slacken the two retaining clips and disconnect the charge air hose from the intercooler and throttle housing.
12 Undo the two bolts and remove the charge air pipe elbow from the throttle housing. Recover the seal.
13 Disconnect the wiring connector from the throttle housing.
14 Undo the three retaining bolts and remove the throttle housing from the inlet manifold. Note the location of any wiring harness support brackets also secured by the retaining bolts.
15 Refitting is a reversal of removal, but thoroughly clean the mating faces and use a new gasket/seal. Tighten the retaining bolts to the specified torque.

Crankshaft speed/position sensor

16 The sensor is located at the rear of the cylinder block, below the starter motor **(see illustration)**. To gain access, firmly apply the handbrake, then jack up the front of the car and support it securely on axle stands (see *Jacking and vehicle support*).

17 Wipe clean the area around the crankshaft sensor then disconnect the wiring connector.
18 Slacken and remove the retaining bolt and remove the sensor from the cylinder block. Recover the sealing ring.
19 Refitting is the reverse of removal, using a new sealing ring. Tighten the sensor retaining bolt to the specified torque.

Camshaft position sensor

Z19DT engines

20 The camshaft sensor is located at the right-hand end of the cylinder head, behind the camshaft sprocket.
21 Remove the timing belt and camshaft sprocket as described in Chapter 2C.
22 Undo the two bolts securing the camshaft sensor bracket to the cylinder head.
23 Disconnect the sensor wiring connector, undo the two bolts and remove the sensor.
24 Refit the sensor using the reverse of removal, tightening the retaining bolts to the specified torque. Refit the camshaft sprocket and timing belt as described in Chapter 2C.

Z19DTH engines

25 The camshaft sensor is located at the right-hand end of the camshaft housing **(see illustration)**. To gain access, remove the plastic cover over the top of the engine.
26 Wipe clean the area around the camshaft sensor then disconnect the wiring connector. Unclip the wiring harness from the support bracket.
27 Slacken and remove the retaining bolt and remove the sensor from the camshaft cover. Recover the sealing ring.
28 Refitting is the reverse of removal, using a new sealing ring. Tighten the sensor retaining bolt to the specified torque.

Coolant temperature sensor

29 Refer to the procedures contained in Chapter 3.

Charge (boost) pressure sensor

30 Remove the plastic cover over the top of the engine.
31 Disconnect the wiring connector from the charge pressure sensor located in the centre of the inlet manifold **(see illustration)**.
32 Slacken and remove the retaining bolt and

13.25 Camshaft sensor location (arrowed) – Z19DTH engines

13.31 Disconnect the wiring connector (arrowed) from the charge pressure sensor

remove the sensor from the manifold. Recover the sealing ring.

33 Refitting is the reverse of removal, using a new sealing ring. Tighten the sensor retaining bolt to the specified torque.

Fuel pressure regulator

34 Disconnect the battery negative terminal (refer to *Disconnecting the battery* in the Reference Chapter).

35 Remove the plastic cover over the top of the engine.

36 On Z19DT engines, remove the fuel rail as described in Section 19.

37 On Z19DTH engines, disconnect the wiring connector from the fuel pressure regulator **(see illustration)**.

38 Remove the regulator from the fuel rail by unscrewing the inner nut (nearest the fuel rail) while counterholding the regulator body with a second spanner. Be prepared for some loss of fuel.

39 Refitting is the reverse of removal, tightening the regulator to the specified torque.

Fuel pressure sensor

Note: *On later models, the fuel pressure sensor is incorporated in the high-pressure fuel pump and a separate sensor on the fuel rail is not fitted.*

40 Disconnect the battery negative terminal (refer to *Disconnecting the battery* in the Reference Chapter).

41 Remove the plastic cover over the top of the engine.

42 Disconnect the wiring connector at the fuel pressure sensor **(see illustration)**.

43 Unscrew the sensor and remove it from the fuel rail. Be prepared for some loss of fuel.

44 Refitting is the reverse of removal, tightening the sensor to the specified torque.

Electronic control unit (ECU)

Note: *If a new ECU is to be fitted, this work must be entrusted to a Vauxhall/Opel dealer or suitably-equipped specialist. It is necessary to initialise the new ECU after installation, which requires the use of dedicated diagnostic equipment.*

45 Disconnect the battery negative terminal (refer to *Disconnecting the battery* in the Reference Chapter).

46 Firmly apply the handbrake, then jack up the front of the car and support it securely on axle stands (see *Jacking and vehicle support*). Remove the left-hand roadwheel.

47 Undo the two bolts, remove the three plastic rivets and detach the front part of the wheel arch liner from the bumper and underbody.

48 Withdraw the locking plates, lift the locking levers and disconnect the two wiring connectors from the ECU.

49 Undo the four nuts securing the ECU to its mounting frame and remove the ECU from under the bumper.

50 Refitting is a reversal of removal, ensuring that the wiring connectors are securely connected and locked with the locking levers.

13.37 Disconnect the wiring connector from the fuel pressure regulator – Z19DTH engines

Turbocharger wastegate solenoid

51 The wastegate (charge pressure) solenoid valve is located under the front bumper on the right-hand side.

52 Firmly apply the handbrake, then jack up the front of the car and support it securely on axle stands (see *Jacking and vehicle support*).

53 Disconnect the wiring connector and the two vacuum hoses from the valve then undo the retaining nuts and remove the valve from its mounting bracket.

54 Refitting is the reverse of removal.

Wheel speed sensors

55 Refer to the anti-lock braking system information contained in Chapter 9.

---

 14 High-pressure fuel pump (1.3 litre engines) – removal and refitting

> ⚠ **Warning: Refer to the information contained in Section 2 before proceeding.**

Note: *A new fuel pump-to-fuel rail high-pressure fuel pipe will be required for refitting.*

Removal

1 Disconnect the battery negative terminal (refer to *Disconnecting the battery* in the Reference Chapter).

14.5 Release the wiring harness and fuel hose (arrowed) from the charge air pipe

13.42 Disconnect the fuel pressure sensor wiring connector

2 Lift off the plastic cover over the top of the engine.

3 Slacken the two retaining clips and disconnect the charge air hose from the intercooler and charge air pipe elbow.

4 Slacken the two retaining clips and disconnect the turbocharger charge air pipe from the flexible upper intake duct and turbocharger.

5 Working along the charge air pipe, release the wiring harness retaining clips from the pipe supports and release the fuel hose from the retaining clips **(see illustration)**.

6 Release the locking clip and disconnect the crankcase breather hose at the quick-release connection on the charge air pipe **(see illustration 11.28)**.

7 Undo the two mounting bolts and remove the charge air pipe from the engine.

8 Disconnect the fuel supply hose at the quick-release connector on the fuel pump. A Vauxhall/Opel special tool is available to release the connector, but provided care is taken, it can be released using a pair of long-nosed pliers, two small screwdrivers, or similar, to depress the retaining tangs. Plug or cover the pump union and hose end to prevent dirt entry.

9 Release the retaining clip and disconnect the fuel return hose at the fuel pump. Plug or cover the pump union and hose end to prevent dirt entry.

10 Thoroughly clean the fuel pipe unions on the fuel pump and fuel rail. Using an open-ended spanner, unscrew the union nuts securing the high-pressure fuel pipe to the fuel pump and fuel rail. Counterhold the union on the pump with a second spanner, while unscrewing the union nut. Withdraw the high-pressure fuel pipe and plug or cover the open unions to prevent dirt entry.

11 Disconnect the pump wiring connector then unscrew the three mounting bolts and withdraw the pump from the camshaft housing. Recover the sealing O-ring **(see illustrations)**.

Caution: The high-pressure fuel pump is manufactured to extremely close tolerances and must not be dismantled in any way. No parts for the pump are available separately and if the unit is in any way suspect, it must be renewed.

14.11a Unscrew the three mounting bolts (arrowed) . . .

14.11b . . . withdraw the fuel pump from the camshaft housing . . .

14.11c . . . and recover the sealing O-ring

Refitting

12 Thoroughly clean the fuel pump and camshaft housing mating faces.

13 Locate a new sealing O-ring on the pump flange and lubricate the O-ring with clean diesel fuel.

14 Align the pump drive dog with the slot on the camshaft, then place the pump in position. Refit the three mounting bolts and tighten them to the specified torque. Reconnect the pump wiring connector.

15 Remove the blanking plugs from the fuel pipe unions on the pump and fuel rail. Locate a new high-pressure fuel pipe over the unions and screw on the union nuts finger-tight at this stage.

16 Using a torque wrench and crow-foot adapter, tighten the fuel pipe union nuts to the specified torque. Counterhold the union on the pump with an open-ended spanner, while tightening the union nut.

17 Reconnect the fuel return hose and secure with the retaining clip.

18 Reconnect the fuel supply hose quick-release connector.

19 Refit the charge air pipe and charge air hose.

20 Observing the precautions listed in Section 2, prime the fuel system as described in Section 5, then start the engine and allow it to idle. Check for leaks at the high-pressure fuel pipe unions with the engine idling. If satisfactory, increase the engine speed to 4000 rpm and check again for leaks. Take the car for a short road test and check for leaks once again on return. If any leaks are detected, obtain and fit a new high-pressure fuel pipe.

21 Refit the engine cover on completion.

15 High-pressure fuel pump (1.7 litre engines) – removal and refitting

⚠ **Warning: Refer to the information contained in Section 2 before proceeding.**

Note: A new fuel pump-to-fuel rail high-pressure fuel pipe will be required for refitting.

Removal

1 Disconnect the battery negative terminal

(refer to *Disconnecting the battery* in the Reference Chapter).

2 Remove the plastic cover over the top of the engine.

3 Remove the timing belt and the high-pressure fuel pump sprocket as described in Chapter 2B.

4 Release the retaining clips and disconnect the fuel supply and return hoses at the high-pressure fuel pump. Suitably plug or cover the open unions to prevent dirt entry.

5 Disconnect the wiring connector from the high-pressure fuel pump.

6 Thoroughly clean the fuel pipe unions on the fuel pump and fuel rail. Using an open-ended spanner, unscrew the union nuts securing the high-pressure fuel pipe to the fuel pump and fuel rail. Counterhold the union on the pump with a second spanner, while unscrewing the union nut. Withdraw the high-pressure fuel pipe and plug or cover the open unions to prevent dirt entry.

7 Unscrew the nut and release the wiring from the high-pressure fuel pump mounting stud bolt. Unscrew the three stud bolts and remove the pump from the engine bracket.

Caution: The high-pressure fuel pump is manufactured to extremely close tolerances and must not be dismantled in any way. No parts for the pump are available separately and if the unit is in any way suspect, it must be renewed.

Refitting

8 Refit the pump to the engine bracket and securely tighten the retaining stud bolts.

9 Remove the blanking plugs from the fuel pipe unions on the pump and fuel rail. Locate a new high-pressure fuel pipe over the unions and screw on the union nuts finger-tight at this stage.

10 Using a torque wrench and crow-foot adapter, tighten the fuel pipe union nuts to the specified torque. Counterhold the union on the pump with an open-ended spanner, while tightening the union nut.

11 Reconnect the pump wiring connector and secure the harness to the pump stud bolt with the retaining nut.

12 Refit the fuel supply and return hoses to the fuel pump and secure with the retaining clips.

13 Refit the high-pressure fuel pump sprocket and the timing belt as described in Chapter 2B.

14 Reconnect the battery negative terminal.

15 Observing the precautions listed in Section 2, prime the fuel system as described in Section 5, then start the engine and allow it to idle. Check for leaks at the high-pressure fuel pipe unions with the engine idling. If satisfactory, increase the engine speed to 4000 rpm and check again for leaks. Take the car for a short road test and check for leaks once again on return. If any leaks are detected, obtain and fit a new high-pressure fuel pipe.

16 Refit the engine cover on completion.

16 High-pressure fuel pump (1.9 litre engines) – removal and refitting

⚠ **Warning: Refer to the information contained in Section 2 before proceeding.**

Z19DT engines

Note: *A complete new set of high-pressure fuel pipes will be required for refitting.*

Removal

1 Disconnect the battery negative terminal (refer to *Disconnecting the battery* in the Reference Chapter).

2 Remove the plastic cover over the top of the engine.

3 Remove the timing belt and the high-pressure fuel pump sprocket as described in Chapter 2C.

4 Remove the fuel rail as described in Section 19.

5 Disconnect the fuel return hose quick-release fitting on the top of the high-pressure fuel pump. Suitably plug or cover the open unions to prevent dirt entry.

6 Disconnect the wiring connector from the high-pressure fuel pump.

7 Unscrew the three retaining nuts and remove the pump from the engine bracket **(see illustrations)**.

Caution: The high-pressure fuel pump is manufactured to extremely close tolerances and must not be dismantled in any way. No parts for the pump are available separately and if the unit is in any way suspect, it must be renewed.

Refitting

8 Refit the pump to the engine bracket and tighten the retaining nuts to the specified torque.

9 Reconnect the pump wiring connector and the fuel return hose quick-release fitting.

10 Refit the fuel rail as described in Section 19.

11 Refit the high-pressure fuel pump sprocket and the timing belt as described in Chapter 2C.

12 Reconnect the battery negative terminal.

13 Observing the precautions listed in Section 2, prime the fuel system as described in Section 5, then start the engine and allow it to idle. Check for leaks at the high-pressure fuel pipe unions with the engine idling. If satisfactory, increase the engine speed to 4000 rpm and check again for leaks. Take the car for a short road test and check for leaks once again on return. If any leaks are detected, obtain and fit a new high-pressure fuel pipe(s).

14 Refit the engine cover on completion.

Z19DTH engines

Note: *A new fuel pump-to-fuel rail high-pressure fuel pipe will be required for refitting.*

Removal

15 Disconnect the battery negative terminal (refer to *Disconnecting the battery* in the Reference Chapter).

16 Remove the plastic cover over the top of the engine.

17 Remove the timing belt and the high-pressure fuel pump sprocket as described in Chapter 2D.

18 Release the retaining clips and disconnect the two fuel return hoses at the fuel return damping chamber **(see illustrations)**. Suitably plug or cover the open unions to prevent dirt entry.

19 Disconnect the injector leak-off pipe and the fuel return quick-release fitting, then undo the two bolts and remove the damping chamber. Suitably plug or cover the open unions to prevent dirt entry.

20 Disconnect the fuel return hose quick-release fitting on the top of the high-pressure fuel pump. Suitably plug or cover the open unions to prevent dirt entry.

16.7a Unscrew the three retaining nuts (arrowed) . . .

21 Disconnect the wiring connector from the high-pressure fuel pump.

22 Thoroughly clean the fuel pipe unions on the fuel pump and fuel rail. Using an open-ended spanner, unscrew the union nuts securing the high-pressure fuel pipe to the fuel pump and fuel rail. Counterhold the union on the pump with a second spanner, while unscrewing the union nut **(see illustration)**. Withdraw the high-pressure fuel pipe and plug or cover the open unions to prevent dirt entry.

23 Unscrew the three retaining nuts and remove the pump from the engine bracket **(see illustrations 16.7a and 16.7b)**.

Caution: The high-pressure fuel pump is manufactured to extremely close tolerances and must not be dismantled in any way. No parts for the pump are available separately and if the unit is in any way suspect, it must be renewed.

Refitting

24 Refit the pump to the engine bracket and tighten the retaining bolts to the specified torque.

25 Remove the blanking plugs from the fuel pipe unions on the pump and fuel rail. Locate a new high-pressure fuel pipe over the unions and screw on the union nuts finger-tight at this stage.

26 Using a torque wrench and crow-foot adapter, tighten the fuel pipe union nuts to the specified torque. Counterhold the union on the pump with an open-ended spanner, while tightening the union nut.

27 Reconnect the pump wiring connector and the fuel return hose quick-release fitting.

16.7b . . . and remove the high-pressure fuel pump from the engine bracket

28 Refit the damping chamber and tighten the retaining bolts securely. Reconnect the injector leak-off pipe, and the two remaining fuel return hoses.

29 Refit the high-pressure fuel pump sprocket and the timing belt as described in Chapter 2D.

30 Reconnect the battery negative terminal.

31 Observing the precautions listed in Section 2, prime the fuel system as described in Section 5, then start the engine and allow it to idle. Check for leaks at the high-pressure fuel pipe unions with the engine idling. If satisfactory, increase the engine speed to 4000 rpm and check again for leaks. Take the car for a short road test and check for leaks once again on return. If any leaks are detected, obtain and fit a new high-pressure fuel pipe(s).

32 Refit the engine cover on completion.

17 Fuel rail (1.3 litre engines) – removal and refitting

⚠️ *Warning: Refer to the information contained in Section 2 before proceeding.*

Note: *A complete new set of high-pressure fuel pipes will be required for refitting.*

Removal

1 Disconnect the battery negative terminal (refer to *Disconnecting the battery* in the Reference Chapter).

2 Lift off the plastic cover over the top of the engine.

16.18a Release the clips and disconnect the upper (arrowed) . . .

16.18b . . . and lower (arrowed) fuel return hoses at the damping chamber

16.22 Counterhold the fuel pipe union on the pump with a second spanner, while unscrewing the union nut

17.8a Disconnect the wiring connector at the at the fuel pressure sensor . . .

17.8b . . . and fuel pressure regulator

17.9a Unscrew the union nuts securing the high pressure fuel pipes to the fuel injectors . . .

17.9b . . . and the fuel rail

3 Slacken the two retaining clips and disconnect the charge air hose from the intercooler and charge air pipe elbow.
4 Slacken the two retaining clips and disconnect the turbocharger charge air pipe from the flexible upper intake duct and turbocharger.

5 Working along the charge air pipe, release the wiring harness retaining clips from the pipe supports and release the fuel hose from the retaining clips **(see illustration 14.5)**.
6 Release the locking clip and disconnect the crankcase breather hose at the quick-release

connection on the charge air pipe **(see illustration 11.28)**.
7 Undo the two mounting bolts and remove the charge air pipe from the engine.
8 Disconnect the wiring connectors at the fuel pressure sensor and fuel pressure regulator on the fuel rail **(see illustrations)**.
9 Thoroughly clean all the high-pressure fuel pipe unions on the fuel rail, fuel pump and injectors. Using two spanners, hold the unions and unscrew the union nuts securing the high-pressure fuel pipes to the fuel injectors. Unscrew the union nuts securing the high-pressure fuel pipes to the fuel rail, withdraw the pipes and plug or cover the open unions to prevent dirt entry **(see illustrations)**. It is advisable to label each fuel pipe (1 to 4) to avoid confusion when refitting.
10 Using an open-ended spanner, unscrew the union nuts securing the high-pressure fuel pipe to the fuel pump and fuel rail. Counterhold the union on the pump with a second spanner, while unscrewing the union nut **(see illustrations)**. Withdraw the high-pressure fuel pipe and plug or cover the open unions to prevent dirt entry.
11 Release the retaining clip and disconnect the fuel return hose at the fuel rail. Cover the hose end to prevent dirt entry.
12 Undo the two retaining bolts and lift the fuel rail off the mounting bracket **(see illustrations)**.
13 If required, the fuel pressure sensor and fuel pressure regulator can be unscrewed from the end of the fuel rail with reference to Section 11. Recover the sealing O-rings from the pressure sensor and pressure regulator.

Refitting

14 If removed, refit the fuel pressure sensor and pressure regulator to the fuel rail using new sealing O-rings lubricated with clean diesel fuel. Tighten the pressure sensor, and the pressure regulator to the specified torque.
15 Locate the fuel rail on the mounting bracket, refit the two retaining bolts and tighten them to the specified torque.
16 Refit the fuel return hose and secure with the retaining clip.
17 Working on one fuel injector at a time, remove the blanking plugs from the fuel pipe unions on the fuel rail and the relevant injector. Locate the new high-pressure fuel

17.10a Unscrew the union nuts securing the high pressure fuel pipe to the fuel pump . . .

17.10b . . . and fuel rail

17.12a Undo the two fuel rail retaining bolts (arrowed) . . .

17.12b . . . and lift the fuel rail off the mounting bracket

17.17 Tighten the fuel pipe union nuts using a torque wrench and crow-foot adapter

18.4 Release the wiring harness support clips from the charge air pipe

18.6 Disconnect the crankcase ventilation hose from the camshaft cover

18.7 Remove the charge air pipe from the top of the engine

pipe over the unions and screw on the union nuts finger-tight. Tighten the union nuts to the specified torque using a torque wrench and crow-foot adapter **(see illustration)**. Counterhold the union on the injector with an open-ended spanner, while tightening the union nut. Repeat this operation for the remaining three injectors.

18 Similarly, fit the new high-pressure fuel pipe to the fuel pump and fuel rail, and tighten the union nuts to the specified torque. Counterhold the union on the pump with an open-ended spanner, while tightening the union nut.

19 Reconnect the wiring connectors at the fuel pressure sensor and pressure regulator.

20 Refit the turbocharger charge air pipe and charge air hose.

21 Observing the precautions listed in Section 2, prime the fuel system as described in Section 5, then start the engine and allow it to

idle. Check for leaks at the high-pressure fuel pipe unions with the engine idling. If satisfactory, increase the engine speed to 4000 rpm and check again for leaks. Take the car for a short road test and check for leaks once again on return. If any leaks are detected, obtain and fit a new high-pressure fuel pipe(s).

22 Refit the engine cover on completion.

18 Fuel rail (1.7 litre engines) – removal and refitting

⚠️ **Warning: Refer to the information contained in Section 2 before proceeding.**
Note: A complete new set of high-pressure fuel pipes will be required for refitting.

Removal

1 Disconnect the battery negative terminal

(refer to *Disconnecting the battery* in the Reference Chapter).

2 Lift off the plastic cover over the top of the engine.

3 Remove the air cleaner assembly and intake duct as described in Section 3.

4 Release the wiring harness support clips from the plastic charge air pipe over the top of the engine **(see illustration)**.

5 Slacken the retaining clips securing the charge air pipe to the turbocharger.

6 Release the retaining clip and disconnect the crankcase ventilation hose from the camshaft cover **(see illustration)**.

7 Open the clip and detach the fuel hose from the charge air pipe, then undo the two charge air pipe retaining bolts. Disengage the pipe from the turbocharger, then remove the pipe from the top of the engine **(see illustration)**.

8 Undo the six bolts securing the rear charge air pipe to the throttle housing and inlet manifold. Remove the charge air pipe and recover the gaskets **(see illustrations)**.

9 Release the locking catches securing the wiring connectors to the four fuel injectors then disconnect the injector wiring **(see illustrations)**.

10 Disconnect the wiring from the glow plugs by squeezing the connectors with thumb and forefinger, and pulling them from the plugs **(see illustration)**.

11 Undo the two bolts securing the wiring harness guide to the camshaft cover, then move the wiring harness to one side **(see illustrations)**.

12 Thoroughly clean the fuel pipe unions on the fuel injectors and fuel rail. Using an

18.8a Undo the six bolts then remove the rear charge air pipe . . .

18.8b . . . and recover the gaskets

18.9a Release the wiring connector locking catches . . .

18.9b . . . and disconnect the wiring connectors at the fuel injectors

18.10 Squeeze the connectors and disconnect the wiring at the four glow plugs

18.11a Undo the two bolts (arrowed) securing the wiring harness guide to the camshaft cover . . .

18.11b . . . then move the wiring harness to one side

18.12a Unscrew the union nuts securing the high pressure fuel pipes to the injectors and fuel rail . . .

18.12b . . . withdraw the high pressure fuel pipes . . .

18.12c . . . and plug or cover the open unions to prevent dirt entry

open-ended spanner, unscrew the union nuts securing the high-pressure fuel pipes to the injectors and fuel rail. Withdraw the high-pressure fuel pipes and plug or cover the open unions to prevent dirt entry **(see illustrations)**.

13 Thoroughly clean the fuel pipe unions on the fuel pump and fuel rail. Using an open-ended spanner, unscrew the union nuts securing the high-pressure fuel pipe to the fuel pump and fuel rail. Counterhold the union on the pump with a second spanner, while unscrewing the union nut. Withdraw the high-pressure fuel pipe and plug or cover the open unions to prevent dirt entry.

14 Disconnect the fuel leak-off hose connection at each injector by pushing in the locking clip and lifting out the hose fitting **(see illustration)**. Suitably plug or cover the open unions to prevent dirt entry.

15 Unscrew the nut and two bolts securing the

injector leak-off hose assembly to the camshaft cover and inlet manifold and move the hose assembly to one side **(see illustration)**.

16 Disconnect the wiring connectors at the charge (boost) pressure sensor, fuel pressure sensor and changeover flap actuator solenoid. Disconnect the vacuum hose from the changeover flap vacuum unit.

17 Unscrew the two nuts and detach the wiring harness support bracket from the fuel rail.

18 Disconnect the fuel leak-off hose at the connector on the fuel rail.

19 Unscrew and remove the two fuel rail retaining stud bolts and recover the spacer sleeves. Note the different lengths of the two bolts and the two spacer sleeves. Lift away the fuel rail and remove it from the engine.

Refitting

20 Locate the spacer sleeves and fuel rail

in position, refit the two retaining bolts and tighten them securely.

21 Reconnect the fuel leak-off hose to the connector on the fuel rail.

22 Refit the wiring harness support bracket and secure with the two nuts.

23 Reconnect the wiring connectors at the charge (boost) pressure sensor, fuel pressure sensor and changeover flap actuator solenoid. Reconnect the vacuum hose from the changeover flap vacuum unit.

24 Refit and tighten the nut and two bolts securing the injector leak-off hose assembly to the camshaft cover and inlet manifold.

25 Reconnect the leak-off hose fittings to the injectors by pushing in the locking clip, attaching the fitting, then releasing the locking clip. Ensure that each fitting is securely connected and retained by the clip.

26 Remove the blanking plugs from the fuel pipe unions on the fuel rail and fuel injectors. Locate the new high-pressure fuel pipes over the unions and screw on the union nuts finger-tight. Tighten the union nuts to the specified torque using a torque wrench and crow-foot adapter. Counterhold the union on the injectors with an open-ended spanner, while tightening the union nuts.

27 Similarly, fit a new high-pressure fuel pipe to the fuel pump and fuel rail, and tighten the union nuts to the specified torque. Counterhold the union on the pump with an open-ended spanner, while tightening the union nut.

28 Place the wiring harness guide back in position on the camshaft cover, then refit and tighten the two retaining bolts.

29 Reconnect the wiring connectors at the glow plugs and fuel injectors.

30 Refit the rear charge air pipe and gaskets, then refit and tighten the six retaining bolts.

31 Locate the upper charge air pipe in position over the turbocharger and secure with the retaining clip and two bolts. Reconnect the crankcase ventilation hose. Clip the wiring harness and fuel hose back into place on the charge air pipe.

32 Refit the air cleaner assembly and intake duct as described in Section 3.

33 Reconnect the battery negative terminal.

34 Observing the precautions listed in Section 2, prime the fuel system as described in Section 5, then start the engine and allow it

18.14 Push in the locking clip and lift out the leak-off hose fitting on each injector

18.15 Unscrew the nut and two bolts (arrowed) and move the leak-off hose assembly to one side

to idle. Check for leaks at the high-pressure fuel pipe unions with the engine idling. If satisfactory, increase the engine speed to 4000 rpm and check again for leaks. Take the car for a short road test and check for leaks once again on return. If any leaks are detected, obtain and fit a new high-pressure fuel pipe(s).

35 Refit the engine cover on completion.

19 Fuel rail (1.9 litre engines) – removal and refitting

  Warning: Refer to the information contained in Section 2 before proceeding.

Note: *A complete new set of high-pressure fuel pipes will be required for refitting.*

Z19DT engines

Removal

1 Disconnect the battery negative terminal (refer to *Disconnecting the battery* in the Reference Chapter).

2 Remove the plastic cover over the top of the engine.

3 Release the locking catches securing the wiring connectors to the four injectors, then disconnect the injector wiring.

4 Undo the two bolts at the top and the two bolts at the front, securing the plastic wiring trough to the inlet manifold **(see illustrations)**. Move the wiring trough and injector wiring harness to one side.

5 Release the retaining clips and disconnect the two fuel return hoses at the fuel return damping chamber. Suitably plug or cover the open unions to prevent dirt entry.

6 Disconnect the injector leak-off pipe and the fuel return quick-release fitting, then undo the two bolts and remove the damping chamber. Suitably plug or cover the open unions to prevent dirt entry.

7 Thoroughly clean the fuel pipe unions on the fuel pump and fuel rail. Using an open-ended spanner, unscrew the union nuts securing the high-pressure fuel pipe to the fuel pump and fuel rail. Counterhold the unions on the pump with a second spanner, while unscrewing the union nuts. Withdraw the high-pressure fuel pipe and plug or cover the open unions to prevent dirt entry.

8 Using two spanners, hold the unions and unscrew the union nuts securing the high-pressure fuel pipes to the fuel injectors. Unscrew the union nuts securing the high-pressure fuel pipes to the fuel rail, withdraw the pipes and plug or cover the open unions to prevent dirt entry.

9 Disconnect the wiring connectors at the fuel pressure regulator and fuel pressure sensor, then undo the two nuts and remove the fuel rail.

Refitting

10 Refit the fuel rail and tighten the retaining

19.4a Undo the two bolts at the top (arrowed) . . .

nuts to the specified torque. Reconnect the fuel pressure regulator and fuel pressure sensor wiring connectors.

11 Working on one fuel injector at a time, remove the blanking plugs from the fuel pipe unions on the fuel rail and the relevant injector. Locate the new high-pressure fuel pipe over the unions and screw on the union nuts finger-tight. Tighten the union nuts to the specified torque using a torque wrench and crow-foot adapter. Counterhold the union on the injector with an open-ended spanner, while tightening the union nut. Repeat this operation for the remaining three injectors.

12 Similarly, fit the new high-pressure fuel pipe to the fuel pump and fuel rail, and tighten the union nuts to the specified torque. Counterhold the union on the pump with an open-ended spanner, while tightening the union nut.

13 Refit the damping chamber and tighten the retaining bolts securely. Reconnect the injector leak-off pipe, and the fuel return hoses.

14 Refit the wiring trough, and secure with the four retaining bolts. Reconnect the wiring connectors to the fuel injectors.

15 Reconnect the battery negative terminal.

16 Observing the precautions listed in Section 2, prime the fuel system as described in Section 5, then start the engine and allow it to idle. Check for leaks at the high-pressure fuel pipe unions with the engine idling. If satisfactory, increase the engine speed to 4000 rpm and check again for leaks. Take

19.20 Unscrew the union nuts securing the high-pressure fuel pipes to the fuel rail and injectors

19.4b . . . and the two bolts at the front (arrowed) and move the wiring trough and harness to one side

the car for a short road test and check for leaks once again on return. If any leaks are detected, obtain and fit a new high-pressure fuel pipe(s).

17 Refit the engine cover on completion.

Z19DTH engines

Removal

18 Disconnect the battery negative terminal (refer to *Disconnecting the battery* in the Reference Chapter).

19 Remove the plastic cover over the top of the engine.

20 Thoroughly clean all the high-pressure fuel pipe unions on the fuel rail, fuel pump and injectors. Using two spanners, hold the unions and unscrew the union nuts securing the high-pressure fuel pipes to the fuel injectors. Unscrew the union nuts securing the high-pressure fuel pipes to the fuel rail, withdraw the pipes and plug or cover the open unions to prevent dirt entry **(see illustration)**.

21 Using an open-ended spanner, unscrew the union nuts securing the high-pressure fuel pipe to the fuel pump and fuel rail **(see illustration)**. Counterhold the unions on the pump with a second spanner, while unscrewing the union nuts. Withdraw the high-pressure fuel pipe and plug or cover the open unions to prevent dirt entry.

22 Disconnect the wiring connectors at the fuel pressure regulator and fuel pressure sensor, then release the clip and disconnect the fuel return hose. Undo the two bolts and remove the fuel rail **(see illustrations)**.

19.21 Unscrew the union nuts securing the high-pressure fuel pipe to the fuel pump and fuel rail

19.22a Disconnect the fuel return hose . . .

19.22b . . . then undo the two bolts (arrowed) and remove the fuel rail

Refitting

23 Refit the fuel rail and tighten the retaining bolts to the specified torque. Reconnect the fuel pressure regulator and fuel pressure sensor wiring connectors, and reconnect the fuel return hose.

24 Working on one fuel injector at a time, remove the blanking plugs from the fuel pipe unions on the fuel rail and the relevant injector. Locate the new high-pressure fuel pipe over the unions and screw on the union nuts finger-tight. Tighten the union nuts to the specified torque using a torque wrench and crow-foot adapter. Counterhold the union on the injector with an open-ended spanner, while tightening the union nut. Repeat this operation for the remaining three injectors.

25 Similarly, fit the new high-pressure

fuel pipe to the fuel pump and fuel rail, and tighten the union nuts to the specified torque. Counterhold the union on the pump with an open-ended spanner, while tightening the union nut.

26 Reconnect the battery negative terminal.

27 Observing the precautions listed in Section 2, prime the fuel system as described in Section 5, then start the engine and allow it to idle. Check for leaks at the high-pressure fuel pipe unions with the engine idling. If satisfactory, increase the engine speed to 4000 rpm and check again for leaks. Take the car for a short road test and check for leaks once again on return. If any leaks are detected, obtain and fit a new high-pressure fuel pipe(s).

28 Refit the engine cover on completion.

20.10 Disconnect the injector wiring, while moving the wiring harness guide forward

20.12a Disconnect the fuel leak-off hose connection at each injector . . .

20.12b . . . and slip a plastic bag over the disconnected leak-off hose to prevent dirt entry

20.13a Unscrew the retaining nut . . .

20 Fuel injectors (1.3 litre engines) – removal and refitting

Warning: Refer to the information contained in Section 2 before proceeding.

Note: The following procedure describes the removal and refitting of the injectors as a complete set, however the injectors may be removed in pairs if required. A new copper sealing washer, camshaft housing seal and high-pressure fuel pipe will be required for each disturbed injector when refitting.

Removal

1 Disconnect the battery negative terminal (refer to Disconnecting the battery in the Reference Chapter).

2 Lift off the plastic cover over the top of the engine.

3 Slacken the two retaining clips and disconnect the turbocharger charge air pipe from the flexible upper intake duct and turbo- charger.

4 Working along the charge air pipe, release the wiring harness retaining clips from the pipe supports and release the fuel hose from the retaining clips (see illustration 14.5).

5 Release the locking clip and disconnect the crankcase breather hose at the quick-release connection on the charge air pipe (see illustration 11.28).

6 Undo the two mounting bolts and remove the charge air pipe from the engine.

7 Thoroughly clean all the high-pressure fuel pipe unions on the fuel rail and injectors.

8 Disconnect the wiring connector at the camshaft position sensor on the top of the camshaft housing.

9 Unscrew the three bolts securing the plastic wiring harness guide to the top of the camshaft housing.

10 Release the locking catches securing the wiring connectors to the four injectors, then disconnect the injector wiring, while at the same time moving the wiring harness guide forward (see illustration).

11 Using two spanners, hold the unions and unscrew the union nuts securing the high-pressure fuel pipes to the fuel injectors. Unscrew the union nuts securing the high-pressure fuel pipes to the fuel rail, withdraw the pipes and plug or cover the open unions to prevent dirt entry (see illustrations 17.9a and 17.9b). It is advisable to label each fuel pipe (1 to 4) to avoid confusion when refitting.

12 Disconnect the fuel leak-off hose connection at each injector by pushing in the locking clip and lifting out the hose fitting. Slip a plastic bag over the disconnected leak-off hose to prevent dirt entry (see illustrations).

13 Unscrew the retaining nut then remove the two washers (where fitted) from the injector clamp brackets (see illustrations). There are two clamp brackets, one securing injectors one and two, and the other securing injectors three and four.

20.13b . . . then remove the upper washer . . .

20.13c . . . and lower washer from the injector clamp brackets

20.14a If necessary, use a slide hammer to free the injectors . . .

20.14b . . . then withdraw the two injectors together with the clamp bracket

20.14c The clamp bracket engages with slots in the injector body

20.15 Remove the copper washer from each injector

14 Working on one pair of injectors at a time (one and two, or three and four) withdraw the two injectors together with the clamp bracket from the camshaft housing and cylinder head. If difficulty is experienced removing the injectors, liberally apply penetrating oil to the base of each injector and allow time for the oil to penetrate. If the injectors are still reluctant to free, it will be necessary to use a small slide hammer engaged under the flange of the injector body casting, and gently tap them free. Note that it is not possible to twist the injectors from side-to-side to free them due to the design of the clamp bracket which positively engages in slots in the injector body **(see illustrations)**.

15 Once the injector pair has been removed, separate them from the clamp bracket and remove the copper washer from each injector **(see illustration)**. The copper washers may have remained in place at the base of the injector orifice in the cylinder head. If so, hook them out with a length of wire. Remove the upper injector seals from the camshaft housing. Label the injectors (1 to 4) so they can be refitted in their original cylinders (unless new injectors are to be fitted).

16 Examine each injector visually for any signs of obvious damage or deterioration. If any defects are apparent, renew the injector(s).

Caution: The injectors are manufactured to extremely close tolerances and must not be dismantled in any way. Do not unscrew the fuel pipe union on the side

of the injector, or separate any parts of the injector body. Do not attempt to clean carbon deposits from the injector nozzle or carry out any form of ultrasonic or pressure testing.

17 If the injectors are in a satisfactory condition, plug the fuel pipe union (if not already done) and suitably cover the electrical element and the injector nozzle.

18 Prior to refitting, obtain a new copper washer and camshaft housing seal for each removed injector.

Refitting

19 Locate a new copper washer on the base of each injector, and fit a new seal to the injector location in the camshaft housing.

20 Place the injector clamp bracket in the slot on each injector body and refit the injectors to the cylinder head in pairs. Guide the clamp bracket over the mounting stud as each injector pair is inserted.

21 Fit the two washers (where applicable) and the injector clamp bracket retaining nut to the mounting stud of each injector pair. Tighten the nuts finger-tight only at this stage.

22 Working on one fuel injector at a time, remove the blanking plugs from the fuel pipe unions on the fuel rail and the relevant injector. Locate the high-pressure fuel pipe over the unions and screw on the union nuts. Take care not to cross-thread the nuts or strain the fuel pipes as they are fitted. Once the union nut threads have started, tighten the nuts moderately tight only at this stage.

23 When all the fuel pipes are in place, tighten the injector clamp bracket retaining nuts to the specified torque.

24 Tighten the fuel pipe union nuts to the specified torque using a torque wrench and crow-foot adapter **(see illustration 17.17)**. Counterhold the union on the injector with an open-ended spanner, while tightening the union nut. Repeat this operation for the remaining three injectors.

25 Reconnect the fuel leak-off hose fittings to the injectors by pushing in the locking clip, attaching the fitting, then releasing the locking clip. Ensure that each fitting is securely connected and retained by the clip.

26 Reconnect the fuel injector wiring connectors and secure with the locking catches.

27 Refit the three bolts securing the plastic wiring harness guide to the top of the camshaft housing.

28 Reconnect the camshaft position sensor wiring connector.

29 Refit the turbocharger charge air pipe.

30 Observing the precautions listed in Section 2, prime the fuel system as described in Section 5, then start the engine and allow it to idle. Check for leaks at the high-pressure fuel pipe unions with the engine idling. If satisfactory, increase the engine speed to 4000 rpm and check again for leaks. Take the car for a short road test and check for leaks once again on return. If any leaks are detected, obtain and fit a new high-pressure fuel pipe(s).

31 Refit the engine cover on completion.

21.2 Mark the position of the injectors on the camshaft housing surface

21.3a Unscrew the retaining bolt . . .

21.3b . . . and remove the the injector clamp bracket

21 Fuel injectors (1.7 litre engines) – removal and refitting

Warning: Refer to the information contained in Section 2 before proceeding.

Note: *A new copper washer, O-ring seal and high-pressure fuel pipe will be required for each removed injector when refitting.*

Removal

1 Remove the camshaft cover as described in Chapter 2B.

2 Before removing the injectors it is advisable to mark their fitted position in relation to the camshaft housing. This will ensure that the injector extension will fit centrally through the outer seal plates in the camshaft cover and will also prevent any difficulties when screwing on the fuel pipe union nuts. Place a square or similar tool on the camshaft housing and in contact with the injector extension. Using a permanent ink marker pen, mark the position of the edge of the square on the camshaft housing surface **(see illustration)**.

3 Starting with injector No 1, unscrew the retaining bolt then remove the injector clamp bracket **(see illustrations)**.

4 Using pointed-nose pliers, lift out the clamp bracket locating dowel from the camshaft housing **(see illustration)**.

5 Withdraw the injector from the cylinder head, twisting it from side-to-side if it is initially tight.

6 Once the injector has been withdrawn, remove the copper washer from the injector base and the O-ring seal from the injector body **(see illustration)**. The copper washer may have remained in place at the base of the injector orifice in the cylinder head. If so, hook it out with a length of wire.

7 Remove the remaining injectors in the same way. Label the injectors (1 to 4) so they can be refitted in their original cylinders (unless new injectors are to be fitted).

8 Examine the injector visually for any signs of obvious damage or deterioration. If any defects are apparent, renew the injector.

Caution: The injectors are manufactured to extremely close tolerances and must not be dismantled in any way. Do not unscrew the fuel pipe union on the side of the injector, or separate any parts of the injector body. Do not attempt to clean carbon deposits from the injector nozzle or carry out any form of ultrasonic or pressure testing.

9 If the injectors are in a satisfactory condition, plug the fuel pipe union (if not already done) and suitably cover the electrical element and the injector nozzle.

10 Prior to refitting, obtain a new copper washer, O-ring seal and high-pressure fuel pipe for each injector.

Refitting

11 Thoroughly clean the injector seat in the cylinder head, ensuring all traces of carbon and other deposits are removed.

12 Locate a new O-ring seal on the injector body and a new copper washer on the base of the injector.

13 Place the injector in position in the cylinder head.

14 Refit the clamp bracket locating dowel to the camshaft housing, then engage the clamp bracket over the injector. Refit the clamp bracket retaining bolt finger-tight only at this stage.

15 Using the square, align the injector with the marks made on the camshaft housing during removal. To be absolutely sure that the injector is correctly aligned, temporarily refit the high-pressure fuel pipe to the injector and fuel rail and lightly tighten the union nuts.

16 Tighten the clamp bracket retaining bolt to the specified torque in the three stages given in the specifications. Remove the high-pressure fuel pipe.

21.4 Lift out the clamp bracket locating dowel from the camshaft housing

21.6 Remove the copper washer (A) from the injector base and the O-ring seal (B) from the injector body

17 Repeat this procedure for the remaining injectors.

18 Once all the injectors are installed, refit the camshaft cover as described in Chapter 2B.

19 Observing the precautions listed in Section 2, prime the fuel system as described in Section 5, then start the engine and allow it to idle. Check for leaks at the high-pressure fuel pipe unions with the engine idling. If satisfactory, increase the engine speed to 4000 rpm and check again for leaks. Take the car for a short road test and check for leaks once again on return. If any leaks are detected, obtain and fit a new high-pressure fuel pipe(s).

20 Refit the engine cover on completion.

22 Fuel injectors (1.9 litre engines) – removal and refitting

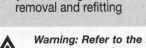

Warning: Refer to the information contained in Section 2 before proceeding.

Note 1: *A new copper washer, retaining nut and high-pressure fuel pipe will be required for each removed injector when refitting.*

Note 2: *The injector is an extremely tight fit in the cylinder head, and it is likely that the special Vauxhall/Opel puller (KM-328-B) and adapter (EN-46786) or suitable alternatives, will be needed.*

Z19DT engines

Removal

1 Disconnect the battery negative terminal (refer to *Disconnecting the battery* in the Reference Chapter).

2 Remove the plastic cover over the top of the engine.

3 Release the locking catches securing the wiring connectors to the four injectors, then disconnect the injector wiring.

4 Undo the two bolts at the top and the two bolts at the front, securing the plastic wiring trough to the inlet manifold **(see illustrations 19.4a and 19.4b)**. Move the wiring trough and injector wiring harness to one side.

5 Thoroughly clean the fuel pipe unions on the fuel rail and injector. Using two spanners, hold the unions and unscrew the union nut securing the high-pressure fuel pipe to the fuel injector. Unscrew the union nut securing the high-pressure fuel pipe to the fuel rail, withdraw the pipe and plug or cover the open unions to prevent dirt entry.

6 Disconnect the fuel leak-off hose connection at each injector by pushing in the locking clip and lifting out the hose fitting. Suitably plug or cap the leak-off hose union on each injector, and slip a plastic bag over the disconnected leak-off hose to prevent dirt entry.

7 Unscrew the retaining nut then remove the washer from the injector clamp bracket.

8 Withdraw the injector together with the clamp bracket from the cylinder head. If difficulty is experienced removing the injector, liberally apply penetrating oil to the base of the injector and allow time for the oil to penetrate. If the injector is still reluctant to free, it will be necessary to use a small slide hammer engaged under the flange of the injector body casting, and gently tap free. If available, use Vauxhall/Opel special tools EN-46786 and KM-328-B for this purpose. Note that it is not possible to twist the injector from side-to-side to free them due to the design of the clamp bracket.

9 Once the injector has been removed, separate it from the clamp bracket and remove the copper washer from the injector base **(see illustration)**. The copper washer may have remained in place at the base of the injector orifice in the cylinder head. If so, hook it out with a length of wire.

10 Remove the remaining injectors in the same way. Label the injectors (1 to 4) so they can be refitted in their original cylinders (unless new injectors are to be fitted).

11 Examine the injector visually for any signs of obvious damage or deterioration. If any defects are apparent, renew the injector.

Caution: The injectors are manufactured to extremely close tolerances and must not be dismantled in any way. Do not unscrew the fuel pipe union on the side of the injector, or separate any parts of the injector body. Do not attempt to clean carbon deposits from the injector nozzle or carry out any form of ultrasonic or pressure testing.

12 If the injectors are in a satisfactory condition, plug the fuel pipe union (if not already done) and suitably cover the electrical element and the injector nozzle.

13 Prior to refitting, obtain a new copper washer a new retaining nut and new high-pressure fuel pipe for each injector.

Refitting

14 Thoroughly clean the injector seat in the cylinder head, ensuring all traces of carbon and other deposits are removed.

15 Locate a new copper washer on the base of the injector.

16 Place the injector clamp bracket in the slot on the injector body and refit the injector to the cylinder head.

17 Fit the washer and the new injector clamp bracket retaining nut and tighten the nut to the specified torque.

18 Remove the blanking plug from the fuel pipe union on the fuel rail and the injector. Locate the new high-pressure fuel pipe over the unions and screw on the union nuts. Take care not to cross-thread the nuts or strain the fuel pipe as it is fitted.

19 Tighten the fuel pipe union nuts to the specified torque using a torque wrench and crow-foot adapter **(see illustration 22.44)**. Counterhold the union on the injector with an open-ended spanner, while tightening the union nut.

20 Repeat this procedure for the remaining injectors.

21 Refit the wiring trough, and secure with

22.9 Remove the copper washer from the injector base

the four retaining bolts. Reconnect the wiring connectors to the fuel injectors.

22 Reconnect the leak-off hose fittings to the injectors by pushing in the locking clip, attaching the fitting, then releasing the locking clip. Ensure that each fitting is securely connected and retained by the clip.

23 Reconnect the battery negative terminal.

24 Observing the precautions listed in Section 2, prime the fuel system as described in Section 5, then start the engine and allow it to idle. Check for leaks at the high-pressure fuel pipe unions with the engine idling. If satisfactory, increase the engine speed to 4000 rpm and check again for leaks. Take the car for a short road test and check for leaks once again on return. If any leaks are detected, obtain and fit a new high-pressure fuel pipe(s).

25 Refit the engine cover on completion.

Z19DTH engines

Removal

26 Disconnect the battery negative terminal (refer to *Disconnecting the battery* in the Reference Chapter).

27 Remove the plastic cover over the top of the engine.

28 Release the retaining clip securing the engine breather hose to the breather pipe adjacent to the engine oil dipstick. Undo the two bolts securing the breather pipe to the cylinder head, and disconnect the pipe from the hose **(see illustration)**.

29 Release the locking catches securing the wiring connectors to the four injectors,

22.28 Undo the two bolts (arrowed) and remove the breather pipe from the cylinder head

22.29a Release the locking catches . . .

22.29b . . . and disconnect the injector wiring connectors

22.30a Disconnect the fuel leak-off hose connection at each injector . . .

22.30b . . . then plug or cap the leak-off hose union on each injector

22.31 Counterhold the injector union when unscrewing the high-pressure fuel pipe unions

22.32 Unscrew the injector clamp bracket retaining nut then remove the washer

then disconnect the injector wiring **(see illustrations)**.

30 Disconnect the fuel leak-off hose connection at each injector by pushing in the locking clip and lifting out the hose fitting. Suitably plug or cap the leak-off hose union on each injector, and slip a plastic bag over the disconnected leak-off hose to prevent dirt entry **(see illustrations)**.

31 Thoroughly clean the fuel pipe unions on the fuel rail and injector. Using two spanners, hold the unions and unscrew the union nut securing the high-pressure fuel pipe to the fuel injector **(see illustration)**. Unscrew the union nut securing the high-pressure fuel pipe to the fuel rail, withdraw the pipe and plug or cover the open unions to prevent dirt entry.

32 Starting with injector No 1, unscrew the retaining nut then remove the washer from the injector clamp bracket **(see illustration)**.

33 Withdraw the injector together with the

clamp bracket from the cylinder head. If difficulty is experienced removing the injector, liberally apply penetrating oil to the base of the injector and allow time for the oil to penetrate. If the injector is still reluctant to free, it will be necessary to use a small slide hammer engaged under the flange of the injector body casting, and gently tap it free **(see illustration)**. If available, use Vauxhall/ Opel special tools EN-46786 and KM-328-B for this purpose. Note that it is not possible to twist the injector from side-to-side to free them due to the design of the clamp bracket.

34 Once the injector has been removed, separate it from the clamp bracket and remove the copper washer from the injector base **(see illustration)**. The copper washer may have remained in place at the base of the injector orifice in the cylinder head. If so, hook it out with a length of wire.

35 Remove the remaining injectors in the

same way. Label the injectors (1 to 4) so they can be refitted in their original cylinders (unless new injectors are to be fitted).

36 Examine the injector visually for any signs of obvious damage or deterioration. If any defects are apparent, renew the injector.

Caution: The injectors are manufactured to extremely close tolerances and must not be dismantled in any way. Do not unscrew the fuel pipe union on the side of the injector, or separate any parts of the injector body. Do not attempt to clean carbon deposits from the injector nozzle or carry out any form of ultrasonic or pressure testing.

37 If the injectors are in a satisfactory condition, plug the fuel pipe union (if not already done) and suitably cover the electrical element and the injector nozzle.

38 Prior to refitting, obtain a new set of copper washers, retaining nuts and high-pressure fuel pipes.

Refitting

39 Thoroughly clean the injector seat in the cylinder head, ensuring all traces of carbon and other deposits are removed.

40 Starting with injector No 4, locate a new copper washer on the base of the injector.

41 Place the injector clamp bracket in the slot on the injector body and refit the injector to the cylinder head.

42 Fit the washer and the injector clamp bracket retaining nut and tighten the nut to the specified torque **(see illustrations)**.

43 Remove the blanking plug from the fuel pipe union on the fuel rail and the injector. Locate the new high-pressure fuel pipe over

22.33 Using a small slide hammer to free the injector body from the cylinder head

22.34 Once the injector has been removed, separate it from the clamp bracket

22.42a Fit the washer . . .

22.42b . . . and the injector clamp bracket retaining nut

22.44 Tighten the fuel pipe union nuts to the specified torque using a torque wrench and crow-foot adapter

the unions and screw on the union nuts. Take care not to cross-thread the nuts or strain the fuel pipe as it is fitted.

44 Tighten the fuel pipe union nuts to the specified torque using a torque wrench and crow-foot adapter **(see illustration)**. Counterhold the union on the injector with an open-ended spanner, while tightening the union nut.

45 Repeat this procedure for the remaining injectors.

46 Reconnect the leak-off hose fittings to the injectors by pushing in the locking clip, attaching the fitting, then releasing the locking clip. Ensure that each fitting is securely connected and retained by the clip.

47 Reconnect the wiring connectors to the fuel injectors.

48 Attach the engine breather hose to the breather pipe and secure with the retaining clip. Secure the breather pipe to the cylinder head with the two bolts securely tightened.

49 Reconnect the battery negative terminal.

50 Observing the precautions listed in Section 2, prime the fuel system as described in Section 5, then start the engine and allow it to idle. Check for leaks at the high-pressure fuel pipe unions with the engine idling. If satisfactory, increase the engine speed to 4000 rpm and check again for leaks. Take the car for a short road test and check for leaks once again on return. If any leaks are detected, obtain and fit a new high-pressure fuel pipe(s).

51 Refit the engine cover on completion.

23 Inlet manifold (1.3 litre engines) – removal and refitting

Removal

1 Disconnect the battery negative terminal (refer to *Disconnecting the battery* in the Reference Chapter).

2 Lift off the plastic cover over the top of the engine.

3 Slacken the two retaining clips and disconnect the turbocharger charge air pipe from the flexible upper intake duct and turbocharger.

4 Working along the charge air pipe, release the wiring harness retaining clips from the pipe supports and release the fuel hose from the retaining clips **(see illustration 14.5)**.

5 Release the locking clip and disconnect the crankcase breather hose at the quick-release connection on the charge air pipe **(see illustration 11.28)**.

6 Undo the two mounting bolts and remove the charge air pipe from the engine.

7 Remove the exhaust gas recirculation (EGR) valve as described in Chapter 4B.

8 Withdraw the engine oil dipstick, then undo the retaining bolt securing the dipstick guide tube to the inlet manifold.

9 Disconnect the fuel supply hose at the quick-release connector on the fuel pump. A Vauxhall/Opel special tool is available to release the connector, but provided care

is taken, it can be released using a pair of long-nosed pliers, two small screwdrivers, or similar, to depress the retaining tangs. Plug or cover the pump union and hose end to prevent dirt entry.

10 Similarly, disconnect the fuel return hose quick-release connector at the leak-off hose adapter adjacent to the fuel pump. Plug or cover the adapter union and hose end to prevent dirt entry.

11 Disconnect the vacuum hose quick-release connector at the vacuum pump.

12 Unclip the fuel supply hose, fuel return hose and the vacuum hose from their support brackets and move the hoses to one side.

13 Disconnect the wiring connectors at the charge (boost) pressure sensor, throttle housing solenoid valve, fuel pressure regulator and fuel pressure sensor. Unclip the wiring harness from the inlet manifold and crankcase ventilation hose bracket.

14 Undo the retaining bolt and detach the crankcase ventilation hose attachment at the timing cover **(see illustration)**.

15 Undo the two retaining bolts and free the crankcase ventilation system oil separator from the inlet manifold **(see illustration)**.

16 Undo the retaining bolt and detach the wiring harness support bracket around the starter motor.

17 Undo the nine retaining bolts (noting their different lengths) and remove the inlet manifold from the cylinder head. Remove the rubber gasket from the manifold flange **(see illustrations)**.

23.14 Undo the retaining bolt and detach the crankcase ventilation hose attachment

23.15 Undo the two bolts (arrowed) and free the oil separator from the inlet manifold

23.17a Undo the retaining bolts (arrowed) and remove the inlet manifold . . .

Refitting

18 Thoroughly clean the inlet manifold and cylinder head mating faces, then locate a new rubber gasket on the inlet manifold flange.

19 Locate the manifold in position and refit the retaining bolts. Diagonally and progressively, tighten the bolts to the specified torque.

20 Refit the retaining bolt and secure the wiring harness support bracket.

21 Refit the crankcase ventilation system oil separator to the inlet manifold.

22 Refit the crankcase ventilation hose attachment to the timing cover and secure with the retaining bolt, securely tightened.

23 Refit the wiring connectors to the charge (boost) pressure sensor, throttle housing solenoid valve, fuel pressure regulator and fuel pressure sensor. Secure the wiring harness to the inlet manifold and crankcase ventilation hose bracket retaining clips.

24 Reconnect the fuel supply hose, fuel return hose and the vacuum hose quick-release connectors and attach the hoses to their support brackets.

25 Refit and tighten the bolt securing the oil dipstick guide tube to the manifold, then re-insert the dipstick.

26 Refit the exhaust gas recirculation (EGR) valve as described in Chapter 4B.

27 Refit the turbocharger charge air pipe.

28 On completion, refit the engine cover and reconnect the battery negative terminal.

24 Inlet manifold (1.7 litre engines) – removal and refitting

Removal

1 Remove the fuel rail as described in Section 18.

2 Undo the eight bolts and two nuts, then remove the inlet manifold from the cylinder head. Recover the gasket.

3 The changeover flap housing can be removed by extracting the circlip and disconnecting the vacuum unit lever from changeover flap linkage. Undo the three bolts and separate the housing from the inlet manifold.

Refitting

4 Thoroughly clean the inlet manifold, cylinder head and, where applicable, the changeover flap housing mating faces.

5 If removed, apply sealant to the changeover flap housing and locate the housing on the manifold. Refit the three bolts and tighten securely. Reconnect the vacuum unit lever to changeover flap linkage.

6 Place a new gasket on the inlet manifold flange, then position the manifold over the cylinder head studs.

7 Refit the retaining bolts and nuts, then diagonally and progressively, tighten the bolts and nuts to the specified torque.

8 Refit the fuel rail as described in Section 18.

23.17b . . . then remove the rubber gasket from the manifold flange

25 Inlet manifold (1.9 litre engines) – removal and refitting

Z19DT engines

Removal

1 Disconnect the battery negative terminal (refer to *Disconnecting the battery* in the Reference Chapter).

2 Remove the plastic cover over the top of the engine.

3 Drain the cooling system as described in Chapter 1.

4 Remove the exhaust gas recirculation (EGR) valve as described in Chapter 4B.

5 Remove the high-pressure fuel pump as described in Section 16.

6 Undo the retaining bolt(s) to release the vacuum lines running over the top of the camshaft cover **(see illustration)**.

7 Remove the throttle housing as described in Section 13.

8 Disconnect the wiring connectors at the four glow plugs.

9 Undo the three retaining bolts and detach the vacuum reservoir from the rear of the cylinder block.

10 Release the retaining clips and disconnect the two coolant hoses at the EGR heat exchanger, and the adjacent hose at the thermostat housing.

11 Unscrew the nut and two bolts securing the coolant pipes to the starter motor bracket.

25.6 Undo the retaining bolt(s) to release the vacuum lines from the camshaft cover

12 Release the clamp and disconnect the metal pipe from the EGR heat exchanger. Undo the retaining nut and bolt and remove the heat exchanger.

13 Remove the alternator as described in Chapter 5.

14 Undo the six bolts securing the alternator and high-pressure fuel pump mounting bracket to the cylinder block and cylinder head. There are five bolts securing the bracket to the block at the rear, and one securing the bracket to the head at the front.

15 Undo the nine retaining nuts and remove the inlet manifold from the cylinder head studs. Recover the gasket.

Refitting

16 Thoroughly clean the inlet manifold and cylinder head mating faces, then locate a new gasket on the inlet manifold flange.

17 Locate the manifold in position and refit the retaining nuts. Diagonally and progressively, tighten the nuts to the specified torque.

18 Refit the alternator and high-pressure fuel pump bracket and tighten the retaining bolts to the specified torque.

19 Refit the alternator as described in Chapter 5.

20 Refit the EGR heat exchanger and securely tighten the retaining nut and bolt. Reconnect the metal EGR pipe and secure with the retaining clamp.

21 Locate the coolant pipe on the starter motor bracket. Refit and securely tighten the retaining nut and bolts.

22 Reconnect the coolant hoses to the EGR heat exchanger and thermostat housing and secure with the retaining clips.

23 Attach the vacuum reservoir to the cylinder block, refit the three retaining bolts and tighten securely.

24 Reconnect the wiring connectors to the glow plugs.

25 Refit the throttle housing as described in Section 13.

26 Refit the vacuum lines running over the top of the camshaft cover and reconnect the vacuum hoses.

27 Refit the high-pressure fuel pump as described in Section 16.

28 Refit the exhaust gas recirculation (EGR) valve as described in Chapter 4B.

29 Refill the cooling system as described in Chapter 1.

30 Reconnect the battery negative terminal.

31 Observing the precautions listed in Section 2, prime the fuel system as described in Section 5, then start the engine and allow it to idle. Check for leaks at the high-pressure fuel pipe unions with the engine idling. If satisfactory, increase the engine speed to 4000 rpm and check again for leaks. Take the car for a short road test and check for leaks once again on return. If any leaks are detected, obtain and fit a new high-pressure fuel pipe.

32 Refit the engine cover on completion.

25.39 Unscrew the two nuts and free the wiring harness and coolant pipes from the starter motor bracket

25.41a Undo the two nuts (arrowed) above the vacuum reservoir . . .

25.41b . . . the bolt at the base of the vacuum reservoir . . .

Z19DTH engines

Removal

33 Disconnect the battery negative terminal (refer to *Disconnecting the battery* in the Reference Chapter).

34 Remove the plastic cover over the top of the engine.

35 Remove the fuel filter crash box as described in Section 9.

36 Remove the high-pressure fuel pump as described in Section 16.

37 Remove the exhaust gas recirculation (EGR) valve as described in Chapter 4B.

38 Disconnect the four vacuum hoses then undo the bolt(s) and remove the two vacuum pipes over the top of the inlet manifold.

39 Unscrew the two nuts securing the wiring harness and coolant pipes to the starter motor bracket. Free the harness and pipes from the bracket **(see illustration)**.

40 Release the clips and disconnect the crankcase breather hoses from the top and bottom of the oil separator.

41 Remove the oil separator and vacuum reservoir mounting bracket by undoing the two nuts above the vacuum reservoir, the bolt at the base of the vacuum reservoir, and the bolt at the right-hand side of the oil separator. Remove the mounting bracket complete with oil separator and vacuum reservoir **(see illustrations)**.

42 Undo the three bolts, release the hose clip, free the wiring harness and detach the coolant pipe from the inlet manifold.

43 Screw two nuts onto the inner high-pressure fuel pump mounting stud. Lock the two nuts together and unscrew the stud from the engine bracket **(see illustration)**.

44 Disconnect the wiring connectors at the throttle housing and charge (boost) pressure sensor.

45 Undo the nine retaining nuts and remove the inlet manifold from the cylinder head studs **(see illustration)**. Recover the gasket.

46 With the manifold removed, if required, remove the throttle housing with reference to Section 13.

47 The changeover flap actuator drive can be removed by disconnecting the drive motor actuating rod ball socket, and undoing the two stud bolts.

25.41c . . . and the bolt at the right-hand side of the oil separator . . .

Refitting

48 If removed, refit the throttle housing with reference to Section 13, then refit the changeover flap actuator drive.

49 Thoroughly clean the inlet manifold and cylinder head mating faces, then locate a new gasket on the inlet manifold flange.

50 Locate the manifold in position and refit the retaining nuts. Diagonally and progressively, tighten the nuts to the specified torque.

51 Reconnect the wiring connectors at the throttle housing and charge (boost) pressure sensor.

52 Refit the high-pressure fuel pump mounting stud, then remove the two nuts used to remove/refit the stud.

53 Refit the coolant pipe to the manifold, and secure with the three bolts tightened securely. Reconnect the coolant pipe and attach the wiring harness.

54 Refit the oil separator and vacuum

25.43 Lock two nuts together and unscrew the fuel pump stud from the engine bracket

25.41d . . . then remove the mounting bracket complete with oil separator and vacuum reservoir

reservoir mounting bracket. Refit and tighten the two bolts and two nuts, then reconnect the crankcase breather hoses.

55 Refit the coolant pipe and wiring harness to the starter motor bracket, then refit and tighten the two nuts.

56 Refit the vacuum pipes over the manifold and reconnect the four vacuum pipes.

57 Refit the exhaust gas recirculation (EGR) valve as described in Chapter 4B.

58 Refit the high-pressure fuel pump as described in Section 16.

59 Refit the fuel filter crash box as described in Section 9.

60 Reconnect the battery negative terminal.

61 Observing the precautions listed in Section 2, prime the fuel system as described in Section 5, then start the engine and allow it to idle. Check for leaks at the high-pressure fuel pipe unions with the engine idling. If satisfactory, increase the engine speed to

25.45 Inlet manifold retaining nuts (arrowed)

26.8 Disconnect the actuating rod ball socket (A), undo the two stud bolts (B) and remove the actuator drive

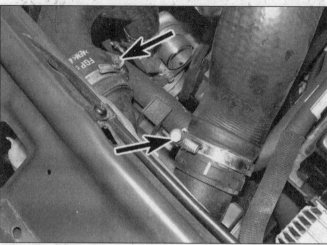

27.5 Slacken the clips (arrowed) and disconnect the two charge air hoses from the intercooler

4000 rpm and check again for leaks. Take the car for a short road test and check for leaks once again on return. If any leaks are detected, obtain and fit a new high-pressure fuel pipe.

62 Refit the engine cover on completion.

26 Inlet manifold changeover flap actuator drive – removal and refitting

Note: *The inlet manifold changeover flap actuator drive is only fitted to Z19DTH engines.*

Removal

1 Disconnect the battery negative terminal (refer to *Disconnecting the battery* in the Reference Chapter).

2 Remove the plastic cover over the top of the engine.

3 Remove the fuel filter crash box as described in Section 9.

4 Disconnect the four vacuum hoses then undo the bolt(s) and remove the two vacuum pipes over the top of the inlet manifold.

5 Unscrew the two nuts securing the wiring harness and coolant pipes to the starter motor

bracket. Free the harness and pipes from the bracket **(see illustration 25.39)**.

6 Release the clips and disconnect the crankcase breather hoses from the top and bottom of the oil separator.

7 Remove the oil separator and vacuum reservoir mounting bracket by undoing the two nuts above the vacuum reservoir, the bolt at the base of the vacuum reservoir, and the bolt at the right-hand side of the oil separator. Remove the mounting bracket complete with oil separator and vacuum reservoir **(see illustrations 25.41a to 25.41d)**.

8 Disconnect the drive motor actuating rod ball socket, and undoing the two stud bolts **(see illustration)**.

9 Withdraw the assembly from the inlet manifold and disconnect the wiring connector.

Refitting

10 Refitting is the reverse of removal.

27 Intercooler – removal and refitting

Note: *On later models, depending on engine*

type and equipment options, it may be necessary to remove the radiator, as described in Chapter 3, to provide sufficient clearance for removal of the intercooler.

Removal

1 Disconnect the battery negative terminal (refer to *Disconnecting the battery* in the Reference Chapter).

2 Remove the plastic cover from the top of the engine

3 Apply the handbrake, then jack up the front of the vehicle and support it on axle stands (see *Jacking and vehicle support*).

4 Remove the front bumper as described in Chapter 11.

5 Slacken the retaining clips and disconnect the two charge air hoses from the top of the intercooler **(see illustration)**.

6 Release the wiring harness from the bracket at the base of the intercooler **(see illustration)**.

7 On models with air conditioning, secure the left-hand side of the condenser to the bonnet crossmember with cable ties. Undo the upper bolt and two lower bolts securing the intercooler and, where fitted, the condenser to the radiator **(see illustrations)**.

27.6 Release the wiring harness from the bracket (arrowed) at the base of the intercooler

27.7a Undo the intercooler upper retaining bolt (arrowed) . . .

27.7b . . . and two lower retaining bolts (arrowed)

27.8 Lower the intercooler and remove it from under the car

8 Carefully lower the intercooler and remove it from under the car **(see illustration)**.

Refitting

9 Refitting is the reverse of removal.

28 Exhaust manifold (1.3 litre engines) – removal and refitting

Note: *New manifold retaining nuts, a new manifold gasket, coolant pipe gasket, catalytic converter gasket, oil filter housing rubber seal, catalytic converter retaining bolt locking plate*

and turbocharger oil supply pipe banjo union copper washers will be required for refitting.

Removal

1 Disconnect the battery negative terminal (refer to *Disconnecting the battery* in the Reference Chapter).

2 Referring to the procedures contained in Section 33, separate the exhaust system front pipe from the catalytic converter.

3 Drain the cooling system as described in Chapter 1.

4 Remove the turbocharger charge air pipe and the charge air hose.

5 Undo the upper nut and two lower bolts and remove the oil filter heat shield **(see illustration)**.

6 Disconnect the wiring connector from the oil pressure switch located at the left-hand end of the cylinder head.

7 Undo the bolt securing the engine lifting bracket to the exhaust manifold and the central nut securing the heat shield to the manifold **(see illustration)**. Remove the lifting bracket, then manipulate the heat shield off the manifold.

8 Undo the two bolts securing the coolant pipe to the heat exchanger on the oil filter housing **(see illustration)**. Release the retaining clip securing the other end of the

pipe to the hose on the thermostat housing. Undo the pipe support bracket bolt, release the wiring harness from the retaining clip and remove the coolant pipe from the engine. Recover the gasket noting that a new one will be required for refitting.

9 Unscrew the banjo union bolt and release the turbocharger oil supply pipe from the oil filter housing **(see illustration)**. Recover the two copper washers from the banjo union, and suitable cover the end of the pipe to prevent dirt entry. Note that new copper washers will be required for refitting.

10 Slacken the retaining clip and disconnect the radiator bottom hose from the outlet at the base of the oil filter housing.

11 Undo the three bolts securing the heat shield support bracket to the heat exchanger on the oil filter housing **(see illustration)**.

12 Undo the remaining bolt and remove the oil filter housing and heat exchanger assembly from the cylinder block. Recover the rubber seal from the rear of the housing. Note that a new seal will be required for refitting.

13 From under the car, undo the bolt securing the catalytic converter support bracket to the sump reinforcement bracket.

14 Suitably support the weight of the catalytic converter on blocks or on a jack. Bend back the locking plate tabs and unscrew the three

28.5 Undo nut and two bolts (arrowed) and remove the oil filter heat shield

28.7 Engine lifting bracket retaining bolt (A) and heat shield centre retaining nut (B)

28.8 Undo the two bolts (arrowed) securing the coolant pipe to the heat exchanger

28.9 Unscrew the turbocharger oil supply pipe banjo union bolt (arrowed) from the oil filter housing

28.11 Undo the three bolts (arrowed) securing the heat shield support bracket to the heat exchanger

28.14 Unscrew the three bolts (arrowed) securing the catalytic converter to the turbocharger

28.15 Separate the catalytic converter from the turbocharger and recover the gasket

28.16 Undo the two bolts securing the turbocharger oil return pipe to the cylinder block

bolts securing the catalytic converter flange to the turbocharger (see illustration). Remove the bolts and locking plate, noting that a new locking plate will be required for refitting.

15 Separate the catalytic converter from the turbocharger and recover the gasket (see illustration). Carefully lower the converter and remove it from under the car. Note that a new gasket will be required for refitting.

16 Undo the two bolts securing the turbocharger oil return pipe to the cylinder block (see illustration). Disconnect the vacuum hose from the turbocharger waste gate actuator.

17 Undo the ten nuts securing the exhaust manifold to the cylinder head. Withdraw the manifold from the cylinder head studs and remove it, complete with turbocharger, from the engine. Recover the manifold gasket and the gasket on the turbocharger oil return pipe flange (see illustrations). Note that a new manifold gasket, oil return pipe gasket and new manifold retaining nuts will be required for refitting.

18 If required, the turbocharger can be removed from the manifold after undoing the three retaining nuts.

Refitting

19 If removed, thoroughly clean the mating faces of the turbocharger and exhaust manifold, then locate the turbocharger over the manifold studs. Refit the three retaining nuts and tighten to the specified torque.

20 Locate a new gasket over the turbocharger oil return pipe flange and bend over the tabs of the gasket to retain it on the flange (see illustrations).

21 Thoroughly clean the mating face of the exhaust manifold and cylinder head, then locate a new gasket over the studs.

28.17a Undo the exhaust manifold retaining nuts . . .

28.17b . . . withdraw the manifold from the cylinder head studs . . .

28.17c . . . and remove the gasket

28.20a Locate a new gasket over the turbocharger oil return pipe . . .

28.20b . . . and bend over the gasket tabs to retain it on the flange

22 Locate the exhaust manifold/turbocharger over the cylinder head studs and secure with the new nuts tightened progressively to the specified torque.
23 Refit the two bolts securing the turbocharger oil return pipe to the cylinder block and tighten them to the specified torque. Reconnect the vacuum hose to the turbocharger waste gate actuator.
24 Using a new gasket, position the catalytic converter on the turbocharger. Insert the three retaining bolts, with a new locking plate and tighten the bolts to the specified torque. Bent over the tabs of the locking plate to retain the bolts.
25 From under the car, refit the bolt securing the catalytic converter support bracket to the sump reinforcement bracket and tighten the bolt to the specified torque.
26 Place a new rubber seal on the oil filter housing, ensuring the seal is fully engaged with the housing grooves (see illustration).
27 Position the oil filter housing on the cylinder block and fit the lower left retaining bolt finger-tight. Place the heat shield support bracket in position and fit the remaining three retaining bolts. Tighten the four bolts to the specified torque.
28 Connect the radiator bottom hose to the outlet at the base of the oil filter housing and secure with the retaining clip.
29 Using a new copper washer on each side of the banjo union, refit the turbocharger oil supply pipe and screw in the banjo union bolt. Tighten the bolt to the specified torque.
30 Locate a new gasket over the heat exchanger coolant pipe and bend over the tabs of the gasket to retain it on the flange (see illustration).
31 Engage the coolant pipe with the hose on the thermostat housing, then position the pipe flange on the heat exchanger. Refit the two bolts and tighten them to the specified torque. At the other end of the pipe, tighten the hose retaining clip, refit and tighten the pipe support bracket bolt and secure the wiring harness with the retaining clip.
32 Place the heat shield in position over the top of the exhaust manifold. Refit the engine lifting bracket and tighten the retaining bolt finger-tight.
33 Place the heat shield over the oil filter, refit the two lower bolts and tighten them finger-tight. Refit the two upper nuts securing the heat shield(s), then tighten the engine lifting bracket bolt, the manifold heat shield upper nuts and the oil filter heat shield lower bolts securely.
34 Reconnect the oil pressure switch wiring connector.
35 Refit the turbocharger charge air pipe and the charge air hose.
36 Refit the exhaust system components with reference to Section 33.
37 Lower the vehicle to the ground, then reconnect the battery negative lead.
38 Refill the cooling system as described in Chapter 1.

28.26 Place a new rubber seal on the oil filter housing, ensuring it fully engages with the housing grooves

29 Exhaust manifold (1.7 litre engines) – removal and refitting

Note: New gaskets for all disturbed joints, and new copper washers for the turbocharger oil supply pipe unions will be required for refitting.

Removal

1 Disconnect the battery negative terminal (refer to *Disconnecting the battery* in the Reference Chapter).
2 Remove the plastic cover from the top of the engine.
3 Remove the air cleaner assembly and intake duct as described in Section 3.
4 Drain the cooling system and the engine oil as described in Chapter 1.
5 Remove the auxiliary drivebelt as described in Chapter 1.
6 Release the refrigerant hoses from the retaining clip on the right-hand side inner wing. Without undoing the refrigerant pipes, disconnect the wiring plug, unbolt the air conditioning compressor from its support bracket (3 bolts), and position it clear of the engine. Use a cable tie or similar to tie the compressor to the bonnet slam panel out of the way. Undo the three bolts and remove the air conditioning compressor support bracket (see illustrations).
7 Release the wiring harness support clips

28.30 Locate a new gasket over the heat exchanger coolant pipe and bend over the tabs to retain it on the flange

from the plastic charge air pipe over the top of the engine (see illustration 18.4).
8 Slacken the retaining clips securing the charge air pipe to the turbocharger.
9 Release the retaining clip and disconnect the crankcase ventilation hose from the camshaft cover (see illustration 18.6).
10 Open the clip and detach the fuel hose from the charge air pipe, then undo the two charge air pipe retaining bolts. Disengage the pipe from the turbocharger, then remove the pipe from the top of the engine (see illustration 18.7).
11 Referring to the procedures contained in Section 33, separate the exhaust system front pipe from the catalytic converter.
12 Undo the two bolts securing the oil dipstick guide tube to the main sump casting.
13 Undo the two bolts securing the turbocharger oil return pipe to the cylinder block.
14 Unscrew the nut and release the turbocharger oil supply pipe from the cylinder block. Recover the two copper washers, and suitable cover the end of the pipe to prevent dirt entry. Note that new copper washers will be required for refitting.
15 Undo the two bolts securing the base of the catalytic converter to the support bracket.
16 Unclip the vacuum hose from the oil dipstick guide tube support bracket, and release the dipstick guide tube from the bracket. Undo the two bolts and remove the bracket from the camshaft cover (see illustrations).
17 Slacken the retaining clips and disconnect

29.6a Tie the compressor to the slam panel . . .

29.6b . . . and remove the compressor mounting bracket

29.16a Unclip the vacuum hose from the oil dipstick guide tube support bracket . . .

the charge air hose from the turbocharger and intercooler.

18 Release the retaining clips and disconnect the upper and lower coolant hoses from the EGR valve heat exchanger. Undo the two bolts at each end of the metal EGR pipe, securing the pipe flanges to the exhaust manifold and EGR valve housing. Undo the retaining bolt and detach the EGR valve heat exchanger bracket from the front of the camshaft housing. Remove the EGR valve heat exchanger/pipe assembly from the engine and collect the two flange gaskets.

19 Disconnect the vacuum hose from the turbocharger wastegate actuator.

20 Unscrew the four bolts and remove the exhaust manifold heat shield.

21 Unscrew the banjo union bolt and release the turbocharger oil supply pipe from the turbocharger. Recover the two copper washers from the banjo union, and suitable cover the end of the pipe to prevent dirt entry. Note that new copper washers will be required for refitting.

22 Undo the two bolts and seven nuts securing the exhaust manifold to the cylinder head. Withdraw the manifold from the cylinder head studs and remove it, complete with turbocharger and catalytic converter, from the engine. Recover the manifold gasket.

23 If required, the catalytic converter and turbocharger can now be removed from the manifold as described in Section 32.

Refitting

24 Refitting is the reverse of removal, noting the following points.

a) If removed, refit the turbocharger and

30.10 Release the retaining clip and disconnect the breather hose from the front of the camshaft cover

29.16b . . . release the dipstick guide tube from the bracket and undo the two bolts (arrowed) . . .

catalytic converter to the manifold as described in Section 32.

b) Ensure all mating surfaces are clean and dry and renew all gaskets, seals and copper washers.

c) Tighten the manifold nuts and bolts evenly and progressively to the specified torque, working in a diagonal sequence.

d) Tighten all other retaining nuts and bolts to the specified torque (where given).

e) Refit the exhaust system front pipe as described in Section 33.

f) Refit the auxiliary drivebelt as described in Chapter 1.

g) On completion refill the cooling system and refill the engine with fresh oil as described in Chapter 1.

h) On starting the engine for the first time, allow the engine to idle for a few minutes before increasing the engine speed; this will allow oil to be circulated around the turbocharger bearings.

30 Exhaust manifold (1.9 litre engines) – removal and refitting

Note: *New manifold retaining nuts, new gaskets for all disturbed joints, and new copper washers for the turbocharger oil supply pipe banjo union will be required for refitting.*

Removal

1 Disconnect the battery negative terminal (refer to *Disconnecting the battery* in the Reference Chapter).

30.13a Undo the turbocharger charge air pipe upper retaining bolt (arrowed) . . .

29.16c . . . then remove the bracket from the camshaft cover

2 Remove the plastic cover from the top of the engine

3 Firmly apply the handbrake, then jack up the front of the car and support it securely on axle stands (see *Jacking and vehicle support*).

4 Drain the cooling system as described in Chapter 1.

5 Remove the exhaust system front pipe as described in Section 33.

6 Remove the air cleaner assembly and air intake duct as described in Section 3.

7 On Z19DT engines, undo the retaining bolt(s) to release the vacuum lines running over the top of the camshaft cover **(see illustration 25.6)**.

8 Release the retaining clips and remove the charge air pipe above the right-hand side of the radiator. Suitably cover the turbocharger air inlet to prevent the entry of dirt and foreign material.

9 On Z19DTH engines, release the retaining clip securing the engine breather hose to the breather pipe adjacent to the engine oil dipstick. Undo the two bolts securing the breather pipe to the cylinder head, and disconnect the pipe from the hose **(see illustration 22.28)**.

10 On Z19DT engines, release the retaining clip and disconnect the breather hose from the front of the camshaft cover **(see illustration)**.

11 Release the two retaining clips and disconnect the charge air hose from the throttle housing, and intercooler.

12 Release the clip and disconnect the radiator top hose from the thermostat housing.

13 Undo the bolt securing the turbocharger charge air pipe to the right-hand end of the camshaft housing (Z19DTH engines) or

30.13b . . . then slacken the clip (arrowed) and move the pipe to one side

30.18 Heat shield retaining nuts and bolts (arrowed)

30.20 Release the EGR pipe clamp from the heat exchanger, separate the pipe and recover the gasket

support bracket (Z19DT engines). Slacken the retaining clip securing the charge air pipe to the turbocharger and move the pipe to one side (see illustrations).

14 Undo the bolt and detach the engine oil dipstick guide tube upper mounting.

15 Release the retaining clip and disconnect the radiator hose from the coolant pipe, then undo the two bolts securing the coolant pipe flange to the right-hand end of the cylinder head.

16 Release the retaining clips securing the heater hose and EGR valve heat exchanger hose at the left-hand end of the pipe assembly.

Undo the bolt securing the heater pipe to the left-hand end of the cylinder head, and the nut securing the pipe to the thermostat housing stud. Remove the pipe assembly from the engine and recover the flange gasket.

17 Undo the nut and bolt and remove the engine lifting bracket from the cylinder head.

18 Undo the three nuts and three bolts securing the heat shield to the exhaust manifold and catalytic converter (see illustration). Manipulate the heat shield off the studs and remove it from the engine.

19 Disconnect the vacuum hose from the turbocharger wastegate actuator.

20 Undo the retaining nut and bolt and release the metal EGR pipe clamp from the EGR valve heat exchanger. Separate the pipe from the heat exchanger and recover the gasket from the pipe fitting (see illustration).

21 Undo the two bolts securing the other end of the pipe to the exhaust manifold. Remove the pipe and recover the gasket (see illustration).

22 Unscrew the two bolts and one nut and remove the catalytic converter lower support bracket.

23 Disconnect the oxygen sensor wiring connector, unscrew the clamp bolt nut and remove the catalytic converter (see illustrations).

24 Unscrew the four bolts securing the oil return pipe to the turbocharger and cylinder block (see illustration). Remove the pipe and recover the gaskets.

25 Unscrew the turbocharger oil supply pipe banjo union from the cylinder block and collect the two copper washers (see illustration).

26 Unscrew the eight nuts securing the exhaust manifold to the cylinder head (see illustration). Note that new nuts will be required for refitting. Withdraw the manifold and turbocharger assembly from the mounting studs, manipulate it sideways, and remove from under the car. Recover the gasket.

30.21 Disconnect the other end of the pipe from the exhaust manifold, then remove the pipe and recover the gasket

30.23a Unscrew the clamp bolt nut (arrowed) . . .

30.23b . . . and remove the catalytic converter

30.24 Unscrew the bolts (arrowed) securing the oil return pipe to the turbocharger and cylinder block

30.25 Unscrew the turbocharger oil supply pipe banjo union (arrowed) and collect the two copper washers

30.26 Exhaust manifold retaining nuts (arrowed)

32.3a Undo the oil return pipe outer bolt, slacken the inner bolt and slide out the pipe flange

Refitting

27 Refitting is the reverse of removal, noting the following points.

a) *Ensure all mating surfaces are clean and dry and renew all gaskets, seals and copper washers.*

b) *Fit the new manifold nuts and tighten them evenly and progressively to the specified torque, working in a diagonal sequence.*

c) *Tighten all other retaining nuts and bolts to the specified torque (where given).*

d) *Refit the exhaust system front pipe as described in Section 33.*

e) *On completion refill the cooling system as described in Chapter 1 and, if necessary, top-up the oil level as described in 'Weekly checks'.*

f) *On starting the engine for the first time, allow the engine to idle for a few minutes before increasing the engine speed; this will allow oil to be circulated around the turbocharger bearings.*

31 Turbocharger – description and precautions

Description

1 The turbocharger increases engine efficiency by raising the pressure in the inlet manifold above atmospheric pressure. Instead of the air simply being sucked into the cylinders, it is forced in.

2 Energy for the operation of the turbocharger comes from the exhaust gas. The gas flows through a specially-shaped housing (the turbine housing) and, in so doing, spins the turbine wheel. The turbine wheel is attached to a shaft, at the end of which is another vaned wheel known as the compressor wheel. The compressor wheel spins in its own housing, and compresses the inlet air on the way to the inlet manifold.

3 The turbochargers operate on the principle of variable vane geometry. At low engine speeds the vanes close to give less flow cross-section, then as the speed increases the vanes open to give an increased flow cross-section. This helps improve the efficiency of the turbocharger.

4 Boost pressure (the pressure in the inlet manifold) is limited by a wastegate, which diverts the exhaust gas away from the turbine wheel in response to a pressure-sensitive actuator.

5 The turbo shaft is pressure-lubricated by an oil feed pipe from the main oil gallery. The shaft 'floats' on a cushion of oil. A drain pipe returns the oil to the sump.

Precautions

6 The turbocharger operates at extremely high speeds and temperatures. Certain precautions must be observed, to avoid premature failure of the turbo, or injury to the operator.

7 Do not operate the turbo with any of its parts exposed, or with any of its hoses removed. Foreign objects falling onto the rotating vanes could cause excessive damage, and (if ejected) personal injury.

8 Do not race the engine immediately after start-up, especially if it is cold. Give the oil a few seconds to circulate.

9 Always allow the engine to return to idle

32.3b Unscrew the return pipe inner bolt and remove the gasket

speed before switching it off – do not blip the throttle and switch off, as this will leave the turbo spinning without lubrication.

10 Allow the engine to idle for several minutes before switching off after a high-speed run.

11 Observe the recommended intervals for oil and filter changing, and use a reputable oil of the specified quality. Neglect of oil changing, or use of inferior oil, can cause carbon formation on the turbo shaft, leading to subsequent failure.

32 Turbocharger – removal and refitting

Note: *On 1.9 litre engines, the turbocharger is an integral part of the exhaust manifold and cannot be separated. The following procedure is therefore only applicable to 1.3 and 1.7 litre engines.*

1.3 litre engines

Removal

1 Carry out the operations described in Section 28, paragraphs 1 to 16.

2 Undo the three retaining nuts, then remove the turbocharger from the exhaust manifold.

3 If required, remove the oil return pipe from the turbocharger as follows. Undo the outer bolt, slacken the inner bolt and slide the pipe out from its location (the inner bolt hole in the pipe flange is slotted to allow removal). With the pipe removed, unscrew the inner bolt and recover the gasket **(see illustrations)**.

4 If required, unscrew the banjo union bolt and release the turbocharger oil supply pipe. Recover the two copper washers from the banjo union, noting that new copper washers will be required for refitting.

Inspection

5 With the turbocharger removed, inspect the housing for cracks or other visible damage.

6 Spin the turbine or the compressor wheel, to verify that the shaft is intact and to feel for

33.5 Removing the exhaust system front pipe from the catalytic converter – two section exhaust systems

33.7 Separate the exhaust front pipe from the catalytic converter and recover the gasket

33.11 Release the exhaust system brackets from the rubber mountings (arrowed)

excessive shake or roughness. Some play is normal, since in use, the shaft is 'floating' on a film of oil. Check that the wheel vanes are undamaged.

7 If oil contamination of the exhaust or induction passages is apparent, it is likely that turbo shaft oil seals have failed.

8 No DIY repair of the turbo is possible and none of the internal or external parts are available separately. If the turbocharger is suspect in any way a complete new unit must be obtained.

Refitting

9 Thoroughly clean the turbocharger and exhaust manifold mating faces.

10 If removed, refit the oil return pipe inner mounting bolt to the turbocharger, together with a new gasket, and screw the bolt in two or three turns. Slide the oil return pipe into place, align the gasket and fit the outer retaining bolt. Tighten both retaining bolts securely.

11 Also, if removed, refit the oil supply pipe, using a new copper washer on each side of the banjo union, refit the banjo union bolt and tighten the bolt to the specified torque.

12 Engage the turbocharger mounting studs with the exhaust manifold, refit the three retaining nuts and tighten to the specified torque.

13 Continue with the exhaust manifold refitting procedures as described in Section 28, paragraphs 20 to 38.

1.7 litre engines

Note: *New turbocharger-to-manifold retaining nuts will be required for refitting.*

Removal

14 Remove the exhaust manifold as described in Section 29.

15 Undo the three bolts and remove the heat shield from the catalytic converter.

16 Undo the four nuts and separate the catalytic converter from the turbocharger. Recover the gasket.

17 Undo the three nuts and remove the turbocharger from the exhaust manifold. Recover the gasket.

Inspection

18 Refer to the information contained in paragraphs 5 to 8.

Refitting

19 Thoroughly clean the turbocharger, catalytic converter and exhaust manifold mating faces.

20 Using a new gasket, refit the turbocharger to the manifold, fit the new retaining nuts and tighten to the specified torque.

21 Refit the catalytic converter to the turbocharger, using a new gasket, then refit and tighten the retaining nuts to the specified torque.

22 Refit the heat shield to the catalytic converter and tighten the bolts to the specified torque.

23 Refit the exhaust manifold as described in Section 29.

33 Exhaust system – general information, removal and refitting

General information

1 According to engine type, the exhaust system consists of two or three main sections. Two section versions utilise a front pipe incorporating the centre silencer, and a tailpipe incorporating the rear silencer. Three section versions utilise a front pipe incorporating an auxiliary catalytic converter, an intermediate pipe incorporating the centre silencer, and a tailpipe incorporating the rear silencer. A primary catalytic converter is fitted between the exhaust manifold and front pipe on all versions.

2 The front pipe is fitted with a flexible section to allow for exhaust system movement and the system is suspended throughout its entire length by rubber mountings.

Removal

3 To remove the various parts of the system, first jack up the front or rear of the car, and support it on axle stands. Alternatively, position the car over an inspection pit, or on car ramps.

Front pipe (two section versions)

4 Remove the tailpipe as described later in this Section.

5 Loosen the clamp securing the exhaust front pipe to the catalytic converter then release the

rubber mountings and slide the front pipe from the catalytic converter **(see illustration)**. While doing this, take care to support the flexible section. **Note:** *Angular movement in excess of 10° can cause permanent damage to the flexible section.* If the front pipe is rusted onto the catalytic converter, apply liberal amounts of penetrating oil and tap around the joint with a hammer to free it. Twist the front pipe in both directions until free.

Front pipe (three section versions)

6 Loosen the clamp securing the front pipe to the intermediate pipe.

7 Undo the three nuts securing the front pipe to the catalytic converter, then free the front pipe from the converter and recover the gasket **(see illustration)**. While doing this, take care to support the flexible section. **Note:** *Angular movement in excess of 10° can cause permanent damage to the flexible section.* On some models, it may be necessary to undo the retaining bolts and release the additional support clamp from the transmission bracket.

8 Slide the front pipe from the intermediate pipe. If the front pipe is rusted onto the intermediate pipe, apply liberal amounts of penetrating oil and tap around the joint with a hammer to free it. Twist the front pipe in both directions until free.

Intermediate pipe

9 Remove the tailpipe as described later in this Section.

10 Undo the three nuts securing the front pipe to the catalytic converter, then free the front pipe from the converter and recover the gasket. While doing this, take care to support the flexible section. **Note:** *Angular movement in excess of 10° can cause permanent damage to the flexible section.* On some models, it may be necessary to undo the retaining bolts and release the additional support clamp from the transmission bracket.

11 Release the rubber mountings and remove the intermediate pipe and front pipe from the car as an assembly **(see illustration)**.

12 Loosen the clamp securing the front pipe to the intermediate pipe. Support the front pipe and slide out the intermediate pipe. If the intermediate pipe is rusted onto the front pipe, apply liberal amounts of penetrating oil and tap around the joint with a hammer to free it.

Twist the intermediate pipe in both directions until free.

Tailpipe

13 Loosen the clamp securing the tail pipe to the front pipe or intermediate pipe.

14 Unhook the tailpipe from its rubber mountings and slide the tailpipe from the front pipe or intermediate pipe. If the tailpipe is rusted onto the front pipe or intermediate pipe, apply liberal amounts of penetrating oil and tap around the joint with a hammer to free it. Twist the tailpipe in both directions until free.

Primary catalytic converter

15 On 1.3 litre engines refer to Section 28, paragraphs 1 to 15.

16 On 1.7 litre engines refer to Section 32, paragraphs 14 to 17.

17 On 1.9 litre engines refer to Section 30, paragraphs 1 to 23.

Heat shield(s)

18 The heat shields are secured to the underside of the body by various nuts and bolts. Each shield can be removed once the relevant exhaust section has been removed. If a shield is being removed to gain access to a component located behind it, it may prove sufficient in some cases to remove the retaining nuts and/or bolts, and simply lower the shield, without disturbing the exhaust system.

Refitting

19 Each section is refitted by reversing the removal sequence, noting the following points:

a) Ensure that all traces of corrosion have been removed from the system joints.

b) When refitting the primary catalytic converter, refer to the Sections indicated in the removal procedures and follow the relevant refitting procedures.

c) When refitting the front pipe to the catalytic converter flange joint, use a new gasket and new retaining nuts, and tighten the nuts to the specified torque.

d) Inspect the rubber mountings for signs of damage or deterioration, and renew as necessary.

e) Prior to tightening the exhaust system fasteners, ensure that all rubber mountings are correctly located, and that there is adequate clearance between the exhaust system and vehicle underbody.

Chapter 4 Part B:
Emissions control systems

Contents

Degrees of difficulty

Easy, suitable for novice with little experience		Fairly easy, suitable for beginner with some experience		Fairly difficult, suitable for competent DIY mechanic		Difficult, suitable for experienced DIY mechanic		Very difficult, suitable for expert DIY or professional	

Specifications

Torque wrench settings	Nm	lbf ft
1.3 litre engines		
EGR valve heat exchanger to EGR valve	25	18
EGR valve mounting bolts	22	16
Oxygen sensor	45	33
1.7 litre engines		
EGR valve heat exchanger pipe flange bolts	28	21
EGR valve housing mounting bolts	25	18
Rear charge air pipe to throttle housing and manifold	25	18
1.9 litre engines		
EGR valve heat exchanger mounting bolt	25	18
EGR valve heat exchanger mounting nut	9	7
EGR valve heat exchanger pipe flange bolts	25	18
EGR valve mounting bolts	25	18
Oxygen sensor	40	30
Vacuum reservoir mounting bracket bolts	25	18

1 General information

1 All models are designed to meet strict emission requirements. The engines are fitted with a crankcase emission control system and a catalytic converter to keep exhaust emissions down to a minimum. An exhaust gas recirculation (EGR) system is also fitted to further decrease exhaust emissions.
2 The emissions control systems function as follows.

Crankcase emission control

3 To reduce the emission of unburned hydrocarbons from the crankcase into the atmosphere, the engine is sealed and the blow-by gases and oil vapour are drawn from inside the crankcase, through an oil separator, into the inlet tract to be burned by the engine during normal combustion.
4 Under all conditions the gases are forced out of the crankcase by the (relatively) higher crankcase pressure; if the engine is worn, the raised crankcase pressure (due to increased blow-by) will cause some of the flow to return under all manifold conditions.

Exhaust emission control

5 To minimise the level of exhaust pollutants released into the atmosphere, one or two catalytic converters are fitted in the exhaust system.
6 The catalytic converter consists of a canister containing a fine mesh impregnated with a catalyst material, over which the hot exhaust gases pass. The catalyst speeds up the oxidation of harmful carbon monoxide, unburned hydrocarbons and soot, effectively reducing the quantity of harmful products

released into the atmosphere via the exhaust gases.
7 On 1.3 and 1.9 litre engines, a heated oxygen sensor is fitted to the exhaust system, upstream of the primary catalytic converter. The sensor monitors the quality of the exhaust gases and provides a signal to the ECU which is then used for mixture correction.

Exhaust gas recirculation (EGR)

8 This system is designed to recirculate small quantities of exhaust gas into the inlet tract, and therefore into the combustion process. This process reduces the level of unburnt hydrocarbons present in the exhaust gas before it reaches the catalytic converter. The system is controlled by the injection system ECU, using the information from its various sensors, via the electrically-operated EGR valve.

2.9 Unscrew the oxygen sensor (arrowed) and remove it from the exhaust manifold

2 Emissions control systems – testing and component renewal

Crankcase emission control

1 The components of this system require no attention other than to check that the hose(s) are clear and undamaged at regular intervals.

Exhaust emission control

Testing

2 The performance of the catalytic converter(s) can be checked only by measuring the exhaust gases using a good-quality, carefully-calibrated exhaust gas analyser.

3 If the catalytic converter(s) is thought to be faulty, before assuming a fault, it is worth checking the problem is not due to a faulty injector(s). Refer to your Vauxhall/Opel dealer for further information.

Catalytic converter renewal

4 On 1.7 and 1.9 litre engines there are two catalytic converters – one fitted between the exhaust manifold and the exhaust front pipe, and a second unit, integral with the exhaust front pipe. On 1.3 litre engines, a single catalytic converter is fitted, between the exhaust manifold and the exhaust front pipe. Refer to Chapter 4A, for removal and refitting details.

Oxygen sensor renewal

Note: *The oxygen sensor is delicate and will*

2.23 Undo the two bolts (arrowed) and remove the EGR valve and heat exchanger assembly – 1.3 litre engines

2.22 Slacken the retaining screw and release the EGR pipe clamp – 1.3 litre engines

not work if it is dropped or knocked, if its power supply is disrupted, or if any cleaning materials are used on it.

5 Warm the engine up to normal operating temperature then stop the engine and disconnect the battery negative terminal (refer to *Disconnecting the battery* in the Reference Chapter). Remove the plastic cover from the top of the engine.

6 Firmly apply the handbrake, then jack up the front of the car and support it securely on axle stands (see *Jacking and vehicle support*).

7 Disconnect the oxygen sensor wiring connector, then unclip the wiring plug from the bracket on the front of the transmission.

8 Trace the wiring back to the sensor and release the wiring from the cable clips.

Caution: Take great care not burn yourself on the hot manifold/sensor.

9 Unscrew the sensor and remove it from the exhaust manifold **(see illustration)**.

10 Refitting is a reverse of the removal procedure. Prior to installing the sensor, apply a smear of high-temperature grease to the sensor threads (Vauxhall/Opel recommend the use of a special grease available from your dealer). Tighten the sensor to the specified torque and ensure that the wiring is correctly routed and in no danger of contacting either the exhaust system or engine.

Exhaust gas recirculation (EGR)

Testing

11 Comprehensive testing of the system can only be carried out using specialist electronic

2.28 Disconnect the air cleaner flexible intake hose from the charge air pipe – 1.7 litre engines

equipment which is connected to the injection system diagnostic wiring connector.

EGR valve renewal – 1.3 litre engines

12 The exhaust gas recirculation valve is bolted to the rear, left-hand side of the cylinder head.

13 Remove the plastic cover over the top of the engine.

14 Drain the cooling system as described in Chapter 1.

15 Remove the battery and battery tray as described in Chapter 5.

16 Remove the air cleaner and relevant air intake ducts as described in Chapter 4A.

17 Remove the fuel filter crash box as described in Chapter 4A.

18 Remove the throttle housing as described in Chapter 4A.

19 Release the retaining clip, withdraw the coolant expansion tank from its location and place it to one side.

20 Slacken the retaining clips, or disconnect the quick-release fittings and detach the two coolant hoses for the EGR valve heat exchanger.

21 Disconnect the wiring connector from the top of the EGR valve.

22 Slacken the retaining screw and release the clamp securing the EGR pipe to the inlet manifold **(see illustration)**.

23 Undo the two mounting bolts and remove the EGR valve and heat exchanger assembly from the engine **(see illustration)**. Recover the gasket.

24 Refit the EGR valve assembly using the reversal of removal, but bearing in mind the following points:

a) *Thoroughly clean the mating faces and use a new gasket. It will be necessary to insert the mounting bolts into the valve prior to refitting, to retain the gasket in position.*

b) *Tighten the mounting bolts to the specified torque.*

c) *Refit the throttle housing as described in Chapter 4A.*

d) *Refit the fuel filter crash box as described in Chapter 4A.*

e) *Refit the air cleaner and relevant air intake ducts as described in Chapter 4A.*

f) *Refit the battery tray and battery as described in Chapter 5.*

g) *Refill the cooling system as described in Chapter 1.*

EGR valve renewal – 1.7 litre engines

25 The exhaust gas recirculation valve is bolted to the rear, left-hand side of the cylinder head.

26 Remove the plastic cover over the top of the engine.

27 Drain the cooling system as described in Chapter 1.

28 Slacken the retaining clip and disconnect the air cleaner flexible intake hose from the charge air pipe **(see illustration)**.

29 Release the wiring harness support clips from the plastic charge air pipe over the top of the engine **(see illustration)**.

2.29 Release the wiring harness support clips from the charge air pipe – 1.7 litre engines

2.31 Disconnect the crankcase ventilation hose from the camshaft cover – 1.7 litre engines

2.32 Remove the charge air pipe from the top of the engine – 1.7 litre engines

30 Slacken the retaining clips securing the charge air pipe to the turbocharger.
31 Release the retaining clip and disconnect the crankcase ventilation hose from the camshaft cover **(see illustration)**.
32 Open the clip and detach the fuel hose from the charge air pipe, then undo the two charge air pipe retaining bolts. Disengage the pipe from the turbocharger, then remove the pipe from the top of the engine **(see illustration)**.
33 Undo the six bolts securing the rear charge air pipe to the throttle housing and inlet manifold. Remove the charge air pipe and recover the gaskets **(see illustrations)**.
34 Remove the battery and battery tray as described in Chapter 5.
35 Remove the throttle housing as described in Chapter 4A.
36 Undo the retaining bolts and remove the engine lifting bracket from the left-hand end of the cylinder head.
37 Disconnect the wiring connector from the top of the EGR valve.
38 Slacken the retaining clip and disconnect the coolant hose from the EGR valve.
39 Undo the two bolts securing the metal EGR pipe flange to the EGR valve housing. Separate the flange from the housing and recover the gasket.
40 Undo the two bolts, noting the different bolt lengths, and remove the EGR valve and housing from the engine. Recover the gasket.
41 Refit the EGR valve assembly using the reversal of removal, but bearing in mind the following points:
 a) Thoroughly clean the mating faces and use a new gasket.
 b) Tighten the mounting bolts to the specified torque.
 c) Refit the throttle housing as described in Chapter 4A.
 d) Refit the charge air pipes using new gaskets.
 e) Refit the battery tray and battery as described in Chapter 5.
 f) Refill the cooling system as described in Chapter 1.

**EGR valve renewal –
1.9 litre Z19DT engines**

42 Disconnect the battery negative terminal

(refer to *Disconnecting the battery* in the Reference Chapter). Remove the plastic cover over the top of the engine.
43 Disconnect the EGR valve wiring connector.
44 Undo the two bolts and disconnect the metal EGR pipe from the throttle housing. Recover the gasket.
45 Undo the two bolts securing the EGR heat exchanger metal pipe to the base of the valve.
46 Undo the three bolts securing the EGR valve to the inlet manifold **(see illustration)**. Remove the valve together with the engine lifting bracket and recover the gasket fitted on each side of the lifting bracket.
47 Refitting is the reverse of removal using new gaskets and tightening the retaining bolts to the specified torque.

2.33a Undo the six bolts then remove the rear charge air pipe . . .

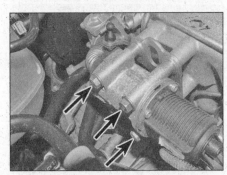

2.46 EGR valve retaining bolts (arrowed) – 1.9 litre Z19DT engines

**EGR valve renewal –
1.9 litre Z19DTH engines**

48 Disconnect the battery negative terminal (refer to *Disconnecting the battery* in the Reference Chapter). Remove the plastic cover over the top of the engine.
49 Disconnect the EGR valve wiring connector.
50 Unscrew the two bolts on the top of the valve and detach the metal EGR pipe flange from the base of the valve. Recover the gasket **(see illustration)**.
51 Unscrew the two nuts and two bolts securing the EGR valve to the inlet manifold and lift off the engine cover bracket **(see illustration)**.
52 To provide sufficient clearance to remove the valve, it will be necessary to unscrew the two mounting studs from the manifold. To do this, lock two nuts together on each stud and

2.33b . . . and recover the gaskets – 1.7 litre engines

2.50 Unscrew the two bolts, detach the metal EGR pipe flange and recover the gasket – 1.9 litre Z19DTH engines

2.51 Unscrew the two nuts and two bolts (arrowed) securing the EGR valve to the inlet manifold – 1.9 litre Z19DTH engines

remove the studs by unscrewing the inner nut.

53 With the studs removed, lift off the valve and recover the gasket **(see illustration)**.

54 Refitting is the reverse of removal using new gaskets and tightening the retaining nuts and bolts to the specified torque.

EGR valve heat exchanger renewal – 1.3 litre engines

55 Remove the EGR valve as described previously.

56 Release the retaining clips and disconnect the two coolant hoses from the heat exchanger.

57 Undo the three bolts and separate the heat exchanger from the EGR valve. Recover the gasket.

58 Refitting is the reverse of removal using a new gasket and tightening the retaining bolts to the specified torque.

EGR valve heat exchanger renewal – 1.7 litre engines

59 Drain the cooling system as described in Chapter 1.

60 Remove the plastic cover over the top of the engine.

61 Slacken the retaining clip and disconnect the air cleaner flexible intake hose from the charge air pipe **(see illustration 2.28)**.

62 Release the wiring harness support clips from the plastic charge air pipe over the top of the engine **(see illustration 2.29)**.

63 Slacken the retaining clips securing the charge air pipe to the turbocharger.

64 Release the retaining clip and disconnect

2.53 Lift off the valve and recover the gasket – 1.9 litre Z19DTH engines

the crankcase ventilation hose from the camshaft cover **(see illustration 2.31)**.

65 Open the clip and detach the fuel hose from the charge air pipe, then undo the two charge air pipe retaining bolts. Disengage the pipe from the turbocharger, then remove the pipe from the top of the engine **(see illustration 2.32)**.

66 Unclip the vacuum hose from the oil dipstick guide tube support bracket, and release the dipstick guide tube from the bracket. Undo the two bolts and remove the bracket from the camshaft cover.

67 Release the retaining clips and disconnect the upper and lower coolant hoses from the EGR valve heat exchanger. Undo the two bolts at each end of the metal EGR pipe, securing the pipe flanges to the exhaust manifold and EGR valve housing. Undo the retaining bolt and detach the EGR valve heat exchanger bracket from the front of the camshaft housing. Remove the EGR valve heat exchanger/pipe assembly from the engine and collect the two flange gaskets.

68 Refitting is the reverse of removal, bearing in mind the following points:

 a) Thoroughly clean the mating faces of the pipe flanges and use new gaskets.

 b) Tighten the flange retaining bolts to the specified torque.

 c) Refill the cooling system as described in Chapter 1.

EGR valve heat exchanger renewal – 1.9 litre Z19DT engines

69 Drain the cooling system as described in Chapter 1.

70 Remove the plastic cover over the top of the engine.

71 Remove the battery and battery tray as described in Chapter 5.

72 Slacken the retaining clips and remove the charge air pipe from the throttle housing and intercooler.

73 Slacken the retaining clips and disconnect the two coolant hoses from the metal coolant pipe assembly at the rear of the engine.

74 Unscrew the two nuts securing the wiring harness and coolant pipe assembly to the starter motor bracket and the nut securing the pipes to the thermostat housing stud. Free the harness and pipes from the bracket.

75 Slacken the retaining clips securing the remaining coolant hoses to the coolant pipe assembly and manoeuvre the pipe assembly from the engine.

76 Undo the two bolts securing the rear metal EGR pipe to the EGR valve. Undo the retaining nut and bolt and release the metal EGR pipe clamp from the EGR valve heat exchanger. Separate the pipe from the heat exchanger and recover the gasket from the pipe fitting.

77 Similarly, undo the retaining nut and bolt and release the front metal EGR pipe clamp from the EGR valve heat exchanger.

78 Free the vacuum reservoir mounting bracket from the rear of the cylinder block by undoing the three mounting bracket retaining bolts.

79 Slacken the retaining clips and disconnect the two coolant hoses from the EGR valve heat exchanger. Undo the retaining nut and bolt securing the heat exchanger to the cylinder head and remove the heat exchanger from the engine.

80 Refitting is the reverse of removal, bearing in mind the following points:

 a) Renew all disturbed gaskets and seals.

 b) Tighten the retaining bolts/nuts to the specified torque.

 c) Refit the battery tray and battery as described in Chapter 5.

 d) Refill the cooling system as described in Chapter 1.

EGR valve heat exchanger renewal – 1.9 litre Z19DTH engines

81 Drain the cooling system as described in Chapter 1.

82 Remove the plastic cover over the top of the engine.

83 Remove the battery and battery tray as described in Chapter 5.

84 Slacken the retaining clips and disconnect the two coolant hoses from the metal coolant pipe assembly at the rear of the engine.

85 Unscrew the two nuts securing the wiring harness and coolant pipe assembly to the starter motor bracket and the nut securing the pipes to the thermostat housing stud. Free the harness and pipes from the bracket.

86 Slacken the retaining clips securing the remaining coolant hoses to the coolant pipe assembly and manoeuvre the pipe assembly from the engine.

87 Remove the thermostat housing as described in Chapter 3.

88 Slacken the retaining clips and remove the charge air hose from the turbocharger and intercooler.

89 Release the retaining clip and disconnect the coolant hose from the metal coolant pipe at the front of the engine.

90 Release the retaining clips and disconnect the coolant hoses from the EGR valve heat exchanger.

91 Undo the two bolts securing the rear metal EGR pipe to the EGR valve. Undo the retaining nut and bolt and release the metal EGR pipe clamp from the EGR valve heat exchanger. Separate the pipe from the heat exchanger and recover the gasket from the pipe fitting.

92 Similarly, undo the two bolts securing the front metal EGR pipe to the exhaust manifold. Undo the retaining nut and bolt and release the metal EGR pipe clamp from the EGR valve heat exchanger. Separate the pipe from the heat exchanger and recover the gasket from the pipe fitting.

93 Undo the two bolts and remove the heat exchanger from the engine.

94 Refitting is the reverse of removal, bearing in mind the following points:

 a) Renew all disturbed gaskets and seals.

 b) Tighten the retaining bolts to the specified torque.

c) *Refit the thermostat housing as described in Chapter 3.*

d) *Refit the battery tray and battery as described in Chapter 5.*

e) *Refill the cooling system as described in Chapter 1.*

3 Catalytic converter – general information and precautions

1 The catalytic converter is a reliable and simple device which needs no maintenance in itself, but there are some facts of which an owner should be aware if the converter is to function properly for its full service life.

a) *DO NOT use fuel or engine oil additives – these may contain substances harmful to the catalytic converter.*

b) *DO NOT continue to use the car if the engine burns oil to the extent of leaving a visible trail of blue smoke.*

c) *Remember that the catalytic converter operates at very high temperatures. DO NOT, therefore, park the car in dry undergrowth, over long grass or piles of dead leaves after a long run.*

d) *Remember that the catalytic converter is FRAGILE – do not strike it with tools during servicing work.*

e) *The catalytic converter, used on a well-maintained and well-driven car, should last for between 50 000 and 100 000 miles – if the converter is no longer effective it must be renewed.*

Notes

Chapter 5
Starting and charging systems

Contents

Degrees of difficulty

Easy, suitable for novice with little experience		**Fairly easy,** suitable for beginner with some experience		**Fairly difficult,** suitable for competent DIY mechanic		**Difficult,** suitable for experienced DIY mechanic		**Very difficult,** suitable for expert DIY or professional	

Specifications

General

Electrical system type .... 12 volt negative earth

Battery

Type .... Lead-acid, 'maintenance-free' (sealed for life)
Charge condition:
  Poor .... 12.5 volts
  Normal .... 12.6 volts
  Good.. 12.7 volts

Torque wrench settings

	Nm	lbf ft
Alternator mounting bolts:		
1.3 litre engines	22	16
1.7 litre engines:		
M8 bolt	19	14
M10 bolt	46	34
1.9 litre engines	70	52
Auxiliary drivebelt tensioner mounting bolt:		
1.3 litre engines	50	37
1.7 litre engines:		
Idler pulley retaining bolt	38	28
Tensioner central mounting bolt	50	37
1.9 litre engines	50	37
Glow plugs:		
1.3 litre engines	10	7
1.7 litre engines	18	13
1.9 litre engines	8	6
Oil pressure warning light switch:		
1.3 litre engines	32	24
1.7 litre engines	20	15
1.9 litre engines	25	18
Roadwheel bolts	110	81
Starter motor mounting bolts:		
1.3 litre engines	25	18
1.7 litre engines:		
Lower bolt	38	28
Upper bolt	60	44
1.9 litre engines	25	18

1 General information, precautions and battery disconnection

General information

The engine electrical system consists mainly of the charging and starting systems, and the diesel engine pre/post-heating system. Because of their engine-related functions, these components are covered separately from the body electrical devices such as the lights, instruments, etc (which are covered in Chapter 12).

The electrical system is of 12 volt negative earth type.

The battery is of the maintenance-free (sealed for life) type, and is charged by the alternator, which is belt-driven from the crankshaft pulley.

The starter motor is of pre-engaged type incorporating an integral solenoid. On starting, the solenoid moves the drive pinion into engagement with the flywheel/driveplate ring gear before the starter motor is energised. Once the engine has started, a one-way clutch prevents the motor armature being driven by the engine until the pinion disengages.

Further details of the various systems are given in the relevant Sections of this Chapter. While some repair procedures are given, the usual course of action is to renew the component concerned. The owner whose interest extends beyond mere component renewal should obtain a copy of the *Automotive Electrical & Electronic Systems Manual*, available from the publishers of this manual.

Precautions

It is necessary to take extra care when working on the electrical system to avoid damage to semi-conductor devices (diodes and transistors), and to avoid the risk of personal injury. In addition to the precautions given in *Safety first!* at the beginning of this manual, observe the following when working on the system:

• Always remove rings, watches, etc, before working on the electrical system. Even with the battery disconnected, capacitive discharge could occur if a component's live terminal is

3.5 Battery charge condition indicator – 'Delco' type battery

earthed through a metal object. This could cause a shock or nasty burn.

• Do not reverse the battery connections. Components such as the alternator, electronic control units, or any other components having semi-conductor circuitry could be irreparably damaged.

• If the engine is being started using jump leads and a slave battery, connect the batteries positive-to-positive and negative-to-negative (see 'Jump starting'). This also applies when connecting a battery charger but in this case both of the battery terminals should first be disconnected.

• Never disconnect the battery terminals, the alternator, any electrical wiring or any test instruments when the engine is running.

• Do not allow the engine to turn the alternator when the alternator is not connected.

• Never test for alternator output by flashing the output lead to earth.

• Never use an ohmmeter of the type incorporating a hand-cranked generator for circuit or continuity testing.

• Always ensure that the battery negative lead is disconnected when working on the electrical system.

• Before using electric-arc welding equipment on the car, disconnect the battery, alternator and components such as the engine electronic control unit to protect them from the risk of damage.

Battery disconnection

Refer to the precautions listed in *Disconnecting the battery* in the Reference Chapter.

2 Electrical fault finding – general information

Refer to Chapter 12.

3 Battery – testing and charging

Testing

Traditional and low maintenance battery

1 If the vehicle covers a small annual mileage, it is worthwhile checking the specific gravity of the electrolyte every three months to determine the state of charge of the battery. Use a hydrometer to make the check and compare the results with the following table. Note that the specific gravity readings assume an electrolyte temperature of 15°C; for every 10°C below 15°C subtract 0.007. For every 10°C above 15°C add 0.007.

	Ambient temperature	
	Above 25°C	Below 25°C
Fully-charged	1.210 to 1.230	1.270 to 1.290
70% charged	1.170 to 1.190	1.230 to 1.250
Discharged	1.050 to 1.070	1.110 to 1.130

2 If the battery condition is suspect, first check the specific gravity of electrolyte in each cell. A variation of 0.040 or more between any cells indicates loss of electrolyte or deterioration of the internal plates.

3 If the specific gravity variation is 0.040 or more, the battery should be renewed. If the cell variation is satisfactory but the battery is discharged, it should be charged as described later in this Section.

Maintenance-free battery

4 Where a 'sealed for life' maintenance-free battery is fitted, topping-up and testing of the electrolyte in each cell is not possible. The condition of the battery can therefore only be tested using a battery condition indicator or a voltmeter.

5 Some models are fitted with a maintenance-free battery with a built-in 'magic-eye' charge condition indicator. The indicator is located in the top of the battery casing, and indicates the condition of the battery from its colour (see illustration). If the indicator shows green, then the battery is in a good state of charge. If the indicator turns darker, eventually to black, then the battery requires charging, as described later in this Section. If the indicator shows clear/yellow, then the electrolyte level in the battery is too low to allow further use, and the battery should be renewed. Do not attempt to charge, load or jump start a battery when the indicator shows clear/yellow.

All battery types

6 If testing the battery using a voltmeter, connect the voltmeter across the battery and compare the result with those given in the Specifications under 'charge condition'. The test is only accurate if the battery has not been subjected to any kind of charge for the previous six hours. If this is not the case, switch on the headlights for 30 seconds, then wait four to five minutes before testing the battery after switching off the headlights. All other electrical circuits must be switched off, so check that the doors and tailgate are fully shut when making the test.

7 If the voltage reading is less than 12.2 volts, then the battery is discharged, whilst a reading of 12.2 to 12.4 volts indicates a partially-discharged condition.

8 If the battery is to be charged, remove it from the vehicle (Section 4) and charge it as described later in this Section.

Charging

Note: *The following is intended as a guide only. Always refer to the manufacturer's recommendations (often printed on a label attached to the battery) before charging a battery.*

Traditional and low maintenance battery

9 Charge the battery at a rate of 3.5 to 4 amps and continue to charge the battery at this rate until no further rise in specific gravity is noted over a four hour period.

4.2 Unscrew the battery negative (–) terminal retaining nut, then lift the terminal clamp off the battery post

4.4 Unscrew the bolt and remove the battery retaining clamp

4.10 Unclip the pre/post-heating system control unit from the front of the battery tray

10 Alternatively, a trickle charger charging at the rate of 1.5 amps can safely be used overnight.
11 Specially rapid 'boost' charges which are claimed to restore the power of the battery in 1 to 2 hours are not recommended, as they can cause serious damage to the battery plates through overheating.
12 While charging the battery, note that the temperature of the electrolyte should never exceed 38ºC.

Maintenance-free battery

13 This battery type takes considerably longer to fully recharge than the standard type, the time taken being dependent on the extent of discharge, but it will take anything up to three days.
14 A constant voltage type charger is required, to be set, when connected, to 13.9 to 14.9 volts with a charger current below 25 amps. Using this method, the battery should be usable within three hours, giving a voltage reading of 12.5 volts, but this is for a partially-discharged battery and, as mentioned, full charging can take considerably longer.
15 If the battery is to be charged from a fully-discharged state (condition reading less than 12.2 volts), have it recharged by your Vauxhall/Opel dealer or local automotive electrician, as the charge rate is higher and constant supervision during charging is necessary.

4 Battery and battery tray – removal and refitting

Note: *Refer to 'Disconnecting the battery' in the Reference Chapter before proceeding.*

Battery

Removal

1 The battery is located at the front, left-hand side of the engine compartment.
2 Open the battery jacket (where fitted) and disconnect the lead at the negative (–) terminal by unscrewing the retaining nut and removing the terminal clamp **(see illustration)**. Note that the battery negative (–) and positive (+) terminal connections are stamped on the battery case.
3 Disconnect the lead at the positive (+) terminal by lifting the plastic terminal cover,

unscrewing the retaining nut and removing the terminal clamp. If necessary, the auxiliary lead may also be unbolted from the terminal.
4 On the inner side of the battery, unscrew the bolt and remove the retaining clamp **(see illustration)**.
5 Carefully lift the battery from its location and remove it from the car. Make sure the battery is kept upright at all times.

Refitting

Note: *As a precaution before refitting the battery, check that all doors are unlocked.*
6 Refitting is a reversal of removal, but smear petroleum jelly on the terminals after reconnecting the leads to reduce corrosion, and always reconnect the positive lead first, followed by the negative lead.

Battery tray

Removal

7 Remove the battery as described previously. Where fitted, remove the battery jacket.
8 Release the wiring harness cable ties from the battery tray and move the harness to one side.
9 Unclip the coolant hose(s) and release it from the battery tray.
10 Unclip the pre/post-heating system control unit from the front of the battery tray and move it to one side **(see illustration)**.
11 Undo the three retaining bolts and remove the battery tray from the engine compartment **(see illustrations)**.

Refitting

12 Refitting is a reversal of removal.

4.11a Undo the three retaining bolts (arrowed) . . .

5 Charging system – testing

Note: *Refer to the precautions given in 'Safety first!' and in Section 1 of this Chapter before starting work.*

1 If the ignition no-charge warning light fails to illuminate when the ignition is switched on, first check the alternator wiring connections for security. If satisfactory, check the condition of all related fuses, fusible links, wiring connections and earthing points. If this fails to reveal the fault, the vehicle should be taken to a Vauxhall/Opel dealer or auto-electrician, as further testing entails the use of specialist diagnostic equipment.
2 If the ignition warning light illuminates when the engine is running, stop the engine and check the condition of the auxiliary drivebelt (see Chapter 1) and the security of the alternator wiring connections. If satisfactory, have the alternator checked by a Vauxhall/Opel dealer or auto-electrician.
3 If the alternator output is suspect even though the warning light functions correctly, the regulated voltage may be checked as follows.
4 Connect a voltmeter across the battery terminals, and start the engine.
5 Increase the engine speed until the voltmeter reading remains steady; the reading should be approximately 12 to 13 volts, and no more than 14 volts.
6 Switch on as many electrical accessories

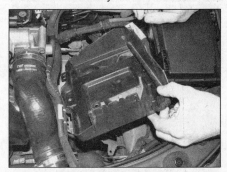

4.11b . . . and remove the battery tray from the engine compartment

7.4 Unscrew the tensioner body retaining bolt and withdraw the tensioner assembly – 1.3 litre engines

(eg, the headlights, heated rear window and heater blower) as possible, and check that the alternator maintains the regulated voltage at around 13.5 to 14.5 volts.

7 If the regulated voltage is not as stated, the fault may be due to worn brushes, weak brush springs, a faulty voltage regulator, a faulty diode, a severed phase winding, or worn or damaged slip-rings. The alternator should be renewed or taken to a Vauxhall/Opel dealer or auto-electrician for testing and repair.

6 Auxiliary drivebelt – removal and refitting

Refer to Chapter 1.

7 Auxiliary drivebelt tensioner – removal and refitting

Removal

1.3 litre engines

1 Firmly apply the handbrake, then jack up the front of the car and support it securely on axle stands (see *Jacking and vehicle support*). Remove the right-hand front roadwheel.
2 Remove the air cleaner assembly and air intake duct as described in Chapter 4A.
3 Remove the auxiliary drivebelt as described in Chapter 1.

7.13 Undo the central mounting bolt (arrowed) and remove the tensioner assembly – 1.9 litre engines

7.9 Remove the auxiliary drivebelt idler pulley retaining bolt (arrowed) – 1.7 litre engines

4 Undo the central mounting bolt, and remove the tensioner assembly from the engine **(see illustration)**.

1.7 litre engines

5 Firmly apply the handbrake, then jack up the front of the car and support it securely on axle stands (see *Jacking and vehicle support*). Remove the right-hand front roadwheel.
6 Remove the air cleaner assembly and air intake duct as described in Chapter 4A.
7 Remove the auxiliary drivebelt as described in Chapter 1.
8 On models equipped with air conditioning, for improved access refer to Chapter 3 and unbolt the air conditioning compressor from its mounting bracket **without disconnecting the refrigerant lines**. Support the compressor to one side for access to the drivebelt tensioner assembly.
9 Undo the auxiliary drivebelt idler pulley retaining bolt and remove the pulley **(see illustration)**.
10 Undo the central mounting bolt and remove the tensioner assembly from the alternator mounting bracket.

1.9 litre engines

11 Firmly apply the handbrake, then jack up the front of the car and support it securely on axle stands (see *Jacking and vehicle support*). Remove the right-hand front roadwheel.
12 Remove the auxiliary drivebelt as described in Chapter 1.
13 Undo the central mounting bolt, and remove the tensioner assembly from the engine **(see illustration)**.

7.14 Ensure that the lug on the tensioner body (arrowed) engages with the cylinder block – 1.3 litre engines

Refitting

1.3 litre engines

14 Place the tensioner assembly in position ensuring that the lug on the tensioner body engages with the corresponding hole on the cylinder block as the tensioner is refitted **(see illustration)**. Tighten the tensioner central mounting bolt to the specified torque.
15 Refit the auxiliary drivebelt as described in Chapter 1.
16 Refit the air cleaner assembly and air intake duct as described in Chapter 4A.
17 Refit the roadwheel then lower the car to the ground. Tighten the roadwheel bolts to the specified torque.

1.7 litre engines

18 Align the tensioner assembly with the alternator mounting bracket, refit the central mounting bolt and tighten the bolt to the specified torque.
19 Refit the auxiliary drivebelt idler pulley and tighten the retaining bolt to the specified torque.
20 Where applicable, refit the air conditioning compressor as described in Chapter 3.
21 Refit the auxiliary drivebelt as described in Chapter 1.
22 Refit the air cleaner assembly and air intake duct as described in Chapter 4A.
23 Refit the roadwheel then lower the car to the ground. Tighten the roadwheel bolts to the specified torque.

1.9 litre engines

24 Place the tensioner assembly in position ensuring that the locating peg on the tensioner mounting surface engages correctly with the corresponding hole in the mounting bracket. Tighten the tensioner central mounting bolt to the specified torque.
25 Refit the auxiliary drivebelt as described in Chapter 1.
26 Refit the roadwheel then lower the car to the ground. Tighten the roadwheel bolts to the specified torque.

8 Alternator – removal and refitting

Removal

1.3 litre engines

1 Disconnect the battery negative terminal (refer to *Disconnecting the battery* in the Reference Chapter).
2 Firmly apply the handbrake, then jack up the front of the vehicle and support it on axle stands (see *Jacking and vehicle support*). Remove the right-hand front roadwheel.
3 Remove the air cleaner assembly and air intake duct as described in Chapter 4A.
4 Remove the auxiliary drivebelt as described in Chapter 1.
5 Unscrew the nuts and disconnect the wires from the rear of the alternator.

8.6 Alternator mounting bolts (arrowed) – 1.3 litre engines

8.11 Disconnect the wiring plug and unbolt the wiring connector (arrowed) – 1.7 litre engines

8.12 Vacuum pump oil feed pipe (A) and return pipe (B) – 1.7 litre engines

6 Unscrew the upper mounting bolt and the two lower mounting bolts, then withdraw the alternator downwards from the block **(see illustration)**.

1.7 litre engines

7 Disconnect the battery negative terminal (refer to *Disconnecting the battery* in the Reference Chapter).
8 Firmly apply the handbrake, then jack up the front of the vehicle and support it on axle stands (see *Jacking and vehicle support*). Remove the right-hand front roadwheel.
9 Remove the auxiliary drivebelt as described in Chapter 1.
10 Remove the horns as described in Chapter 12.
11 Disconnect the alternator wiring plug, then undo the nut and disconnect the wiring connector **(see illustration)**.
12 Unscrew the oil feed pipe to the vacuum pump on the rear of the alternator, and unclip the oil return pipe **(see illustration)**. Be prepared for oil spillage.
13 Disconnect the vacuum pipes for the EGR solenoid valve and brake servo from the vacuum pump.
14 Unscrew the upper and lower alternator mounting bolts and manoeuvre the alternator, complete with vacuum pump, out through the aperture created by removing the horns **(see illustrations)**.

1.9 litre engines

15 Disconnect the battery negative terminal (refer to *Disconnecting the battery* in the Reference Chapter).
16 Firmly apply the handbrake, then jack up the front of the car and support it securely on axle stands (see *Jacking and vehicle support*). Remove the right-hand front roadwheel.
17 Remove the auxiliary drivebelt as described in Chapter 1.
18 Undo the alternator lower front mounting bolt **(see illustration)**.
19 Remove the fuel filter crash box as described in Chapter 4A.
20 On Z19DTH engines, undo the two bolts securing the wiring harness support bracket to the high-pressure fuel pump mounting bracket. Unclip the wiring harness as necessary and move it clear of the alternator.
21 Unscrew the three retaining nuts and

disconnect the wiring connectors from the alternator terminals.
22 Undo the alternator upper rear mounting bolts and manoeuvre the alternator upwards and out of position **(see illustration)**.

Refitting

1.3 litre engines

23 Manoeuvre the alternator into position and refit the upper and lower mounting bolts. Tighten the bolts to the specified torque.
24 Reconnect the wiring to the alternator terminals and tighten the retaining nuts securely.
25 Refit the auxiliary drivebelt as described in Chapter 1.
26 Refit the air cleaner assembly and air intake duct as described in Chapter 4A.
27 Refit the roadwheel then lower the car to the ground. Tighten the roadwheel bolts to the specified torque.

8.14a Alternator upper mounting bolt . . .

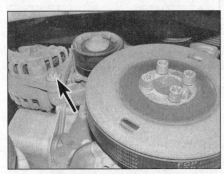

8.18 Alternator lower front mounting bolt (arrowed) – 1.9 litre engines

28 On completion, reconnect the battery negative terminal.

1.7 litre engines

29 Manoeuvre the alternator into position and refit the upper and lower mounting bolts. Tighten the bolts to the specified torque.
30 Reconnect the EGR solenoid valve and brake servo vacuum pipes to the vacuum pump.
31 Refit the oil feed pipe to the vacuum pump using new copper washers on the banjo bolt. Refit and secure the oil return pipe to the vacuum pump.
32 Reconnect the alternator wiring plug and wiring connector. Tighten the connector retaining nut securely.
33 Refit the horns as described in Chapter 12.
34 Refit the auxiliary drivebelt as described in Chapter 1.
35 Refit the roadwheel then lower the car to the ground. Tighten the roadwheel bolts to the specified torque.

8.14b . . . and lower mounting bolt – 1.7 litre engines

8.22 Alternator upper rear mounting bolts (arrowed) – 1.9 litre engines

11.4 Working through the access hole, unscrew and remove the starter upper mounting bolt – 1.3 litre engines

36 On completion, reconnect the battery negative terminal, then check and if necessary, top-up the engine oil as described in *Weekly checks*.

1.9 litre engines

37 Manoeuvre the alternator into position and refit the upper rear retaining bolt(s). Tighten the bolt(s) finger-tight only at this stage.

38 Reconnect the wiring to the alternator terminals and tighten the retaining nuts securely.

39 On Z19DTH engines, refit the wiring harness support bracket to the fuel pump mounting bracket and secure with the two bolts. Clip the wiring harness back into position in the bracket.

40 Refit the alternator lower front mounting bolt, then tighten the upper and lower mounting bolts to the specified torque.

41 Refit the auxiliary drivebelt as described in Chapter 1.

42 Refit the fuel filter crash box as described in Chapter 4A.

43 Refit the roadwheel then lower the car to the ground. Tighten the roadwheel bolts to the specified torque.

44 On completion, reconnect the battery negative terminal.

9 Alternator – testing and overhaul

If the alternator is thought to be suspect,

11.8 Battery positive cable connection on the starter motor (arrowed) – 1.3 litre engines

it should be removed from the vehicle and taken to an auto-electrician for testing. Most auto-electricians will be able to supply and fit brushes at a reasonable cost. However, check on the cost of repairs before proceeding as it may prove more economical to obtain a new or exchange alternator.

10 Starting system – testing

Note: *Refer to the precautions given in 'Safety first!' and in Section 1 of this Chapter before starting work.*

1 If the starter motor fails to operate during the normal starting procedure, the possible causes are as follows:
   a) The engine immobiliser is faulty.
   b) The battery is faulty.
   b) The electrical connections between the switch, solenoid, battery and starter motor are somewhere failing to pass the necessary current from the battery through the starter to earth.
   c) The solenoid is faulty.
   d) The starter motor is mechanically or electrically defective.

2 To check the battery, switch on the headlights. If they dim after a few seconds, this indicates that the battery is discharged – recharge (see Section 3) or renew the battery. If the headlights glow brightly, operate the starter switch while watching the headlights. If they dim, then this indicates that current is reaching the starter motor, therefore the fault must lie in the starter motor. If the lights continue to glow brightly (and no clicking sound can be heard from the starter motor solenoid), this indicates that there is a fault in the circuit or solenoid – see the following paragraphs. If the starter motor turns slowly when operated, but the battery is in good condition, then this indicates either that the starter motor is faulty, or there is considerable resistance somewhere in the circuit.

3 If a fault in the circuit is suspected, disconnect the battery leads (including the earth connection to the body), the starter/solenoid wiring and the engine/transmission earth strap. Thoroughly clean the connections, and reconnect the leads and wiring. Use a voltmeter or test light to check that full battery voltage is available at the battery positive lead connection to the solenoid. Smear petroleum jelly around the battery terminals to prevent corrosion – corroded connections are among the most frequent causes of electrical system faults.

4 If the battery and all connections are in good condition, check the circuit by disconnecting the ignition switch supply wire from the solenoid terminal. Connect a voltmeter or test lamp between the wire end and a good earth (such as the battery negative terminal), and check that the wire is live when the ignition switch is turned to the 'start' position, or the

'start/stop' button is depressed. If it is, then the circuit is sound – if not the circuit wiring can be checked as described in Chapter 12.

5 The solenoid contacts can be checked by connecting a voltmeter or test light between the battery positive feed connection on the starter side of the solenoid and earth. When the ignition switch is turned to the 'start' position, or the 'start/stop' button is depressed, there should be a reading or lighted bulb, as applicable. If there is no reading or lighted bulb, the solenoid is faulty and should be renewed.

6 If the circuit and solenoid are proved sound, the fault must lie in the starter motor. In this event, it may be possible to have the starter motor overhauled by a specialist, but check on the cost of spares before proceeding, as it may prove more economical to obtain a new or exchange motor.

11 Starter motor – removal and refitting

Removal

1.3 litre engines

1 Remove the battery and battery tray as described in Section 4.

2 Using a suitable forked tool, release the gear selector inner cable end fittings from the transmission selector levers. Pull back the retaining sleeves and detach the outer cables from the mounting bracket on the transmission.

3 Extract the rubber plug (where fitted) at the top of the transmission bellhousing for access to the starter upper mounting bolt.

4 Using a long socket bit inserted through the access hole, unscrew and remove the upper mounting bolt **(see illustration)**. Take great care not to drop the bolt in the bellhousing!

5 Apply the handbrake, then jack up the front of the vehicle and support it on axle stands (see *Jacking and vehicle support*).

6 Disconnect the two vacuum hoses from the vacuum reservoir at the rear of the cylinder block.

7 Unscrew the nut and detach the earth cable, then undo the two bolts and remove the vacuum reservoir complete with its mounting bracket.

8 Undo the two nuts and disconnect the wiring from the starter solenoid **(see illustration)**.

9 Unscrew the lower mounting bolt and withdraw the starter motor from the engine.

1.7 litre engines

10 Remove the battery and battery tray as described in Section 4.

11 Firmly apply the handbrake, then jack up the front of the car and support it securely on axle stands (see *Jacking and vehicle support*).

12 Detach the oil filter housing-to-cylinder block oil return hose from the rear of the engine. Be prepared for fluid spillage.

11.13 Disconnect the starter solenoid wiring connections (arrowed) – 1.7 litre engines

11.15 Slacken and remove the starter motor retaining bolts (arrowed) – 1.7 litre engines

11.18a Remove the oil filler cap . . .

11.18b . . . unscrew the two bolts (arrowed) . . .

11.18c . . . release the engine breather hose . . .

11.18d . . . and lift off the plastic engine cover – 1.9 litre (Z19DT) engines

13 Slacken and remove the retaining nut and screw, and disconnect the wiring from the starter motor solenoid. Recover the washers under the nut **(see illustration)**.

14 Unscrew the retaining nut and disconnect the earth lead from the starter motor lower bolt.

15 Slacken and remove the retaining bolts, then manoeuvre the starter motor out from underneath the engine. Note the dissimilar lengths of the securing bolts – the lower bolt is the longer **(see illustration)**.

1.9 litre engines

16 Disconnect the battery negative terminal (refer to *Disconnecting the battery* in the Reference Chapter).

17 Firmly apply the handbrake, then jack up the front of the car and support it securely on axle stands (see *Jacking and vehicle support*).

18 On Z19DT engines, remove the oil filler cap and unscrew the two bolts securing the plastic cover over the top of the engine. Release the engine breather hose, then lift off the cover and refit the oil filler cap **(see illustrations)**. On Z19DTH engines, remove the plastic cover by pulling it upwards off the mounting studs.

19 Slacken and remove the two retaining nuts and disconnect the wiring from the starter motor solenoid **(see illustration)**. Recover the washers under the nuts.

20 Unscrew the retaining nut and disconnect the earth lead from the starter motor lower stud bolt **(see illustration)**.

21 Open the retaining clips and release

the two heater hoses from the coolant pipe support bracket.

22 Undo the two nuts and release the wiring harness from the support bracket above the starter motor **(see illustration)**.

11.19 Undo the nuts (arrowed) and disconnect the starter solenoid wiring connectors – 1.9 litre engines

11.22 Undo the nuts and release the wiring harness from the support bracket – 1.9 litre engines

23 Unscrew the starter motor lower stud bolt and the two upper mounting bolts **(see illustration)**. Collect the wiring harness support bracket then manoeuvre the starter motor upwards and out of position.

11.20 Unscrew the nut (arrowed) and disconnect the earth lead from the starter motor stud bolt – 1.9 litre engines

11.23 Unscrew the bolts (arrowed), collect the wiring harness bracket and remove the starter from above – 1.9 litre engines

14.5 Oil pressure warning light switch – 1.7 litre engines

14.6 Oil pressure warning light switch (arrowed) – 1.9 litre engines

5 Disconnect the wiring connector by pulling, then unscrew the switch. Be prepared for oil spillage, and if the switch is to be left removed from the engine for any length of time, plug the switch aperture **(see illustration)**.

1.9 litre engines

6 The oil pressure warning light switch is screwed into the oil filter housing at the rear of the engine **(see illustration)**.

7 Firmly apply the handbrake, then jack up the front of the car and support it securely on axle stands (see *Jacking and vehicle support*).

8 Disconnect the wiring connector then unscrew the switch and recover the sealing washer. Be prepared for oil spillage, and if the switch is to be left removed from the engine for any length of time, plug the switch aperture.

Refitting

9 Examine the sealing washer for signs of damage or deterioration and if necessary renew.

10 Refit the switch and washer, tightening it to the specified torque, and reconnect the wiring connector.

11 Lower the vehicle to the ground then check, and if necessary, top-up the engine oil as described in *Weekly checks*.

Refitting

24 Refitting is a reversal of removal tightening the retaining bolts to the specified torque. Ensure all wiring is correctly routed and its retaining nuts are securely tightened.

12 Starter motor – testing and overhaul

If the starter motor is thought to be suspect, it should be removed from the vehicle and taken to an auto-electrician for testing. Most auto-electricians will be able to supply and fit brushes at a reasonable cost. However, check on the cost of repairs before proceeding as it may prove more economical to obtain a new or exchange motor.

13 Ignition switch – removal and refitting

The switch is integral with the steering column lock, and removal and refitting is described in Chapter 10.

14 Oil pressure warning light switch – removal and refitting

Removal

1.3 litre engines

1 The oil pressure warning light switch is screwed into the front left-hand end of the cylinder head. To gain access, remove the plastic cover from the top of the engine.

2 Pull back the cover and disconnect the wiring from the switch.

3 Place some cloth rags beneath the switch, then unscrew the switch from the block. Be prepared for oil spillage, and if the switch is to be left removed from the engine for any length of time, plug the switch aperture

1.7 litre engines

4 The oil pressure warning light switch is screwed into the left-hand end of the cylinder block, below and slightly to the rear of the thermostat housing. To improve access to the switch, remove the battery and battery tray as described in Section 4.

15 Oil level sensor – removal and refitting

Removal

1.3 and 1.9 litre engines

1 The oil level sensor is located inside the sump which must first be removed (see the relevant Part of Chapter 2).

2 With the sump removed, slide off the retaining clip and free the sensor wiring connector from the sump **(see illustration)**.

3 Where fitted, undo the retaining bolts and remove the oil baffle plate from inside the sump **(see illustration)**.

4 Note the correct routing of the wiring then undo the retaining bolts and remove the sensor assembly from the sump **(see illustration)**. Check the wiring connector seal for signs or damage and renew if necessary.

1.7 litre engines

5 The oil level sensor is located inside the sump main casting. To gain access, remove the sump lower pan from the main casting as described in Chapter 2B.

6 Disconnect the sensor wiring connector, then slide off the external retaining clip and free the sensor wiring connector from the sump main casting.

7 Note the correct routing of the wiring then undo the retaining bolts and remove the sensor assembly from the sump main casting. Check the wiring connector seal for signs or damage and renew if necessary.

15.2 Slide off the retaining clip (arrowed) and free the oil level sensor wiring connector from the sump

15.3 Where fitted, undo the retaining bolts and remove the oil baffle plate

15.4 Undo the two bolts (arrowed) and remove the oil level sensor from the sump

Refitting

8 Prior to refitting remove all traces of locking compound from the sensor retaining bolt and sump threads. Apply a drop of fresh locking compound to the bolt threads and lubricate the wiring connector seal with a smear of engine oil.

9 Fit the sensor, making sure the wiring is correctly routed, and securely tighten its retaining bolts. Ease the wiring connector through the sump, taking care not to damage its seal, and secure it in position with the retaining clip.

10 Ensure the sensor is correctly refitted then, where applicable, refit the oil baffle plate.

11 Refit the sump as described in the appropriate Part of Chapter 2.

16 Pre/post-heating system – description and testing

Description

1 Each cylinder of the engine is fitted with a heater plug (commonly called a glow plug) screwed into it. The plugs are electrically-operated before and during start-up when the engine is cold. Electrical feed to the glow plugs is controlled via the pre/post-heating system control unit.

2 A warning light in the instrument panel tells the driver that pre/post-heating is taking place. When the light goes out, the engine is ready to be started. The voltage supply to the glow plugs continues for several seconds after the light goes out. If no attempt is made to start, the timer then cuts off the supply, in order to avoid draining the battery and overheating the glow plugs.

3 The glow plugs also provide a 'post-heating' function, whereby the glow plugs remain switched on after the engine has started. The length of time 'post-heating' takes place is also determined by the control unit, and is dependent on engine temperature.

4 The fuel filter is fitted with a heating element to prevent the fuel 'waxing' in extreme cold temperature conditions and to improve combustion. The heating element is an integral part of the fuel filter housing and is controlled by the pre/post-heating system control unit.

Testing

5 If the system malfunctions, testing is ultimately by substitution of known good units, but some preliminary checks may be made as follows.

6 Connect a voltmeter or 12 volt test lamp between the glow plug supply cable and earth (engine or vehicle metal). Make sure that the live connection is kept clear of the engine and bodywork.

7 Have an assistant switch on the ignition, and check that voltage is applied to the glow plugs. Note the time for which the warning light is lit, and the total time for which voltage is applied before the system cuts out. Switch off the ignition.

8 At an underbonnet temperature of 20°C, typical times noted should be approximately 3 seconds for warning light operation. Warning light time will increase with lower temperatures and decrease with higher temperatures.

9 If there is no supply at all, the control unit or associated wiring is at fault.

10 To locate a defective glow plug, disconnect the wiring connector from each plug.

11 Use a continuity tester, or a 12 volt test lamp connected to the battery positive terminal, to check for continuity between each glow plug terminal and earth. The resistance of a glow plug in good condition is very low (less than 1 ohm), so if the test lamp does not light or the continuity tester shows a high resistance, the glow plug is certainly defective.

12 If an ammeter is available, the current draw of each glow plug can be checked. After an initial surge of 15 to 20 amps, each plug should draw 12 amps. Any plug which draws much more or less than this is probably defective.

13 As a final check, the glow plugs can be removed and inspected as described in the following Section.

17 Glow plugs – removal, inspection and refitting

Caution: If the pre/post-heating system has just been energised, or if the engine has been running, the glow plugs will be very hot.

Removal

1.3 litre engines

1 The glow plugs are located at the front of the cylinder head above the exhaust manifold.

2 Lift off the engine cover, then slacken the retaining clips and remove the charge air hose from the turbocharger and charge air pipe.

3 Disconnect the wiring from the glow plugs by squeezing the connectors with thumb and forefinger, and pulling them from the plugs **(see illustration)**.

4 Unscrew the glow plugs and remove them from the cylinder head.

1.7 litre engines

5 The glow plugs are located at the rear of the cylinder head above the inlet manifold.

6 Remove the oil filler cap and lift off the plastic cover over the top of the engine by pulling it upwards off the mounting studs. Refit the oil filler cap.

7 Release the wiring harness support clips from the plastic charge air pipe over the top of the engine.

8 Slacken the retaining clips securing the

17.3 Disconnect the wiring from the glow plugs (No 1 glow plug arrowed) – 1.3 litre engines

charge air pipe to the turbocharger and air cleaner intake duct.

9 Release the retaining clip and disconnect the crankcase ventilation hose from the camshaft cover.

10 Open the clip and detach the fuel hose from the charge air pipe, then undo the two charge air pipe retaining bolts. Disengage the pipe from the air cleaner intake duct and turbocharger, then remove the pipe from the top of the engine.

11 Disconnect the wiring from the glow plugs by squeezing the connectors with thumb and forefinger, and pulling them from the plugs.

12 Unscrew the glow plugs and remove them from the cylinder head **(see illustration)**.

1.9 litre engines

13 The glow plugs are located at the rear of the cylinder head above the inlet manifold.

14 On Z19DT engines, remove the oil filler cap and unscrew the two bolts securing the plastic cover over the top of the engine. Release the engine breather hose, then lift off the cover and refit the oil filler cap **(see illustrations 11.18a to 11.18d)**. On Z19DTH engines, remove the plastic cover by pulling it upwards off the mounting studs.

15 On Z19DT engines, undo the two retaining bolts, disconnect the four vacuum hoses and remove the vacuum pipe assembly from the top of the camshaft cover.

16 Disconnect the wiring from the glow plugs by squeezing the connectors with thumb and forefinger, and pulling them from the plugs.

17.12 Remove the glow plug from the cylinder head – 1.7 litre engines

17.17 Unscrew the glow plugs and remove them from the cylinder head – 1.9 litre engines

17 Unscrew the glow plugs and remove them from the cylinder head **(see illustration)**.

Inspection

18 Inspect each glow plug for physical damage. Burnt or eroded glow plug tips can be caused by a bad injector spray pattern. Have the injectors checked if this type of damage is found.

19 If the glow plugs are in good physical condition, check them electrically using a 12 volt test lamp or continuity tester as described in the previous Section.

20 The glow plugs can be energised by applying 12 volts to them to verify that they heat up evenly and in the required time. Observe the following precautions.

a) *Support the glow plug by clamping it carefully in a vice or self-locking pliers. Remember it will become red-hot.*

b) *Make sure that the power supply or test lead incorporates a fuse or overload trip to protect against damage from a short-circuit.*

c) *After testing, allow the glow plug to cool for several minutes before attempting to handle it.*

21 A glow plug in good condition will start to glow red at the tip after drawing current for 5 seconds or so. Any plug which takes much longer to start glowing, or which starts glowing in the middle instead of at the tip, is defective.

Refitting

22 Carefully refit the plugs and tighten to the specified torque. Do not overtighten, as this can damage the glow plug element. Push the electrical connectors firmly onto the glow plugs.

23 The remainder of refitting is a reversal of removal, checking the operation of the glow plugs on completion.

---

18 Pre/post-heating system control unit – removal and refitting

Removal

1 The pre/post-heating system control unit is located on the left-hand side of the engine compartment where it is mounted onto the front of the battery tray.

2 Disconnect the battery negative terminal (refer to *Disconnecting the battery* in the Reference Chapter).

3 Unclip the control unit and slide it up and off the battery tray **(see illustration 4.10)**.

4 Disconnect the wiring connector from the base of the control unit and remove the unit from the engine compartment.

Refitting

5 Refitting is a reversal of removal.

Chapter 6
Clutch

Contents

Degrees of difficulty

Easy, suitable for novice with little experience	**Fairly easy,** suitable for beginner with some experience	**Fairly difficult,** suitable for competent DIY mechanic	**Difficult,** suitable for experienced DIY mechanic	**Very difficult,** suitable for expert DIY or professional

Specifications

Type .... Single dry plate with diaphragm spring, hydraulically-operated

Friction disc
Diameter:

1.3 litre engines	216 mm
1.7 litre engines:	
Z17DTL engines	205 mm
Z17DTH engines	228 mm
1.9 litre engines	239 mm

New lining thickness:

1.3 litre engines	7.20 mm
1.7 litre engines:	
Z17DTL engines	7.65 mm
Z17DTH engines	8.40 mm
1.9 litre engines	7.80 mm

Torque wrench settings

	Nm	lbf ft
ABS hydraulic modulator mounting bracket bolts	20	15
Clutch master cylinder retaining nuts*	20	15
Clutch pedal bracket nut/bolts*	20	15
Pressure plate retaining bolts:		
M7 bolts	15	11
M8 bolts	28	21
Release cylinder mounting bolts	5	4

* Use new nuts/bolts

1 General information

The clutch consists of a friction disc, a pressure plate assembly, and the hydraulic release cylinder (which incorporates the release bearing); all of these components are contained in the large cast-aluminium alloy bellhousing, sandwiched between the engine and the transmission.

The friction disc is fitted between the engine flywheel and the clutch pressure plate, and is allowed to slide on the transmission input shaft splines.

The pressure plate assembly is bolted to the engine flywheel. When the engine is running, drive is transmitted from the crankshaft, via the flywheel, to the friction disc (these components being clamped securely together by the pressure plate assembly) and from the friction disc to the transmission input shaft.

To interrupt the drive, the spring pressure must be relaxed. This is achieved using a hydraulic release mechanism which consists of the master cylinder, the release cylinder and the pipe/hose linking the two components. Depressing the pedal pushes on the master cylinder pushrod which hydraulically forces the release cylinder piston against the pressure plate spring fingers. This causes the springs to deform and releases the clamping force on the friction disc.

The clutch is self-adjusting and requires no manual adjustment.

2.8 Clutch bleed screw (arrowed)

2 Clutch hydraulic system – bleeding

⚠️ **Warning: Hydraulic fluid is poisonous; wash off immediately and thoroughly in the case of skin contact, and seek immediate medical advice if any fluid is swallowed or gets into the eyes. Certain types of hydraulic fluid are flammable, and may ignite when allowed into contact with hot components; when servicing any hydraulic system, it is safest to assume that the fluid is flammable, and to take precautions against the risk of fire as though it is petrol that is being handled. Hydraulic fluid is also an effective paint stripper, and will attack plastics; if any is spilt, it should be washed off immediately, using copious quantities of fresh water. Finally, it is hygroscopic (it absorbs moisture from the air) – old fluid may be contaminated and unfit for further use. When topping-up or renewing the fluid, always use the recommended type, and ensure that it comes from a freshly-opened sealed container.**

General information

1 The correct operation of any hydraulic system is only possible after removing all air from the components and circuit; this is achieved by bleeding the system.

2 The manufacturer's stipulate that the system must be initially bled by the 'back-bleeding' method using Vauxhall/Opel special bleeding equipment. This entails connecting a pressure bleeding unit containing fresh brake fluid, to the release cylinder bleed screw, with a collecting vessel connected to the brake fluid master cylinder reservoir. The pressure bleeding unit is then switched on, the bleed screw is opened and hydraulic fluid is delivered under pressure, backwards, to be expelled from the reservoir into the collecting vessel. Final bleeding is then carried out in the conventional way.

3 In practice, this method would normally only be required if new hydraulic components have been fitted, or if the system has been completely drained of hydraulic fluid. If the system has only been disconnected to allow

component removal and refitting procedures to be carried out, such as removal and refitting of the transmission (for example for clutch renewal) or engine removal and refitting, then it is quite likely that normal bleeding will be sufficient.

4 Our advice would therefore be as follows:
  a) *If the hydraulic system has only been partially disconnected, try bleeding by the conventional methods described in paragraphs 10 to 15, or 16 to 19.*
  b) *If the hydraulic system has been completely drained and new components have been fitted, try bleeding by using the pressure bleeding method described in paragraphs 20 to 22.*
  c) *If the above methods fail to produce a firm pedal on completion, it will be necessary to 'back-bleed' the system using Vauxhall/Opel bleeding equipment, or suitable alternative equipment as described in paragraphs 23 to 28.*

5 During the bleeding procedure, add only clean, unused hydraulic fluid of the recommended type; never re-use fluid that has already been bled from the system. Ensure that sufficient fluid is available before starting work.

6 If there is any possibility of incorrect fluid being already in the system, the hydraulic circuit must be flushed completely with uncontaminated, correct fluid.

7 If hydraulic fluid has been lost from the system, or air has entered because of a leak, ensure that the fault is cured before continuing further.

8 The bleed screw is located in the hose end fitting which is situated on the top of the transmission housing **(see illustration)**. On some models access to the bleed screw is limited and it may be necessary to jack up the front of the vehicle and support it on axle stands so that the screw can be reached from below, or remove the battery and battery tray as described in Chapter 5, so that the screw can be reached from above.

9 Check that all pipes and hoses are secure, unions tight and the bleed screw is closed. Clean any dirt from around the bleed screw.

Bleeding procedure

Conventional method

10 Collect a clean glass jar, a suitable length of plastic or rubber tubing which is a tight fit over the bleed screw, and a ring spanner to fit the screw. The help of an assistant will also be required.

11 Unscrew the master cylinder fluid reservoir cap (the clutch shares the same fluid reservoir as the braking system), and top the master cylinder reservoir up to the upper (MAX) level line. Ensure that the fluid level is maintained at least above the lower level line in the reservoir throughout the procedure.

12 Remove the dust cap from the bleed screw. Fit the spanner and tube to the screw, place the other end of the tube in the jar, and

pour in sufficient fluid to cover the end of the tube.

13 Have the assistant fully depress the clutch pedal several times to build-up pressure, then maintain it on the final down stroke.

14 While pedal pressure is maintained, unscrew the bleed screw (approximately one turn) and allow the compressed fluid and air to flow into the jar. The assistant should maintain pedal pressure and should not release it until instructed to do so. When the flow stops, tighten the bleed screw again, have the assistant release the pedal slowly, and recheck the reservoir fluid level.

15 Repeat the steps given in paragraphs 13 and 14 until the fluid emerging from the bleed screw is free from air bubbles. If the master cylinder has been drained and refilled allow approximately five seconds between cycles for the master cylinder passages to refill.

Using a one-way valve kit

16 As their name implies, these kits consist of a length of tubing with a one-way valve fitted, to prevent expelled air and fluid being drawn back into the system; some kits include a translucent container, which can be positioned so that the air bubbles can be more easily seen flowing from the end of the tube.

17 The kit is connected to the bleed screw, which is then opened.

18 The user returns to the driver's seat, depresses the clutch pedal with a smooth, steady stroke, and slowly releases it; this is repeated until the expelled fluid is clear of air bubbles.

19 Note that these kits simplify work so much that it is easy to forget the clutch fluid reservoir level; ensure that this is maintained at least above the lower level line at all times.

Pressure-bleeding method

20 These kits are usually operated by the reservoir of pressurised air contained in the spare tyre. However, note that it will probably be necessary to reduce the pressure to a lower level than normal; refer to the instructions supplied with the kit.

21 By connecting a pressurised, fluid-filled container to the clutch fluid reservoir, bleeding can be carried out simply by opening the bleed screw and allowing the fluid to flow out until no more air bubbles can be seen in the expelled fluid.

22 This method has the advantage that the large reservoir of fluid provides an additional safeguard against air being drawn into the system during bleeding.

'Back-bleeding' method

23 The following procedure describes the bleeding method using Vauxhall/Opel equipment. Alternative equipment is available and should be used in accordance with the maker's instructions.

24 Connect the pressure hose (MKM-6174-1) to the bleed screw located in the hose end fitting situated on the top of the transmission housing **(see illustration 2.8)**. Connect the other end of the hose to a suitable pressure bleeding device set to operate at approximately 2.0 bar.

25 Attach the cap (MKM-6174-2) to the master cylinder reservoir, and place the hose in a collecting vessel.

26 Switch on the pressure bleeding equipment, open the bleed screw, and allow fresh hydraulic fluid to flow from the pressure bleeding unit, through the system and out through the top of the reservoir and into the collecting vessel. When fluid, free from air bubbles appears in the reservoir, close the bleed screw and switch off the bleeding equipment.

27 Disconnect the bleeding equipment from the bleed screw and reservoir.

28 Carry out a final conventional bleeding procedure as described in paragraphs 10 to 15, or 16 to 19.

All methods

29 When bleeding is complete, no more bubbles appear and correct pedal feel is restored, tighten the bleed screw securely (do not overtighten). Remove the tube and spanner, and wash off any spilt fluid. Refit the dust cap to the bleed screw.

30 Check the hydraulic fluid level in the master cylinder reservoir, and top-up if necessary (see *Weekly checks*).

31 Discard any hydraulic fluid that has been bled from the system; it will not be fit for re-use.

32 Check the operation of the clutch pedal. If the clutch is still not operating correctly, air must still be present in the system, and further bleeding is required. Failure to bleed satisfactorily after a reasonable repetition of the bleeding procedure may be due to worn master cylinder/release cylinder seals.

3 Master cylinder – removal and refitting

Note: *New master cylinder retaining nuts will be required for refitting.*

Removal

Right-hand drive models

1 Unscrew the brake/clutch hydraulic fluid reservoir filler cap, and top-up the reservoir to the MAX mark (see *Weekly checks*). Place a piece of polythene over the filler neck, and secure the polythene with the filler cap. This will minimise brake fluid loss during subsequent operations.

2 Remove all traces of dirt from the outside of the master cylinder and the brake/clutch hydraulic fluid reservoir, then position some cloth beneath the cylinder to catch any spilt fluid.

3 Extract the retaining clip and disconnect the hydraulic pipe from the connector on the end of the master cylinder **(see illustration)**. Plug the pipe end and master cylinder port

3.3 Extract the retaining clip (arrowed) and disconnect the hydraulic pipe from the master cylinder connector

to minimise fluid loss and prevent the entry of dirt. Gently squeeze the two legs of the retaining clip together, and re-insert the clip into the master cylinder connector.

4 Release the retaining clip (where fitted) and disconnect the fluid supply hose from the brake/clutch hydraulic fluid reservoir **(see illustration)**.

5 From inside the car, remove the lower facia panel on the driver's side as described in Chapter 11.

6 Disconnect the return spring from the clutch pedal, then slide off the spring clip and withdraw the clevis pin securing the master cylinder pushrod to the clutch pedal.

7 Unscrew the two nuts securing the master cylinder to the pedal support bracket, then return to the engine compartment and remove the master cylinder from the vehicle. If the master cylinder is faulty it must be renewed; overhaul of the unit is not possible.

Left-hand drive models

8 Remove the battery and battery tray as described in Chapter 5.

9 Lift the coolant expansion tank up and out of its mounting bracket and place it to one side.

10 Undo the two upper bolts and one lower bolt securing the ABS hydraulic modulator mounting bracket to the bulkhead and body. Taking great care not to strain the hydraulic brake pipes, carefully move the assembly to one side as far as the brake pipes will allow and support it in this position.

11 Continue with the removal procedure as described in paragraphs 1 to 7.

Refitting

Right-hand drive models

12 Manoeuvre the master cylinder into position whilst ensuring that the pushrod aligns correctly with the pedal. Fit two new master cylinder retaining nuts and tighten them to the specified torque.

13 Refit the master cylinder pushrod-to-clutch pedal clevis pin, and secure it in position with the spring clip.

14 Refit the return spring to the clutch pedal.

15 Refit the lower facia panel on the driver's side as described in Chapter 11.

16 Connect the fluid supply hose to the

3.4 Disconnect the fluid supply hose (arrowed) from the reservoir

brake/clutch hydraulic fluid reservoir and, where applicable, secure with the retaining clip.

17 Press the hydraulic pipe back into the connector on the end of the master cylinder ensuring that the pipe audibly engages and is securely retained.

18 Bleed the clutch hydraulic system as described in Section 2.

Left-hand drive models

19 Carry out the operations described in paragraphs 12 to 17.

20 Carefully locate the ABS hydraulic modulator mounting bracket back into position and secure with the three bolts, tightened to the specified torque.

21 Refit the coolant expansion back into its mounting bracket.

22 Refit the battery tray and battery described in Chapter 5.

23 Bleed the clutch hydraulic system as described in Section 2.

4 Release cylinder – removal and refitting

Note 1: *Due to the amount of work necessary to remove and refit clutch components, it is usually considered good practice to renew the clutch friction disc, pressure plate assembly and release cylinder as a matched set, even if only one of these is actually worn enough to require renewal. It is also worth considering the renewal of the clutch components on a preventative basis if the engine and/or transmission have been removed for some other reason.*

Note 2: *Refer to the warning concerning the dangers of asbestos dust at the beginning of Section 6.*

Removal

1 Unless the complete engine/transmission unit is to be removed from the car and separated for major overhaul (see Chapter 2E), the clutch release cylinder can be reached by removing the transmission only, as described in Chapter 7A.

2 Wipe clean the outside of the release cylinder then slacken the union nut and disconnect the

4.2 Clutch release cylinder hydraulic pipe union nut (arrowed)

4.3 Clutch release cylinder retaining bolts (arrowed)

hydraulic pipe **(see illustration)**. Wipe up any spilt fluid with a clean cloth.

3 Unscrew the three retaining bolts and slide the release cylinder off from the transmission input shaft **(see illustration)**. Remove the sealing ring which is fitted between the cylinder and transmission housing and discard it; a new one must be used on refitting. Whilst the cylinder is removed, take care not to allow any debris to enter the transmission unit.

4 The release cylinder is a sealed unit and cannot be overhauled. If the cylinder seals are leaking or the release bearing is noisy or rough in operation, then the complete unit must be renewed.

5 To remove the hydraulic pipe, extract the retaining clip and remove the hydraulic hose end fitting from the fastening sleeve on top of the transmission housing **(see illustration)**. Gently squeeze the legs of the retaining clip together and re-insert the clip back into position in the end fitting.

6 Using a small screwdriver, carefully spread the retaining lugs of the fastening sleeve to release the hydraulic pipe connection, and remove the pipe from inside the transmission housing. Check the condition of the sealing ring on the hydraulic pipe and renew if necessary.

7 If required, the fastening sleeve can be removed by squeezing the lower retaining lugs together with pointed-nose pliers, then withdrawing the sleeve upwards and out of the transmission. Note that if the fastening sleeve is removed, a new one must be obtained for refitting.

Refitting

8 Ensure the release cylinder and transmission mating surfaces are clean and dry and fit the new sealing ring to the transmission recess.

9 Lubricate the release cylinder seal with a smear of transmission oil then carefully ease the cylinder along the input shaft and into position. **Note:** *Vauxhall/Opel technicians use a special tapered sleeve on the input shaft to prevent damage to the seal. If necessary, wrap suitable tape around the end of the shaft.* Ensure the sealing ring is still correctly seated in its groove then refit the release cylinder retaining bolts and tighten them to the specified torque.

10 If removed, fit the new fastening sleeve, engaging the lug on the sleeve with the cut-out in the housing **(see illustration)**. Ensure that the sleeve can be felt to positively lock in position.

11 Insert the hydraulic pipe into the fastening sleeve until the end fitting can be felt to positively lock in position.

12 Reconnect the hydraulic pipe to the release cylinder, tightening its union nut to the specified torque.

13 Refit the hydraulic hose end fitting to the fastening sleeve ensuring that it is positively retained by its clip.

14 Refit the transmission unit as described in Chapter 7A.

15 Bleed the clutch hydraulic system as described in Section 2.

4.5 Extract the retaining clip (arrowed) and remove the hydraulic hose end fitting from the fastening sleeve

4.10 Make sure the lug (arrowed) on the fastening sleeve is located correctly in the transmission housing

5 Clutch pedal – removal and refitting

Note: *New master cylinder retaining nuts and pedal bracket retaining nut/bolts will be required for refitting.*

Removal

1 Remove the lower facia panel on the driver's side, and the steering column lower shroud, as described in Chapter 11.

2 Where fitted (according to model), remove the clutch switch from the pedal bracket.

3 Disconnect the return spring from the clutch pedal, then slide off the spring clip and withdraw the clevis pin securing the master cylinder pushrod to the clutch pedal.

4 Unscrew the upper nut (right-hand drive models), or the two upper bolts (left-hand drive models), securing the pedal bracket to the facia crossmember.

5 Unscrew the two nuts securing the clutch master cylinder to the pedal bracket, then carefully withdraw the clutch pedal and bracket from inside the vehicle. Make sure that all wiring is moved to one side as the pedal and bracket are removed.

6 Check the pedal and bracket for excessive wear and damage. It is not possible to renew the pedal pivot bushes separately, so if they are worn, the complete assembly must be renewed.

Refitting

7 Manoeuvre the pedal and bracket assembly into position, making sure that the surrounding wiring is not trapped. Screw on the new retaining nuts/bolts, including those for the master cylinder, and tighten to the specified torque.

8 Refit the master cylinder pushrod-to-clutch pedal clevis pin, and secure it in position with the spring clip.

9 Refit the return spring to the clutch pedal then, where applicable, refit the clutch switch.

10 Refit the steering column lower shroud and the lower facia panel as described in Chapter 11.

6 Clutch assembly – removal, inspection and refitting

⚠ *Warning: Dust created by clutch wear and deposited on the clutch components may contain asbestos, which is a health hazard. DO NOT blow it out with compressed air, or inhale any of it. DO NOT use petrol or petroleum-based solvents to clean off the dust. Brake system cleaner or methylated spirit should be used to flush the dust into a suitable receptacle. After the clutch components are wiped clean with rags, dispose of the contaminated rags and cleaner in a sealed, marked container.*

Note: *To prevent possible damage to the ends of the pressure plate diaphragm spring fingers, Vauxhall/Opel recommend the use of a special jig (KM-6263) to remove the clutch assembly, however, with care it is possible to carry out the work without the jig.*

Removal

1 Unless the complete engine/transmission unit is to be removed from the car and separated for major overhaul (see Chapter 2E), the clutch can be reached by removing the transmission as described in Chapter 7A.

2 Before disturbing the clutch, use chalk or a marker pen to mark the relationship of the pressure plate assembly to the flywheel.

3 At this stage, Vauxhall/Opel technicians fit the special jig KM-6263 to the engine and compress the diaphragm spring fingers until the friction disc is released **(see illustrations)**. The pressure plate mounting bolts are then unscrewed, and the jig spindle backed off.

4 If the jig is not available, progressively unscrew the pressure plate retaining bolts in diagonal sequence by half a turn at a time, until spring pressure is released and the bolts can be unscrewed by hand.

5 Remove the pressure plate assembly and collect the friction disc, noting which way round the disc is fitted. It is recommended that new pressure plate retaining bolts are obtained.

Inspection

Note: *Due to the amount of work necessary to remove and refit clutch components, it is usually considered good practice to renew the clutch friction disc, pressure plate assembly and release cylinder as a matched set, even*

if only one of these is actually worn enough to require renewal. It is also worth considering the renewal of the clutch components on a preventative basis if the engine and/or transmission have been removed for some other reason.

6 When cleaning clutch components, read first the warning at the beginning of this Section; remove dust using a clean, dry cloth, and working in a well-ventilated atmosphere.

7 Check the friction disc facings for signs of wear, damage or oil contamination. If the friction material is cracked, burnt, scored or damaged, or if it is contaminated with oil or grease (shown by shiny black patches), the friction disc must be renewed.

8 If the friction material is still serviceable, check that the centre boss splines are unworn, that the torsion springs are in good condition and securely fastened, and that all the rivets are tight. If any wear or damage is found, the friction disc must be renewed.

9 If the friction material is fouled with oil, this must be due to an oil leak from the crankshaft oil seal, from the sump-to-cylinder block joint, or from the release cylinder assembly (either the main seal or the sealing ring). Renew the crankshaft oil seal or repair the sump joint as described in the appropriate Part of Chapter 2, before installing the new friction disc. The clutch release cylinder is covered in Section 4.

10 Check the pressure plate assembly for obvious signs of wear or damage; shake it to check for loose rivets, or worn or damaged fulcrum rings, and check that the drive straps securing the pressure plate to the cover do not show signs of overheating (such as a deep yellow or blue discoloration). If the diaphragm spring is worn or damaged, or if its pressure

is in any way suspect, the pressure plate assembly should be renewed.

11 Examine the machined bearing surfaces of the pressure plate and of the flywheel; they should be clean, completely flat, and free from scratches or scoring. If either is discoloured from excessive heat, or shows signs of cracks, it should be renewed – although minor damage of this nature can sometimes be polished away using emery paper.

12 Check that the release cylinder bearing rotates smoothly and easily, with no sign of noise or roughness. Also check that the surface itself is smooth and unworn, with no signs of cracks, pitting or scoring. If there is any doubt about its condition, the clutch release cylinder should be renewed (it is not possible to renew the bearing separately).

Refitting

13 On 1.9 litre models, the clutch pressure plate is unusual, as there is a pre-adjustment mechanism to compensate for wear in the friction disc (this is termed by Vauxhall/Opel as a self-adjusting clutch (SAC), which is slightly ambiguous as all clutches fitted to these models are essentially self-adjusting). However, this mechanism must be reset before refitting the pressure plate. A new plate may be supplied preset, in which case this procedure can be ignored.

14 A large diameter bolt (M14 at least) long enough to pass through the pressure plate, a matching nut, and several large diameter washers, will be needed for this procedure. Mount the bolt head in the jaws of a sturdy bench vice, with one large washer fitted.

15 Offer the plate over the bolt, friction disc surface facing down, and locate it centrally

H44610

6.3a Vauxhall special jig KM-6263 for removing the clutch pressure plate and friction disc

1, 3 and 6   Bolts securing the jig to the engine
2 and 5   Bolts for adjusting the jig to the centre of the crankshaft

J44724

6.3b Thrust piece (1) in contact with the diaphragm spring fingers (3) of the pressure plate (2)

6.15 Mount a large bolt and washer into a vice, then fit the pressure plate over it

6.16 Fit large washers and a nut to the bolt and hand-tighten

6.17a Tighten the nut until the spring adjuster is free to turn . . .

over the bolt and washer – the washer should bear on the centre hub **(see illustration)**.

16 Fit several further large washers over the bolt, so that they bear on the ends of the spring fingers, then add the nut and tighten by hand to locate the washers **(see illustration)**.

17 The purpose of the procedure is to turn the plate's internal adjuster disc so that the three small coil springs visible on the plate's outer surface are fully compressed. Tighten the nut just fitted until the adjuster disc is free to turn. Using a pair of thin-nosed, or circlip pliers, in one of the three windows in the top surface, open the jaws of the pliers to turn the adjuster disc anti-clockwise, so that the springs are fully compressed **(see illustrations)**.

18 Hold the pliers in this position, then unscrew the centre nut. Once the nut is released, the adjuster disc will be gripped in

6.17b . . . then open up the jaws of suitable pliers to compress the springs

position, and the pliers can be removed. Take the pressure plate from the vice, and it is ready to fit.

19 On reassembly, ensure that the friction surfaces of the flywheel and pressure plate are completely clean, smooth, and free from oil or grease. Use solvent to remove any protective grease from new components.

20 Lightly grease the teeth of the friction disc hub with high melting-point grease. Do not apply too much, otherwise it may eventually contaminate the friction disc linings.

Using the Vauxhall jig

21 Fit the special Vauxhall guide bush to the centre of the crankshaft, and locate the friction disc on it, making sure that the lettering 'transmission side' or 'Getriebeseite' points towards the transmission **(see illustration)**.

22 Locate the pressure plate on the special centring pins on the flywheel, then compress the diaphragm spring fingers with the jig, until the friction disc is in full contact with the flywheel.

23 Insert new pressure plate retaining bolts, and progressively tighten them to the specified torque. If necessary, hold the flywheel stationary while tightening the bolts, using a screwdriver engaged with the teeth of the starter ring gear.

24 Back off the jig spindle so that the diaphragm spring forces the pressure plate against the friction disc and flywheel, then remove the jig and guide bush from the engine.

25 Refit the transmission as described in Chapter 7A.

Without using the Vauxhall jig

26 Locate the friction disc on the flywheel, making sure that the lettering 'transmission side' or 'Getriebeseite' points towards the transmission **(see illustration 6.21)**.

27 Refit the pressure plate assembly, aligning the marks made on dismantling (if the original pressure plate is re-used). Fit new pressure plate bolts, but tighten them only finger-tight so that the friction disc can still be moved **(see illustration)**.

28 The friction disc must now be centralised so that, when the transmission is refitted, its input shaft will pass through the splines at the centre of the friction disc.

29 Centralisation can be achieved by passing a screwdriver or other long bar through the friction disc and into the hole in the crankshaft. The friction disc can then be moved around until it is centred on the crankshaft hole. Alternatively, a clutch-aligning tool can be used to eliminate the guesswork; these can be obtained from most accessory shops **(see illustration)**.

30 When the friction disc is centralised, tighten the pressure plate bolts evenly and in a diagonal sequence to the specified torque setting.

31 Refit the transmission as described in Chapter 7A.

6.21 The lettering 'transmission side' or 'Getriebeseite' on the friction disc must point towards the transmission

6.27 Fit the pressure plate assembly over the friction disc

6.29 Centralise the friction disc using a clutch aligning tool or similar

Chapter 7 Part A:
Manual transmission

Contents

Degrees of difficulty

Easy, suitable for novice with little experience	Fairly easy, suitable for beginner with some experience	Fairly difficult, suitable for competent DIY mechanic	Difficult, suitable for experienced DIY mechanic	Very difficult, suitable for expert DIY or professional

Specifications

General

Type:
  1.7 litre models..   Five forward speeds and reverse. Synchromesh on all forward speeds
  1.3 and 1.9 litre models ....   Six forward speeds and reverse. Synchromesh on all forward speeds
Manufacturer's designation:
  1.3 litre models.......................................   M20
  1.7 litre:
    Z17DTL engine models...........................   F17+
    Z17DTH engine models F23
  1.9 litre models......................................   M32

Gear ratios

M20 transmissions:
  1st.......................................   3.81:1
  2nd......................................   2.15:1
  3rd......................................   1.30:1
  4th.......................................   0.95:1
  5th.......................................   0.74:1
  6th.......................................   0.61:1
  Reverse..................................   3.81:1
F17+ transmissions:
  1st.......................................   3.72:1
  2nd......................................   2.13:1
  3rd......................................   1.41:1
  4th.......................................   1.12:1
  5th.......................................   0.89:1
  Reverse..................................   3.30:1
F23 transmissions:
  1st.......................................   3.57:1
  2nd......................................   1.88:1
  3rd......................................   1.19:1
  4th.......................................   0.84:1
  5th.......................................   0.68:1
  Reverse..................................   3.30:1
M32 transmissions:
  1st.......................................   3.81:1
  2nd......................................   2.15:1
  3rd......................................   1.46:1
  4th.......................................   1.07:1
  5th.......................................   0.86:1
  6th.......................................   0.74:1
  Reverse..................................   3.72:1

Final drive ratios

M20 transmissions	3.72:1
F17+ transmissions	3.74:1
F23 transmissions	3.95:1
M32 transmissions	3.65:1

Lubrication

Lubricant type	See *Lubricants and fluids* on page 0•18
Lubricant capacity	See Chapter 1

Torque wrench settings

	Nm	lbf ft
Differential lower cover plate bolts (F17+ transmissions).	18	13
Engine/transmission mountings.	See the relevant Part of Chapter 2	
Engine-to-transmission bolts	See the relevant Part of Chapter 2	
Gearchange mechanism selector rod clamp bolt:		
Stage 1	12	9
Stage 2	Angle tighten a further 225°	
Oil drain plug:		
F23 transmissions	35	26
M20 and M32 transmissions	20	15
Oil filler plug:		
F23 transmissions	35	26
M20 and M32 transmissions	30	22
Oil level plug:		
F17+ transmissions:		
Stage 1	4	3
Stage 2	Angle-tighten a further 45° to 135°	
F23 transmissions	35	26
Oil seal carrier to differential (M20 and M32 transmissions):		
Stage 1	20	15
Stage 2	Angle-tighten a further 45°	
Reversing light switch	20	15
Roadwheel bolts.	110	81

1 General information

The transmission is contained in a cast-aluminium alloy casing bolted to the engine's left-hand end, and consists of the gearbox and final drive differential – often called a transaxle.

Drive is transmitted from the crankshaft via the clutch to the input shaft, which has a splined extension to accept the clutch friction disc, and rotates in sealed ball-bearings. From the input shaft, drive is transmitted to the output shaft, which rotates in a roller bearing at its right-hand end, and a sealed ball-bearing at its left-hand end. From the output shaft, the drive is transmitted to the differential crownwheel, which rotates with the differential case and planetary gears, thus driving the sun gears and driveshafts. The rotation of the planetary gears on their shaft allows the inner roadwheel to rotate at a slower speed than the outer roadwheel when the car is cornering.

The input and output shafts are arranged side-by-side, parallel to the crankshaft and driveshafts, so that their gear pinion teeth are in constant mesh. In the neutral position, the output shaft gear pinions rotate freely, so that drive cannot be transmitted to the crownwheel.

Gear selection is via a floor-mounted lever and either a rod-operated, or cable-operated selector linkage mechanism. The selector linkage cause the appropriate selector fork to move its respective synchro-sleeve along the shaft, to lock the gear pinion to the synchro-hub. Since the synchro-hubs are splined to the output shaft, this locks the pinion to the shaft, so that drive can be transmitted. To ensure that gearchanging can be made quickly and quietly, a synchromesh system is fitted to all forward gears, consisting of baulk rings and spring-loaded fingers, as well as the gear pinions and synchro-hubs. The synchromesh cones are formed on the mating faces of the baulk rings and gear pinions.

2 Transmission oil – draining and refilling

1 This operation is much more efficient if the car is first taken on a journey of sufficient length to warm the engine/transmission up to normal operating temperature.

Caution: If the procedure is to be carried out on a hot transmission unit, take care not to burn yourself on the hot exhaust or the transmission/engine unit.

2 Position the vehicle over an inspection pit, on vehicle ramps, or jack it up and support it securely on axle stands (see *Jacking and vehicle support*), but make sure that it is level. Where fitted, remove the clips and bolts and remove the undertray from beneath the engine.

F17+ transmissions

Note: *A new differential lower cover plate gasket will be required for this operation.*

Draining

3 Since the transmission oil is not renewed as part of the manufacturer's maintenance schedule, no drain plug is fitted to the transmission. If for any reason the transmission needs to be drained, the only way of doing so is to remove the differential lower cover plate.

4 Wipe clean the area around the differential cover plate and position a suitable container underneath the cover.

5 Evenly and progressively slacken and remove the retaining bolts then withdraw the cover plate and allow the transmission oil to drain into the container **(see illustration)**. Remove the gasket and discard it; a new one should be used on refitting.

6 Allow the oil to drain completely into the container. If the oil is hot, take precautions against scalding. Remove all traces of dirt and oil from the cover and transmission mating surfaces and wipe clean the inside of the cover plate.

7 Once the oil has finished draining, ensure the mating surfaces are clean and dry then

2.5 Differential cover plate securing bolts (arrowed)

2.8 Transmission oil level plug (arrowed) – F17+ transmissions

2.9 Fill the transmission through the reversing light switch aperture – F17+ transmissions

refit the cover plate to the transmission unit, complete with a new gasket. Refit the retaining bolts and evenly and progressively tighten them to the specified torque.

Refilling

8 Wipe clean the area around the level plug. The level plug is located behind the driveshaft inner joint on the left-hand side of the transmission **(see illustration)**. Unscrew the plug and clean it.

9 The transmission is refilled via the reversing light switch aperture **(see illustration)**. Wipe clean the area around the reversing light switch, and remove the switch as described in Section 7. Refill the transmission with the specified grade of oil given in *Lubricants and fluids*, until it reaches the bottom of the level plug aperture. Allow any excess oil to drain, then refit and tighten the level plug to the specified torque.

10 Refit the reversing light switch with reference to Section 7, then lower the vehicle to the ground.

F23 transmissions

Draining

11 Wipe clean the area around the drain plug, located below the left-hand driveshaft, and position a suitable container under the plug.

12 Undo the drain plug and allow the oil to drain.

13 Once the oil has finished draining, refit the drain plug with a new sealing washer where applicable, and tighten the plug to the specified torque.

Refilling

14 Wipe clean the area around the level plug located on the rear of the differential housing **(see illustration)**. Unscrew the plug and clean it.

15 The transmission is refilled via the oil filler plug on the top of the casing **(see illustration)**. To gain access to the plug, remove the battery and battery tray as described in Chapter 5.

16 Wipe clean the area around the plug and unscrew it. Refill the transmission with the specified grade of oil given in *Lubricants and fluids*, until it reaches the bottom of the level plug aperture. Allow any excess oil to drain,

then refit and tighten the level plug to the specified torque.

17 Refit the oil filler plug and tighten it to the specified torque. Where applicable, refit the engine undertray, then lower the vehicle to the ground.

18 Refit the battery tray and battery as described in Chapter 5.

M20 and M32 transmissions

Note: *A new transmission oil drain plug will be required.*

Draining

19 Wipe clean the area around the drain plug, located on the lower left-hand side of the differential housing, and position a suitable container under the plug.

20 Undo the drain plug and allow the oil to drain.

2.14 Transmission oil level plug (arrowed) – F23 transmissions

2.22 Transmission oil filler plug (arrowed) – M20 and M32 transmissions

21 Once the oil has finished draining, fit the new drain plug and tighten the plug to the specified torque.

Refilling

22 The transmission is refilled via the oil filler plug on the top of the casing **(see illustration)**. To gain access to the plug, remove the battery and battery tray as described in Chapter 5.

23 Wipe clean the area around the plug and unscrew it. Refill the transmission with *exactly* 2.2 litres of the specified grade of oil given in *Lubricants and fluids*, then refit and tighten the oil filler plug to the specified torque **(see illustration)**.

24 Where applicable, refit the engine undertray, then lower the vehicle to the ground.

25 Refit the battery tray and battery as described in Chapter 5.

2.15 Transmission oil filler plug (arrowed) – F23 transmissions

2.23 Use a graduated container to fill the transmission with the specified quantity of oil – M20 and M32 transmissions

3.4 Gearchange selector rod clamp bolt and nut (arrowed) – F17+ transmissions

3.5 Unclip and remove the access panel in the centre console

3.6 Carefully prise up and remove the ashtray from the centre console

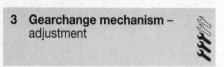

3 Gearchange mechanism – adjustment

F17+ transmissions

Note: *A 5 mm drill or metal rod will be required to carry out this procedure.*

1 Adjustment of the gearchange linkage/ mechanism should only be needed if the mechanism has been disconnected or removed. The mechanism is adjusted at the clamp bolt which secures the selector rod to the transmission linkage at the rear of the engine compartment. Access is best from under the vehicle.

2 Remove the battery and battery tray as described in Chapter 5.

3.7a Undo the two screws (arrowed) securing the gear lever gaiter trim panel to the centre console . . .

3.8 Insert a 5 mm drill or punch through the lever base and into the locating hole – F17+ transmissions

3 Apply the handbrake, then jack up the front of the vehicle and support it on axle stands (see *Jacking and vehicle support*). Remove the engine undertray where fitted.

4 Slacken the gearchange selector rod clamp bolt which is situated at the front of the rod **(see illustration)**. Do not remove the bolt completely.

5 From inside the vehicle, unclip and remove the access panel in the centre console, beneath the handbrake lever **(see illustration)**.

6 Using a small screwdriver, carefully prise up the right-hand side of the ashtray, withdraw the ashtray from the centre console and disconnect the wiring connector **(see illustration)**.

7 Undo the two screws securing the rear of the gear lever gaiter trim panel to the centre console. Lift the panel up at the rear and

3.7b . . . then lift the panel up and disengage it from the centre console at the front

3.9 Lock the selector mechanism by pressing in the spring-loaded locking pin (arrowed) – F17+ transmissions

disengage it from the centre console at the front **(see illustrations)**. Fold the gaiter up the gear lever for access to the gear lever housing.

8 Push the gear lever to the left in neutral, then insert a 5 mm drill or metal rod through the special hole in the lever housing to lock it in the adjusting position **(see illustration)**.

9 Working in the engine compartment, with the selector mechanism in neutral, turn the selector shaft anti-clockwise against the spring pressure towards the third gear position, and lock the selector mechanism by pressing in the spring-loaded locking pin which is located on the top of the transmission unit **(see illustration)**. Ensure that the locking pin is pressed fully in so that the spring is completely compressed.

10 With both the lever and transmission locked in position, tighten the selector rod clamp bolt to the specified Stage 1 torque, then through the Stage 2 angle.

11 Remove the locking rod from the gear lever and check the operation of the gearchange mechanism; the transmission locking pin will automatically release when the lever is moved into the reverse position.

12 Ensure the transmission locking pin has released, then refit the engine undertray (where necessary) and lower the vehicle to the ground.

13 Refit the battery tray and battery as described in Chapter 5.

14 Check that all gears can be engaged easily, first with the engine off, then with the engine running and the clutch disengaged.

15 On completion, refit the gear lever gaiter trim panel, ashtray, and access panel to the centre console.

F23 transmissions

16 Carry out the operations described in paragraphs 5 to 7 above.

17 Using a small screwdriver, open the clamping piece on the end of each selector cable as far as the notch. Opening them any further may damage the clamping pieces **(see illustrations)**.

18 In the engine compartment, set the gearchange selector on the transmission to the 'neutral' position.

19 Working back inside the car, position

3.17a Using a small screwdriver, open the clamping piece on the end of each selector cable . . .

3.17b . . . until the lug (arrowed) rests on the notch – F23 transmissions

3.19 Lock the gear lever in 'neutral' by pushing in the clamp with a screwdriver – F23 transmissions

3.24 Pull up the reverse gear detent on the gear lever to expose the two tabs (arrowed) on the locking block – M20 and M32 transmissions

3.25 Engage the lug (arrowed) at the base of the locking block with the slot on the side of the gear lever housing – M20 and M32 transmissions

3.27 Using a 5 mm drill bit (arrowed) to lock the selector mechanism in the adjustment position – M20 and M32 transmissions

the gear lever in the 'neutral' position, and lock it there by pushing in the clamp **(see illustration)**.

20 Lock both gearshift cable clamping pieces by pushing them down, then pull out the clamp to unlock the gear lever.

21 Check that all gears can be engaged easily, first with the engine off, then with the engine running and the clutch disengaged.

22 On completion, refit the gear lever gaiter trim panel, ashtray, and access panel to the centre console.

M20 and M32 transmissions

Note: *A 5 mm drill bit or dowel rod will be required to carry out this procedure.*

23 Carry out the operations described in paragraphs 16 and 17 above.

24 Pull up the reverse gear detent on the gear lever to expose the two tabs on the locking block **(see illustration)**. Using a screwdriver, depress the right-hand tab, then depress the left-hand tab while carefully turning the screwdriver, until the locking block releases and moves down the lever.

25 Move the gear lever to the left and engage the lug at the base of the locking block with the slot on the side of the gear lever housing **(see illustration)**. The lever is now locked in the adjustment position.

26 Remove the battery and battery tray as described in Chapter 5.

27 Set the gearchange selector on the transmission to the 'neutral' position. Pull

the selector up and lock it in the adjustment position by inserting a 5 mm drill bit or dowel rod through the hole in the side of the housing **(see illustration)**. Ensure that the drill bit or dowel rod fully engages with the selector.

28 Working back inside the car, lock both gearshift cable clamping pieces by pushing them down.

29 Remove the drill bit or dowel rod used to lock the gearchange selector on the transmission.

30 Lift the locking block on the gear lever out of the slot on the lever housing, and slide it fully up the lever until it locks back in its original position.

31 Refit the battery tray and battery as described in Chapter 5.

32 Check that all gears can be engaged easily, first with the engine off, then with the engine running and the clutch disengaged.

33 On completion, refit the gear lever gaiter trim panel, ashtray, and access panel to the centre console.

4 Gearchange mechanism (F17+ transmissions) – removal and refitting

1 The gearchange mechanism consists of the gear lever housing and selector rod, and the linkage assembly on the transmission. The lever housing and selector rod, and the linkage assembly can be removed separately.

Gear lever housing and selector rod

Removal

2 Apply the handbrake, then jack up the front of the vehicle and support it on axle stands (see *Jacking and vehicle support*). Where fitted, remove the engine undertray.

3 Reach up behind the transmission and slacken the gearchange selector rod clamp bolt which is situated at the front of the rod **(see illustration 3.4)**. Do not remove the bolt completely. Push the selector rod rearwards and separate it from the shift guide.

4 Prise the gaiter from the bulkhead and withdraw from the selector rod.

5 Remove the centre console as described in Chapter 11.

6 Unscrew the four bolts, then withdraw the gear lever housing and selector rod assembly from the vehicle.

Refitting

7 Refitting is a reversal of removal, tightening the housing mounting bolts securely. Adjust the linkage as described in Section 3 before refitting the centre console.

Linkage assembly

Removal

8 Apply the handbrake, then jack up the front of the vehicle and support it on axle stands (see *Jacking and vehicle support*). Where fitted, remove the engine undertray.

4.11 Gearchange universal joint removal

Arrow shows position of hollow pin retaining spring

9 Reach up behind the transmission and slacken the gearchange selector rod clamp bolt which is situated at the front of the rod **(see illustration 3.4)**. Do not remove the bolt completely. Push the selector rod rearwards and separate it from the shift guide.

10 Remove the two clips and disconnect the linkage from the shift guide brackets.

11 Depress the retaining spring and lever out the pin. Detach the universal joint from the shift rod **(see illustration)**.

12 Withdraw the linkage assembly upwards and out of position.

5.3 Depress the lugs on the sides of the outer cable ends and lift the cables from the gear lever housing

5.5 Undo the four retaining bolts (arrowed) and lift the gear lever housing from the floor

5.15 Release the inner cable end fittings from the transmission selector levers

5.16 Pull back the retaining sleeves and detach the outer cables from the transmission mounting bracket

Refitting

13 Refitting is a reversal of removal, but adjust the linkage as described in Section 3.

5 Gearchange mechanism (F23, M20 and M32 transmissions) – removal and refitting

Gear lever housing

Removal

1 Remove the centre console as described in Chapter 11.

2 Using a small screwdriver, open the clamping piece on the end of each selector cable as far as the notch. Opening them any further may damage the clamping pieces **(see illustrations 3.17a and 3.17b)**.

3 Note the fitted locations of the two cables, then depress the lugs on the sides of the outer cable ends and lift the outer cables from the gear lever housing **(see illustration)**.

4 Move the two selector cables forward to disengage the inner cables from the gear lever clamping pieces.

5 Undo the four retaining bolts and lift the gear lever housing from the floor **(see illustration)**.

6 If required, the cable clamping pieces attached to the gear lever can be carefully prised from their position using a forked tool. No further dismantling of the assembly is recommended.

Refitting

7 If previously removed, attached the cable clamping pieces to the base of the lever using a pair of pliers.

8 Position the gear lever housing on the floor, insert the securing bolts and tighten securely.

9 Engage the selector inner cables with the clamping pieces, then refit the outer cables to the gear lever housing. Do not lock the clamping pieces at this stage.

10 Carry out the gearchange mechanism adjustment procedure, as described in Section 3.

11 Refit the centre console as described in Chapter 11.

Selector cables

Removal

12 Carry out the operations described in paragraphs 1 to 4 above.

13 Remove the battery and battery tray as described in Chapter 5.

14 Working in the engine compartment, note the fitted locations of the cables at their transmission attachments.

15 Using a suitable forked tool, release the inner cable end fittings from the transmission selector levers **(see illustration)**.

16 Pull back the retaining sleeves and detach the outer cables from the mounting bracket on the transmission **(see illustration)**.

17 Apply the handbrake, then jack up the front of the vehicle and support it on axle

stands (see *Jacking and vehicle support*). Where fitted, remove the engine undertray.

18 Release the rubber grommet at the cable entry point on the engine compartment bulkhead, then pull the cables (complete with grommet) out of the bulkhead and into the engine compartment.

Refitting

19 Push the selector cables through the bulkhead passage from the engine compartment and locate the rubber grommet back into position in the bulkhead.

20 Refit the engine undertray (where necessary) and lower the vehicle to the ground.

21 Refit the outer cables to the mounting bracket on the transmission.

22 Engage the inner cable end fittings with the transmission selector levers, squeezing them together with pliers if necessary.

23 Engage the selector inner cables with the clamping pieces, then refit the outer cables to the gear lever housing. Do not lock the clamping pieces at this stage.

24 Carry out the gearchange mechanism adjustment procedure, as described in Section 3.

25 If not already done, refit the battery tray and battery as described in Chapter 5.

26 Refit the centre console as described in Chapter 11.

6 Oil seals – renewal

Driveshaft oil seals

F17+ and F23 transmissions

1 Firmly apply the handbrake, then jack up the front of the car and support it securely on axle stands (see *Jacking and vehicle support*). Where fitted, remove the engine undertray.

2 Drain the transmission oil as described in Section 2.

3 Remove the driveshaft/intermediate shaft as described in Chapter 8.

4 Note the correct fitted depth of the seal in its housing then carefully prise it out of position using a large flat-bladed screwdriver **(see illustration)**.

5 Remove all traces of dirt from the area around the oil seal aperture, then apply a smear of grease to the outer lip of the new oil seal. Ensure the seal is correctly positioned, with its sealing lip facing inwards, and tap it squarely into position, using a suitable tubular drift (such as a socket) which bears only on the hard outer edge of the seal **(see illustration)**. Ensure the seal is fitted at the same depth in its housing that the original was.

6 Refit the driveshaft/intermediate shaft as described in Chapter 8.

7 Refill the transmission with the specified type and amount of oil, as described in Section 2.

6.4 Prising out a driveshaft oil seal

M20 and M32 transmissions – right-hand oil seal

8 Proceed as described above in paragraphs 1 to 7.

M20 and M32 transmissions – left-hand oil seal

Note: *A hydraulic press, together with tubes and mandrels of suitable diameters will be needed for this operation.*

9 Firmly apply the handbrake, then jack up the front of the car and support it securely on axle stands (see *Jacking and vehicle support*). Where fitted, remove the engine undertray.

10 Drain the transmission oil as described in Section 2.

11 Remove the driveshaft as described in Chapter 8.

12 Undo the four bolts and remove the oil seal carrier from the side of the differential housing.

13 Place the oil seal carrier on the press bed with its outer surface facing down. Using a suitable mandrel, press the oil seal out of the carrier.

14 Using a small screwdriver, remove the sealing O-ring from the oil seal carrier.

15 Support the inner surface of the oil seal carrier on the press bed. Lubricate the new oil seal with transmission oil, then press it fully into position in the carrier using a suitable tube which bears only on the hard outer edge of the seal.

16 Fit a new O-ring to the oil seal carrier, then refit the carrier to the differential housing, tightening the retaining bolts to the specified torque.

7.4 Unscrew and remove the reversing light switch together with its sealing washer – F17+ transmissions

6.5 Fitting a new driveshaft oil seal using a socket as a tubular drift

17 Refit the driveshaft as described in Chapter 8.

18 Refill the transmission with the specified type and amount of oil, as described in Section 2.

Input shaft oil seal

19 The input shaft oil seal is an integral part of the clutch release cylinder; if the seal is leaking the complete release cylinder assembly must be renewed. Before condemning the release cylinder, check that the leak is not coming from the sealing ring which is fitted between the cylinder and the transmission housing; the sealing ring can be renewed once the release cylinder assembly has been removed. Refer to Chapter 6 for removal and refitting details.

7 Reversing light switch – testing, removal and refitting

F17+ transmissions

1 The reversing light circuit is controlled by a plunger-type switch screwed into the top of the transmission towards the front of the housing.

Testing

2 If a fault develops in the circuit, first ensure that the circuit fuse has not blown and that the reversing light bulbs are sound.

3 To test the switch, disconnect the wiring connector. Use a multimeter (set to the resistance function) or a battery-and-bulb test circuit to check that there is continuity between the switch terminals only when reverse gear is selected. If this is not the case, and there are no obvious breaks or other damage to the wires, the switch is faulty, and must be renewed.

Removal

4 Disconnect the wiring connector, then unscrew the switch and remove it from the transmission casing along with its sealing washer **(see illustration)**.

Refitting

5 Fit a new sealing washer to the switch, then screw it back into position in the top of the transmission housing and tighten it to

7.9 The reversing light switch (arrowed) is positioned above the left-hand driveshaft – F23 transmissions

the specified torque. Reconnect the wiring connector, then test the operation of the circuit.

F23 transmissions

6 The reversing light circuit is controlled by a plunger-type switch screwed into the rear of the transmission above the left-hand driveshaft.

7 To gain access to the switch, firmly apply the handbrake, then jack up the front of the car and support it securely on axle stands (see *Jacking and vehicle support*). Where fitted, remove the engine undertray.

Testing

8 Proceed as described in paragraphs 2 and 3 above.

Removal

9 Disconnect the wiring connector, then unscrew the switch and remove it from the transmission casing along with its sealing washer **(see illustration)**.

Refitting

10 Fit a new sealing washer to the switch, then screw it back into position in the rear of the transmission housing and tighten it to the specified torque. Reconnect the wiring connector, then test the operation of the circuit.

11 On completion, refit the engine undertray (where applicable) and lower the vehicle to the ground.

M20 and M32 transmissions

12 The reversing light circuit is controlled by

8.6 Prise out the clip to disconnect the clutch hydraulic hose from the release cylinder pipe

a plunger-type switch screwed into the front of the transmission casing.

13 To gain access to the switch, firmly apply the handbrake, then jack up the front of the car and support it securely on axle stands (see *Jacking and vehicle support*). Where fitted, remove the engine undertray.

Testing

14 Proceed as described in paragraphs 2 and 3 above.

Removal

15 Disconnect the wiring connector, then unscrew the switch and remove it from the transmission casing along with its sealing washer.

Refitting

16 Fit a new sealing washer to the switch, then screw it back into position in the transmission casing and tighten it to the specified torque. Reconnect the wiring connector, then test the operation of the circuit.

17 On completion, refit the engine undertray (where applicable) and lower the vehicle to the ground.

8 Transmission – removal and refitting

Removal

1 Apply the handbrake, then jack up the front of the vehicle and support it on axle stands (see *Jacking and vehicle support*). Allow sufficient working room to remove the transmission from under the left-hand side of the engine compartment. Remove both front roadwheels then, where necessary, undo the retaining clips/screws and remove the engine undertray. Also remove the engine top cover where fitted.

2 Remove the battery and battery tray as described in Chapter 5.

3 Drain the transmission oil as described in Section 2.

4 Disconnect the wiring connectors from the reversing light switch and oxygen sensor and free the wiring from the transmission unit and retaining brackets.

5 Remove the filler cap from the brake/clutch fluid reservoir on the bulkhead, then tighten it onto a piece of polythene. This will reduce the loss of fluid when the clutch hydraulic hose is disconnected. Alternatively, fit a hose clamp to the flexible hose next to the clutch hydraulic connection on the transmission housing.

6 Place some cloth rags beneath the hose, then prise out the retaining clip securing the clutch hydraulic pipe/hose end fitting to the top of the transmission bellhousing and detach the end fitting from the transmission **(see illustration)**. Gently squeeze the two legs of the retaining clip together and re-insert the retaining clip back into position in the end fitting. Discard the sealing ring from the

pipe end; a new sealing ring must be used on refitting. Plug/cover both the union and pipe ends to minimise fluid loss and prevent the entry of dirt into the hydraulic system. **Note:** *Whilst the hose/pipe is disconnected, do not depress the clutch pedal.*

7 On F17+ transmissions, refer to Section 4 and disconnect the gearchange/selector rod from the transmission linkage assembly. On F23, M20 and M32 transmissions, refer to Section 5 and disconnect the gearchange selector cables at their transmission attachments.

8 On M32 transmissions, remove the EGR valve heat exchanger as described in Chapter 4B.

9 Working as described in Chapter 8, disconnect the inner ends of both driveshafts from the differential and intermediate shaft, then remove the intermediate shaft. There is no need to disconnect the driveshafts from the swivel hub. Support the driveshafts by suspending them with wire or string – do not allow the driveshafts to hang down under their own weight, or the joints may be damaged.

10 Remove the front subframe assembly as described in Chapter 10, ensuring that the engine unit is securely supported by connecting a hoist to the engine assembly. If available, the type of support bar which locates in the engine compartment side channels is to be preferred.

11 Unscrew and remove the upper bolts securing the transmission to the rear of the engine. Where necessary, pull up the coolant hoses and secure them away from the transmission using plastic cable ties. On M20 transmissions, undo and remove the starter motor lower mounting bolt.

12 Place a jack with a block of wood beneath the transmission, and raise the jack to take the weight of the transmission.

13 Unbolt the left-hand engine/transmission mounting bracket from the transmission with reference to the relevant Part of Chapter 2.

14 Lower the left-hand side of the engine/transmission making sure that the coolant hoses and wiring harnesses are not stretched.

15 Slacken and remove the remaining bolts securing the transmission to the engine and sump flange. Note the correct fitted positions of each bolt, and the relevant brackets, as they are removed to use as a reference on refitting. Make a final check that all components have been disconnected, and are positioned clear of the transmission so that they will not hinder the removal procedure.

16 With the bolts removed, move the trolley jack and transmission, to free it from its locating dowels. Once the transmission is free, lower the jack and manoeuvre the unit out from under the car. Remove the locating dowels from the transmission or engine if they are loose, and keep them in a safe place.

Refitting

17 The transmission is refitted by a reversal of the removal procedure, bearing in mind the following points.

a) Ensure the locating dowels are correctly positioned prior to installation.

b) Tighten all nuts and bolts to the specified torque (where given).

c) Renew the driveshaft oil seals (see Section 6) before refitting the driveshafts/ intermediate shaft.

d) Refit the front subframe assembly as described in Chapter 10.

e) Fit a new sealing ring to the clutch hydraulic hose before clipping the hose into the end fitting. Ensure the hose is securely retained by its clip then bleed the hydraulic system as described in Chapter 6.

f) On M32 transmissions, refit the EGR valve heat exchanger as described in Chapter 4B.

g) Refill the transmission with the specified type and quantity of oil, as described in Section 2.

h) On completion, adjust the gearchange mechanism as described in Section 3.

9 Transmission overhaul – general information

1 Overhauling a manual transmission unit is a difficult and involved job for the DIY home mechanic. In addition to dismantling and reassembling many small parts, clearances must be precisely measured and, if necessary, changed by selecting shims and spacers. Internal transmission components are also often difficult to obtain, and in many instances, extremely expensive. Because of this, if the transmission develops a fault or becomes noisy, the best course of action is to have the unit overhauled by a specialist repairer, or to obtain an exchange reconditioned unit.

2 Nevertheless, it is not impossible for the more experienced mechanic to overhaul the transmission, provided the special tools are available, and the job is done in a deliberate step-by-step manner, so that nothing is overlooked.

3 The tools necessary for an overhaul include internal and external circlip pliers, bearing pullers, a slide hammer, a set of pin punches, a dial test indicator, and possibly a hydraulic press. In addition, a large, sturdy workbench and a vice will be required.

4 During dismantling of the transmission, make careful notes of how each component is fitted, to make reassembly easier and more accurate.

5 Before dismantling the transmission, it will help if you have some idea what area is malfunctioning. Certain problems can be closely related to specific areas in the transmission, which can make component examination and renewal easier. Refer to the Fault finding Section of this manual for more information.

10 Transmission oil level check

1 Position the vehicle over an inspection pit, on vehicle ramps, or jack it up and support it securely on axle stands (see Jacking and vehicle support), but make sure that it is level. The oil must be checked before the car is driven, or at least 5 minutes after the engine has been switched off. If the oil is checked immediately after driving the car, some of the oil will remain distributed around the transmission components, resulting in an inaccurate level reading.

F17+ transmissions

2 Where fitted, undo the retaining clips/ screws and remove the engine undertray.

3 Wipe clean the area around the level plug. The level plug is located behind the driveshaft inner joint on the left-hand side of the transmission (see illustration 2.8). Unscrew the plug and clean it.

4 The oil level should reach the lower edge of the level plug aperture. If topping-up is necessary, wipe clean the area around the reversing light switch, and remove the switch as described in Section 7.

5 Add the specified grade of oil given in Lubricants and fluids, through the reversing light switch aperture, until it reaches the bottom of the level plug aperture. Allow any excess oil to drain, then refit and tighten the level plug to the specified torque.

6 Refit the reversing light switch with reference to Section 7.

7 Where applicable, refit the engine undertray, then lower the vehicle to the ground.

F23 transmissions

8 Where fitted, undo the retaining clips/ screws and remove the engine undertray.

9 Wipe clean the area around the level plug located on the rear of the differential housing (see illustration 2.14). Unscrew the plug and clean it.

10 The oil level should reach the lower edge of the level plug aperture. If topping-up is necessary, wipe clean the area around the filler plug on the top of the casing and unscrew the plug (see illustration 2.15). To gain access to the plug, remove the battery and battery tray as described in Chapter 5.

11 Add the specified grade of oil given in Lubricants and fluids, through the filler plug aperture, until it reaches the bottom of the level plug aperture. Allow any excess oil to drain, then refit and tighten the level plug to the specified torque.

12 Refit the oil filler plug and tighten it to the specified torque. Where applicable, refit the engine undertray, then lower the vehicle to the ground. If removed, refit the battery tray and battery with reference to Chapter 5.

M20 and M32 transmissions

13 On the M20 and M32 transmissions, there is no provision for oil level checking once the transmission has been initially filled. If for any reason it is thought that the oil level may be low, the transmission oil must be completely drained, then refilled with an exact specified quantity of oil as described in Section 2.

Chapter 7 Part B:
Automatic transmission

Contents

Degrees of difficulty

Easy, suitable for novice with little experience	**Fairly easy,** suitable for beginner with some experience	**Fairly difficult,** suitable for competent DIY mechanic	**Difficult,** suitable for experienced DIY mechanic	**Very difficult,** suitable for expert DIY or professional

Specifications

General

Type	Electronically-controlled adaptive automatic, six forward speeds and reverse, with sequential manual gear selection capability
Manufacturer's designation	AF40

Lubrication

Lubricant type	See *Lubricants and fluids* on page 0•18
Lubricant capacity	See Chapter 1

Torque wrench settings

	Nm	lbf ft
Automatic transmission fluid drain/filler plugs:		
Drain plug	50	37
Filler plug	40	30
Level checking plug	8	6
Electronic control unit mounting bolts	25	18
Engine/transmission mountings	See Chapter 2C	
Engine-to-transmission bolts	See Chapter 2C	
Fluid cooler pipes to transmission	7	5
Roadwheel bolts	110	81
Selector lever to transmission selector shaft	15	11
Torque converter-to-driveplate bolts*	30	22

* Use new bolts

1 General information

1.9 litre SOHC engine models are optionally available with a six-speed, electronically-controlled automatic transmission. The transmission consists of a torque converter, an epicyclic geartrain, and hydraulically-operated clutches and brakes. The unit is controlled by the electronic control unit (ECU) via electrically-operated solenoid valves. The transmission unit has three driving modes; normal, sport and winter modes. In addition to the fully automatic operation, the transmission can also be operated manually with a six-speed sequential gear selection.

The torque converter provides a fluid coupling between engine and transmission, which acts as an automatic clutch, and also provides a degree of torque multiplication when accelerating. The torque converter incorporates a lock-up function whereby the engine and transmission can be directly coupled by means of a clutch unit inside the torque converter. The lock-up function is controlled by the ECU according to operating conditions.

The epicyclic geartrain provides either of the six forward or one reverse gear ratios, according to which of its component parts

are held stationary or allowed to turn. The components of the geartrain are held or released by hydraulically actuated brakes and clutches. A fluid pump within the transmission provides the necessary hydraulic pressure to operate the brakes and clutches.

In automatic mode, the transmission is fully adaptive, whereby the shift points are dependent on driver input, roadspeed, engine speed and vehicle operating conditions. The ECU receives inputs from various engine and drivetrain related sensors, and determines the appropriate shift point for each gear. If the transmission unit is switched into sport mode, using the button on the facia, the transmission shifts up only at high engine speeds, giving improved acceleration and overtaking performance. When the transmission is in sport mode, the indicator light in the instrument panel is illuminated. If the transmission is switched into winter mode, using the button on the selector lever indicator panel, the transmission will select third gear as the vehicle pulls away from a standing start; this helps to maintain traction on very slippery surfaces.

Driver control of the transmission is by a four-position selector lever. The drive D position, allows automatic changing throughout the range of forward gear ratios. An automatic kickdown facility shifts the transmission down a gear if the accelerator pedal is fully depressed. If the selector lever is moved to the left from the D position, the transmission enters manual mode. In manual mode the gear selector lever can be used to shift the transmission up or down each gear sequentially.

Due to the complexity of the automatic transmission, any repair or overhaul work must be left to a Vauxhall/Opel dealer or transmission specialist with the necessary special equipment for fault diagnosis and repair. The contents of the following Sections are therefore confined to supplying general information, and any service information and instructions that can be used by the owner.

2 Transmission fluid – draining and refilling

Draining

1 Position the vehicle over an inspection pit, on vehicle ramps, or jack it up and support it securely on axle stands (see *Jacking and vehicle support*), but make sure that it is level. Where fitted, remove the clips and bolts and remove the undertray from beneath the engine.

2 Position a container under the combined drain plug/level checking plug at the base of the transmission. Note that the drain plug and level checking plug are incorporated into one unit – the drain plug is the larger of the two plugs, with the level checking plug screwed into the centre of it **(see illustration)**.

3 Unscrew the level checking plug and remove it, along with its sealing washer, from the centre of the drain plug. Now unscrew the drain plug and remove it, along with its sealing washer, from the transmission. Allow the fluid to drain completely into the container.

4 When the fluid has finished draining, clean the drain plug threads and those of the transmission casing, fit a new sealing washer and refit the drain plug, tightening it to the specified torque.

Refilling

5 Wipe clean the area around the transmission fluid filler plug, located on the top of the transmission housing, adjacent to the selector cable **(see illustration)**. Unscrew and remove the filler plug along with its sealing washer.

6 Slowly refill the transmission with the specified type of fluid, via the filler plug aperture until fluid just starts to drip out of the level checking plug aperture. Use a funnel with a fine mesh gauze, to avoid spillage, and to ensure that no foreign matter enters the transmission.

7 Refit the level checking plug and tighten it securely.

8 Add a further 0.5 litre of fluid via the filler plug aperture.

9 Start the engine and allow it to idle. With the footbrake firmly applied, slowly move the selector lever from position P to position D and back to position P, stopping at each position for at least two seconds. Repeat this procedure twice.

10 With the engine still idling, unscrew the fluid level checking plug once more. Allow the excess fluid to run from the level checking plug aperture until it is only dripping out. Refit the level checking plug with a new sealing washer, and tighten the plug to the specified torque.

11 If no fluid runs from the level checking plug aperture, switch the engine off and repeat paragraphs 8 to 10.

12 Once the fluid level is correct, refit the filler plug with a new sealing washer, and tighten the plug to the specified torque.

13 On completion, refit the engine undertray and lower the vehicle to the ground.

3 Selector cable – adjustment

Note: *If the battery is disconnected with the selector lever in the P (park) position, the lever will be locked in position. To manually release the lever, use a small screwdriver to carefully prise up the right-hand side of the ashtray. Withdraw the ashtray from the centre console and move it to one side. Using a flat-bladed screwdriver, push the yellow emergency release lever, located at the front of the selector housing, forward whilst moving the selector lever to the N (neutral) position.*

1 Operate the selector lever throughout its entire range and check that the transmission engages the correct gear indicated on the

2.2 Transmission fluid level checking plug (1) and drain plug (2)

2.5 Transmission fluid filler plug (1)

3.5a Use a small screwdriver to open the clamping piece (1) on the selector cable . . .

selector lever position indicator. If adjustment is necessary, continue as follows.

2 Position the selector lever in the N (neutral) position.

3 Using a small screwdriver, carefully prise up the right-hand side of the ashtray, withdraw the ashtray from the centre console and disconnect the wiring connector.

4 Position the selector lever in the P (park) position.

5 Working in the ashtray aperture, use a small screwdriver to open the clamping piece on the selector cable as far as the notch **(see illustrations)**. Opening any further may damage the clamping piece.

6 Working in the engine compartment, remove the battery and battery tray as described in Chapter 5. Move the lever on the transmission selector lever position switch fully forwards so that the transmission is also positioned in the P position **(see illustration)**. With both the selector lever and transmission correctly positioned, lock the clamping piece on the selector cable by pushing it down until it clicks in position.

7 Refit the battery tray and battery as described in Chapter 5.

8 Check the operation of the selector lever and, if necessary, repeat the adjustment procedure. On completion, refit the ashtray to the centre console.

4	Selector cable – removal and refitting

Removal

1 Remove the centre console as described in Chapter 11 then position the selector lever in the P (park) position.

2 Using a small screwdriver, open the clamping piece on the end of the selector cable as far as the notch. Opening any further may damage the clamping piece **(see illustration 3.5b)**.

3 Again using a small screwdriver, lift up the

3.5b . . . until the lug (arrowed) rests on the notch

locking clip securing the outer cable to the selector lever housing **(see illustration)**.

4 Move the selector cable forward to disengage the inner cable from the selector lever clamping piece.

5 Working in the engine compartment, remove the battery and battery tray as described in Chapter 5. Use a forked tool or flat-bladed screwdriver, and carefully lever the selector inner cable end fitting off the balljoint on the selector lever position switch. Pull back the retaining sleeve and detach the outer cable from the mounting bracket on the transmission **(see illustration)**.

6 Release the rubber grommet at the cable entry point on the engine compartment bulkhead, then pull the cable (complete with grommet) out of the bulkhead and into the engine compartment.

Refitting

7 Push the selector cable through the bulkhead passage from the engine compartment and locate the rubber grommet back into position in the bulkhead.

8 Refit the outer cable to the mounting bracket on the transmission.

9 Engage the inner cable end fitting with

4.3 Lift up the locking clip securing the outer cable to the selector lever housing

3.6 Move the lever on the selector lever position switch fully forwards so the transmission is in the P position

the balljoint on the selector lever position switch, squeezing them together with pliers if necessary.

10 Move the lever on the selector lever position switch fully forwards so that the transmission is positioned in the P position.

11 From inside the car, position the selector lever in the P position and guide the cable back into its location in the selector lever housing, engaging the inner cable with the clamping piece. Push down the outer cable locking clip and the inner cable clamping piece ensuring they both lock fully into position.

12 Refit the centre console as described in Chapter 11.

13 Refit the battery tray and battery as described in Chapter 5.

4.5 Selector inner cable end fitting (1) and outer cable retaining sleeve (2)

5 Selector lever assembly – removal and refitting

Removal

1 Carry out the operations described in Section 4, paragraphs 1 to 4.
2 Disconnect the selector lever assembly wiring connector and release the wiring harness from the retaining clips and ties.
3 Undo the four mounting bolts and lift the selector lever assembly from the floor.

Refitting

4 Working in the engine compartment, check that the transmission is in the P (park) position by moving the lever on the selector lever position switch fully forwards **(see illustration 3.6)**.
5 From inside the car, position the selector lever in the P position, then manoeuvre the selector lever assembly into place, engaging it with the selector cable. Refit the mounting bolts and tighten them securely.
6 Reconnect the selector lever assembly wiring connector and secure the wiring harness with the retaining clips and ties.
7 Push down the selector outer cable locking clip and the inner cable clamping piece ensuring they both lock fully into position.
8 Refit the centre console as described in Chapter 11.

6 Selector lever assembly components – removal and refitting

Selector lever knob

Removal

1 Move the selector lever to the D (drive) position.
2 Rotate the locking sleeve, located directly beneath the lever knob, clockwise, approximately 30°.
3 Depress the release button on the lever knob and pull the knob up and off the selector lever.

Refitting

4 Make sure the selector lever is still in the D position, then place the knob on the selector lever, press the release button on the front of the knob, and push the knob fully into position.
5 Turn the locking sleeve anti-clockwise to secure.

Selector lever position indicator

Removal

6 Remove the selector lever knob as described previously.
7 Using a small screwdriver, carefully prise up the right-hand side of the ashtray, withdraw the ashtray from the centre console and disconnect the wiring connector.

6.8 Unclip and remove the access panel in the centre console, beneath the handbrake lever

8 Unclip and remove the access panel in the centre console, beneath the handbrake lever **(see illustration)**.
9 Undo the two screws securing the rear of the selector lever trim panel to the centre console **(see illustration)**. Lift the panel up at the rear and disengage it from the centre console at the front.
10 Carefully unclip the intermediate frame around the edge of the position indicator panel and remove the frame rearward.
11 Release the wiring harness at the front of the selector lever housing from its retaining clips and ties, and disconnect the wiring harness connector.
12 Lift the position indicator assembly and withdraw the unit up and off the selector lever.

Refitting

13 Reconnect the wiring harness, then refit the position indicator assembly and intermediate frame to the selector lever housing.
14 Refit the selector lever trim panel to the centre console and secure with the two screws.
15 Refit the centre console access panel and ashtray, then refit the selector lever knob as described previously.

Selector lever control unit

Removal

16 Remove the selector lever assembly as described in Section 5.

6.9 Undo the two screws (arrowed) securing the rear of the selector lever trim panel to the centre console

17 Disconnect the selector lever lock switch wiring connector from the control unit mounted on the side of the selector lever assembly.
18 Release the retaining tab and remove the control unit from the selector lever assembly.

Refitting

19 Refitting is a reversal of removal.

Selector lever lock switch

Removal

20 Remove the selector lever assembly as described in Section 5.
21 Carefully unclip the selector emergency release lever from its guides on the side of the selector lever housing.
22 Disconnect the selector lever lock switch wiring connector from the control unit mounted on the side of the selector lever assembly.
23 Withdraw the lock switch from the side of the selector lever housing.

Refitting

24 Refitting is a reversal of removal.

7 Mode switches – removal and refitting

Winter mode switch

1 The winter mode switch is an integral part of the selector lever position indicator and cannot be individually removed. If the switch is faulty, the complete position indicator panel must be renewed. Removal and refitting procedures for the selector lever position indicator are contained in Section 6.

Sport mode switch

2 The sport mode switch is an integral part of the facia centre switch panel and cannot be individually removed. If the switch is faulty, the complete switch panel must be renewed. Removal and refitting procedures for the facia centre switch panel are contained in Chapter 12.

8 Oil seals – renewal

Driveshaft oil seals

1 Firmly apply the handbrake, then jack up the front of the car and support it securely on axle stands (see *Jacking and vehicle support*). Where fitted, remove the engine undertray.
2 Drain the transmission oil as described in Section 2.
3 Remove the driveshaft/intermediate shaft as described in Chapter 8.
4 Note the correct fitted depth of the seal in its housing then carefully prise it out of position using a large flat-bladed screwdriver **(see illustration)**.

5 Remove all traces of dirt from the area around the oil seal aperture, then lubricate the new oil seal with automatic transmission fluid. Ensure the seal is correctly positioned, with its sealing lip facing inwards, and tap it squarely into position, using a suitable tubular drift (such as a socket) which bears only on the hard outer edge of the seal **(see illustration)**. Ensure the seal is fitted at the same depth in its housing that the original was.

6 Refit the driveshaft/intermediate shaft as described in Chapter 8.

7 Refill the transmission with the specified type and amount of oil, as described in Section 2.

Torque converter oil seal

8 Remove the transmission as described in Section 13.

9 Carefully slide the torque converter off of the transmission shaft whilst being prepared for fluid spillage.

10 Note the correct fitted position of the seal in the oil pump housing then carefully lever the seal out of position taking care not to mark the housing or input shaft.

11 Remove all traces of dirt from the area around the oil seal aperture then press the new seal into position, ensuring its sealing lip is facing inwards.

12 Lubricate the seal with clean transmission fluid then carefully ease the torque converter into position. Slide the torque converter onto the transmission shaft by turning it until it fully engages with the oil pump.

13 Refit the transmission as described in Section 13.

9 Fluid cooler – general information

The transmission fluid cooler is an integral part of the radiator assembly. Refer to Chapter 3 for removal and refitting details, if the cooler is damaged the complete radiator assembly must be renewed.

10 Selector lever position switch – removal and refitting

The selector lever position switch is an integral part of the transmission electronic control unit and cannot be separated. Removal and refitting procedures for the electronic control unit are contained in Section 12.

11 Transmission input/ output speed sensors – removal and refitting

The input and output shaft speed sensors are located internally within the transmission

8.4 Prising out a driveshaft oil seal

and are not individually available. If one or both speed sensors are diagnosed as faulty, it will be necessary to obtain a complete new transmission.

12 Electronic control unit – removal and refitting

Note: *If a new ECU is to be fitted, this work must be entrusted to a Vauxhall/Opel dealer or suitably-equipped specialist. It is necessary to reset the transmission electronic control system prior to removal, and to programme the new ECU after installation. This work requires the use of dedicated Vauxhall/ Opel diagnostic equipment or a compatible alternative.*

Removal

1 The combined ECU and selector lever position switch are located on the top of the transmission housing.

2 Ensure the handbrake is fully applied, then move the gear selector lever to the N (neutral) position.

3 Remove the battery and battery tray as described in Chapter 5.

4 Unclip the pre/post-heating system control unit wiring harness from the battery tray support.

5 Release the ECU wiring harness from its retaining clips, then disconnect the wiring harness connector from the ECU.

6 Using a forked tool or flat-bladed screwdriver, carefully lever the selector inner cable end fitting off the balljoint on the selector lever position switch. Pull back the retaining sleeve and detach the outer cable from the mounting bracket on the transmission **(see illustration 4.5)**.

7 Unscrew the retaining nut and remove the lever from the transmission selector shaft.

8 Unscrew and remove the three mounting bolts, then carefully lift the ECU upwards and remove it from the transmission **(see illustration)**. Take great care not to damage the wiring connector pins on the underside of the ECU as it is lifted off.

Refitting

9 Prior to refitting, first make sure that the

8.5 Fitting a new driveshaft oil seal using a socket as a tubular drift

transmission selector shaft is still in the N (neutral) position. If there is any doubt, temporarily engage the selector shaft lever with the transmission selector shaft and move the lever fully forwards (to the P position) then move it two notches backwards.

10 Set the selector lever position switch on the ECU to the N position by turning the switch until the two arrows are aligned.

11 Check that the transmission wiring harness is correctly located, then carefully place the ECU in position. Take great care not to damage the wiring connector pins as the ECU is fitted.

12 Refit the three bolts and tighten to the specified torque.

13 Refit the selector lever to the shaft and tighten its retaining nut to the specified torque.

14 Refit the selector outer cable to the mounting bracket on the transmission. Engage the selector inner cable end fitting with the balljoint on the selector lever, squeezing them together with pliers if necessary.

15 Reconnect the ECU wiring harness connector, then secure the harness in its retaining clips.

16 Clip the pre/post-heating system control unit wiring harness to the battery tray support.

17 Refit the battery tray and battery as described in Chapter 5.

12.8 Electronic control unit mounting bolts (arrowed)

13 Automatic transmission – removal and refitting

Note: *New torque converter-to-driveplate bolts will be required for refitting.*

Removal

1 Apply the handbrake, place the selector lever in the N (Neutral) position. then jack up the front of the vehicle and support it on axle stands (see *Jacking and vehicle support*). Allow sufficient working room to remove the transmission from under the left-hand side of the engine compartment. Remove both front roadwheels then, where necessary, undo the retaining clips/screws and remove the engine undertray. Also remove the engine top cover where fitted.

2 Drain the transmission fluid as described in Section 2, then refit the drain plug and tighten it to the specified torque.

3 Remove the battery and battery tray as described in Chapter 5.

4 Release the transmission ECU wiring harness from its retaining clips, then disconnect the wiring harness connector from the ECU.

5 Using a forked tool or flat-bladed screwdriver, carefully lever the selector inner cable end fitting off the balljoint on the selector lever position switch. Pull back the retaining sleeve and detach the outer cable from the mounting bracket on the transmission.

6 Release the battery wiring harness from the clips or ties securing it to the engine/transmission unit.

7 Undo the retaining nut and detach the transmission ECU wiring harness support bracket from the transmission.

8 Release the retaining clip and free the engine management ECU wiring harness from the front of the transmission.

9 Disconnect the inner ends of both driveshafts/intermediate shaft from the differential as described in Chapter 8. There is no need to disconnect the driveshafts from the swivel hub. Support the driveshafts by suspending them with wire or string – do not allow the driveshafts to hang down under their own weight, or the joints may be damaged.

10 Unscrew and remove the upper bolts securing the transmission to the rear of the engine. Where necessary, pull up the coolant hoses and secure them away from the transmission using plastic cable ties.

11 Remove the front subframe assembly as described in Chapter 10, ensuring that the engine unit is securely supported by connecting a hoist to the engine assembly. If available, the type of support bar which locates in the engine compartment side channels is to be preferred.

12 Disconnect the wiring connector, then undo the retaining bolt and release the wiring harness support bracket from the engine/transmission rear mounting/torque link. Similarly disconnect and separate the remaining wiring harness connector from the rear mounting/torque link.

13 Undo the three retaining bolts and remove the engine/transmission rear mounting/torque link from the rear of the transmission housing.

14 Unscrew the central retaining nut and

detach the fluid cooler pipes from the transmission. Suitably cover the pipe ends and plug the transmission orifices to prevent dirt entry.

15 Undo the two retaining bolts and remove the engine/transmission front mounting/torque link from the front of the transmission housing.

16 Remove the starter motor as described in Chapter 5.

17 Using a socket and extension bar, turn the crankshaft pulley until one of the bolts securing the torque converter to the driveplate becomes accessible through the starter motor aperture. Slacken and remove the bolt, then turn the crankshaft pulley as necessary, and undo the remaining bolts as they become accessible. There are six securing bolts in total. Discard the bolts, new ones must be used on refitting.

18 Unscrew the retaining bolt and detach the engine management ECU wiring harness support bracket from the front of the transmission.

19 Disconnect the breather hose from the top of the transmission.

20 Place a jack with a block of wood beneath the transmission, and raise the jack to take the weight of the transmission.

21 Mark the bolt positions for correct refitting, then unscrew the three bolts securing the left-hand engine/transmission mounting to the transmission casing.

22 By manipulating the engine hoist and the jack under the transmission, lower the engine/transmission approximately 50 mm. Ensure that the various coolant hoses and wiring harnesses are not stretched.

23 Slacken and remove the remaining bolts securing the transmission to the engine and sump flange. Note the correct fitted positions of each bolt, and the relevant brackets, as they are removed to use as a reference on refitting. Make a final check that all components have been disconnected, and are positioned clear of the transmission so that they will not hinder the removal procedure.

24 With all the bolts removed, move the trolley jack and transmission, to free it from its locating dowels. Once the transmission is free, lower the jack and manoeuvre the unit out from under the car, taking care to ensure that the torque converter does not fall off. Remove the locating dowels from the transmission or engine if they are loose, and keep them in a safe place. Retain the torque converter while the transmission is removed by bolting a strip of metal across the transmission bellhousing end face.

Refitting

25 The transmission is refitted by a reversal of the removal procedure, bearing in mind the following points.

a) Prior to refitting, remove all traces of old locking compound from the torque converter threads by running a tap of the correct thread diameter and pitch down

J44609

13.25 Check that the torque converter is fully entered

1 *Straight-edge*
2 *Vernier calipers on bolt hole*
3 *Torque converter centre stub*

the holes. In the absence of a suitable tap, use one of the old bolts with slots cut in its threads.

b) Ensure the engine/transmission locating dowels are correctly positioned and apply a smear of molybdenum disulphide grease to the torque converter locating pin and its centering bush in the crankshaft end.

c) Check that the torque converter is fully entered inside the transmission bellhousing by measuring the distance from the flange to the bolt holes in the torque converter, using a straight-edge and vernier calipers **(see illustration)**. The distance must measure approximately 20.0 mm.

d) Once the transmission and engine are correctly joined, refit the securing bolts, tightening them to the specified torque setting.

e) Fit the new torque converter-to-driveplate bolts and tighten them lightly only to start then go around and tighten them to the specified torque setting in a diagonal sequence.

f) Tighten all nuts and bolts to the specified torque (where given).

g) Renew the driveshaft oil seals (see Section 8) and refit the driveshafts/intermediate shaft to the transmission as described in Chapter 8.

h) Refit the front subframe assembly as described in Chapter 10.

i) On completion, refill the transmission with the specified type and quantity of fluid as described in Section 2 and adjust the selector cable as described in Section 3.

14 Automatic transmission overhaul – general information

1 In the event of a fault occurring with the transmission, it is first necessary to determine whether it is of a mechanical, electrical or hydraulic nature, and to do this, special test equipment is required. It is therefore essential to have the work carried out by a Vauxhall/Opel dealer or suitably equipped specialist if a transmission fault is suspected.

2 Do not remove the transmission from the car for possible repair before professional fault diagnosis has been carried out, since most tests require the transmission to be in the vehicle.

Chapter 8
Driveshafts

Contents

Degrees of difficulty

Easy, suitable for novice with little experience	Fairly easy, suitable for beginner with some experience	Fairly difficult, suitable for competent DIY mechanic	Difficult, suitable for experienced DIY mechanic	Very difficult, suitable for expert DIY or professional

Specifications

General
Driveshaft type . . . . Solid steel shafts with inner and outer constant velocity (CV) joints. Right-hand driveshaft incorporating intermediate shaft

Lubrication (overhaul only – see text)
Lubricant type/specification . . . . Use only special grease supplied in sachets with gaiter kits – joints are otherwise pre-packed with grease and sealed

Torque wrench settings

	Nm	lbf ft
Anti-roll bar connecting link retaining nut*	55	41
Driveshaft retaining nut*:		
Stage 1	150	111
Stage 2	Slacken the nut by 45°	
Stage 3	250	185
Intermediate shaft bearing housing to support bracket	18	13
Lower arm balljoint clamp bolt nut*	50	37
Roadwheels	110	81
Track rod end to swivel hub*:		
Stage 1	30	22
Stage 2	Angle-tighten a further 90°	
Stage 3	Angle-tighten a further 15°	

Use new nuts/bolts.

1 General information

Drive is transmitted from the differential to the front wheels by means of two, solid steel driveshafts.

Both driveshafts are splined at their outer ends to accept the wheel hubs, and are threaded so that each hub can be fastened by a large nut. The inner end of each driveshaft is splined to accept the intermediate shaft and is held in place by an internal circlip.

Constant velocity (CV) joints are fitted to each end of the driveshafts, to ensure the smooth and efficient transmission of drive at all the angles possible as the roadwheels move up-and-down with the suspension, and as they turn from side-to-side under steering. On 1.3 and 1.7 litre models, both inner and outer constant velocity joints are of the ball-and-cage type. On 1.9 litre models, the outer constant velocity joints are of the ball-and-cage type and the inner joints are of the tripod type.

The right-hand driveshaft on all models has an intermediate shaft attached to the rear of the cylinder block.

2 Driveshaft – removal and refitting

Note: *A new driveshaft retaining nut, inner joint circlip, lower arm balljoint clamp bolt and nut, anti-roll bar connecting link retaining nut and a new track rod end retaining nut will be needed for refitting. The driveshaft outer joint splines may be a tight fit in the hub and it is possible that a puller/extractor will be required to draw the hub assembly off the driveshaft during removal.*

TOOL TiP

A tool to hold the wheel hub stationary whilst the driveshaft retaining nut is slackened can be fabricated from two lengths of steel strip (one long, one short) and a nut an bolt; the nut and bolt forming the pivot of a forked tool.

Removal

1 Firmly apply the handbrake, then jack up the front of the car and support it securely on axle stands (see *Jacking and vehicle support*). Remove the relevant front roadwheel.

2 To prevent rotation of the wheel hub as the driveshaft retaining nut is slackened, make up a holding tool and bolt the tool to the wheel hub using two wheel bolts **(see Tool Tip)**.

3 With the holding tool in place, slacken and remove the driveshaft retaining nut using a socket and long bar. Where necessary, support the socket on an axle stand to prevent it slipping off the nut. This nut is very tight; make

2.6 Unscrew the retaining nut and withdraw the clamp bolt from the swivel hub

2.8 Push down the lower suspension arm to free the balljoint from the swivel hub

2.4 Unscrew the retaining nut, then use a balljoint separator tool to remove the track rod end from the swivel hub

sure that there is no risk of pulling the car off the axle stands as the nut is slackened.

4 Unscrew the nut securing the track rod end to the steering arm on the swivel hub, then use a balljoint separator tool to remove the track rod end **(see illustration)**.

5 Unscrew and remove the nut securing the anti-roll bar connecting link to the suspension strut, while holding the link stub on the flats provided with a further spanner **(see illustration)**. Release the link from the strut and move it to one side.

6 Unscrew the nut and remove the clamp bolt securing the front suspension lower arm to the swivel hub. Note that the bolt head faces the front of the vehicle **(see illustration)**.

7 Use a chisel or screwdriver as a wedge to expand the lower portion of the swivel hub **(see illustration)**.

2.7 Use a chisel or screwdriver as a wedge to expand the lower portion of the swivel hub

2.9a Use a soft-faced hammer to drive the driveshaft from the hub splines . . .

2.5 Unscrew the nut securing the connecting link to the anti-roll bar, while holding the link stub with a further spanner

8 Using a lever, push down on the suspension lower arm to free the balljoint from the swivel hub, then move the swivel hub to one side and release the arm, taking care not to damage the balljoint rubber boot **(see illustration)**. It is advisable to place a protective cover over the rubber boot such as the plastic cap from an aerosol can, suitably cut to fit.

9 The hub must now be freed from the end of the driveshaft. It may be possible to pull the hub off the driveshaft, but if the end of the driveshaft is tight in the hub, temporarily refit the driveshaft retaining nut to protect the driveshaft threads, then tap the end of the driveshaft with a soft-faced hammer while pulling outwards on the swivel hub **(see illustrations)**. Alternatively, use a suitable puller to press the driveshaft through the hub.

10 With the driveshaft detached from the swivel hub, tie the suspension strut to one side and support the driveshaft on an axle stand.

11 If working on the left-hand driveshaft, place a suitable container beneath the differential, to collect escaping transmission oil/fluid when the driveshaft is withdrawn.

12 Using a stout bar, release the inner end of the driveshaft from the differential or intermediate shaft. Lever between the constant velocity joint and differential housing, or between the constant velocity joint and intermediate shaft bearing housing, to release the driveshaft retaining circlip **(see illustration)**.

2.9b . . . then pull the swivel hub outwards

13 Withdraw the driveshaft, ensuring that the constant velocity joints are not placed under excessive strain, and remove the driveshaft from beneath the vehicle. Whilst the driveshaft is removed, plug or tape over the differential aperture to prevent dirt entry.

Caution: Do not allow the vehicle to rest on its wheels with one or both driveshafts removed, as damage to the wheel bearings(s) may result. If the vehicle must be moved on its wheels, clamp the wheel bearings using spacers and a long threaded rod to take the place of the driveshaft.

Refitting

14 Before refitting the driveshaft, examine the oil seal in the transmission housing and renew it if necessary as described in the relevant Part of Chapter 7.

15 Remove the circlip from the end of the driveshaft inner joint splines or intermediate shaft and discard it. Fit a new circlip, making sure it is correctly located in the groove.

16 Thoroughly clean the driveshaft splines, intermediate shaft splines (where applicable), and the apertures in the transmission and hub assembly. Apply a thin film of grease to the oil seal lips, and to the driveshaft splines and shoulders. Check that all gaiter clips are securely fastened.

17 Offer up the driveshaft, and engage the inner joint splines with those of the differential sun gear or intermediate shaft, taking care not to damage the oil seal. Push the joint fully into position, then check that the circlip is correctly located and securely holds the joint in position. If necessary, use a soft-faced mallet or drift to drive the driveshaft inner joint fully into position.

18 Align the outer constant velocity joint splines with those of the hub, and slide the joint back into position in the hub.

19 Using a lever, push down on the lower suspension arm, then relocate the balljoint and release the arm. Make sure that the balljoint stub is fully entered in the swivel hub.

20 Insert a new lower arm balljoint clamp bolt with its head facing the front of the vehicle, fit a new retaining nut and tighten the nut to the specified torque.

21 Refit the track rod end to the steering arm on the swivel hub and tighten the new nut to the specified torque in the stages given in the Specifications.

22 Locate the anti-roll bar connecting link on the suspension strut, fit a new retaining nut and tighten the nut to the specified torque.

23 Lubricate the inner face and threads of the new driveshaft retaining nut with clean engine oil, and refit it to the end of the driveshaft. Use the method employed on removal to prevent the hub from rotating, and tighten the driveshaft retaining nut to the specified torque in the stages given in the Specifications. Check that the hub rotates freely.

24 Refit the roadwheel, lower the vehicle to the ground and tighten the roadwheel bolts to the specified torque.

25 Check and if necessary top-up the transmission oil/fluid level, using the information given in the relevant Part of Chapter 7.

3 Intermediate shaft – removal and refitting

Removal

1 Remove the right-hand driveshaft as described in Section 2.

2 Place a suitable container beneath the differential, to collect escaping transmission oil/fluid when the intermediate shaft is withdrawn.

3 Undo the three bolts securing the intermediate shaft bearing housing to the support bracket on the cylinder block **(see illustration)**. Pull the intermediate shaft out of the transmission, slide it through the support bracket and remove the shaft from under the car.

Refitting

4 Before refitting the intermediate shaft, examine the oil seal in the transmission housing and renew it if necessary as described in the relevant Part of Chapter 7.

5 Remove the circlip from the end of the intermediate shaft and discard it. Fit a new circlip, making sure it is correctly located in the groove.

6 Thoroughly clean the driveshaft splines, intermediate shaft splines, and the aperture in the transmission. Apply a thin film of grease to the oil seal lips, and to the driveshaft and intermediate shaft splines and shoulders.

7 Insert the intermediate shaft into the transmission, engaging the splines with the differential sun gear, taking care not to damage the oil seal.

8 Refit the three bolts securing the intermediate shaft bearing housing to the support bracket on the cylinder block. Tighten the bolts to the specified torque.

9 Refit the right-hand driveshaft as described in Section 2.

2.12 Using a stout bar, release the inner end of the driveshaft from the differential or intermediate shaft

4 Intermediate shaft bearing – renewal

Note: *A hydraulic press, together with tubes and mandrels of suitable diameters will be needed for this operation. A new intermediate shaft circlip and, where fitted, a new O-ring will also be required.*

1 Remove the intermediate shaft as described in Section 3.

2 Where fitted, remove the O-ring from the end of the intermediate shaft.

3 Using circlip pliers, or a small screwdriver, extract the circlip securing the intermediate shaft in the bearing **(see illustration)**.

4 Support the underside of the bearing housing on the press bed and press the intermediate shaft downwards out of the bearing.

5 With the intermediate shaft removed, press the bearing out of the housing using a suitable mandrel.

6 Locate the new bearing in the housing and press it fully into position using a suitable tube in contact with the bearing outer race.

7 With the bearing supported on its inner race, press the intermediate shaft back into the bearing until it is fully engaged.

8 Secure the intermediate shaft with a new circlip then, where applicable, fit a new O-ring to the end of the shaft.

9 On completion, refit the intermediate shaft as described in Section 3.

3.3 Intermediate shaft bearing housing retaining bolts (arrowed)

4.3 Extract the circlip (arrowed) securing the intermediate shaft in the bearing

5.2 Release the rubber gaiter retaining clips by cutting through them using a hacksaw

5.3 Cut the gaiter open using a suitable knife and remove it from the driveshaft

5.5 Outer CV joint snap-ring (arrowed)

5 Driveshaft joint gaiters – renewal

Outer CV joint

1 Remove the driveshaft from the car as described in Section 2, then secure the shaft in a vice equipped with soft jaws.

2 Release the rubber gaiter inner and outer retaining clips by cutting through them using a junior hacksaw **(see illustration)**. Spread the clips and remove them from the gaiter.

3 Slide the rubber gaiter down the shaft to expose the CV joint or, alternatively, cut the gaiter open using a suitable knife and remove it from the driveshaft **(see illustration)**.

4 Using old rags, clean away as much of the old grease as possible from the CV joint. It is advisable to wear disposable rubber gloves during this operation.

5 The outer CV joint will be retained on the driveshaft either by an external snap-ring, or by an internal circlip **(see illustration)**. If an external snap-ring is fitted, use circlip pliers to expand the snap-ring as the CV joint is removed.

6 Using a mallet, sharply strike the edge of the outer joint to drive it off the end of the shaft **(see illustrations)**.

7 Once the joint has been removed, extract the snap-ring from the joint, or remove the circlip from the groove in the driveshaft splines **(see illustration)**. A new snap-ring or circlip must be fitted on reassembly.

8 If still in place, withdraw the rubber gaiter from the driveshaft.

9 With the CV joint removed from the driveshaft, wipe away the remaining grease (do not use any solvent) to allow the joint components to be inspected.

10 Move the inner splined driving member from side-to-side, to expose each ball in turn at the top of its track. Examine the balls for cracks, flat spots, or signs of surface pitting.

11 Inspect the ball tracks on the inner and outer members. If the tracks have widened, the balls will no longer be a tight fit. At the same time, check the ball cage windows for wear or cracking between the windows.

12 If on inspection any of the constant velocity joint components are found to be worn or damaged, it will be necessary to renew the complete joint assembly. If the joint is in satisfactory condition, obtain a repair kit consisting of a new gaiter and retaining clips, a constant velocity joint snap-ring or circlip, and the correct type and quantity of grease **(see illustration)**.

13 Slide the new rubber gaiter and retaining clips onto the driveshaft **(see illustration)**.

14 Fit a new snap-ring to the constant velocity joint, or a new circlip to the groove in the driveshaft, as applicable **(see illustrations)**.

15 Pack the joint with the grease supplied in the repair kit **(see illustration)**. Work the grease well into the bearing tracks whilst twisting the joint, and fill the rubber gaiter with any excess.

16 Screw on the driveshaft retaining nut two or three turns to protect the threads, then engage the joint with the driveshaft splines. Tap the joint onto the driveshaft until the

5.6a Sharply strike the edge of the outer joint to drive it off the end of the shaft

5.6b If an external snap-ring is fitted, use circlip pliers to expand the snap-ring as the joint is removed

5.7 Removing the circlip from the groove in the driveshaft splines

5.12 Components required for driveshaft gaiter renewal

5.13 Slide the new rubber gaiter and retaining clips onto the driveshaft

5.14a Fit a new snap-ring to the constant velocity joint . . .

5.14b . . . or a new circlip to the groove in the driveshaft

5.15 Pack the joint with the grease supplied in the repair kit

5.16 Tap the joint onto the driveshaft until the snap-ring or circlip engages in its groove

5.18a Secure the large gaiter retaining clip in position by compressing the raised section of the clip

5.18b The small inner retaining clip is secured in the same way

snap-ring or circlip engages in its groove **(see illustration)**. Make sure that the joint is securely retained, by pulling on the joint, not the shaft.

17 Ease the gaiter over the joint, and ensure that the gaiter lips are correctly located in the grooves on both the driveshaft and constant velocity joint. Lift the outer sealing lip of the gaiter, to equalise air pressure within the gaiter.

18 Pull the large gaiter retaining clip as tight as possible, and locate the hooks on the clip in their slots. Remove any slack in the gaiter retaining clip by carefully compressing the raised section of the clip. In the absence of the special tool, a pair of side-cutters may be used. Secure the small retaining clip using the same procedure **(see illustrations)**.

19 Check that the constant velocity joint moves freely in all directions, then refit the driveshaft to the car as described in Section 2.

Inner CV joint

Note: On 1.9 litre models the inner tripod type CV joint cannot be detached from the driveshaft. If inner CV joint gaiter renewal is required, it will be necessary to remove the outer CV joint as described previously and slide the inner joint gaiter off the outer end of the driveshaft.

20 Remove the driveshaft from the car as described in Section 2, then secure the shaft in a vice equipped with soft jaws.

21 Remove the circlip from the groove in the CV joint splines then, where fitted, slide off the rubber dust cover **(see illustrations)**. Note that a new circlip must be fitted on reassembly.

22 Release the rubber gaiter inner and outer retaining clips by cutting through them using a junior hacksaw **(see illustration)**. Spread the clips and remove them from the gaiter.

23 Slide the rubber gaiter down the shaft to expose the CV joint.

5.21a Remove the circlip from the groove in the inner CV joint splines . . .

5.22 Cut off the rubber gaiter retaining clips, then slide the gaiter down the shaft

24 Using old rags, clean away as much of the old grease as possible from the CV joint **(see illustration)**. It is advisable to wear disposable rubber gloves during this operation.

25 Expand the CV joint retaining snap-ring using circlip pliers, then remove the joint by

5.21b . . . then, where fitted, slide off the rubber dust cover

5.24 Clean away as much of the old grease as possible from the CV joint

5.25a Expand the joint retaining snap-ring using circlip pliers . . .

5.25b . . . then remove the joint by tapping it off the driveshaft with a hammer and punch

tapping it off the driveshaft with a hammer and punch in contact with the joint inner member **(see illustrations)**.

26 Once the joint has been removed, extract the snap-ring noting that a new snap-ring must be fitted on reassembly.

27 Withdraw the rubber gaiter from the drive-shaft.

28 With the CV joint removed from the driveshaft, wipe away the remaining grease (do not use any solvent) and inspect the joint components as described previously in paragraphs 10 and 11.

29 If on inspection any of the constant velocity joint components are found to be worn or damaged, it will be necessary to renew the complete joint assembly. If the joint is in satisfactory condition, obtain a repair kit consisting of a new gaiter and retaining clips, a constant velocity joint

snap-ring and circlip, and the correct type and quantity of grease.

30 Slide the new rubber gaiter and retaining clips onto the driveshaft **(see illustration)**.

31 Fit a new snap-ring to the constant velocity joint, then engage the joint with the driveshaft splines. Tap the joint onto the driveshaft until the snap-ring engages in its groove **(see illustration)**. Make sure that the joint is securely retained, by pulling on the joint, not the shaft.

32 Pack the joint with the grease supplied in the repair kit **(see illustration)**. Work the grease well into the bearing tracks whilst twisting the joint, and fill the rubber gaiter with any excess.

33 Ease the gaiter over the joint, and ensure that the gaiter lips are correctly located in the grooves on both the driveshaft and constant velocity joint. Lift the outer sealing lip of the gaiter, to equalise air pressure within the gaiter.

34 Pull the large gaiter retaining clip as tight as possible, and locate the hooks on the clip in their slots. Remove any slack in the gaiter retaining clip by carefully compressing the raised section of the clip. In the absence of the special tool, a pair of side-cutters may be used. Secure the small retaining clip using the same procedure **(see illustrations)**.

35 Where applicable, slide the rubber dust cover onto the CV joint, then fit a new circlip to the groove in the joint splines.

36 Check that the constant velocity joint moves freely in all directions, then refit the driveshaft to the car as described in Section 2.

6 Driveshaft overhaul – general information

1 If any of the checks described in Chapter 1 reveal possible wear in any driveshaft joint, carry out the following procedures to identify the source of the problem.

2 Firmly apply the handbrake, then jack up the front of the vehicle and support it securely on axle stands (see *Jacking and vehicle support*).

3 Referring to the information contained in Section 2, make up a tool to hold the wheel hub, and bolt the tool to the hub. Use a torque wrench to check that the driveshaft retaining nut is securely fastened, then repeat this check on the remaining driveshaft nut.

4 Road test the vehicle, and listen for a metallic clicking from the front as the vehicle is driven slowly in a circle on full-lock. If a clicking noise is heard, this indicates wear in the outer constant velocity joint.

5 If vibration, consistent with roadspeed, is felt through the car when accelerating, there is a possibility of wear in the inner constant velocity joints.

6 To check the joints for wear, remove the driveshafts, then dismantle them as described in Section 3; if any wear or free play is found, the affected joint must be renewed. Note that if renewal of the inner joint on 1.9 litre models is required, it will be necessary to obtain a new inner joint complete with driveshaft, then transfer the existing outer joint to the new driveshaft.

5.30 Slide the new rubber gaiter and retaining clips onto the driveshaft

5.31 Tap the joint onto the driveshaft until the snap-ring engages in its groove

5.32 Pack the joint with the grease supplied in the repair kit

5.34a Secure the large gaiter retaining clip in position by compressing the raised section of the clip

5.34b The small inner retaining clip is secured in the same way

Chapter 9
Braking system

Contents

Degrees of difficulty

Easy, suitable for novice with little experience	**Fairly easy,** suitable for beginner with some experience	**Fairly difficult,** suitable for competent DIY mechanic	**Difficult,** suitable for experienced DIY mechanic	**Very difficult,** suitable for expert DIY or professional

Specifications

Front brakes

Type	Ventilated disc, with single-piston sliding caliper
Disc diameter	280.0 mm
Disc thickness:	
New	25.0 mm
Minimum.......................................	22.0 mm
Maximum disc run-out.......................................	0.11 mm
Brake pad friction material minimum thickness..................	2.0 mm
Brake caliper piston diameter	57.0 mm

Rear Brakes

Type	Solid disc, with single-piston sliding caliper
Disc diameter	264.0 mm
Disc thickness:	
New	10.0 mm
Minimum.......................................	8.0 mm
Maximum disc run-out.......................................	0.13 mm
Brake pad friction material minimum thickness..................	2.0 mm
Brake caliper piston diameter	38.0 mm

ABS system type

Standard ABS system	ATE Mk 70
ABS with traction control and electronic stability programme........	ATE Mk 60 ESP

Torque wrench settings

	Nm	lbf ft
ABS hydraulic modulator mounting bracket bolts	20	15
ABS hydraulic modulator to mounting bracket	8	6
Air conditioning refrigerant pipe block connection	20	15
Brake caliper bleed screws	6	4
Brake caliper guide bolts:		
Front caliper	28	21
Rear caliper	25	18
Brake caliper mounting bracket bolts	100	74
Brake fluid pipe unions.	14	10
Brake hydraulic hose banjo union bolts.	40	30
Brake pedal mounting bracket bolts/nuts	20	15
Handbrake lever retaining nuts	10	7
High-pressure fuel pump mounting bracket bolts (1.9 litre engines) . . .	25	18
Master cylinder retaining nuts:		
1.3 and 1.7 litre engines	15	11
1.9 litre engines	21	15
Roadwheel bolts.	110	81
Vacuum pump mounting bolts:		
1.3 litre engines:		
Stage 1	6	4
Stage 2	20	15
1.9 litre engines:*		
Stage 1	6	4
Stage 2	Angle-tighten a further 50°	
Vacuum servo unit mounting nuts	20	15

* Use new fasteners

1 General information

The braking system is of servo-assisted, dual-circuit hydraulic type split diagonally. The arrangement of the hydraulic system is such that each circuit operates one front and one rear brake from a tandem master cylinder. Under normal circumstances, both circuits operate in unison. However, in the event of hydraulic failure in one circuit, full braking force will still be available at two wheels.

All models are fitted with front and rear disc brakes. The disc brakes are actuated by single-piston sliding type calipers, which ensure that equal pressure is applied to each disc pad.

An Anti-lock Braking System (ABS) is fitted as standard equipment to all vehicles covered in this manual. On higher specification models, the ABS may also incorporate traction control or an electronic stability programme. Refer to Section 17 for further information on ABS operation.

The cable-operated handbrake provides an independent mechanical means of rear brake application.

On diesel engines, since there is no throttling as such of the inlet manifold, the manifold is not a suitable source of vacuum to operate the vacuum servo unit. The servo unit is therefore connected to a separate, engine mounted vacuum pump. On 1.3 and 1.9 litre engines, the pump is bolted to the left-hand end of the cylinder head and driven by the camshaft. On 1.7 litre engines, the pump is attached to the rear of the alternator and driven by the auxiliary drivebelt, via the alternator.

⚠ **Warning: When servicing any part of the system, work carefully and methodically; also observe scrupulous cleanliness when overhauling any part of the hydraulic system. Always renew components (in axle sets, where applicable) if in doubt about their condition, and use only genuine Vauxhall/Opel parts, or at least those of known good quality. Note the warnings given in 'Safety first!' and at relevant points in this Chapter concerning the dangers of asbestos dust and hydraulic fluid.**

2 Hydraulic system – bleeding

⚠ **Warning: Hydraulic fluid is poisonous; wash off immediately and thoroughly in the case of skin contact, and seek immediate medical advice if any fluid is swallowed or gets into the eyes. Certain types of hydraulic fluid are inflammable, and may ignite when allowed into contact with hot components; when servicing any hydraulic system, it is safest to assume that the fluid is inflammable, and to take precautions against the risk of fire as though it is petrol that is being handled. Hydraulic fluid is also an effective paint stripper, and will attack plastics; if any is spilt, it should be washed off immediately, using copious quantities of fresh water. Finally, it is hygroscopic (it absorbs moisture from the air) – old fluid may be contaminated and unfit for further use. When topping-up or renewing the fluid, always use the recommended type, and ensure that it comes from a freshly-opened sealed container.**

General

1 The correct operation of any hydraulic system is only possible after removing all air from the components and circuit; this is achieved by bleeding the system.

2 During the bleeding procedure, add only clean, unused hydraulic fluid of the recommended type; never re-use fluid that has already been bled from the system. Ensure that sufficient fluid is available before starting work.

3 If there is any possibility of incorrect fluid being already in the system, the brake components and circuit must be flushed completely with uncontaminated, correct fluid, and new seals should be fitted to the various components.

4 If hydraulic fluid has been lost from the system, or air has entered because of a leak, ensure that the fault is cured before proceeding further.

5 Park the vehicle over an inspection pit or on car ramps. Alternatively, apply the handbrake then jack up the front and rear of the vehicle and support it on axle stands (see *Jacking and vehicle support*). For improved access with the vehicle jacked up, remove the roadwheels.

6 Check that all pipes and hoses are secure, unions tight and bleed screws closed. Clean any dirt from around the bleed screws.

7 Unscrew the master cylinder reservoir cap, and top the master cylinder reservoir up to the MAX level line; refit the cap loosely, and remember to maintain the fluid level at least above the MIN level line throughout the

procedure, otherwise there is a risk of further air entering the system.

8 There is a number of one-man, do-it-yourself brake bleeding kits currently available from motor accessory shops. It is recommended that one of these kits is used whenever possible, as they greatly simplify the bleeding operation, and also reduce the risk of expelled air and fluid being drawn back into the system. If such a kit is not available, the basic (two-man) method must be used, which is described in detail below.

Caution: Vauxhall recommend using a pressure bleeding kit for this operation (see paragraphs 24 to 27).

9 If a kit is to be used, prepare the vehicle as described previously, and follow the kit manufacturer's instructions, as the procedure may vary slightly according to the type being used; generally, they are as outlined below in the relevant sub-section.

10 Whichever method is used, the same sequence should be followed (paragraphs 11 and 12) to ensure the removal of all air from the system.

Bleeding sequence

11 If the system has been only partially disconnected, and suitable precautions were taken to minimise fluid loss, it should only be necessary to bleed that part of the system (ie, the primary or secondary circuit). If the master cylinder or main brake lines have been disconnected, then the complete system must be bled.

12 If the complete system is to be bled, then it should be done in the following sequence:

Right-hand drive models

a) Left-hand rear brake.
b) Right-hand rear brake.
c) Left-hand front brake.
d) Right-hand front brake.

Left-hand drive models

a) Right-hand rear brake.
b) Left-hand rear brake.
c) Right-hand front brake.
d) Left-hand front brake.

Bleeding

Basic (two-man) method

13 Collect together a clean glass jar, a suitable length of plastic or rubber tubing which is a tight fit over the bleed screw, and a ring spanner to fit the screw. The help of an assistant will also be required.

14 Remove the dust cap from the first bleed screw in the sequence **(see illustrations)**. Fit the spanner and tube to the screw, place the other end of the tube in the jar, and pour in sufficient fluid to cover the end of the tube.

15 Ensure that the master cylinder reservoir fluid level is maintained at least above the MIN level line throughout the procedure.

16 Have the assistant fully depress the brake pedal several times to build-up pressure, then maintain it on the final downstroke.

2.14a Remove the dust caps from the front . . .

2.14b . . . and rear bleed screws

17 While pedal pressure is maintained, unscrew the bleed screw (approximately one turn) and allow the compressed fluid and air to flow into the jar. The assistant should maintain pedal pressure, following it down to the floor if necessary, and should not release it until instructed to do so. When the flow stops, tighten the bleed screw again, have the assistant release the pedal slowly, and recheck the reservoir fluid level.

18 Repeat the steps given in paragraphs 16 and 17 until the fluid emerging from the bleed screw is free from air bubbles. If the master cylinder has been drained and refilled, and air is being bled from the first screw in the sequence, allow approximately five seconds between cycles for the master cylinder passages to refill.

19 When no more air bubbles appear, securely tighten the bleed screw, remove the tube and spanner, and refit the dust cap. Do not overtighten the bleed screw.

20 Repeat the procedure on the remaining screws in the sequence, until all air is removed from the system and the brake pedal feels firm again.

Using a one-way valve kit

21 As the name implies, these kits consist of a length of tubing with a one-way valve fitted, to prevent expelled air and fluid being drawn back into the system; some kits include a translucent container, which can be positioned so that the air bubbles can be more easily seen flowing from the end of the tube.

22 The kit is connected to the bleed screw, which is then opened. The user returns to the driver's seat, depresses the brake pedal with a smooth, steady stroke, and slowly releases it; this is repeated until the expelled fluid is clear of air bubbles.

23 Note that these kits simplify work so much that it is easy to forget the master cylinder reservoir fluid level; ensure that this is maintained at least above the MIN level line at all times.

Using a pressure-bleeding kit

24 These kits are usually operated by a reservoir of pressurised air contained in the spare tyre. However, note that it will probably be necessary to reduce the pressure to a lower level than normal; refer to the instructions supplied with the kit.

25 By connecting a pressurised, fluid-filled

container to the master cylinder reservoir, bleeding can be carried out simply by opening each screw in turn (in the specified sequence), and allowing the fluid to flow out until no more air bubbles can be seen in the expelled fluid.

26 This method has the advantage that the large reservoir of fluid provides an additional safeguard against air being drawn into the system during bleeding.

27 Pressure-bleeding is particularly effective when bleeding 'difficult' systems, or when bleeding the complete system at the time of routine fluid renewal.

All methods

28 When bleeding is complete, and firm pedal feel is restored, wash off any spilt fluid, securely tighten the bleed screws, and refit the dust caps.

29 Check the hydraulic fluid level in the master cylinder reservoir, and top-up if necessary (see *Weekly checks*).

30 Discard any hydraulic fluid that has been bled from the system; it will not be fit for re-use.

31 Check the feel of the brake pedal. If it feels at all spongy, air must still be present in the system, and further bleeding is required. Failure to bleed satisfactorily after a reasonable repetition of the bleeding procedure may be due to worn master cylinder seals.

3 Hydraulic pipes and hoses – renewal

Note: *Before starting work, refer to the note at the beginning of Section 2 concerning the dangers of hydraulic fluid.*

1 If any pipe or hose is to be renewed, minimise fluid loss by first removing the master cylinder reservoir cap and screwing it down onto a piece of polythene. Alternatively, flexible hoses can be sealed, if required, using a proprietary brake hose clamp. Metal brake pipe unions can be plugged (if care is taken not to allow dirt into the system) or capped immediately they are disconnected. Place a wad of rag under any union that is to be disconnected, to catch any spilt fluid.

2 If a flexible hose is to be disconnected, unscrew the brake pipe union nut before removing the spring clip which secures the

3.2a Pull out the spring clip . . .

3.2b . . . and disconnect the hydraulic hose from the strut bracket

hose to its mounting bracket. Where applicable, unscrew the banjo union bolt securing the hose to the caliper and recover the copper washers. When removing the front flexible hose, pull out the spring clip and disconnect it from the strut **(see illustrations)**.

3 To unscrew union nuts, it is preferable to obtain a brake pipe spanner of the correct size; these are available from most motor accessory shops. Failing this, a close-fitting open-ended spanner will be required, though if the nuts are tight or corroded, their flats may be rounded-off if the spanner slips. In such a case, a self-locking wrench is often the only way to unscrew a stubborn union, but it follows that the pipe and the damaged nuts must be renewed on reassembly. Always clean a union and surrounding area before disconnecting it. If disconnecting a component with more than one union, make a careful note of the connections before disturbing any of them.

4 If a brake pipe is to be renewed, it can be obtained, cut to length and with the union nuts and end flares in place, from Vauxhall/Opel dealers. All that is then necessary is to bend it to shape, following the line of the original, before fitting it to the car. Alternatively, most motor accessory shops can make up brake pipes from kits, but this requires very careful measurement of the original, to ensure that the replacement is of the correct length. The safest answer is usually to take the original to the shop as a pattern.

5 On refitting, do not overtighten the union nuts.

6 When refitting hoses to the calipers, always use new copper washers and tighten the banjo union bolts to the specified torque. Make sure that the hoses are positioned so that they will not touch surrounding bodywork or the roadwheels.

7 Ensure that the pipes and hoses are correctly routed, with no kinks, and that they

are secured in the clips or brackets provided. After fitting, remove the polythene from the reservoir, and bleed the hydraulic system as described in Section 2. Wash off any spilt fluid, and check carefully for fluid leaks.

4 Front brake pads – renewal

⚠️ *Warning: Renew BOTH sets of front brake pads at the same time – NEVER renew the pads on only one wheel, as uneven braking may result. Note that the dust created by wear of the pads may contain asbestos, which is a health hazard. Never blow it out with compressed air, and do not inhale any of it. An approved filtering mask should be worn when working on the brakes. DO NOT use petroleum-based solvents to clean brake parts – use brake cleaner or methylated spirit only.*

1 Apply the handbrake, then jack up the front of the vehicle and support it on axle stands (see *Jacking and vehicle support*). Remove the front roadwheels.

2 Follow the accompanying photos **(illustrations 4.2a to 4.2y)** for the actual pad renewal procedure, bearing in mind the additional points listed below. Be sure to stay in order and read the caption under each illustration. Note that if the old pads are to be refitted, ensure that they are identified so that they can be returned to their original positions.

4.2a Push in the caliper piston by levering the caliper body towards the outside of the vehicle

4.2b Unclip the wiring guide from the brake hose. Where fitted, detach the pad wear warning indicator wire from the inner pad

4.2c Release the legs of the retaining spring from the caliper body . . .

4.2d . . . then remove the spring from the caliper mounting bracket

4.2e Remove the dust caps from the upper and lower guide bolts

4.2f Unscrew the upper guide bolt . . .

4.2g . . . and remove it from the caliper

4.2h Similarly unscrew the lower guide bolt and remove it from the caliper

4.2i Lift the caliper and brake pads off the mounting bracket

4.2j Remove the outer pad from the caliper body . . .

4.2k . . . and the inner pad from the caliper piston, noting that it is retained by a spring clip attached to the pad backing plate

4.2l Measure the thickness of the pad friction material. If any are worn down to the specified minimum, or fouled with oil or grease, all four pads must be renewed

4.2m Brush the dust and dirt from the caliper piston and mounting bracket

4.2n Apply a little high melting-point copper brake grease to the pad backing plate contact areas on the mounting bracket

4.2o If new pads are to be fitted, before refitting the caliper, push back the caliper piston whilst opening the bleed screw. This is to prevent any dirt/debris being forced back up the hydraulic circuit in the ABS modulator

4.2p The brake pads are 'handed' for each side. Make sure the arrow on the backing plate points in the direction of forward rotation of the brake disc

4.2q Fit the inner pad to the caliper, ensuring that its clip is correctly located in the caliper piston

4.2r Fit the outer pad to the caliper mounting bracket, ensuring that its friction material is facing the brake disc

4.2s Slide the caliper into position in the mounting bracket

4.2t Fit the guide bolts . . .

4.2u . . . tighten the guide bolts to the specified torque . . .

4.2v . . . then refit the dust caps

4.2w Locate the retaining spring legs into the holes in the caliper . . .

4.2x . . . then hold the legs in place and locate the spring behind the lugs on the mounting bracket

4.2y Clip the wiring guide back onto the brake hose. Where fitted, attach the pad wear warning indicator wire to the inner pad

3 After removing the caliper from the mounting bracket, support it on top of the brake disc. Do not allow the caliper to hang unsupported on the flexible brake hose.

4 If the original brake pads are still serviceable, carefully clean them using a clean, fine wire brush or similar, paying particular attention to the sides and back of the metal backing plate. Clean out the grooves in the friction material, and pick out any large embedded particles of dirt or debris. Carefully clean the pad locations in the caliper body/mounting bracket.

5 Prior to fitting the pads, check that the guide bolts are a snug fit in the caliper mounting bracket. Inspect the dust seal around the piston for damage, and the piston for evidence of fluid leaks, corrosion or damage. If attention to any of these components is necessary, refer to Section 7.

6 If new brake pads are to be fitted, the caliper piston must be pushed back into the cylinder to allow for the extra pad thickness. Either use a G-clamp or similar tool, or use suitable pieces of wood as levers. Clamp off the flexible brake hose leading to the caliper then connect a brake bleeding kit to the caliper bleed screw. Open the bleed screw as the piston is retracted, the surplus brake fluid will then be collected in the bleed kit vessel (see illustration 4.2o). Close the bleed screw just before the caliper piston is pushed fully into the caliper. This should ensure no air enters the hydraulic system. Note: *The ABS unit contains hydraulic components that are very sensitive to impurities in the brake fluid. Even the smallest particles can cause the system to fail through blockage. The pad retraction method described here prevents any debris in the brake fluid expelled from the caliper from being passed back to the ABS hydraulic unit, as well as preventing any chance of damage to the master cylinder seals.*

7 With the brake pads installed, depress the brake pedal repeatedly, until normal (non-assisted) pedal pressure is restored, and the pads are pressed into firm contact with the brake disc.

8 Repeat the above procedure on the remaining front brake caliper.

9 Refit the roadwheels, then lower the vehicle to the ground and tighten the roadwheel bolts to the specified torque setting.

10 Check the hydraulic fluid level as described in *Weekly checks*.

Caution: New pads will not give full braking

efficiency until they have bedded-in. Be prepared for this, and avoid hard braking as far as possible for the first hundred miles or so after pad renewal.

5 Rear brake pads – renewal

⚠ *Warning: Renew BOTH sets of rear brake pads at the same time – NEVER renew the pads on only one wheel, as uneven braking may result. Note that the dust created by wear of the pads may contain asbestos, which is a health hazard. Never blow it out with compressed air, and do not inhale any of it. An approved filtering mask should be worn when working on the brakes. DO NOT use petroleum-based solvents to clean brake parts – use brake cleaner or methylated spirit only.*

1 Chock the front wheels then jack up the rear of the car and securely support it on axle stands (see *Jacking and vehicle support*). Remove the rear roadwheels.

2 Slacken the handbrake cable adjuster at the handbrake lever as described in Section 14, paragraphs 11 to 13.

3 Follow the accompanying photos (illustrations 5.3a to 5.3u) for the actual pad renewal procedure, bearing in mind the additional points listed below. Be sure to stay in order and read the caption under each illustration. Note that if the old pads are to be refitted, ensure that they are identified so that they can be returned to their original positions.

5.3a Using a screwdriver, push the handbrake operating lever downwards, and detach the cable end fitting from the lever

5.3b Prise out the handbrake outer cable retaining clip . . .

5.3c . . . and withdraw the handbrake cable from the caliper bracket

5.3d Unscrew the upper guide pin bolt while counterholding the guide pin with a second spanner

5.3e Unscrew the lower guide pin bolt in the same way

5.3f Lift the caliper off the mounting bracket and suspend it from a suitable place under the wheel arch using a cable tie or similar

5.3g Remove the inner pad . . .

5.3h . . . and outer pad from the caliper mounting bracket

5.3i Remove the lower guide plate . . .

5.3j . . . and upper guide plate from the caliper mounting bracket

5.3k Measure the thickness of the pad friction material. If any are worn down to the specified minimum, or fouled with oil or grease, all four pads must be renewed

5.3l Using a caliper retracting tool to retract the piston as far as the stop

5.3m Once the piston is fully retracted, unscrew it slightly until the next piston cut-out (arrowed) is visible through the caliper

5.3n Brush the dust and dirt from the caliper, piston and mounting bracket, then fit the lower guide plate . . .

5.3o . . . and upper guide plate to the caliper mounting bracket

5.3p Apply a little high melting-point copper brake grease to the pad backing plate contact areas on the guide plates

5.3q If present remove the protective film from the pad backing plate, then fit the inner pad to the caliper mounting bracket . . .

5.3r . . . followed by the outer pad

5.3s Slide the caliper into position in the mounting bracket

5.3t Refit the upper and lower guide pin bolts and tighten them to the specified torque

5.3u Refit the handbrake cable to the mounting bracket and secure with the retaining clip, then reconnect the cable end to the caliper lever

4 If the original brake pads are still serviceable, carefully clean them using a clean, fine wire brush or similar, paying particular attention to the sides and back of the metal backing plate. Clean out the grooves in the friction material, and pick out any large embedded particles of dirt or debris. Carefully clean the pad locations in the caliper body/mounting bracket.

5 Prior to fitting the pads, check that the guide bolts are a snug fit in the caliper mounting bracket. Brush the dust and dirt from the caliper and piston, but do not inhale it, as it is injurious to health. Inspect the dust seal around the piston for damage, and the piston for evidence of fluid leaks, corrosion or damage. If attention to any of these components is necessary, refer to Section 8.

6 If new brake pads are to be fitted, it will be necessary to retract the piston fully into the caliper bore by rotating it in a clockwise direction. This can be achieved by using sturdy circlip pliers, noting that as well as being turned, the piston has to be pressed in very firmly. Special tools are readily available to achieve this with less effort. While the caliper is being retracted, clamp off the flexible brake hose leading to the caliper then connect a brake bleeding kit to the caliper bleed screw. Open the bleed screw as the piston is retracted, the surplus brake fluid will then be collected in the bleed kit vessel (see illustration 5.3l). Close the bleed screw just before the caliper piston is pushed fully into the caliper. This should ensure no air enters the hydraulic system. Note: *The ABS unit contains hydraulic components that are very sensitive to impurities in the brake fluid. Even the smallest particles can cause the system to fail through blockage. The pad retraction method described here prevents any debris in the brake fluid expelled from the caliper from being passed back to the ABS hydraulic unit, as well as preventing any chance of damage to the master cylinder seals.*

7 With the brake pads installed, depress the brake pedal repeatedly, until normal (non-assisted) pedal pressure is restored, and the pads are pressed into firm contact with the brake disc.

8 Repeat the above procedure on the remaining rear brake caliper.

6.9a Unclip the ABS wheel speed sensor wiring guide from the brake hydraulic hose . . .

6.9b . . . pull out the spring clip . . .

6.9c . . . and disconnect the hydraulic hose from the strut bracket

9 Adjust the handbrake cable as described in Chapter 1 after fitting both sets of brake pads.

10 Refit the roadwheels, then lower the vehicle to the ground and tighten the roadwheel bolts to the specified torque setting.

11 Check the hydraulic fluid level as described in *Weekly checks.*

Caution: New pads will not give full braking efficiency until they have bedded-in. Be prepared for this, and avoid hard braking as far as possible for the first hundred miles or so after pad renewal.

6 Front/rear brake disc – inspection, removal and refitting

Note: *Before starting work, refer to the warning at the beginning of Section 4 or 5 concerning the dangers of asbestos dust. If either disc requires renewal, both should be renewed at the same time together with new pads, to ensure even and consistent braking.*

Inspection

1 Remove the wheel trim, then loosen the roadwheel bolts. If checking a front disc, apply the handbrake, and if checking a rear disc, chock the front wheels and release the handbrake, then jack up the relevant end of the vehicle and support on axle stands (see *Jacking and vehicle support*). Remove the roadwheel.

2 Check that the brake disc securing screw is tight, then fit a spacer approximately 10.0 mm thick to one of the roadwheel bolts, and refit and tighten the bolt in the hole opposite the disc securing screw.

3 Rotate the brake disc, and examine it for deep scoring or grooving. Light scoring is normal, but if excessive, the disc should be removed and either renewed or machined (within the specified limits) by an engineering works. The minimum thickness is given in the Specifications at the start of this Chapter.

4 Using a dial gauge, or a flat metal block and feeler blades, check that the disc run-out does not exceed the figure given in the Specifications. Measure the run-out 10.0 mm in from the outer edge of the disc.

5 If the disc run-out is excessive, remove the disc as described later, and check that the disc-to-hub surfaces are perfectly clean. Refit the disc and check the run-out again.

6 If the run-out is still excessive, the disc should be renewed.

7 To remove a disc, proceed as follows.

Front disc

Removal

8 Remove the roadwheel bolt and spacer used when checking the disc.

9 Unclip the ABS wheel speed sensor wiring guide from the brake hydraulic hose, then extract the retaining clip and release the hydraulic hose from the suspension strut **(see illustrations).**

10 Unbolt and remove the front brake caliper complete with disc pads and mounting

6.10a Unbolt and remove the front brake caliper complete with disc pads and mounting bracket . . .

6.11a Remove the securing screw . . .

bracket and suspend it from the coil spring using a cable tie **(see illustrations).**

11 Remove the securing screw and withdraw the disc from the hub **(see illustrations).**

Refitting

12 Refit the disc, making sure that the mating faces of the disc and hub are perfectly clean, and apply a little locking fluid to the threads of the securing screw.

13 Refit the caliper mounting bracket complete with caliper and pads and tighten the bolts to the specified torque.

Rear disc

Removal

14 Where applicable, remove the roadwheel bolt and spacer used when checking the disc.

15 Remove the rear brake pads as described in Section 5.

6.10b . . . and suspend it from the coil spring using a cable tie

6.11b . . . and withdraw the disc from the hub

6.17a Remove the securing screw (arrowed)

6.17b . . . and withdraw the disc from the hub

16 Undo the two bolts securing the caliper mounting bracket to the hub carrier and remove the mounting bracket.

17 Remove the securing screw and withdraw the disc from the hub (see illustrations).

Refitting

18 Refit the disc, making sure that the mating faces of the disc and hub are perfectly clean, and apply a little locking fluid to the threads of the securing screw.

19 Refit the caliper mounting bracket and tighten the bolts to the specified torque.

20 Refit the brake pads as described in Section 5.

7 Front brake caliper – removal, overhaul and refitting

Note: *New brake hose copper washers will be required when refitting. Before starting work, refer to the note at the beginning of Section 2 concerning the dangers of hydraulic fluid, and to the warning at the beginning of Section 4 concerning the dangers of asbestos dust.*

Removal

1 Apply the handbrake, then jack up the front of the vehicle and support it on axle stands (see *Jacking and vehicle support*). Remove the roadwheel.

2 Minimise fluid loss by first removing the master cylinder reservoir cap and screwing it down onto a piece of polythene. Alternatively, use a brake hose clamp to clamp the flexible hose leading to the brake caliper.

3 Clean the area around the caliper brake hose union. Unscrew and remove the union bolt, and recover the copper sealing washer from each side of the hose union. Discard the washers; new ones must be used on refitting. Plug the hose end and caliper hole, to minimise fluid loss and prevent the ingress of dust and dirt into the hydraulic system.

4 Remove the brake pads as described in Section 4, then remove the caliper from the vehicle.

Overhaul

5 With the caliper on the bench, wipe it clean with a cloth rag.

6 Withdraw the partially-ejected piston

from the caliper body, and remove the dust seal. The piston can be withdrawn by hand, or if necessary pushed out by applying compressed air to the brake hose union hole. Only low pressure should be required, such as is generated by a foot pump.

7 Using a small screwdriver, carefully remove the piston seal from the groove in the caliper, taking care not to mark the bore (see illustration).

8 Carefully press the guide bushes out of the caliper body.

9 Thoroughly clean all components, using only methylated spirit or clean hydraulic fluid. Never use mineral-based solvents such as petrol or paraffin, which will attack the rubber components of the hydraulic system. Dry the components using compressed air or a clean, lint-free cloth. If available, use compressed air to blow clear the fluid passages.

> ⚠ **Warning: Wear eye protection when using compressed air.**

10 Check all components, and renew any that are worn or damaged. If the piston and/or cylinder bore are scratched excessively, renew the complete caliper body. Similarly check the condition of the guide bushes and bolts; both bushes and bolts should be undamaged and (when cleaned) a reasonably tight sliding fit. If there is any doubt about the condition of any component, renew it.

11 If the caliper is fit for further use, obtain the necessary components from your Vauxhall/

7.7 Removing the piston seal from the caliper body

Opel dealer. Renew the caliper seals and dust covers as a matter of course; these should never be re-used.

12 On reassembly, ensure that all components are absolutely clean and dry.

13 Dip the piston and the new piston seal in clean hydraulic fluid, and smear clean fluid on the cylinder bore surface.

14 Locate the new seal in the cylinder bore groove, using only the fingers to manipulate it into position.

15 Fit the new dust seal to the piston, then insert the piston into the cylinder bore using a twisting motion to ensure it enters the seal correctly. Locate the dust seal in the body groove, and push the piston fully into the caliper bore.

16 Insert the guide bushes into position in the caliper body.

Refitting

17 Refit the brake pads as described in Section 4, together with the caliper which at this stage will not have the hose attached.

18 Position a new copper sealing washer on each side of the hose union, and connect the brake hose to the caliper. Ensure that the hose is correctly positioned against the caliper body lug, then install the union bolt and tighten it to the specified torque setting.

19 Remove the brake hose clamp or polythene, and bleed the hydraulic system as described in Section 2. Note that, providing the precautions described were taken to minimise brake fluid loss, it should only be necessary to bleed the relevant front brake circuit.

20 Refit the roadwheel, then lower the vehicle to the ground and tighten the roadwheel bolts to the specified torque.

8 Rear brake caliper – removal, overhaul and refitting

Note 1: *Before starting work, refer to the note at the beginning of Section 2 concerning the dangers of hydraulic fluid, and to the warning at the beginning of Section 5 concerning the dangers of asbestos dust.*

Note 2: *Due to the integral handbrake operating mechanism incorporated in the caliper piston, it is not possible to fully dismantle the caliper. Only the guide bushes and dust seal can be individually renewed. Check the availability of parts before proceeding.*

Removal

1 Chock the front wheels, then jack up the rear of the vehicle and support on axle stands (see *Jacking and vehicle support*). Remove the roadwheel.

2 Minimise fluid loss by first removing the master cylinder reservoir cap and screwing it down onto a piece of polythene. Alternatively, use a brake hose clamp to clamp the flexible hose leading to the brake caliper.

3 Clean the area around the caliper brake hose union. Unscrew and remove the union bolt, and recover the copper sealing washer from each side of the hose union **(see illustration)**. Discard the washers; new ones must be used on refitting. Plug the hose end and caliper hole, to minimise fluid loss and prevent the ingress of dust and dirt into the hydraulic system.

4 Remove the brake pads as described in Section 5, then remove the caliper from the vehicle.

Overhaul

5 With the caliper on the bench, wipe it clean with a cloth rag.

6 Using a small screwdriver, carefully prise out the dust seal from the caliper, taking care not to damage the piston.

7 Carefully press the guide bushes out of the caliper body.

8 Further dismantling of the caliper is not possible as individual parts are not available separately.

9 Thoroughly clean all components, using only methylated spirit or clean hydraulic fluid. Dry the components using a clean, lint-free cloth.

10 Check the condition of the exposed portion of the caliper piston. If the piston and/or cylinder bore are scratched excessively or corroded, renew the complete caliper body. Similarly check the condition of the guide bushes and bolts; both bushes and bolts should be undamaged and (when cleaned) a reasonably tight sliding fit. If there is any doubt about the condition of any component, renew it.

11 If the caliper is fit for further use, obtain the necessary components from your Vauxhall/Opel dealer. Renew the caliper dust cover as a matter of course; it should never be re-used.

12 Fit the new dust seal to the piston, then locate the dust seal in the caliper body groove.

13 Insert the guide bushes into position in the caliper body.

Refitting

14 Refit the brake pads as described in Section 5, together with the caliper which at this stage will not have the hose attached.

15 Position a new copper sealing washer on each side of the hose union, and connect the brake hose to the caliper. Ensure that the hose is correctly positioned against the caliper body lug, then install the union bolt and tighten it to the specified torque setting.

16 Remove the brake hose clamp or polythene, and bleed the hydraulic system as described in Section 2. Note that, providing the precautions described were taken to minimise brake fluid loss, it should only be necessary to bleed the relevant front brake circuit.

17 Refit the roadwheel, then lower the vehicle to the ground and tighten the roadwheel bolts to the specified torque.

8.3 Rear caliper brake hose union bolt (arrowed)

9 Master cylinder – removal, overhaul and refitting

Note: *Before starting work, refer to the warning at the beginning of Section 2 concerning the dangers of hydraulic fluid.*

Removal

1 Remove the master cylinder reservoir cap, and syphon the hydraulic fluid from the reservoir. **Note:** *Do not syphon the fluid by mouth, as it is poisonous; use a syringe or an old hydrometer.* Alternatively, open any convenient bleed screw in the system, and gently pump the brake pedal to expel the fluid through a plastic tube connected to the screw (see Section 2).

2 Disconnect the wiring connector from the brake fluid level sensor at the base of the reservoir.

3 On models with manual transmission, release the clip and disconnect the clutch hydraulic pipe from the fluid reservoir **(see illustration)**. Tape over or plug the outlet.

4 Place cloth rags beneath the fluid reservoir then undo the reservoir retaining bolt and carefully prise the reservoir from the top of the master cylinder and remove it from the engine compartment. If necessary, prise the reservoir seals from the top of the cylinder.

5 Place cloth rags beneath the master cylinder to collect escaping brake fluid. Identify the brake lines for position, then unscrew the union nuts and move the lines to one side. Tape over or plug the line outlets.

6 Unscrew the mounting nuts and withdraw

9.3 Disconnect the clutch hydraulic pipe (arrowed) from the fluid reservoir

the master cylinder from the vacuum servo unit **(see illustration)**. Take care not to spill fluid on the vehicle paintwork.

Overhaul

7 At the time of writing, master cylinder overhaul is not possible as no spares are available.

8 The only parts available individually are the fluid reservoir and its mounting seals and the filler cap.

9 If the master cylinder is worn excessively, it must be renewed.

10 Remove the reservoir seals from the master cylinder body and obtain new seals for reassembly.

11 Lubricate the new seals with clean brake hydraulic fluid and push the new seals into position.

Refitting

12 Fit the master cylinder to the servo unit, ensuring that the servo unit pushrod enters the master cylinder piston centrally. Fit the retaining nuts and tighten them to the specified torque setting.

13 Refit the brake lines and tighten the union nuts securely.

14 On manual transmission models, reconnect the clutch hydraulic pipe.

15 Reconnect the wiring connector to the brake fluid level sensor.

16 Remove the reservoir filler cap and polythene, then top-up the reservoir with fresh hydraulic fluid to the MAX mark (see *Weekly checks*).

17 Bleed the hydraulic systems as described in Section 2 and Chapter 6 then refit the filler cap. Thoroughly check the operation of the brakes and clutch before using the vehicle on the road.

10 Brake pedal – removal and refitting

Removal

1 Remove the lower trim panel beneath the facia on the driver's side as described in Chapter 11.

2 Release the two retaining clips and remove the facia lower panel above the pedals.

9.6 Master cylinder mounting nuts (arrowed)

10.5 Unhook the pedal return spring (A) then slide off the spring clip (B) and withdraw the clevis pin

11.8 Undo the bolt (arrowed) and withdraw the refrigerant pipes from the expansion valve

3 Release the expanding rivet and remove the driver's side footwell air duct.

4 Disconnect the wiring connector at the stop-light switch and release the wiring harness from the support clips.

5 Unhook the return spring from the brake pedal, then slide off the spring clip, and withdraw the clevis pin securing the pedal to the servo unit pushrod **(see illustration)**.

6 On left-hand drive models, remove the steering column intermediate shaft as described in Chapter 10.

7 Undo the six mounting bracket retaining nuts (right-hand drive models) or the four nuts and two bolts (left-hand drive models) and remove the pedal and support bracket assembly from the vehicle.

8 Check the pedal and bracket for excessive wear and damage. It is not possible to renew the pedal pivot bushes separately, so if they are worn, the complete assembly must be renewed.

Refitting

9 Manoeuvre the pedal and support bracket assembly into place making sure the brake servo pushrod fits correctly over the brake pedal.

10 Refit the pedal mounting bracket bolts/ nuts and tighten to the specified torque.

11 Align the pedal hole with the pushrod end,

11.11 Carefully ease the vacuum hose (arrowed) out of the servo unit rubber grommet

and insert the clevis pin. Secure the pin in position with the spring clip.

12 Refit the return spring to the brake pedal.

13 Reconnect the stop-light switch wiring connector.

14 On left-hand drive models, refit the steering column intermediate shaft as described in Chapter 10.

15 Refit the driver's side footwell air duct, then refit the facia trim panels as described in Chapter 11.

11 Vacuum servo unit –
testing, removal and refitting

Testing

1 To test the operation of the servo unit, with the engine off, depress the footbrake several times to exhaust the vacuum. Now start the engine, keeping the pedal firmly depressed. As the engine starts, there should be a noticeable 'give' in the brake pedal as the vacuum builds-up. Allow the engine to run for at least two minutes, then switch it off. The brake pedal should now feel normal, but further applications should result in the pedal feeling firmer, the pedal stroke decreasing with each application.

2 If the servo does not operate as described, first inspect the servo unit check valve as described in Section 12.

3 If the servo unit still fails to operate satisfactorily, the fault lies within the unit itself. Repairs to the unit are not possible; if faulty, the servo unit must be renewed.

Removal

Right-hand drive models

Note: *On models equipped with air conditioning, refer to the air conditioning system precautionary information contained in Chapter 3.*

4 On models equipped with air conditioning, have the refrigerant discharged at a dealer

service department or an automotive air conditioning repair facility.

5 Remove the windscreen wiper motor and linkage as described in Chapter 12.

6 On 1.9 litre engines, carry out the following operations as described in the Chapters indicated:

   a) *Remove the auxiliary drivebelt (Chapter 1).*
   b) *Remove the auxiliary drivebelt tensioner (Chapter 5).*
   c) *Remove the alternator (Chapter 5).*
   d) *Remove the high-pressure fuel pump (Chapter 4A).*

7 On 1.9 litre engines, after removal of the components listed in paragraph 6, undo the six bolts, noting the different bolt lengths, securing the high-pressure fuel pump mounting bracket to the cylinder block and cylinder head. Remove the bracket from the engine.

8 On models equipped with air conditioning, undo the bolt securing the refrigerant pipe block connection to the expansion valve and withdraw the refrigerant pipes from the valve **(see illustration)**. Note that new seals for the refrigerant pipes will be required for refitting. Suitably plug or cover the disconnected pipes.

9 On models equipped with air conditioning, unscrew the retaining nut, release the two clips and free the refrigerant pipes from the vicinity of the servo unit.

10 Remove the master cylinder as described in Section 9.

11 Carefully ease the vacuum hose out of the servo unit, taking care not to displace the sealing grommet **(see illustration)**.

12 Remove the lower trim panel beneath the facia on the driver's side as described in Chapter 11.

13 Release the two retaining clips and remove the facia lower panel above the pedals.

14 Release the expanding rivet and remove the driver's side footwell air duct.

15 Unhook the return spring from the brake pedal, then slide off the spring clip, and withdraw the clevis pin securing the pedal to the servo unit pushrod **(see illustration 10.5)**.

16 Slacken and remove the two diagonally opposite nuts securing the servo unit to the pedal mounting bracket.

17 Return to the engine compartment, and lift the servo unit out of position.

Left-hand drive models

18 Remove the battery and battery tray as described in Chapter 5.

19 Release the locking clip, then lift up the cooling system expansion tank and remove it from the mounting bracket. Place the tank to one side.

20 Remove the ABS hydraulic modulator as described in Section 18, then undo the three retaining bolts and remove the modulator mounting bracket.

21 Remove the master cylinder as described in Section 9.

22 Carefully ease the vacuum hose out of the servo unit, taking care not to displace the sealing grommet.

23 Remove the lower trim panel beneath the facia on the driver's side as described in Chapter 11.

24 Release the two retaining clips and remove the facia lower panel above the pedals.

25 Release the expanding rivet and remove the driver's side footwell air duct.

26 Unhook the return spring from the brake pedal, then slide off the spring clip, and withdraw the clevis pin securing the pedal to the servo unit pushrod **(see illustration 10.5)**.

27 Slacken and remove the two diagonally opposite nuts securing the servo unit to the pedal mounting bracket.

28 Return to the engine compartment, and lift the servo unit out of position.

Refitting

Right-hand drive models

29 Locate the vacuum servo unit in position on the bulkhead ensuring that the servo unit pushrod locates correctly around the brake pedal. Refit the two nuts and tighten them to the specified torque.

30 Apply a smear of multi-purpose grease to the clevis pin then align the servo unit pushrod with the brake pedal hole and insert the pin. Secure the pin in position with the retaining clip, making sure it is correctly located in the groove.

31 Refit the driver's side footwell air duct, then refit the facia trim panels as described in Chapter 11.

32 Refit the vacuum hose to the servo grommet, ensuring that the hose is correctly seated.

33 Refit the brake master cylinder as described in Section 9.

34 On models equipped with air conditioning, resecure the refrigerant pipes in the vicinity of the servo unit.

35 On models equipped with air conditioning, refit the refrigerant pipe block connection to the expansion valve using new seals and secure with the retaining bolt, tightened to the specified torque.

12.3 Disconnect the vacuum hose quick-release fitting at the vacuum pump

36 On 1.9 litre engines, refit the high-pressure fuel pump mounting bracket and tighten the retaining bolts to the specified torque.

37 On 1.9 litre engines, refit the components listed in paragraph 6, as described in the Chapters indicated.

38 Refit the windscreen wiper motor and linkage as described in Chapter 12.

39 On models with air conditioning, on completion, have the system evacuated, charged and leak-tested by the specialist who discharged it.

Left-hand drive models

40 Locate the vacuum servo unit in position on the bulkhead ensuring that the servo unit pushrod locates correctly around the brake pedal. Refit the two nuts and tighten them to the specified torque.

41 Apply a smear of multi-purpose grease to the clevis pin then align the servo unit pushrod with the brake pedal hole and insert the pin. Secure the pin in position with the retaining clip, making sure it is correctly located in the groove.

42 Refit the driver's side footwell air duct, then refit the facia trim panels as described in Chapter 11.

43 Refit the vacuum hose to the servo grommet, ensuring that the hose is correctly seated.

44 Refit the brake master cylinder as described in Section 9, but don't bleed the hydraulic circuits at this stage.

45 Refit the ABS hydraulic modulator mounting bracket, then refit the hydraulic modulator as described in Section 18.

13.4 Disconnect the wiring connector (arrowed) from the handbrake lever warning light switch

46 Refit the cooling system expansion tank and secure with the locking clip.

47 Refit the battery and battery tray as described in Chapter 5.

48 Remove the master cylinder reservoir filler cap and polythene, then top-up the reservoir with fresh hydraulic fluid to the MAX mark (see *Weekly checks*).

49 Bleed the hydraulic systems as described in Section 2 and Chapter 6 then refit the filler cap. Thoroughly check the operation of the brakes and clutch before using the vehicle on the road.

12 Vacuum servo unit check valve and hose – removal, testing and refitting

Removal

1 Carefully ease the vacuum hose out of the servo unit, taking care not to displace the sealing grommet **(see illustration 11.11)**.

2 Remove the plastic cover over the top of the engine.

3 Disconnect the hose quick-release fitting from the vacuum pump **(see illustration)**.

4 Unclip the vacuum hose from its supports on the bulkhead and engine, then remove the hose and check valve from the car.

Testing

5 Examine the check valve and hose for signs of damage, and renew if necessary. The valve may be tested by blowing through it in both directions. Air should flow through the valve in one direction only – when blown through from the servo unit end. If air flows in both directions, or not at all, renew the valve and hose as an assembly.

6 Examine the servo unit rubber sealing grommet for signs of damage or deterioration, and renew as necessary.

Refitting

7 Refitting is a reversal of removal ensuring that the quick-release connector audibly locks in position, and that the hose is correctly seated in the servo grommet.

8 On completion, start the engine and check that there are no air leaks.

13 Handbrake lever – removal and refitting

Removal

1 Disconnect the battery negative terminal (refer to *Disconnecting the battery* in the Reference Chapter).

2 Remove the centre console as described in Chapter 11.

3 Ensure that the handbrake lever is released (off).

4 Disconnect the wiring connector from the handbrake lever warning light switch **(see illustration)**.

5 Disconnect the two wiring connectors at the airbag ECU located at the rear of the handbrake lever. Unclip the wiring harness from both sides of the handbrake lever frame.
6 Undo the handbrake cable adjuster nut and release the cable from the handbrake lever **(see illustration)**.
7 Undo the three retaining nuts and remove the handbrake lever assembly from inside the car.

Refitting

8 Refitting is the reverse of removal, but adjust the handbrake as described in Chapter 1, and refit the centre console as described in Chapter 11.

14 Handbrake cables –
removal and refitting

Removal

1 The handbrake cable consists of two sections, a short front (primary) section which connects the lever to the compensator plate, and the main cables (secondary) section which links the compensator plate to the rear brake calipers. Each section can be removed individually as follows.

Primary (front) cable

2 Chock the front wheels then jack up the rear of the car and securely support it on axle stands (see *Jacking and vehicle support*). Ensure that the handbrake lever is released (off).

14.11 Unclip and remove the centre console access panel

14.14 Push the handbrake operating lever on the brake caliper downwards, and detach the cable end fitting from the lever

13.6 Undo the handbrake cable adjuster nut (arrowed) and release the cable from the handbrake lever

3 Remove the centre console as described in Chapter 11.
4 Undo the handbrake cable adjuster nut and release the cable from the handbrake lever **(see illustration 13.6)**.
5 Release the cable from the guide on the mounting plate where necessary.
6 Remove the exhaust front pipe and intermediate pipe with reference to Chapter 4A.
7 Unscrew the nuts and remove the exhaust heat shield from the underbody.
8 Detach the front cable from the compensator plate by twisting it through 90°.
9 Release the grommet from the lever mounting plate, and withdraw the front cable from inside the vehicle. Remove the grommet from the cable.

Secondary (main) cable

Note: *The secondary cables are supplied as one part, together with the compensator plate.*

14.12 Unclip the cover from around the handbrake lever

14.15a Prise out the handbrake outer cable retaining clip . . .

10 Chock the front wheels then jack up the rear of the car and securely support it on axle stands (see *Jacking and vehicle support*). Remove both rear roadwheels.
11 From inside the vehicle, unclip and remove the access panel in the centre console, beneath the handbrake lever **(see illustration)**.
12 Unclip the cover from around the handbrake lever **(see illustration)**.
13 Move the handbrake lever to the fully released position, then turn the cable adjuster nut anti-clockwise to remove all tension from the cables **(see illustration 13.6)**.
14 Working on each side in turn, use a screwdriver to push the handbrake operating lever on the brake caliper downwards, and detach the cable end fitting from the lever **(see illustration)**.
15 Prise out the handbrake outer cable retaining clip and withdraw the handbrake cable from the caliper bracket **(see illustrations)**.
16 Remove the exhaust front pipe and intermediate pipe with reference to Chapter 4A.
17 Unscrew the nuts and remove the exhaust heat shield from the underbody.
18 Detach the front cable from the compensator plate by twisting it through 90°.
19 Release the main cable sections from the supports on the rear axle and fuel tank, and withdraw the cable from under the vehicle.

Refitting

20 Refitting is a reversal of the removal procedure, but adjust the handbrake as described in Chapter 1. Where applicable, make sure that the fitting on the rear of the front cable locates correctly in the compensator plate. Also make sure that the protective sleeve on the front cable is firmly located over the bead next to the compensator plate.

15 Stop-light switch –
removal, refitting and adjustment

Removal

1 The stop-light switch is located on the brake pedal bracket in the driver's footwell.
2 Remove the lower trim panel beneath the

14.15b . . . and withdraw the handbrake cable from the caliper bracket

facia on the driver's side as described in Chapter 11.

3 Release the two retaining clips and remove the facia lower panel above the pedals.

4 Release the expanding rivet and remove the driver's side footwell air duct.

5 Disconnect the wiring connector at the stop-light switch.

6 Push the brake pedal down, pull out the brake switch actuating pin, then unclip the locking sleeve from around the actuating pin **(see illustrations)**.

7 Release the securing clips and pull the switch to disengage it from the pedal mounting bracket.

Refitting and adjustment

8 With the actuating pin pulled out, and the locking sleeve unclipped, refit the switch to the pedal bracket.

9 Secure the switch with the locking sleeve.

10 Release the brake pedal and the pedal will automatically adjust the position of the actuating pin.

11 Reconnect the wiring connector, then refit the facia footwell trim panel as described in Chapter 11.

16 Handbrake warning light switch – removal and refitting

Removal

1 Remove the centre console as described in Chapter 11.

2 Disconnect the wiring connector from the warning light switch on the side of the handbrake lever **(see illustration 13.4)**.

3 Unscrew the mounting bolt and remove the switch from the handbrake lever bracket.

Refitting

4 Refitting is a reversal of removal.

17 Anti-lock braking and traction control systems – general information

ABS is fitted as standard to all models. On higher specification models, the ABS may also incorporate traction control or an electronic stability programme as additional safety features.

The ABS system comprises a hydraulic modulator and electronic control unit together with four wheel speed sensors. The hydraulic modulator contains the electronic control unit (ECU), the hydraulic solenoid valves (one set for each brake) and the electrically-driven pump. The purpose of the system is to prevent the wheel(s) locking during heavy braking. This is achieved by automatic release of the brake on the relevant wheel, followed by re-application of the brake.

The solenoid valves are controlled by the ECU, which itself receives signals from the four

15.6a Pull out the centre actuating pin arrowed (switch removed for clarity) . . .

15.6b . . . and unclip the locking sleeve

wheel speed sensors which monitor the speed of rotation of each wheel. By comparing these signals, the ECU can determine the speed at which the vehicle is travelling. It can then use this speed to determine when a wheel is decelerating at an abnormal rate, compared to the speed of the vehicle, and therefore predicts when a wheel is about to lock. During normal operation, the system functions in the same way as a conventional braking system.

If the ECU senses that a wheel is about to lock, it operates the relevant solenoid valve(s) in the hydraulic unit, which then isolates from the master cylinder the relevant brake(s) on the wheel(s) which is/are about to lock, effectively sealing-in the hydraulic pressure.

If the speed of rotation of the wheel continues to decrease at an abnormal rate, the ECU operates the electrically-driven pump which pumps the hydraulic fluid back into the master cylinder, releasing the brake. Once the speed of rotation of the wheel returns to an acceptable rate, the pump stops, and the solenoid valves switch again, allowing the hydraulic master cylinder pressure to return to the caliper, which then re-applies the brake. This cycle can be carried out many times a second.

The action of the solenoid valves and return pump creates pulses in the hydraulic circuit. When the ABS system is functioning, these pulses can be felt through the brake pedal.

On models with traction control, the ABS hydraulic modulator incorporates an additional set of solenoid valves which operate the traction control system. The system operates at speeds up to approximately 30 mph using the signals supplied by the wheel speed sensors. If the ECU senses that a driving wheel is about to lose traction, it prevents this by momentarily applying the relevant front brake. The ABS ECU also communicates with the engine management ECU during traction control operation. In severe cases of traction loss the engine management ECU will reduce engine power to assist with traction recovery.

The electronic stability programme (ESP) is a further development of ABS and traction control. Using additional sensors to monitor steering wheel position, vehicle yaw rate, acceleration and deceleration, in conjunction with the ABS sensors, the ECU can intervene under conditions of vehicle instability. Using

the signals from the various sensors, the ECU can determine driver intent (steering wheel position, throttle position, vehicle speed and engine speed). From the sensor inputs from the wheel speed sensors, yaw rate sensors and acceleration sensors the ECU can calculate whether the vehicle is responding to driver input, or whether an unstable driving situation is occurring. If instability is detected, the ECU will intervene by applying or releasing the relevant front or rear brake, in conjunction with a power reduction, until vehicle stability returns.

The operation of the ABS, traction control, and stability programmes is entirely dependent on electrical signals. To prevent the system responding to any inaccurate signals, a built-in safety circuit monitors all signals received by the ECU. If an inaccurate signal or low battery voltage is detected, the system is automatically shut down, and the relevant warning light on the instrument panel is illuminated, to inform the driver that the system is not operational. Normal braking is still available, however.

If a fault develops in the ABS/traction control/ESP system, the vehicle must be taken to a Vauxhall/Opel dealer for fault diagnosis and repair.

18 Anti-lock Braking and Traction Control system components – removal and refitting

Note 1: *Faults on the ABS system can only be diagnosed using Vauxhall/Opel diagnostic equipment or compatible alternative equipment.*

Note 2: *Before starting work, refer to the note at the beginning of Section 2 concerning the dangers of hydraulic fluid.*

Hydraulic modulator

1 Remove the battery and battery tray as described in Chapter 5.

2 Release the locking clip, then lift up the cooling system expansion tank and remove it from the mounting bracket. Place the tank to one side.

3 Minimise fluid loss by first removing the master cylinder reservoir cap and screwing it down onto a piece of polythene.

18.4 Disconnect the wiring harness plug (arrowed) from the ECU

4 Pull out the locking bar and disconnect the wiring harness plug from the ECU **(see illustration)**.

5 Note and record the fitted position of the brake pipes at the modulator, then unscrew the union nuts and release the pipes. As a precaution, place absorbent rags beneath the brake pipe unions when unscrewing them. Suitably plug or cap the disconnected unions to prevent dirt entry and fluid loss.

6 Unscrew the three retaining bolts and remove the hydraulic modulator from the mounting bracket.

7 Refitting is the reverse of the removal procedure, noting the following points:

a) Tighten the modulator retaining bolts to the specified torque.

b) Refit the brake pipes to their respective locations, and tighten the union nuts to the specified torque.

c) Ensure that the wiring is correctly routed, and that the ECU wiring harness plug is firmly pressed into position and secured with the locking bar.

d) Refit the battery tray and battery as described in Chapter 5.

e) On completion, bleed the complete hydraulic system as described in Section 2. Ensure that the system is bled in the correct order, to prevent air entering the modulator return pump.

Electronic control unit (ECU)

Note: At the time of writing, no information was available for removal and refitting of the ECU on systems incorporating an electronic stability programme (ESP). This work should therefore be entrusted to a Vauxhall/Opel dealer.

8 Remove the hydraulic modulator from the car as described previously in this Section.

9 Undo the three retaining bolts and carefully withdraw the ECU from the base of the hydraulic modulator. Note that new retaining bolts will be required for refitting.

10 Carefully remove the eight sealing rings from the modulator valves and obtain new sealing rings for refitting.

11 Locate the new sealing rings over the solenoid valves, then carefully place the ECU in position, keeping it square and level.

12 Fit the three new retaining bolts and tighten securely.

13 On completion, refit the hydraulic modulator as described previously in this Section.

Wheel speed sensors

14 The front and rear wheel speed sensors are an integral part of the hub bearings and cannot be separated.

15 Refer to Chapter 10 for front and rear hub bearing removal and refitting procedures.

19 Vacuum pump – removal and refitting

Removal

1.3 litre engines

1 Disconnect the battery negative terminal (refer to *Disconnecting the battery* in the Reference Chapter).

2 Remove the plastic cover over the top of the engine.

3 Slacken the two retaining clips and disconnect the charge air hose from the intercooler and charge air pipe elbow.

4 Disconnect the quick-release fitting and detach the vacuum servo unit vacuum hose from the pump **(see illustration)**. Disconnect the smaller vacuum hose from the outlet on the side of the pump.

5 Release the retaining clips and disconnect the fuel return hoses at the fuel pump and at the fuel leak-off hose adaptor pipe. Plug or cover the pump union and hose ends to prevent dirt entry.

6 Undo the retaining bolt and free the leak-off hose adaptor pipe from its location.

7 Disconnect the wiring connector at the EGR valve.

8 Undo the two mounting bolts and remove the pump from the camshaft housing **(see illustration)**. Recover the gasket.

1.7 litre engines

9 Remove the alternator as described in Chapter 5.

10 Undo the three retaining bolts and remove the vacuum pump from the rear of the alternator. Remove the O-ring seal.

1.9 litre engines

11 Disconnect the battery negative terminal (refer to *Disconnecting the battery* in the Reference Chapter).

12 Remove the plastic cover over the top of the engine.

13 Slacken the two retaining clips and disconnect the charge air hose from the intercooler and charge air pipe elbow.

14 Disconnect the quick-release fitting and detach the vacuum servo unit vacuum hose from the pump **(see illustration)**. Disconnect the smaller vacuum hose from the outlet on the side of the pump.

15 Undo the four mounting bolts and remove the pump from the cylinder head/camshaft housing **(see illustrations)**. Recover the gasket. Note that new mounting bolts will be required for refitting.

19.4 Disconnect the quick-release fitting (arrowed) and detach the servo unit vacuum hose – 1.3 litre engines

19.8 Undo the two mounting bolts (arrowed) and remove the pump from the camshaft housing – 1.3 litre engines

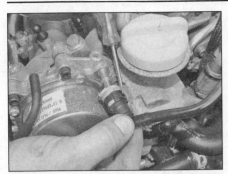

19.14 Disconnect the quick-release fitting and detach the vacuum hose from the pump – 1.9 litre engines

19.15a Undo the four mounting bolts (arrowed) . . .

19.15b . . . and remove the vacuum pump from the cylinder head/camshaft housing – 1.9 litre engines

Refitting

16 Refitting is a reversal of removal, but clean the mating faces of the pump and cylinder head/camshaft housing or alternator, and fit a new gasket or O-ring as applicable. Tighten the mounting bolts to the specified torque (where given).

Chapter 10
Suspension and steering

Contents

Degrees of difficulty

Easy, suitable for novice with little experience	**Fairly easy,** suitable for beginner with some experience	**Fairly difficult,** suitable for competent DIY mechanic	**Difficult,** suitable for experienced DIY mechanic	**Very difficult,** suitable for expert DIY or professional

Specifications

Front suspension
Type . . . . Independent, with MacPherson struts, gas-filled shock absorbers and anti-roll bar

Rear suspension
Type . . . . Semi-independent torsion beam, with trailing arms, coil springs and telescopic shock absorbers

Steering
Type . . . . Rack and pinion with electro-hydraulic power steering (EHPS)

Front and rear hub bearings
Bearing play (maximum). . . . . 0.1 mm
Bearing radial run-out. . . . . 0.04 mm
Bearing lateral run-out . . . . 0.05 mm

Torque wrench settings

	Nm	lbf ft
Front suspension		
Anti-roll bar connecting link retaining nut*	55	41
Anti-roll bar to subframe	20	15
Driveshaft retaining nut*:		
Stage 1	150	111
Stage 2	Slacken the nut by 45°	
Stage 3	250	185
Front engine mounting/torque link to subframe	55	41
Hub bearing assembly to swivel hub*:		
Stage 1	90	66
Stage 2	Angle-tighten a further 30°	
Stage 3	Angle-tighten a further 15°	
Stage 1	90	66
Stage 2	Angle-tighten a further 75°	
Stage 3	Angle-tighten a further 15°	
Lower arm balljoint clamp bolt nut*:	50	37
Lower arm to subframe*:		
Lower balljoint to lower arm	35	26
Rear engine mounting/torque link bracket to subframe	55	41
Rear engine mounting/torque link bracket to transmission	80	59
Subframe mounting bolts:		
Stage 1	90	66
Stage 2	Angle-tighten a further 45°	
Stage 3	Angle-tighten a further 15°	
Suspension strut piston rod nut*	80	59
Swivel hub to strut*:		
Stage 1	85	63
Stage 2	Angle-tighten a further 75°	
Stage 3	Angle-tighten a further 15°	
Rear suspension		
Brake hydraulic line union nuts	16	12
Hub bearing assembly to trailing arm*:		
Stage 1	50	37
Stage 2	Angle-tighten a further 30°	
Stage 3	Angle-tighten a further 15°	
Shock absorber:		
To body	90	66
To trailing arm	130	96
Torsion beam front mounting bracket*:		
Centre bolt:		
Stage 1	90	66
Stage 2	Angle-tighten a further 60°	
Stage 3	Angle-tighten a further 15°	
Bracket-to-underbody bolts:		
Stage 1	90	66
Stage 2	Angle-tighten a further 30°	
Stage 3	Angle-tighten a further 15°	
Steering		
Electro-hydraulic pump to steering gear and subframe	22	16
Hydraulic pressure and return line union nuts:		
TRW steering gear	30	22
ZF steering gear	16	12
Intermediate shaft to steering gear pinion and steering column*	24	18
Steering column mounting bolts*	22	16
Steering gear to subframe*:		
Stage 1	45	33
Stage 2	Angle-tighten a further 45°	
Stage 3	Angle-tighten a further 15°	
Steering wheel retaining bolt*	30	22
Track rod end locking nut	60	44
Track rod end to swivel hub*:		
Stage 1	30	22
Stage 2	Angle-tighten a further 90°	
Stage 3	Angle-tighten a further 15°	
Track rod to steering rack	90	66
Roadwheels		
All models	110	81

* Use new fasteners

1 General information

The independent front suspension is of the MacPherson strut type, incorporating coil springs and integral telescopic shock absorbers. The MacPherson struts are located by transverse lower suspension arms, which utilise rubber inner mounting bushes, and incorporate a balljoint at the outer ends. The front swivel hubs, which carry the hub bearings, brake calipers and disc assemblies, are bolted to the MacPherson struts, and connected to the lower arms via the balljoints. A front anti-roll bar is fitted, which has link rods with balljoints at each end to connect it to the strut.

The rear suspension is of semi-independent type, consisting of a torsion beam and trailing arms, with double-conical coil springs and telescopic shock absorbers. The front ends of the trailing arms are attached to the vehicle underbody by horizontal bushes, and the rear ends are located by the shock absorbers, which are bolted to the underbody at their upper ends. The coil springs are mounted independently of the shock absorbers, and act directly between the trailing arms and the underbody. Each rear wheel bearing, hub and stub axle assembly is manufactured as a sealed unit, and cannot be dismantled.

The steering system is of the electro-hydraulic power steering (EHPS) type. This system utilises a conventional rack-and-pinion type steering gear mounted on the front subframe, with variable power assistance generated by a hydraulic pump, driven by an electric motor. The degree of power assistance available is governed by the speed of the electric motor which is controlled by the steering system electronic control unit. The ECU receives input signals on steering wheel position (from a steering angle sensor) and roadspeed (from the ABS wheel speed sensors) and calculates the amount of power assistance required. The hydraulic pump, electric motor and hydraulic fluid reservoir are mounted above the rack-and-pinion steering gear on the front subframe.

The steering column is linked to the steering gear by an intermediate shaft. The intermediate shaft has a universal joint fitted to its upper end, and is secured to the column by a clamp bolt. The lower end of the intermediate shaft is attached to the steering gear pinion by means of a clamp bolt.

2 Front swivel hub – removal and refitting

Caution: The front wheel camber setting is controlled by the bolts securing the swivel hub to the front suspension strut. Before removing the bolts, mark the swivel

2.3a Depress the retaining tab and release the wheel speed sensor wiring connector from the strut bracket – models without a brake pad wear indicator

hub in relation to the strut accurately. On completion, the camber setting must be checked and adjusted by a suitably-equipped garage.

Note: *A new driveshaft retaining nut, lower arm balljoint clamp bolt and nut, suspension strut-to-swivel hub nuts and bolts and a new track rod end retaining nut will be needed for refitting. The driveshaft outer joint splines may be a tight fit in the hub and it is possible that a puller/extractor will be required to draw the hub assembly off the driveshaft during removal.*

Removal

1 Firmly apply the handbrake, then jack up the front of the car and support it securely on axle stands (see *Jacking and vehicle support*). Remove the relevant front roadwheel.

2.4a Depress the locking tab and release the wiring connector from the suspension strut

2.4c . . . then hold the upper part of the connector and twist the lower part in the direction of the arrow

2.3b Push the locking tab downward and disconnect the wheel speed sensor wiring from the connector – models without a brake pad wear indicator

2 Remove the front brake disc as described in Chapter 9.

3 On models without a front brake pad wear indicator, depress the retaining tab and release the ABS wheel speed sensor wiring connector from the suspension strut bracket. Push the locking tab downward and disconnect the wheel speed sensor wiring from the connector **(see illustrations)**.

4 On models with a front brake pad wear indicator depress the locking tab and release the wiring connector from the suspension strut. Slide the locking bar on the connector downward, then hold the upper part of the connector and twist the lower part to open the connector. Disconnect the ABS wheel speed sensor wire from the connector and also disconnect the brake pad wear warning indicator wire **(see illustrations)**.

2.4b Slide the locking bar on the wiring connector downward . . .

2.4d Disconnect the wires from the connector – models with a brake pad wear indicator

TOOL TiP

A tool to hold the wheel hub stationary whilst the driveshaft retaining nut is slackened can be fabricated from two lengths of steel strip (one long, one short) and a nut an bolt; the nut and bolt forming the pivot of a forked tool.

5 To prevent rotation of the wheel hub as the driveshaft retaining nut is slackened, make up a holding tool and bolt the tool to the wheel hub using two wheel bolts **(see Tool Tip)**.

6 With the holding tool in place, slacken and remove the driveshaft retaining nut using a socket and long bar. Where necessary, support the socket on an axle stand to prevent it slipping off the nut. This nut is very tight; make sure that there is no risk of pulling the car off the axle stands as the nut is slackened.

7 Unscrew the nut securing the track rod end to the steering arm on the swivel hub, then use a balljoint separator tool to remove the track rod end **(see illustration)**.

8 Unscrew the nut and remove the clamp

2.9 Use a chisel or screwdriver as a wedge to expand the lower portion of the swivel hub

2.11b . . . then free the driveshaft from the swivel hub

2.7 Use a balljoint separator tool to remove the track rod end

bolt securing the front suspension lower arm balljoint to the swivel hub **(see illustration)**. Note that a new clamp bolt and nut will be required for refitting.

9 Use a chisel or screwdriver as a wedge to expand the lower portion of the swivel hub **(see illustration)**.

10 Using a lever, push down on the suspension lower arm to free the balljoint from the swivel hub, then move the swivel hub to one side and release the arm, taking care not to damage the balljoint rubber boot. It is advisable to place a protective cover over the rubber boot such as the plastic cap from an aerosol can, suitably cut to fit.

11 The hub must now be freed from the end of the driveshaft. It may be possible to pull the hub off the driveshaft, but if the end of the driveshaft is tight in the hub, temporarily refit the driveshaft retaining nut to protect the

2.11a Tap the end of the driveshaft with a soft-faced hammer . . .

2.13 Slacken and remove the two nuts and bolts securing the suspension strut to the swivel hub

2.8 Unscrew the nut and remove the clamp bolt securing the lower arm balljoint to the swivel hub

driveshaft threads, then tap the end of the driveshaft with a soft-faced hammer while pulling outwards on the swivel hub **(see illustrations)**. Alternatively, use a suitable puller to press the driveshaft through the hub.

12 Mark the position of the suspension strut on the swivel hub by drawing a circle around the heads of the two retaining bolts. **Note:** *This is important to maintain the camber setting*.

13 Slacken and remove the two nuts and bolts securing the suspension strut to the swivel hub, noting that new nuts and bolts will be required for refitting **(see illustration)**. Disengage the swivel hub from the strut and remove it from the car.

Refitting

14 Ensure that the driveshaft outer constant velocity joint and hub splines are clean, then slide the hub onto the driveshaft splines. Fit the new driveshaft retaining nut, tightening it by hand only at this stage.

15 Engage the swivel hub with the suspension strut, and insert the new bolts from the front of the strut so that their threads are facing to the rear. Fit the new nuts, tightening them by hand only at this stage.

16 Locate the lower arm balljoint in the swivel hub. Insert the new clamp bolt from the front of the swivel hub, so that its threads are facing to the rear. Fit the new nut to the clamp bolt, and tighten it to the specified torque.

17 With the hub correctly located, align the strut-to-swivel hub bolt heads with the marks made on the strut during removal. Tighten the bolts to the specified torque and through the specified angles given in the Specifications, using a torque wrench and angle-tightening gauge.

18 Engage the track rod balljoint in the swivel hub, then fit the new retaining nut and tighten it to the specified torque setting.

19 Refit the brake disc together with the brake caliper and pads as described in Chapter 9.

20 Reconnect the ABS wheel speed sensor wiring connector and, where applicable, the break pad wear warning indicator wire. Secure the wiring in the relevant support brackets and clips.

21 Refit the brake hydraulic hose to the suspension strut and secure with the retaining clip.

22 Using the method employed on removal to prevent rotation, tighten the driveshaft retaining nut through the stages given in the Specifications.

23 Refit the roadwheel, then lower the vehicle to the ground and tighten the roadwheel bolts to the specified torque.

3 Front hub bearings – checking and renewal

Note: *The front hub bearing and integral ABS wheel speed sensor is a sealed unit and no repairs are possible. If the bearing is worn or the speed sensor is faulty, a new bearing assembly must be obtained.*

Checking

1 Firmly apply the handbrake, then jack up the front of the car and support it securely on axle stands (see *Jacking and vehicle support*). Remove the roadwheel.

2 A dial test indicator (DTI) will be required to measure the amount of play in the bearing. Locate the DTI on the suspension strut and zero the probe on the brake disc.

3 Lever the hub in and out and measure the amount of play in the bearing.

4 To measure the bearing lateral and radial run-out, undo the two bolts securing the brake caliper mounting bracket to the swivel hub. Slide the mounting bracket, complete with brake caliper and pads off the brake disc, and tie it to the coil spring using wire or a cable tie.

5 Undo the securing screw and remove the brake disc from the wheel hub.

6 To check the lateral run-out, locate the DTI on the suspension strut and zero the probe on the front face of the hub flange. Rotate the hub and measure the run-out.

7 To check the radial run-out, zero the DTI probe on the upper face of the extended portion at the centre of the hub. Rotate the hub and measure the run-out.

8 If the play or run-out exceeds the specified amount, renew the hub bearing as described below.

9 If the bearing is satisfactory, refit the brake disc and tighten its retaining screw securely.

10 Slide the brake pads, caliper and mounting bracket over the disc and into position on the swivel hub. Fit the two caliper mounting bracket retaining bolts and tighten them to the specified torque (see Chapter 9).

11 Refit the roadwheel, then lower the vehicle to the ground and tighten the roadwheel bolts to the specified torque.

Renewal

Note: *New hub bearing retaining bolts will be required for refitting.*

12 Carry out the operations described in Section 2, paragraphs 1 to 11.

13 Undo the three bolts securing the bearing assembly to the swivel hub **(see illustration)**.

3.13 Undo the three bolts (arrowed) securing the bearing assembly to the swivel hub . . .

14 Remove the bearing and the brake shield from the swivel hub **(see illustration)**.

15 Thoroughly clean the swivel hub and brake shield, then place the shield in position on the swivel hub.

16 Locate the wheel bearing over the brake shield and into the swivel hub. Position the bearing so that the wheel speed sensor wiring connector is toward the brake caliper side of the swivel hub (ie, towards the front of the vehicle). Align the retaining bolt holes and fit the three new bolts.

17 Tighten the retaining bolts progressively to the specified Stage 1 torque setting using a torque wrench, and then through the specified Stage 2 and Stage 3 angles, using an angle tightening gauge **(see illustrations)**.

18 Ensure that the driveshaft outer constant velocity joint and hub splines are clean, then slide the hub onto the driveshaft splines. Fit the new driveshaft retaining nut, tightening it by hand only at this stage.

19 Locate the lower arm balljoint in the swivel hub. Insert the clamp bolt from the front of the swivel hub, so that its threads are facing to the rear. Fit the new nut to the clamp bolt, and tighten it to the specified torque.

20 Engage the track rod balljoint in the swivel hub, then fit the new retaining nut and tighten it to the specified torque setting.

21 Refit the brake disc together with the brake caliper and pads as described in Chapter 9.

22 Reconnect the ABS wheel speed sensor wiring connector and, where applicable, the brake pad wear warning indicator wire. Secure

3.17a Tighten the retaining bolts to the Stage 1 torque setting using a torque wrench . . .

3.14 . . . then remove the bearing assembly and brake shield from the hub

the wiring in the relevant support brackets and clips.

23 Refit the brake hydraulic hose to the suspension strut and secure with the retaining clip.

24 Using the method employed on removal to prevent rotation, tighten the driveshaft retaining nut through the stages given in the Specifications.

25 Refit the roadwheel, then lower the vehicle to the ground and tighten the roadwheel bolts to the specified torque.

4 Front suspension strut – removal, overhaul and refitting

Note: *New strut-to-swivel hub bolts and nuts, strut retaining clamp and strut-to-anti-roll bar link rod nut, will be required for refitting. Ideally, both front suspension struts should be renewed at the same time in order to maintain good steering and suspension characteristics.*

Removal

1 Apply the handbrake, then jack up the front of the vehicle and support it on axle stands (see *Jacking and vehicle support*). Remove the front roadwheel.

2 Unclip the ABS wheel speed sensor wiring guide from the brake hydraulic hose, then extract the retaining clip and release the hydraulic hose from the suspension strut **(see illustrations)**.

3.17b . . . and then through the Stage 2 and 3 angles, using an angle tightening gauge

4.2a Unclip the ABS wheel speed sensor wiring guide from the hydraulic hose . . .

4.2b . . . then extract the retaining clip . . .

4.2c . . . and release the hydraulic hose from the suspension strut

3 On models without a front brake pad wear indicator, depress the retaining tab and release the ABS wheel speed sensor wiring connector from the suspension strut bracket. Push the locking tab downward and disconnect the wheel speed sensor wiring from the connector **(see illustrations 2.3a and 2.3b)**.

4 On models with a front brake pad wear indicator depress the locking tab and release the wiring connector from the suspension strut. Slide the locking bar on the connector downward, then hold the upper part of the connector and twist the lower part to open the connector. Disconnect the ABS wheel speed sensor wire from the connector and also disconnect the brake pad wear warning indicator wire **(see illustrations 2.4a to 2.4d)**.

5 Unscrew the nut and disconnect the anti-roll bar link rod from the strut. Use a spanner on the special flats to hold the link while the nut is being loosened **(see illustration)**.

6 Mark the position of the suspension strut on the swivel hub by drawing a circle around the heads of the two retaining bolts. **Note:** *This is important to maintain the camber setting.*

7 Slacken and remove the two nuts and bolts securing the suspension strut to the swivel hub, noting that new nuts and bolts will be required for refitting. Disengage the top of the swivel hub from the strut **(see illustrations)**.

8 Engage the help of an assistant to support the strut beneath the front wing. From within the engine compartment, prise apart the two halves of the strut retaining clamp by spreading open the serrations **(see illustration)**. Push up on the strut to relieve the tension on the clamp, and remove the two clamp halves from the strut tower. Note that the retaining clamp will be destroyed during removal and a new clamp must be obtained for refitting.

9 Lower the strut and withdraw it from under the front wing.

Overhaul

Note 1: *A spring compressor tool will be required for this operation. Before overhaul, mark the position of each component in relationship with each other for reassembly.*
Note 2: *A new piston rod nut will be required for reassembly.*

10 With the suspension strut resting on a bench, or clamped in a vice, fit a spring compressor tool, and compress the coil spring to relieve the pressure on the spring seats **(see illustration)**. Ensure that the compressor tool is securely located on the spring, in accordance with the tool manufacturer's instructions.

11 Using a screwdriver, prise out the plastic cap from the upper mounting **(see illustration)**.

12 Mark the position of the spring on the top and bottom mountings, then counterhold the strut piston rod with an Allen key or suitable

4.5 Unscrew the nut and disconnect the anti-roll bar link rod from the strut

4.7a Undo the two nuts and bolts securing the suspension strut to the swivel hub . . .

4.7b . . . then disengage the top of the swivel hub from the strut

4.8 Prise apart the two halves of the strut retaining clamp by spreading open the serations

4.10 Fit a spring compressor tool, and compress the coil spring

4.11 Prise out the plastic cap from the upper mounting

4.12 Counterhold the strut piston rod with an Allen key or suitable bit, and unscrew the piston rod nut

4.13a Remove the strut upper mounting . . .

4.13b . . . upper spring seat with rubber gaiter . . .

4.13c . . . spring . . .

4.13d . . . and buffer, from the strut

bit, and unscrew the piston rod nut **(see illustration)**.

13 Remove the strut upper mounting, upper spring seat with rubber gaiter, spring and buffer from the strut **(see illustrations)**.

14 With the strut assembly now completely dismantled, examine all the components for wear, damage or deformation. Renew any of the components as necessary.

15 Examine the strut for signs of fluid leakage. Check the strut piston for signs of pitting along its entire length, and check the strut body for signs of damage. While holding it in an upright position, test the operation of the strut by moving the piston through a full stroke, and then through short strokes of 50 to 100 mm. In both cases, the resistance felt should be smooth and continuous. If the resistance is jerky or uneven or if there is any visible sign of wear or damage to the strut, renewal is necessary.

16 If any doubt exists as to the condition of the coil spring, carefully remove the spring compressors and check the spring for distortion and signs of cracking. Renew the spring if it is damaged or distorted, or if there is any doubt as to its condition.

17 Inspect all other components for damage or deterioration, and renew any that are suspect.

18 With the spring compressed with the compressor tool, locate the spring on the strut making sure that it is correctly seated with its lower end against the raised stop **(see illustration)**.

19 Refit the buffer, rubber gaiter, upper spring seat and the upper mounting.

20 Refit the new piston rod nut and tighten it to the specified torque while counterholding the piston rod. Refit the plastic cap to the upper mounting.

21 Slowly slacken the spring compressor tool to relieve the tension in the spring. Check that the ends of the spring locate correctly against the stops on the spring seats. If necessary,

turn the spring and the upper seat so that the components locate correctly before the compressor tool is removed. Remove the compressor tool when the spring is fully seated.

Refitting

22 Locate the strut in position under the front wing and engage the help of an assistant to retain it in place. Engage the two halves of the new strut retaining clamp with the strut upper mounting and push the two halves together so that the serrations engage. Using a pair of wide-opening grips or similar, squeeze the two clamp halves fully together **(see illustration)**.

4.18 Locate the spring on the strut making sure that its lower end (A) is against the raised stop (B)

4.22 Engage the two halves of the strut retaining clamp with the strut upper mounting and squeze the two clamp halves fully together

5.5 Front suspension lower arm inner mounting located on the subframe

23 Engage the swivel hub with the suspension strut, and insert the new bolts from the front of the strut so that their threads are facing to the rear. Fit the new nuts, tightening them by hand only at this stage.

24 Align the strut-to-swivel hub bolt heads with the marks made on the strut during removal. Tighten the bolts to the specified torque and through the specified angles given in the Specifications, using a torque wrench and angle-tightening gauge.

25 Locate the hydraulic hose in the strut bracket and secure with the retaining clip. Refit the ABS wheel speed sensor wiring guide to the brake hydraulic hose.

26 Reconnect the ABS wheel speed sensor wiring connector and, where applicable, the brake pad wear warning indicator wire. Secure the wiring in the relevant support brackets and clips.

27 Connect the anti-roll bar link rod to the strut and use a spanner on the flats to hold the link while tightening the nut to the specified torque.

28 Refit the roadwheel, then lower the vehicle to the ground and tighten the roadwheel bolts to the specified torque.

5 Front suspension lower arm – removal, overhaul and refitting

Note: *New lower arm inner pivot bolts and lower arm balljoint clamp bolt and nut will be needed for refitting.*

Removal

1 Firmly apply the handbrake, then jack up

6.2 Front suspension lower balljoint showing rivets securing it to the lower arm

the front of the car and support it securely on axle stands (see *Jacking and vehicle support*). Remove the front roadwheel.

2 Unscrew the nut and remove the clamp bolt securing the front suspension lower arm balljoint to the swivel hub (see illustration 2.8). Note that a new clamp bolt and nut will be required for refitting.

3 Use a chisel or screwdriver as a wedge to expand the lower portion of the swivel hub (see illustration 2.9).

4 Using a lever, push down on the suspension lower arm to free the balljoint from the swivel hub, then move the swivel hub to one side and release the arm, taking care not to damage the balljoint rubber boot. It is advisable to place a protective cover over the rubber boot such as the plastic cap from an aerosol can, suitably cut to fit.

5 Note that the lower arm inner retaining bolt heads are facing the front of the vehicle. Unscrew and remove the bolts and withdraw the lower arm from the subframe (see illustration). It will be necessary to slightly press the arms to release the rubber mountings.

Overhaul

6 The lower balljoint may be renewed as described in Section 6. The rubber bushes are a tight fit in the arm and must be pressed out. If a press is not available, the bushes can be drawn out using a long bolt, nut, washers and a socket or length of metal tubing.

7 Prior to fitting the new bushes, coat them with silicone grease or soapy water. Press both bushes fully into the lower arm.

Refitting

8 Locate the lower arm on the subframe and fit the retaining bolts from the front of the vehicle. Hand-tighten the bolts at this stage.

9 Locate the lower arm balljoint in the swivel hub. Insert the new clamp bolt from the front of the swivel hub, so that its threads are facing to the rear. Fit the new nut to the clamp bolt, and tighten it to the specified torque.

10 Refit the front wheel and lower the vehicle to the ground.

11 With the weight of the vehicle on the suspension, tighten the lower arm inner pivot bolts to the specified torque and in the stages given.

12 Have the front wheel alignment settings checked on completion.

6 Front suspension lower balljoint – renewal

Note: *The original balljoint is riveted to the lower arm; service replacements are bolted in position.*

1 Remove the front suspension lower arm as described in Section 5. **Note:** *If the fitted balljoint is a service replacement, it is not necessary to completely remove the arm but only to disconnect the balljoint from the*

bottom of the swivel hub then unbolt the old balljoint.

2 Mount the lower arm in a vice, then drill the heads from the three rivets that secure the balljoint to the lower arm, using a 12.0 mm diameter drill (see illustration).

3 If necessary, tap the rivets from the lower arm, then remove the balljoint.

4 Clean any rust from the rivet holes, and apply rust inhibitor.

5 The new balljoint must be fitted using three special bolts, spring washers and nuts, available from a Vauxhall/Opel parts stockists.

6 Ensure that the balljoint is fitted the correct way up, noting that the securing nuts are positioned on the underside of the lower arm. Tighten the nuts to the specified torque.

7 Refit the front suspension lower arm as described in Section 5.

7 Front subframe – removal and refitting

Note: *Vauxhall/Opel technicians use special jigs to ensure that the subframe is correctly aligned. Without the use of these tools it is important to note the position of the subframe accurately before removal.*

Removal

1 Jack up the front and rear of the car and support it securely on axle stands (see *Jacking and vehicle support*). Preferably, position the car over an inspection pit, or on a lift. The help of an assistant will be needed for this procedure.

2 Set the front wheels in the straight-ahead position, then remove the ignition key and lock the column by turning the steering wheel as required. Remove both front roadwheels and remove the lower liner from the right-hand wheel arch.

3 Remove the front bumper as described in Chapter 11.

4 Remove the plastic cover over the top of the engine.

5 Remove the complete exhaust system as described in Chapter 4A.

6 In the driver's footwell, unscrew the bolt securing the bottom of the steering column intermediate shaft to the steering gear pinion. Use paint or a suitable marker pen to make

7.6 Unscrew the clamp bolt, then disconnect the intermediate shaft from the steering gear pinion

alignment marks between the intermediate shaft and the steering gear pinion, then pull the shaft from the pinion and position to one side **(see illustration)**.

7 Release the locking clip, then lift up the cooling system expansion tank and remove it from the mounting bracket. Place the tank to one side.

8 Retain the radiator in position by inserting a drill bit, or similar, through the holes provided on each of the radiator upper mounting brackets **(see illustration)**. This is necessary as the radiator bottom mounting rubbers are located in the subframe.

9 Lift off the cover from the wiring junction box at the left-hand rear corner of the engine compartment. Undo the nut and disconnect the electro-hydraulic power steering system positive cable from the junction box terminal **(see illustration)**.

10 Disconnect the wiring connector for the electro-hydraulic power steering system at the block connector adjacent to the ABS hydraulic modulator **(see illustration)**.

11 Undo the bolt and disconnect the electro-hydraulic power steering system earth cable from the battery negative terminal clamp.

12 Working under the car, release the cable ties and retaining clips and release the power steering wiring harness from its body attachments. The wiring harness must be free to be removed with the subframe.

13 Connect a hoist to the engine/transmission assembly and support its weight. If available, the type of support bar which locates in the engine compartment side channels is to be preferred,

7.8 Insert a drill bit (arrowed) or similar, through the holes provided on the radiator mounting brackets (shown with radiator removed)

as this will ensure correct repositioning during refitting. Connect the hoist chains to the lifting brackets on the cylinder head.

14 Unscrew the nut and disconnect the anti-roll bar link rod from the strut. Use a spanner on the special flats to hold the link while the nut is being loosened **(see illustration 4.5)**.

15 Unscrew the nut securing the track rod end to the steering arm on the swivel hub, then use a balljoint separator tool to remove the track rod end **(see illustration 2.7)**.

16 Unscrew the nut and remove the clamp bolt securing the front suspension lower arm balljoint to the swivel hub **(see illustration 2.8)**. Note that a new clamp bolt and nut will be required for refitting.

17 Use a chisel or screwdriver as a wedge to expand the lower portion of the swivel hub **(see illustration 2.9)**.

7.9 Disconnect the power steering positive cable (arrowed) from the junction box terminal

18 Using a lever, push down on the suspension lower arm to free the balljoint from the swivel hub, then move the swivel hub to one side and release the arm, taking care not to damage the balljoint rubber boot. It is advisable to place a protective cover over the rubber boot such as the plastic cap from an aerosol can, suitably cut to fit.

19 On manual transmission models with a rod-type gearchange mechanism, note the position of the gearchange linkage located above the engine rear mounting, then disconnect it from the support bracket on the subframe (refer to Chapter 7A if necessary).

20 Undo the three bolts and detach the rear engine mounting/torque link bracket from the transmission.

21 Slacken and remove the nut securing the front engine mounting/torque link to the subframe bracket. Withdraw the through-bolt **(see illustration)**.

22 Support the subframe with a length of wood on a trolley jack. Ideally, a purpose-made cradle should be used. Enlist the help of an assistant.

23 Accurately mark the position of the subframe and mounting bolts to ensure correct refitting. Note that Vauxhall/Opel technicians use a special jig with guide pins located through the alignment holes in the subframe and underbody.

24 Unscrew and remove the subframe mounting bolts, noting the position of each bolt, as they are of different lengths **(see illustrations)**. There are two bolts at the front,

7.10 Disconnect the power steering wiring at the block connector (arrowed)

7.21 Undo the nut (arrowed) and remove the bolt securing the front engine mounting/torque link to the subframe bracket

7.24a Unscrew the subframe front mounting bolts . . .

7.24b . . . side mounting bolts . . .

7.24c . . . and rear support bracket bolts

7.25 Guide the steering gear pinion through the rubber grommet when lowering the subframe

two bolts located above the lower suspension arms, and six bolts located on the triangular rear support brackets.

25 With the help of an assistant, carefully lower the subframe taking care not to damage the wiring harness for the power steering. As it is being lowered, guide the steering gear pinion through the rubber grommet in the floor **(see illustrations)**.

26 Remove the steering gear, front suspension lower arms and anti-roll bar with reference to Sections 18, 5 and 8. If necessary, the subframe mounting rubbers may be renewed, however, they must be renewed in pairs only (ie, left and right together). Use a metal tube, a long threaded bar, and two nuts and washers to force out the rubbers. If necessary, unbolt and remove the gearchange bracket (where fitted).

Refitting

27 Refitting is a reversal of removal, bearing in mind the following points:

a) *Ensure that the radiator lower mounting pegs engage correctly in the subframe brackets as the subframe is refitted.*

b) *Tighten all nuts and bolts to the specified torque and, where necessary, in the stages given. Note that new nuts/ bolts should be used on all disturbed fittings.*

c) *Make sure that the subframe is correctly aligned with the underbody before fully tightening the mounting bolts.*

8.4 Anti-roll bar clamp mounting bolts (arrowed)

8 Front anti-roll bar – removal and refitting

Note: *It is recommended that all mounting nuts and bolts are renewed when refitting.*

Removal

1 Remove the front subframe assembly as described in Section 7.

2 Prior to removal of the anti-roll bar, mark the position of each anti-roll bar mounting clamp rubber.

3 Unscrew the retaining nut and disconnect the link rod from the ends of the anti-roll bar, discard the retaining nut; a new one should be used on refitting. Use a spanner on the flats to hold the link while the nut is being loosened.

4 Unscrew the two bolts from each mounting clamp, and remove the clamp **(see illustration)**. As the last clamp is removed, support the anti-roll bar and remove it from the subframe.

5 Inspect the mounting clamp rubbers for signs of damage and deterioration, and renew if necessary **(see illustrations)**. **Note:** *On later models, the mounting clamp rubbers are a modified two-piece design and cannot be renewed separately. If the rubbers are worn, a complete new anti-roll bar complete with integral mounting clamps will be required. Consult a Vauxhall/Opel dealer for further information.*

Refitting

6 Align the mounting rubbers with the marks made on the anti-roll bar prior to removal.

7 Refit the anti-roll bar to the subframe, and fit the mounting clamps. Ensure that the clamp half is correctly engaged with the anti-roll bar rubbers, then tighten each clamp retaining bolt, by hand only at this stage.

8 With the two clamps loosely installed, check the position of the anti-roll bar to the marks made on removal, then tighten the clamp bolts to the specified torque setting.

9 Refit the link rods to the ends of the anti-roll bar using new retaining nuts, tighten to the specified torque setting.

10 Refit the front subframe assembly as described in Section 7.

8.5a Remove the clamps from the rubber bushes . . .

11 Refit the roadwheels if not already done, then lower the vehicle to the ground and tighten the roadwheel bolts to the specified torque setting.

9 Rear hub bearings – checking and renewal

Note: *The rear hub bearing and integral ABS wheel speed sensor is a sealed unit and no repairs are possible. If the bearing is worn or the speed sensor is faulty, a new bearing assembly must be obtained.*

Checking

1 Chock the front wheels then jack up the rear of the car and securely support it on axle stands (see *Jacking and vehicle support*). Remove the roadwheel.

2 Remove the brake disc as described in Chapter 9.

3 A dial test indicator (DTI) will be required to measure the amount of radial and lateral run-out in the bearing. Zero the indicator on the outer edge of the hub flange.

4 Lever the hub in and out and measure the amount of play in the bearing.

5 To measure lateral run-out, locate the probe on the surface of the hub which contacts the disc. To measure radial run-out, locate the probe on the outer perimeter of the hub so that it is pointing towards the centre of the hub.

6 Slowly turn the hub and note the maximum amount of run-out. If the run-out exceeds the amount given in the Specifications, renew the hub bearing unit as described below.

7 Remove the indicator and refit the brake disc with reference to Chapter 9.

8 Refit the roadwheel, then lower the vehicle to the ground and tighten the roadwheel bolts to the specified torque.

Renewal

Note: *New hub bearing retaining nuts will be required for refitting.*

9 Chock the front wheels then jack up the rear of the car and securely support it on axle stands (see *Jacking and vehicle support*). Remove the roadwheel.

8.5b . . . then remove the bushes and inspect for wear

10 Remove the rear brake disc as described in Chapter 9.

11 Disconnect the wiring for the ABS wheel speed sensor located on the inside of the bearing assembly **(see illustration)**.

12 Attach the brake caliper carrier plate to the rear coil spring with a plastic cable tie to prevent straining the hydraulic brake line.

13 Support the bearing assembly and unscrew the four mounting nuts on the inside of the trailing arm. Withdraw the bearing and brake shield from the rear trailing arm. Note that the locating studs are spaced so that the bearing will only fit in one position.

14 Thoroughly clean the trailing arm, bearing unit and brake shield mating faces, then place the shield in position on the bearing unit.

15 Refit the bearing unit and brake shield to the trailing arm, and screw on four new retaining nuts.

16 Tighten the retaining nuts progressively to the specified Stage 1 torque setting using a torque wrench, and then through the specified Stage 2 and Stage 3 angles, using an angle tightening gauge.

17 Reconnect the ABS wheel speed sensor wiring connector.

18 Refit the rear brake disc as described in Chapter 9.

10 Rear shock absorber – removal, inspection and refitting

Note: *Always renew shock absorbers in pairs to maintain good road handling.*

Removal

1 Chock the front wheels then jack up the rear of the car and securely support it on axle stands (see *Jacking and vehicle support*). Remove the rear roadwheels.

2 Using a trolley jack, slightly raise the trailing arm on the relevant side.

3 Unscrew and remove the shock absorber lower mounting bolt from the trailing arm **(see illustration)**.

4 Support the shock absorber, then unscrew and remove the upper mounting bolt and withdraw the shock absorber from the underbody bracket **(see illustration)**.

Inspection

5 The shock absorber can be tested by clamping the lower mounting eye in a vice, then fully extending and compressing the shock absorber several times. Any evidence of jerky movement or lack of resistance indicates the need for renewal.

6 Examine the mounting rubbers in the shock absorber for excessive wear.

7 If the shock absorber or its mounting rubbers are worn excessively, renew the complete shock absorber.

Refitting

8 Refitting is a reversal of removal, but tighten the mounting bolts to the specified torque.

11 Rear suspension coil spring – removal and refitting

Note: *Due to the design of the rear suspension, it is important to note that only one coil spring should be removed at a time. Note that the rear springs should be renewed in pairs.*

Removal

1 Chock the front wheels then jack up the rear of the car and securely support it on axle stands (see *Jacking and vehicle support*). Remove the rear roadwheels.

2 Using a trolley jack, slightly raise the trailing arm on the relevant side.

3 Unscrew and remove the shock absorber lower mounting bolt from the trailing arm **(see illustration 10.3)**.

9.11 Disconnecting the ABS wiring from the inside of the rear hub

4 Carefully lower the trailing arm as far as possible without straining the brake flexible hoses leading to the rear brakes.

5 Remove the coil spring and spring seats from the underbody and trailing arm, and withdraw from under the vehicle. Note that the upper spring seat incorporates a damper buffer **(see illustrations)**.

Refitting

6 Refitting is a reversal of removal, but note the following points.

a) Ensure that the spring locates correctly on the upper and lower seats, as well as on the trailing arm and underbody.

b) Tighten the shock absorber lower mounting bolt to the specified torque.

c) If both springs are being renewed, repeat the procedure on the remaining side of the vehicle.

10.3 Unscrew and remove the shock absorber lower mounting bolt from the trailing arm . . .

10.4 . . . and the upper mounting bolt from the underbody bracket

11.5a Remove the rear coil spring, together with the spring seats . . .

11.5b . . . then remove the upper spring seat . . .

11.5c . . . and lower spring seat

12.2 Unclip and remove the centre console access panel

12.3 Unclip the cover from around the handbrake lever

12.4 Handbrake cable adjuster nut (arrowed)

12 Rear suspension torsion beam and trailing arms – removal and refitting

Note: *New front mounting bracket retaining bolts will be required for refitting.*

Removal

1 Chock the front wheels then jack up the rear of the car and securely support it on axle stands (see *Jacking and vehicle support*). Remove the rear roadwheels.
2 From inside the vehicle, unclip and remove the access panel in the centre console, beneath the handbrake lever **(see illustration)**.
3 Unclip the cover from around the handbrake lever **(see illustration)**.
4 Move the handbrake lever to the fully released position, then turn the cable adjuster nut anti-clockwise to remove all tension from the cables **(see illustration)**.
5 Working on each side in turn, use a screwdriver to push the handbrake operating lever on the brake caliper downwards, and detach the cable end fitting from the lever **(see illustration)**.
6 Prise out the handbrake outer cable retaining clip and withdraw the handbrake cable from the caliper bracket **(see illustrations)**.
7 Remove the clips and disconnect the handbrake outer cables from the support brackets on the trailing arms. Also release the handbrake cables from the supports on the torsion beam.
8 Disconnect the ABS rear wheel speed sensor wiring from the rear hubs, and unclip the wiring from the torsion beam.
9 Remove the filler cap from the brake hydraulic fluid reservoir in the engine compartment, then tighten the cap down onto a piece of polythene sheeting. This will help prevent the fluid from draining from the system when the rear brake flexible hoses are disconnected.
10 Unscrew the union nuts and disconnect the rear brake hydraulic pipes from the flexible hoses at the support brackets on the trailing arms on each side. Recover the retaining plates. Be prepared for some loss of brake fluid, and plug or tape over the ends of the lines and hoses to prevent entry of dust and dirt.
11 Support the weight of the torsion beam and trailing arms using two trolley jacks. Alternatively, one trolley jack and a length of wood may be used, but the help of an assistant will be required.
12 Unscrew the lower mounting bolts and detach both shock absorbers from the torsion beam.
13 Carefully lower the torsion beam until it is possible to remove the coil springs and spring seats. Note that the upper spring seats incorporate buffers.
14 Make sure that the torsion beam is supported, then unscrew and remove the front mounting bracket bolts from the underbody **(see illustration)**. Note that new bolts will be required for refitting.
15 Lower the torsion beam to the ground and remove it from under the vehicle.
16 The brake components can be removed from the trailing arms, referring to the relevant Sections of Chapter 9. The hub bearing units can be removed with reference to Section 9.
17 If necessary, the front mounting brackets can be removed after unscrewing the retaining nut and withdrawing the centre through bolt. Note that a new nut and bolt will be required for refitting. Renewal of the front mounting bushes is a complex operation requiring numerous special tools and a hydraulic press. Bush renewal should therefore be entrusted to a Vauxhall/Opel dealer.

Refitting

18 Refit any components that were removed from the torsion beam, referring to the relevant Sections of this Chapter and Chapter 9, as applicable. If the front mounting brackets were removed from the trailing arms, refit the brackets using new nuts and bolts, but only tighten the nuts lightly at this stage.

12.5 Push the handbrake operating lever on the brake caliper downwards, and detach the cable end fitting from the lever

12.6a Prise out the handbrake outer cable retaining clip . . .

12.6b . . . and withdraw the handbrake cable from the caliper bracket

12.14 Rear suspension torsion beam front mounting bracket

19 Check the condition of the threads in the front mounting bracket captive nuts on the underbody. If necessary, use a tap to clean out the threads.
20 Support the torsion beam on the trolley jacks, and position the assembly under the rear of the vehicle.
21 Raise the jacks, and fit the new mounting bracket bolts. Do not fully tighten the bolts at this stage.
22 If the front mounting brackets have been removed from the trailing arms, position the torsion beam so that the distance between the coil spring contact surfaces on the trailing arms and underbody is 173.0 ± 10.0 mm. With the torsion beam in this position, tighten the front mounting bracket centre bolts on each side to the specified torque and angle settings in the stages given.
23 Fully tighten the front mounting bracket-to-underbody bolts to the specified torque and angle settings in the stages given.
24 Locate the upper and lower seats on the coil springs, then refit the springs on the torsion beam.
25 Raise the torsion beam until the shock absorber lower mounting bolts can be inserted. Tighten the bolts to the specified torque.
26 Refit the brake hydraulic pipes and flexible hoses together with the retaining plates and tighten the union nuts to the specified torque.
27 Clip the wiring to the torsion beam and reconnect it to the ABS wheel speed sensors.
28 Reconnect the handbrake cables to the caliper levers and fit the cables in the supports.
29 Bleed the complete brake hydraulic system, as described in Chapter 9.
30 Adjust the handbrake cable as described in Chapter 1, then refit the handbrake lever cover and centre console access panel.
31 Refit the roadwheels and lower the vehicle to the ground.

13 Steering wheel – removal and refitting

Warning: Make sure that the airbag safety recommendations given in Chapter 12 are followed to prevent personal injury.
Note: *A new steering wheel retaining bolt will be required for refitting.*

Removal

1 Remove the airbag as described in Chapter 12.
2 Set the front wheels in the straight-ahead position, then lock the column in position after removing the ignition key.
3 Disconnect the wiring harness connector for the steering wheel switches **(see illustration)**.
4 Unscrew the Torx retaining bolt securing the steering wheel to the column **(see illustration)**.

13.3 Disconnect the wiring harness connector for the steering wheel switches

13.5 Alignment marks (arrowed) between the steering column shaft and steering wheel

5 Check that there are alignment marks between the steering column shaft and steering wheel **(see illustration)**. If no marks are visible, centre punch the wheel and column shaft to ensure correct alignment when refitting.
6 Grip the steering wheel with both hands and carefully rock it from side-to-side to release it from the splines on the steering column. As the steering wheel is being removed, guide the wiring for the airbag through the aperture in the wheel, taking care not to damage the wiring connectors **(see illustration)**.

Refitting

7 Refit the steering wheel, aligning the marks made prior to removal. Route the airbag wiring connectors through the steering wheel aperture. **Note:** *Make sure the guide pin on the steering wheel centre hub locates correctly with the contact unit on the steering column,*

14.4 Insert a thin rod into the lock housing hole, press the rod to release the detent spring, and pull out the lock cylinder

13.4 Unscrew the steering wheel retaining bolt (arrowed)

13.6 Guide the wiring for the airbag through the aperture in the wheel

and that the two arrows on the contact unit are aligned.
8 Clean the threads in the steering column, coat the new retaining bolt threads with locking compound, then fit the bolt and tighten to the specified torque.
9 Reconnect the wiring connector for the steering wheel switches.
10 Release the steering lock, and refit the airbag as described in Chapter 12.

14 Ignition switch/ steering column lock – removal and refitting

Removal

1 Disconnect the battery negative terminal (refer to *Disconnecting the battery* in the Reference Chapter).
2 Remove the steering column shrouds as described in Chapter 11.
3 Insert the ignition key into the ignition switch/lock, and turn it to position I.
4 Insert a thin rod into the hole in the lock housing, press the rod to release the detent spring, and pull out the lock cylinder using the key **(see illustration)**.

Refitting

5 Insert the ignition switch/lock into the lock housing, while the key is in position I. Remove the rod from the lock housing.
6 Refit steering column shrouds as described in Chapter 11, then reconnect the battery.

15.9a Unscrew the steering column lower fastening clamp bolt . . .

15.9b . . . and the two upper mounting bolts (arrowed) . . .

15.9c . . . then slide the column upward to disengage the locating tongue (arrowed)

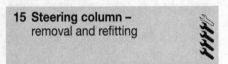

15 Steering column –
removal and refitting

Note: *It is recommended that all mounting nuts and bolts are renewed when refitting.*

Removal

1 Remove the steering wheel as described in Section 13.
2 Remove the steering column shrouds as described in Chapter 11.
3 Remove the lower trim panel beneath the facia on the driver's side as described in Chapter 11.
4 Release the two retaining clips and remove the facia lower panel above the pedals.
5 Remove the steering column electronics module as described in Chapter 12.

6 If applicable, make sure the steering column adjustment handle is in the locked position.
7 In the driver's footwell, unscrew the bolt securing the bottom of the steering column intermediate shaft to the steering gear pinion. Use paint or a suitable marker pen to make alignment marks between the intermediate shaft and the steering gear pinion, then pull the shaft from the pinion and position to one side **(see illustration 7.6)**.
8 Undo the retaining bolt and disconnect the earth cable from the column. Unscrew the plastic retainer and release the wiring harness from the side of the column.
9 Unscrew the steering column lower fastening clamp bolt, and the two upper mounting bolts. Slide the column upward to disengage the locating tongue, then withdraw the steering column from the facia crossmember, and remove the column from inside the vehicle **(see illustrations)**.

Refitting

10 Refitting is a reversal of removal, bearing in mind the following points:
 a) *Tighten all nuts and bolts to the specified torque. Note that new nuts/bolts should be used on all disturbed fittings.*
 b) *Ensure that the marks made on the steering column and intermediate shaft are correctly aligned.*
 c) *Refit the steering column electronics module as described in Chapter 12.*
 d) *Refit the steering column shrouds and facia footwell trim panel as described in Chapter 11.*
 e) *Refit the steering wheel as described in Section 13.*

16 Steering column intermediate shaft –
removal and refitting

Note: *New intermediate shaft upper and lower clamp bolts will be required for refitting.*

Removal

1 Set the front wheels in the straight-ahead position. Remove the ignition key and allow the steering lock to engage.
2 Remove the steering column shrouds as described in Chapter 11.
3 Remove the lower trim panel beneath the facia on the driver's side as described in Chapter 11.
4 Release the two retaining clips and remove the facia lower panel above the pedals.
5 Mark the steering column intermediate shaft upper and lower joints in relation to the steering column and steering gear pinion as an aid to refitting, then unscrew both clamp bolts **(see illustrations)**.
6 Compress the telescopic intermediate shaft and slide the joints from the column and pinion **(see illustration)**. Withdraw the intermediate shaft from inside the vehicle.
7 Inspect the intermediate shaft universal joints for excessive wear or damage. If either joint is worn or damaged, the complete shaft assembly must be renewed.

Refitting

8 Check that the front wheels and steering

16.5a Unscrew the intermediate shaft upper clamp bolt (arrowed) . . .

16.5b . . . and lower clamp bolt (arrowed) . . .

16.6a Separate the intermediate shaft from the steering column . . .

16.6b . . . and steering gear pinion

wheel are still in the straight-ahead position, and that the steering wheel is still locked.

9 Slide the intermediate shaft lower joint onto the steering gear pinion, aligning the previously-made marks. Note that it will not be possible to insert the clamp bolt if the splines are not correctly aligned. Insert the new clamp bolt and tighten to the specified torque.

10 Slide the upper end of the intermediate shaft onto the column splines, aligning the previously-made marks. Insert the new clamp bolt and tighten to the specified torque.

11 Refit the steering column shrouds and facia footwell trim panel as described in Chapter 11.

17 Steering gear rubber gaiters – renewal

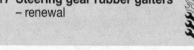

1 Remove the relevant track rod end as described in Section 21.

2 Remove the inner and outer securing clips **(see illustration)**, then slide the gaiter off the end of the track rod.

3 Thoroughly clean the track rod, then slide the new gaiter into position. Note that a groove is provided in the track rod for the outer end of the gaiter to locate in.

4 Fit the gaiter securing clips, using new clips if necessary, making sure that the gaiter is not twisted.

5 Refit the track rod end as described in Section 21.

6 Have the front wheel toe setting checked and adjusted at the earliest opportunity.

18 Steering gear – removal and refitting

Note: *New steering gear mounting bolts will be required for refitting.*

Removal

1 Set the front wheels in the straight-ahead position. Remove the ignition key and allow the steering lock to engage.

2 Remove the front subframe as described in Section 7.

3 On left-hand drive models, unbolt the rear engine mounting/torque link bracket from the subframe.

4 Where fitted, unbolt the support bracket for the pressure and return lines from the subframe.

5 Position a suitable container beneath the steering gear fluid unions to catch spilt hydraulic fluid.

6 Unscrew the union nuts and disconnect the fluid pressure and return lines from the steering gear **(see illustration)**.

7 Note the routing of the wiring loom then either disconnect it from the electro-hydraulic pump (where possible) or release it from the subframe. **Note:** *On pumps supplied by TRW,*

the wiring loom is supplied together with the pump and cannot be separated.

8 Unscrew the mounting nuts and withdraw the electro-hydraulic pump together with the fluid reservoir and pressure/return lines from the subframe and steering gear.

9 Unscrew the mounting bolts and remove the steering gear from the subframe **(see illustration)**. If necessary, remove the anti-roll bar first with reference to Section 8. The manufacturers recommend that the mounting bolts are renewed whenever removed.

10 If necessary, remove the track rod ends and track rods with reference to Sections 21 and 22. **Note:** *New steering gear assemblies are available from Vauxhall/Opel either with or without the track rods fitted. Also remove the rubber grommets from the pinion.*

Refitting

11 Refit the track rods and track rod ends with reference to Sections 22 and 21. Also refit the rubber grommets to the pinion.

12 Clean any dirt from the steering gear and subframe, then locate the steering gear in position. Insert the new mounting bolts and tighten to the specified torque, then through the specified angles.

13 Where removed, refit the anti-roll bar with reference to Section 8.

14 Refit the electro-hydraulic pump, together with the fluid reservoir and pressure/return lines to the subframe and steering gear, and tighten the mounting nuts to the specified torque.

15 Reconnect the wiring loom to the electro-hydraulic pump and attach it to the subframe.

16 Fit new rubber sealing rings to the pressure and return lines, then refit the lines to the steering gear and tighten the union nuts to the specified torque.

17 Where fitted, refit the support bracket for the pressure and return lines to the subframe and tighten the mounting bolts securely.

18 On left-hand drive models, refit the rear engine mounting/torque link bracket to the subframe and tighten to the specified torque.

19 Refit the front subframe as described in Section 7.

20 Bleed the power steering hydraulic system as described in Section 20.

21 Have the front wheel toe setting checked and adjusted at the earliest opportunity.

18.6 Hydraulic fluid line connections on the steering gear

17.2 Steering gear rubber gaiter outer securing clip

19 Electro-hydraulic power steering pump – removal and refitting

Removal

1 Remove the front subframe as described in Section 7.

2 Position a suitable container beneath the power steering pump fluid unions to catch spilt hydraulic fluid.

3 Disconnect the pressure and return lines from the power steering pump. Use a spanner to unscrew the pressure line union nut. If necessary, cut free the return line clip and update it with a screw-type clip.

4 Note the routing of the wiring loom then either disconnect it from the electro-hydraulic pump (where possible) or release it from the subframe. **Note:** *On pumps supplied by TRW, the wiring loom is supplied together with the pump and cannot be separated.*

5 Unscrew the mounting nuts and withdraw the electro-hydraulic pump, together with the bracket, wiring and fluid reservoir from the subframe and steering gear.

6 Unscrew the mounting nuts and remove the electro-hydraulic pump and mounting bushes from the bracket. Check the rubber mounting bushes for wear and damage and renew them if necessary.

Refitting

7 Refit the pump and bushes to the bracket and tighten the mounting nuts.

8 Refit the electro-hydraulic pump and

18.9 Steering gear mounting bolt retaining nut (arrowed)

21.2 Hold the track rod stationary while loosening the track rod end securing locknut

21.3 Unscrew the balljoint nut securing the track rod end to the steering arm on the swivel hub

21.4 Disconnect the track rod end from the steering arm on the swivel hub using a balljoint separator tool

bracket on the subframe and steering gear and tighten the mounting nuts to the specified torque.

9 Reconnect the wiring loom (where applicable) and secure it to the subframe. Make sure that the loom is routed as noted during removal.

10 Fit a new rubber sealing ring to the pressure line, then reconnect the pressure and return lines to the power steering pump. Tighten the pressure line union nut securely, and fit a new clip to the return line.

11 Refit the front subframe as described in Section 7

12 Bleed the power steering hydraulic system as described in Section 20.

20 Power steering hydraulic system – bleeding

Note: *The system must be bled at room temperature – do not bleed the system immediately after using the vehicle on the road.*

1 Check and top-up the power steering fluid level in the reservoir to the MAX mark on the dipstick as described in Chapter 1. If the system regularly requires more fluid, check the hoses for leaks.

2 Start the engine, then switch it off again after approximately five seconds. Repeat this procedure two more times, pausing briefly between each stop/start and maintaining the fluid level in the reservoir.

3 Now start the engine again and allow it to idle. Turn the steering to full left lock, then full right lock five times. Switch the engine off.

4 Recheck the fluid level in the reservoir and top-up if necessary. Remove the funnel and tube and refit the reservoir filler cap.

5 It is possible that some air may still remain in the system after bleeding but this will be expelled when the car is driven on the road.

21 Track rod end – removal and refitting

Note: *A new track rod end retaining nut will be needed for refitting.*

Removal

1 Apply the handbrake, then jack up the front of the vehicle, and support securely on axle stands (see *Jacking and vehicle support*). Remove the relevant roadwheel.

2 Loosen the track rod end securing locknut on the track rod a quarter turn, while holding the track rod stationary with a second spanner on the flats provided **(see illustration)**. If necessary, use a wire brush to remove rust from the nut and threads and lubricate the threads with penetrating oil before unscrewing the nut. As an additional check, measure the visible amount of threads on the track rod using vernier calipers. This will ensure the track rod end is refitted in the same position.

3 Unscrew and remove the balljoint nut securing the track rod end to the steering arm on the swivel hub **(see illustration)**.

4 Disconnect the track rod end balljoint from the steering arm on the swivel hub using a balljoint separator tool, taking care not to damage the balljoint boot **(see illustration)**.

5 Unscrew the track rod end from the track rod, counting the number of turns necessary to remove it and taking care not to disturb the locknut. **Note:** *The track rod ends are handed side-for-side. The right-hand track rod end is marked with an R and has a right-hand thread, whereas the left-hand one is marked with an L and has a **left-hand thread**.*

Refitting

6 Screw the track rod end onto the track rod the number of turns noted during removal. Check that the visible amount of threads on the track rod is as previously noted.

7 Insert the track rod end balljoint in the steering arm on the swivel hub, then fit the nut and tighten to the specified torque, then through the angles given. If the balljoint stud turns as the nut is being tightened, press down on the track rod end to force the stud into the arm.

8 Tighten the track rod end securing locknut on the track rod while holding the track rod stationary with a second spanner on the flats provided. If possible, tighten the nut to the specified torque using a special crow-foot adapter for the torque wrench.

9 Refit the roadwheel, then lower the vehicle to the ground, and tighten the wheelbolts.

10 Have the front wheel alignment checked and adjusted at the earliest opportunity.

22 Track rod – removal and refitting

Removal

1 Remove the track rod end from the relevant track rod as described in Section 21. Note, however, that on right-hand drive models it is necessary to remove both track rod ends and bellows when removing the left-hand track rod. Conversely, on left-hand drive models it is necessary to remove both track rod ends and bellows when removing the right-hand track rod.

2 Where necessary, remove the wheel arch liner or trim from under the wheel arch by removing the fasteners (see Chapter 11).

3 Release the clips and slide the rubber bellows from the steering gear and track rod. Remove the bellows from both sides where necessary (see paragraph 1). Where metal clips are fitted, either prise them free with a screwdriver, or carefully cut them off with a hacksaw.

4 Turn the steering on full lock so that the rack protrudes from the steering gear on the relevant side. Mark the inner joint housing and rack in relation to each other to indicate how tight it is (see paragraph 6).

5 Hold the rack stationary with a spanner on the flats provided, then unscrew and remove the track rod inner joint housing. Use either a large adjustable spanner or grips.

Refitting

6 Clean the threads and apply a little locking fluid to them, then screw the track rod inner joint housing into the rack and tighten to the specified torque. Because of its size and design, using a torque wrench may be difficult, in which case the joint housing should be tightened until the previously-made marks are aligned with each other.

7 Refit the bellows making sure that the inner end is pushed fully onto the steering gear and the outer end is seated in the groove on the track rod. Use new clips if necessary.

8 Where necessary, refit the wheel arch liner or trim.

9 Refit the track rod end(s) as described in Section 21.

10 Have the front wheel alignment checked and adjusted at the earliest opportunity.

23 Wheel alignment and steering angles – general information

Definitions

1 A car's steering and suspension geometry is defined in four basic settings – all angles are expressed in degrees (toe settings are also expressed as a measurement); the steering axis is defined as an imaginary line drawn through the axis of the suspension strut, extended where necessary to contact the ground.

2 Camber is the angle between each roadwheel and a vertical line drawn through its centre and tyre contact patch, when viewed from the front or rear of the car. Positive camber is when the roadwheels are tilted outwards from the vertical at the top; negative camber is when they are tilted inwards. Slight adjustment of the front camber angle is possible, by altering the position of the swivel hub at its attachment to the front suspension strut. The rear camber angle is not adjustable.

3 Castor is the angle between the steering axis and a vertical line drawn through each roadwheel's centre and tyre contact patch, when viewed from the side of the car. Positive castor is when the steering axis is tilted so that it contacts the ground ahead of the vertical; negative castor is when it contacts the ground behind the vertical. The castor angle is not adjustable.

4 Toe is the difference, viewed from above, between lines drawn through the roadwheel centres and the car's centre-line. 'Toe-in' is when the roadwheels point inwards, towards each other at the front, while 'toe-out' is when they splay outwards from each other at the front.

5 The front wheel toe setting is adjusted by screwing the track rod in or out of its balljoints, to alter the effective length of the track rod assembly. The rear wheel toe setting is not adjustable.

Checking and adjustment

6 Due to the special measuring equipment necessary to check the wheel alignment and steering angles, and the skill required to use it properly, the checking and adjustment of these settings is best left to a Vauxhall/ Opel dealer or similar expert. Note that most tyre-fitting shops now possess sophisticated checking equipment.

Chapter 11
Bodywork and fittings

Contents

Degrees of difficulty

Easy, suitable for novice with little experience 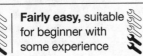	Fairly easy, suitable for beginner with some experience	Fairly difficult, suitable for competent DIY mechanic	Difficult, suitable for experienced DIY mechanic	Very difficult, suitable for expert DIY or professional

Specifications

Torque wrench settings	Nm	lbf ft
Front seat belt anchorage bolts	25	18
Front seat belt inertia reel nut	20	15
Front seat belt stalk and tensioner bolt	35	26
Front seat mounting bolts	35	26
Rear seat belt anchorage bolts	35	26
Rear seat belt inertia reel bolt	35	26
Rear seat belt stalk retaining bolts	35	26
Seat belt-to-height adjuster mounting bolts	30	22

1 General information

The bodyshell is made of pressed-steel sections, and is available in three- and five-door Hatchback, and Estate versions. Most components are welded together, but some use is made of structural adhesives; the front wings are bolted on.

The bonnet is made of aluminium, whereas the doors, and some other vulnerable panels, are made of zinc-coated metal. These are further protected by being coated with an anti-chip primer, prior to being sprayed.

Extensive use is made of plastic materials, mainly on the interior, but also in exterior components. The front and rear bumpers are injection-moulded from a synthetic material which is very strong and yet light. Plastic components such as wheel arch liners are fitted to the underside of the vehicle, to improve the body's resistance to corrosion.

2 Maintenance –
bodywork and underframe

The general condition of a vehicle's body-work is the one thing that significantly affects its value. Maintenance is easy, but needs to be regular. Neglect, particularly after minor damage, can lead quickly to further deterioration and costly repair bills. It is important also to keep watch on those parts of the vehicle not immediately visible, for instance the underside, inside all the wheel arches, and the lower part of the engine compartment.

The basic maintenance routine for the bodywork is washing – preferably with a lot of water, from a hose. This will remove all the loose solids which may have stuck to the vehicle. It is important to flush these off in such a way as to prevent grit from scratching the finish. The wheel arches and underframe need washing in the same way, to remove any accumulated mud, which will retain moisture and tend to encourage rust. Paradoxically enough, the best time to clean the underframe and wheel arches is in wet weather, when the mud is thoroughly wet and soft. In very wet weather, the underframe is usually cleaned of large accumulations automatically, and this is a good time for inspection.

Periodically, except on vehicles with a wax-based underbody protective coating, it is a good idea to have the whole of the underframe of the vehicle steam-cleaned, engine compartment included, so that a thorough inspection can be carried out to see what minor repairs and renovations are necessary. Steam-cleaning is available at many garages, and is necessary for the removal of the accumulation of oily grime, which sometimes is allowed to become thick

in certain areas. If steam-cleaning facilities are not available, there are some excellent grease solvents available which can be brush-applied; the dirt can then be simply hosed off. Note that these methods should not be used on vehicles with wax-based underbody protective coating, or the coating will be removed. Such vehicles should be inspected annually, preferably just prior to Winter, when the underbody should be washed down, and any damage to the wax coating repaired. Ideally, a completely fresh coat should be applied. It would also be worth considering the use of such wax-based protection for injection into door panels, sills, box sections, etc, as an additional safeguard against rust damage, where such protection is not provided by the vehicle manufacturer.

After washing paintwork, wipe off with a chamois leather to give an unspotted clear finish. A coat of clear protective wax polish will give added protection against chemical pollutants in the air. If the paintwork sheen has dulled or oxidised, use a cleaner/polisher combination to restore the brilliance of the shine. This requires a little effort, but such dulling is usually caused because regular washing has been neglected. Care needs to be taken with metallic paintwork, as special non-abrasive cleaner/polisher is required to avoid damage to the finish. Always check that the door and ventilator opening drain holes and pipes are completely clear, so that water can be drained out. Brightwork should be treated in the same way as paintwork. Windscreens and windows can be kept clear of the smeary film which often appears, by the use of proprietary glass cleaner. Never use any form of wax or other body or chromium polish on glass.

3 Maintenance of
upholstery and carpets –
general

Mats and carpets should be brushed or vacuum-cleaned regularly, to keep them free of grit. If they are badly stained, remove them from the vehicle for scrubbing or sponging, and make quite sure they are dry before refitting. Seats and interior trim panels can be kept clean by wiping with a damp cloth. If they do become stained (which can be more apparent on light-coloured upholstery), use a little liquid detergent and a soft nail brush to scour the grime out of the grain of the material. Do not forget to keep the headlining clean in the same way as the upholstery. When using liquid cleaners inside the vehicle, do not over-wet the surfaces being cleaned. Excessive damp could get into the seams and padded interior, causing stains, offensive odours or even rot.

If the inside of the vehicle gets wet accidentally, it is worthwhile taking some trouble to dry it out properly, particularly where carpets are involved. Do not leave oil or electric heaters inside the vehicle for this purpose.

4 Minor body damage –
repair

Minor scratches

If the scratch is very superficial, and does not penetrate to the metal of the bodywork, repair is very simple. Lightly rub the area of the scratch with a paintwork renovator, or a very fine cutting paste, to remove loose paint from the scratch, and to clear the surrounding bodywork of wax polish. Rinse the area with clean water.

Apply touch-up paint to the scratch using a fine paint brush; continue to apply fine layers of paint until the surface of the paint in the scratch is level with the surrounding paintwork. Allow the new paint at least two weeks to harden, then blend it into the surrounding paintwork by rubbing the scratch area with a paintwork renovator or a very fine cutting paste. Finally, apply wax polish.

Where the scratch has penetrated right through to the metal of the bodywork, causing the metal to rust, a different repair technique is required. Remove any loose rust from the bottom of the scratch with a penknife, then apply rust-inhibiting paint to prevent the formation of rust in the future. Using a rubber or nylon applicator, fill the scratch with bodystopper paste. If required, this paste can be mixed with cellulose thinners to provide a very thin paste which is ideal for filling narrow scratches. Before the stopper-paste in the scratch hardens, wrap a piece of smooth cotton rag around the top of a finger. Dip the finger in cellulose thinners, and quickly sweep it across the surface of the stopper-paste in the scratch; this will ensure that the surface of the stopper-paste is slightly hollowed. The scratch can now be painted over as described earlier in this Section.

Dents

When deep denting of the vehicle's bodywork has taken place, the first task is to pull the dent out, until the affected bodywork almost attains its original shape. There is little point in trying to restore the original shape completely, as the metal in the damaged area will have stretched on impact, and cannot be reshaped fully to its original contour. It is better to bring the level of the dent up to a point which is about 3 mm below the level of the surrounding bodywork. In cases where the dent is very shallow anyway, it is not worth trying to pull it out at all. If the underside of the dent is accessible, it can be hammered out gently from behind, using a mallet with a wooden or plastic head. Whilst doing this, hold a suitable block of wood firmly against the outside of the panel, to absorb the impact from the hammer blows and thus prevent a large area of the bodywork from being 'belled-out'.

Should the dent be in a section of the

bodywork which has a double skin, or some other factor making it inaccessible from behind, a different technique is called for. Drill several small holes through the metal inside the area – particularly in the deeper section. Then screw long self-tapping screws into the holes, just sufficiently for them to gain a good purchase in the metal. Now the dent can be pulled out by pulling on the protruding heads of the screws with a pair of pliers.

The next stage of the repair is the removal of the paint from the damaged area, and from an inch or so of the surrounding 'sound' bodywork. This is accomplished most easily by using a wire brush or abrasive pad on a power drill, although it can be done just as effectively by hand, using sheets of abrasive paper. To complete the preparation for filling, score the surface of the bare metal with a screwdriver or the tang of a file, or alternatively, drill small holes in the affected area. This will provide a really good 'key' for the filler paste.

To complete the repair, see the Section on filling and respraying.

Rust holes or gashes

Remove all paint from the affected area, and from an inch or so of the surrounding 'sound' bodywork, using an abrasive pad or a wire brush on a power drill. If these are not available, a few sheets of abrasive paper will do the job most effectively. With the paint removed, you will be able to judge the severity of the corrosion, and therefore decide whether to renew the whole panel (if this is possible) or to repair the affected area. New body panels are not as expensive as most people think, and it is often quicker and more satisfactory to fit a new panel than to attempt to repair large areas of corrosion.

Remove all fittings from the affected area, except those which will act as a guide to the original shape of the damaged bodywork (eg headlight shells etc). Then, using tin snips or a hacksaw blade, remove all loose metal and any other metal badly affected by corrosion. Hammer the edges of the hole inwards, in order to create a slight depression for the filler paste.

Wire-brush the affected area to remove the powdery rust from the surface of the remaining metal. Paint the affected area with rust-inhibiting paint, if the back of the rusted area is accessible, treat this also.

Before filling can take place, it will be necessary to block the hole in some way. This can be achieved by the use of aluminium or plastic mesh, or aluminium tape.

Aluminium or plastic mesh, or glass-fibre matting, is probably the best material to use for a large hole. Cut a piece to the approximate size and shape of the hole to be filled, then position it in the hole so that its edges are below the level of the surrounding bodywork. It can be retained in position by several blobs of filler paste around its periphery.

Aluminium tape should be used for small or very narrow holes. Pull a piece off the roll,

trim it to the approximate size and shape required, then pull off the backing paper (if used) and stick the tape over the hole; it can be overlapped if the thickness of one piece is insufficient. Burnish down the edges of the tape with the handle of a screwdriver or similar, to ensure that the tape is securely attached to the metal underneath.

Filling and respraying

Before using this Section, see the Sections on dent, deep scratch, rust holes and gash repairs.

Many types of bodyfiller are available, but generally speaking, those proprietary kits which contain a tin of filler paste and a tube of resin hardener are best for this type of repair. A wide, flexible plastic or nylon applicator will be found invaluable for imparting a smooth and well-contoured finish to the surface of the filler.

Mix up a little filler on a clean piece of card or board – measure the hardener carefully (follow the maker's instructions on the pack), otherwise the filler will set too rapidly or too slowly. Using the applicator, apply the filler paste to the prepared area; draw the applicator across the surface of the filler to achieve the correct contour and to level the surface. As soon as a contour that approximates to the correct one is achieved, stop working the paste – if you carry on too long, the paste will become sticky and begin to 'pick-up' on the applicator. Continue to add thin layers of filler paste at 20-minute intervals, until the level of the filler is just proud of the surrounding bodywork.

Once the filler has hardened, the excess can be removed using a metal plane or file. From then on, progressively-finer grades of abrasive paper should be used, starting with a 40-grade production paper, and finishing with a 400-grade wet-and-dry paper. Always wrap the abrasive paper around a flat rubber, cork, or wooden block – otherwise the surface of the filler will not be completely flat. During the smoothing of the filler surface, the wet-and-dry paper should be periodically rinsed in water. This will ensure that a very smooth finish is imparted to the filler at the final stage.

At this stage, the 'dent' should be surrounded by a ring of bare metal, which in turn should be encircled by the finely 'feathered' edge of the good paintwork. Rinse the repair area with clean water, until all of the dust produced by the rubbing-down operation has gone.

Spray the whole area with a light coat of primer – this will show up any imperfections in the surface of the filler. Repair these imperfections with fresh filler paste or bodystopper, and once more smooth the surface with abrasive paper. Repeat this spray-and-repair procedure until you are satisfied that the surface of the filler, and the feathered edge of the paintwork, are perfect. Clean the repair area with clean water, and allow to dry fully.

The repair area is now ready for final spraying. Paint spraying must be carried out in a warm, dry, windless and dust-free atmosphere. This condition can be created artificially if you have access to a large indoor working area, but if you are forced to work in the open, you will have to pick your day very carefully. If you are working indoors, dousing the floor in the work area with water will help to settle the dust which would otherwise be in the atmosphere. If the repair area is confined to one body panel, mask off the surrounding panels; this will help to minimise the effects of a slight mis-match in paint colours. Bodywork fittings (eg chrome strips, door handles etc) will also need to be masked off. Use genuine masking tape, and several thicknesses of newspaper, for the masking operations.

Before commencing to spray, agitate the aerosol can thoroughly, then spray a test area (an old tin, or similar) until the technique is mastered. Cover the repair area with a thick coat of primer; the thickness should be built up using several thin layers of paint, rather than one thick one. Using 400-grade wet-and-dry paper, rub down the surface of the primer until it is really smooth. While doing this, the work area should be thoroughly doused with water, and the wet-and-dry paper periodically rinsed in water. Allow to dry before spraying on more paint.

Spray on the top coat, again building up the thickness by using several thin layers of paint. Start spraying at one edge of the repair area, and then, using a side-to-side motion, work until the whole repair area and about 2 inches of the surrounding original paintwork is covered. Remove all masking material 10 to 15 minutes after spraying on the final coat of paint.

Allow the new paint at least two weeks to harden, then, using a paintwork renovator, or a very fine cutting paste, blend the edges of the paint into the existing paintwork. Finally, apply wax polish.

Plastic components

With the use of more and more plastic body components by the vehicle manufacturers (eg bumpers. spoilers, and in some cases major body panels), rectification of more serious damage to such items has become a matter of either entrusting repair work to a specialist in this field, or renewing complete components. Repair of such damage by the DIY owner is not really feasible, owing to the cost of the equipment and materials required for effecting such repairs. The basic technique involves making a groove along the line of the crack in the plastic, using a rotary burr in a power drill. The damaged part is then welded back together, using a hot-air gun to heat up and fuse a plastic filler rod into the groove. Any excess plastic is then removed, and the area rubbed down to a smooth finish. It is important that a filler rod of the correct plastic is used, as body components can be made of a variety of different types (eg polycarbonate, ABS, polypropylene).

6.2a Undo the upper screw . . .

6.2b . . . and lower screw each side securing the bumper to the wheel arch

6.3 Release the three plastic rivets (arrowed) securing the lower centre of the bumper to the subframe

6.4 Pull out the centre pin and extract the expanding rivet each side

Damage of a less serious nature (abrasions, minor cracks etc) can be repaired by the DIY owner using a two-part epoxy filler repair material. Once mixed in equal proportions, this is used in similar fashion to the bodywork filler used on metal panels. The filler is usually cured in twenty to thirty minutes, ready for sanding and painting.

If the owner is renewing a complete component himself, or if he has repaired it with epoxy filler, he will be left with the problem of finding a suitable paint for finishing which is compatible with the type of plastic used. At one time, the use of a universal paint was not possible, owing to the complex range of plastics encountered in body component applications. Standard paints, generally speaking, will not bond to plastic or rubber satisfactorily. However, it is now possible to obtain a plastic body parts finishing kit which

consists of a pre-primer treatment, a primer and coloured top coat. Full instructions are normally supplied with a kit, but basically, the method of use is to first apply the pre-primer to the component concerned, and allow it to dry for up to 30 minutes. Then the primer is applied, and left to dry for about an hour before finally applying the special-coloured top coat. The result is a correctly-coloured component, where the paint will flex with the plastic or rubber, a property that standard paint does not normally possess.

5 Major body damage repair – general

Where serious damage has occurred, or large areas need renewal due to neglect, it means that

complete new panels will need welding-in, and this is best left to professionals. If the damage is due to impact, it will also be necessary to check completely the alignment of the bodyshell, and this can only be carried out accurately by a Vauxhall/Opel dealer, or accident repair specialist, using special jigs. If the body is left misaligned, it is primarily dangerous as the car will not handle properly, and secondly, uneven stresses will be imposed on the steering, suspension and possibly transmission, causing abnormal wear, or complete failure, particularly to such items as the tyres.

6 Front bumper – removal and refitting

Removal

1 Remove the radiator grille as described in Section 20.
2 Working under the wheel arch, undo the four retaining screws (two on each side) securing the wheel arch liner to the bumper (see illustrations).
3 Release the three plastic rivets securing the lower centre of the bumper to the front subframe (see illustration).
4 Pull out the centre pin and extract the expanding rivet each side, adjacent to the headlight (see illustration).
5 Where applicable, disconnect the foglight wiring connectors and headlight washer hoses from the rear of the bumper. Unclip the outside temperature sensor from the centre ventilation grille.
6 With the aid of an assistant, pull the bumper upward and outward at the sides to disengage the guide rails (see illustration).
7 Unclip the bumper from the four front guide rails and carefully lift it off the car (see illustration).

Refitting

8 Refitting is a reversal of the removal procedure, ensuring that all bumper fasteners are securely tightened.

7 Rear bumper – removal and refitting

Removal

Saloon and Hatchback models

1 Remove the rear light cluster each side as described in Chapter 12.
2 Remove the rear number plate.
3 Push out the centre pin and extract the expanding rivet each side securing the lower inner corner of the mudflap to the base of the bumper on each side (see illustration).
4 From under the wheel arch undo the three screws on each side and remove both mudflaps (see illustrations).

6.6 Pull the bumper upward and outward at the sides to disengage the guide rails

6.7 Unclip the bumper from the four front guide rails and lift it off the car

7.3 Push out the centre pin and extract the expanding rivet securing the mudflaps to the base of the bumper

5 Undo the screw on each side above the mudflap location, securing the wheel arch liner to the bumper **(see illustration)**.
6 Undo the two bumper rear retaining screws in the number plate aperture **(see illustration)**.
7 Release the tailgate weatherstrip from the upper edge of the bumper **(see illustration)**.
8 On models with parking distance sensors, disconnect the distance sensor main wiring connector from the underside of the bumper.
9 With the aid of an assistant, pull the bumper upward and outward at the sides to disengage the side guide rails **(see illustration)**.
10 Pull the bumper rearwards to disengage the rear guide rails and centre guide rails **(see illustration)**.
11 When sufficient clearance exists, release the number plate light bulbholders from the light units. The bulbholders are a bayonet fitting in the light units **(see illustration)**.

7.7 Release the tailgate weatherstrip from the upper edge of the bumper

7.11 Release the number plate light bulbholders from the light units

7.4a Undo the three screws (arrowed) on each side . . .

7.5 Undo the screw each side (arrowed) securing the wheel arch liner to the bumper

12 Carefully lift the bumper off the car **(see illustration)**.

Estate models

13 Remove the rear light cluster each side as described in Chapter 12.

7.9 Pull the bumper upward and outward at the sides to disengage the side guide rails

7.12 Carefully lift the bumper off the car

7.4b . . . and remove both mudflaps

7.6 Undo the two screws in the number plate aperture

14 Undo the retaining screw each side in the rear light cluster aperture **(see illustration)**.
15 Working under the wheel arch, undo the four retaining screws (two on each side)

7.10 Pull the bumper rearwards to disengage the rear guide rails and centre guide rails

7.14 Undo the retaining screw (arrowed) each side in the rear light cluster aperture

7.15a Undo the lower screw . . .

7.15b . . . and the upper screw each side, securing the wheel arch liner to the bumper

7.16 Pull out the centre pin and extract the expanding rivet each side securing the bumper to the underbody brackets

7.18 Pull the bumper upward and outward at the sides to disengage the side guide rails

7.19 Pull the bumper rearwards to disengage the rear guide rails and carefully lift it off the car

securing the wheel arch liner to the bumper **(see illustrations)**.

16 Pull out the centre pin and extract the expanding rivet each side securing the lower centre of the bumper to the underbody brackets **(see illustration)**.

17 Release the tailgate weatherstrip from the upper edge of the bumper.

18 With the aid of an assistant, pull the bumper upward and outward at the sides to disengage the side guide rails **(see illustration)**.

19 Pull the bumper rearwards to disengage the rear guide rails and carefully lift it off the car **(see illustration)**.

Refitting

20 Refitting is a reversal of the removal procedure, ensuring that all bumper fasteners are securely tightened.

9.4a Insert a small screwdriver through the gap between the release handle and mounting bracket . . .

8 Bonnet and support strut – removal, refitting and adjustment

Bonnet

Removal

1 Open the bonnet, and have an assistant support it.

2 Using a marker pen or paint, mark around the hinge positions on the bonnet.

3 Using a screwdriver prise out the retaining spring clip and disconnect the support strut from the bonnet.

4 With the aid of the assistant, unscrew the bolts securing the bonnet to the hinges on both sides.

5 Lift off the bonnet taking care not to damage the vehicle paintwork.

Refitting

6 Align the marks made on the bonnet before removal with the hinges, then refit and tighten the bonnet securing bolts.

7 Check the bonnet adjustment as follows.

Adjustment

8 Close the bonnet, and check that there is an equal gap (approximately 4.0 mm) at each side, between the bonnet and the wing panels. Check also that the bonnet sits flush in relation to the surrounding body panels.

9 The bonnet should close smoothly and positively without excessive pressure. If this is not the case, adjustment will be required.

10 To adjust the bonnet alignment, loosen the bonnet-to-hinge mounting bolts, and move the bonnet on the bolts as required (the bolt holes in the hinges are enlarged). If necessary, the scissor-type hinge mounting bolts may be loosened as well. Access to the hinge retaining bolts can be gained after removing the water deflector (see Section 20). To adjust the bonnet front height in relation to the front wings, adjustable rubber bump stops are fitted to the front corners of the bonnet. These may be screwed in or out as necessary. After making an adjustment, the bonnet striker must be adjusted so that the lock spring holds the bonnet firmly against the rubber bump stops. Loosen the locknut and screw the striker in or out as necessary.

Support strut

Removal

11 Open the bonnet, and have an assistant support it.

12 Using a screwdriver prise out the retaining spring clips and disconnect the strut from the bonnet and body. Note which way round the strut is fitted.

Refitting

13 Refitting is a reversal of removal.

9 Bonnet release cable – removal and refitting

Removal

1 Remove the driver's side lower trim panel as described in Section 26.

2 Remove the water deflector as described in Section 20.

3 Remove the bonnet lock spring as described in Section 10.

4 Insert a small screwdriver through the gap between the release handle and mounting bracket, to depress the detent lug **(see illustrations)**. With the lug depressed, lift the release handle off the mounting bracket.

5 Detach the outer cable from the release handle frame, then slip the inner cable end fitting out of the lever **(see illustrations)**.

6 Release the cable from the support clips

9.4b . . . to depress the detent lug (arrowed)

9.5a Detach the outer cable from the release handle frame . . .

9.5b . . . then slip the inner cable end fitting out of the lever

and brackets in the engine compartment, then withdraw the cable through the rubber grommet and into the passenger compartment. As an aid to refitting, tie a length of string to the cable before removing it and leave the string in position ready for refitting.

Refitting

7 Refitting is a reversal of removal, but tie the string to the end of the cable, and use the string to pull the cable into position. Ensure that the cable is routed as noted before removal, and make sure that the grommet is correctly seated. On completion, refit the water deflector and the interior trim panels as described in Section 20 and 26.

10 Bonnet lock spring – removal and refitting

Removal

1 The bonnet is held in its locked position with a strong spring which engages with the striker on the front edge of the bonnet. The release cable is connected to the end of the spring.

2 The striker may be removed from the bonnet by unscrewing the locknut, however measure its fitted length first as a guide to refitting it.

3 To remove the lock spring, disengage the spring leg from the front crossmember, slide the other end of the spring off the release cable and remove the spring from the crossmember **(see illustrations)**.

Refitting

4 Refitting is a reversal of removal.

11 Door – removal, refitting and adjustment

Front door

Removal

1 To remove a door, open it fully and support it under its lower edge on blocks or axle stands covered with pads of rag.

10.3a Disengage the bonnet lock spring leg from the front crossmember . . .

2 Disconnect the wiring connector from the front edge of the door. To release the connector, pull out the locking clip, then twist the collar and pull the connector from the socket in the door **(see illustrations)**.

11.2a Pull out the locking clip . . .

11.3 The front door check arm pivot is attached to the A-pillar with a Torx bolt

10.3b . . . slide the other end off the release cable and remove the spring from the crossmember

3 Unscrew the Torx bolt securing the door check arm pivot to the A-pillar **(see illustration)**.

4 Where applicable, remove the plastic covers from the hinge pins **(see illustration)**,

11.2b . . . then twist the collar and pull the connector from the socket

11.4 Removing the plastic covers from the front door hinge pins

11.8 Front door lock striker on the B-pillar

11.9 Disconnecting the wiring from the front edge of the rear door

11.10 Rear door check arm

11.11 Removing the plastic covers from the rear door hinge pins

11.15 Rear door lock striker on the C-pillar

then drive out the pins using a punch. Have an assistant support the door as the pins are driven out, then withdraw the door from the vehicle. If renewing a door, transfer all the serviceable fixings to the new door.

Refitting

5 Refitting is a reversal of removal.

Adjustment

6 The door hinges are welded onto the door frame and the body pillar, so that there is no provision for adjustment or alignment.

7 If the door can be moved up and down on its hinges due to wear in the hinge pins or their holes, it may be possible to drill out the holes and fit slightly oversize pins. Consult a Vauxhall/Opel dealer for further advice.

8 Door closure may be adjusted by altering the position of the lock striker on the body pillar, using an Allen key or a hexagon bit (see illustration).

Rear door

Removal

9 Disconnect the wiring connector from the front edge of the door (see illustration). To release the connector, twist the locking collar, then pull the connector from the socket in the door.

10 Unscrew the Torx bolt securing the door check arm pivot to the B-pillar (see illustration).

11 Where applicable, remove the plastic covers from the hinge pins (see illustration), then drive out the pins using a punch. Have an assistant support the door as the pins are driven out, then withdraw the door from the vehicle. If renewing a door, transfer all the serviceable fixings to the new door.

Refitting

12 Refitting is a reversal of removal.

Adjustment

13 The door hinges are welded onto the door frame and the body pillar, so that there is no provision for adjustment or alignment.

14 If the door can be moved up and down on its hinges due to wear in the hinge pins or their holes, it may be possible to drill out the holes and fit slightly oversize pins. Consult a Vauxhall/Opel dealer for further advice.

15 Door closure may be adjusted by altering the position of the lock striker on the body pillar, using an Allen key or a hexagon bit (see illustration).

12 Door inner trim panel – removal and refitting

Front door

Removal

1 Carefully prise off the door mirror interior trim panel to release the three retaining clips (see illustration).

2 Remove the foam insulation from the mirror interior trim panel and disconnect the speaker wiring connector (see illustrations).

3 Using a plastic wedge or similar tool, carefully prise off the door grab handle plastic cover and undo the two screws now exposed (see illustrations).

4 Pull open the door interior handle and prise off the trim plate using a small screwdriver. Undo the screw in the trim panel aperture (see illustrations).

12.1 Carefully prise off the door mirror interior trim panel

12.2a Remove the foam insulation from the mirror interior trim panel . . .

12.2b . . . and disconnect the speaker wiring connector

12.3a Prise off the door grab handle plastic cover . . .

12.3b . . . and undo the two screws (arrowed) now exposed

12.4a Pull open the door interior handle and prise off the trim plate . . .

12.4b . . . then undo the screw (arrowed) in the trim panel aperture

12.5a Undo the lower screws (arrowed) . . .

12.5b . . . and rear screws (arrowed) securing the edge of the trim panel to the door

5 Undo the two lower screws (3 lower screws on 3-door Hatchback models) and two rear screws securing the edge of the trim panel to the door **(see illustrations)**.

6 Using a wide-bladed screwdriver or removal tool, carefully prise the bottom and sides of the panel away from door to release the internal clips **(see illustration)**. Lift the panel upward to release it from the window aperture.

7 Once the panel is free, reach behind and release the door lock operating cable from the interior handle. Disengage the inner cable end from the handle lever **(see illustration)**.

8 Disconnect the wiring connectors from the window control switch and door interior handle, then remove the trim panel from the car **(see illustrations)**.

Refitting

9 Refitting is a reversal of removal.

Rear door

Removal

10 Where a manual window regulator is fitted, locate a cloth rag between the handle and the trim panel and pull it to one side to release the spring clip. Remove the handle from the splined shaft and refit the spring clip to the handle.

11 Using a plastic wedge or similar tool, carefully prise off the door grab handle plastic cover and undo the two screws now exposed **(see illustrations 12.3a and 12.3b)**.

12 Pull open the door interior handle and prise off the trim plate using a small screwdriver.

Undo the screw in the trim panel aperture **(see illustrations 12.4a and 12.4b)**.

13 Undo the screw securing the lower edge

12.6 Carefully prise the bottom and sides of the panel away from door to release the internal clips

12.8a Disconnect the wiring connectors from the window control switch . . .

of the trim panel to the door **(see illustration)**.

14 Using a wide-bladed screwdriver or removal

12.7 Reach behind the panel and release the door lock operating cable from the interior handle

12.8b . . . and door interior handle

12.13 Undo the screw (arrowed) securing the lower edge of the rear trim panel to the door

12.14 Carefully prise the bottom and sides of the panel away from door to release the internal clips

13.3a Remove the screw (arrowed) from the rear edge of the door . . .

13.3b . . . to gain access to the handle locking screw (arrowed)

tool, carefully prise the bottom and sides of the panel away from door to release the internal clips. Lift the panel upward to release it from the window aperture **(see illustration)**.

15 Once the panel is free, reach behind and release the door lock operating cable from the

interior handle. Disengage the inner cable end from the handle lever **(see illustration 12.7)**.

16 On models with electric windows, disconnect the wiring connector from the window control switch, then remove the trim panel from the car.

13.4 With the exterior door handle held open, turn the handle locking screw anti-clockwise until it reaches its stop

13.5 Withdraw the fixed part of the handle, containing the lock cylinder, from the door

13.6 Disengage the exterior handle front pivot from the frame and remove the handle from the door

13.12a Prise out the blanking cap from the rear edge of the door . . .

Refitting

17 Refitting is a reversal of removal.

13 Door handles and lock components – removal and refitting

Door interior handle

Removal

1 The door interior handle is an integral part of the door inner trim panel and cannot be individually removed. If there are any problems with the interior handle, a new inner trim panel will be required.

Front door exterior handle

Removal

2 On vehicles with the 'Open and Start' system, remove the door inner trim panel as described in Section 12, and disconnect the 'Open and Start' wiring harness connector.

3 Open the door and remove the screw from the rear edge of the door to gain access to the handle locking screw **(see illustrations)**.

4 Pull the exterior door handle outwards and hold it in that position. With the exterior door handle held in the open position, turn the handle locking screw anti-clockwise until it reaches its stop **(see illustration)**. The exterior door handle should now be fixed in the open position.

5 Withdraw the fixed part of the handle, containing the lock cylinder, from the door **(see illustration)**.

6 Slide the exterior door handle to the rear, disengage the front pivot from the handle frame and remove the handle from the door **(see illustration)**.

Refitting

7 Engage the handle front pivot with the frame and move the handle back into position.

8 Refit the fixed part of the handle with the lock cylinder to the door.

9 Hold the exterior handle and turn the handle locking screw clockwise to retain the handle.

10 Check the operation of the handle then refit the blanking cap to the edge of the door.

11 On vehicles with the 'Open and Start' system, reconnect the wiring connector then refit the door inner trim panel as described in Section 12.

Rear door exterior handle

Removal

12 Open the door and carefully prise out the blanking cap from the rear edge of the door to gain access to the handle locking screw **(see illustrations)**.

13 Pull the exterior door handle outwards and hold it in that position. With the exterior door handle held in the open position, turn the handle locking screw anti-clockwise until it reaches its stop **(see illustration)**. The exterior door handle should now be fixed in the open position.

13.12b ... to gain access to the handle locking screw (arrowed)

13.13 With the exterior door handle held open, turn the handle locking screw anti-clockwise until it reaches its stop

13.14 Withdraw the fixed part of the handle from the door

14 Withdraw the fixed part of the handle from the door **(see illustration)**.
15 Slide the exterior door handle to the rear, disengage the front pivot from the handle frame and remove the handle from the door **(see illustration 13.6)**.

Refitting

16 Engage the handle front pivot with the frame and move the handle back into position.
17 Refit the fixed part of the handle to the door.
18 Hold the exterior handle and turn the handle locking screw clockwise to retain the handle.
19 Check the operation of the handle then refit the blanking cap to the edge of the door.

Front door lock cylinder

Removal

20 Remove the exterior handle as described previously in this Section.

21 Unclip the trim cap and remove the cap from the lock cylinder housing.
22 The lock cylinder body is an integral part of the housing and no further dismantling is possible.

Refitting

23 Refitting is a reversal of removal.

Front door exterior handle frame

Note: *A pop-rivet gun and suitable rivets will be required when refitting. The rivet heads should be approximately 4.8 mm in diameter and 11 mm in length.*

Removal

24 Disconnect the battery negative terminal (refer to *Disconnecting the battery* in the Reference Chapter).
25 Remove the exterior handle as described previously in this Section.
26 Pull out the centre pin and remove the

inner trim panel plastic guides from the door panel **(see illustration)**.
27 Release the clips securing the wiring harness to the door **(see illustration)**.
28 Carefully peel back the protective plastic sheet and remove the sheet from the door **(see illustration 13.58)**.
29 Using an 8.5 mm drill bit, drill out the two rivets securing the window rear guide rail to the door, taking great care not to damage the door panel **(see illustration)**.
30 Remove the guide rail through the door aperture **(see illustration)**.
31 Undo the two screws securing the security cover to the exterior handle frame and door lock, and remove the cover through the door aperture **(see illustrations)**.
32 Release the retaining clip and disconnect the lock operating rod from the lever on the exterior handle frame **(see illustration)**.
33 Slacken the exterior handle frame front

13.26 Pull out the centre pin and remove the inner trim panel plastic guides from the door panel

13.27 Release the clips (arrowed) securing the wiring harness to the door

13.29 Drill out the two rivets (arrowed) securing the window rear guide rail to the door

13.30 Remove the guide rail through the door aperture

13.31a Undo the two screws (arrowed) securing the security cover to the exterior handle frame and door lock ...

13.31b ... and remove the cover through the door aperture

13.32 Release the retaining clip (arrowed) and disconnect the lock operating rod from the lever on the exterior handle frame

13.33b ... extract the rear guide clip, then slide the handle frame forward ...

retaining screw approximately five turns. Extract the rear guide clip, then slide the handle frame forward to release the rear locating lugs. Disengage the lock cylinder operating rod and remove the frame through the door aperture **(see illustrations)**.

13.53 Undo the three screws (arrowed) securing the lock to the door

13.55a Release the locking clip and disconnect the outer cable ...

13.33a Slacken the exterior handle frame front retaining screw approximately five turns ...

13.33c ... disengage the lock cylinder operating rod and remove the frame through the door aperture

34 Clean out the remains of the old rivets from inside the door.

Refitting

35 Connect the lock cylinder operating rod, then place the exterior handle frame in

13.54 Disconnect the wiring connector, then remove the lock assembly through the upper door aperture

13.55b ... and inner cable from the lock

position in the door. Refit the rear guide clip, then tighten the front retaining screw securely.

36 Engage the lock operating rod with the lever on the exterior handle frame and push the retaining clip back into position on the rod.

37 Refit the security cover and secure with the two screws.

38 Position the window guide rail in the door and secure the guide rail with new pop rivets.

39 Refit the protective plastic sheet to the door ensuring it is firmly stuck with no air bubbles. If the sheet was damaged during removal it should be renewed. This entails cutting a new sheet to the correct size and shape using the old sheet as a template. The new sheet can then be attached to the door with fresh adhesive.

40 Refit the wiring harness clips and inner trim panel plastic guides to the door, ensuring they are firmly attached.

41 Refit the door inner trim panel as described in Section 12.

42 Refit the exterior handle as described previously in this Section, then reconnect the battery negative terminal.

Rear door exterior handle frame

Removal

43 Disconnect the battery negative terminal (refer to *Disconnecting the battery* in the Reference Chapter).

44 Remove the exterior handle as described previously in this Section.

45 Remove the door inner trim panel as described in Section 12.

46 Remove the rear door lock as described later in this Section.

47 Slacken the exterior handle frame front retaining screw approximately five turns. Extract the rear guide clip, then slide the handle frame forward to release the rear locating lugs. Disengage the lock cylinder operating rod and remove the frame through the door aperture **(see illustrations 13.33a to 13.33c)**.

Refitting

48 Place the exterior handle frame in position in the door. Refit the rear guide clip, then tighten the front retaining screw securely.

49 Refit the rear door lock as described later in this Section.

50 Refit the door inner trim panel as described in Section 12.

51 Refit the exterior handle as described previously in this Section, then reconnect the battery negative terminal.

Front door lock

Removal

52 Remove the front door exterior handle frame as described earlier in this Section.

53 Undo the three screws securing the lock to the door **(see illustration)**.

54 Withdraw the lock from its location, then lift the locking bar and disconnect the wiring connector. Remove the lock assembly through the upper door aperture **(see illustration)**.

13.58 Carefully peel back the protective plastic sheet and remove the sheet from the door

13.59 Release the retaining clip (arrowed) and disconnect the lock operating rod from the lever on the exterior handle frame

13.61 Withdraw the lock from its location, then lift the locking bar and disconnect the wiring connector

55 If required, disconnect the operating cables from the lock linkage and bracket **(see illustrations)**.

Refitting

56 Refitting is a reversal of removal.

Rear door lock

Removal

57 Remove the door inner trim panel as described in Section 12.

58 Carefully peel back the protective plastic sheet and remove the sheet from the door **(see illustration)**.

59 Release the retaining clip and disconnect the lock operating rod from the lever on the exterior handle frame **(see illustration)**.

60 Undo the three screws securing the lock to the door **(see illustration 13.53)**.

61 Withdraw the lock from its location, then lift the locking bar and disconnect the wiring connector **(see illustration)**.

62 Remove the lock assembly through the door aperture.

63 If required, disconnect the operating cables from the lock linkage and bracket **(see illustrations 13.55a and 13.55b)**.

Refitting

64 If removed, reconnect the operating cables to the lock linkage and bracket.

65 Insert the lock assembly into the door and reconnect the wiring connector.

66 Position the lock assembly in its location, refit the three retaining screws and tighten securely.

67 Engage the lock operating rod with the lever on the exterior handle frame, and push the retaining clip back into position on the rod.

68 Refit the protective plastic sheet to the door ensuring it is firmly stuck with no air bubbles. If the sheet was damaged during removal it should be renewed. This entails cutting a new sheet to the correct size and shape using the old sheet as a template. The new sheet can then be attached to the door with fresh adhesive.

69 Refit the door inner trim panel as described in Section 12.

14 Door window glass and regulator – removal and refitting

Front door window glass

Note: *A pop-rivet gun and suitable rivets will be required when refitting. The rivet heads should be approximately 4.8 mm in diameter and 11 mm in length.*

Removal

1 Open the door window fully.

2 Remove the door inner trim panel as described in Section 12.

3 Pull out the centre pin and remove the inner trim panel plastic guides from the door panel **(see illustration 13.26)**.

14.6 Tap up the door window inner waist seal from the door aperture, then lift the seal up and remove it from the door

14.8a Drill out the two rivets (arrowed) securing the window rear guide rail to the door . . .

4 Release the clips securing the wiring harness to the door **(see illustration 13.27)**.

5 Carefully peel back the protective plastic sheet and remove the sheet from the door **(see illustration 13.58)**.

6 Using a plastic wedge or similar tool, starting from the rear, tap up the door window inner waist seal from the door aperture. Lift the seal up and remove it from the door **(see illustration)**.

7 Similarly, tap up the door window outer waist seal from the door aperture. Lift the seal up and remove it from the door **(see illustration)**.

8 Using an 8.5 mm drill bit, drill out the two rivets securing the window rear guide rail to the door, taking great care not to damage the door panel. Remove the guide rail through the door aperture **(see illustrations)**.

14.7 Similarly, tap up the outer waist seal and remove it from the door

14.8b . . . then remove the guide rail through the door aperture

14.9 Undo the two bolts (arrowed) securing the window glass lower frame to the regulator front lifting arm

14.10a Disengage the window glass lower frame from the regulator rear lifting arm (arrowed) . . .

14.10b . . . and lift the glass up and out of the door

9 Undo the two bolts securing the window glass lower frame to the regulator front lifting arm **(see illustration)**.

10 Disengage the window glass lower frame from the regulator rear lifting arm and lift the glass up and out of the door **(see illustrations)**.

11 Clean out the remains of the old rivets from inside the door.

Refitting

12 Carefully lower the window glass into the door and engage the lower frame with the regulator rear lifting arm.

13 Locate the regulator front lifting arm over the window glass lower frame, refit the two retaining bolts and tighten securely.

14 Refit the window rear guide rail to the door and secure the guide rail with new pop rivets.

15 Refit the window inner and outer waist seals to the door aperture, ensuring that the retaining clips securely engage.

16 Refit the protective plastic sheet to the door ensuring it is firmly stuck with no air bubbles. If the sheet was damaged during removal it should be renewed. This entails cutting a new sheet to the correct size and shape using the old sheet as a template. The new sheet can then be attached to the door with fresh adhesive.

17 Refit the inner trim panel plastic guides and the wiring harness retaining clips.

18 Refit the door inner trim panel as described in Section 12.

Rear door window glass

Removal

19 Open the door window fully.

20 Remove the door inner trim panel as described in Section 12.

21 On models with manual window regulators, remove the rubber seal from the regulator shaft.

22 On models with electric window regulators, release the clips securing the wiring harness to the door **(see illustration)**.

23 Carefully peel back the protective plastic sheet and remove the sheet from the door **(see illustration 13.58)**.

24 Using a plastic wedge or similar tool, starting from the rear, tap up the door window inner waist seal from the door aperture. Lift the seal up and remove it from the door.

25 Similarly, tap up the door window outer waist seal from the door aperture. Lift the seal up and remove it from the door **(see illustration)**.

26 Carefully pull away the window guide channel from the rear guide rail **(see illustration)**.

27 Undo the screws securing the upper and lower ends of the window rear guide rail to the door, then remove the guide rail **(see illustrations)**.

14.22 On models with electric window regulators, release the clips (arrowed) securing the wiring harness to the door

14.25 Tap up the door window outer waist seal, then lift the seal up and remove it from the door

14.26 Carefully pull away the window guide channel from the rear guide rail

14.27a Undo the screws securing the upper . . .

14.27b . . . and lower ends of the window rear guide rail to the door . . .

14.27c . . . then remove the guide rail

14.28a Disengage the window glass lower frame from the regulator lifting arms (arrowed) . . .

14.28b . . . and lift the glass up and out of the door

14.36 Remove the fixed window glass from the door

28 Disengage the window glass lower frame from the regulator lifting arms and lift the glass up and out of the door (see illustrations).

Refitting

29 Carefully lower the window glass into the door and engage the lower frame with the regulator lifting arms.

30 Refit the window rear guide rail to the door and secure the guide rail with the two screws.

31 Refit the window inner and outer waist seals to the door aperture, ensuring that the retaining clips securely engage.

32 Refit the protective plastic sheet to the door ensuring it is firmly stuck with no air bubbles. If the sheet was damaged during removal it should be renewed. This entails cutting a new sheet to the correct size and shape using the old sheet as a template. The new sheet can then be attached to the door with fresh adhesive.

33 Refit the wiring harness retaining clips or regulator shaft rubber seal, as applicable.

34 Refit the door inner trim panel as described in Section 12.

Rear door fixed window glass

Removal

35 Carry out the operations described previously in paragraphs 19 to 27.

36 Remove the fixed window glass from the door (see illustration).

Refitting

37 Locate the fixed window glass in the guide channel.

38 Carry out the operations described in paragraphs 30 to 34.

Front and rear door window regulator

Note: *A pop-rivet gun and suitable rivets will be required when refitting. The rivet heads should be approximately 4.8 mm in diameter and 11 mm in length.*

Removal

39 Remove the front or rear door window glass as described previously in this Section.

40 Where applicable, disconnect the wiring connector from the window regulator motor (see illustration).

41 Using an 8.5 mm drill bit, drill out the six rivets securing the window regulator to the door, taking great care not to damage the door panel (see illustration).

42 Remove the regulator through the door aperture.

43 Clean out the remains of the old rivets from inside the door.

Refitting

44 Refit the regulator to the door and secure the regulator with new pop rivets.

45 Reconnect the regulator wiring connector, where applicable.

46 Refit the front or rear door window glass as described previously in this Section.

15 Tailgate and support struts – removal, refitting and adjustment

Tailgate

Removal

1 On Hatchback models, unhook the lifting cords and remove the parcel shelf from the luggage compartment. Unscrew the parcel shelf lifting pins on each side.

2 Remove the tailgate upper side trim panel, by prising it free at the sides, then at the centre to release the internal retaining clips. On some models, the panel is in two parts with a join at the centre. In this case, remove the left-hand panel first, followed by the right-hand panel. (see illustrations).

3 Disconnect the tailgate main wiring harness connector, then release the grommet and pull

14.40 Disconnect the wiring connector from the window regulator motor

14.41 Drill out the six rivets (arrowed) securing the window regulator to the door

15.2a Remove the tailgate upper side trim panel, by prising it free at the sides . . .

15.2b . . . then at the centre to release the internal retaining clips

15.3a Disconnect the tailgate main wiring harness connector . . .

15.3b . . . then release the grommet and pull the wiring connector out of the tailgate

15.6 Extract the clips (arrowed) and carefully drive out the hinge pins, from outside to inside

15.9 Prise the spring clip from the top of the support strut and disconnect it from the ball on the tailgate

the wiring connector out of the tailgate **(see illustrations)**.

4 Disconnect the tailgate washer hose from the jet and pull the hose out of the tailgate.

5 Have an assistant support the tailgate, then

disconnect the tops of the support struts by prising out the spring clips with a small screwdriver. Lower the struts to the body.

6 Extract the clips and carefully drive out the hinge pins, from outside to inside, using a small drift, while the assistant supports the tailgate **(see illustration)**. Withdraw the tailgate from the body.

Refitting

7 Refitting is a reversal of removal, but apply a little grease to the pivots, and check that when closed the tailgate is positioned centrally within the body aperture and flush with the surrounding bodywork. If necessary, adjust the position of the rubber supports so that the tailgate is flush with the surrounding bodywork. After making adjustments, check that the striker enters the lock centrally and if necessary loosen the striker bolts to reposition it. Tighten the bolts on completion.

Support struts

Removal

8 Open the tailgate and note which way round the struts are fitted. Have an assistant support the tailgate in its open position.

9 Using a small screwdriver, prise the spring clip from the top of the strut and disconnect it from the ball on the tailgate **(see illustration)**.

10 Similarly prise the spring clip from the bottom of the strut and disconnect it from the ball on the body. Withdraw the strut.

Refitting

11 Refitting is a reversal of removal.

16 Tailgate lock components – removal and refitting

16.3 Pull out the expanding rivet (A) and undo the retaining screw (B) (where fitted)

16.4a On Estate models, pull out the expanding rivet each side . . .

16.4b . . . and unscrew the two screws at the top of the panel

Removal

1 On Hatchback models, unhook the lifting cords and remove the parcel shelf from the luggage compartment. Unscrew the parcel shelf lifting pins on each side.

2 Remove the tailgate upper side trim panel, by prising it free at the sides, then at the centre to release the internal retaining clips. On some models, the panel is in two parts with a join at the centre. In this case, remove the left-hand panel first, followed by the right-hand panel. **(see illustrations 15.2a and 15.2b)**.

3 Pull out the expanding rivet and undo the retaining screw (where fitted), securing the lock cover panel to the base of the tailgate **(see illustration)**. Remove the panel.

16.5 Pull the lower trim panel away from the tailgate to release the remaining internal clips

16.6 Undo the three lock assembly retaining screws (arrowed)

16.7 Withdraw the lock through the tailgate aperture and disconnect the wiring connector

4 On Estate models, pull out the expanding rivet each side, securing the tailgate lower trim panel to the tailgate, and unscrew the two screws at the top of the panel (**see illustrations**).

5 On all models, pull the lower trim panel away from the tailgate to release the remaining internal clips and remove the panel from the tailgate (**see illustration**).

6 Undo the three lock assembly retaining screws (**see illustration**).

7 Withdraw the lock through the tailgate aperture and disconnect the wiring connector (**see illustration**).

Refitting

8 Refitting is a reversal of removal.

---

17 Exterior mirrors and associated components – removal and refitting

Exterior mirror

Removal

1 Carefully prise off the door mirror interior trim panel to release the three retaining clips (**see illustration**).

2 Remove the foam insulation from the mirror interior trim panel and disconnect the speaker wiring connector (**see illustrations**).

3 On electrically operated mirrors, disconnect the wiring connector from the mirror (**see illustration**).

4 Undo the three retaining bolts and remove the mirror assembly from the door (**see illustration**).

Refitting

5 Refitting is a reversal of removal.

Mirror glass

Removal

6 Push in the upper inner (nearest the door) corner of the glass so that the lower outer corner of the glass is forced out from the centre.

7 Using a plastic wedge, prise the outer edge of the glass outwards to release the internal retaining clips (**see illustration**).

8 Withdraw the mirror glass and, where applicable, disconnect the wiring connectors (**see illustration**).

17.1 Carefully prise off the door mirror interior trim panel to release the three retaining clips

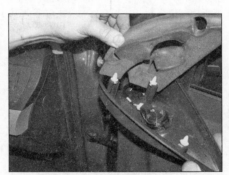

17.2a Remove the foam insulation from the mirror interior trim panel . . .

17.2b . . . and disconnect the speaker wiring connector

17.3 On electrically operated mirrors, disconnect the wiring connector from the mirror

17.4 Undo the three retaining bolts (arrowed) and remove the mirror assembly from the door

17.7 Using a plastic wedge, prise the outer edge of the glass outwards to release the internal retaining clips

17.8 Withdraw the mirror glass and, where applicable, disconnect the wiring connectors (arrowed)

17.10 Prise the upper edge of the outer cover away from the mirror body to release the four upper clips (arrowed)

Refitting

9 Refitting is a reversal of removal. Carefully press the mirror glass into the housing until the centre retainer clips are engaged.

Outer cover

Removal

10 Carefully prise the upper edge of the outer cover away from the mirror body to release the four upper clips **(see illustration)**.
11 Unhook the four lower clips and remove the outer cover from the mirror body **(see illustration)**.

Refitting

12 Refitting is a reversal of removal.

18 Windscreen and fixed window glass – general information

The windscreen, tailgate and rear quarter window glasses are cemented in position with a special adhesive and require the use of specialist equipment for their removal and refitting. Renewal of such fixed glass is considered beyond the scope of the home mechanic. Owners are strongly advised to have the work carried out by one of the many specialist windscreen fitting specialists.

19 Sunroof – general information

An electric sunroof was offered as an optional extra on most models, and is fitted as standard equipment on some models.

Due to the complexity of the sunroof mechanism, considerable expertise is needed to repair, renew or adjust the sunroof components successfully. Removal of the roof first requires the headlining to be removed, which is a complex and tedious operation in itself, and not a task to be undertaken lightly. Therefore, any problems with the sunroof should be referred to a Vauxhall/Opel dealer.

20 Body exterior fittings – removal and refitting

Radiator grille

1 Push in the centre pins and extract the four expanding rivets securing the upper edge of the radiator grille to the body panel **(see illustration)**. Note that the expanding rivet centre pins are likely to be lost when doing this

and new expanding rivets may be required for refitting.
2 Disengage the six lower lugs and remove the radiator grille from the car **(see illustration)**.

Wheel arch liners and body under-panels

3 The various plastic covers fitted to the underside of the vehicle are secured in position by a mixture of screws, nuts and retaining clips, and removal will be fairly obvious on inspection. Work methodically around the liner/panel, removing its retaining screws and releasing its retaining clips until it is free to be removed from the underside of the vehicle. Most clips used on the vehicle, with the exception of the fasteners which are used to secure the wheel arch liners, are simply prised out of position. The wheel arch liner clips are released by tapping their centre pins through the clip, and then removing the outer section of the clip; new clips will be required on refitting if the centre pins are not recovered.
4 When refitting, renew any retaining clips that may have been broken on removal, and ensure that the panel is securely retained by all the relevant clips, nuts and screws. Vauxhall/Opel also recommend that plastic nuts (where used) are renewed, regardless of their apparent condition, whenever they are disturbed.

17.11 Unhook the four lower clips (arrowed) and remove the outer cover from the mirror body

20.1 Push in the centre pins and extract the expanding rivets securing the upper edge of the radiator grille to the body panel

20.2 Disengage the six lower lugs and remove the radiator grille from the car

Water deflector

Note: *The water deflector retaining clips, and the water deflector itself, are manufactured from extremely brittle plastic and are likely to break during the following operations. Be prepared to obtain new clips, and possibly a new water deflector!*

5 Remove the windscreen wiper arms as described in Chapter 12.

6 Open the bonnet, and pull up the rubber weatherseal from the flange at the rear of the engine compartment **(see illustration)**.

7 Carefully prise free the water deflector from the base of the windscreen to release the five retaining clips **(see illustration)**.

8 Disconnect the windscreen washer hose and remove the water deflector from the car.

9 Refit the water deflector using a reversal of the removal procedure. Refit the wiper arms as described in Chapter 12.

Body trim strips and badges

10 The various body trim strips and badges are held in position with a special adhesive tape. Removal requires the trim/badge to be heated, to soften the adhesive, and then cut away from the surface. Due to the high risk of damage to the vehicle's paintwork during this operation, it is recommended that this task should be entrusted to a Vauxhall/Opel dealer.

21 Seats –
removal and refitting

Warning: The front seats are equipped with seat belt tensioners, and side airbags may be built into the outer sides of the seats. The seat belt tensioners and side airbags may cause injury if triggered accidentally. If the tensioner has been triggered due to a sudden impact or accident, the unit must be renewed, as it cannot be reset. If a seat is to be disposed of, the tensioner must be triggered before the seat is removed from the vehicle. Due to safety considerations, tensioner renewal or seat disposal must be entrusted to a Vauxhall/ Opel dealer. Where side airbags are fitted, refer to Chapter 12 for the precautions

21.5 Slacken and remove the seat retaining bolts (arrowed) from the rear of the guide rails

20.6 Pull up the rubber weatherseal from the flange at the rear of the engine compartment

which should be observed when dealing with an airbag system.

1 Disconnect the battery negative terminal (refer to *Disconnecting the battery* in the Reference Chapter). Wait 2 minutes for the capacitors to discharge, before working on the seat electrics.

Front seat removal

2 Slide the seat adjustment fully forward.

3 Unclip the cover over the seat belt mounting, by releasing it at the rear, then disengaging the front locating tabs **(see illustration)**.

4 Undo the seat belt retaining bolt **(see illustration)**.

5 Slacken and remove the seat retaining bolts from the rear of the guide rails **(see illustration)**.

6 Pull the seat backwards to disengage the guide rail front mounting lugs from the floor.

21.3 Unclip the cover over the seat belt mounting

21.8 Pull out the two release straps, while at the same time lifting the rear seat cushion up at the front

20.7 Carefully prise free the water deflector from the base of the windscreen to release the five retaining clips

7 Pull out the locking bar and disconnect the wiring connector from the underside of the seat, then remove the seat from the car.

Rear seat removal

Cushion – Hatchback models

8 Pull out the two release straps, while at the same time lifting the cushion up at the front **(see illustration)**.

9 Push the cushion rearwards and upwards to disengage it at the rear and remove the cushion from the car.

Cushion – Estate models

10 Pull out the two release straps, while at the same time lifting the cushion up at the front.

11 Tip the cushion fully forward, then disengage the pivot arms from the brackets on the floor **(see illustration)**. Remove the cushion from the car.

21.4 Undo the seat belt retaining bolt (arrowed)

21.11 Tip the cushion fully forward, then disengage the pivot arms from the brackets on the floor

21.13a Undo the bolts (arrowed) securing the centre . . .

21.13b . . . and side seat belt buckles and seat hinge to the floor

21.14 Seat hinge rear securing bolts (arrowed)

21.15a Press the outer hinge pin locking collar in, to free the hinge pin . . .

21.15b . . . while at the same time pulling upward to release the backrest

Backrest

12 Remove the rear seat cushion as described previously in this Section.
13 Undo the three bolts securing the seat belt buckles and seat hinge to the floor (see illustrations).
14 Fold the backrest forward and undo the three rear bolts securing the seat hinge to the floor (see illustration).
15 Using a screwdriver, press the outer hinge pin locking collar in, to free the hinge pin, while at the same time pulling upward to release the backrest (see illustrations). Remove the backrest from the car.

Front seat refitting

16 Refitting is a reverse of the removal procedure, noting the following points:
  a) *Remove all traces of old thread-locking compound from the threads of the seat retaining bolts, and clean the threaded holes*

in the vehicle floor, ideally by running a tap of the correct size and pitch down them.
  b) *Apply a suitable thread-locking compound to the threads of the seat bolts. Refit the bolts, and tighten them to the specified torque setting.*
  c) *Reconnect the seat wiring connector making sure it has locked securely, then reconnect the battery negative terminal.*

Rear seat refitting

17 Refitting is a reverse of the removal procedure.

22 Seat belt tensioning mechanism – general information

All models covered in this manual are fitted with a front seat belt pyrotechnic tensioner system. The system is designed to

instantaneously take up any slack in the seat belt in the case of a sudden frontal impact, therefore reducing the possibility of injury to the front seat occupants. Each front seat is fitted with its own system, the components of which are mounted on the seat frame.

The seat belt tensioner is triggered by a frontal impact causing a deceleration of six times the force of gravity or greater. Lesser impacts, including impacts from behind, will not trigger the system.

When the system is triggered, a pretensioned spring draws back the seat belt via a cable which acts on the seat belt stalk. The cable can move by up to 80.0 mm, which therefore reduces the slack in the seat belt around the shoulders and waist of the occupant by a similar amount.

There is a risk of injury if the system is triggered inadvertently when working on the vehicle, and it is therefore strongly recommended that any work involving the seat belt tensioner system is entrusted to a Vauxhall/Opel dealer. Refer to the warning given at the beginning of Section 23 before contemplating any work on the front seats.

23 Seat belt components – removal and refitting

⚠️ *Warning: The front seats are fitted with pyrotechnic seat belt tensioners which are triggered by the airbag control system. Before removing a seat belt, disconnect the battery and wait at least 2 minutes to allow the system capacitors to discharge.*

Front belt and reel

Removal

1 Unclip the cover over the seat belt mounting on the front seat, by releasing it at the rear, then disengaging the front locating tabs (see illustration 21.3).
2 Undo the seat belt retaining bolt (see illustration 21.4).
3 Remove the B-pillar inner trim panel and sill trim panel as described in Section 24.
4 Undo the seat belt upper mounting bolt.
5 Prise the cover from the lower outside of

23.5a Prise the cover from the lower outside of the B-pillar . . .

23.5b . . . for access to the front seat belt reel mounting nut

23.10 Undo the retaining bolt (arrowed) and withdraw the tensioner from the seat

23.11 Release the cable retaining clip (arrowed) and remove the tensioner

23.15 Undo the seat belt lower mounting bolt (arrowed)

the B-pillar for access to the front seat belt reel mounting nut **(see illustrations)**. Using a 13 mm socket, 65 mm deep on the inside, unscrew the nut taking care not to drop it inside the B-pillar. Note that an extension pin is provided to enable the nut to be removed safely.

6 With the nut removed, remove the reel from the inside of the pillar.

Refitting

7 Refitting is a reversal of removal, but tighten the mounting bolts to the specified torque.

Front belt stalk and tensioner

Removal

8 Remove the front seat as described in Section 21.

9 From underneath the seat, slide out the wiring connector locking bar and disconnect the wiring connector. Unclip the wiring harness from the seat.

10 Undo the retaining bolt and withdraw the tensioner from the seat **(see illustration)**.

11 Release the cable retaining clip and remove the tensioner **(see illustration)**.

Refitting

12 Refitting is a reverse of the removal procedure, noting the following points:

a) *Remove all traces of old thread-locking compound from the thread of the tensioner retaining bolt, and clean the threaded hole in the seat, ideally by running a tap of the correct size and pitch down it.*

b) *Apply a suitable thread-locking compound to the thread of the tensioner retaining bolt. Refit the bolt, and tighten it to the specified torque setting.*

Rear outer belt and reel

Removal

13 Remove the rear seat cushion as described in Section 21.

14 Remove the relevant luggage compartment side trim panels as described in Section 24.

15 Undo the seat belt lower mounting bolt **(see illustration)**.

16 Undo the seat belt reel mounting bolt and remove the reel and belt from the car **(see illustration)**.

23.16 Undo the seat belt reel mounting bolt (arrowed) and remove the reel and belt from the car

Refitting

17 Refitting is a reversal of removal, but tighten the mounting bolts to the specified torque.

Rear centre belt and reel

18 The inertia reel for the centre rear seat belt is located internally within the rear seat backrest. To gain access, the backrest must be removed and completely dismantled. This is a complex operation and considerable expertise is needed to remove and refit the seat upholstery and internal components without damage. Therefore, any problems with the centre seat belt and reel should be referred to a Vauxhall/Opel dealer.

Rear belt stalk

Removal

19 Remove the rear seat cushion as described in Section 21.

20 Undo the retaining bolt and remove the relevant stalk from the floor **(see illustration)**.

Refitting

21 Refitting is a reversal of removal, but tighten the mounting bolts to the specified torque.

24 Interior trim –
removal and refitting

1 The interior trim panels are secured by a combination of clips and screws. Removal

23.20 Rear seat belt stalk retaining bolts

and refitting is generally self-explanatory, noting that it may be necessary to remove or loosen surrounding panels to allow a particular panel to be removed. The following paragraphs describe the general removal and refitting details of the major panels on 5-door Hatchback and Estate models. The procedures are generally similar on 3-door Hatchback models, although some differences will be encountered in the luggage compartment area.

A-pillar trim panel

2 Pull off the front door weather strip in the vicinity of the A-pillar trim panel.

3 On models equipped with curtain airbags, pull out the airbag positioning clip from the trim panel **(see illustration)**.

4 Pull the trim panel away from the A-pillar and remove it from the car **(see illustration)**.

24.3 Pull out the airbag positioning clip from the trim panel

24.4 Pull the trim panel away from the A-pillar and remove it from the car

24.9 Prise out the plastic cover at the top of the panel

24.10 Prise the upper and lower parts of the trim panel away from the B-pillar

24.11a Feed the seat belt through the opening . . .

24.11b . . . and remove the panel from the car

24.12 Lift the tongue at the base of the upper panel, then release the retaining pegs (arrowed) while pulling the panels apart

5 Refitting is a reversal of removal.

B-pillar trim panel

6 Unclip the cover over the seat belt mounting on the front seat, by releasing it at the rear, then disengaging the front locating tabs **(see illustration 21.3)**.
7 Undo the seat belt retaining bolt **(see illustration 21.4)**.
8 Remove the side sill inner trim panel as described later in this Section.
9 Prise out the plastic cover at the top of the panel **(see illustration)**.
10 Starting at the top, prise the upper and lower parts of the trim panel away from the B-pillar **(see illustration)**.
11 Feed the seat belt through the opening and remove the panel from the car **(see illustrations)**.
12 To separate the upper and lower parts of

the panel, lift the tongue at the base of the upper panel, then release the retaining peg at each side, while pulling the panels apart **(see illustration)**.
13 Refitting is a reversal of removal, but tighten the seat belt retaining bolt to the specified torque.

Side sill inner trim panel

14 Open the front and rear doors and pull the weatherstrip away from the B-pillar and the lower part of the door apertures.
15 Using a small screwdriver, carefully disengage the sill trim panel from the B-pillar lower trim **(see illustration)**.
16 Lift the panel upwards to unclip it from the sill and remove the panel from the car **(see illustration)**.
17 Refitting is a reversal of removal.

Tailgate aperture upper centre trim panel

18 Open the tailgate.
19 Pull the panel away to release the internal clips, and remove the panel from the car **(see illustration)**.
20 Refitting is a reversal of removal.

Tailgate aperture lower centre trim panel

21 Open the tailgate.
22 Remove the luggage compartment floor covering.
23 Undo the four panel retaining screws **(see illustration)**.
24 Pull the panel away to release the internal clips, and remove the panel from the car.
25 Refitting is a reversal of removal.

24.15 Disengage the side sill trim panel from the B-pillar lower trim

24.16 Lift the panel upwards to unclip it from the sill

24.19 Pull the tailgate aperture panel away to release the internal clips, and remove the panel from the car

24.23 Undo the four lower panel retaining screws

24.27a Pull the upper part of the panel away from the C-pillar and roof . . .

24.27b . . . then disengage the panel from the lower side trim

24.31 Pull out the centre pin and extract the expanding rivet

24.32 Pull the panel away from the pillar to release the internal clips

24.33 Slide the seat belt out through the slot in the panel, then remove the panel from the car

D-pillar trim panel – Estate models

26 Remove the tailgate aperture upper centre trim panel as described previously.

27 Pull the upper part of the panel away from the C-pillar and roof to release the internal clips. Disengage the panel from the lower side trim panel and remove it from the car (see illustration).

28 Refitting is a reversal of removal.

C-pillar lower trim panel

29 Remove the rear seat cushion and rear seat backrest as described in Section 21.

30 Remove the side sill inner trim panel as described previously.

31 Pull out the centre pin and extract the expanding rivet securing the base of the panel to the C-pillar (see illustration).

32 Pull the panel away from the pillar to release the internal clips (see illustration).

33 Slide the seat belt out through the slot in the panel, then remove the panel from the car (see illustration).

34 Refitting is a reversal of removal.

Luggage compartment side trim panel – Hatchback models

35 Remove the luggage compartment floor covering.

36 Remove the C-pillar lower trim panel as described previously.

37 Undo the rear seat belt lower mounting bolt.

38 Prise out the plastic cover at the top of the panel upper part (see illustration).

39 Pull the panel out to disengage the retaining clips and release the panel from the pillar (see illustration).

40 Feed the seat belt through the panel opening and remove the panel from the car (see illustration).

41 Undo the three screws securing the panel lower part to the pillar (see illustration).

24.38 Prise out the plastic cover at the top of the panel upper part

24.39 Pull the panel out to disengage the retaining clips

24.40 Feed the seat belt through the panel opening and remove the panel from the car

24.41 Undo the three screws (arrowed) securing the panel lower part to the pillar

24.42 Pull the panel out to disengage the retaining clips and release the panel from the pillar

24.46 Remove the rear light cluster access panel from the lower part of the side trim panel

24.47 Carefully prise out the luggage compartment light, disconnect the wiring and remove the light

42 Pull the panel out to disengage the retaining clips and release the panel from the pillar (see illustration).
43 Refitting is a reversal of removal, but tighten the seat belt mounting bolt to the specified torque.

Luggage compartment side trim panel – Estate models

44 Remove the luggage compartment floor covering.
45 Remove the D-pillar trim panel and the C-pillar lower trim panel as described previously.
46 Remove the rear light cluster access panel from the lower part of the side trim panel (see illustration).
47 Carefully prise out the luggage compart-

ment light, disconnect the wiring connector and remove the light (see illustration).
48 Using a forked tool, prise out the retaining plates at the front and rear of the upper part of the panel (see illustration).
49 Undo the retaining screw located at the front and rear corners of the panel upper part (see illustrations).
50 Lift the front end of the panel upper part, pull the panel out to disengage the retaining clips and remove the upper part from the car (see illustration).
51 Using a forked tool, prise out the retaining plates at the base of the lower part of the panel (see illustration).
52 Pull the panel out to disengage the retaining clips and remove the lower part from the car (see illustration).

53 Refitting is a reversal of removal.

C-pillar upper trim panel – Estate models

54 Remove the luggage compartment side trim panel as described previously.
55 Undo the rear seat belt lower mounting bolt.
56 Prise out the plastic cover at the top of the panel (see illustration).
57 Pull the panel out to disengage the retaining clips and release the panel from the C-pillar (see illustration).
58 Feed the seat belt through the panel opening and remove the panel from the car (see illustration).
59 Refitting is a reversal of removal, but tighten the seat belt mounting bolt to the specified torque.

24.48 Prise out the retaining plates at the front and rear of the upper part of the panel

24.49a Undo the retaining screw located at the front corner . . .

24.49b . . . and rear corner (arrowed) of the panel upper part

24.50 Lift the front end of the panel upper part, then pull the panel out to disengage the retaining clips

24.51 Prise out the retaining plates at the base of the lower part of the panel

24.52 Pull the panel out to disengage the retaining clips and remove the lower part from the car

24.56 Prise out the plastic cover at the top of the panel

24.57 Pull the panel out to disengage the retaining clips and release the panel from the C-pillar

24.58 Feed the seat belt through the panel opening and remove the panel from the car

Interior mirror

60 On models fitted with a rain sensor, unclip and remove the sensor trim panel, then release the retaining clip(s) and disconnect the wiring connectors from the mirror assembly.

61 Press the retaining clip at the top of the interior mirror mounting bracket, then carefully release the interior mirror in the downwards direction to remove it from the windscreen.

62 Refitting is the reverse of removal.

25 Centre console – removal and refitting

Removal

1 Disconnect the battery negative terminal (refer to *Disconnecting the battery* in the Reference Chapter).

2 Unclip and remove the access panel in the centre console, beneath the handbrake lever **(see illustration)**.

3 Unclip the cover from around the handbrake lever **(see illustration)**.

4 At the rear of the console, remove the stowage box by pulling it upward to release the retaining clips **(see illustration)**.

5 Unscrew the nut, now exposed, securing the rear of the console to the floor **(see illustration)**.

6 Move both front seats fully forward and undo the console rear retaining screws on both sides.

7 Undo the screw below the handbrake lever

securing the console to the support bracket **(see illustration)**.

8 At the front of the console, prise out the trim caps and undo the screw each side securing

the console to the base of the facia **(see illustrations)**.

9 Using a small screwdriver, carefully prise up the right-hand side of the ashtray, withdraw the

25.2 Unclip and remove the access panel beneath the handbrake lever

25.3 Unclip the cover from around the handbrake lever

25.4 Remove the stowage box by pulling it upward to release the retaining clips

25.5 Console rear retaining nut (A) and left-hand side retaining screw (B)

25.7 Undo the screw (arrowed) below the handbrake lever

25.8a Prise out the trim caps . . .

25.8b . . . and undo the screw (arrowed) each side

25.9a Carefully prise up the right-hand side of the ashtray . . .

25.9b . . . then withdraw the ashtray and disconnect the wiring connector

25.10a Undo the two screws securing the rear of the gear lever gaiter trim panel to the console . . .

25.10b . . . lift the panel up at the rear and disengage it from the console at the front

25.11 Undo the two screws (arrowed) securing the front of the console to the facia

ashtray from the centre console and disconnect the wiring connector **(see illustrations)**.

10 Undo the two screws securing the rear of the gear lever gaiter trim panel to the centre console. Lift the panel up at the rear and disengage it from the centre console at the front **(see illustrations)**.

11 Undo the two screws securing tne front of the console to the centre of the facia **(see illustration)**.

12 Lift the console up and slide it to the rear to disengage the front guides from the lugs on the facia **(see illustrations)**.

13 Feed the gear lever gaiter trim panel through the console aperture and remove the console from the car.

Refitting

14 Refitting is a reversal of removal.

26 Facia panel components – removal and refitting

Glovebox

Removal

1 Open the glovebox lid and undo the four screws securing the glovebox to the facia **(see illustration)**.

25.12a Lift the console up and slide it to the rear . . .

25.12b . . . to disengage the front guides (arrowed) from the lugs on the facia

26.1 Undo the four screws (arrowed) securing the glovebox to the facia

26.2 Withdraw the glovebox from the facia and disconnect the glovebox light wiring connector

26.8a Undo the two centre panel lower retaining screws (arrowed) . . .

26.8b . . . then pull the panel away from the facia to release the upper retaining lugs (arrowed)

26.9 Lift up the locking bar and disconnect the wiring connector

2 Withdraw the glovebox from the facia, disconnect the glovebox light wiring connector and remove the glovebox from the car **(see illustration)**.

Refitting

3 Refitting is a reversal of removal.

Facia centre panel

Removal

4 Disconnect the battery negative terminal (refer to *Disconnecting the battery* in the Reference Chapter).
5 Remove the centre console as described in Section 25.
6 Remove the radio/cassette/CD player as described in Chapter 12.
7 Remove the heater control assembly as described in Chapter 3.
8 Undo the two centre panel lower retaining screws, then pull the panel away from the facia to release the upper retaining lugs **(see illustrations)**.
9 Lift up the locking bar and disconnect the wiring connector, then remove the panel from the car **(see illustration)**.

Refitting

10 Refitting is a reversal of removal.

Driver's side lower trim panel

Removal

11 Remove the headlight switch as described in Chapter 12.
12 Remove the steering column shrouds as described later in this Section.
13 Working in the headlight switch aperture, undo the two screws securing the upper part of the panel to the facia **(see illustration)**.
14 Undo the two panel lower securing screws beneath the steering column.
15 Swivel the panel down and detach the lower lugs from the facia tube **(see illustration)**. Remove the panel from the car.

Refitting

16 Refitting is a reversal of removal.

Steering column shrouds

Removal

17 Turn the steering wheel as necessary to access the left and right front retaining screws.

26.13 Undo the two screws (arrowed) in the switch aperture securing the lower trim panel to the facia

18 Carefully prise off the screw trim cap and undo the front retaining screw now exposed **(see illustrations)**. Repeat this procedure on the other side of the shroud.

26.18a Carefully prise off the screw trim cap . . .

26.19 Undo the lower shroud lower retaining screw

26.15 Swivel the panel down and detach the lower lugs from the facia tube

19 Undo the lower shroud lower retaining screw **(see illustration)**.
20 Carefully prise free the circular trim panel around the ignition switch **(see illustration)**.

26.18b . . . and undo the front retaining screw now exposed

26.20 Carefully prise free the circular trim panel around the ignition switch

26.21a Lift up the upper column shroud and undo the right-hand retaining screw (arrowed) . . .

26.21b . . . and left-hand retaining screw (arrowed) securing the lower shroud to the steering column

26.22 Remove the lower shroud from the steering column

26.23 Unclip the upper shroud from the instrument panel and remove it from the car

21 Lift up the upper column shroud and undo the two screws securing the lower shroud to the steering column (see illustrations).
22 Remove the lower shroud from the steering column (see illustration).
23 Unclip the upper shroud from the instrument panel and remove it from the car (see illustration).

Refitting

24 Refitting is a reversal of removal.

Complete facia assembly

Note: *This is an involved operation entailing the removal of numerous components and assemblies, and the disconnection of a multitude of wiring connectors. Make notes on the location of all disconnected wiring, or attach labels to the connectors, to avoid confusion when refitting.*

26.36 Remove the trim caps at the left-hand and right-hand ends of the facia

26.33 Carefully release the facia decorative strip using a plastic spatula or similar tool

Removal

25 Disconnect the battery negative terminal (refer to *Disconnecting the battery* in the Reference Chapter).
26 Remove the A-pillar trim panels on both sides as described in Section 24.
27 Remove the side sill inner trim panel on both sides as described in Section 24.
28 Remove the centre console as described in Section 25.
29 Remove the steering wheel as described in Chapter 10.
30 Remove the following facia panels as described previously in this Section:
a) Glovebox.
b) Facia centre panel.
c) Driver's side lower trim panel.
d) Steering column shrouds.
31 Remove the following components as described in Chapter 12:

26.37a Undo the bolt in the sun sensor aperture

26.35 Carefully prise out the sun sensor panel from the top of the facia

a) *Steering column electronics module.*
b) *Instrument panel.*
c) *Information display.*
32 Remove the steering column as described in Chapter 10.
33 Carefully release the facia decorative strip on the passenger's side using a plastic spatula or similar tool (see illustration).
34 Extract the plastic rivets and remove the footwell air duct on the driver's and passenger's side.
35 Carefully prise out the sun sensor panel from the top of the facia and disconnect the wiring connector (where fitted) (see illustration).
36 Remove the trim caps at the left-hand and right-hand ends of the facia (see illustration).
37 Undo the following fasteners securing the facia to the mounting brackets (see illustrations):
a) *1 bolt in the sun sensor aperture.*
b) *1 bolt at the left-hand and right-hand end.*

26.37b Undo the bolt (arrowed) at each end of the facia

26.37c Undo the bolt (arrowed) at the left-hand floor bracket . . .

26.37d . . . and the three bolts (arrowed) at the right-hand floor bracket

26.37e Undo the bolt (arrowed) at the lower corner of the facia each side

c) 4 bolts at the centre floor brackets.
d) 1 bolt each side at the lower left-hand and right-hand corners of the facia.

38 With the help of an assistant, carefully lift the facia from its location. Check that all wiring has been disconnected, then remove the facia from the car.

Refitting

39 Refitting is a reversal of removal ensuring that all wiring is correctly reconnected and all mountings securely tightened.

Facia crossmember

Note: *This is an involved operation entailing the disconnection of a multitude of wiring connectors. Make notes on the location of all disconnected wiring, or attach labels to the connectors, to avoid confusion when refitting.*

Removal

40 Remove the facia as described previously in this Section.

41 Remove the steering column as described in Chapter 10.
42 Remove the passenger's airbag as described in Chapter 12.
43 Remove the front doors as described in Section 11.
44 Remove the brake pedal as described in Chapter 9.
45 Remove the clutch pedal as described in Chapter 6.
46 Undo the bolts securing the crossmember centre supports to the floor brackets.
47 Disconnect all remaining earth cables and wiring connections, making careful notes as to their locations.
48 From outside the car, undo the two bolts securing the crossmember to the A-pillar on each side **(see illustration)**.
49 With the help of an assistant, check that all wiring has been disconnected, then remove the crossmember from the car.

26.48 Undo the two bolts (arrowed) securing the crossmember to the A-pillar on each side

Refitting

50 Refitting is a reversal of removal ensuring that all wiring is correctly reconnected and all mountings securely tightened.

Notes

Chapter 12
Body electrical systems

Contents

Degrees of difficulty

Easy, suitable for novice with little experience	Fairly easy, suitable for beginner with some experience	Fairly difficult, suitable for competent DIY mechanic	Difficult, suitable for experienced DIY mechanic	Very difficult, suitable for expert DIY or professional

Specifications

System type . . . . 12 volt negative earth

Bulbs   **Wattage**

Direction indicator side repeater	5
Direction indicator	21
Front foglight	55
Headlight	55
Interior lights.	10
Number plate light	10
Rear foglight	21
Reversing light	21
Sidelight	5
Stop/tail-light	21/5

1 General information and precautions

⚠️ **Warning: Before carrying out any work on the electrical system, read through the precautions given in 'Safety first!' at the beginning of this manual, and in Chapter 5.**

1 The electrical system is of the 12 volt negative earth type. Power for the lights and all electrical accessories is supplied by a lead-acid type battery, which is charged by the engine-driven alternator.

2 This Chapter covers repair and service procedures for the various electrical components not associated with the engine. Information on the battery, alternator and starter motor can be found in Chapter 5.

3 It should be noted that, prior to working on any component in the electrical system, the battery negative terminal should first be disconnected, to prevent the possibility of electrical short-circuits and/or fires.

Caution: Before proceeding, refer to 'Disconnecting the battery' in the Reference Chapter for further information.

2 Electrical fault finding – general information

Note: *Refer to the precautions given in 'Safety first!' and in Section 1 before starting work. The following tests relate to testing of the main electrical circuits, and should not be used to test delicate electronic circuits (such as the anti-lock braking system or fuel injection system), particularly where an electronic control unit is used.*

General

1 A typical electrical circuit consists of an electrical component, any switches, relays, motors, fuses, fusible links or circuit breakers related to that component, and the wiring and connectors which link the component to both the battery and the vehicle body. To help to pinpoint a problem in an electrical circuit, wiring diagrams are shown at the end of this Chapter.

2 Before attempting to diagnose an electrical fault, first study the appropriate wiring diagram to obtain a complete understanding of the components included in the particular circuit concerned. The possible sources of a fault can be narrowed down by noting if other components related to the circuit are operating properly. If several components or circuits fail at one time, the problem is likely to be related to a shared fuse or earth connection.

3 Electrical problems usually stem from simple causes, such as loose or corroded connections, a faulty earth connection, a blown fuse, a melted fusible link, or a faulty relay (refer to Section 3 for details of testing relays). Inspect the condition of all fuses, wires and connections in a problem circuit before testing the components. Use the wiring diagrams to determine which terminal connections will need to be checked in order to pinpoint the trouble-spot.

4 The basic tools required for electrical fault finding include a circuit tester or voltmeter (a 12 volt bulb with a set of test leads can also be used for certain tests); a self-powered test light (sometimes known as a continuity tester); an ohmmeter (to measure resistance); a battery and set of test leads; and a jumper wire, preferably with a circuit breaker or fuse incorporated, which can be used to bypass suspect wires or electrical components. Before attempting to locate a problem with test instruments, use the wiring diagram to determine where to make the connections.

5 To find the source of an intermittent wiring fault (usually due to a poor or dirty connection, or damaged wiring insulation), a 'wiggle' test can be performed on the wiring. This involves wiggling the wiring by hand to see if the fault occurs as the wiring is moved. It should be possible to narrow down the source of the fault to a particular section of wiring. This method of testing can be used in conjunction with any of the tests described in the following sub-Sections.

6 Apart from problems due to poor connections, two basic types of fault can occur in an electrical circuit – open-circuit, or short-circuit.

7 Open-circuit faults are caused by a break somewhere in the circuit, which prevents current from flowing. An open-circuit fault will prevent a component from working, but will not cause the relevant circuit fuse to blow.

8 Short-circuit faults are caused by a 'short' somewhere in the circuit, which allows the current flowing in the circuit to 'escape' along an alternative route, usually to earth. Short-circuit faults are normally caused by a breakdown in wiring insulation, which allows a feed wire to touch either another wire, or an earthed component such as the bodyshell. A short-circuit fault will normally cause the relevant circuit fuse to blow.

Finding an open-circuit

9 To check for an open-circuit, connect one lead of a circuit tester or voltmeter to either the negative battery terminal or a known good earth.

10 Connect the other lead to a connector in the circuit being tested, preferably nearest to the battery or fuse.

11 Switch on the circuit, bearing in mind that some circuits are live only when the ignition switch is turned to a particular position.

12 If voltage is present (indicated either by the tester bulb lighting or a voltmeter reading, as applicable), this means that the section of the circuit between the relevant connector and the battery is problem-free.

13 Continue to check the remainder of the circuit in the same fashion.

14 When a point is reached at which no voltage is present, the problem must lie between that point and the previous test point with voltage. Most problems can be traced to a broken, corroded or loose connection.

Finding a short-circuit

15 To check for a short-circuit, first disconnect the load(s) from the circuit (loads are the components which draw current from a circuit, such as bulbs, motors, heating elements, etc).

16 Remove the relevant fuse from the circuit, and connect a circuit tester or voltmeter to the fuse connections.

17 Switch on the circuit, bearing in mind that some circuits are live only when the ignition switch is turned to a particular position.

18 If voltage is present (indicated either by the tester bulb lighting or a voltmeter reading, as applicable), this means that there is a short-circuit.

19 If no voltage is present, but the fuse still blows with the load(s) connected, this indicates an internal fault in the load(s).

Finding an earth fault

20 The battery negative terminal is connected to 'earth' – the metal of the engine/transmission unit and the car body – and most systems are wired so that they only receive a positive feed, the current returning via the metal of the car body. This means that the component mounting and the body form part of that circuit. Loose or corroded mountings can therefore cause a range of electrical faults, ranging from total failure of a circuit, to a puzzling partial fault. In particular, lights may shine dimly (especially when another circuit sharing the same earth point is in operation), motors (eg, wiper motors or the radiator cooling fan motor) may run slowly, and the operation of one circuit may have an apparently-unrelated effect on another. Note that on many vehicles, earth straps are used between certain components, such as the engine/transmission and the body, usually where there is no metal-to-metal contact between components, due to flexible rubber mountings, etc.

21 To check whether a component is properly earthed, disconnect the battery, and connect one lead of an ohmmeter to a known good earth point. Connect the other lead to the wire or earth connection being tested. The resistance reading should be zero; if not, check the connection as follows.

22 If an earth connection is thought to be faulty, dismantle the connection, and clean back to bare metal both the bodyshell and the wire terminal or the component earth connection mating surface. Be careful to remove all traces of dirt and corrosion, then use a knife to trim away any paint, so that a clean metal-to-metal joint is made. On reassembly, tighten the joint fasteners securely; if a wire terminal is being refitted, use serrated washers between the terminal

3.2 Access to the fuses in the luggage compartment can be gained by opening the stowage compartment cover

3.3 Release the catches and lift off the fuse/relay box cover for access to the engine compartment fuses

3.4 Pull the fuse out of its terminals using the plastic removal tool provided

and the bodyshell, to ensure a clean and secure connection. When the connection is remade, prevent the onset of corrosion in the future by applying a coat of petroleum jelly or silicone-based grease. Alternatively, at regular intervals, spray on a proprietary ignition sealer or a water-dispersant lubricant.

3   Fuses and relays – general information

Fuses

1 The main fuses are located behind the trim panel on the left-hand side of the luggage compartment, with additional fuses and relays located in the fuse/relay box on the left-hand side of the engine compartment.
2 To gain access to the luggage compartment fuses, turn the catches and open the cover **(see illustration)**.
3 To gain access to the engine compartment fuses, release the catches using a small screwdriver and lift off the fuse/relay box cover **(see illustration)**.
4 To remove a fuse, first switch off the circuit concerned (or the ignition), then pull the fuse out of its terminals using the plastic removal tool provided **(see illustration)**. The wire within the fuse is clearly visible; if the fuse is blown, it will be broken or melted.
5 Always renew a fuse with one of an identical rating; never use a fuse with a different rating from the original, nor substitute anything else. Never renew a fuse more than once without tracing the source of the trouble. The fuse rating is stamped on top of the fuse; note that the fuses are also colour-coded for easy recognition.
6 If a new fuse blows immediately, find the cause before renewing it again; a short to earth as a result of faulty insulation is most likely. Where a fuse protects more than one circuit, try to isolate the defect by switching on each circuit in turn (if possible) until the fuse blows again. Always carry a supply of spare fuses of each relevant rating on the vehicle, a spare of each rating should be clipped into the base of the fuse/relay box.

Relays

7 Most of the relays are located in the fuse/relay boxes in the luggage compartment and engine compartment **(see illustrations 3.2 and 3.3)**.
8 If a circuit or system controlled by a relay develops a fault and the relay is suspect, operate the system; if the relay is functioning, it should be possible to hear it click as it is energised. If this is the case, the fault lies with the components or wiring of the system. If the relay is not being energised, then either the relay is not receiving a main supply or a switching voltage, or the relay itself is faulty. Testing is by the substitution of a known good unit, but be careful; while some relays are identical in appearance and in operation, others look similar but perform different functions.
9 To renew a relay, first ensure that the ignition switch is off. The relay can then simply be pulled out from the socket and the new relay pressed in.

4   Switches – removal and refitting

Note: *Disconnect the battery negative terminal (refer to 'Disconnecting the battery' in the Reference Chapter) before removing any switch, and reconnect the terminal after refitting.*

Ignition switch/ steering column lock

1 Refer to Chapter 10.

Steering column switches

2 The direction indicator and windscreen wiper switches are an integral part of the steering column electronics module, and cannot be individually renewed.
3 To remove the steering column electronics module, which also contains the airbag rotary connector, proceed as described in Section 17.

Lighting switch assembly

4 With the light switch knob in the off position, press the knob in and turn it to the AUTO position (vehicles with automatic dipped beam activation), or to the vertical position (sidelights 'on'). The switch assembly internal catch is now unlocked and the switch assembly can be withdrawn from the facia **(see illustrations)**. Once the switch is released, turn the switch off.
5 Release the locking catch and disconnect the switch wiring connector.
6 Note that the switch assembly cannot be dismantled; if any of its functions are faulty, the complete assembly must be renewed.
7 Reconnect the wiring connector and push the switch back into the facia.

Facia centre switches

8 The facia centre switches are contained in the switch strip assembly located in the facia

4.4a Press the switch knob in and turn it to the appropriate position . . .

4.4b . . . then withdraw the switch assembly from the facia

4.9a Turn the switch strip retaining catches a quarter of a turn . . .

4.9b . . . and withdraw the switch strip from the centre panel

4.16 Release the retaining clip and push the rear of the switch out of the trim panel

4.17 Disengage the control switch front locating tab (arrowed) and remove the switch

4.19a Carefully prise out the rear control switch assembly . . .

4.19b . . . and disconnect the wiring connector

centre panel. If an individual switch is faulty the complete switch strip must be renewed. To gain access to the switch, remove the facia centre panel as described in Chapter 11, Section 26.

9 With the facia centre panel removed, turn the switch strip retaining catches a quarter of a turn and withdraw the switch strip from the centre panel **(see illustration)**.

10 Refit the switch strip and turn the retaining catches back a quarter of a turn to lock the assembly in position.

11 Refit the facia centre panel as described in Chapter 11, Section 26.

Heated rear window/ blower motor switch

12 The heated rear window and blower motor switches are an integral part of the heater control assembly. Removal and refitting procedures are contained in Chapter 3.

Handbrake warning light switch

13 Refer to Chapter 9.

Stop-light switch

14 Refer to Chapter 9.

Electric window/mirror switches

Front door

15 Remove the front door inner trim panel as described in Chapter 11, Section 12.

16 Carefully release the retaining clip and push the rear of the switch out of the trim panel **(see illustration)**.

17 Disengage the switch front locating tab and remove the switch from the panel **(see illustration)**.

18 Refitting is the reverse of removal.

Rear door

19 Carefully prise out the switch assembly

and disconnect the wiring connector **(see illustrations)**.

20 Refitting is the reverse of removal.

Air conditioning system switch

21 The air conditioning system control switch is an integral part of the heating/ventilation control unit, and cannot be removed. Should the switch become faulty, the complete control unit assembly must be renewed (see Chapter 3).

Steering wheel switches

22 Turn the steering wheel so that the switch retaining screw opening is accessible, then undo the retaining screw from the rear of the steering wheel **(see illustration)**.

23 Unclip the switch surround from the steering wheel, then disconnect the wiring connector from the switch **(see illustration)**.

24 Refitting is the reverse of removal.

5 Bulbs (exterior lights) – renewal

General

1 Whenever a bulb is renewed, note the following points:

a) *Make sure the switch is in the OFF position, for the respective bulb you are working on.*

b) *Remember that if the light has just been in use, the bulb may be extremely hot.*

c) *Always check the bulb contacts and*

4.22 Undo the retaining screw from the rear of the steering wheel to release the switches

4.23 Unclip the switch surround from the steering wheel, then disconnect the switch wiring connector

5.1 Open the flap in the wheel arch liner for access to the outer bulbs in the headlight unit

5.2 Remove the outer plastic cover from the rear of the headlight

5.3 Rotate the dipped beam bulbholder anti-clockwise to release the bayonet fitting

holder, ensuring that there is clean metal-to-metal contact between the bulb and its live(s) and earth. Clean off any corrosion or dirt before fitting a new bulb.

d) Wherever bayonet-type bulbs are fitted, ensure that the live contact(s) bear firmly against the bulb contact.

e) Always ensure that the new bulb is of the correct rating, and that it is completely clean before fitting it; this applies particularly to headlight/foglight bulbs.

Halogen type headlight unit

Note 1: If working on the outer bulb in the headlight unit, turn the steering on to full lock for access under the wheel arch. Open the flap in the wheel arch liner for access to the rear of the headlight unit **(see illustration)**.

Note 2: If working on the inner bulb in the headlight unit, remove the air intake duct at the front of the air cleaner housing (right-hand side) or unclip the wiring harness connector from the front of the fuse/relay box (left-hand side).

Note 3: The outer bulb in the headlight unit is the dipped beam bulb and the inner bulb is the main beam bulb.

Dipped beam

2 Remove the plastic cover from the rear of the headlight unit **(see illustration)**.

3 Rotate the bulbholder anti-clockwise to release the bayonet fitting, then withdraw the bulbholder from the light unit **(see illustration)**.

4 Hold the bulb by its base and withdraw it

from the bulbholder **(see illustration)**. When handling the new bulb, use a tissue or clean cloth to avoid touching the glass with the fingers; moisture and grease from the skin can cause blackening and rapid failure of this type of bulb. If the glass is accidentally touched, wipe it clean using methylated spirit.

5 Fit the new bulb to the bulbholder, then refit the bulbholder to the headlight unit. Turn the bulbholder clockwise to lock it in position.

6 Refit the plastic cover to the rear of the headlight unit, then refit any components removed for access.

Main beam

7 Remove the plastic cover from the rear of the headlight unit **(see illustration)**.

8 Disconnect the wiring connector from the rear of the bulb **(see illustration)**.

9 Compress the legs of the retaining spring

clip and pivot the clip off the bulb. Lift the bulb out of the light unit **(see illustrations)**. When handling the new bulb, use a tissue or clean cloth to avoid touching the glass with the fingers; moisture and grease from the skin can cause blackening and rapid failure of this type of bulb. If the glass is accidentally touched, wipe it clean using methylated spirit.

10 Fit the new bulb to the headlight unit and secure with the spring clip. Reconnect the wiring connector.

11 Refit the plastic cover to the rear of the headlight unit, then refit any components removed for access.

Front sidelight

12 Remove the main beam plastic cover from the rear of the headlight unit **(see illustration 5.7)**.

13 Withdraw the sidelight bulbholder from the

5.4 Hold the bulb by its base and withdraw it from the bulbholder

5.7 Remove the inner plastic cover from the rear of the headlight

5.8 Disconnect the wiring connector (arrowed) from the rear of the bulb

5.9a Compress the legs of the retaining spring clip (arrowed) and pivot the clip off the bulb . . .

5.9b . . . then lift the bulb out of the light unit

5.13a Withdraw the sidelight bulbholder from the rear of the headlight unit

5.13b The bulb is a push-fit in the bulbholder

5.15 Twist the indicator bulbholder anti-clockwise, and remove it from the rear of the headlight unit

5.16 The bulb is a bayonet fit in the bulbholder

rear of the headlight unit. The bulb is of the capless (push-fit) type, and can be removed by simply pulling it out of the bulbholder **(see illustrations)**.

14 Refitting is the reverse of the removal procedure, ensuring that the bulbholder is fully engaged. On completion, refit any components removed for access.

Front indicator

15 Twist the indicator bulbholder anti-clockwise, and remove it from the rear of the headlight unit **(see illustration)**.

16 The bulb is a bayonet fit in the holder, and can be removed by pressing it and twisting in an anti-clockwise direction **(see illustration)**.

17 Refitting is a reverse of the removal procedure. On completion, refit any components removed for access.

Xenon type headlight unit

⚠️ *Warning: Xenon dipped beam headlights operate at very high voltage. Do not touch the associated wiring when the headlights are switched on.*

Note: *The outer bulb in the headlight unit is the main beam bulb and the inner bulb is the dipped beam bulb.*

Dipped beam

18 Remove the headlight unit as described in Section 7.

19 Undo the three screws and lift off the plastic cover at the rear of the headlight unit.

20 Disconnect the xenon starter unit from the bulb by turning it anti-clockwise.

21 Compress the legs of the retaining spring clip and pivot the clip off the bulb. Withdraw the bulb from the rear of the headlight unit.

22 When handling the new bulb, use a tissue or clean cloth to avoid touching the glass with the fingers; moisture and grease from the skin can cause blackening and rapid failure of this type of bulb. If the glass is accidentally touched, wipe it clean using methylated spirit.

23 Install the new bulb, ensuring that its locating tabs are correctly located in the headlight unit cut-outs. Secure the bulb with the retaining spring clip and reconnect the starter unit. Turn the starter unit clockwise to lock it in position

24 Refit the plastic cover to the rear of the unit, then refit the headlight unit as described in Section 7.

Main beam

25 Renewal of the main beam bulb is as described previously in this Section for the halogen type headlight unit.

Front sidelight

26 Renewal of the front sidelight bulb is as described previously in this Section for the halogen type headlight unit.

Front indicator

27 Renewal of the front indicator bulb is as described previously in this Section for the halogen type headlight unit.

Indicator side repeater

28 Push the light unit toward the front door, and release the front edge of the unit from the wing. If necessary, assist removal using a suitable plastic wedge, taking great care not to damage the painted finish of the wing.

29 Withdraw the light unit from the wing, and pull the bulbholder out of the light unit. The bulb is of the capless (push-fit) type, and can be removed by simply pulling it out of the bulbholder.

30 Refitting is a reverse of the removal procedure.

Front foglight

31 Reach up under the front bumper, twist the cover and free it from the foglight unit **(see illustration)**.

32 Release the spring clip and withdraw the foglight bulb from the light unit **(see illustration)**.

33 Disconnect the wiring connector and remove the bulb **(see illustration)**.

5.31 Twist the cover and free it from the foglight unit

5.32 Release the spring clip and withdraw the foglight bulb from the light unit

5.33 Disconnect the wiring connector and remove the bulb

5.39 Disconnect the wiring connector from the bulbholder

5.40 Release the sealing grommet from the top of the light cluster

5.42 Unscrew the plastic nuts and withdraw the light cluster from the rear wing

5.43 On 5-door models, undo the three screws (arrowed) securing the bulbholder to the light cluster

5.44a On 5-door models, depress the two locking tabs on the side of the bulbholder . . .

5.44b . . . and withdraw the bulbholder from the light cluster

34 When handling the new bulb, use a tissue or clean cloth to avoid touching the glass with the fingers; moisture and grease from the skin can cause blackening and rapid failure of this type of bulb. If the glass is accidentally touched, wipe it clean using methylated spirit.

35 Connect the wiring connector to the new bulb.

36 Insert the new bulb, making sure it is correctly located, and secure it in position with the spring clip.

37 Refit the cover to the rear of the unit.

Rear light cluster

Hatchback models

38 Turn the catch(es), where applicable, and remove the access cover from the luggage compartment trim panel.

39 Reach in through the trim panel opening and disconnect the wiring connector from the bulbholder **(see illustration)**.

40 Using a small screwdriver, release the sealing grommet from the top of the light cluster **(see illustration)**.

41 Use the wheelbrace from the tool kit to slacken the two light cluster plastic retaining nuts.

42 Hold the light cluster from the outside and unscrew the plastic nuts by hand the rest of the way. Withdraw the light cluster from the rear wing **(see illustration)**.

43 On 5-door models, undo the three screws securing the bulbholder to the rear of the light cluster **(see illustration)**.

44 On 5-door models, depress the two locking tabs on the side of the bulbholder and withdraw the bulbholder from the light cluster. **(see illustrations)**. On 3-door models, release the four retaining clips and withdraw the bulbholder from the light cluster.

45 The relevant bulb can then be renewed; all bulbs have a bayonet fitting **(see illustration)**.

Note that the stop/tail-light bulb has offset locating pins, to prevent it being installed incorrectly.

46 Refitting is the reverse of the removal sequence, bearing in mind the following points:

a) Ensure that the bulbholder locates securely in position on the light cluster.

b) Ensure that the rubber seals are in place on the bulbholder, locating pegs and retaining studs before refitting the light cluster.

c) Re-engage the sealing grommet with the top of the light cluster after refitting.

Estate models

47 Press the catches and remove the access cover from the luggage compartment trim panel **(see illustration)**.

48 Reach in through the trim panel opening and use the wheelbrace from the tool kit to slacken the three light cluster plastic retaining nuts **(see illustration)**.

5.45 The relevant bulb can then be renewed

5.47 Remove the access cover from the luggage compartment trim panel

5.48 Slacken the three light cluster plastic nuts (arrowed)

5.50 Withdraw the light cluster and disconnect the wiring connector

5.51a Lift off the rubber seal from the rear of the bulbholder . . .

5.51b . . . undo the three retaining screws (arrowed) . . .

5.51c . . . and separate the bulbholder from the light cluster

5.52 The relevant bulb can then be renewed

5.54 Carefully prise the number plate light unit out from its location

49 Hold the light cluster from the outside and unscrew the plastic nuts by hand the rest of the way.

50 Withdraw the light cluster from the rear wing and disconnect the wiring connector **(see illustration)**.

51 Lift off the rubber seal from the rear of the bulbholder, then undo the three retaining screws and separate the bulbholder from the light cluster **(see illustrations)**.

52 The relevant bulb can then be renewed; all bulbs have a bayonet fitting **(see illustration)**.

Note that the stop/tail-light bulb has offset locating pins, to prevent it being installed incorrectly.

53 Refitting is the reverse of the removal sequence.

Number plate light

54 Using a small flat-bladed screwdriver, carefully prise the light unit out from its location **(see illustration)**.

55 Twist the bulbholder to remove it from the light unit, and remove the bulb **(see illustrations)**.

56 Refitting is a reverse of the removal procedure.

High-level stop-light

57 The high-level stop-light bulbs are of the LED (light emitting diode) type and cannot be individually renewed. Remove the complete light unit as described in Section 7.

5.55a Twist the bulbholder to remove it from the light unit . . .

5.55b . . . and remove the push-fit bulb

6 Bulbs (interior lights) – renewal

General

1 Refer to Section 5, paragraph 1.

Front courtesy light

2 Using a small screwdriver, carefully prise the light unit lens from the overhead console **(see illustration)**.

3 Pull the relevant bulb from its socket **(see illustration)**.

6.2 Carefully prise the light unit lens from the overhead console

6.3 Pull the relevant bulb from its socket

6.8 Carefully prise the luggage compartment light unit out of position and release the bulb from the contacts

6.10a Carefully prise up the right-hand side of the ashtray . . .

6.10b . . . withdraw the ashtray from the centre console and disconnect the wiring connector

6.13a Carefully prise the glovebox light unit out of position . . .

6.13b . . . then release the bulb from its contacts

6.16 Twist and remove the relevant bulb-holder from the rear of the information display

4 Install the new bulb, ensuring that it is securely held in position by the contacts, and clip the light unit lens back into position.

Rear courtesy light

5 Using a suitable screwdriver, carefully prise the right-hand side of the light unit out of position, and withdraw the light unit.
6 Release the locking plate and disconnect the wiring connector. Remove the relevant bulb from the light unit.
7 Install the new bulb, ensuring that it is securely held in position by the contacts. Refit the wiring connector and locking plate, then clip the light unit back into position.

Luggage compartment light

8 Using a suitable screwdriver, carefully prise the light unit out of position, and release the bulb from the light unit contacts **(see illustration)**.
9 Install the new bulb, ensuring that it is securely held in position by the contacts, and clip the light unit back into position.

Cigarette lighter/ ashtray illumination

10 Using a small screwdriver, carefully prise up the right-hand side of the ashtray, withdraw the ashtray from the centre console and disconnect the wiring connector at the rear of the cigarette lighter socket **(see illustrations)**.
11 Using a small screwdriver, depress the retaining lug and withdraw the bulbholder from the lighter socket. Remove the bulb from the bulbholder.
12 Refitting is a reverse of the removal procedure.

Glovebox light

13 Open the glovebox. Using a small flat-bladed screwdriver, carefully prise the light unit out of position, then release the bulb from its contacts **(see illustrations)**. Install the new bulb, ensuring it is securely held in position by the contacts, and clip the light unit back into position.

Switch illumination

14 All the switches are fitted with illumination bulbs; some are also fitted with a bulb to show when the circuit concerned is operating. These bulbs are an integral part of the switch assembly, and cannot be obtained separately.

Information display illumination

15 Remove the information display unit as described in Section 10.
16 Twist and remove the relevant bulbholder

7.2a Undo the lower retaining bolt (arrowed) . . .

from the rear of the unit **(see illustration)**. The bulbs are integral with the bulbholders.
17 Fit the new bulbholder and bulb, then refit the information display unit as described in Section 10.

---

7 Exterior light units – removal and refitting

Note: *Disconnect the battery negative terminal (refer to 'Disconnecting the battery' in the Reference Chapter) before removing any light unit, and reconnect the terminal after refitting.*

Headlight

⚠️ **Warning: Xenon dipped beam headlights operate at very high voltage. Do not touch the associated wiring when the headlights are switched on.**

1 Remove the front bumper as described in Chapter 11, Section 6.
2 Undo the three retaining bolts and withdraw the headlight unit from the vehicle. Disconnect the wiring connectors from rear of the headlight unit as it is withdrawn **(see illustrations)**.
3 On models fitted with halogen type headlight units, the headlight beam adjustment motor can be removed and refitted as follows. Note that a new adjustment motor cover will be required to carry out this procedure.
4 Using a suitable knife cut around the circumference of the adjustment motor cover at the joint between the cover and the rear of the headlight unit. Remove and discard the

7.2b ... the upper outer retaining bolt (arrowed) ...

7.2d ... then withdraw the headlight unit ...

cover. Rotate the adjustment motor clockwise to free the motor from the rear of the headlight unit. Unclip the balljoint from the rear of the light reflector and disconnect the wiring connector.

5 On refitting, align the motor balljoint with the light unit socket, and clip it into position. Engage the motor assembly with the light, and twist it anti-clockwise to secure it in position. Obtain a new adjustment motor cover and secure it to the headlight unit using three self-tapping screws in the holes provided.

6 Refitting is a reverse of the removal procedure. On completion, check the headlight beam alignment using the information given in Section 8.

Front indicator light

7 The front direction indicator lights are integral with the headlight units. Removal and refitting is as described above.

7.28a Using a thin tool, depress the retaining clips while at the same time pulling up on the light unit ...

7.2c ... and the upper inner retaining bolt (arrowed)

7.2e ... and disconnect the wiring connector

Indicator side repeater light

8 Push the light unit toward the front door, and release the front edge of the unit from the wing. If necessary, assist removal using a suitable plastic wedge, taking great care not damage the painted finish of the wing.

9 Withdraw the light unit from the wing, and disconnect its wiring connector. Tie a piece of string to the wiring, to prevent it falling back into the wing.

10 On refitting, connect the wiring connector, and clip the light unit back into position.

Front foglight

11 Working under the front bumper, undo the three foglight retaining bolts, disconnect the wiring connector and remove the light unit from the bumper.

12 Refit the light unit to the bumper, and securely tighten its retaining bolts.

13 Reconnect the wiring connector.

7.28b ... then withdraw the unit from the tailgate

Rear light cluster

Hatchback models

14 Turn the catch (es), where applicable, and remove the access cover from the luggage compartment trim panel.

15 Reach in through the trim panel opening and disconnect the wiring connector from the bulbholder **(see illustration 5.39)**.

16 Using a small screwdriver, release the sealing grommet from the top of the light cluster **(see illustration 5.40)**.

17 Use the wheelbrace from the tool kit to slacken the two light cluster plastic retaining nuts.

18 Hold the light cluster from the outside and unscrew the plastic nuts by hand the rest of the way. Withdraw the light cluster from the rear wing **(see illustration 5.42)**.

19 Refitting is the reverse of the removal sequence, bearing in mind the following points:

a) Ensure that the rubber seals are in place on the bulbholder, locating pegs and retaining studs before refitting the light cluster.

b) Re-engage the sealing grommet with the top of the light cluster after refitting.

Estate models

20 Press the catches and remove the access cover from the luggage compartment trim panel **(see illustration 5.47)**.

21 Reach in through the trim panel opening and use the wheelbrace from the tool kit to slacken the three light cluster plastic retaining nuts **(see illustration 5.48)**.

22 Hold the light cluster from the outside and unscrew the plastic nuts by hand the rest of the way.

23 Withdraw the light cluster from the rear wing and disconnect the wiring connector **(see illustration 5.50)**.

24 Refitting is the reverse of the removal sequence.

Number plate light

25 Using a small flat-bladed screwdriver, carefully prise the light unit out from its location **(see illustration 5.54)**.

26 Twist the bulbholder to remove it from the light unit.

27 Refitting is the reverse of the removal sequence.

High-level stop-light

28 Using a suitably protected spatula or similar thin tool, insert the tool between the light unit and tailgate at the lower right-hand corner. Push up on the tool, while at the same time pulling up on the light unit, to release the first of the six retaining clips. Work around the light unit to release the remaining clips and withdraw the unit from the tailgate **(see illustrations)**.

29 Disconnect the wiring connector, and on Hatchback models, also disconnect the tailgate washer hose from the jet **(see**

7.29a Disconnect the wiring connector . . .

illustrations). Remove the stop-light unit from the tailgate.

30 Reconnect the wiring connector and, where applicable, the washer hose, then push the light unit into the tailgate until it locks in position.

8 Headlight beam alignment – general information

1 Accurate adjustment of the headlight beam is only possible using optical beam-setting equipment, and this work should therefore be carried out by a Vauxhall/Opel dealer or suitably-equipped workshop.

2 For reference, the headlights can be adjusted using the adjuster assemblies fitted to the top of each light unit. The inner adjuster, alters the vertical position of the beam. The

9.3a Undo the instrument panel left-hand lower retaining screw (arrowed) . . .

10.3a Undo the two screws (arrowed) . . .

7.29b . . . and on Hatchback models, also disconnect the tailgate washer hose from the jet

outer adjuster alters the horizontal aim of the beam.

3 Most models have an electrically-operated headlight beam adjustment system, controlled via a switch in the facia. The recommended settings are as follows.

- 0 Front seat(s) occupied
- 1 All seats occupied
- 2 All seats occupied, and load in luggage compartment
- 3 Driver's seat occupied and load in the luggage compartment

Note: *When adjusting the headlight aim, ensure that the switch is set to position 0.*

9 Instrument panel – removal and refitting

Note: *The instrument panel is a complete*

9.3b . . . and right-hand lower retaining screw (arrowed)

10.3b . . . and withdraw the information display unit from the facia

sealed assembly, and no dismantling of the instrument panel is possible.

Removal

1 Disconnect the battery negative terminal (refer to *Disconnecting the battery* in the Reference Chapter).

2 Remove the steering column shrouds as described in Chapter 11, Section 26.

3 Undo the two lower retaining screws, then pull the panel away from the facia at the bottom **(see illustrations)**.

4 Disengage the top of the panel from the facia, disconnect the wiring connector and remove the panel from the car **(see illustration)**.

Refitting

5 Refitting is a reversal of removal.

10 Information display unit – removal and refitting

Removal

1 Disconnect the battery negative terminal (refer to *Disconnecting the battery* in the Reference Chapter).

2 Remove the facia centre panel as described in Chapter 11, Section 26.

3 Undo the two lower retaining screws and withdraw the information display unit from the facia **(see illustrations)**.

4 Disconnect the wiring connector and remove the unit from the car **(see illustration)**.

9.4 Disengage the top of the panel from the facia and disconnect the wiring connector

10.4 Disconnect the wiring connector and remove the unit from the car

12.2 The horns are located under the front bumper on the right-hand side

Refitting

5 Refitting is a reversal of removal.

11 Cigarette lighter – removal and refitting

The cigarette lighter is an integral part of the ashtray. Proceed as described in Section 6, paragraphs 10 to 12.

12 Horn – removal and refitting

Removal

1 Firmly apply the handbrake, then jack up the front of the car and support it securely on axle stands (see *Jacking and vehicle support*). Remove the wheel arch lower panel on the right-hand side.

2 Working under the bumper on the right-hand side, undo the retaining nut/bolt and remove the horn(s), disconnecting the wiring connector as it becomes accessible **(see illustration)**.

Refitting

3 Refitting is the reverse of removal.

13 Wiper arm – removal and refitting

Removal

1 Operate the wiper motor, then switch it off so that the wiper arm returns to the at-rest (parked) position.

 HAYNES HiNT *Stick a piece of masking tape along the edge of the wiper blade, to use as an alignment aid on refitting.*

2 Unclip the wiper arm spindle nut cover (windscreen wiper arm), or pivot the cover up (tailgate wiper arm), then slacken and remove the spindle nut and washer **(see illustrations)**.

3 Using a suitable puller, free the wiper arm from the spindle and remove the arm **(see illustration)**. Note: *If both windscreen wiper arms are to be removed at the same time, mark them for identification. The arms are not interchangeable; the passenger-side wiper arm is longer than the driver's-side arm, and its shaft is also cranked slightly.*

Refitting

4 Ensure that the wiper arm and spindle splines are clean and dry, then refit the arm to the spindle, aligning the wiper blade with the tape fitted on removal. Refit the spindle nut, tightening it securely, and clip the nut cover back in position.

14 Windscreen wiper motor and linkage – removal and refitting

Removal

1 Disconnect the battery negative terminal (refer to *Disconnecting the battery* in the Reference Chapter).

2 Remove the wiper arms as described in Section 13.

3 Remove the water deflector as described in Chapter 11, Section 20.

4 Undo the three retaining bolts, and withdraw the wiper motor and linkage assembly from the scuttle **(see illustrations)**.

5 Disconnect the wiring connector from the wiper motor and remove the assembly from the car **(see illustration)**.

6 If necessary, mark the relative positions of the motor shaft and linkage arm, then unscrew the retaining nut from the motor spindle. Free

13.2a Unclip the windscreen wiper arm spindle nut cover . . .

13.2b . . . then slacken and remove the spindle nut . . .

13.2c . . . and collect the washer

13.3 Using a suitable puller, free the wiper arm from the spindle

14.4a Undo the four retaining bolts (arrowed) . . .

14.4b . . . and withdraw the wiper motor and linkage assembly

the wiper linkage from the spindle, then remove the three motor retaining bolts, and separate the motor and linkage **(see illustration)**.

Refitting

7 Where necessary, assemble the motor and linkage, and securely tighten the motor retaining bolts. Locate the linkage arm on the motor spindle, aligning the marks made prior to removal, and securely tighten its retaining nut.

8 Reconnect the wiper motor wiring connector, then manoeuvre the motor assembly back into position in the vehicle. Refit the retaining bolts, and tighten them securely.

9 Refit the water deflector as described in Chapter 11, Section 20.

10 Install both the wiper arms as described in Section 13, and reconnect the battery negative terminal.

---

15 Tailgate wiper motor –
removed and refitting

Removal

1 On Hatchback models, unhook the lifting cords and remove the parcel shelf from the luggage compartment. Unscrew the parcel shelf lifting pins on each side.

2 Remove the tailgate upper side trim panel, by prising it free at the sides, then at the centre to release the internal retaining clips. On some models, the panel is in two parts with a join at the centre. In this case, remove the left-hand panel first, followed by the right-hand panel. **(see illustrations)**.

3 Pull out the expanding rivet and undo the retaining screw (where fitted), securing the lock cover panel to the base of the tailgate **(see illustration)**. Remove the panel.

4 On Estate models, pull out the expanding rivet each side, securing the tailgate lower trim panel to the tailgate, and unscrew the two screws at the top of the panel **(see illustrations)**.

5 On all models, pull the lower trim panel away from the tailgate to release the remaining internal clips and remove the panel from the tailgate **(see illustration)**.

6 Remove the wiper arm as described in Section 13.

15.4b ... and unscrew the two screws at the top of the panel

14.5 Disconnect the wiper motor wiring connector and remove the assembly from the car

15.2a Remove the tailgate upper side trim panel, by prising it free at the sides ...

7 Disconnect the wiring connector, then slacken and remove the three wiper motor mounting bolts and remove the wiper motor **(see illustration)**.

15.3 Pull out the expanding rivet (A) and undo the retaining screw (B) (where fitted)

15.5 Pull the lower trim panel away from the tailgate to release the remaining internal clips

14.6 Wiper motor retaining bolts (arrowed)

15.2b ... then at the centre to release the internal retaining clips

Refitting

8 Refitting is the reverse of removal, ensuring the wiper motor retaining bolts are securely tightened.

15.4a On Estate models, pull out the expanding rivet each side ...

15.7 Tailgate wiper motor mounting bolts (arrowed)

16.2 Unscrew the bolt (arrowed) securing the filler neck to the bonnet crossmember

16.3 Disconnect the wiring connector (A) and washer hoses at the washer pump (B)

16.4 Washer reservoir retaining bolt (arrowed)

16.7 Ease the pump out from the reservoir and recover its sealing grommet

16 Windscreen/tailgate washer system components – removal and refitting

Washer system reservoir

1 Remove the front bumper as described in Chapter 11, Section 6.

2 Unscrew the bolt securing the filler neck to the bonnet crossmember **(see illustration)**.

3 Disconnect the wiring connector(s) and washer hoses at the washer pump(s), then release the wiring and hoses from the side of the reservoir **(see illustration)**.

4 Undo the retaining bolt (two bolts on some models, according to equipment) and lower the reservoir out from under the car **(see illustration)**.

5 Refitting is the reverse of removal, ensuring that the washer hose(s) are securely connected.

Washer pump

6 Remove the front bumper as described in Chapter 11, Section 6.

7 Disconnect the pump washer hoses, then carefully ease the pump out from the reservoir and recover its sealing grommet **(see illustration)**.

8 Refitting is the reverse of removal, using a new sealing grommet if the original one shows signs of damage or deterioration.

Windscreen washer jets

9 Remove the water deflector as described in Chapter 11, Section 20

16.10 Depress the retaining clip, then prise the washer nozzle from the water deflector panel

10 Depress the retaining clip, then carefully prise the nozzle from the water deflector panel **(see illustration)**.

11 Disconnect the nozzle from its fluid hose(s), and remove it from the vehicle.

12 On refitting, securely connect the nozzle to the hose, and clip it into position in the water deflector panel. Refit the water deflector panel, then check the operation of the jet. If necessary, adjust the nozzle using a pin, aiming the spray to a point slightly above the centre of the swept area.

Tailgate washer jet

Hatchback models

13 Remove the high-level stop-light as described in Section 7.

14 Release the two retaining lugs and remove the washer jet from the stop-light unit.

15 When refitting, ensure that the jet is clipped securely in position. Check the operation of

17.6 Undo the three bolts (arrowed) securing the electronics module to the steering column

16.16 Carefully extract the washer jet from the tailgate

the jet. If necessary, adjust the nozzle using a pin, aiming the spray to a point slightly above the centre of the swept area.

Estate models

16 Carefully extract the washer jet from the tailgate **(see illustration)**.

17 Disconnect the fluid hose and remove the jet from the car.

18 When refitting, ensure that the jet is clipped securely in position. Check the operation of the jet. If necessary, adjust the nozzle using a pin, aiming the spray to a point slightly above the centre of the swept area.

17 Steering column electronics module – removal and refitting

Removal

1 Disconnect the battery negative terminal (refer to *Disconnecting the battery* in the Reference Chapter) and wait for 2 minutes.

2 Remove the driver's airbag as described in Section 24.

3 Set the roadwheels in the straight-ahead position and ensure they remain in that position during the removal and refitting procedures.

4 Remove the steering wheel as described in Chapter 10.

5 Remove the steering column shrouds as described in Chapter 11, Section 26.

6 Undo the three bolts securing the module to the steering column **(see illustration)**.

7 Withdraw the module from the steering

17.7 Withdraw the module from the steering column and disconnect the wiring connector

17.8a Insert a thin rod down the slot on the side of the stalk to depress the internal retaining lug . . .

17.8b . . . then withdraw the stalk from the electronics module

column, disconnect the wiring connector and remove the module **(see illustration)**.

8 If required the direction indicator and wiper switch stalks can be removed from the module as follows. Insert a 1.5 mm diameter rod down the slot on the side of the stalk. Push the rod in fully, to depress the internal retaining lug and withdraw the stalk from the module **(see illustrations)**. Note that this procedure merely allows the stalks to be removed, the actual direction indicator and wiper switches themselves are an integral part of the electronics module and cannot be removed.

Refitting

9 If removed, push the switch stalks back into position in the module until they lock into place.

10 Refit the electronics module to the steering wheel using a reverse of the removal procedure.

---

18 Radio/cassette/CD player –
removal and refitting

Note: *The following removal and refitting procedure is for the range of radio/cassette/CD units which Vauxhall/Opel fit as standard equipment. Removal and refitting procedures of non-standard units may differ slightly.*

Removal

1 All the radio/cassette/CD players fitted by Vauxhall have DIN standard fixings. Two

special tools, obtainable from most car accessory shops, are required for removal. Alternatively, suitable tools can be fabricated from 3 mm diameter wire, such as welding rod.

2 Disconnect the battery negative terminal (refer to *Disconnecting the battery* in the Reference Chapter).

3 Insert the tools into the holes on the front of the unit, and push them until they snap into place. The radio/cassette/CD player can then be slid out of the facia **(see illustration)**.

4 Disconnect the wiring and aerial connections at the rear of the unit, and remove the unit from the car.

Refitting

5 To refit the radio/cassette player/CD, reconnect the wiring and simply push the unit into the facia until the retaining lugs snap into

18.3 Removing the radio/cassette/CD player using welding rod to compress the internal clips

place. On completion, reconnect the battery and enter the radio security code, where applicable.

---

19 Speakers –
removal and refitting

Front door small (tweeter) speaker

1 Carefully prise off the door mirror interior trim panel to release the three retaining clips **(see illustration)**.

2 Remove the foam insulation from the mirror interior trim panel and disconnect the speaker wiring connector **(see illustrations)**.

3 Withdraw the speaker from the panel **(see illustration)**.

4 Refitting is the reverse of removal.

19.1 Carefully prise off the door mirror interior trim panel to release the three retaining clips

19.2a Remove the foam insulation from the mirror interior trim panel . . .

19.2b . . . and disconnect the speaker wiring connector

19.3 Withdraw the speaker from the mirror trim panel

19.6 Door loudspeaker retaining screws (arrowed)

Door main speaker

Note: *On 3-door Hatchback models, a rear speaker is fitted behind the rear interior trim panel. Remove the trim panel and proceed as described in paragraphs 6 and 7.*

5 Remove the door inner trim panel as described in Chapter 11.

6 Undo the retaining screws, then free the speaker from its location **(see illustration)**. Disconnect the wiring connectors and remove the speaker.

7 Refitting is the reverse of removal.

20 Radio aerial – general information

1 Where required, the aerial mast can be unscrewed from the base unit.

2 Removal of the base unit entails removal of the headlining, which is a complicated operation, considered to be outside the scope of this manual. Therefore, any problems relating to the aerial base unit or wiring should be entrusted to a Vauxhall/Opel dealer.

21 Anti-theft alarm system – general information

Note: *This information is applicable only to the anti-theft alarm system fitted by Vauxhall/Opel as standard equipment.*

1 Most models in the range are fitted with an anti-theft alarm system as standard equipment. The alarm is automatically armed and disarmed when the deadlocks are operated using the driver's door lock or remote control key. The alarm has switches on all the doors (including the tailgate), the bonnet, the radio/cassette/CD player and the ignition and starter circuits. If the tailgate, bonnet or any of the doors are opened whilst the alarm is set, the alarm horn will sound and the hazard warning lights will flash. The alarm also has an immobiliser function which makes the ignition and starter circuits inoperable whilst the alarm is triggered.

2 The alarm system performs a self-test every time it is switched on; this test takes approximately 10 seconds. During the self-test, the LED (light emitting diode) in the hazard warning light switch will come on. If the LED flashes, then either the tailgate, bonnet or one of the doors is open, or there is a fault in the circuit. After the initial 10-second period, the LED will flash to indicate that the alarm is switched on. On unlocking the driver's door lock, the LED will illuminate for approximately 1 second, then go out, indicating that the alarm has been switched off.

3 With the alarm set, if the tailgate is unlocked, the tailgate switch sensing will automatically be switched off, but the door and bonnet switches will still be active. Once the tailgate is shut and locked again, the tailgate switch sensing will be switched back on after approximately 10 seconds.

4 Should the alarm system develop a fault, the vehicle should be taken to a Vauxhall/Opel dealer for examination.

22 Heated seat components – general information

On models with heated seats, a heater mat is fitted to both the seat back and seat cushion. Renewal of either heater mat involves peeling back the upholstery, removing the old mat, sticking the new mat in position and then refitting the upholstery. Note that upholstery removal and refitting requires considerable skill and experience if it is to be carried out successfully, and is therefore best entrusted to your Vauxhall/Opel dealer. In practice, it will be very difficult for the home mechanic to carry out the job without ruining the upholstery.

23 Airbag system – general information and precautions

General information

A driver's airbag is fitted as standard equipment on all models. The airbag is fitted in the steering wheel centre pad. Additionally, a passenger's airbag located in the facia, side airbags located in the front seats, and curtain airbags located in the headlining are optionally available.

The system is armed only when the ignition is switched on, however, a reserve power source maintains a power supply to the system in the event of a break in the main electrical supply. The steering wheel and facia airbags are activated by a 'g' sensor (deceleration sensor), and controlled by an electronic control unit located under the centre console. The side airbags and curtain airbags are activated by severe side impact and operate independently of the main system. A separate electrical supply, control unit and sensor is provided for the side/curtain airbags on each side of the car.

The airbags are inflated by a gas generator, which forces the bag out from its location in the steering wheel, facia, seat back frame, or headlining.

Precautions

Warning: The following precautions must be observed when working on vehicles equipped with an airbag system, to prevent the possibility of personal injury.

General precautions

The following precautions **must** be observed when carrying out work on a vehicle equipped with an airbag:

a) *Do not disconnect the battery with the engine running.*
b) *Before carrying out any work in the vicinity of the airbag, removal of any of the airbag components, or any welding work on the vehicle, de-activate the system as described in the following sub-Section.*
c) *Do not attempt to test any of the airbag system circuits using test meters or any other test equipment.*
d) *If the airbag warning light comes on, or any fault in the system is suspected, consult a Vauxhall/Opel dealer without delay. Do not attempt to carry out fault diagnosis, or any dismantling of the components.*

Precautions when handling an airbag

a) *Transport the airbag by itself, bag upward.*
b) *Do not put your arms around the airbag.*
c) *Carry the airbag close to the body, bag outward.*
d) *Do not drop the airbag or expose it to impacts.*
e) *Do not attempt to dismantle the airbag unit.*
f) *Do not connect any form of electrical equipment to any part of the airbag circuit.*

Precautions when storing an airbag

a) *Store the unit in a cupboard with the airbag upward.*
b) *Do not expose the airbag to temperatures above 80ºC.*
c) *Do not expose the airbag to flames.*
d) *Do not attempt to dispose of the airbag – consult a Vauxhall/Opel dealer.*
e) *Never refit an airbag which is known to be faulty or damaged.*

De-activation of airbag system

The system must be de-activated before carrying out any work on the airbag components or surrounding area:

a) *Switch on the ignition and check the operation of the airbag warning light on the instrument panel. The light should illuminate when the ignition is switched on, then extinguish.*
b) *Switch off the ignition.*
c) *Remove the ignition key.*
d) *Switch off all electrical equipment.*
e) *Disconnect the battery negative terminal (refer to 'Disconnecting the battery' in the Reference Chapter).*

24.2a Insert a screwdriver into the holes at the rear of the steering wheel (shown with steering wheel removed) . . .

24.2b . . . to depress the airbag internal spring retainers (arrowed – shown with airbag removed)

24.3 Release the locking clips, then disconnect the wiring connectors

24.6 Passenger's airbag retaining bolt (arrowed)

f) Insulate the battery negative terminal and the end of the battery negative lead to prevent any possibility of contact.

g) Wait for at least two minutes before carrying out any further work. Wait at least ten minutes if the airbag warning light did not operate correctly.

Activation of airbag system

To activate the system on completion of any work, proceed as follows:

a) Ensure that there are no occupants in the vehicle, and that there are no loose objects around the vicinity of the steering wheel. Close the vehicle doors and windows.

b) Ensure that the ignition is switched off then reconnect the battery negative terminal.

c) Open the driver's door and switch on the ignition, without reaching in front of the steering wheel. Check that the airbag warning light illuminates briefly then extinguishes.

d) Switch off the ignition.

e) If the airbag warning light does not operate as described in paragraph c), consult a Vauxhall/Opel dealer before driving the vehicle.

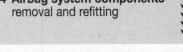

24 Airbag system components – removal and refitting

Warning: Refer to the precautions given in Section 23 before attempting to carry out work on any of the airbag components.

1 De-activate the airbag system as described in the previous Section, then proceed as described under the relevant heading.

Driver's airbag

2 Turn the steering wheel through 90° so that the two holes at the rear of the steering wheel spokes are accessible. Insert a screwdriver into the holes, one at a time, to depress the internal spring retainers, and at the same time pull the airbag unit away from the steering wheel to release it **(see illustrations)**.

3 Release the locking clips, then disconnect the wiring connectors at the rear of the airbag unit **(see illustration)**. Remove the airbag unit. Note that the airbag must not be knocked or dropped, and should be stored the correct way up, with its padded surface uppermost.

4 Refitting is a reversal of the removal procedure.

Passenger's airbag

5 Remove the complete facia assembly as described in Chapter 11, Section 26.

6 Undo the bolt securing the airbag to the facia crossmember **(see illustration)**. Withdraw the airbag and disconnect the wiring connector(s). Note that the airbag must not be knocked or dropped, and should be stored the correct way up (as mounted in the vehicle).

7 Refitting is a reversal of the removal procedure, tightening the retaining bolt securely.

Side airbags

8 The side airbags are located internally within the front seat back and no attempt should be made to remove them. Any suspected

problems with the side airbag system should be referred to a Vauxhall/Opel dealer.

Curtain airbags

9 The curtain airbags are located behind the headlining above the doors on each side and no attempt should be made to remove them. Any suspected problems with the curtain airbag system should be referred to a Vauxhall/Opel dealer.

Airbag control unit

10 The airbag control unit is located beneath the centre console and no attempt should be made to remove it. Any suspected problems with the control unit should be referred to a Vauxhall/Opel dealer.

Airbag rotary connector

11 The airbag rotary connector is an integral part of the steering column electronics module. Removal and refitting procedures for the module are contained in Section 17.

VAUXHALL ASTRA wiring diagrams

Diagram 1

Key to symbols

Dashed outline denotes part of a larger item, containing in this case an electronic or solid state device.
XE2/11 - Connector No. **XE2**, pin No. **11**

Solenoid actuator

Heating element

Earth point & location

Wire colour (red with yellow tracer)

Bulb

Switch

Fuse/fusible link

Resistor

Variable resistor

Variable resistor

Wire splice, soldered joint, or unspecified connector

Connecting wires

Diode

Light-emitting diode

Item number

Motor/pump

Engine fusebox ④
(without rear electronic control unit)

Fuse	Rating	Circuit protected
F1	20A	ABS
F2	30A	ABS
F3	30A	Heater blower, climate control system
F4	30A	Heater blower, heating, air conditioning
F5	30A	Engine cooling fan
	40A	Engine cooling fan
F6	20A	Engine cooling fan
	30A	Engine cooling fan
	40A	Engine cooling fan
F7	20A	Central locking
F8	10A	Front washer, tailgate
F9	30A	Heated rear window, heated mirrors
F10	7.5A	Diagnostic connector
F11	7.5A	Instruments
F12	7.5A	Mobile telephone, audio system, display
F13	5A	Interior light
F14	30A	Front wiper
F15	30A	Front wiper
F16	5A	Horn, ABS, stop light switch, air conditioning
F17	25A	Diesel filter or air conditioning
F18	25A	Starter
F19	30A	Transmission electronics
F20	15A	Horn
F21	20A	Engine electronics
F22	7.5A	Engine electronics
F23	5A	Headlight levelling
F24	15A	Fuel pump
F25	5A	Reversing lights
F26	10A	Engine electronics
F27	7.5A	Heating, air conditioning, air quality sensor
F28	-	Spare
F29	5A	Power steering
F30	10A	Engine electronics
F31	15A	Rear wiper
F32	5A	Stop light switch
F33	5A	Headlight levelling, light switch, clutch switch, instrument cluster, driver's door control unit
F34	7.5A	Steering column control unit
F35	20A	Infotainment system
F36	15A	Cigar lighter, front accessory socket

Engine fusebox ④
(with rear electronic control unit)

Fuse	Rating	Circuit protected
F1	20A	ABS
F2	30A	ABS
F3	30A	Heater blower, climate control system
F4	30A	Heater blower, heating, air conditioning
F5	30A	Engine cooling fan
	40A	Engine cooling fan
F6	20A	Engine cooling fan
	30A	Engine cooling fan
	40A	Engine cooling fan
F7	10A	Front washer
F8	15A	Horn
F9	25A	Headlight washer
F10	-	Spare
F11	-	Spare
F12	-	Spare
F13	15A	Front foglights
F14	30A	Front wiper
F15	30A	Front wiper
F16	5A	Electronic control units, open & start system, ABS, stop light switch, TwinTop
F17	25A	Diesel filter heater
F18	25A	Starter
F19	30A	Transmission electronics
F20	10A	Air conditioning
F21	20A	Engine electronics
F22	7.5A	Engine electronics
F23	10A	Adaptive forward lighting, headlight levelling
F24	15A	Fuel pump
F25	15A	Transmission electronics
F26	10A	Engine electronics
F27	5A	Power steering
F28	5A	Transmission electronics
F29	7.5A	Transmission electronics
F30	10A	Engine electronics
F31	10A	Adaptive forward lighting
F32	5A	Stop light switch, air conditioning, clutch switch
F33	5A	Adaptive forward lighting, headlight levelling, light switch
F34	7.5A	Steering column control unit
F35	20A	Infotainment system
F36	7.5A	Mobile telephone, audio system, display

H33731

VAUXHALL ASTRA wiring diagrams

Diagram 2

Rear fusebox ⑭
(without rear electronic control unit)

Fuse	Rating	Circuit protected
F1	15A	Luggage compartment accessory socket
F2	15A	Rear accessory socket
F3	30A	Front electic windows
F4	30A	Rear electric windows
F5	7.5A	Heated mirrors
F6	10A	Air conditioning

Rear fusebox ⑭
(with rear electronic control unit)

Fuse	Rating	Circuit protected
F1	25A	Front electric windows
F2	-	Spare
F3	7.5A	Instrument cluster
F4	5A	Heating, air conditioning, climate control
F5	7.5A	Airbags
F6	-	Spare
F7	-	Spare
F8	-	Spare
F9	-	Spare
F10	-	Spare
F11	25A	Heated rear window
F12	15A	Rear wiper
F13	5A	Parking distance sensors
F14	7.5A	Heating, air conditioning
F15	-	Spare
F16	5A	Seat occupancy recognition, open & start system
F17	5A	Rain sensor, air quality sensor, tyre pressure monitor, interior mirror
F18	5A	Instruments, switches
F19	-	Spare
F20	10A	CDC
F21	7.5A	Heated mirrors
F22	20A	Sunroof
F23	25A	Rear electric windows
F24	7.5A	Diagnostic connector
F25	-	Spare
F26	7.5A	Retractable mirrors
F27	5A	Ultrasonic alarm sensor
F28	-	Spare
F29	15A	Cigar lighter, front accessory socket
F30	15A	Rear accessory socket
F31	-	Spare
F32	-	Spare
F33	15A	Open & start
F34	25A	Sunroof, TwinTop
F35	15A	Rear accessory socket
F36	20A	Towing equipment
F37	5A	Interior light
F38	25A	Central locking
F39	15A	LH seat heater
F40	15A	RH seat heater
F41	-	Spare
F42	-	Spare
F43	-	Spare
F44	-	Spare

Earth locations

E1	Battery -ve terminal
E2	On rear of engine
E3	LH front wheel arch
E4	LH front chassis leg
E5	RH front chassis leg
E6	LH front inner wing
E7	LH front inner wing
E8	Base of LH 'A' pillar
E9	LH dashboard crossmember
E10	Bracket on steering column
E11	RH dashboard crossmember
E12	Centre dashboard crossmember
E13	Base of RH 'A' pillar
E14	Transmission tunnel
E15	Transmission tunnel
E16	LH 'C' pillar
E17	Near LH rear light
E18	Below battery
E19	Not used
E20	Below battery
E21	Near battery
E22	Lh rear of engine
E23	LH rear of engine
E24	LH rear of engine
E25	RH rear compartment (Twin Top only)

Key to circuits

Diagram 1	Information for wiring diagrams
Diagram 2	Information for wiring diagrams
Diagram 3	Typical starting, charging & engine cooling fans
Diagram 4	Typical horn, stop & reversing lights, sidelights, tail lights, number plate lights, headlights
Diagram 5	Typical foglights, direction indicators & hazard warning lights, trailer socket, headlight levelling (without xenon headlights)
Diagram 6	Typical headlight levelling (with xenon headlights), interior lighting, cigar lighter & accessory socket, heated rear window
Diagram 7	Typical heater & wash/wipe
Diagram 8	Typical audio system, sunroof & electric mirrors
Diagram 9	Typical electric windows, central locking

H33732

Wire colours

Bk	Black	**Pk**	Pink
Ye	Yellow	**Vt**	Violet
Bu	Blue	**Og**	Orange
Bn	Brown	**Wh**	White
Gn	Green	**Lgn**	Light Green
Gy	Grey	**Lbu**	Light Blue
Pu	Purple	**Dgn**	Dark Green
Bg	Beige	**DBu**	Dark Blue
Rd	Red		

Key to items

1 Battery
2 Alternator
3 Starter motor
4 Engine fusebox
  a = under bonnet control unit
  k1 = starter relay
  k3 = terminal 15 relay
  k11 = engine cooling fan relay
  k12 = engine cooling fan relay
  k13 = engine cooling fan relay

5 Steering column control unit
6 Engine cooling fan
7 Engine cooling fan relay

Diagram 3

H33733

Typical starting & charging

Typical engine cooling fan - dual fan

Typical engine cooling fan - single fan

Wire colours

Bk	Black	**Pk**	Pink
Ye	Yellow	**Vt**	Violet
Bu	Blue	**Og**	Orange
Bn	Brown	**Wh**	White
Gn	Green	**Lgn**	Light Green
Gy	Grey	**Lbu**	Light Blue
Pu	Purple	**Dgn**	Dark Green
Bg	Beige	**DBu**	Dark Blue
Rd	Red		

* 5 door hatch
** 3 door hatch
*** Estate

Key to items

1 Battery
4 Engine fusebox
  a = under bonnet control unit
  k2 = engine control relay
5 Steering column control unit
10 Horn
11 Horn switch
12 Stop light switch
13 Reversing light switch
14 Rear fusebox
  a = rear control unit
15 LH rear light unit
  a = stop/tail light
  b = reversing light
  c = tail light
16 RH rear light unit
  (as above)
17 High level stop light
18 Number plate light
19 Instrument cluster
20 Light switch
  a = auto/side/headlights
21 LH headlight
  a = sidelight
  b = main beam
  c = main beam aperture actuator
  d = xenon control unit
  e = xenon ignition unit
  f = dip beam
22 RH headlight
  (as above)

Diagram 4

H33734

Typical horn

Typical stop & reversing lights

Typical side, tail & number plate lights

Typical headlights

Wire colours

Bk	Black	**Pk**	Pink
Ye	Yellow	**Vt**	Violet
Bu	Blue	**Og**	Orange
Bn	Brown	**Wh**	White
Gn	Green	**Lgn**	Light Green
Gy	Grey	**Lbu**	Light Blue
Pu	Purple	**Dgn**	Dark Green
Bg	Beige	**DBu**	Dark Blue
Rd	Red		

* 5 door hatch
** 3 door hatch
*** Estate

Key to items

1 Battery
4 Engine fusebox
   a = under bonnet control unit
   k3 = terminal 15 relay
   k16 = front foglight relay
5 Steering column control unit
14 Rear fusebox
   a = rear control unit
   b = trailer control unit
15 LH rear light unit
   d = direction indicator
16 RH rear light unit
   d = direction indicator
   e = foglight

19 Instrument cluster
20 Light switch
   b = front foglight
   c = rear foglight
   d = headlight levelling adjuster
21 LH headlight
   g = hazard warning
   h = headlight levelling adjuster
22 RH headlight
   (as above)
25 LH front foglight
26 RH front foglight

27 Centre console switch
   a = hazard warning switch
28 LH indicator side repeater
29 RH indicator side repeater
30 Engine maxifusebox
31 Trailer socket

Diagram 5

H33735

Typical foglights

Typical trailer socket

Typical headlight levelling – without xenon headlights

Typical direction indicators & hazard warning lights

Wire colours

Bk	Black	**Pk**	Pink
Ye	Yellow	**Vt**	Violet
Bu	Blue	**Og**	Orange
Bn	Brown	**Wh**	White
Gn	Green	**Lgn**	Light Green
Gy	Grey	**Lbu**	Light Blue
Pu	Purple	**Dgn**	Dark Green
Bg	Beige	**DBu**	Dark Blue
Rd	Red		

Key to items

1 Battery
4 Engine fusebox
  a = under bonnet control unit
  k3 = terminal 15 relay
5 Steering column control unit
14 Rear fusebox
  a = rear control unit
  k1 = terminal 15 relay
  K3 = heated rear window relay
19 Instrument cluster
20 Light switch
  e = interior lighting dimmer
21 LH headlight
  h = headlight levelling adjuster
22 RH headlight
  h = headlight levelling adjuster
30 Engine maxifusebox
35 Headlight levelling control unit
36 Vehicle level sensor
37 Driver's door courtesy light
41 Glovebox light
42 Luggage compartment light
43 LH vanity mirror light
44 RH vanity mirror light
45 Front accessory socket/cigar lighter
46 Rear accessory socket
47 Heated rear window
38 Passenger's door courtesy light
39 Front interior light
40 Rear interior light

Diagram 6

H33736

Typical headlight levelling - with xenon headlights

Typical interior lighting

Typical cigar lighter & accessory sockets

Typical heated rear window

Wire colours

Bk	Black	**Pk**	Pink
Ye	Yellow	**Vt**	Violet
Bu	Blue	**Og**	Orange
Bn	Brown	**Wh**	White
Gn	Green	**Lgn**	Light Green
Gy	Grey	**Lbu**	Light Blue
Pu	Purple	**Dgn**	Dark Green
Bg	Beige	**DBu**	Dark Blue
Rd	Red		

Key to items

1 Battery
4 Engine fusebox
  a = under bonnet control unit
  k5 = front wiper relay (low/hi speed)
  k6 = front wiper relay (on/off)
  k7 = headlight washer relay
  k15 = heater blower relay
5 Steering column control unit
14 Rear fusebox
  a = rear control unit
  k1 = terminal 15 relay

19 Instrument cluster
30 Engine maxifusebox
50 Heater unit
  a = control unit
  b = heater blower resistors
  c = heater blower motor
  d = recirculation flap motor
  e = air distribution flap motor
  f = mixed air flap motor
51 Front and rear washer pump
52 Headlight washer pump

53 Rain sensor
54 Front wiper motor
55 Rear wiper motor
56 Wash/wipe switch

Diagram 7

H33737

Typical heater

Typical wash/wipe

Wire colours

Bk	Black	**Pk**	Pink
Ye	Yellow	**Vt**	Violet
Bu	Blue	**Og**	Orange
Bn	Brown	**Wh**	White
Gn	Green	**Lgn**	Light Green
Gy	Grey	**Lbu**	Light Blue
Pu	Purple	**Dgn**	Dark Green
Bg	Beige	**DBu**	Dark Blue
Rd	Red		

Key to items

1 Battery
4 Engine fusebox
14 Rear fusebox
   a = under bonnet control unit
19 Instrument cluster
30 Engine maxifusebox
60 Audio unit
61 Antenna module
62 Instrument panel centre speaker
63 LH front door speaker
64 LH front tweeter
65 RH front door speaker

66 RH front tweeter
67 LH rear speaker
68 RH rear speaker
69 Sunroof switch
70 Sunroof motor
71 Sunscreen switch
72 Sunscreen motor
73 LH door mirror assembly
   a = heating element
   b = mirror retraction
   c = mirror adjustment

74 RH door mirror assembly
   (as above)
75 Driver's door switch
   a = control unit
   b = mirror retraction control
   c = switch illumination
   d = mirror control

Diagram 8

H33738

Typical audio system

Typical sunroof

Typical electric mirrors

Wire colours

Bk	Black	**Pk**	Pink
Ye	Yellow	**Vt**	Violet
Bu	Blue	**Og**	Orange
Bn	Brown	**Wh**	White
Gn	Green	**Lgn**	Light Green
Gy	Grey	**Lbu**	Light Blue
Pu	Purple	**Dgn**	Dark Green
Bg	Beige	**DBu**	Dark Blue
Rd	Red		

Key to items

1 Battery
14 Rear fusebox
 a = under bonnet control unit
19 Instrument cluster
27 Centre console switch
30 Engine maxifusebox
75 Driver's door switch
 e = rear window isolation
 f = LH front window
 g = LH rear window
 h = RH rear window
 i = RH front window

80 Front passenger door switch
81 LH rear door switch
82 RH rear door switch
83 Driver's window motor
84 Passenger's window motor
85 LH rear window motor
86 RH rear window motor
87 Driver's door lock motor
88 Passenger's door lock motor
89 LH rear door lock motor
90 RH rear door lock motor
91 Tailgate lock motor

92 Tailgate lock switch
93 Fuel filler flap lock

Diagram 9

H33739

Typical electric windows

Typical central locking

Dimensions and Weights

Note: *All figures are approximate and may vary according to model. Refer to manufacturer's data for exact figures.*

Dimensions

Overall length:
    3-door Hatchback . . . . 4290 mm
    5-door Hatchback . . . . 4249 mm
    Estate . . . . 4515 mm
Overall width (including door mirrors) . . . . 2032 mm
Overall height (unladen):
    3-door Hatchback . . . . 1435 mm
    5-door Hatchback . . . . 1460 mm
    Estate . . . . 1500 mm
Wheelbase:
    Hatchback . . . . 2614 mm
    Estate . . . . 2703 mm
Turning circle diameter (wall to wall) . . . . 11.20 metres
Front track . . . . 1488 mm
Rear track . . . . 1488 mm

Weights

Kerb weight:
    1.3 litre models:
        Hatchback . . . . 1320 to 1355 kg
        Estate . . . . 1380 to 1395 kg
    1.7 litre models:
        Hatchback . . . . 1345 to 1380 kg
        Estate . . . . 1393 to 1408 kg
    1.9 litre models:
        Hatchback . . . . 1375 to 1410 kg
        Estate . . . . 1435 to 1465 kg
Gross vehicle weight . . . . Refer to information contained on the vehicle identification plate
Maximum roof load (including weight of rack):
    Hatchback . . . . 75 kg
    Estate . . . . 100 kg

Conversion factors

Length (distance)

Inches (in)	x 25.4	= Millimetres (mm)	x 0.0394	= Inches (in)	
Feet (ft)	x 0.305	= Metres (m)	x 3.281	= Feet (ft)	
Miles	x 1.609	= Kilometres (km)	x 0.621	= Miles	

Volume (capacity)

Cubic inches (cu in; in³)	x 16.387	= Cubic centimetres (cc; cm³)	x 0.061	= Cubic inches (cu in; in³)	
Imperial pints (Imp pt)	x 0.568	= Litres (l)	x 1.76	= Imperial pints (Imp pt)	
Imperial quarts (Imp qt)	x 1.137	= Litres (l)	x 0.88	= Imperial quarts (Imp qt)	
Imperial quarts (Imp qt)	x 1.201	= US quarts (US qt)	x 0.833	= Imperial quarts (Imp qt)	
US quarts (US qt)	x 0.946	= Litres (l)	x 1.057	= US quarts (US qt)	
Imperial gallons (Imp gal)	x 4.546	= Litres (l)	x 0.22	= Imperial gallons (Imp gal)	
Imperial gallons (Imp gal)	x 1.201	= US gallons (US gal)	x 0.833	= Imperial gallons (Imp gal)	
US gallons (US gal)	x 3.785	= Litres (l)	x 0.264	= US gallons (US gal)	

Mass (weight)

Ounces (oz)	x 28.35	= Grams (g)	x 0.035	= Ounces (oz)	
Pounds (lb)	x 0.454	= Kilograms (kg)	x 2.205	= Pounds (lb)	

Force

Ounces-force (ozf; oz)	x 0.278	= Newtons (N)	x 3.6	= Ounces-force (ozf; oz)	
Pounds-force (lbf; lb)	x 4.448	= Newtons (N)	x 0.225	= Pounds-force (lbf; lb)	
Newtons (N)	x 0.1	= Kilograms-force (kgf; kg)	x 9.81	= Newtons (N)	

Pressure

Pounds-force per square inch (psi; lbf/in²; lb/in²)	x 0.070	= Kilograms-force per square centimetre (kgf/cm²; kg/cm²)	x 14.223	= Pounds-force per square inch (psi; lbf/in²; lb/in²)	
Pounds-force per square inch (psi; lbf/in²; lb/in²)	x 0.068	= Atmospheres (atm)	x 14.696	= Pounds-force per square inch (psi; lbf/in²; lb/in²)	
Pounds-force per square inch (psi; lbf/in²; lb/in²)	x 0.069	= Bars	x 14.5	= Pounds-force per square inch (psi; lbf/in²; lb/in²)	
Pounds-force per square inch (psi; lbf/in²; lb/in²)	x 6.895	= Kilopascals (kPa)	x 0.145	= Pounds-force per square inch (psi; lbf/in²; lb/in²)	
Kilopascals (kPa)	x 0.01	= Kilograms-force per square centimetre (kgf/cm²; kg/cm²)	x 98.1	= Kilopascals (kPa)	
Millibar (mbar)	x 100	= Pascals (Pa)	x 0.01	= Millibar (mbar)	
Millibar (mbar)	x 0.0145	= Pounds-force per square inch (psi; lbf/in²; lb/in²)	x 68.947	= Millibar (mbar)	
Millibar (mbar)	x 0.75	= Millimetres of mercury (mmHg)	x 1.333	= Millibar (mbar)	
Millibar (mbar)	x 0.401	= Inches of water (inH₂O)	x 2.491	= Millibar (mbar)	
Millimetres of mercury (mmHg)	x 0.535	= Inches of water (inH₂O)	x 1.868	= Millimetres of mercury (mmHg)	
Inches of water (inH₂O)	x 0.036	= Pounds-force per square inch (psi; lbf/in²; lb/in²)	x 27.68	= Inches of water (inH₂O)	

Torque (moment of force)

Pounds-force inches (lbf in; lb in)	x 1.152	= Kilograms-force centimetre (kgf cm; kg cm)	x 0.868	= Pounds-force inches (lbf in; lb in)	
Pounds-force inches (lbf in; lb in)	x 0.113	= Newton metres (Nm)	x 8.85	= Pounds-force inches (lbf in; lb in)	
Pounds-force inches (lbf in; lb in)	x 0.083	= Pounds-force feet (lbf ft; lb ft)	x 12	= Pounds-force inches (lbf in; lb in)	
Pounds-force feet (lbf ft; lb ft)	x 0.138	= Kilograms-force metres (kgf m; kg m)	x 7.233	= Pounds-force feet (lbf ft; lb ft)	
Pounds-force feet (lbf ft; lb ft)	x 1.356	= Newton metres (Nm)	x 0.738	= Pounds-force feet (lbf ft; lb ft)	
Newton metres (Nm)	x 0.102	= Kilograms-force metres (kgf m; kg m)	x 9.804	= Newton metres (Nm)	

Power

Horsepower (hp)	x 745.7	= Watts (W)	x 0.0013	= Horsepower (hp)	

Velocity (speed)

Miles per hour (miles/hr; mph)	x 1.609	= Kilometres per hour (km/hr; kph)	x 0.621	= Miles per hour (miles/hr; mph)	

Fuel consumption*

Miles per gallon, Imperial (mpg)	x 0.354	= Kilometres per litre (km/l)	x 2.825	= Miles per gallon, Imperial (mpg)	
Miles per gallon, US (mpg)	x 0.425	= Kilometres per litre (km/l)	x 2.352	= Miles per gallon, US (mpg)	

Temperature

Degrees Fahrenheit = (°C x 1.8) + 32   Degrees Celsius (Degrees Centigrade; °C) = (°F - 32) x 0.56

It is common practice to convert from miles per gallon (mpg) to litres/100 kilometres (l/100km), where mpg x l/100 km = 282

Spare parts are available from many sources, including maker's appointed garages, accessory shops, and motor factors. To be sure of obtaining the correct parts, it will sometimes be necessary to quote the vehicle identification number. If possible, it can also be useful to take the old parts along for positive identification. Items such as starter motors and alternators may be available under a service exchange scheme – any parts returned should be clean.

Our advice regarding spare parts is as follows.

Officially appointed garages

This is the best source of parts which are peculiar to your car, and which are not otherwise generally available (eg, badges, interior trim, certain body panels, etc). It is also the only place at which you should buy parts if the vehicle is still under warranty.

Accessory shops

These are very good places to buy materials and components needed for the maintenance of your car (oil, air and fuel filters, light bulbs, drivebelts, greases, brake pads, touch-up paint, etc). Components of this nature sold by a reputable shop are of the same standard as those used by the car manufacturer.

Besides components, these shops also sell tools and general accessories, usually have convenient opening hours, charge lower prices, and can often be found close to home. Some accessory shops have parts counters where components needed for almost any repair job can be purchased or ordered.

Motor factors

Good factors will stock all the more important components which wear out comparatively quickly, and can sometimes supply individual components needed for the overhaul of a larger assembly (eg, brake seals and hydraulic parts, bearing shells, pistons, valves). They may also handle work such as cylinder block reboring, crankshaft regrinding, etc.

Tyre and exhaust specialists

These outlets may be independent, or members of a local or national chain. They frequently offer competitive prices when compared with a main dealer or local garage, but it will pay to obtain several quotes before making a decision. When researching prices, also ask what 'extras' may be added – for instance fitting a new valve and balancing the wheel are both commonly charged on top of the price of a new tyre.

Other sources

Beware of parts or materials obtained from market stalls, car boot sales or similar outlets. Such items are not invariably sub-standard, but there is little chance of compensation if they do prove unsatisfactory. In the case of safety-critical components such as brake pads, there is the risk not only of financial loss, but also of an accident causing injury or death.

Second-hand components or assemblies obtained from a car breaker can be a good buy in some circumstances, but his sort of purchase is best made by the experienced DIY mechanic.

Vehicle identification

Modifications are a continuing and unpublished process in vehicle manufacture, quite apart from major model changes. Spare parts manuals and lists are compiled upon a numerical basis, the individual vehicle numbers being essential to correct identification of the component required.

When ordering spare parts, always give as much information as possible. Quote the car model, year of manufacture and vehicle identification and/or engine numbers as appropriate.

The *vehicle identification plate* is attached to the front right-hand side door pillar **(see illustration)** and includes the Vehicle Identification Number (VIN), vehicle weight information and paint and trim colour codes.

The *Vehicle Identification Number (VIN)* is given on the vehicle identification plate and is also stamped into the body floor panel between the right-hand front seat and the door sill panel **(see illustration)**; lift the flap in the carpet to see it.

The engine number is stamped on a horizontal flat located on the front of the cylinder block, at the transmission end. The first part of the engine number gives the engine code – eg Z13DTH.

Engine codes are as follows:
1.3 litre (1248 cc) DOHC 16-valve engine (66 kW) Z13DTH
1.7 litre (1686 cc) DOHC 16-valve engine (59 kW) Z17DTL
1.7 litre (1686 cc) DOHC 16-valve engine (74 kW) Z17DTH
1.9 litre (1910 cc) SOHC 8-valve diesel engine (74 kW) Z19DTL
1.9 litre (1910 cc) SOHC 8-valve diesel engine (88 kW) Z19DT
1.9 litre (1910 cc) DOHC 16-valve diesel engine (88/110 kW) . .Z19DTH

Vauxhall/Opel use a 'Car pass' scheme for vehicle identification. This is a card which is issued to the customer when the car is first purchased. It contains important information, eg, VIN number, key number and radio code. It also includes a special code for diagnostic equipment, therefore it must be kept in a secure place and not in the vehicle.

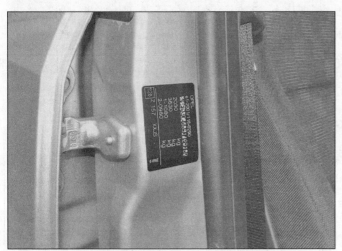

Vehicle Identification Number (VIN) plate attached to the front right-hand side door pillar

The VIN number is stamped into the body floor next to the right-hand front seat

Whenever servicing, repair or overhaul work is carried out on the car or its components, observe the following procedures and instructions. This will assist in carrying out the operation efficiently and to a professional standard of workmanship.

Joint mating faces and gaskets

When separating components at their mating faces, never insert screwdrivers or similar implements into the joint between the faces in order to prise them apart. This can cause severe damage which results in oil leaks, coolant leaks, etc upon reassembly. Separation is usually achieved by tapping along the joint with a soft-faced hammer in order to break the seal. However, note that this method may not be suitable where dowels are used for component location.

Where a gasket is used between the mating faces of two components, a new one must be fitted on reassembly; fit it dry unless otherwise stated in the repair procedure. Make sure that the mating faces are clean and dry, with all traces of old gasket removed. When cleaning a joint face, use a tool which is unlikely to score or damage the face, and remove any burrs or nicks with an oilstone or fine file.

Make sure that tapped holes are cleaned with a pipe cleaner, and keep them free of jointing compound, if this is being used, unless specifically instructed otherwise.

Ensure that all orifices, channels or pipes are clear, and blow through them, preferably using compressed air.

Oil seals

Oil seals can be removed by levering them out with a wide flat-bladed screwdriver or similar implement. Alternatively, a number of self-tapping screws may be screwed into the seal, and these used as a purchase for pliers or some similar device in order to pull the seal free.

Whenever an oil seal is removed from its working location, either individually or as part of an assembly, it should be renewed.

The very fine sealing lip of the seal is easily damaged, and will not seal if the surface it contacts is not completely clean and free from scratches, nicks or grooves. If the original sealing surface of the component cannot be restored, and the manufacturer has not made provision for slight relocation of the seal relative to the sealing surface, the component should be renewed.

Protect the lips of the seal from any surface which may damage them in the course of fitting. Use tape or a conical sleeve where possible. Lubricate the seal lips with oil before fitting and, on dual-lipped seals, fill the space between the lips with grease.

Unless otherwise stated, oil seals must be fitted with their sealing lips toward the lubricant to be sealed.

Use a tubular drift or block of wood of the appropriate size to install the seal and, if the seal housing is shouldered, drive the seal down to the shoulder. If the seal housing is unshouldered, the seal should be fitted with its face flush with the housing top face (unless otherwise instructed).

Screw threads and fastenings

Seized nuts, bolts and screws are quite a common occurrence where corrosion has set in, and the use of penetrating oil or releasing fluid will often overcome this problem if the offending item is soaked for a while before attempting to release it. The use of an impact driver may also provide a means of releasing such stubborn fastening devices, when used in conjunction with the appropriate screwdriver bit or socket. If none of these methods works, it may be necessary to resort to the careful application of heat, or the use of a hacksaw or nut splitter device.

Studs are usually removed by locking two nuts together on the threaded part, and then using a spanner on the lower nut to unscrew the stud. Studs or bolts which have broken off below the surface of the component in which they are mounted can sometimes be removed using a stud extractor. Always ensure that a blind tapped hole is completely free from oil, grease, water or other fluid before installing the bolt or stud. Failure to do this could cause the housing to crack due to the hydraulic action of the bolt or stud as it is screwed in.

When tightening a castellated nut to accept a split pin, tighten the nut to the specified torque, where applicable, and then tighten further to the next split pin hole. Never slacken the nut to align the split pin hole, unless stated in the repair procedure.

When checking or retightening a nut or bolt to a specified torque setting, slacken the nut or bolt by a quarter of a turn, and then retighten to the specified setting. However, this should not be attempted where angular tightening has been used.

For some screw fastenings, notably cylinder head bolts or nuts, torque wrench settings are no longer specified for the latter stages of tightening, "angle-tightening" being called up instead. Typically, a fairly low torque wrench setting will be applied to the bolts/nuts in the correct sequence, followed by one or more stages of tightening through specified angles.

Locknuts, locktabs and washers

Any fastening which will rotate against a component or housing during tightening should always have a washer between it and the relevant component or housing.

Spring or split washers should always be renewed when they are used to lock a critical component such as a big-end bearing retaining bolt or nut. Locktabs which are folded over to retain a nut or bolt should always be renewed.

Self-locking nuts can be re-used in non-critical areas, providing resistance can be felt when the locking portion passes over the bolt or stud thread. However, it should be noted that self-locking stiffnuts tend to lose their effectiveness after long periods of use, and should then be renewed as a matter of course.

Split pins must always be replaced with new ones of the correct size for the hole.

When thread-locking compound is found on the threads of a fastener which is to be re-used, it should be cleaned off with a wire brush and solvent, and fresh compound applied on reassembly.

Special tools

Some repair procedures in this manual entail the use of special tools such as a press, two or three-legged pullers, spring compressors, etc. Wherever possible, suitable readily-available alternatives to the manufacturer's special tools are described, and are shown in use. In some instances, where no alternative is possible, it has been necessary to resort to the use of a manufacturer's tool, and this has been done for reasons of safety as well as the efficient completion of the repair operation. Unless you are highly-skilled and have a thorough understanding of the procedures described, never attempt to bypass the use of any special tool when the procedure described specifies its use. Not only is there a very great risk of personal injury, but expensive damage could be caused to the components involved.

Environmental considerations

When disposing of used engine oil, brake fluid, antifreeze, etc, give due consideration to any detrimental environmental effects. Do not, for instance, pour any of the above liquids down drains into the general sewage system, or onto the ground to soak away. Many local council refuse tips provide a facility for waste oil disposal, as do some garages. If none of these facilities are available, consult your local Environmental Health Department, or the National Rivers Authority, for further advice.

With the universal tightening-up of legislation regarding the emission of environmentally-harmful substances from motor vehicles, most vehicles have tamperproof devices fitted to the main adjustment points of the fuel system. These devices are primarily designed to prevent unqualified persons from adjusting the fuel/air mixture, with the chance of a consequent increase in toxic emissions. If such devices are found during servicing or overhaul, they should, wherever possible, be renewed or refitted in accordance with the manufacturer's requirements or current legislation.

OIL CARE
FOLLOW THE CODE
OIL BANK LINE
0800 66 33 66
www.oilbankline.org.uk

Note: It is antisocial and illegal to dump oil down the drain. To find the location of your local oil recycling bank, call this number free.

The jack supplied with the vehicle tool kit should only be used for changing roadwheels – see *Wheel changing* at the front of this manual. Ensure the jack head is correctly engaged before attempting to raise the vehicle. When carrying out any other kind of work, raise the vehicle using a hydraulic jack, and always supplement the jack with axle stands positioned under the vehicle jacking points.

When jacking up the vehicle with a trolley jack, position the jack head under one of the relevant jacking points. Use a block of wood between the jack or axle stand and the sill – the block of wood should have a groove cut into it , in which the welded flange of the sill will locate. **Do not** jack the vehicle under the sump or any of the steering or suspension components. Supplement the jack using axle stands **(see illustrations)**.

 Warning: Never work under, around, or near a raised vehicle, unless it is adequately supported in at least two places.

Front jacking point for hydraulic jack or axle stands

Rear jacking point for hydraulic jack or axle stands

Axle stands should be placed under, or adjacent to the jacking point (arrowed)

Disconnecting the battery

Numerous systems fitted to the vehicle require battery power to be available at all times, either to ensure their continued operation (such as the clock) or to maintain control unit memories which would be erased if the battery were to be disconnected. Whenever the battery is to be disconnected therefore, first note the following, to ensure that there are no unforeseen consequences of this action:

a) First, on any vehicle with central locking, it is a wise precaution to remove the key from the ignition, and to keep it with you, so that it does not get locked in, if the central locking should engage accidentally when the battery is reconnected.

b) Depending on model and specification, the Vauxhall/Opel anti-theft alarm system may be of the type which is automatically activated when the vehicle battery is disconnected and/or reconnected. To prevent the alarm sounding on models so equipped, switch the ignition on, then off, and disconnect the battery within15 seconds. If the alarm is activated when the battery is reconnected, switch the ignition on then off to deactivate the alarm.

c) If a security-coded audio unit is fitted, and the unit and/or the battery is disconnected, the unit will not function again on reconnection until the correct security code is entered. Details of this procedure, which varies according to the unit fitted, are given in the vehicle audio system operating instructions. Ensure you have the correct code before you disconnect the battery. If you do not have the code or details of the correct procedure, but can supply proof of ownership and a legitimate reason for wanting this information, a Vauxhall/Opel dealer may be able to help.

d) The engine management electronic control unit is of the 'self-learning' type, meaning that as it operates, it also monitors and stores the settings which give optimum engine performance under all operating conditions. When the battery is disconnected, these settings are lost and the ECU reverts to the base settings programmed into its memory at the factory. On restarting, this may lead to the engine running/idling roughly for a short while, until the ECU has re-learned the optimum settings. This process is best accomplished by taking the vehicle on a road test (for approximately 15 minutes), covering all engine speeds and loads, concentrating mainly in the 2500 to 3500 rpm region.

e) On models equipped with automatic transmission, the transmission selector lever assembly incorporates an electrically-operated selector lever lock mechanism that prevents the lever being moved out of the P position unless the ignition is switched on and the brake pedal is depressed. If the selector lever is in the P position and the battery is disconnected, it will not be possible to move the selector lever out of position P by the normal means. Although it is possible to manually override the system (see Chapter 7B), it is sensible to move the selector lever to the N position before disconnecting the battery.

f) On models with electric windows, it will be necessary to reprogramme the motors to restore the one-touch function of the buttons, after reconnection of the battery. To do this, fully close both front windows. With the windows closed, depress the up button of the driver's side window for approximately 5 seconds, then release it and depress the passenger side window up button for approximately 5 seconds.

g) On models with an electric sliding sunroof, it will be necessary to fully open and fully close the sunroof after battery reconnection, to recalibrate the sensors.

h) On all models, when reconnecting the battery after disconnection, switch on the ignition and wait 10 seconds to allow the electronic vehicle systems to stabilise and re-initialise.

Introduction

A selection of good tools is a fundamental requirement for anyone contemplating the maintenance and repair of a motor vehicle. For the owner who does not possess any, their purchase will prove a considerable expense, offsetting some of the savings made by doing-it-yourself. However, provided that the tools purchased meet the relevant national safety standards and are of good quality, they will last for many years and prove an extremely worthwhile investment.

To help the average owner to decide which tools are needed to carry out the various tasks detailed in this manual, we have compiled three lists of tools under the following headings: *Maintenance and minor repair, Repair and overhaul*, and *Special*. Newcomers to practical mechanics should start off with the *Maintenance and minor repair* tool kit, and confine themselves to the simpler jobs around the vehicle. Then, as confidence and experience grow, more difficult tasks can be undertaken, with extra tools being purchased as, and when, they are needed. In this way, a *Maintenance and minor repair* tool kit can be built up into a *Repair and overhaul* tool kit over a considerable period of time, without any major cash outlays. The experienced do-it-yourselfer will have a tool kit good enough for most repair and overhaul procedures, and will add tools from the *Special* category when it is felt that the expense is justified by the amount of use to which these tools will be put.

Maintenance and minor repair tool kit

The tools given in this list should be considered as a minimum requirement if routine maintenance, servicing and minor repair operations are to be undertaken. We recommend the purchase of combination spanners (ring one end, open-ended the other); although more expensive than open-ended ones, they do give the advantages of both types of spanner.

- ☐ *Combination spanners:*
  Metric - 8 to 19 mm inclusive
- ☐ *Adjustable spanner - 35 mm jaw (approx.)*
- ☐ *Spark plug spanner (with rubber insert) - petrol models*
- ☐ *Spark plug gap adjustment tool - petrol models*
- ☐ *Set of feeler gauges*
- ☐ *Brake bleed nipple spanner*
- ☐ *Screwdrivers:*
  Flat blade - 100 mm long x 6 mm dia
  Cross blade - 100 mm long x 6 mm dia
  Torx - various sizes (not all vehicles)
- ☐ *Combination pliers*
- ☐ *Hacksaw (junior)*
- ☐ *Tyre pump*
- ☐ *Tyre pressure gauge*
- ☐ *Oil can*
- ☐ *Oil filter removal tool*
- ☐ *Fine emery cloth*
- ☐ *Wire brush (small)*
- ☐ *Funnel (medium size)*
- ☐ *Sump drain plug key (not all vehicles)*

Repair and overhaul tool kit

These tools are virtually essential for anyone undertaking any major repairs to a motor vehicle, and are additional to those given in the *Maintenance and minor repair* list. Included in this list is a comprehensive set of sockets. Although these are expensive, they will be found invaluable as they are so versatile - particularly if various drives are included in the set. We recommend the half-inch square-drive type, as this can be used with most proprietary torque wrenches.

The tools in this list will sometimes need to be supplemented by tools from the *Special* list:

- ☐ *Sockets (or box spanners) to cover range in previous list (including Torx sockets)*
- ☐ *Reversible ratchet drive (for use with sockets)*
- ☐ *Extension piece, 250 mm (for use with sockets)*
- ☐ *Universal joint (for use with sockets)*
- ☐ *Flexible handle or sliding T "breaker bar" (for use with sockets)*
- ☐ *Torque wrench (for use with sockets)*
- ☐ *Self-locking grips*
- ☐ *Ball pein hammer*
- ☐ *Soft-faced mallet (plastic or rubber)*
- ☐ *Screwdrivers:*
  Flat blade - long & sturdy, short (chubby), and narrow (electrician's) types
  Cross blade - long & sturdy, and short (chubby) types
- ☐ *Pliers:*
  Long-nosed
  Side cutters (electrician's)
  Circlip (internal and external)
- ☐ *Cold chisel - 25 mm*
- ☐ *Scriber*
- ☐ *Scraper*
- ☐ *Centre-punch*
- ☐ *Pin punch*
- ☐ *Hacksaw*
- ☐ *Brake hose clamp*
- ☐ *Brake/clutch bleeding kit*
- ☐ *Selection of twist drills*
- ☐ *Steel rule/straight-edge*
- ☐ *Allen keys (inc. splined/Torx type)*
- ☐ *Selection of files*
- ☐ *Wire brush*
- ☐ *Axle stands*
- ☐ *Jack (strong trolley or hydraulic type)*
- ☐ *Light with extension lead*
- ☐ *Universal electrical multi-meter*

Sockets and reversible ratchet drive

Brake bleeding kit

Torx key, socket and bit

Hose clamp

Angular-tightening gauge

Special tools

The tools in this list are those which are not used regularly, are expensive to buy, or which need to be used in accordance with their manufacturers' instructions. Unless relatively difficult mechanical jobs are undertaken frequently, it will not be economic to buy many of these tools. Where this is the case, you could consider clubbing together with friends (or joining a motorists' club) to make a joint purchase, or borrowing the tools against a deposit from a local garage or tool hire specialist. It is worth noting that many of the larger DIY superstores now carry a large range of special tools for hire at modest rates.

The following list contains only those tools and instruments freely available to the public, and not those special tools produced by the vehicle manufacturer specifically for its dealer network. You will find occasional references to these manufacturers' special tools in the text of this manual. Generally, an alternative method of doing the job without the vehicle manufacturers' special tool is given. However, sometimes there is no alternative to using them. Where this is the case and the relevant tool cannot be bought or borrowed, you will have to entrust the work to a dealer.

☐ Angular-tightening gauge
☐ Valve spring compressor
☐ Valve grinding tool
☐ Piston ring compressor
☐ Piston ring removal/installation tool
☐ Cylinder bore hone
☐ Balljoint separator
☐ Coil spring compressors (where applicable)
☐ Two/three-legged hub and bearing puller
☐ Impact screwdriver
☐ Micrometer and/or vernier calipers
☐ Dial gauge
☐ Stroboscopic timing light
☐ Dwell angle meter/tachometer
☐ Fault code reader
☐ Cylinder compression gauge
☐ Hand-operated vacuum pump and gauge
☐ Clutch plate alignment set
☐ Brake shoe steady spring cup removal tool
☐ Bush and bearing removal/installation set
☐ Stud extractors
☐ Tap and die set
☐ Lifting tackle
☐ Trolley jack

Buying tools

Reputable motor accessory shops and superstores often offer excellent quality tools at discount prices, so it pays to shop around.

Remember, you don't have to buy the most expensive items on the shelf, but it is always advisable to steer clear of the very cheap tools. Beware of 'bargains' offered on market stalls or at car boot sales. There are plenty of good tools around at reasonable prices, but always aim to purchase items which meet the relevant national safety standards. If in doubt, ask the proprietor or manager of the shop for advice before making a purchase.

Care and maintenance of tools

Having purchased a reasonable tool kit, it is necessary to keep the tools in a clean and serviceable condition. After use, always wipe off any dirt, grease and metal particles using a clean, dry cloth, before putting the tools away. Never leave them lying around after they have been used. A simple tool rack on the garage or workshop wall for items such as screwdrivers and pliers is a good idea. Store all normal spanners and sockets in a metal box. Any measuring instruments, gauges, meters, etc, must be carefully stored where they cannot be damaged or become rusty.

Take a little care when tools are used. Hammer heads inevitably become marked, and screwdrivers lose the keen edge on their blades from time to time. A little timely attention with emery cloth or a file will soon restore items like this to a good finish.

Working facilities

Not to be forgotten when discussing tools is the workshop itself. If anything more than routine maintenance is to be carried out, a suitable working area becomes essential.

It is appreciated that many an owner-mechanic is forced by circumstances to remove an engine or similar item without the benefit of a garage or workshop. Having done this, any repairs should always be done under the cover of a roof.

Wherever possible, any dismantling should be done on a clean, flat workbench or table at a suitable working height.

Any workbench needs a vice; one with a jaw opening of 100 mm is suitable for most jobs. As mentioned previously, some clean dry storage space is also required for tools, as well as for any lubricants, cleaning fluids, touch-up paints etc, which become necessary.

Another item which may be required, and which has a much more general usage, is an electric drill with a chuck capacity of at least 8 mm. This, together with a good range of twist drills, is virtually essential for fitting accessories.

Last, but not least, always keep a supply of old newspapers and clean, lint-free rags available, and try to keep any working area as clean as possible.

Micrometers

Dial test indicator ("dial gauge")

Strap wrench

Compression tester

Fault code reader

This is a guide to getting your vehicle through the MOT test. Obviously it will not be possible to examine the vehicle to the same standard as the professional MOT tester. However, working through the following checks will enable you to identify any problem areas before submitting the vehicle for the test.

It has only been possible to summarise the test requirements here, based on the regulations in force at the time of printing. Test standards are becoming increasingly stringent, although there are some exemptions for older vehicles.

An assistant will be needed to help carry out some of these checks.

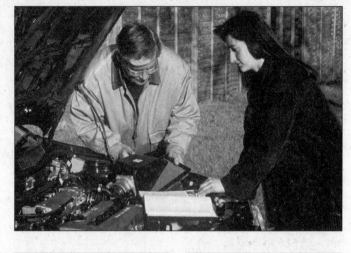

The checks have been sub-divided into four categories, as follows:

1 Checks carried out **FROM THE DRIVER'S SEAT**

2 Checks carried out **WITH THE VEHICLE ON THE GROUND**

3 Checks carried out **WITH THE VEHICLE RAISED AND THE WHEELS FREE TO TURN**

4 Checks carried out on **YOUR VEHICLE'S EXHAUST EMISSION SYSTEM**

---

1 Checks carried out **FROM THE DRIVER'S SEAT**

Handbrake

☐ Test the operation of the handbrake. Excessive travel (too many clicks) indicates incorrect brake or cable adjustment.
☐ Check that the handbrake cannot be released by tapping the lever sideways. Check the security of the lever mountings.

Footbrake

☐ Depress the brake pedal and check that it does not creep down to the floor, indicating a master cylinder fault. Release the pedal, wait a few seconds, then depress it again. If the pedal travels nearly to the floor before firm resistance is felt, brake adjustment or repair is necessary. If the pedal feels spongy, there is air in the hydraulic system which must be removed by bleeding.

☐ Check that the brake pedal is secure and in good condition. Check also for signs of fluid leaks on the pedal, floor or carpets, which would indicate failed seals in the brake master cylinder.
☐ Check the servo unit (when applicable) by operating the brake pedal several times, then keeping the pedal depressed and starting the engine. As the engine starts, the pedal will move down slightly. If not, the vacuum hose or the servo itself may be faulty.

Steering wheel and column

☐ Examine the steering wheel for fractures or looseness of the hub, spokes or rim.
☐ Move the steering wheel from side to side and then up and down. Check that the steering wheel is not loose on the column, indicating wear or a loose retaining nut. Continue moving the steering wheel as before, but also turn it slightly from left to right.
☐ Check that the steering wheel is not loose on the column, and that there is no abnormal

movement of the steering wheel, indicating wear in the column support bearings or couplings.

Windscreen, mirrors and sunvisor

☐ The windscreen must be free of cracks or other significant damage within the driver's field of view. (Small stone chips are acceptable.) Rear view mirrors must be secure, intact, and capable of being adjusted.

☐ The driver's sunvisor must be capable of being stored in the "up" position.

Seat belts and seats

Note: *The following checks are applicable to all seat belts, front and rear.*

☐ Examine the webbing of all the belts (including rear belts if fitted) for cuts, serious fraying or deterioration. Fasten and unfasten each belt to check the buckles. If applicable, check the retracting mechanism. Check the security of all seat belt mountings accessible from inside the vehicle.

☐ Seat belts with pre-tensioners, once activated, have a "flag" or similar showing on the seat belt stalk. This, in itself, is not a reason for test failure.

☐ The front seats themselves must be securely attached and the backrests must lock in the upright position.

Doors

☐ Both front doors must be able to be opened and closed from outside and inside, and must latch securely when closed.

2 Checks carried out WITH THE VEHICLE ON THE GROUND

Vehicle identification

☐ Number plates must be in good condition, secure and legible, with letters and numbers correctly spaced – spacing at (A) should be at least twice that at (B).

☐ The VIN plate and/or homologation plate must be legible.

Electrical equipment

☐ Switch on the ignition and check the operation of the horn.

☐ Check the windscreen washers and wipers, examining the wiper blades; renew damaged or perished blades. Also check the operation of the stop-lights.

☐ Check the operation of the sidelights and number plate lights. The lenses and reflectors must be secure, clean and undamaged.

☐ Check the operation and alignment of the headlights. The headlight reflectors must not be tarnished and the lenses must be undamaged.

☐ Switch on the ignition and check the operation of the direction indicators (including the instrument panel tell-tale) and the hazard warning lights. Operation of the sidelights and stop-lights must not affect the indicators - if it does, the cause is usually a bad earth at the rear light cluster.

☐ Check the operation of the rear foglight(s), including the warning light on the instrument panel or in the switch.

☐ The ABS warning light must illuminate in accordance with the manufacturers' design. For most vehicles, the ABS warning light should illuminate when the ignition is switched on, and (if the system is operating properly) extinguish after a few seconds. Refer to the owner's handbook.

Footbrake

☐ Examine the master cylinder, brake pipes and servo unit for leaks, loose mountings, corrosion or other damage.

☐ The fluid reservoir must be secure and the fluid level must be between the upper (**A**) and lower (**B**) markings.

☐ Inspect both front brake flexible hoses for cracks or deterioration of the rubber. Turn the steering from lock to lock, and ensure that the hoses do not contact the wheel, tyre, or any part of the steering or suspension mechanism. With the brake pedal firmly depressed, check the hoses for bulges or leaks under pressure.

Steering and suspension

☐ Have your assistant turn the steering wheel from side to side slightly, up to the point where the steering gear just begins to transmit this movement to the roadwheels. Check for excessive free play between the steering wheel and the steering gear, indicating wear or insecurity of the steering column joints, the column-to-steering gear coupling, or the steering gear itself.

☐ Have your assistant turn the steering wheel more vigorously in each direction, so that the roadwheels just begin to turn. As this is done, examine all the steering joints, linkages, fittings and attachments. Renew any component that shows signs of wear or damage. On vehicles with power steering, check the security and condition of the steering pump, drivebelt and hoses.

☐ Check that the vehicle is standing level, and at approximately the correct ride height.

Shock absorbers

☐ Depress each corner of the vehicle in turn, then release it. The vehicle should rise and then settle in its normal position. If the vehicle continues to rise and fall, the shock absorber is defective. A shock absorber which has seized will also cause the vehicle to fail.

Exhaust system

☐ Start the engine. With your assistant holding a rag over the tailpipe, check the entire system for leaks. Repair or renew leaking sections.

3 Checks carried out **WITH THE VEHICLE RAISED AND THE WHEELS FREE TO TURN**

Jack up the front and rear of the vehicle, and securely support it on axle stands. Position the stands clear of the suspension assemblies. Ensure that the wheels are clear of the ground and that the steering can be turned from lock to lock.

Steering mechanism

☐ Have your assistant turn the steering from lock to lock. Check that the steering turns smoothly, and that no part of the steering mechanism, including a wheel or tyre, fouls any brake hose or pipe or any part of the body structure.
☐ Examine the steering rack rubber gaiters for damage or insecurity of the retaining clips. If power steering is fitted, check for signs of damage or leakage of the fluid hoses, pipes or connections. Also check for excessive stiffness or binding of the steering, a missing split pin or locking device, or severe corrosion of the body structure within 30 cm of any steering component attachment point.

Front and rear suspension and wheel bearings

☐ Starting at the front right-hand side, grasp the roadwheel at the 3 o'clock and 9 o'clock positions and rock gently but firmly. Check for free play or insecurity at the wheel bearings, suspension balljoints, or suspension mountings, pivots and attachments.
☐ Now grasp the wheel at the 12 o'clock and 6 o'clock positions and repeat the previous inspection. Spin the wheel, and check for roughness or tightness of the front wheel bearing.

☐ If excess free play is suspected at a component pivot point, this can be confirmed by using a large screwdriver or similar tool and levering between the mounting and the component attachment. This will confirm whether the wear is in the pivot bush, its retaining bolt, or in the mounting itself (the bolt holes can often become elongated).

☐ Carry out all the above checks at the other front wheel, and then at both rear wheels.

Springs and shock absorbers

☐ Examine the suspension struts (when applicable) for serious fluid leakage, corrosion, or damage to the casing. Also check the security of the mounting points.
☐ If coil springs are fitted, check that the spring ends locate in their seats, and that the spring is not corroded, cracked or broken.
☐ If leaf springs are fitted, check that all leaves are intact, that the axle is securely attached to each spring, and that there is no deterioration of the spring eye mountings, bushes, and shackles.

☐ The same general checks apply to vehicles fitted with other suspension types, such as torsion bars, hydraulic displacer units, etc. Ensure that all mountings and attachments are secure, that there are no signs of excessive wear, corrosion or damage, and (on hydraulic types) that there are no fluid leaks or damaged pipes.
☐ Inspect the shock absorbers for signs of serious fluid leakage. Check for wear of the mounting bushes or attachments, or damage to the body of the unit.

Driveshafts (fwd vehicles only)

☐ Rotate each front wheel in turn and inspect the constant velocity joint gaiters for splits or damage. Also check that each driveshaft is straight and undamaged.

Braking system

☐ If possible without dismantling, check brake pad wear and disc condition. Ensure that the friction lining material has not worn excessively, (A) and that the discs are not fractured, pitted, scored or badly worn (B).

☐ Examine all the rigid brake pipes underneath the vehicle, and the flexible hose(s) at the rear. Look for corrosion, chafing or insecurity of the pipes, and for signs of bulging under pressure, chafing, splits or deterioration of the flexible hoses.
☐ Look for signs of fluid leaks at the brake calipers or on the brake backplates. Repair or renew leaking components.
☐ Slowly spin each wheel, while your assistant depresses and releases the footbrake. Ensure that each brake is operating and does not bind when the pedal is released.

□ Examine the handbrake mechanism, checking for frayed or broken cables, excessive corrosion, or wear or insecurity of the linkage. Check that the mechanism works on each relevant wheel, and releases fully, without binding.

□ It is not possible to test brake efficiency without special equipment, but a road test can be carried out later to check that the vehicle pulls up in a straight line.

Fuel and exhaust systems

□ Inspect the fuel tank (including the filler cap), fuel pipes, hoses and unions. All components must be secure and free from leaks.

□ Examine the exhaust system over its entire length, checking for any damaged, broken or missing mountings, security of the retaining clamps and rust or corrosion.

Wheels and tyres

□ Examine the sidewalls and tread area of each tyre in turn. Check for cuts, tears, lumps, bulges, separation of the tread, and exposure of the ply or cord due to wear or damage. Check that the tyre bead is correctly seated on the wheel rim, that the valve is sound and properly seated, and that the wheel is not distorted or damaged.

□ Check that the tyres are of the correct size for the vehicle, that they are of the same size

and type on each axle, and that the pressures are correct.

□ Check the tyre tread depth. The legal minimum at the time of writing is 1.6 mm over at least three-quarters of the tread width. Abnormal tread wear may indicate incorrect front wheel alignment.

Body corrosion

□ Check the condition of the entire vehicle structure for signs of corrosion in load-bearing areas. (These include chassis box sections, side sills, cross-members, pillars, and all suspension, steering, braking system and seat belt mountings and anchorages.) Any corrosion which has seriously reduced the thickness of a load-bearing area is likely to cause the vehicle to fail. In this case professional repairs are likely to be needed.

□ Damage or corrosion which causes sharp or otherwise dangerous edges to be exposed will also cause the vehicle to fail.

4 Checks carried out on YOUR VEHICLE'S EXHAUST EMISSION SYSTEM

Petrol models

□ The engine should be warmed up, and running well (ignition system in good order, air filter element clean, etc).

□ Before testing, run the engine at around 2500 rpm for 20 seconds. Let the engine drop to idle, and watch for smoke from the exhaust. If the idle speed is too high, or if dense blue or black smoke emerges for more than 5 seconds, the vehicle will fail. Typically, blue smoke signifies oil burning (engine wear); black smoke means unburnt fuel (dirty air cleaner element, or other fuel system fault).

□ An exhaust gas analyser for measuring carbon monoxide (CO) and hydrocarbons (HC) is now needed. If one cannot be hired or borrowed, have a local garage perform the check.

CO emissions (mixture)

□ The MOT tester has access to the CO limits for all vehicles. The CO level is measured at idle speed, and at 'fast idle' (2500 to 3000 rpm). The following limits are given as a general guide:

At idle speed – Less than 0.5% CO
At 'fast idle' – Less than 0.3% CO
Lambda reading – 0.97 to 1.03

□ If the CO level is too high, this may point to poor maintenance, a fuel injection system problem, faulty lambda (oxygen) sensor or catalytic converter. Try an injector cleaning treatment, and check the vehicle's ECU for fault codes.

HC emissions

□ The MOT tester has access to HC limits for all vehicles. The HC level is measured at 'fast idle' (2500 to 3000 rpm). The following limits are given as a general guide:

At 'fast idle' – Less then 200 ppm

□ Excessive HC emissions are typically caused by oil being burnt (worn engine), or by a blocked crankcase ventilation system ('breather'). If the engine oil is old and thin, an oil change may help. If the engine is running badly, check the vehicle's ECU for fault codes.

Diesel models

□ The only emission test for diesel engines is measuring exhaust smoke density, using a calibrated smoke meter. The test involves accelerating the engine at least 3 times to its maximum unloaded speed.

Note: *On engines with a timing belt, it is VITAL that the belt is in good condition before the test is carried out.*

□ With the engine warmed up, it is first purged by running at around 2500 rpm for 20 seconds. A governor check is then carried out by slowly accelerating the engine to its maximum speed. After this, the smoke meter is connected, and the engine is accelerated quickly to maximum speed three times. If the smoke density is less than the limits given below, the vehicle will pass:

Non-turbo vehicles: 2.5m-1
Turbocharged vehicles: 3.0m-1

□ If excess smoke is produced, try fitting a new air cleaner element, or using an injector cleaning treatment. If the engine is running badly, where applicable, check the vehicle's ECU for fault codes. Also check the vehicle's EGR system, where applicable. At high mileages, the injectors may require professional attention.

Engine

- [ ] Engine fails to rotate when attempting to start
- [ ] Engine rotates, but will not start
- [ ] Engine difficult to start when cold
- [ ] Engine difficult to start when hot
- [ ] Starter motor noisy or excessively-rough in engagement
- [ ] Engine starts, but stops immediately
- [ ] Engine idles erratically
- [ ] Engine misfires at idle speed
- [ ] Engine misfires throughout the driving speed range
- [ ] Engine hesitates on acceleration
- [ ] Engine stalls
- [ ] Engine lacks power
- [ ] Engine backfires
- [ ] Oil pressure warning light illuminated with engine running
- [ ] Engine runs-on after switching off
- [ ] Engine noises

Cooling system

- [ ] Overheating
- [ ] Overcooling
- [ ] External coolant leakage
- [ ] Internal coolant leakage
- [ ] Corrosion

Fuel and exhaust systems

- [ ] Excessive fuel consumption
- [ ] Fuel leakage and/or fuel odour
- [ ] Excessive noise or fumes from exhaust system

Clutch

- [ ] Pedal travels to floor – no pressure or very little resistance
- [ ] Clutch fails to disengage (unable to select gears)
- [ ] Clutch slips (engine speed increases, with no increase in vehicle speed)
- [ ] Judder as clutch is engaged
- [ ] Noise when depressing or releasing clutch pedal

Manual transmission

- [ ] Noisy in neutral with engine running
- [ ] Noisy in one particular gear
- [ ] Difficulty engaging gears
- [ ] Jumps out of gear
- [ ] Vibration
- [ ] Lubricant leaks

Automatic transmission

- [ ] Fluid leakage
- [ ] Transmission fluid brown, or has burned smell
- [ ] General gear selection problems
- [ ] Transmission will not downshift (kickdown) with accelerator pedal fully depressed
- [ ] Engine will not start in any gear, or starts in gears other than Park or Neutral
- [ ] Transmission slips, shifts roughly, is noisy, or has no drive in forward or reverse gears

Driveshafts

- [ ] Vibration when accelerating or decelerating
- [ ] Clicking or knocking noise on turns (at slow speed on full-lock)

Braking system

- [ ] Vehicle pulls to one side under braking
- [ ] Noise (grinding or high-pitched squeal) when brakes applied
- [ ] Excessive brake pedal travel
- [ ] Brake pedal feels spongy when depressed
- [ ] Excessive brake pedal effort required to stop vehicle
- [ ] Judder felt through brake pedal or steering wheel when braking
- [ ] Brakes binding
- [ ] Rear wheels locking under normal braking

Suspension and steering

- [ ] Vehicle pulls to one side
- [ ] Wheel wobble and vibration
- [ ] Excessive pitching and/or rolling around corners, or during braking
- [ ] Wandering or general instability
- [ ] Excessively-stiff steering
- [ ] Excessive play in steering
- [ ] Lack of power assistance
- [ ] Tyre wear excessive

Electrical system

- [ ] Battery will not hold a charge for more than a few days
- [ ] Ignition/no-charge warning light remains illuminated with engine running
- [ ] Ignition/no-charge warning light fails to come on
- [ ] Lights inoperative
- [ ] Instrument readings inaccurate or erratic
- [ ] Horn inoperative, or unsatisfactory in operation
- [ ] Windscreen wipers inoperative, or unsatisfactory in operation
- [ ] Windscreen washers inoperative, or unsatisfactory in operation
- [ ] Electric windows inoperative, or unsatisfactory in operation
- [ ] Central locking system inoperative, or unsatisfactory in operation

Introduction

The vehicle owner who does his or her own maintenance according to the recommended service schedules should not have to use this section of the manual very often. Modern component reliability is such that, provided those items subject to wear or deterioration are inspected or renewed at the specified intervals, sudden failure is comparatively rare. Faults do not usually just happen as a result of sudden failure, but develop over a period of time. Major mechanical failures in particular are usually preceded by characteristic symptoms over hundreds or even thousands of miles.

Those components which do occasionally fail without warning are often small and easily carried in the vehicle.

With any fault-finding, the first step is to decide where to begin investigations. Sometimes this is obvious, but on other occasions, a little detective work will be necessary. The owner who makes half a dozen haphazard adjustments or replacements may be successful in curing a fault (or its symptoms), but will be none the wiser if the fault recurs, and ultimately may have spent more time and money than was necessary.

A calm and logical approach will be found to be more satisfactory in the long run. Always take into account any warning signs or abnormalities that may have been noticed in the period preceding the fault – power loss, high or low gauge readings, unusual smells, etc – and remember that failure of components such as fuses may only be pointers to some underlying fault.

The pages which follow provide an easy-reference guide to the more common problems which may occur during the operation of the vehicle. These problems and their possible causes are grouped under headings denoting various components or systems, such as Engine, Cooling system, etc. The general Chapter which deals with the problem is also shown in brackets; refer to the relevant part of that Chapter for system-specific information. Whatever the fault, certain basic principles apply. These are as follows:

Verify the fault. This is simply a matter of being sure that you know what the symptoms are before starting work. This is particularly important if you are investigating a fault for someone else, who may not have described it very accurately.

Don't overlook the obvious. For example, if the vehicle won't start, is there fuel in the tank? (Don't take anyone else's word on this particular point, and don't trust the fuel gauge either!) If an electrical fault is indicated, look for loose or broken wires before digging out the test gear.

Cure the disease, not the symptom. Substituting a flat battery with a fully-charged one will get you off the hard shoulder, but if the underlying cause is not attended to, the new battery will go the same way.

Don't take anything for granted. Particularly, don't forget that a 'new' component may itself be defective (especially if it's been rattling around in the boot for months), and don't leave components out of a fault diagnosis sequence just because they are new or recently-fitted.

When you do finally diagnose a difficult fault, you'll probably realise that all the evidence was there from the start.

Consider what work, if any, has recently been carried out. Many faults arise through careless or hurried work. For instance, if any work has been performed under the bonnet, could some of the wiring have been dislodged or incorrectly routed, or a hose trapped? Have all the fasteners been properly tightened? Were new, genuine parts and new gaskets used? There is often a certain amount of detective work to be done in this case, as an apparently-unrelated task can have far-reaching consequences.

Engine

Engine fails to rotate when attempting to start
- [ ] Battery terminal connections loose or corroded (see *Weekly checks*)
- [ ] Battery discharged or faulty (Chapter 5)
- [ ] Broken, loose or disconnected wiring in the starting circuit (Chapter 5)
- [ ] Defective starter solenoid or ignition switch (Chapter 5 or 12)
- [ ] Defective starter motor (Chapter 5)
- [ ] Starter pinion or flywheel ring gear teeth loose or broken (Chapter 2A, 2B, 2C, 2D or 5)
- [ ] Engine earth strap broken or disconnected (Chapter 5)
- [ ] Engine suffering 'hydraulic lock' (eg from water drawn into the engine after traversing flooded roads, or from a serious internal coolant leak) – consult a main dealer for advice
- [ ] Automatic transmission not in position P or N (Chapter 7B)

Engine rotates, but will not start
- [ ] Fuel tank empty
- [ ] Battery discharged (engine rotates slowly) (Chapter 5)
- [ ] Battery terminal connections loose or corroded (see *Weekly checks*)
- [ ] Immobiliser fault, or 'uncoded' ignition key being used (Chapter 12 or Roadside repairs)
- [ ] Preheating system faulty (Chapter 5)
- [ ] Fuel injection/engine management system fault (Chapter 4A or 4B)
- [ ] Air in fuel system (Chapter 4A)
- [ ] Major mechanical failure (eg timing /beltchain snapped) (Chapter 2A, 2B, 2C or 2B)

Engine difficult to start when cold
- [ ] Battery discharged (Chapter 5A)
- [ ] Battery terminal connections loose or corroded (see *Weekly checks*)
- [ ] Preheating system faulty (Chapter 5)
- [ ] Fuel injection/engine management system fault (Chapter 4A or 4B)
- [ ] Wrong grade of engine oil used (*Weekly checks*, Chapter 1)
- [ ] Low cylinder compression (Chapter 2A, 2B, 2C or 2D)

Engine difficult to start when hot
- [ ] Air filter element dirty or clogged (Chapter 1)
- [ ] Fuel injection/engine management system fault (Chapter 4A or 4B)
- [ ] Low cylinder compression (Chapter 2A, 2B, 2C or 2D)

Starter motor noisy or excessively-rough in engagement
- [ ] Starter pinion or flywheel ring gear teeth loose or broken (Chapter 2A, 2B, 2C, 2D or 5)
- [ ] Starter motor mounting bolts loose or missing (Chapter 5)
- [ ] Starter motor internal components worn or damaged (Chapter 5)

Engine starts, but stops immediately
- [ ] Fuel injection/engine management system fault (Chapter 4A or 4B)

Engine idles erratically
- [ ] Air filter element clogged (Chapter 1)
- [ ] Uneven or low cylinder compression (Chapter 2A, 2B, 2C or 2D)
- [ ] Camshaft lobes worn (Chapter 2A, 2B, 2C or 2D)
- [ ] Fuel injection/engine management system fault (Chapter 4A or 4B)

Engine misfires at idle speed
- [ ] Faulty injector(s) (Chapter 4A)
- [ ] Uneven or low cylinder compression (Chapter 2A, 2B, 2C or 2D)
- [ ] Disconnected, leaking, or perished crankcase ventilation hoses (Chapter 4B)
- [ ] Fuel injection/engine management system fault (Chapter 4A or 4B)

Engine misfires throughout the driving speed range
- [ ] Fuel filter choked (Chapter 1)
- [ ] Fuel tank vent blocked, or fuel pipes restricted (Chapter 4A or 4B)
- [ ] Faulty injector(s) (Chapter 4A)
- [ ] Uneven or low cylinder compression (Chapter 2A, 2B, 2C or 2D)
- [ ] Blocked catalytic converter (Chapter 4A or 4B)
- [ ] Fuel injection/engine management system fault (Chapter 4A or 4B)
- [ ] Engine overheating (Chapter 3)

Engine hesitates on acceleration
- [ ] Faulty injector(s) (Chapter 4A)
- [ ] Fuel injection/engine management system fault (Chapter 4A or 4B)

Engine stalls
- [ ] Fuel filter choked (Chapter 1)
- [ ] Fuel tank vent blocked, or fuel pipes restricted (Chapter 4A or 4B)
- [ ] Faulty injector(s) (Chapter 4A)
- [ ] Fuel injection/engine management system fault (Chapter 4A or 4B)

Engine lacks power
- [ ] Air filter element blocked (Chapter 1)
- [ ] Fuel filter choked (Chapter 1)
- [ ] Fuel pipes blocked or restricted (Chapter 4A or 4B)
- [ ] Engine overheating (Chapter 3)
- [ ] Accelerator pedal position sensor faulty (Chapter 4A)
- [ ] Faulty injector(s) (Chapter 4A)
- [ ] Uneven or low cylinder compression (Chapter 2A, 2B, 2C or 2D)
- [ ] Fuel injection/engine management system fault (Chapter 4A or 4B)
- [ ] Blocked catalytic converter (Chapter 4A or 4B)
- [ ] Brakes binding (Chapter 1 or 9)
- [ ] Clutch slipping (Chapter 6)

Engine (continued)

Engine backfires

- [ ] Fuel injection/engine management system fault (Chapter 4A or 4B)
- [ ] Blocked catalytic converter (Chapter 4A or 4B)

Oil pressure warning light illuminated with engine running

- [ ] Low oil level, or incorrect oil grade (see *Weekly checks*)
- [ ] Faulty oil pressure sensor, or wiring damaged (Chapter 5)
- [ ] Worn engine bearings and/or oil pump (Chapter 2A, 2B, 2C, 2D or 2E)
- [ ] High engine operating temperature (Chapter 3)
- [ ] Oil pump pressure relief valve defective (Chapter 2A, 2B, 2C or 2D)
- [ ] Oil pump pick-up strainer clogged (Chapter 2A, 2B, 2C or 2D)

Engine runs-on after switching off

- [ ] Excessive carbon build-up in engine (Chapter 2A, 2B, 2C, 2D or 2E)
- [ ] High engine operating temperature (Chapter 3)
- [ ] Fuel injection/engine management system fault (Chapter 4A or 4B)

Engine noises

Pre-ignition (pinking) or knocking during acceleration or under load

- [ ] Excessive carbon build-up in engine (Chapter 2A, 2B, 2C, 2D or 2E)
- [ ] Fuel injection/engine management system fault (Chapter 4A or 4B)
- [ ] Faulty injector(s) (Chapter 4A)

Whistling or wheezing noises

- [ ] Leaking exhaust manifold gasket or pipe-to-manifold joint (Chapter 4A)
- [ ] Leaking vacuum hose (Chapter 4A, 4B or 9)
- [ ] Blowing cylinder head gasket (Chapter 2A, 2B, 2C or 2D)
- [ ] Partially blocked or leaking crankcase ventilation system (Chapter 4B)

Tapping or rattling noises

- [ ] Worn valve gear or camshaft (Chapter 2A, 2B, 2C or 2D)
- [ ] Ancillary component fault (coolant pump, alternator, etc) (Chapter 3, 5, etc)

Knocking or thumping noises

- [ ] Worn big-end bearings (regular heavy knocking, perhaps less under load) (Chapter 2E)
- [ ] Worn main bearings (rumbling and knocking, perhaps worsening under load) (Chapter 2E)
- [ ] Piston slap – most noticeable when cold, caused by piston/bore wear (Chapter 2E)
- [ ] Ancillary component fault (coolant pump, alternator, etc) (Chapter 3, 5, etc)
- [ ] Engine mountings worn or defective (Chapter 2A, 2B, 2C or 2D)
- [ ] Front suspension or steering components worn (Chapter 10)

Cooling system

Overheating

- [ ] Insufficient coolant in system (see *Weekly checks*)
- [ ] Thermostat faulty (Chapter 3)
- [ ] Radiator core blocked, or grille restricted (Chapter 3)
- [ ] Cooling fan or cooling module faulty (Chapter 3)
- [ ] Inaccurate coolant temperature sensor (Chapter 3)
- [ ] Airlock in cooling system (Chapter 1 or 3)
- [ ] Expansion tank pressure cap faulty (Chapter 1 or 3)
- [ ] Engine management system fault (Chapter 4A or 4B)

Overcooling

- [ ] Thermostat faulty (Chapter 3)
- [ ] Inaccurate coolant temperature sensor (Chapter 3)
- [ ] Cooling fan faulty (Chapter 3)
- [ ] Engine management system fault (Chapter 4A or 4B)

External coolant leakage

- [ ] Deteriorated or damaged hoses or hose clips (Chapter 1)
- [ ] Radiator core or heater matrix leaking (Chapter 3)
- [ ] Expansion tank pressure cap faulty (Chapter 1 or 3)
- [ ] Coolant pump internal seal leaking (Chapter 3)
- [ ] Coolant pump gasket leaking (Chapter 3)
- [ ] Boiling due to overheating (Chapter 3)
- [ ] Cylinder block core plug leaking (Chapter 2E)

Internal coolant leakage

- [ ] Leaking cylinder head gasket (Chapter 2A, 2B, 2C or 2D)
- [ ] Cracked cylinder head or cylinder block (Chapter 2A, 2B, 2C or 2D)

Corrosion

- [ ] Infrequent draining and flushing (Chapter 1)
- [ ] Incorrect coolant mixture or inappropriate coolant type (see *Weekly checks*)

Fuel and exhaust systems

Excessive fuel consumption

☐ Air filter element dirty or clogged (Chapter 1)
☐ Fuel injection system fault (Chapter 4A or 4B)
☐ Engine management system fault (Chapter 4A or 4B)
☐ Crankcase ventilation system blocked (Chapter 4B)
☐ Tyres under-inflated (see *Weekly checks*)
☐ Brakes binding (Chapter 1 or 9)
☐ Fuel leak, causing apparent high consumption (Chapter 1, 4A or 4B)

Fuel leakage and/or fuel odour

☐ Damaged or corroded fuel tank, pipes or connections (Chapter 4A or 4B)

Excessive noise or fumes from exhaust system

☐ Leaking exhaust system or manifold joints (Chapter 1 or 4A)
☐ Leaking, corroded or damaged silencers or pipe (Chapter 1 or 4A)
☐ Broken mountings causing body or suspension contact (Chapter 1 or 4A)

Clutch

Pedal travels to floor – no pressure or very little resistance

☐ Air in hydraulic system/faulty master or slave cylinder (Chapter 6)
☐ Faulty hydraulic release system (Chapter 6)
☐ Clutch pedal return spring detached or broken (Chapter 6)
☐ Faulty clutch release cylinder (Chapter 6)
☐ Broken diaphragm spring in clutch pressure plate (Chapter 6)

Clutch fails to disengage (unable to select gears)

☐ Air in hydraulic system/faulty master or slave cylinder (Chapter 6)
☐ Faulty hydraulic release system (Chapter 6)
☐ Clutch disc sticking on transmission input shaft splines (Chapter 6)
☐ Clutch disc sticking to flywheel or pressure plate (Chapter 6)
☐ Faulty pressure plate assembly (Chapter 6)
☐ Clutch release mechanism worn or incorrectly assembled (Chapter 6)

Clutch slips (engine speed increases, with no increase in vehicle speed)

☐ Faulty hydraulic release system (Chapter 6)
☐ Clutch disc linings excessively worn (Chapter 6)
☐ Clutch disc linings contaminated with oil or grease (Chapter 6)
☐ Faulty pressure plate or weak diaphragm spring (Chapter 6)

Judder as clutch is engaged

☐ Clutch disc linings contaminated with oil or grease (Chapter 6)
☐ Clutch disc linings excessively worn (Chapter 6)
☐ Faulty or distorted pressure plate or diaphragm spring (Chapter 6).
☐ Worn or loose engine or transmission mountings (Chapter 2A, 2B, 2C or 2D)
☐ Clutch disc hub or transmission input shaft splines worn (Chapter 6)

Noise when depressing or releasing clutch pedal

☐ Faulty clutch release cylinder (Chapter 6)
☐ Worn or dry clutch pedal bushes (Chapter 6)
☐ Faulty pressure plate assembly (Chapter 6)
☐ Pressure plate diaphragm spring broken (Chapter 6)
☐ Broken clutch disc cushioning springs (Chapter 6)

Manual transmission

Noisy in neutral with engine running

- ☐ Lack of oil (Chapter 7A)
- ☐ Input shaft bearings worn (noise apparent with clutch pedal released, but not when depressed) (Chapter 7A)*
- ☐ Clutch release cylinder faulty (noise apparent with clutch pedal depressed, possibly less when released) (Chapter 6)

Noisy in one particular gear

- ☐ Worn, damaged or chipped gear teeth (Chapter 7A)*

Difficulty engaging gears

- ☐ Clutch fault (Chapter 6)
- ☐ Worn, damaged, or poorly-adjusted gearchange (Chapter 7A)
- ☐ Lack of oil (Chapter 7A)
- ☐ Worn synchroniser units (Chapter 7A)*

Jumps out of gear

- ☐ Worn, damaged, or poorly-adjusted gearchange (Chapter 7A)
- ☐ Worn synchroniser units (Chapter 7A)*
- ☐ Worn selector forks (Chapter 7A)*

Vibration

- ☐ Lack of oil (Chapter 7A)
- ☐ Worn bearings (Chapter 7A)*

Lubricant leaks

- ☐ Leaking driveshaft or selector shaft oil seal (Chapter 7A)
- ☐ Leaking housing joint (Chapter 7A)*
- ☐ Leaking input shaft oil seal (Chapter 7A)*

*Although the corrective action necessary to remedy the symptoms described is beyond the scope of the home mechanic, the above information should be helpful in isolating the cause of the condition, so that the owner can communicate clearly with a professional mechanic.

Automatic transmission

Note: Due to the complexity of the automatic transmission, it is difficult for the home mechanic to properly diagnose and service this unit. For problems other than the following, the vehicle should be taken to a dealer service department or automatic transmission specialist. Do not be too hasty in removing the transmission if a fault is suspected, as most of the testing is carried out with the unit still fitted. Remember that, besides the sensors specific to the transmission, many of the engine management system sensors described in Chapter 4 are essential to the correct operation of the transmission.

Fluid leakage

- ☐ Automatic transmission fluid is usually dark red in colour. Fluid leaks should not be confused with engine oil, which can easily be blown onto the transmission by airflow.
- ☐ To determine the source of a leak, first remove all built-up dirt and grime from the transmission housing and surrounding areas using a degreasing agent, or by steam-cleaning. Drive the vehicle at low speed, so airflow will not blow the leak far from its source. Raise and support the vehicle, and determine where the leak is coming from. The following are common areas of leakage:
  - a) Fluid pan
  - b) Dipstick tube (Chapter 7B)
  - c) Transmission-to-fluid cooler unions (Chapter 7B)

Transmission fluid brown, or has burned smell

- ☐ Transmission fluid level low (Chapter 7B)

General gear selection problems

- ☐ Chapter 7B deals with checking the selector cable on automatic transmissions. The following are common problems which may be caused by a faulty cable or sensor:

a) Engine starting in gears other than Park or Neutral.
b) Indicator panel indicating a gear other than the one actually being used.
c) Vehicle moves when in Park or Neutral.
d) Poor gear shift quality or erratic gear changes.

Transmission will not downshift (kickdown) with accelerator pedal fully depressed

- ☐ Low transmission fluid level (Chapter 7B)
- ☐ Engine management system fault (Chapter 4A)
- ☐ Faulty transmission sensor or wiring (Chapter 7B)
- ☐ Incorrect selector cable adjustment (Chapter 7B)

Engine will not start in any gear, or starts in gears other than Park or Neutral

- ☐ Faulty transmission sensor or wiring (Chapter 7B)
- ☐ Engine management system fault (Chapter 4A)
- ☐ Incorrect selector cable adjustment (Chapter 7B)

Transmission slips, shifts roughly, is noisy, or has no drive in forward or reverse gears

- ☐ Transmission fluid level low (Chapter 7B)
- ☐ Faulty transmission sensor or wiring (Chapter 7B)
- ☐ Engine management system fault (Chapter 4A)

Note: There are many probable causes for the above problems, but diagnosing and correcting them is considered beyond the scope of this manual. Having checked the fluid level and all the wiring as far as possible, a dealer or transmission specialist should be consulted if the problem persists.

Driveshafts

Vibration when accelerating or decelerating

☐ Worn inner constant velocity joint (Chapter 8)
☐ Bent or distorted driveshaft (Chapter 8)
☐ Worn intermediate bearing (Chapter 8)

Clicking or knocking noise on turns (at slow speed on full-lock)

☐ Worn outer constant velocity joint (Chapter 8)
☐ Lack of constant velocity joint lubricant, possibly due to damaged gaiter (Chapter 8)

Braking system

Note: *Before assuming that a brake problem exists, make sure that the tyres are in good condition and correctly inflated, that the front wheel alignment is correct, and that the vehicle is not loaded with weight in an unequal manner. Apart from checking the condition of all pipe and hose connections, any faults occurring on the anti-lock braking system should be referred to a Vauxhall/Opel dealer for diagnosis.*

Vehicle pulls to one side under braking

☐ Worn, defective, damaged or contaminated brake pads on one side (Chapter 1 or 9)
☐ Seized or partially-seized brake caliper piston (Chapter 1 or 9)
☐ A mixture of brake pad lining materials fitted between sides (Chapter 1 or 9)
☐ Brake caliper mounting bolts loose (Chapter 9)
☐ Worn or damaged steering or suspension components (Chapter 1 or 10)

Noise (grinding or high-pitched squeal) when brakes applied

☐ Brake pad friction lining material worn down to wear sensor or metal backing (Chapter 1 or 9)
☐ Excessive corrosion of brake disc (may be apparent after the vehicle has been standing for some time (Chapter 1 or 9)
☐ Foreign object (stone chipping, etc) trapped between brake disc and shield (Chapter 1 or 9)

Excessive brake pedal travel

☐ Faulty master cylinder (Chapter 9)
☐ Air in hydraulic system (Chapter 1 or 9)
☐ Faulty vacuum servo unit (Chapter 9)

Brake pedal feels spongy when depressed

☐ Air in hydraulic system (Chapter 1 or 9)
☐ Deteriorated flexible rubber brake hoses (Chapter 1 or 9)
☐ Master cylinder mounting nuts loose (Chapter 9)
☐ Faulty master cylinder (Chapter 9)

Excessive brake pedal effort required to stop vehicle

☐ Faulty vacuum servo unit (Chapter 9)
☐ Faulty vacuum pump (Chapter 9)
☐ Disconnected, damaged or insecure brake servo vacuum hose (Chapter 9)
☐ Primary or secondary hydraulic circuit failure (Chapter 9)
☐ Seized brake caliper piston (Chapter 9)
☐ Brake pads incorrectly fitted (Chapter 9)
☐ Incorrect grade of brake pads fitted (Chapter 9)
☐ Brake pad linings contaminated (Chapter 1 or 9)

Judder felt through brake pedal or steering wheel when braking

Note: *Under heavy braking on models equipped with ABS, vibration may be felt through the brake pedal. This is a normal feature of ABS operation, and does not constitute a fault*

☐ Excessive run-out or distortion of discs (Chapter 1 or 9)
☐ Brake pad linings worn (Chapter 1 or 9)
☐ Brake caliper mounting bolts loose (Chapter 9)
☐ Wear in suspension or steering components or mountings (Chapter 1 or 10)
☐ Front wheels out of balance (see *Weekly checks*)

Brakes binding

☐ Seized brake caliper piston (Chapter 9)
☐ Faulty master cylinder (Chapter 9)

Rear wheels locking under normal braking

☐ Rear brake pad linings contaminated or damaged (Chapter 1 or 9)
☐ Rear brake discs warped (Chapter 1 or 9)

Suspension and steering

Note: *Before diagnosing suspension or steering faults, be sure that the trouble is not due to incorrect tyre pressures, mixtures of tyre types, or binding brakes.*

Vehicle pulls to one side

- ☐ Defective tyre (see *Weekly checks*)
- ☐ Excessive wear in suspension or steering components (Chapter 1 or 10)
- ☐ Incorrect front wheel alignment (Chapter 10)
- ☐ Accident damage to steering or suspension components (Chapter 1 or 10)

Wheel wobble and vibration

- ☐ Front wheels out of balance (vibration felt mainly through the steering wheel) (see *Weekly checks*)
- ☐ Rear wheels out of balance (vibration felt throughout the vehicle) (see *Weekly checks*)
- ☐ Roadwheels damaged or distorted (see *Weekly checks*)
- ☐ Faulty or damaged tyre (see *Weekly checks*)
- ☐ Worn steering or suspension joints, bushes or components (Chapter 1 or 10)
- ☐ Wheel bolts loose (Chapter 1)

Excessive pitching and/or rolling around corners, or during braking

- ☐ Defective shock absorbers (Chapter 1 or 10)
- ☐ Broken or weak spring and/or suspension component (Chapter 1 or 10)
- ☐ Worn or damaged anti-roll bar or mountings (Chapter 1 or 10)

Wandering or general instability

- ☐ Incorrect front wheel alignment (Chapter 10)
- ☐ Worn steering or suspension joints, bushes or components (Chapter 1 or 10)
- ☐ Roadwheels out of balance (see *Weekly checks*)
- ☐ Faulty or damaged tyre (see *Weekly checks*)
- ☐ Wheel bolts loose (Chapter 1)
- ☐ Defective shock absorbers (Chapter 1 or 10)
- ☐ Power steering system fault (Chapter 10)

Excessively-stiff steering

- ☐ Seized steering linkage balljoint or suspension balljoint (Chapter 1 or 10)
- ☐ Incorrect front wheel alignment (Chapter 10)
- ☐ Steering rack damaged (Chapter 10)
- ☐ Power steering system fault (Chapter 10)

Excessive play in steering

- ☐ Worn steering column/intermediate shaft joints (Chapter 10)
- ☐ Worn track rod balljoints (Chapter 1 or 10)
- ☐ Worn steering rack (Chapter 10)
- ☐ Worn steering or suspension joints, bushes or components (Chapter 1 or 10)

Lack of power assistance

- ☐ Power steering system fault (Chapter 10)
- ☐ Faulty steering rack (Chapter 10)

Tyre wear excessive

Tyres worn on inside or outside edges

- ☐ Tyres under-inflated (wear on both edges) (see *Weekly checks*)
- ☐ Incorrect camber or castor angles (wear on one edge only) (Chapter 10)
- ☐ Worn steering or suspension joints, bushes or components (Chapter 1 or 10)
- ☐ Excessively-hard cornering or braking
- ☐ Accident damage

Tyre treads exhibit feathered edges

- ☐ Incorrect toe-setting (Chapter 10)

Tyres worn in centre of tread

- ☐ Tyres over-inflated (see *Weekly checks*)

Tyres worn on inside and outside edges

- ☐ Tyres under-inflated (see *Weekly checks*)

Tyres worn unevenly

- ☐ Tyres/wheels out of balance (see *Weekly checks*)
- ☐ Excessive wheel or tyre run-out
- ☐ Worn shock absorbers (Chapter 1 10)
- ☐ Faulty tyre (see *Weekly checks*)

Electrical system

Note: *For problems associated with the starting system, refer to the faults listed under 'Engine' earlier in this Section.*

Battery will not hold a charge for more than a few days

- [ ] Battery defective internally (Chapter 5)
- [ ] Battery terminal connections loose or corroded (see *Weekly checks*)
- [ ] Auxiliary drivebelt worn or faulty automatic adjuster (Chapter 1)
- [ ] Alternator not charging at correct output (Chapter 5)
- [ ] Alternator or voltage regulator faulty (Chapter 5)
- [ ] Short-circuit causing continual battery drain (Chapter 5 or 12)

Ignition/no-charge warning light remains illuminated with engine running

- [ ] Auxiliary drivebelt broken, worn, or or faulty automatic adjuster (Chapter 1)
- [ ] Internal fault in alternator or voltage regulator (Chapter 5)
- [ ] Broken, disconnected, or loose wiring in charging circuit (Chapter 5 or 12)

Ignition/no-charge warning light fails to come on

- [ ] Warning light bulb blown (Chapter 12)
- [ ] Broken, disconnected, or loose wiring in warning light circuit (Chapter 5 or 12)
- [ ] Alternator faulty (Chapter 5)

Lights inoperative

- [ ] Bulb blown (Chapter 12)
- [ ] Corrosion of bulb or bulbholder contacts (Chapter 12)
- [ ] Blown fuse (Chapter 12)
- [ ] Faulty relay (Chapter 12)
- [ ] Broken, loose, or disconnected wiring (Chapter 12)
- [ ] Faulty switch (Chapter 12)

Instrument readings inaccurate or erratic

Fuel or temperature gauges give no reading

- [ ] Faulty gauge sender unit (Chapter 3 or 4A)
- [ ] Wiring open-circuit (Chapter 12)
- [ ] Faulty gauge (Chapter 12)

Fuel or temperature gauges give continuous maximum reading

- [ ] Faulty gauge sender unit (Chapter 3 or 4A)
- [ ] Wiring short-circuit (Chapter 12)
- [ ] Faulty gauge (Chapter 12)

Horn inoperative, or unsatisfactory in operation

Horn operates all the time

- [ ] Horn push either earthed or stuck down (Chapter 12)
- [ ] Horn cable-to-horn push earthed (Chapter 12)

Horn fails to operate

- [ ] Blown fuse (Chapter 12)
- [ ] Cable or connections loose, broken or disconnected (Chapter 12)
- [ ] Faulty horn (Chapter 12)

Horn emits intermittent or unsatisfactory sound

- [ ] Cable connections loose (Chapter 12)
- [ ] Horn mountings loose (Chapter 12)
- [ ] Faulty horn (Chapter 12)

Windscreen wipers inoperative, or unsatisfactory in operation

Wipers fail to operate, or operate very slowly

- [ ] Wiper blades stuck to screen, or linkage seized or binding (Chapter 12)
- [ ] Blown fuse (Chapter 12)
- [ ] Battery discharged (Chapter 5)
- [ ] Cable or connections loose, broken or disconnected (Chapter 12)
- [ ] Faulty relay (Chapter 12)
- [ ] Faulty wiper motor (Chapter 12)

Wiper blades sweep over too large or too small an area of the glass

- [ ] Wiper blades incorrectly fitted, or wrong size used (see *Weekly checks*)
- [ ] Wiper arms incorrectly positioned on spindles (Chapter 12)
- [ ] Excessive wear of wiper linkage (Chapter 12)
- [ ] Wiper motor or linkage mountings loose or insecure (Chapter 12)

Wiper blades fail to clean the glass effectively

- [ ] Wiper blade rubbers dirty, worn or perished (see *Weekly checks*)
- [ ] Wiper blades incorrectly fitted, or wrong size used (see *Weekly checks*)
- [ ] Wiper arm tension springs broken, or arm pivots seized (Chapter 12)
- [ ] Insufficient windscreen washer additive to adequately remove road film (see *Weekly checks*)

Electrical system (continued)

Windscreen washers inoperative, or unsatisfactory in operation

One or more washer jets inoperative

- ☐ Blocked washer jet
- ☐ Disconnected, kinked or restricted fluid hose (Chapter 12)
- ☐ Insufficient fluid in washer reservoir (see *Weekly checks*)

Washer pump fails to operate

- ☐ Broken or disconnected wiring or connections (Chapter 12)
- ☐ Blown fuse (Chapter 12)
- ☐ Faulty washer switch (Chapter 12)
- ☐ Faulty washer pump (Chapter 12)

Washer pump runs for some time before fluid is emitted from jets

- ☐ Faulty one-way valve in fluid supply hose (Chapter 12)

Electric windows inoperative, or unsatisfactory in operation

Window glass will only move in one direction

- ☐ Faulty switch (Chapter 12)

Window glass slow to move

- ☐ Battery discharged (Chapter 5)
- ☐ Regulator seized or damaged, or in need of lubrication (Chapter 11)
- ☐ Door internal components or trim fouling regulator (Chapter 11)
- ☐ Faulty motor (Chapter 11)

Window glass fails to move

- ☐ Blown fuse (Chapter 12)
- ☐ Faulty relay (Chapter 12)
- ☐ Broken or disconnected wiring or connections (Chapter 12)
- ☐ Faulty motor (Chapter 11)

Central locking system inoperative, or unsatisfactory in operation

Complete system failure

- ☐ Remote handset battery discharged, where applicable (Chapter 1)
- ☐ Blown fuse (Chapter 12)
- ☐ Faulty relay (Chapter 12)
- ☐ Broken or disconnected wiring or connections (Chapter 12)
- ☐ Faulty motor (Chapter 11)

Latch locks but will not unlock, or unlocks but will not lock

- ☐ Remote handset battery discharged, where applicable (Chapter 1)
- ☐ Faulty master switch (Chapter 12)
- ☐ Broken or disconnected latch operating rods or levers (Chapter 11)
- ☐ Faulty relay (Chapter 12)
- ☐ Faulty motor (Chapter 11)

One solenoid/motor fails to operate

- ☐ Broken or disconnected wiring or connections (Chapter 12)
- ☐ Faulty operating assembly (Chapter 11)
- ☐ Broken, binding or disconnected latch operating rods or levers (Chapter 11)
- ☐ Fault in door latch (Chapter 11)

A

ABS (Anti-lock brake system) A system, usually electronically controlled, that senses incipient wheel lockup during braking and relieves hydraulic pressure at wheels that are about to skid.

Air bag An inflatable bag hidden in the steering wheel (driver's side) or the dash or glovebox (passenger side). In a head-on collision, the bags inflate, preventing the driver and front passenger from being thrown forward into the steering wheel or windscreen.

Air cleaner A metal or plastic housing, containing a filter element, which removes dust and dirt from the air being drawn into the engine.

Air filter element The actual filter in an air cleaner system, usually manufactured from pleated paper and requiring renewal at regular intervals.

Air filter

Allen key A hexagonal wrench which fits into a recessed hexagonal hole.

Alligator clip A long-nosed spring-loaded metal clip with meshing teeth. Used to make temporary electrical connections.

Alternator A component in the electrical system which converts mechanical energy from a drivebelt into electrical energy to charge the battery and to operate the starting system, ignition system and electrical accessories.

Alternator (exploded view)

Ampere (amp) A unit of measurement for the flow of electric current. One amp is the amount of current produced by one volt acting through a resistance of one ohm.

Anaerobic sealer A substance used to prevent bolts and screws from loosening. Anaerobic means that it does not require oxygen for activation. The Loctite brand is widely used.

Antifreeze A substance (usually ethylene glycol) mixed with water, and added to a vehicle's cooling system, to prevent freezing of the coolant in winter. Antifreeze also contains chemicals to inhibit corrosion and the formation of rust and other deposits that

would tend to clog the radiator and coolant passages and reduce cooling efficiency.

Anti-seize compound A coating that reduces the risk of seizing on fasteners that are subjected to high temperatures, such as exhaust manifold bolts and nuts.

Anti-seize compound

Asbestos A natural fibrous mineral with great heat resistance, commonly used in the composition of brake friction materials. Asbestos is a health hazard and the dust created by brake systems should never be inhaled or ingested.

Axle A shaft on which a wheel revolves, or which revolves with a wheel. Also, a solid beam that connects the two wheels at one end of the vehicle. An axle which also transmits power to the wheels is known as a live axle.

Axle assembly

Axleshaft A single rotating shaft, on either side of the differential, which delivers power from the final drive assembly to the drive wheels. Also called a driveshaft or a halfshaft.

B

Ball bearing An anti-friction bearing consisting of a hardened inner and outer race with hardened steel balls between two races.

Bearing

Bearing The curved surface on a shaft or in a bore, or the part assembled into either, that permits relative motion between them with minimum wear and friction.

Big-end bearing The bearing in the end of the connecting rod that's attached to the crankshaft.

Bleed nipple A valve on a brake wheel cylinder, caliper or other hydraulic component that is opened to purge the hydraulic system of air. Also called a bleed screw.

Brake bleeding

Brake bleeding Procedure for removing air from lines of a hydraulic brake system.

Brake disc The component of a disc brake that rotates with the wheels.

Brake drum The component of a drum brake that rotates with the wheels.

Brake linings The friction material which contacts the brake disc or drum to retard the vehicle's speed. The linings are bonded or riveted to the brake pads or shoes.

Brake pads The replaceable friction pads that pinch the brake disc when the brakes are applied. Brake pads consist of a friction material bonded or riveted to a rigid backing plate.

Brake shoe The crescent-shaped carrier to which the brake linings are mounted and which forces the lining against the rotating drum during braking.

Braking systems For more information on braking systems, consult the *Haynes Automotive Brake Manual*.

Breaker bar A long socket wrench handle providing greater leverage.

Bulkhead The insulated partition between the engine and the passenger compartment.

C

Caliper The non-rotating part of a disc-brake assembly that straddles the disc and carries the brake pads. The caliper also contains the hydraulic components that cause the pads to pinch the disc when the brakes are applied. A caliper is also a measuring tool that can be set to measure inside or outside dimensions of an object.

Camshaft A rotating shaft on which a series of cam lobes operate the valve mechanisms. The camshaft may be driven by gears, by sprockets and chain or by sprockets and a belt.

Canister A container in an evaporative emission control system; contains activated charcoal granules to trap vapours from the fuel system.

Canister

Carburettor A device which mixes fuel with air in the proper proportions to provide a desired power output from a spark ignition internal combustion engine.

Carburettor

Castellated Resembling the parapets along the top of a castle wall. For example, a castellated balljoint stud nut.

Castellated nut

Castor In wheel alignment, the backward or forward tilt of the steering axis. Castor is positive when the steering axis is inclined rearward at the top.

Catalytic converter A silencer-like device in the exhaust system which converts certain pollutants in the exhaust gases into less harmful substances.

Catalytic converter

Circlip A ring-shaped clip used to prevent endwise movement of cylindrical parts and shafts. An internal circlip is installed in a groove in a housing; an external circlip fits into a groove on the outside of a cylindrical piece such as a shaft.

Clearance The amount of space between two parts. For example, between a piston and a cylinder, between a bearing and a journal, etc.

Coil spring A spiral of elastic steel found in various sizes throughout a vehicle, for example as a springing medium in the suspension and in the valve train.

Compression Reduction in volume, and increase in pressure and temperature, of a gas, caused by squeezing it into a smaller space.

Compression ratio The relationship between cylinder volume when the piston is at top dead centre and cylinder volume when the piston is at bottom dead centre.

Constant velocity (CV) joint A type of universal joint that cancels out vibrations caused by driving power being transmitted through an angle.

Core plug A disc or cup-shaped metal device inserted in a hole in a casting through which core was removed when the casting was formed. Also known as a freeze plug or expansion plug.

Crankcase The lower part of the engine block in which the crankshaft rotates.

Crankshaft The main rotating member, or shaft, running the length of the crankcase, with offset "throws" to which the connecting rods are attached.

Crankshaft assembly

Crocodile clip See Alligator clip

D

Diagnostic code Code numbers obtained by accessing the diagnostic mode of an engine management computer. This code can be used to determine the area in the system where a malfunction may be located.

Disc brake A brake design incorporating a rotating disc onto which brake pads are squeezed. The resulting friction converts the energy of a moving vehicle into heat.

Double-overhead cam (DOHC) An engine that uses two overhead camshafts, usually one for the intake valves and one for the exhaust valves.

Drivebelt(s) The belt(s) used to drive accessories such as the alternator, water pump, power steering pump, air conditioning compressor, etc. off the crankshaft pulley.

Accessory drivebelts

Driveshaft Any shaft used to transmit motion. Commonly used when referring to the axleshafts on a front wheel drive vehicle.

Driveshaft

Drum brake A type of brake using a drum-shaped metal cylinder attached to the inner surface of the wheel. When the brake pedal is pressed, curved brake shoes with friction linings press against the inside of the drum to slow or stop the vehicle.

Drum brake assembly

E

EGR valve A valve used to introduce exhaust gases into the intake air stream.

EGR valve

Electronic control unit (ECU) A computer which controls (for instance) ignition and fuel injection systems, or an anti-lock braking system. For more information refer to the *Haynes Automotive Electrical and Electronic Systems Manual*.

Electronic Fuel Injection (EFI) A computer controlled fuel system that distributes fuel through an injector located in each intake port of the engine.

Emergency brake A braking system, independent of the main hydraulic system, that can be used to slow or stop the vehicle if the primary brakes fail, or to hold the vehicle stationary even though the brake pedal isn't depressed. It usually consists of a hand lever that actuates either front or rear brakes mechanically through a series of cables and linkages. Also known as a handbrake or parking brake.

Endfloat The amount of lengthwise movement between two parts. As applied to a crankshaft, the distance that the crankshaft can move forward and back in the cylinder block.

Engine management system (EMS) A computer controlled system which manages the fuel injection and the ignition systems in an integrated fashion.

Exhaust manifold A part with several passages through which exhaust gases leave the engine combustion chambers and enter the exhaust pipe.

Exhaust manifold

F

Fan clutch A viscous (fluid) drive coupling device which permits variable engine fan speeds in relation to engine speeds.

Feeler blade A thin strip or blade of hardened steel, ground to an exact thickness, used to check or measure clearances between parts.

Feeler blade

Firing order The order in which the engine cylinders fire, or deliver their power strokes, beginning with the number one cylinder.

Flywheel A heavy spinning wheel in which energy is absorbed and stored by means of momentum. On cars, the flywheel is attached to the crankshaft to smooth out firing impulses.

Free play The amount of travel before any action takes place. The "looseness" in a linkage, or an assembly of parts, between the initial application of force and actual movement. For example, the distance the brake pedal moves before the pistons in the master cylinder are actuated.

Fuse An electrical device which protects a circuit against accidental overload. The typical fuse contains a soft piece of metal which is calibrated to melt at a predetermined current flow (expressed as amps) and break the circuit.

Fusible link A circuit protection device consisting of a conductor surrounded by heat-resistant insulation. The conductor is smaller than the wire it protects, so it acts as the weakest link in the circuit. Unlike a blown fuse, a failed fusible link must frequently be cut from the wire for replacement.

G

Gap The distance the spark must travel in jumping from the centre electrode to the side

Adjusting spark plug gap

electrode in a spark plug. Also refers to the spacing between the points in a contact breaker assembly in a conventional points-type ignition, or to the distance between the reluctor or rotor and the pickup coil in an electronic ignition.

Gasket Any thin, soft material - usually cork, cardboard, asbestos or soft metal - installed between two metal surfaces to ensure a good seal. For instance, the cylinder head gasket seals the joint between the block and the cylinder head.

Gasket

Gauge An instrument panel display used to monitor engine conditions. A gauge with a movable pointer on a dial or a fixed scale is an analogue gauge. A gauge with a numerical readout is called a digital gauge.

H

Halfshaft A rotating shaft that transmits power from the final drive unit to a drive wheel, usually when referring to a live rear axle.

Harmonic balancer A device designed to reduce torsion or twisting vibration in the crankshaft. May be incorporated in the crankshaft pulley. Also known as a vibration damper.

Hone An abrasive tool for correcting small irregularities or differences in diameter in an engine cylinder, brake cylinder, etc.

Hydraulic tappet A tappet that utilises hydraulic pressure from the engine's lubrication system to maintain zero clearance (constant contact with both camshaft and valve stem). Automatically adjusts to variation in valve stem length. Hydraulic tappets also reduce valve noise.

I

Ignition timing The moment at which the spark plug fires, usually expressed in the number of crankshaft degrees before the piston reaches the top of its stroke.

Inlet manifold A tube or housing with passages through which flows the air-fuel mixture (carburettor vehicles and vehicles with throttle body injection) or air only (port fuel-injected vehicles) to the port openings in the cylinder head.

J

Jump start Starting the engine of a vehicle with a discharged or weak battery by attaching jump leads from the weak battery to a charged or helper battery.

L

Load Sensing Proportioning Valve (LSPV) A brake hydraulic system control valve that works like a proportioning valve, but also takes into consideration the amount of weight carried by the rear axle.

Locknut A nut used to lock an adjustment nut, or other threaded component, in place. For example, a locknut is employed to keep the adjusting nut on the rocker arm in position.

Lockwasher A form of washer designed to prevent an attaching nut from working loose.

M

MacPherson strut A type of front suspension system devised by Earle MacPherson at Ford of England. In its original form, a simple lateral link with the anti-roll bar creates the lower control arm. A long strut - an integral coil spring and shock absorber - is mounted between the body and the steering knuckle. Many modern so-called MacPherson strut systems use a conventional lower A-arm and don't rely on the anti-roll bar for location.

Multimeter An electrical test instrument with the capability to measure voltage, current and resistance.

N

NOx Oxides of Nitrogen. A common toxic pollutant emitted by petrol and diesel engines at higher temperatures.

O

Ohm The unit of electrical resistance. One volt applied to a resistance of one ohm will produce a current of one amp.

Ohmmeter An instrument for measuring electrical resistance.

O-ring A type of sealing ring made of a special rubber-like material; in use, the O-ring is compressed into a groove to provide the sealing action.

O-ring

Overhead cam (ohc) engine An engine with the camshaft(s) located on top of the cylinder head(s).

Overhead valve (ohv) engine An engine with the valves located in the cylinder head, but with the camshaft located in the engine block.

Oxygen sensor A device installed in the engine exhaust manifold, which senses the oxygen content in the exhaust and converts this information into an electric current. Also called a Lambda sensor.

P

Phillips screw A type of screw head having a cross instead of a slot for a corresponding type of screwdriver.

Plastigage A thin strip of plastic thread, available in different sizes, used for measuring clearances. For example, a strip of Plastigage is laid across a bearing journal. The parts are assembled and dismantled; the width of the crushed strip indicates the clearance between journal and bearing.

Plastigage

Propeller shaft The long hollow tube with universal joints at both ends that carries power from the transmission to the differential on front-engined rear wheel drive vehicles.

Proportioning valve A hydraulic control valve which limits the amount of pressure to the rear brakes during panic stops to prevent wheel lock-up.

R

Rack-and-pinion steering A steering system with a pinion gear on the end of the steering shaft that mates with a rack (think of a geared wheel opened up and laid flat). When the steering wheel is turned, the pinion turns, moving the rack to the left or right. This movement is transmitted through the track rods to the steering arms at the wheels.

Radiator A liquid-to-air heat transfer device designed to reduce the temperature of the coolant in an internal combustion engine cooling system.

Refrigerant Any substance used as a heat transfer agent in an air-conditioning system. R-12 has been the principle refrigerant for many years; recently, however, manufacturers have begun using R-134a, a non-CFC substance that is considered less harmful to the ozone in the upper atmosphere.

Rocker arm A lever arm that rocks on a shaft or pivots on a stud. In an overhead valve engine, the rocker arm converts the upward movement of the pushrod into a downward movement to open a valve.

Rotor In a distributor, the rotating device inside the cap that connects the centre electrode and the outer terminals as it turns, distributing the high voltage from the coil secondary winding to the proper spark plug. Also, that part of an alternator which rotates inside the stator. Also, the rotating assembly of a turbocharger, including the compressor wheel, shaft and turbine wheel.

Runout The amount of wobble (in-and-out movement) of a gear or wheel as it's rotated. The amount a shaft rotates "out-of-true." The out-of-round condition of a rotating part.

S

Sealant A liquid or paste used to prevent leakage at a joint. Sometimes used in conjunction with a gasket.

Sealed beam lamp An older headlight design which integrates the reflector, lens and filaments into a hermetically-sealed one-piece unit. When a filament burns out or the lens cracks, the entire unit is simply replaced.

Serpentine drivebelt A single, long, wide accessory drivebelt that's used on some newer vehicles to drive all the accessories, instead of a series of smaller, shorter belts. Serpentine drivebelts are usually tensioned by an automatic tensioner.

Serpentine drivebelt

Shim Thin spacer, commonly used to adjust the clearance or relative positions between two parts. For example, shims inserted into or under bucket tappets control valve clearances. Clearance is adjusted by changing the thickness of the shim.

Slide hammer A special puller that screws into or hooks onto a component such as a shaft or bearing; a heavy sliding handle on the shaft bottoms against the end of the shaft to knock the component free.

Sprocket A tooth or projection on the periphery of a wheel, shaped to engage with a chain or drivebelt. Commonly used to refer to the sprocket wheel itself.

Starter inhibitor switch On vehicles with an automatic transmission, a switch that prevents starting if the vehicle is not in Neutral or Park.

Strut See MacPherson strut.

T

Tappet A cylindrical component which transmits motion from the cam to the valve stem, either directly or via a pushrod and rocker arm. Also called a cam follower.

Thermostat A heat-controlled valve that regulates the flow of coolant between the cylinder block and the radiator, so maintaining optimum engine operating temperature. A thermostat is also used in some air cleaners in which the temperature is regulated.

Thrust bearing The bearing in the clutch assembly that is moved in to the release levers by clutch pedal action to disengage the clutch. Also referred to as a release bearing.

Timing belt A toothed belt which drives the camshaft. Serious engine damage may result if it breaks in service.

Timing chain A chain which drives the camshaft.

Toe-in The amount the front wheels are closer together at the front than at the rear. On rear wheel drive vehicles, a slight amount of toe-in is usually specified to keep the front wheels running parallel on the road by offsetting other forces that tend to spread the wheels apart.

Toe-out The amount the front wheels are closer together at the rear than at the front. On front wheel drive vehicles, a slight amount of toe-out is usually specified.

Tools For full information on choosing and using tools, refer to the *Haynes Automotive Tools Manual.*

Tracer A stripe of a second colour applied to a wire insulator to distinguish that wire from another one with the same colour insulator.

Tune-up A process of accurate and careful adjustments and parts replacement to obtain the best possible engine performance.

Turbocharger A centrifugal device, driven by exhaust gases, that pressurises the intake air. Normally used to increase the power output from a given engine displacement, but can also be used primarily to reduce exhaust emissions (as on VW's "Umwelt" Diesel engine).

U

Universal joint or U-joint A double-pivoted connection for transmitting power from a driving to a driven shaft through an angle. A U-joint consists of two Y-shaped yokes and a cross-shaped member called the spider.

V

Valve A device through which the flow of liquid, gas, vacuum, or loose material in bulk may be started, stopped, or regulated by a movable part that opens, shuts, or partially obstructs one or more ports or passageways. A valve is also the movable part of such a device.

Valve clearance The clearance between the valve tip (the end of the valve stem) and the rocker arm or tappet. The valve clearance is measured when the valve is closed.

Vernier caliper A precision measuring instrument that measures inside and outside dimensions. Not quite as accurate as a micrometer, but more convenient.

Viscosity The thickness of a liquid or its resistance to flow.

Volt A unit for expressing electrical "pressure" in a circuit. One volt that will produce a current of one ampere through a resistance of one ohm.

W

Welding Various processes used to join metal items by heating the areas to be joined to a molten state and fusing them together. For more information refer to the *Haynes Automotive Welding Manual.*

Wiring diagram A drawing portraying the components and wires in a vehicle's electrical system, using standardised symbols. For more information refer to the *Haynes Automotive Electrical and Electronic Systems Manual.*

Note: *References throughout this index are in the form* **"Chapter number"** • **"Page number".** *So, for example, 2C•15 refers to page 15 of Chapter 2C.*

Note: *References throughout this index are in the form* "**Chapter number**" • "**Page number**". *So, for example, 2C•15 refers to page 15 of Chapter 2C.*

Haynes Manuals – The Complete **UK Car** List

Title	Book No.
ALFA ROMEO Alfasud/Sprint (74 - 88) up to F *	0292
Alfa Romeo Alfetta (73 - 87) up to E *	0531
AUDI 80, 90 & Coupe Petrol (79 - Nov 88) up to F	0605
Audi 80, 90 & Coupe Petrol (Oct 86 - 90) D to H	1491
Audi 100 & 200 Petrol (Oct 82 - 90) up to H	0907
Audi 100 & A6 Petrol & Diesel (May 91 - May 97) H to P	3504
Audi A3 Petrol & Diesel (96 - May 03) P to 03	4253
Audi A4 Petrol & Diesel (95 - 00) M to X	3575
Audi A4 Petrol & Diesel (01 - 04) X to 54	4609
AUSTIN A35 & A40 (56 - 67) up to F *	0118
Austin/MG/Rover Maestro 1.3 & 1.6 Petrol (83 - 95) up to M	0922
Austin/MG Metro (80 - May 90) up to G	0718
Austin/Rover Montego 1.3 & 1.6 Petrol (84 - 94) A to L	1066
Austin/MG/Rover Montego 2.0 Petrol (84 - 95) A to M	1067
Mini (59 - 69) up to H *	0527
Mini (69 - 01) up to X	0646
Austin/Rover 2.0 litre Diesel Engine (86 - 93) C to L	1857
Austin Healey 100/6 & 3000 (56 - 68) up to G *	0049
BEDFORD CF Petrol (69 - 87) up to E	0163
Bedford/Vauxhall Rascal & Suzuki Supercarry (86 - Oct 94) C to M	3015
BMW 316, 320 & 320i (4-cyl) (75 - Feb 83) up to Y *	0276
BMW 320, 320i, 323i & 325i (6-cyl) (Oct 77 - Sept 87) up to E	0815
BMW 3- & 5-Series Petrol (81 - 91) up to J	1948
BMW 3-Series Petrol (Apr 91 - 99) H to V	3210
BMW 3-Series Petrol (Sept 98 - 03) S to 53	4067
BMW 520i & 525e (Oct 81 - June 88) up to E	1560
BMW 525, 528 & 528i (73 - Sept 81) up to X *	0632
BMW 5-Series 6-cyl Petrol (April 96 - Aug 03) N to 03	4151
BMW 1500, 1502, 1600, 1602, 2000 & 2002 (59 - 77) up to S *	0240
CHRYSLER PT Cruiser Petrol (00 - 03) W to 53	4058
CITROËN 2CV, Ami & Dyane (67 - 90) up to H	0196
Citroën AX Petrol & Diesel (87 - 97) D to P	3014
Citroën Berlingo & Peugeot Partner Petrol & Diesel (96 - 05) P to 55	4281
Citroën BX Petrol (83 - 94) A to L	0908
Citroën C15 Van Petrol & Diesel (89 - Oct 98) F to S	3509
Citroën C3 Petrol & Diesel (02 - 05) 51 to 05	4197
Citroën CX Petrol (75 - 88) up to F	0528
Citroën Saxo Petrol & Diesel (96 - 04) N to 54	3506
Citroën Visa Petrol (79 - 88) up to F	0620
Citroën Xantia Petrol & Diesel (93 - 01) K to Y	3082
Citroën XM Petrol & Diesel (89 - 00) G to X	3451
Citroën Xsara Petrol & Diesel (97 - Sept 00) R to W	3751
Citroën Xsara Picasso Petrol & Diesel (00 - 02) W to 52	3944
Citroën ZX Diesel (91 - 98) J to S	1922
Citroën ZX Petrol (91 - 98) H to S	1881
Citroën 1.7 & 1.9 litre Diesel Engine (84 - 96) A to N	1379
FIAT 126 (73 - 87) up to E *	0305
Fiat 500 (57 - 73) up to M *	0090
Fiat Bravo & Brava Petrol (95 - 00) N to W	3572
Fiat Cinquecento (93 - 98) K to R	3501
Fiat Panda (81 - 95) up to M	0793
Fiat Punto Petrol & Diesel (94 - Oct 99) L to V	3251
Fiat Punto Petrol (Oct 99 - July 03) V to 03	4066
Fiat Regata Petrol (84 - 88) A to F	1167
Fiat Tipo Petrol (88 - 91) E to J	1625
Fiat Uno Petrol (83 - 95) up to M	0923
Fiat X1/9 (74 - 89) up to G *	0273
FORD Anglia (59 - 68) up to G *	0001
Ford Capri II (& III) 1.6 & 2.0 (74 - 87) up to E *	0283
Ford Capri II (& III) 2.8 & 3.0 V6 (74 - 87) up to E	1309

Title	Book No.
Ford Cortina Mk I & Corsair 1500 ('62 - '66) up to D*	0214
Ford Cortina Mk III 1300 & 1600 (70 - 76) up to P *	0070
Ford Escort Mk I 1100 & 1300 (68 - 74) up to N *	0171
Ford Escort Mk I Mexico, RS 1600 & RS 2000 (70 - 74) up to N *	0139
Ford Escort Mk II Mexico, RS 1800 & RS 2000 (75 - 80) up to W *	0735
Ford Escort (75 - Aug 80) up to V *	0280
Ford Escort Petrol (Sept 80 - Sept 90) up to H	0686
Ford Escort & Orion Petrol (Sept 90 - 00) H to X	1737
Ford Escort & Orion Diesel (Sept 90 - 00) H to X	4081
Ford Fiesta (76 - Aug 83) up to Y	0334
Ford Fiesta Petrol (Aug 83 - Feb 89) A to F	1030
Ford Fiesta Petrol (Feb 89 - Oct 95) F to N	1595
Ford Fiesta Petrol & Diesel (Oct 95 - Mar 02) N to 02	3397
Ford Fiesta Petrol & Diesel (Apr 02 - 05) 02 to 54	4170
Ford Focus Petrol & Diesel (98 - 01) S to Y	3759
Ford Focus Petrol & Diesel (Oct 01 - 05) 51 to 05	4167
Ford Galaxy Petrol & Diesel (95 - Aug 00) M to W	3984
Ford Granada Petrol (Sept 77 - Feb 85) up to B *	0481
Ford Granada & Scorpio Petrol (Mar 85 - 94) B to M	1245
Ford Ka (96 - 02) P to 52	3570
Ford Mondeo Petrol (93 - Sept 00) K to X	1923
Ford Mondeo Petrol & Diesel (Oct 00 - Jul 03) X to 03	3990
Ford Mondeo Petrol & Diesel (July 03 - 07) 03 to 56	4619
Ford Mondeo Diesel (93 - 96) L to N	3465
Ford Orion Petrol (83 - Sept 90) up to H	1009
Ford Sierra 4-cyl Petrol (82 - 93) up to K	0903
Ford Sierra V6 Petrol (82 - 91) up to J	0904
Ford Transit Petrol (Mk 2) (78 - Jan 86) up to C	0719
Ford Transit Petrol (Mk 3) (Feb 86 - 89) C to G	1468
Ford Transit Diesel (Feb 86 - 99) C to T	3019
Ford 1.6 & 1.8 litre Diesel Engine (84 - 96) A to N	1172
Ford 2.1, 2.3 & 2.5 litre Diesel Engine (77 - 90) up to H	1606
FREIGHT ROVER Sherpa Petrol (74 - 87) up to E	0463
HILLMAN Avenger (70 - 82) up to Y	0037
Hillman Imp (63 - 76) up to R *	0022
HONDA Civic (Feb 84 - Oct 87) A to E	1226
Honda Civic (Nov 91 - 96) J to N	3199
Honda Civic Petrol (Mar 95 - 00) M to X	4050
Honda Civic Petrol & Diesel (01 - 05) X to 55	4611
Honda Jazz (01 - Feb 08) 51 - 57	4735
HYUNDAI Pony (85 - 94) C to M	3398
JAGUAR E Type (61 - 72) up to L *	0140
Jaguar MkI & II, 240 & 340 (55 - 69) up to H *	0098
Jaguar XJ6, XJ & Sovereign; Daimler Sovereign (68 - Oct 86) up to D	0242
Jaguar XJ6 & Sovereign (Oct 86 - Sept 94) D to M	3261
Jaguar XJ12, XJS & Sovereign; Daimler Double Six (72 - 88) up to F	0478
JEEP Cherokee Petrol (93 - 96) K to N	1943
LADA 1200, 1300, 1500 & 1600 (74 - 91) up to J	0413
Lada Samara (87 - 91) D to J	1610
LAND ROVER 90, 110 & Defender Diesel (83 - 07) up to 56	3017
Land Rover Discovery Petrol & Diesel (89 - 98) G to S	3016
Land Rover Discovery Diesel (Nov 98 - Jul 04) S to 04	4606
Land Rover Freelander Petrol & Diesel (97 - Sept 03) R to 53	3929
Land Rover Freelander Petrol & Diesel (Oct 03 - Oct 06) 53 to 56	4623
Land Rover Series IIA & III Diesel (58 - 85) up to C	0529
Land Rover Series II, IIA & III 4-cyl Petrol (58 - 85) up to C	0314

Title	Book No.
MAZDA 323 (Mar 81 - Oct 89) up to G	1608
Mazda 323 (Oct 89 - 98) G to R	3455
Mazda 626 (May 83 - Sept 87) up to E	0929
Mazda B1600, B1800 & B2000 Pick-up Petrol (72 - 88) up to F	0267
Mazda RX-7 (79 - 85) up to C *	0460
MERCEDES-BENZ 190, 190E & 190D Petrol & Diesel (83 - 93) A to L	3450
Mercedes-Benz 200D, 240D, 240TD, 300D & 300TD 123 Series Diesel (Oct 76 - 85)	1114
Mercedes-Benz 250 & 280 (68 - 72) up to L *	0346
Mercedes-Benz 250 & 280 123 Series Petrol (Oct 76 - 84) up to B *	0677
Mercedes-Benz 124 Series Petrol & Diesel (85 - Aug 93) C to K	3253
Mercedes-Benz C-Class Petrol & Diesel (93 - Aug 00) L to W	3511
MGA (55 - 62) *	0475
MGB (62 - 80) up to W	0111
MG Midget & Austin-Healey Sprite (58 - 80) up to W *	0265
MINI Petrol (July 01 - 05) Y to 05	4273
MITSUBISHI Shogun & L200 Pick-Ups Petrol (83 - 94) up to M	1944
MORRIS Ital 1.3 (80 - 84) up to B	0705
Morris Minor 1000 (56 - 71) up to K	0024
NISSAN Almera Petrol (95 - Feb 00) N to V	4053
Nissan Almera & Tino Petrol (Feb 00 - 07) V to 56	4612
Nissan Bluebird (May 84 - Mar 86) A to C	1223
Nissan Bluebird Petrol (Mar 86 - 90) C to H	1473
Nissan Cherry (Sept 82 - 86) up to D	1031
Nissan Micra (83 - Jan 93) up to K	0931
Nissan Micra (93 - 02) K to 52	3254
Nissan Primera Petrol (90 - Aug 99) H to T	1851
Nissan Stanza (82 - 86) up to D	0824
Nissan Sunny Petrol (May 82 - Oct 86) up to D	0895
Nissan Sunny Petrol (Oct 86 - Mar 91) D to H	1378
Nissan Sunny Petrol (Apr 91 - 95) H to N	3219
OPEL Ascona & Manta (B Series) (Sept 75 - 88) up to F *	0316
Opel Ascona Petrol (81 - 88)	3215
Opel Astra Petrol (Oct 91 - Feb 98)	3156
Opel Corsa Petrol (83 - Mar 93)	3160
Opel Corsa Petrol (Mar 93 - 97)	3159
Opel Kadett Petrol (Nov 79 - Oct 84) up to B	0634
Opel Kadett Petrol (Oct 84 - Oct 91)	3196
Opel Omega & Senator Petrol (Nov 86 - 94)	3157
Opel Rekord Petrol (Feb 78 - Oct 86) up to D	0543
Opel Vectra Petrol (Oct 88 - Oct 95)	3158
PEUGEOT 106 Petrol & Diesel (91 - 04) J to 53	1882
Peugeot 205 Petrol (83 - 97) A to P	0932
Peugeot 206 Petrol & Diesel (98 - 01) S to X	3757
Peugeot 206 Petrol & Diesel (02 - 06) 51 to 06	4613
Peugeot 306 Petrol & Diesel (93 - 02) K to 02	3073
Peugeot 307 Petrol & Diesel (01 - 04) Y to 54	4147
Peugeot 309 Petrol (86 - 93) C to K	1266
Peugeot 405 Petrol (88 - 97) E to P	1559
Peugeot 405 Diesel (88 - 97) E to P	3198
Peugeot 406 Petrol & Diesel (96 - Mar 99) N to T	3394
Peugeot 406 Petrol & Diesel (Mar 99 - 02) T to 52	3982
Peugeot 505 Petrol (79 - 89) up to G	0762
Peugeot 1.7/1.8 & 1.9 litre Diesel Engine (82 - 96) up to N	0950
Peugeot 2.0, 2.1, 2.3 & 2.5 litre Diesel Engines (74 - 90) up to H	1607
PORSCHE 911 (65 - 85) up to C	0264

* Classic reprint

Title	Book No.
Porsche 924 & 924 Turbo (76 - 85) up to C	0397
PROTON (89 - 97) F to P	3255
RANGE ROVER V8 Petrol (70 - Oct 92) up to K	0606
RELIANT Robin & Kitten (73 - 83) up to A *	0436
RENAULT 4 (61 - 86) up to D *	0072
Renault 5 Petrol (Feb 85 - 96) B to N	1219
Renault 9 & 11 Petrol (82 - 89) up to F	0822
Renault 18 Petrol (79 - 86) up to D	0598
Renault 19 Petrol (89 - 96) F to N	1646
Renault 19 Diesel (89 - 96) F to N	1946
Renault 21 Petrol (86 - 94) C to M	1397
Renault 25 Petrol & Diesel (84 - 92) B to K	1228
Renault Clio Petrol (91 - May 98) H to R	1853
Renault Clio Diesel (91 - June 96) H to N	3031
Renault Clio Petrol & Diesel (May 98 - May 01) R to Y	3906
Renault Clio Petrol & Diesel (June 01 - '05) Y to 55	4168
Renault Espace Petrol & Diesel (85 - 96) C to N	3197
Renault Laguna Petrol & Diesel (94 - 00) L to W	3252
Renault Laguna Petrol & Diesel (Feb 01 - Feb 05) X to 54	4283
Renault Mégane & Scénic Petrol & Diesel (96 - 99) N to T	3395
Renault Mégane & Scénic Petrol & Diesel (Apr 99 - 02) T to 52	3916
Renault Megane Petrol & Diesel (Oct 02 - 05) 52 to 55	4284
Renault Scenic Petrol & Diesel (Sept 03 - 06) 53 to 06	4297
ROVER 213 & 216 (84 - 89) A to G	1116
Rover 214 & 414 Petrol (89 - 96) G to N	1689
Rover 216 & 416 Petrol (89 - 96) G to N	1830
Rover 211, 214, 216, 218 & 220 Petrol & Diesel (Dec 95 - 99) N to V	3399
Rover 25 & MG ZR Petrol & Diesel (Oct 99 - 04) V to 54	4145
Rover 414, 416 & 420 Petrol & Diesel (May 95 - 98) M to R	3453
Rover 45 / MG ZS Petrol & Diesel (99 - 05) V to 55	4384
Rover 618, 620 & 623 Petrol (93 - 97) K to P	3257
Rover 75 / MG ZT Petrol & Diesel (99 - 06) S to 06	4292
Rover 820, 825 & 827 Petrol (86 - 95) D to N	1380
Rover 3500 (76 - 87) up to E *	0365
Rover Metro, 111 & 114 Petrol (May 90 - 98) G to S	1711
SAAB 95 & 96 (66 - 76) up to R *	0198
Saab 90, 99 & 900 (79 - Oct 93) up to L	0765
Saab 900 (Oct 93 - 98) L to R	3512
Saab 9000 (4-cyl) (85 - 98) C to S	1686
Saab 9-3 Petrol & Diesel (98 - Aug 02) R to 02	4614
Saab 9-5 4-cyl Petrol (97 - 04) R to 54	4156
SEAT Ibiza & Cordoba Petrol & Diesel (Oct 93 - Oct 99) L to V	3571
Seat Ibiza & Malaga Petrol (85 - 92) B to K	1609
SKODA Estelle (77 - 89) up to G	0604
Skoda Fabia Petrol & Diesel (00 - 06) W to 06	4376
Skoda Favorit (89 - 96) F to N	1801
Skoda Felicia Petrol & Diesel (95 - 01) M to X	3505
Skoda Octavia Petrol & Diesel (98 - Apr 04) R to 04	4285
SUBARU 1600 & 1800 (Nov 79 - 90) up to H *	0995
SUNBEAM Alpine, Rapier & H120 (67 - 74) up to N *	0051
SUZUKI SJ Series, Samurai & Vitara (4-cyl) Petrol (82 - 97) up to P	1942
Suzuki Supercarry & Bedford/Vauxhall Rascal (86 - Oct 94) C to M	3015
TALBOT Alpine, Solara, Minx & Rapier (75 - 86) up to D	0337

Title	Book No.
Talbot Horizon Petrol (78 - 86) up to D	0473
Talbot Samba (82 - 86) up to D	0823
TOYOTA Avensis Petrol (98 - Jan 03) R to 52	4264
Toyota Carina E Petrol (May 92 - 97) J to P	3256
Toyota Corolla (80 - 85) up to C	0683
Toyota Corolla (Sept 83 - Sept 87) A to E	1024
Toyota Corolla (Sept 87 - Aug 92) E to K	1683
Toyota Corolla Petrol (Aug 92 - 97) K to P	3259
Toyota Corolla Petrol (July 97 - Feb 02) P to 51	4286
Toyota Hi-Ace & Hi-Lux Petrol (69 - Oct 83) up to A	0304
Toyota Yaris Petrol (99 - 05) T to 05	4265
TRIUMPH GT6 & Vitesse (62 - 74) up to N *	0112
Triumph Herald (59 - 71) up to K *	0010
Triumph Spitfire (62 - 81) up to X	0113
Triumph Stag (70 - 78) up to T *	0441
Triumph TR2, TR3, TR3A, TR4 & TR4A (52 - 67) up to F *	0028
Triumph TR5 & 6 (67 - 75) up to P *	0031
Triumph TR7 (75 - 82) up to Y *	0322
VAUXHALL Astra Petrol (80 - Oct 84) up to B	0635
Vauxhall Astra & Belmont Petrol (Oct 84 - Oct 91) B to J	1136
Vauxhall Astra Petrol (Oct 91 - Feb 98) J to R	1832
Vauxhall/Opel Astra & Zafira Petrol (Feb 98 - Apr 04) R to 04	3758
Vauxhall/Opel Astra & Zafira Diesel (Feb 98 - Apr 04) R to 04	3797
Vauxhall/Opel Astra Petrol (04 - 07) 04 - 07	4732
Vauxhall/Opel Astra Diesel (04 - 07) 04 - 07	4733
Vauxhall/Opel Calibra (90 - 98) G to S	3502
Vauxhall Carlton Petrol (Oct 78 - Oct 86) up to D	0480
Vauxhall Carlton & Senator Petrol (Nov 86 - 94) D to L	1469
Vauxhall Cavalier Petrol (81 - Oct 88) up to F	0812
Vauxhall Cavalier Petrol (Oct 88 - 95) F to N	1570
Vauxhall Chevette (75 - 84) up to B	0285
Vauxhall/Opel Corsa Diesel (Mar 93 - Oct 00) K to X	4087
Vauxhall Corsa Petrol (Mar 93 - 97) K to R	1985
Vauxhall/Opel Corsa Petrol (Apr 97 - Oct 00) P to X	3921
Vauxhall/Opel Corsa Petrol & Diesel (Oct 00 - Sept 03) X to 53	4079
Vauxhall/Opel Corsa Petrol & Diesel (Oct 03 - Aug 06) 53 to 06	4617
Vauxhall/Opel Frontera Petrol & Diesel (91 - Sept 98) J to S	3454
Vauxhall Nova Petrol (83 - 93) up to K	0909
Vauxhall/Opel Omega Petrol (94 - 99) L to T	3510
Vauxhall/Opel Vectra Petrol & Diesel (95 - Feb 99) N to S	3396
Vauxhall/Opel Vectra Petrol & Diesel (Mar 99 - May 02) T to 02	3930
Vauxhall/Opel Vectra Petrol & Diesel (June 02 - Sept 05) 02 to 55	4618
Vauxhall/Opel 1.5, 1.6 & 1.7 litre Diesel Engine (82 - 96) up to N	1222
VW 411 & 412 (68 - 75) up to P *	0091
VW Beetle 1200 (54 - 77) up to S	0036
VW Beetle 1300 & 1500 (65 - 75) up to P	0039
VW 1302 & 1302S (70 - 72) up to L *	0110
VW Beetle 1303, 1303S & GT (72 - 75) up to P	0159
VW Beetle Petrol & Diesel (Apr 99 - 01) T to 51	3798
VW Golf & Jetta Mk 1 Petrol 1.1 & 1.3 (74 - 84) up to A	0716
VW Golf, Jetta & Scirocco Mk 1 Petrol 1.5, 1.6 & 1.8 (74 - 84) up to A	0726

Title	Book No.
VW Golf & Jetta Mk 1 Diesel (78 - 84) up to A	0451
VW Golf & Jetta Mk 2 Petrol (Mar 84 - Feb 92) A to J	1081
VW Golf & Vento Petrol & Diesel (Feb 92 - Mar 98) J to R	3097
VW Golf & Bora Petrol & Diesel (April 98 - 00) R to X	3727
VW Golf & Bora 4-cyl Petrol & Diesel (01 - 03) X to 53	4169
VW Golf & Jetta Petrol & Diesel (04 - 07) 53 to 07	4610
VW LT Petrol Vans & Light Trucks (76 - 87) up to E	0637
VW Passat & Santana Petrol (Sept 81 - May 88) up to E	0814
VW Passat 4-cyl Petrol & Diesel (May 88 - 96) E to P	3498
VW Passat 4-cyl Petrol & Diesel (Dec 96 - Nov 00) P to X	3917
VW Passat Petrol & Diesel (Dec 00 - May 05) X to 05	4279
VW Polo & Derby (76 - Jan 82) up to X	0335
VW Polo (82 - Oct 90) up to H	0813
VW Polo Petrol (Nov 90 - Aug 94) H to L	3245
VW Polo Hatchback Petrol & Diesel (94 - 99) M to S	3500
VW Polo Hatchback Petrol (00 - Jan 02) V to 51	4150
VW Polo Petrol & Diesel (02 - May 05) 51 to 05	4608
VW Scirocco (82 - 90) up to H *	1224
VW Transporter 1600 (68 - 79) up to V	0082
VW Transporter 1700, 1800 & 2000 (72 - 79) up to V *	0226
VW Transporter (air-cooled) Petrol (79 - 82) up to Y *	0638
VW Transporter (water-cooled) Petrol (82 - 90) up to H	3452
VW Type 3 (63 - 73) up to M *	0084
VOLVO 120 & 130 Series (& P1800) (61 - 73) up to M *	0203
Volvo 142, 144 & 145 (66 - 74) up to N *	0129
Volvo 240 Series Petrol (74 - 93) up to K	0270
Volvo 262, 264 & 260/265 (75 - 85) up to C *	0400
Volvo 340, 343, 345 & 360 (76 - 91) up to J	0715
Volvo 440, 460 & 480 Petrol (87 - 97) D to P	1691
Volvo 740 & 760 Petrol (82 - 91) up to J	1258
Volvo 850 Petrol (92 - 96) J to P	3260
Volvo 940 petrol (90 - 98) H to R	3249
Volvo S40 & V40 Petrol (96 - Mar 04) N to 04	3569
Volvo S40 & V50 Petrol & Diesel (Mar 04 - Jun 07) 04 to 07	4731
Volvo S70, V70 & C70 Petrol (96 - 99) P to V	3573
Volvo V70 / S80 Petrol & Diesel (98 - 05) S to 55	4263

AUTOMOTIVE TECHBOOKS

Title	Book No.
Automotive Electrical and Electronic Systems Manual	3049
Automotive Gearbox Overhaul Manual	3473
Automotive Service Summaries Manual	3475
Automotive Timing Belts Manual – Austin/Rover	3549
Automotive Timing Belts Manual – Ford	3474
Automotive Timing Belts Manual – Peugeot/Citroën	3568
Automotive Timing Belts Manual – Vauxhall/Opel	3577

DIY MANUAL SERIES

Title	Book No.
The Haynes Air Conditioning Manual	4192
The Haynes Car Electrical Systems Manual	4251
The Haynes Manual on Bodywork	4198
The Haynes Manual on Brakes	4178
The Haynes Manual on Carburettors	4177
The Haynes Manual on Diesel Engines	4174
The Haynes Manual on Engine Management	4199
The Haynes Manual on Fault Codes	4175
The Haynes Manual on Practical Electrical Systems	4267
The Haynes Manual on Small Engines	4250
The Haynes Manual on Welding	4176

* Classic reprint

Preserving Our Motoring Heritage

< The Model J Duesenberg Derham Tourster. Only eight of these magnificent cars were ever built – this is the only example to be found outside the United States of America

Almost every car you've ever loved, loathed or desired is gathered under one roof at the Haynes Motor Museum. Over 300 immaculately presented cars and motorbikes represent every aspect of our motoring heritage, from elegant reminders of bygone days, such as the superb Model J Duesenberg to curiosities like the bug-eyed BMW Isetta. There are also many old friends and flames. Perhaps you remember the 1959 Ford Popular that you did your courting in? The magnificent 'Red Collection' is a spectacle of classic sports cars including AC, Alfa Romeo, Austin Healey, Ferrari, Lamborghini, Maserati, MG, Riley, Porsche and Triumph.

A Perfect Day Out

Each and every vehicle at the Haynes Motor Museum has played its part in the history and culture of Motoring. Today, they make a wonderful spectacle and a great day out for all the family. Bring the kids, bring Mum and Dad, but above all bring your camera to capture those golden memories for ever. You will also find an impressive array of motoring memorabilia, a comfortable 70 seat video cinema and one of the most extensive transport book shops in Britain. The Pit Stop Cafe serves everything from a cup of tea to wholesome, home-made meals or, if you prefer, you can enjoy the large picnic area nestled in the beautiful rural surroundings of Somerset.

> John Haynes O.B.E., Founder and Chairman of the museum at the wheel of a Haynes Light 12.

< Graham Hill's Lola Cosworth Formula 1 car next to a 1934 Riley Sports.

The Museum is situated on the A359 Yeovil to Frome road at Sparkford, just off the A303 in Somerset. It is about 40 miles south of Bristol, and 25 minutes drive from the M5 intersection at Taunton.

Open 9.30am - 5.30pm (10.00am - 4.00pm Winter) 7 days a week, *except Christmas Day, Boxing Day and New Years Day*

Special rates available for schools, coach parties and outings Charitable Trust No. 292048